Contents

‖‖‖ ‖ ‖‖‖‖‖‖‖‖‖‖‖‖‖‖‖‖‖‖‖‖ ‖‖‖ ‖ ‖‖‖

✔ **KU-528-462**

OPPOSITE *OMOIDE YOKOCHŌ*, SHINJUKU **PREVIOUS PAGE** SHIBUYA CROSSING

Introduction to
Tokyo

With its sushi and sumo, geisha and gardens, neon and noodles, it may seem that Tokyo is in danger of collapsing under the weight of its own stereotypes. Yet ticking off a bunch of travel clichés is rarely this much fun, and as you might expect of the planet's largest metropolis, there's also enough nuance here to keep you entertained for a lifetime. Ordered yet bewildering, Japan's pulsating capital will lead you a merry dance: this is Asia at its weirdest, straightest, prettiest, sleaziest and coolest, all at the same time.

Caught up in an untidy web of overhead cables, plagued by seemingly incessant noise, the concrete and steel conurbation may seem the stereotypical urban nightmare. Yet step back from the frenetic main roads and chances are you'll find yourself in tranquil backstreets, where dinky **wooden houses** are fronted by neatly clipped bonsai trees; wander beyond the high-tech emporia, and you'll discover charming fragments of the old city such as **temples** and **shrines** wreathed in wisps of smoking incense.

Centuries of organizing itself around the daily demands of millions of inhabitants have made Tokyo something of a **model metropolitan environment**. Trains run on time and to practically every corner of the city, **crime** is hardly worth worrying about, and convenience stores and vending machines provide everything you could need (and many things you never thought you did) 24 hours a day.

With so much going on, just walking the streets of this hyperactive city can be an energizing experience. It need not be an expensive one, either. You'll be pleasantly surprised by how **affordable** many things are. Cheap-and-cheerful *izakaya* – bars that serve food – and casual cafés serving noodles and rice dishes are plentiful, the metro is a bargain, and tickets for a sumo tournament or a kabuki play can be bought for the price of a few drinks.

Browsing the **shops** and marvelling at the passing parade is mesmerizing – the next best thing to having a ringside seat at the hippest of catwalk shows. The city's great wealth and relative lack of planning restrictions have given **architects** almost unparalleled freedom to

ABOVE HIE-JINJA, AKASAKA

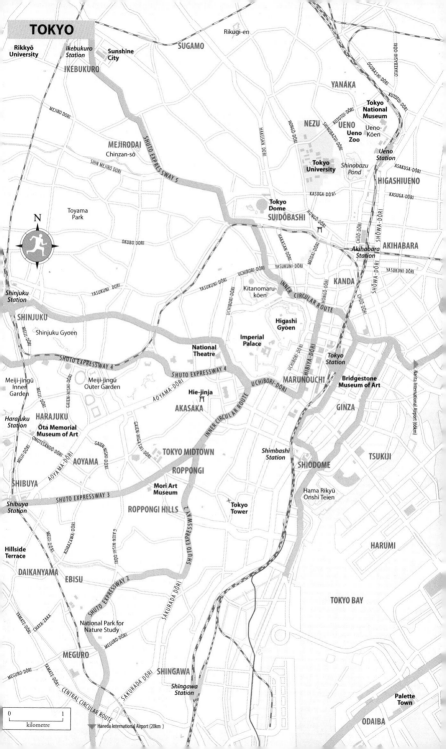

realize their wildest dreams. Likewise, in über-chic bars, restaurants and clubs you'll see today what the rest of the world will get tomorrow. You may not figure out exactly what makes Tokyo tick – and you're sure to get a little confused while trying – but the conclusion is inescapable: Japan's powerhouse capital is a seductive and addictive experience.

What to see

One way to ease yourself into the city is by taking a relatively crowd-free turn around the **Imperial Palace** – the inviolate home of the emperor and a tangible link to the past. From here it's a quick hop to **Marunouchi** which has been busily restyling itself as a chic shopping and dining destination to rival glitzy **Ginza**.

High on your sightseeing agenda should also be the evocative **Shitamachi** area, Tokyo's northeast quarter, where the Edo-era spirit of the city remains. **Asakusa**'s primary focus is the major Buddhist temple of **Sensō-ji**, surrounded by a plethora of traditional craft shops. The leafy precincts of **Ueno Park** contain several major museums, including the **Tokyo National Museum**. From here it's an easy stroll to the charming and tranquil districts of **Nezu**, **Sendagi** and **Yanaka**, packed with small temples, shrines and shops.

The weird, wired and wonderful **Akihabara** area – famous worldwide for its electronics stores – has recently rebooted as the focus of Tokyo's dynamic manga and anime scene; nearby you'll find the **Kanda Myōjin**, one of Tokyo's oldest shrines and host to one of the city's top three festivals, the **Kanda Matsuri**. Across the Sumida-gawa is **Ryōguku**, home to the colossal **Edo-Tokyo Museum** and the **National Sumo Stadium**.

LEFT-FIELD TOKYO

Many visitors to Tokyo expect to see something a little quirky during their stay – here are a few places to sample the city's more intriguing facets.

Capsule hotels The rooms at capsule hotels are pretty darn small – there's no more characteristic Japanese sleeping experience (see box, p.150).

Robot Restaurant Seeing is believing at this zany attraction, where performances feature dozens of dancing girls and robots (see box, p.190).

Game centres Bash the hell out of the world's weirdest arcade machines in one of the city's many game centres (see p.90).

Oddball cafés Have your coffee served by costumed girls, fawning guys in dicky-bows, or surrounded by owls, cats or snakes (see box, p.160).

Golden Gai Tokyo drinking at its most atmospheric, this is a warren of minuscule bars in neon-drenched Shinjuku (see p.130).

Shibuya crossing It's amazing to see just how many people can cross a road at the same time; take in the spectacle over a coffee at *L'Occitane* (see p.170).

Standing noodle bars Eat like a horse, standing up at one of the city's umpteen cheap and cheerful *soba-ya* or *udon-ya* (see box, p.158).

The frenetic early-morning fish market has long been the draw at **Tsukiji**, on the edge of **Tokyo Bay**. Across the water from here, and linked to the main city by the impressive Rainbow Bridge, is **Odaiba**, a futuristic man-made island, where you'll find the **Miraikan**, Tokyo's most fascinating science museum, and the touristy, fun public **bathhouse** Ōedo Onsen Monogatari.

Roppongi's nightlife can exhaust the most committed hedonist, but save some energy to return by day to explore the **Roppongi Art Triangle** formed by the **National Art Center**, housed in one of the city's most dazzling architectural spaces; the **Suntory Museum of Art**; and the excellent Mori Art Museum, atop the **Roppongi Hills** complex.

The southern part of central Tokyo is a slightly unwieldy mishmash of districts revolving around **Ebisu** and **Meguro**; highlights here include the calmer, boutique-filled **Daikanyama** and **Nakameguro** neighbourhoods.

Fashionistas should head towards on-trend **Shibuya** and **Harajuku**, and the super-chic, boutique-lined boulevards of **Aoyama**. When you've reached consumer saturation point, retreat to the wooded grounds of nearby **Meiji-jingū**, the city's most venerable Shinto shrine, or peruse the delicate woodblock prints and crafts and artworks in the **Nezu Museum**, the **Ōta Memorial Museum of Art** or the **Japan Folk Crafts Museum**. This area will also be the hub of the **2020 Summer Olympics** (see box, p.120), which will be the second Games to be held in Tokyo.

Also on the west side of the city lies **Shinjuku**, bursting with towering skyscrapers, endless amounts of neon, TV screens several storeys tall, and arguably the world's most complicated railway station. Attractions here include the monumental **Tokyo Metropolitan Government Building**, the beautiful gardens of **Shinjuku Gyoen** and the lively and raffish **Kabukichō** entertainment area; the hipster paradise of **Shimokitazawa** is a short trip to the west.

In the north of Tokyo, offbeat pleasures include the rickety **Toden-Arakawa Line**, the city centre's last tramway; the Frank Lloyd Wright-designed Myonichi-kan in Ikebukuro; and a trio of pretty Japanese **gardens**.

OPPOSITE SENSŌ-JI, ASAKUSA

TOP 5 URBAN GREEN ESCAPES

Look at any map of central Tokyo and you'll quickly realize that there isn't much in the way of parkland – just 5.3 square metres of park per resident compared to 29 square metres in New York and 26 square metres in Paris. Then factor in that two of the biggest central patches of greenery (those immediately around the Imperial Palace and the Akasaka Detached Palace) are largely off-limits to the general public. Here are five bona fide urban green escapes; see ⓦ tokyo-park.or.jp for further suggestions.

Hama Rikyū Onshi Teien Once the duck-hunting grounds of the shogun, now a beautiful bayside retreat (see p.53).

Higashi Gyoen The east garden of the Imperial Palace, an oasis of tranquillity in the heart of the city (see p.43).

Meiji-jingū Inner Garden Peaceful grounds surrounding Tokyo's most important Shinto shrine (see p.116).

National Park for Nature Study A slightly inconvenient location helps to preserve this park's natural serenity (see p.109).

Shinjuku Gyoen English, French and Japanese garden styles combine harmoniously at this spacious park (see p.131).

High-speed trains put several important sights within **day-trip** range of Tokyo, including the ancient temple and shrine towns of **Kamakura** to the south and **Nikkō** to the north. **Mount Fuji**, 100km southwest of the capital, can be climbed in July and August, while the adjoining national park area of **Hakone** offers relaxed hiking amid beautiful lakeland scenery and the chance to take a dip in an onsen – a Japanese mineral bath.

When to go

One of the best times to visit is in the spring, from April to early May. At the start of this period (known as *hanami*) flurries of falling cherry blossom give the city a soft pink hue and by the end the temperatures are pleasant. October and November are also good months to come; this is when you'll catch the fireburst of **autumn** leaves in Tokyo's parks and gardens.

Avoid the steamy height of **summer** (late July to early Sept), when the city's humidity sees its citizens scurrying from one air-conditioned haven to another. From January through to March temperatures can dip to freezing, but the crisp blue **winter** skies are rarely disturbed by rain or snow showers. Carrying an umbrella in any season is a good idea but particularly so during *tsuyu*, the rainy season in June and July, and in September, when typhoons occasionally strike the coast.

When planning your visit also check the city's calendar of **festivals** and special events (see p.25) for any that may interest you. Note also that many attractions shut for several days around New Year when Tokyo becomes a ghost town, as many people return to their family homes elsewhere in the country.

AVERAGE MONTHLY TEMPERATURES AND RAINFALL

	Jan	Feb	March	April	May	June	July	Aug	Sept	Oct	Nov	Dec
Max/min (°C)	10/1	10/1	13/4	18/10	23/15	25/18	29/22	31/24	27/20	21/14	17/8	12/3
Max/min (°F)	49/33	50/34	55/40	65/50	73/58	78/65	84/72	87/75	80/68	70/57	62/47	58/38
Rainfall (mm)	110	155	228	254	244	305	254	203	279	228	162	96

Author picks

Our intrepid author has explored every corner of Tokyo in a quest to better understand the machinations of this fascinating city. Here are some of his favourite places and experiences.

Nakameguro This charming neighbourhood remains more popular with expats than visitors – pop by for a meal, a coffee or a stroll along the banks of the Meguro-gawa (p.108), and see what the tourists are missing.

Sake This Japanese rice-booze is a delight to drink in all its forms: head to an *izakaya* and have it served hot, housed in a lacquered box; take your pick of the stylish range of "cup sake" jars on offer at a specialist bar like *Buri* (p.178); or select one of the beautiful sake bottles (or even a simple carton) on sale at any convenience store.

Sky restaurants Many of Tokyo's tallest towers are topped with restaurants: head to Hibiki (p.157) or Hokkaidō (p.166) for cheap meals with gargantuan views.

Sumo This sport is often ridiculed by foreigners – until they visit a tournament for themselves, and witness the brute force and centuries-old pageantry on display. Even if you can't get to an event, it's on local TV from 4pm to 6pm during tournament time (p.208).

Tsukemen Most foreigners have heard of soba, udon and ramen, but relatively few know about *tsukemen*, Tokyo's own creation, and just the treat during the city's steamy summer – these springy noodles are served lukewarm, to be dipped into and then slurped from a side bowl of broth (box, p.155).

Odaiba beach Perhaps the best sunset view in the city: watch the distant skyscrapers fade to grey, then freckle with lights, behind the gleaming Rainbow Bridge (p.93).

> Our author recommendations don't end here. We've flagged up our favourite places – a perfectly sited hotel, an atmospheric café, a special restaurant – throughout the Guide, highlighted with the ★ symbol.

FROM TOP SAKE BOTTLES; ODAIBA BEACH; MEGURO-GAWA, NAKAMEGURO

17

things not to miss

It's impossible to see everything that Tokyo has to offer in one trip – and we don't suggest you try. What follows, in no particular order, is a selective and subjective taste of the city's highlights, from the most impressive museums to tranquil gardens, and the best day-trip destinations around the city. All highlights are colour-coded by chapter and have a page reference to take you straight into the Guide, where you can find out more.

1 SUMO
Page 208

Witness the titanic clashes of wrestling giants at the National Sumo Stadium in Ryōgoku.

2 ASAKUSA
Page 73

Home to old craft shops, traditional inns and the bustling Sensō-ji.

3 NATIONAL ART CENTER
Page 100

Set aside a chunk of time to explore this enormous gallery, a highlight of the so-called Roppongi Art Triangle.

4 MOUNT FUJI
Page 223

The stunning symmetry of this Japanese icon is visible from Tokyo, if you're in luck, and it's quite possible to climb it on a day-trip from the capital.

5 TRADITIONAL PERFORMING ARTS
Page 188

Enjoy kabuki, nō and *bunraku* puppetry at the National Theatre, Kabukiza Theatre or Shimbashi Embujō.

6 SUSHI
Box, page 155

There are innumerable places in which to scoff delectable raw fish – don't leave without giving it a try.

7 RIKUGI-EN
Page 140

A quintessential Japanese-style garden designed to reflect scenes from ancient Japanese poetry.

8 MATSURI
Page 25

Your visit may well coincide with one of the capital's umpteen *matsuri* (traditional festivals) – a slice of quintessential Japan.

9 NIKKŌ
Page 211

The dazzling Tōshō-gū is the star turn of this quiet mountain town, surrounded by some of the most beautiful countryside in the land.

10 GOLDEN GAI
Page 130

It's amazing how many bars are squeezed into this corner of neon-soaked Kabukichō – getting to and from your seat can resemble a game of Twister.

11 HANAMI PARTIES
Box, page 26

Pack a picnic and sit under the cherry blossoms in Ueno Park, around the Imperial Palace moat or along the Meguro-gawa.

12 ONSEN BATHING
Box, page 207

Soak in an old neighbourhood bathhouse such as Jakotsu-yu in Asakusa, or at the resort-like spa complex of Ōedo Onsen Monogatari in Tokyo Bay.

13 MEIJI-JINGŪ
Page 116

Enjoy one of the many annual festivals or regular wedding ceremonies held at Tokyo's most venerable Shinto shrine.

14 HARAJUKU
Page 113

Trawl the boutiques of Cat Street, dive into crowded Takeshita-dōri or simply sit and watch the weekend human circus spool by outside Harajuku station.

15 GHIBLI MUSEUM
Page 132

Most visitors will have seen at least one Studio Ghibli anime – get behind the scenes at this imaginative museum.

16 NEZU MUSEUM
Page 118

Housed in one of Tokyo's most impressive pieces of modern architecture, this repository of Asian arts also has a magnificent garden.

17 WATER BUSES
Page 24

Cruise down the Sumida-gawa or across Tokyo Bay on one of the city's ferry services, including the manga-inspired *Himiko* sightseeing boat.

Itineraries

The Japanese tend to holiday with their every second mapped out beforehand, but it's hard to do the same in their own capital city – it's a gigantic place whose every neighbourhood can eat up a full day of your time, if not several. If time is an issue, these itineraries will give you at least a taster of what Tokyo is all about, lassoing together some of its most spellbinding districts and enchanting sights.

THE YAMANOTE LINE

Japan Rail has an astonishing 32 separate lines crisscrossing the capital (and that's not even counting private lines, or those of the metro system), but most famous of all is the Yamanote-sen, which encircles central Tokyo and links some of its most significant neighbourhoods. The following itinerary takes you anticlockwise around the line.

Shinjuku Perhaps the most famous Tokyo neighbourhood of all, a high-rise, high-octane mishmash of pulsating neon, teeming crowds and hundreds upon hundreds of bars and restaurants. **See p.124**

Harajuku See the city's most colourful youngsters dressed up to the nines in outlandish attire. **See p.113**

Shibuya Just as madcap as Shinjuku – the sheer number of people making their way across the road when the traffic lights change outside Shibuya station is absolutely mind-boggling. **See p.121**

Ginza Head east from the newly revamped Tokyo station and you're in this classic shopping neighbourhood. **See p.54**

Akihabara Famed as the capital's capital of electronics, head here to get your fix of arcade games, maid cafés, manga-character stores and much more. **See p.58**

Ueno Stroll around Ueno Park's lily-filled lake, visit the zoo, experience a couple of temples and gardens, or hit a few excellent museums. **See p.64**

Ikebukuro Though off the regular tourist radar, there's plenty to like about Ikebukuro – nearby sights include a retro-futurist cathedral, several onsen and one of architect Frank Lloyd Wright's most famous creations. **See p.135**

THE BEST OF MODERN TOKYO

You only really need to walk down the street to get a handle on Tokyo's contemporary delights, but tracking down the sights on the following itinerary will give you a great introduction to the quirkiness of modern Tokyo.

Maid café Enjoy a coffee served by cartoon-character-costumed maids at *Maidreamin* in the neon-soaked mega-district of Shibuya. **See p.170**

Takeshita-dōri, Harajuku Kit yourself out in the latest weird and wonderful Tokyo styles along this fun, hip shopping alley. **See p.113**

Tokyo Metropolitan Government Building This twin-towered beast is one of the most astonishing looking buildings in the otherworldly neon craziness of Shinjuku. Head to its lofty observation decks for one of Tokyo's best sunset views. **See p.127**

Shimokitazawa A short way west of Shinjuku, the popularity of this relatively low-rise hipster hangout has ballooned of late – leave "regular" Tokyo behind and go shopping for some vintage clothes. **See p.132**

Contemporary art Top-rate galleries abound across the capital, with a particularly strong concentration of small, independent affairs in the Ginza and Roppongi neighbourhoods. **See box, p.54 & box, p.99**

Robot Restaurant It would spoil the surprise to describe this wacky performance venue in full. Pop along for an evening show and see what all the fuss is about. **See box, p.190**

Karaoke Japan blessed the world with this wonderful concept, so it would be a pity to leave the country without letting it hear your own crimes against music. **See box, p.181**

Jicoo Take an evening trip down to Tokyo Bay on this space-age floating bar. **See p.177**

THE BEST OF TRADITIONAL TOKYO

Though relentlessly modern, Tokyo wears its history and traditions with pride, and there are innumerable ways to get into the old-fashioned spirit of things – dip in and out of the following itinerary to explore the best of traditional Tokyo.

Hot springs If you're willing to bare all to total strangers, Tokyo is a great place to do it – there are several great bathhouses dotted around the city. **See box, p.207**

Sensō-ji This charming temple is the focus of the traditional Asakusa neighbourhood; try to visit it in the early evening, then head to nearby *Bar Six* to see the illuminations come on after sundown. **See p.75 & p.176**

Traditional gardens A whole host of immaculately sculpted gardens keep things natural amid the all-pervasive high-rise, with Rikugi-en a particularly appealing example. **See p.140**

Yushima Seidō Just west of Akihabara, this black-laquered shrine receives relatively few visitors, but scores highly on the atmosphere front. **See p.60**

Izakaya These traditional drinking dens also function as superbly atmospheric places to eat and make new friends. Try sticks of *yakitori* or deep-fried *kushiage*, give some bubbling *oden* a go, and wash the lot down with sake or a cold beer. **See p.175**

Traditional theatre Pop along to Kabukiza Theatre for a spellbinding kabuki performance. **See p.188**

TAXI, SHINJUKU

Basics

Getting there

If you're flying to Tokyo, note that airfares are at their highest around the Japanese holiday periods of Golden Week (early May) and the O-bon festival in mid-August, as well as at Christmas and New Year, when seats are at a premium. Flying at weekends is also generally more expensive; you may end up paying more than the prices quoted below.

Tokyo isn't a difficult city for the independent traveller to negotiate, nor need it be horrendously expensive. However, if you're worried about the cost or potential language problems, a **package tour** is worth considering. Flight-and-accommodation packages can be cheaper than booking the two separately, particularly if you want to stay in the more upmarket hotels. Prices for a return flight, five nights' accommodation at a three- or four-star hotel and airport transfers begin at around £800 from the UK, US$1000 from the US and Aus$1800 from Australia, based on double occupancy.

Flights from the UK and Ireland

All Nippon Airways (ANA; Ⓦana.co.jp), British Airways (Ⓦbritishairways.com) and Japan Airlines (Ⓦjal.co.jp) all fly nonstop **from London** to Tokyo, with the trip taking about 12hr. Return fares start from around £500 direct if you're very lucky, but you'll usually have to transfer (usually in Russia or the Middle East) to get prices like this; fares can fall as low as £400, so it pays to shop around and be flexible with your schedule. There are no direct flights **from Dublin**; again, transferring in the Middle East can bring return prices as low as €600, though it's always worth considering a budget flight to London or mainland Europe if you can find a good deal from there.

Flights from the US and Canada

A number of airlines fly nonstop **from the US and Canada** to Tokyo, including Air Canada (Ⓦaircanada.com), All Nippon Airways (ANA), American Airlines (Ⓦaa.com), Japan Airlines (JAL) and United (Ⓦunited.com), with connections from virtually every regional airport. Flying time is around 15hr from New York, 13hr from Chicago and 10hr from Los Angeles.

Many flights are offered at substantial discounts, so keep an eye out for special offers. In general, return fares to Tokyo start at around US$700 from Chicago or New York, US$550 from Los Angeles and Can$700 from Vancouver. However, be prepared to pay up to double these fares (especially for direct flights), and note that to get the cheapest deals you may have to transfer in China – which, unfortunately, involves looping back on yourself.

Flights from Australia, New Zealand and South Africa

Qantas (Ⓦqantas.com), Japan Airlines (JAL) and Air New Zealand (Ⓦairnewzealand.com) operate nonstop flights to Tokyo **from Australia and New Zealand**. Flying time is around 10hr from Australia and 12hr from New Zealand. Return fares from Australia to Tokyo sometimes go under Aus$500 with Jetstar (Ⓦjetstar.com), who fly direct from Cairns, the Gold Coast, Melbourne and Sydney. From New Zealand direct routings cost NZ$1100 and up, though you can lop a fair bit off this by flying with Jetstar, via Australia.

Flying **from South Africa**, you'll be routed through Southeast Asia or the Middle East. Promotional fares can be as cheap as R8000, though you're more likely to be paying in the region of R11,000 and above.

Flights from other Asian countries

If you're already in Asia, it can be quite cheap to fly to Tokyo with **low-cost regional carriers**. Air Asia (Ⓦairasia.com) have flights from Kuala Lumpur and Bangkok; Cebu Pacific (Ⓦcebupacificair.com) fly from Cebu and Manila; Eastar (Ⓦeastarjet.com), Jeju Air (Ⓦjejuair.net) and Jin (Ⓦjinair.com) each

---

A BETTER KIND OF TRAVEL

At Rough Guides we are passionately committed to travel. We believe it helps us understand the world we live in and the people we share it with – and of course tourism is vital to many developing economies. But the scale of modern tourism has also damaged some places irreparably, and climate change is accelerated by most forms of transport, especially flying. All Rough Guides' flights are carbon-offset, and every year we donate money to a variety of environmental charities.

run flights from Seoul; HK Express (**W**hkexpress .com) make the run from Hong Kong; and Scoot (**W**flyscoot.com) scoot over from Bangkok, Singapore and Taipei. Japanese operations include Peach (**W**flypeach.com), who offer flights from Seoul, Shanghai and Taipei; and Vanilla Air (**W**vanilla-air.com), who connect to Ho Chi Minh City, Hong Kong and Taipei.

Flights from within Japan

For flights to Tokyo from within Japan, the big two **domestic airlines** are All Nippon Airways (ANA; **W**ana.co.jp) and Japan Airlines (JAL; **W**jal.co.jp). Both carriers offer substantial discounts for advance bookings, with an extra discount if the booking is made entirely online. There's little to choose between the two as far as prices and quality of service are concerned.

Local **low-cost airlines** have ballooned of late, providing much-needed competition to the rail operators; these include Jetstar (**W**jetstar.com), Peach (**W**flypeach.com), Skymark (**W**skymark.co.jp), Solaseed Air (**W**solaseedair.jp) and Vanilla Air (**W**vanilla-air.com). Services are usually fine, though with the usual restrictions on baggage allowance.

AGENTS AND INTERNATIONAL TOUR OPERATORS

Artisans of Leisure US ☎ 1 800 214 8144, **W** artisansofleisure.com. Luxury private tours, including ones focused on food, art, gardens and even ceramics.

IACE Travel US ☎ 1 866 735 4223, **W** iace-asia.com. US-based Japan specialist with many packages and themed tours to Tokyo.

Inside Japan UK ☎ 0117 370 9751, US ☎ 1 303 952 0379, Australia ☎ 07 3703 3838; **W** insidejapantours.com. Great range of well-designed small-group, self-guided and fully tailored trips, ranging from Tokyo stopovers to Mount Fuji climbs.

Into Japan UK ☎ 01865 841 443, **W** intojapan.co.uk. Upmarket tailor-made and special-interest tours, plus off-the-peg fifteen-day Luxury Japan packages.

Japan Journeys UK ☎ 020 7766 5267, **W** japanjourneys.co.uk. Tokyo options include an anime- and manga- themed tour.

Japan Package Australia ☎ 02 9264 7384, **W** www.japan package.com.au. Sydney-based agent offering a variety of Japan packages (including plenty of anime tours) as well as Japan Rail Passes.

Japan Travel Bureau (JTB) US ☎ 1 877 798 9808, **W** online .jtbusa.com; Canada ☎ 416 367 5824, **W** jtb.ca; Australia ☎ 1300 739 330, **W** japantravel.com.au. The various wings of this Japanese operation offer tours of the capital, Fuji, Nikkō and beyond; they also handle Sunrise Tours (see p.25).

Japan Travel Centre UK ☎ 020 7611 0150, **W** www.japantravel -centre.com. Offers flights, accommodation packages, Japan Rail Passes and guided tours.

Magical Japan UK ☎ 0161 440 7332, **W** magicaljapan.co.uk. Various guided tours, all offering at least three days in and around Tokyo; customized packages possible.

Mitsui Travel Australia ☎ 02 9232 2720, **W** mitsuitravel.com.au. Specializing in shorter tours, including a two-day onsen stay in Tokyo and Hakone.

Travel Japan Australia ☎ 02 9267 0555, **W** traveljapan.com.au. Provides everything from flights to Tokyo to packages and customized itineraries.

Travel Wright **W** wrightwaytravel.org. An annual tour to Japan (usually Sept) focused around the work and legacy of architect Frank Lloyd Wright.

Arrival

Tokyo boasts two major international airports: Narita, the old stalwart out east; and Haneda, far more central, recently upgraded, and hosting an ever-greater range of international connections. Other access points to the city include a slew of train stations, long-distance bus terminals and ferry points, all for domestic connections only.

By plane to Narita

Narita International Airport (成田空港; ☎0476 34-8000, **W**www.narita-airport.jp) is some 66km east of the city centre. There are three terminals; T3 is a new wing used by low-cost carriers and designed with a nod to the 2020 Olympics, while the other two both have **tourist information** and **accommodation-booking** booths. If you have a **Japan Rail Pass** (see p.23) exchange order, you can arrange to use your pass immediately (it's valid on JR services from the airport); pick it up at the JR travel agencies – not the ticket offices – in the basement, though be aware the queues can be very long. Alternatively, you can collect it later from any major JR station.

Trains to Tokyo

The fastest way into Tokyo **from Narita** is on the **Skyliner** (1–3 hourly, 7.30am–10.30pm; 41min to Ueno; ¥2470) express train operated by Keisei (**W**keisei.co.jp), who also offer the cheapest train connection into town in the form of the *tokkyū* (limited express) service (every 30min; 6am–11pm; 1hr 11min to Ueno; ¥1030). Both services stop at Nippori (same prices), where it's easy to transfer to the Yamanote or the Keihin Tōhoku lines.

JR's **Narita Express**, also known as the **N'EX** (**W**www.jreast.co.jp/e/nex), runs to several city stations. The cheapest fare is ¥3020 to Tokyo station (every 30min, 7.45am–9.45pm; 1hr), and there are also frequent direct N'EX services to Shinjuku (hourly; 1hr 20min) for ¥3190. N'EX services to Ikebukuro (1hr 20min; ¥3190) and Yokohama (1hr 30min; ¥4290) via Shinagawa are much less frequent. JR usually run some kind of **discount scheme** for foreign passport holders; at the time of writing, return tickets valid for two weeks were available to all stations (even Yokohama) for ¥4000. You can save some money by taking the slightly slower, but far less comfortable, JR *kaisoku* (rapid) train to Tokyo station (hourly; 1hr 25min; ¥1320).

Buses and taxis to Tokyo

The cheapest way into Tokyo is on the **Access Narita buses** (Ⓦaccessnarita.jp), which head to Ginza and Tokyo station, and cost just ¥1000; departing every 15min at peak times, they even have toilets on board, but they can be prone to traffic delays. You can pay with cash on the bus; check the website for boarding points.

Alternatively, the more costly **Airport Limousine buses** (Ⓣ03 3665 7220, Ⓦwww.limousinebus.co.jp) can be useful if you're weighed down by luggage and staying at or near a major hotel. Tickets are sold in each of the arrival lobbies; the buses depart directly outside (check which platform you need) and stop at many major hotels and train stations around the city. Journeys to central Tokyo typically cost ¥3100, and take at least ninety minutes. Once you factor in the cost of a taxi from one of the train stations to your hotel, these buses can be a good deal; as with JR trains, it's worth keeping an eye out for discounts. The ¥3400 **Limousine & Metro Pass** combines a one-way bus trip from Narita to central Tokyo and a 24-hour metro pass valid on nine of Tokyo's thirteen subway lines.

Lastly, **taxis** to the city centre cost around ¥30,000, and are little faster than going by bus.

By plane to Haneda

Jutting into Tokyo Bay just 20km south of the Imperial Palace, **Haneda Airport** (羽田空港; flight information Ⓣ03 5757 8111, Ⓦhaneda-airport.jp) is where most domestic flights touch down, as well as an ever-increasing roster of international services, including some long-haul destinations.

From Haneda Airport, it's a short monorail journey (every 5–10min, 5.20am–11.15pm; 13–19min; ¥490) to Hamamatsuchō station on the Yamanote line. Alternatively, you can board a Keihin Kūkō-line train to Shinagawa or Sengakuji and connect directly with other rail and subway lines. A limousine bus

(Ⓣ03 3665 7220, Ⓦwww.limousinebus.co.jp) to the city centre will set you back ¥1030–1230, depending upon your destination, and take around an hour; the same goes for the Haneda Airport Express services (Ⓦhnd-bus.com). A taxi from Haneda to central Tokyo costs ¥4000–8000.

By train

Shinkansen trains from western Japan pull in to **Tokyo station** (東京駅) and **Shinagawa station** (品川駅), around 6km southwest. Most Shinkansen services from the north arrive at Tokyo station, though a few services go only as far as **Ueno station** (上野駅), some 4km northeast of the Imperial Palace. Tokyo, Shinagawa and Ueno stations are all on the Yamanote line and are connected to several subway lines, putting them within reach of most of the capital. Other long-distance JR services stop at Tokyo and Ueno stations, Shinjuku station on Tokyo's west side and Ikebukuro station in the city's northwest corner.

Non-JR trains terminate at different stations: the Tōkyū Tōyoko line from Yokohama ends at **Shibuya station** (渋谷駅), though some services carry on to Ikebukuro and beyond after they magically turn into the Fukutōshin subway line; the Tōbu Nikkō line runs from Nikkō to **Asakusa station** (浅草駅), east of Ueno; and the Odakyū line from Hakone finishes at **Shinjuku station** (新宿駅), which is also the terminus for the Seibu Shinjuku line from Kawagoe. All these stations have subway connections and (apart from Asakusa) are on the Yamanote rail line.

By bus

Long-distance buses pull in at several major stations around the city, making transport connections straightforward. The main overnight services from Kyoto and Ōsaka arrive at the eastern Yaesu exit of Tokyo station; other buses arrive at Ikebukuro, Shibuya, Shinagawa and Shinjuku.

By boat

Long-distance **ferries** from Tokushima in Shikoku and in Kyūshū arrive at Tokyo Ferry Terminal (東京フェリーターミナル) at Ariake, on the man-made island of Odaiba (see p.89) in Tokyo Bay; for details, see Ocean Tōkyū Ferry (Ⓣ03 3528 1011, Ⓦwww.otf.jp). Buses run from the port to Shin-Kiba station, from which you can catch the metro or the overland JR Keiyō line. A taxi from the port to central Tokyo costs around ¥2000.

City transport

Tokyo's public transport system is efficient, clean and safe, with trains and subways the best way of getting around; a lack of signs in English makes the bus system a lot more challenging. For short, cross-town journeys, taxis are handy and, if shared by a group of people, not all that expensive. Sightseeing tours are also worth considering if you are pushed for time or would like a guided commentary.

By subway

Its colourful map may look daunting, but Tokyo's **subway** is relatively easy to negotiate: the simple colour-coding on trains and maps, as well as clear signposts (many also in English), directional arrows and alpha-numeric station codes, make this by far the most *gaijin*-friendly form of transport. You'll have a much less crowded journey if you avoid travelling at rush hour (7.30–9am & 5.30–7.30pm).

There are two systems, the nine-line **Tokyo Metro** (Ⓦ www.tokyometro.jp) and the four-line **Toei** (Ⓦ www.kotsu.metro.tokyo.jp). The systems share some stations, but unless you buy a special ticket from the vending machines that specifies your route from one system to the other, or you have a pass (see box below), you cannot switch mid-journey between the two sets of lines without paying extra

at the ticket barrier. Subways also connect to overland train lines, such as the Yamanote. A colour **map** of the subway system appears at the back of this book (see pp.298–299).

Tickets are bought at the vending machines beside the electronic ticket gates (ticket sales windows are only found at major stations). Most trips across central Tokyo cost no more than ¥200. Ticket machines generally have multi-language functions, but if you're fazed by the wide range of price buttons, buy the cheapest ticket (usually ¥170) and sort out the difference with the gatekeeper at the other end.

Trains run daily from around 5am to just after midnight, and during peak daytime hours as frequently as every five minutes (and at least every fifteen minutes at other times). Maps close to the ticket barriers (usually outside them, annoyingly) indicate where the exits emerge.

For **planning journeys** on both subway and regular trains, the route function on Google Maps (Ⓦ maps.google.com) usually works like a charm. A local alternative is Hyperdia (Ⓦ www.hyperdia .com), which also offers a helpful smartphone app.

By train

Japan Railways East (Ⓦ jreast.co.jp), part of the national rail network, runs the main overland services in and around Tokyo, and there are also several **private railways**, including lines run by Odakyū,

---

TOKYO TRANSPORT PASSES AND TRAVEL CARDS

A useful alternative to buying individual tickets is to get one of the many types of pass available, or to use a prepaid travel card.

PASSES

Both Tokyo Metro and Toei have **24-hour tickets** for use on their respective subway systems (¥600 and ¥700 respectively), with the Toei pass also covering the city's buses; depending upon your precise plans, it may work out better to get a one-day **economy pass** covering both systems (¥1000).

JR has its own one-day **Tokunai Pass** (¥750), which gives unlimited travel on JR trains within the Tokyo Metropolitan District Area.

For day-use of the city's subways, JR trains and buses there's the **Tokyo Free Ticket** (¥1590), but you'd really have to be tearing all over town to get your money's worth.

PREPAID CARDS

Although they don't save you any money, the most convenient way to travel is to use a **Pasmo** (Ⓦ www.pasmo.co.jp) or JR **Suica** stored-value card. Both can be used on all subways, many buses and both JR and private trains in the wider Tokyo area. The card can be recharged at ticket machines and ticket offices. To get either card (available from ticket machines in metro and JR stations), you need to spend a minimum of ¥2000, of which ¥500 is a deposit, which will be returned to you, plus any remaining value (minus a small processing fee) when you cash in the card before leaving Tokyo.

JAPANESE ADDRESSES

Japanese **addresses** are, frankly, a little bit ridiculous – when it's impossible to find the building you're looking for even when you're standing right in front of it, it's clear that there are some major system failures. This stems from the fact that in many places, including Tokyo, **few roads have names**; instead, city districts are split into numbered blocks, on which the numbers themselves are usually not visible.

Addresses start with the largest **administrative district** – in Tokyo's case it's Tōkyō-*to* (metropolis), but elsewhere most commonly it's the *ken* (prefecture) accompanied by a seven-digit postcode – for example, Saitama-ken 850-0072. Next comes the *ku* (ward; for example Shinjuku-ku), followed by the *chō* (district), then three numbers representing the *chōme* (local neighbourhood), block and individual building. Finally there might come the building name and the floor on which the business or person is located – much like the American system, 1F is the ground floor, 2F the first floor above ground, and B1F the first floor below ground.

Japanese addresses are therefore written in **reverse order** from the Western system. However, when written in English, they usually follow the Western order; this is the system we adopt in this guide. For example, the address 2-12-7 Roppongi, Minato-ku identifies building number 7, somewhere on block 12 of number 2 *chōme* in Roppongi district, in the Minato ward of Tokyo (this can also be written as 12-7 Roppongi, 2-chōme, Minato-ku). Where the block is entirely taken up by one building, the address will have only two numbers.

Actually **locating an address** on the ground can be frustrating – even Japanese people find it tough. The old-fashioned way is to have the address written down, preferably in Japanese, and then get to the nearest train or bus station; once in the neighbourhood, find a local police box (*kōban*), which will have a detailed local map. The modern-day solution is, inevitably, Google Maps, on which the results of address searches are usually accurate. If all else fails, don't be afraid to phone – often someone will come to meet you.

Tōbu, Seibu and Tōkyū. They all have their own colour coding on maps, with the various JR lines coming in many different shades – take care not to confuse these with those of the subway network. The famous JR **Yamanote train line** (shown in green on network maps, and indicated by green flashes on the trains) loops around the city centre. Another useful JR route is the orange **Chūō line**, which starts at Tokyo station and runs west to Shinjuku and the suburbs beyond; rapid services (look for the red *kanji* characters on the side of the train, or on the platform displays) miss out some stations. JR's yellow **Sōbu line** goes from Chiba in the east to Mitaka in the west, and runs parallel to the Chūō line in the centre of Tokyo. The blue JR **Keihin Tōhoku line** runs from Ōmiya in the north through Tokyo station, and on to Yokohama and beyond. It's fine to transfer between JR lines on the same ticket.

The lowest **fare** on JR lines is ¥140. Ticket machines are easy to operate if buying single tickets, if you can find your destination on the network maps above. Both Pasmo and JR Suica prepaid cards (see box opposite) work at the ticket gates.

If you're planning a lot of train travel around Japan in a short period of time, the **Japan Rail Pass** (🌐japanrailpass.net) can be a good deal, though you have to buy this outside Japan; prepare for giant queues if picking it up at the airport, though

note that you can also pick it up from any major JR station. JR East (🌐www.jreast.co.jp) offers its own cheaper versions of the pass, covering its network in the Tokyo region and northern Japan; these can be purchased in Japan from JR ticket offices.

By monorail

Tokyo has a couple of monorail systems: the **Tokyo monorail**, which runs from Hamamatsuchō to Haneda Airport (see p.21); and the **Yurikamome monorail**, which connects Shimbashi with Toyosu via Odaiba (see p.89). These services operate like the city's private rail lines – you buy separate tickets for journeys on them or travel using the various stored-value cards, such as Pasmo and Suica (see box opposite).

By bus

Buses are a good way of cutting across the few areas of Tokyo not served by a subway or train line, though they're little used by overseas visitors. Compared to the subway there's little information in English; you may have to get used to recognizing *kanji* place names, or memorize the numbers of useful bus routes. The final destination is listed on the front of the bus, along with the route number. You pay on entry, by dropping the flat rate (¥210) into the fare box by the driver (there's a machine in the box for changing notes); travel cards are also accepted.

By bicycle

You'll see people **cycling** all over Tokyo, but despite this it's not a terribly bike-friendly city. Most locals cycle on the pavement, there being very few dedicated bike lanes, and Japanese rules of courtesy dictate that even though every bike has a bell, absolutely nobody uses them – even if they're coming up behind you, at speed, on a narrow path, in the rain. In addition to the bike **rental outfits** listed here, check out Ⓦcycle-tokyo.cycling.jp, which has lots of useful information about bike rental and cycling in the city. Note that there's a free bike-rental scheme in operation on Sundays around the Imperial Palace (see p.41).

BIKE RENTAL

Community Cycle Ⓦ docomo-cycle.jp. One of the easiest means of getting hold of a bike, with cycle docks across the city; after registering online (you pay with your bank card) and receiving a pass code, it's ¥150 for the first half-hour, then ¥100 for each subsequent one.
Muji The Ginza outlet of this huge Japanese chain (see map, p.52) rents out bikes out for ¥1000 a day (¥3000 deposit required); daily 10am–8pm.
Sumida Park One of the cheapest rental operations in the city, enabling you to see the Asakusa area at leisure (see p.73 for details).
Tokyobike Ⓦ tokyobike.com. Without doubt the coolest bike store and the coolest rental spot in the city, if a little expensive; it's good if you're in the Ueno and Yanaka area (see p.64 for details).

By ferry

The Tokyo Cruise Ship Company (Ⓦsuijobus.co.jp) runs several **ferry** services, known as *suijō basu* (water buses), in and around Tokyo Bay. The popular Sumida-gawa service (every 30–50min, 10am–6.30pm; 40min; ¥780) plies the route between **Hinode Pier** on Tokyo Bay and **Asakusa** to the northeast of the city centre. Some boats call at the **Hama Rikyū Teien** (see p.53), entry to which is often included with the ticket price; you can also head to Hinode from Odaiba (20min; ¥480). The ferries' large picture windows give a completely different view of the city from the one you'll get on the streets – reason enough for hopping aboard.

For a little more you can travel on the *Himiko* or the *Hotaluna*, near-identical space-age ferries that run from Asakusa to Odaiba (6 daily; ¥1560), sometimes via Hinode. Designed by Matsumoto Reiji, a famous manga artist, these silver-painted ships become floating bars at night (see p.177).

Hinode Pier (close by Hinode station on the Yurikamome monorail or a 10min walk from Hamamatsuchō station on the Yamanote line) is also the jumping-off point for several good daily **cruises** around Tokyo Bay, and for ferries to various points around the island of Odaiba, or across to Kasai Rinkai-kōen on the east side of the bay.

By taxi

For short hops, **taxis** are often the best option. The basic rate is ¥730 for the first 2km, after which the meter racks up ¥80 every 275m, plus a time charge when the taxi is moving at less than 10km per hour. Between 11pm and 5am, rates are twenty to thirty percent higher.

Most taxis have a limit of four passengers. There's never any need to open or close the passenger doors, which are operated by the taxi driver – trying to do it manually can damage the mechanism, and will get your driver seething. This is just one reason why some taxis refuse to take foreigners; communication difficulties are another, bigger reason, and as such it's always a good idea to have the name and address of your destination clearly written on a piece of paper (in Japanese, if possible). If your driver doesn't know exactly where your destination is, a stop at a local police box may be necessary to locate the exact address.

When flagging down a taxi, a red light next to the driver means the cab is free; green means it's occupied. There are designated stands in the busiest parts of town; after the trains stop at night, be prepared for long queues, especially in areas such as Roppongi and Shinjuku. Major taxi firms include Hinomaru Limousine (☎03 3212 0505, Ⓦhinomaru.co.jp) and Nippon Kōtsū (☎03 3799 9220, Ⓦwww.nihon-kotsu.co.jp/en).

Those who have sworn off licenced taxis forever will be glad to know that **Uber** (Ⓦuber.com) is functional in Tokyo, though it's still not in common use among locals. It's not all that much cheaper than the regular cabs (and quite often more expensive), though there are no late-night surcharges, and drivers are more likely to speak at least a little English.

Sightseeing tours

For a quick overview of Tokyo there are the usual **bus tours**, offered by operations such as Hato Bus (Ⓦwww.hatobus.com), Japan Grey Line (Ⓦwww.jgl.co.jp/inbound) and Sky Bus (see opposite), ranging from half-day jaunts around the central sights (around ¥4500, excluding lunch) to visits out to

Kamakura, Nikkō and Hakone. If the sky's the limit on your budget, go for a spin in a **helicopter** instead: Excel Air Service (Ⓦ excel-air.com) will take you for a fifteen-minute flight for around ¥20,000.

If bus tours are not your cup of tea, but you still fancy having a guide on hand, you might consider one of the various **walking** or **cycling** tours (see below), **culinary** tours and activities (see box, p.170) or sightseeing **ferries** (see opposite). Free walking tours are available on selected days of the week around the Imperial Palace (see p.41), Ueno (see p.64) and Asakusa (see p.73). Finally, there's even a go-kart tour inspired by the Mario Kart game (see box, p.110).

LOCAL TOUR OPERATORS

Eyexplore Tokyo Ⓦ eyexploretokyo.com. Small outfit running a few photo-tours of the city (¥9900).

Haunted Tokyo Ⓦ hauntedtokyotours.com. Interesting English-language tours focusing on the spookier parts of Tokyo's history (usually 2–3hr; ¥4500).

His Go ☎ 080 4869 0514, Ⓦ hisgo.com. Try your hand at calligraphy, *taiko* drumming or wielding a samurai sword, or one of the many other cultural experiences offered by this wing of local tour company HIS. Small-group and customized options available.

Sky Bus ☎ 03 3215 0008, Ⓦ skybus.jp. Offers four tours, most in open-top double-decker buses, including a route around the Imperial Palace grounds and through Ginza and Marunouchi (50min; ¥1600), and an Odaiba night tour (2hr; ¥2100). They also have three hop-on, hop-off routes (¥3500), with tickets valid for 24hr.

Sunrise Tours ☎ 03 5796 5454, Ⓦ www.jtb-sunrisetours.jp. Affiliated to JTB (see p.20), this operator has various Tokyo programmes on offer, including sumo and maid-café tours.

Tokyo Great Cycling Tour ☎ 03 4590 2995, Ⓦ tokyocycling.jp. See the capital on a couple of guided bike tours (6hr; ¥10,000 including lunch) that run on Tuesdays, Thursdays and weekends.

The media

English newspapers and magazines are readily available, while on TV and radio there are some programmes presented in English or with an alternative English soundtrack, such as the main news bulletins on NHK. Throughout this guide we list English-language websites wherever useful; most places also have Japanese-only websites.

Newspapers and magazines

The English-language daily **newspaper** you'll most commonly find at Tokyo's newsstands is *The Japan Times* (Ⓦ japantimes.co.jp). It has comprehensive coverage of national and international news, as well as occasionally interesting features, some culled from the world's media; the online sumo coverage is good when there's a tournament on. There's also the *Daily Yomiuri* (Ⓦ yomiuri.co.jp) newspaper, as well as English-language magazines including *Time* and *The Economist*.

The free monthly **magazine** *Metropolis* (Ⓦ metropolisjapan.com) is packed with interesting features, reviews, and listings of film, music and other events, as is their website; the same can be said for *Time Out* (Ⓦ timeout.com/tokyo), whose magazine comes out every two months. The twice-yearly publication *KIE* (Kateigahō International Edition; Ⓦ int.kateigaho.com) is a gorgeous, glossy magazine covering cultural matters, with many travel features and in-depth profiles of areas of Tokyo and other parts of Japan. Also worth a look is *Tokyo Notice Board* (Ⓦ tokyonoticeboard.co.jp), a freesheet devoted almost entirely to classifieds.

You'll find all these at the tourist information centres, larger hotels, foreign-language bookstores (see p.197) and bars or restaurants frequented by *gaijin*.

Television

Funded much like Britain's BBC, the state broad-caster **NHK** (Ⓦ nhk.or.jp) has two **TV channels** – the regular NHK, and NHK–Educational – as well as three satellite channels, and NHK World, an inter-national channel which often veers towards propa-ganda. Many TV sets can access a bilingual soundtrack, and it's thus possible to tune into English-language commentary for NHK's nightly 7pm news; films and imported TV shows on both NHK and the commercial channels are also sometimes broadcast with an alternative English soundtrack. **Digital, satellite and cable** channels available in all top-end hotels include BBC World, CNN and MTV.

Festivals and events

No matter when you visit Tokyo, chances are there'll be a religious festival (*matsuri*) taking place somewhere – fantastic fun for first-time visitors and old Tokyo hands alike. You'll find details of upcoming events online; try the official city site (Ⓦ www.gotokyo.org), or

those of the main expat magazines (see p.25). The dates given in the festival listings here can vary according to the lunar calendar, so check ahead if you wish to attend a particular event.

Of the major events listed, by far the most important is **New Year**, when most of the city closes down for a week (roughly Dec 28–Jan 3). Tokyo also hosts three grand **sumo tournaments** each year (see p.208), as well as film, theatre and music festivals. Several non-Japanese festivals which have also caught on include **Valentine's Day** (Feb 14), when women give men gifts of chocolate; on **White Day** (March 14) men get their turn (white chocolates, of course). Later in the year, **Pocky Day** (November 11) is an even more overtly commercial affair, even by Japanese standards – people give their loved ones boxes of Pocky, sweet breadsticks whose skinny nature vaguely resembles the date (eleven-eleven). **Christmas** is also commercial, and celebrated with glee; Christmas Eve, in particular, is one of the most popular date nights of the year, and all fancy restaurants are booked solid. By contrast, **New Year's Eve** is a fairly subdued, family-oriented event.

For details of public holidays, see p.37.

JANUARY

Ganjitsu (or Gantan) January 1. The *hatsu-mōde* – the first shrine visit of the year – draws the crowds to Meiji-jingū, Hie-jinja, Kanda Myōjin and other city shrines to pray for good fortune. Performances of traditional dance and music take place at Yasukuni-jinja. National holiday.

Kōkyo Ippan Sanga January 2. Thousands of loyal Japanese – and a few curious foreigners – troop into the Imperial Palace grounds to greet the emperor. The royal family appear on the balcony several times from 9.30am to 3pm.

Dezomeshiki January 6. At Tokyo Big Sight in Odaiba, firemen in Edo-period costume pull off dazzling stunts atop long bamboo ladders.

Seijin-no-hi (Coming-of-Age Day) Second Monday in January. A colourful pageant of 20-year-old women, and a few men, visit city shrines in traditional dress to celebrate their entry into adulthood. At Meiji-jingū various ancient rituals are observed, including a ceremonial archery contest. National holiday.

FEBRUARY

Setsubun February 3 or 4. On the last day of winter by the lunar calendar, people scatter lucky beans around their homes and at shrines or temples, to drive out evil and welcome in the year's good luck. The liveliest festivities take place at Sensō-ji, Kanda Myōjin, Zōjō-ji and Hie-jinja.

MARCH

Hina Matsuri (Doll Festival) March 3. Families with young girls display beautiful dolls of the emperor, empress and their courtiers dressed in ancient costume. Department stores, hotels and museums often put on special displays at this time.

Hi Watari Second Sunday in March. A spectacular fire-walking ceremony held at the foot of Mount Takao.

Anime Japan Late March ⓦ www.anime-japan.jp. Three-day event during which Japan's anime industry displays its shows and films for the coming year.

Cherry Blossoms Usually late March to early April. Not a festival as such, and the precise dates are dictated by the weather, but the coming of the cherry blossoms is *huge* in Tokyo, with hordes gathering to eat, drink and be merry in picnic-like affairs known as *hanami* (see box below).

APRIL

Art Fair Tokyo Early April ⓦ artfairtokyo.com. Tokyo International Forum is the focus for Japan's largest commercial art event, with around a hundred local and national galleries participating.

Hana Matsuri April 8. The Buddha's birthday is celebrated in all Tokyo's temples with either parades or quieter celebrations, during which a small statue of Buddha is sprinkled with sweet tea.

Jibeta Matsuri Mid-April. In this celebration of fertility, an iron phallus is forged and giant wooden phalluses are paraded around Kanayama-jinja, in the southern Tokyo suburb of Kawasaki, amid dancing crowds, including a group of demure transvestites.

Kamakura Matsuri Mid-April. Kamakura's week-long festival includes traditional dances, costume parades and horseback archery.

Earth Day Tokyo Around 22 April ⓦ earthday-tokyo.org. The capital joins in global celebrations of our planet's environment with big events in Yoyogi Park and elsewhere.

MAY

Design Festa May and November ⓦ designfesta.com. Thousands of young and aspiring artists converge on Tokyo Big Sight in Odaiba for this twice-yearly weekend celebration of design.

Kodomo-no-hi (Children's Day) May 5. Families fly carp banners, symbolizing strength, outside their homes. National holiday.

Rainbow Pride Early May ⓦ tokyorainbowpride.com. The largest Pride event in the country, usually followed one day later by a suitably colourful parade.

Kanda Matsuri Mid-May. One of the city's top three festivals, taking place in odd-numbered years at Kanda Myōjin, during which people in

---

HANAMI PARTIES

With the arrival of spring in late March or early April, a pink tide of **cherry blossom** washes north over Tokyo, lasting little more than a week. The finest displays are along the moat around the Imperial Palace (particularly the section close by Yasukuni-jinja), in Ueno-kōen, Aoyama Cemetery, Shinjuku Gyoen, the riverside Sumida-kōen and on the banks of the Meguro-gawa by Nakameguro station, where every tree shelters a blossom-viewing (**hanami**) party.

Heian-period costume escort eighty gilded *mikoshi* (portable shrines) through the streets.

Tōshō-gū Haru Matsuri May 17–18. Huge procession of one thousand armour-clad warriors and three *mikoshi*, commemorating the burial of Shogun Tokugawa Ieyasu in Nikkō in 1617; takes place outside the eponymous shrine (see p.66).

Sanja Matsuri Third weekend in May. Tokyo's most boisterous festival, when over one hundred *mikoshi* are jostled through the streets of Asakusa, accompanied by lion dancers, geisha and musicians.

JUNE

Sannō Matsuri Mid-June. In even-numbered years the last of the big three *matsuri* (after Kanda and Sanja) takes place, focusing on colourful processions of *mikoshi* through Akasaka.

JULY

Rainbow Reel Tokyo Mid-July Ⓦ rainbowreeltokyo.com. One of the best Tokyo film festivals, dedicated to queer movies.

Fuji Rock Late July. The biggest event on the Japanese musical calendar, and a major draw for both bands and festival-goers from overseas (see box, p.185).

Lantern Festivals Late July and early August. Connected to O-bon (see below), this tradition sees paper lanterns floated down various waterways, including the Imperial Palace moat.

Hanabi Taikai Late July and early August. The summer skies explode with thousands of fireworks, harking back to traditional "river-opening" ceremonies to mark the start of the summer boating season. The Sumida-gawa display is the most spectacular (view it from river boats or Asakusa's Sumida-kōen on the last Sat in July), but those in Edogawa, Tamagawa, Arakawa and Harumi come close. Kamakura has its *hanabi taikai* on August 10.

AUGUST

Fukagawa Matsuri Mid-August. Every three years Tomioka Hachiman-gū, a shrine in Fukagawa (east across the Sumida River from central Tokyo), hosts the city's wettest festival, when spectators throw buckets of water over a hundred *mikoshi* being shouldered through the streets.

O-bon Mid-August. Families gather around their ancestral graves and much of Tokyo closes down, while many neighbourhoods stage dances in honour of the deceased.

Summer Sonic Mid-August Ⓦ summersonic.com. Two-day rock festival (see box, p.185).

Asakusa Samba Carnival Last Saturday in August. Rio comes to the streets of Asakusa with this spectacular parade of sequinned and feathered dancers – it might sound a bit random, but there are over 200,000 Brazilians living in Japan.

SEPTEMBER

Tsurugaoka Hachiman-gū Matsuri September 14–16. Annual shrine festival of Tsurugaoka Hachiman-gū in Kamakura. The highlight is a demonstration of horseback archery on the final day.

Ningyō Kuyō September 25. A funeral service for unwanted dolls is held at Kiyomizu Kannon-dō in Ueno-kōen, after which they are cremated.

OCTOBER

Festival/Tokyo October to December Ⓦ festival-tokyo.jp. Major theatre and performing arts events are held at various venues across the city.

Kawagoe Grand Matsuri October 14–15. One of the liveliest festivals in the Tokyo area, involving some 25 ornate floats and hundreds of costumed revellers.

Tōshō-gū Aki Matsuri October 17. Repeat of Nikkō's fabulous procession held for the spring festival, minus the horseback archery displays.

Roppongi Art Night Late October Ⓦ roppongiartnight.com. Dusk-to-dawn street performances and art events are held across Tokyo's party district.

Tokyo Design Week Late October and early November Ⓦ tdwa.com. Catch the best of contemporary Japanese design at this event, held at a variety of venues, generally around Aoyama and Odaiba.

Tokyo International Film Festival Late October and early November Ⓦ tiff-jp.net. Major film festival at which a slew of works from Japan and beyond are shown on screens around the city.

NOVEMBER

Daimyō Gyōretsu November 3. Re-enactment of a feudal lord's procession along the Tōkaidō (the great road linking Tokyo and Kyoto), accompanied by his doctor, accountant, tea master and road sweepers. At Sōun-ji, near Hakone-Yumoto.

Shichi-go-san-no-hi November 15. Children aged seven, five and three ("*shichi-go-san*") don traditional garb to visit the shrines, particularly Meiji-jingū, Hie-jinja and Yasukuni-jinja.

Tori-no-ichi Mid-November. Fairs selling *kumade* (bamboo rakes decorated with lucky charms) are held at shrines on "rooster days" in the zodiacal calendar. The main fair is at Ōtori-jinja (Iriya station).

Tokyo Filmex Late November Ⓦ filmex.net. Film festival focusing on pieces from emerging Asian directors.

DECEMBER

Gishi-sai December 14. Costume parade in Nihombashi re-enacting the famous vendetta of the 47 *rōnin* (see box, p.111), followed by a memorial service for them at Sengaku-ji.

Hagoita-ichi December 17–19. The build-up to New Year begins with a battledore fair outside Asakusa's Sensō-ji.

Ōmisoka December 31. Leading up to midnight, temple bells ring out 108 times (the number of human frailties according to Buddhist thinking), while thousands gather at Meiji-jingū, Hie-jinja and other major shrines to honour the gods with the first visit of the New Year. If you don't like crowds, head for a small local shrine.

Culture and etiquette

Japan is famous for its complex web of social conventions and rules of behaviour. Fortunately, allowances are made for befuddled foreigners, but it will be greatly appreciated – and even draw gasps of astonishment – if you show a grasp of the basic principles. The two main danger areas are to do with footwear and bathing which, if you get them wrong, can cause great offence. There are also etiquette points to bear in mind around eating (see p.154) and drinking (see p.175).

Japan is a strictly hierarchical society where men generally take precedence, so women shouldn't expect doors to be held open or seats vacated. **Sexual discrimination** remains widespread, and foreign women working in Japan can find the predominantly male business culture hard going.

Pushing and shoving on crowded trains or buses is not uncommon. Never respond by getting angry or showing **aggression**, as this is considered a complete loss of face. By the same token, don't make your **opinions** known too forcefully or contradict people outright; it's more polite to say "maybe" than a direct "no", so if you get a vague answer to a question don't push for confirmation unless it's important.

Note that it's particularly unwise to criticize any aspect of Japanese society, however small, to a local; in a land where people tend to describe themselves as a "we", it's often taken as a personal insult.

Blowing your nose in public is also considered rude – locals keep sniffing until they find somewhere private (this can continue for hours on end, which is great fun if you're sat next to a sniffler on a long train ride). An even more common agony for visitors is having to **sit on the floor** at people's houses and certain restaurants – excruciatingly uncomfortable for people who aren't used to it. If you're wearing trousers, sitting cross-legged is fine; otherwise, tuck your legs to one side.

Meetings and greetings

Some visitors to Japan complain that it's difficult to **meet local people** – the Japanese themselves famously have problems meeting each other, as evidenced by regular pay-for-company stories in the international press, and the legion of "snack" bars (where local men essentially pay to have their egos massaged). It's also true that many Japanese are shy of foreigners, mainly through a fear of being unable to communicate. A few words of Japanese will help enormously, and there are various opportunities for fairly formal contact, such as through the Goodwill Guides (see p.38). Otherwise, try popping into a local bar, a *yakitori* joint or suchlike;

with everyone crammed in like sardines, and emboldened by alcohol, it's far easier to strike up a conversation.

Whenever Japanese meet, express thanks or say goodbye, there's a flurry of **bowing** – and, between friends, an energetic waving of hands. The precise depth of the bow and the length of time it's held for depend on the relative status of the two individuals; foreigners aren't expected to bow, but it's terribly infectious and you'll soon find yourself bobbing with the best of them. The usual compromise is a slight nod or a quick half-bow. Japanese more familiar with Western customs might offer you a hand to shake, in which case treat it gently – they won't be expecting a firm grip.

Japanese **names** are traditionally written with the family name first, followed by a given name, which is the practice used throughout this book (except where the Western version has become famous, such as Issey Miyake). When dealing with foreigners, however, they may well write their name the other way round. Check if you're not sure because, when **addressing people**, it's normal to use the family name plus -*san*: for example, Suzuki-san. *San* is an honorific term applied to others, so you do not use it when introducing yourself or your family. As a foreigner, you can choose whichever of your names you feel comfortable with; you'll usually have a -*san* tacked onto the end of your given name. You'll also often hear -*chan* or -*kun* as a form of address; these are diminutives reserved for very good friends, young children and pets. The suffix -*sama* is the most polite form of address.

Japanese people tend to **dress** smartly, especially in Tokyo. Tourists don't have to go overboard, but will be better received if they look neat and tidy, while for anyone hoping to do business, a snappy suit (any colour, as long as it's black) is *de rigueur*. It's also important to be **punctual** for social and business appointments.

An essential part of any **business meeting** is the swapping of *meishi* (**name cards**); if you're doing business here, it's a very good idea to have them printed in Japanese as well as English. Always carry a copious supply, since you'll be expected to exchange a card with everyone present. *Meishi* are offered with both hands, held so that the recipient can read the writing. It's polite to read the card and then place it on the table beside you, face up. Never write on a *meishi*, at least not in the owner's presence, and never shove it in a pocket – pop it into your wallet, a dedicated card-holder, or somewhere suitably respectful.

Hospitality, gifts and tips

Entertaining, whether it's business or purely social, usually takes place in bars and restaurants. The host generally orders and, if it's a Japanese-style meal, will keep passing you different things to try. You'll also find your glass continually topped up. It's polite to return the gesture but if you don't drink, or don't want any more, leave it full.

It's a rare honour to be invited to someone's home in Japan, and if this happens you should always take a **gift**, which should always be wrapped, using plenty of fancy paper and ribbon if possible. Most shops gift-wrap purchases automatically, and anything swathed in paper from a big department store has extra cachet.

Japanese people love giving gifts (in fact, they are more-or-less obliged to give souvenirs known as *omiyage* to friends and colleagues following any holiday), and you should never refuse one if offered, though it's good manners to protest at their generosity first. Again, it's polite to give and receive with both hands, and to belittle your humble donation while giving profuse thanks for the gift you receive. It's the custom not to open gifts in front of the donor, thus avoiding potential embarrassment.

Tipping is not expected in Japan. If someone's been particularly helpful, the best approach is to give a small present, or offer some money discreetly in an envelope.

Shoes and slippers

It's customary to change into **slippers** when entering a Japanese home or a ryokan, and not uncommon in traditional restaurants, temples and, occasionally, museums and art galleries. If you come across a slightly raised floor and a row of slippers, then use them; leave your shoes either on the lower floor (the *genkan*) or on the shelves (sometimes lockers) provided. Also try not to step on the *genkan* with bare or stockinged feet. Once inside, remove your slippers before stepping onto tatami (the rice-straw flooring), and remember to change into the special **toilet slippers** kept inside the bathroom when you go to the toilet.

Toilets

Although you'll still come across traditional Japanese squat-style **toilets** (*toire* or *otearai*; トイレ／お手洗い), Western sit-down toilets are becoming the norm. Look out for nifty enhancements such as a heated seat and those that flush automatically as you walk away. Another handy device plays the sound of flushing water to cover embarrassing noises.

High-tech toilets, with a control panel to one side, are very common. Finding the flush button can be a challenge – they're often tiny things on wall panels, marked with the *kanji* for large (大) or small (小), used for number twos and ones respectively.

Most public toilets now provide **paper** (often extremely thin), though not always soap for washing your hands. There are public toilets at most train and subway stations, department stores, and city parks. They're generally pretty clean.

Bathing

Taking a traditional Japanese **bath**, whether in an onsen, a *sentō* or a ryokan (see box, p.149), is a ritual that's definitely worth mastering. Everyone uses the same water, and the golden rule is to wash and rinse the soap off thoroughly before stepping into the bath – showers and bowls are provided, as well as soap and shampoo in most cases. Ryokan and the more upmarket public bathhouses provide small towels (bring your own or buy one on the door if using a cheaper *sentō*), though no one minds full nudity. Baths are typically **segregated**, so memorize the *kanji* for female (女), which looks a little like a woman; and male (男), which looks sort of like a chap with a box on his head.

Note that **tattoos** – which are associated with the *yakuza* in Japan – are a big issue when it comes to public bathing. Even if you look nothing like a member of the local mafia, you may be asked to cover up the offending image, or even denied access to the baths entirely. If you're intending to visit any particular bathing establishment, the best course of action is to get your accommodation (or a local tourist office) to call ahead for verification of their tattoo regulations.

LGBT Tokyo

LGBT travellers should have few concerns about visiting Tokyo and are unlikely to encounter any problems. Japan has no laws against homosexual activity and outward discrimination is very rare, including at hotels and ryokan where two people of the same sex sharing a room will hardly raise an eyebrow.

That said, marriage remains an almost essential step on the career ladder, keeping many Japanese gays in the closet, often leading double lives and/or being apathetic to concepts of gay liberation and rights. General codes of behaviour mean that public displays of affection between any couple, gay or straight, are very rare – so don't expect a warm welcome if you walk down the street hand in hand or kiss in public. In recent times being gay has come to be seen as more acceptable – and among young people it's rarely an issue – but Tokyo has a long way to go before it can be considered truly gay-friendly.

There's a decent number of gay and lesbian venues, particularly in the Shinjuku Nichōme area (see p.185).

ONLINE RESOURCES

Fridae ⓦ fridae.com. Asia-wide site with some good Tokyo info.
Tokyo Wrestling ⓦ tokyowrestling.com. Trilingual (it's in French too) lesbian-focused website.
Utopia ⓦ utopia-asia.com. Pan-Asian site with good Japan specifics.

Kids' Tokyo

What with Japan being the land of anime, manga and a treasure chest of must-have toys and computer games, you'll have no problem selling the kids on a trip to Tokyo. It's a safe, child-friendly city that offers a vast number of ways to distract and entertain kids of every age. For families who don't mind bedding down together, a ryokan or Japanese-style room in a hotel, where you can share a big tatami room, is ideal (see pp.142–152).

Essentials

At most attractions, school-age children get **reduced rates**, typically half the adult price. Children under 6 ride free on trains, subways and buses, while those aged 6–11 pay half fare. **Nappies**, **baby food** and pretty much anything else you may need are widely available in supermarkets and pharmacies, though not necessarily your favourite brand. While **breast-feeding** in public is generally accepted, it's best to be as discreet as possible. Most Japanese women who breast-feed use the private rooms provided in department stores and public buildings and in many shops. Only at the more upmarket Western-

style hotels will you be able to arrange **babysitting**; Poppins (ⓦ poppins.co.jp) is one reputable baby-sitting service.

Sights and activities

We've listed a selection of amusement and **theme parks** (see box, p.191), and there's also the wonderful Ghibli Museum in Mitaka (see p.132), which is part gallery and part theme park. To give children their **animal** fix, try Tokyo Sea Life Park (see p.93) or Ueno Zoo (see p.66). The best **museums** for kids include Ueno's National Science Museum (see p.67), Odaiba's Miraikan (see p.92) and the Edo-Tokyo Museum in Ryōgoku (see p.83).

Other family-friendly outings to consider include taking a **boat trip** across Tokyo Bay (see p.89), learning how to make **origami** cranes at the Origami Kaikan (see p.60), or visiting the PUK **puppet theatre** (see p.189).

Chances are that near most hotels will be a small **playground**; if your kids need more room to burn off steam, head to the open spaces of Yoyogi-kōen (see p.117) or Shinjuku Gyoen (see p.131).

Also check out the listings for **toyshops** and those specializing in manga, anime and character product goods (see p.204 & p.194). The showrooms for products by Sony (see p.54) and Panasonic (see p.89) will be appealing to **teenagers**, as will spending time exploring electronic, anime and manga hotspot Akihabara (see p.58).

Finally, you'll find local-authority-managed **children's halls** (*jidokan*) throughout the city, which are free to long-term Tokyo residents and provide a whole range of activities and classes for school-age kids and younger. Most central is the National Children's Castle (5-53-1 Jingūmae, Shibuya-ku; ☎03 3797 5666, ⓦ kodomono-shiro .com/english; Omotesandō subway), which houses a large playground, a jungle gym, a lobby packed with musical instruments, a good-value family hotel and a swimming pool.

Dining

The hazy situation with regard to **smoking** in Tokyo restaurants (most still allow it), combined with uncommon dishes and Japanese-language menus, will provide parents trying to feed fussy kids with certain challenges. One solution is to ask your hotel to point you in the direction of the nearest **"family restaurant" chain**, such as *Denny's, Royal Host* or *Jonathan's*; all have children's menus including Western and Japanese dishes with pictures of each dish, as well as nonsmoking sections. Tokyo's **vegetarian** cafés and restaurants (see box, p.168) are another option.

Travel essentials

Costs

Despite its reputation as an outrageously expensive city, prices in Tokyo have dropped or at least stabilized in recent years, and with a little planning it is a manageable destination even for those on a fairly modest budget. The key is to do what the majority of Japanese do: eat in local restaurants, avoid the ritzier bars and take advantage of any available discounts. There's also a surprising amount you can do in Tokyo without spending any money at all (see box below).

By staying in hostels and eating in the cheapest local restaurants, the absolute minimum **daily budget** for food and accommodation is ¥4000–7000. By the time you've added in some transport costs, a few entry tickets, meals in classier restaurants and one or two nights in a ryokan or business hotel, you'll be reaching an expenditure of at least ¥15,000 per day.

Holders of the **International Student Identity Card** (ISIC; ⓦ isic.org) are eligible for discounts on some transport and admission fees, as are children.

Crime and personal safety

Tokyo boasts one of the lowest crime rates in the world. On the whole, the Japanese are honest and law-abiding, there's little theft, and drug-related crimes are relatively rare. Nonetheless, it always pays to be careful in crowds, and to keep money and important documents stowed in an inside pocket or money belt, or in your hotel safe.

> ### GRUTT PASS
> One of the best deals on offer in Tokyo is the **Grutt Pass**. For ¥2000 you get a ticket booklet which allows free or discounted entry to seventy attractions, including all major museums. Valid for two months after first being used, the ticket can be bought at participating venues and at the Tokyo Metropolitan Government tourist information centre in Shinjuku (see p.125), among other outlets.

The presence of **police boxes** (*kōban*) in every neighbourhood helps to discourage petty crime, and the local police seem to spend the majority of their time dealing with stolen bikes and helping bemused visitors – Japanese and foreigners – find addresses. In theory, you should carry your **passport** or ID at all times; the police have the right to arrest anyone who fails to do so. In practice they rarely stop foreigners, but if you're found without ID, you'll most likely be escorted back to your hotel or apartment to collect it. Anyone found with **drugs** will be treated less leniently; if you're lucky, you'll simply be fined and deported, rather than sent to prison.

The generally low status of women in Japan is reflected in the amount of **groping** that goes on in crowded commuter trains. If you do have the misfortune to be groped, the best solution is to grab the offending hand, yank it high in the air and embarrass the guy as much as possible. Fortunately, more violent **sexual attacks** are rare, though harassment, stalking and rape are seriously under-reported. Women should exercise the same caution about being alone with a man as they would anywhere – violent crimes against women are rare, but they do occur. Tokyo Metropolitan Police run an **English-language hotline** (☎03 3501 0110;

> ### TOKYO FOR FREE
> Bear in mind that many of the best things to do in Tokyo are absolutely **free**. Some of the top places in town – in a very literal sense – won't set you back a single yen; most popular are the **observatories** at the Tokyo Metropolitan Government Building (see p.127), while those heading to the restaurant levels in the Caretta Building in Shidome (home to *Hibiki*; see p.157) or Ebisu Garden Place (home to *Hokkaido*; p.166) will get an eyeful even if they're not eating. The majority of **temples and shrines** are free, as are many **museums and galleries** – and a whole bunch more become so if you invest in a Grutt Pass (see box above). Lastly, there are free **walking tours** around Asakusa (see p.73), Ueno (see p.64) and the Imperial City area (see p.41), and free **bike rental** around the Imperial Palace on Sundays.

EMERGENCY NUMBERS

Police ☎ 110
Fire or ambulance ☎ 119

Mon–Fri 8.30am–5.15pm). Another useful option is **Tokyo English Language Lifeline** (TELL; ☎ 03 5774 0992, Ⓦ telljp.com; daily 9am–11pm).

Earthquakes

Japan is home to one-tenth of the world's active volcanoes; it's also the site of one-tenth of its major earthquakes (over magnitude 7 on the Richter scale). At least one quake is recorded every day somewhere in the country (see Ⓦ www.jma .go.jp/en/quake for details of the most recent), though fortunately the vast majority consist of **minor tremors** that you probably won't even notice. One that the whole world noticed occurred off the country's east coast in March 2011 (see p.258). The fifth most powerful earthquake in recorded history, it unleashed a **tsunami** of prodigious force; the combined effect killed almost 16,000 people, and caused a meltdown at the nuclear power plant in Fukushima, where the effects will be felt for decades. Do note, however, that since the 1980s buildings have been designed to withstand even the most powerful 'quakes. Tokyo is equipped with some of the world's most **sophisticated sensors**, and architects employ mind-boggling techniques to try to ensure the city's high-rises remain upright.

If you do have the misfortune to experience more than a minor rumble, follow the **safety procedures** listed below:

- Extinguish any fires and turn off electrical appliances.
- Open any doors leading out of the room, as they often get jammed shut, blocking your exit later.
- Stay away from windows because of splintering glass. If you have time, draw the curtains to contain the glass.
- Don't rush outside (many people are injured by falling masonry), but get under something solid, such as a ground-floor doorway, or a desk.
- If you are outside when the quake hits, beware of falling objects and head for the nearest park or other open space.
- If the earthquake occurs at night, make sure you've got a torch (all hotels and ryokan provide flashlights in the rooms).

- When the tremors have died down, go to the nearest park, playing field or open space, taking your documents and other valuables with you. If available, take a cushion or pillow to protect your head against falling glass.
- Eventually, make your way to the designated neighbourhood emergency centre for information, food and shelter.
- Ultimately, get in touch with your embassy.

Beware of aftershocks, which may go on for a long time and can topple structures that are already weakened; also note that most casualties are caused by fire and traffic accidents, rather than collapsing buildings. In the aftermath of a major earthquake, it may be impossible to contact friends and relatives for a while, since the phone lines are likely to be down or reserved for emergency services, while internet servers may be hit by power cuts.

Climate

The **summer** months in Tokyo are hot and humid, while **winters** are cold but drier; the rainy season – known as *tsuyu* – is in June and July, but rain can fall at any time, especially between March and October. The most pleasant seasons to visit are **spring** (April to early May) and **autumn** (Oct and Nov). There's more advice on the best time to visit the city, as well as information on average temperatures and rainfall, in the Introduction (see p.8).

Electricity

Mains **electricity** in Tokyo is 100V, 50Hz AC. Japanese plugs have two flat pins or, less commonly, three pins (two flat and one rounded, earth pin). If you are arriving from North America or Canada, the voltage difference should cause no problems with computers, digital cameras, cell phones and the like. Appliances such as hair dryers, curling irons and travel kettles should also work, but not quite as efficiently, in which case you may need a converter. Large hotels can often provide voltage converters and adaptors.

Entry requirements

All visitors to Japan must have a passport valid for the duration of their stay. Citizens of Ireland, the UK and certain other European countries can stay in Japan for up to ninety days without a visa provided they are visiting for tourism or business purposes;

this stay can be **extended** for another three months (see below). Citizens of Australia, Canada, New Zealand and the US can also stay for up to ninety days without a visa, though this is not extendable and you are required to be in possession of a return air ticket. Anyone from these countries wishing to stay longer will have to leave Japan and then re-enter.

Citizens of certain other countries must apply for a **visa** in advance in their own country. Visas are usually free, though in certain circumstances you may be charged a fee of around ¥3000 for a single-entry visa. The rules on visas do change from time to time, so check first with the nearest Japanese embassy or consulate, or on the Japanese Ministry of Foreign Affairs website ⓦ www.mofa.go.jp.

To get a **visa extension** you'll need to fill in two copies of an "Application for Extension of Stay", available from the **Tokyo Regional Immigration Bureau** at 5-5-30 Kōnan, Minato-ku (Mon–Fri 9am–noon & 1–4pm; ☎03 5796 7111, ⓦwww.immi-moj .go.jp), a short walk from Tennozu Isle station. Go early in the day, since the process takes forever; note that your application may not be confirmed for two weeks. Bring along passport photos (and your passport, of course), a letter explaining your reasons for wanting to extend your stay, and a fee of ¥4000. In addition, you may be asked to show proof of **sufficient funds** to support your stay, and a valid onward ticket out of the country. If you're not a national of one of the few countries with six-month reciprocal visa exemptions (these include Ireland and the UK), expect a thorough grilling from the immigration officials. An easier option – and the only alternative available to nationals of those countries who are not eligible for an extension – may be a short trip out of the country, say to South Korea or Hong Kong, though you may still have to run the gauntlet of immigration officials on your return.

Citizens of the UK, Ireland, Canada, Australia and New Zealand, among other countries, can apply for a **working holiday visa** if they are aged between 18 and 30 (officially up to 25 for Canadians and Australians, though there are often ways around this); this grants a stay of up to one year and entitles the holder to take paid employment so long as your stay is "primarily deemed to be a holiday". Full details of the scheme can be found at ⓦmofa.go.jp.

British nationals are also eligible for the **volunteer visa scheme**, which allows holders to undertake voluntary work for charitable organizations in Japan for up to one year. Your application must include a letter from the host organization confirming details of the voluntary work to be undertaken and the treatment the volunteer will receive (pocket money and board and lodging are allowed, but formal remuneration is not). You must also be able to show evidence of sufficient funds for your stay in Japan. Contact your local embassy or consulate to check the current details of the scheme.

Foreigners legally allowed to stay in Japan for more than ninety days – basically those with legal employment or married to a Japanese citizen – must obtain **residency status** before their first ninety days is up. Resident cards can be issued, with prior arrangement, at the main international airports, though most people end up applying at their local government office. The resident cards (Zairyū kādo; 在留カード) include your photograph and must (legally speaking) be carried at all times, though they're rarely checked.

In addition, if you're on any sort of working visa and you leave Japan temporarily, you must get a **re-entry visa** before you leave if you wish to continue working on your return. Re-entry visas are available from local immigration bureaus.

EMBASSIES IN TOKYO

Australia 2-1-14 Mita, Minato-ku ☎ 03 5232 4111, ⓦ japan .embassy.gov.au.

Canada 7-3-38 Akasaka, Minato-ku ☎ 03 5412 6200, ⓦ japan .gc.ca.

China 3-4-33 Moto-Azabu, Minato-ku ☎ 03 3403 3064, ⓦ www .china-embassy.or.jp.

Ireland 2-10-7 Kōjimachi, Chiyoda-ku ☎ 03 3263 0695, ⓦ irishembassy.jp.

New Zealand 20-40 Kamiyamachō, Shibuya-ku ☎ 03 3467 2271, ⓦ nzembassy.com/japan.

Russian Federation 2-1-1 Azabudai, Minato-ku ☎ 03 3583 4224, ⓦ russia-emb.jp.

South Africa 4F 1-4 Kojimachi, Chiyoda-ku ☎ 03 3265 3366, ⓦ sajapan.org.

South Korea 1-2-5 Minami-Azabu, Minato-ku ☎ 03 3452 7611.

UK 1 Ichibanchō, Chiyoda-ku ☎ 03 5211 1100, ⓦ ukinjapan.fco .gov.uk.

USA 1-10-5 Akasaka, Minato-ku ☎ 03 3224 5000, ⓦ japan .usembassy.gov.

JAPANESE EMBASSIES AND CONSULATES ABROAD

You'll find a full list on ⓦ www.mofa.go.jp.

Australia 112 Empire Circuit, Yarralumla, Canberra ☎ 02 6273 3244, ⓦ au.emb-japan.go.jp.

Canada 255 Sussex Drive, Ottawa ☎ 613 241 8541, ⓦ ca.emb-japan .go.jp.

China 1 Liangmaqiao Dongjie, Chaoyang, Beijing ☎ 010 8531 9800, ⓦ cn.emb-japan.go.jp.

Ireland Nutley Building, Merrion Centre, Nutley Lane, Dublin ☎ 01 202 8300, ⓦ ie.emb-japan.go.jp.

New Zealand Level 18, Majestic Centre, 100 Willis St, Wellington ☎ 04 473 1540, ⓦ nz.emb-japan.go.jp.

Singapore 16 Nassim Rd ☎ 65 235 8855, ⓦ sg.emb-japan.go.jp.

South Africa 259 Baines St, Groenkloof, Pretoria ☎ 012 452 1500, ⓦ japan.org.za.

South Korea Twin Tree Tower A, 6 Yulgok-ro, Jongno-gu, Seoul ☎ 02 2170 5200, ⓦ kr.emb-japan.go.jp.

UK 101–104 Piccadilly, London ☎ 020 7465 6500, ⓦ uk.emb-japan.go.jp; 2 Melville Crescent, Edinburgh ☎ 0131 225 4777, ⓦ edinburgh.uk.emb-japan.go.jp.

US 2520 Massachusetts Ave NW, Washington DC ☎ 202 238 6700, ⓦ us.emb-japan.go.jp.

Health

To find an English-speaking doctor and the hospital or clinic best suited to your needs, contact the **Tokyo Medical Information Service** (Mon–Fri 9am–8pm; ☎ 03 5285 8181, ⓦ www.himawari.metro.tokyo.jp); they can also provide emergency medical translation services over the phone. Major hotels usually stock a limited array of common medicines. You should find English-speaking staff at the establishments below.

Note that certain medications that are commonplace outside Japan are actually **illegal** here – some of the more prominent prescription drugs on the no-no list are codeine and some ADHD medication. The health ministry website (ⓦ www.mhlw.go.jp) has more specific details on these, and the forms you'll need to fill in if you're to bring these meds into Japan legally.

HOSPITALS, CLINICS AND PHARMACIES

American Pharmacy Marunouchi Building, 2-4-1 Marunouchi, Chiyoda-ku ☎ 03 5220 7716; Tokyo station. Has English-speaking pharmacists and a good range of drugs and general medical supplies. Mon–Fri 9am–9pm, Sat 10am–9pm, Sun 10am–8pm.

National Azabu Pharmacy Above the National Azabu supermarket ☎ 03 3442 3495; Hiro-o station.

St Luke's International Hospital 9-1 Akashichō, Chūō-ku ☎ 03 3541 5151, ⓦ hospital.luke.or.jp. Reception desk open Mon–Fri 8.30–11am for non-emergency cases.

Tokyo Adventist Hospital 3-17-3 Amanuma, Suginami-ku ☎ 03 3392 6151. Open 24hr for emergencies.

Tokyo Medical and Surgical Clinic 32 Shiba-kōen Building, 3-4-30 Shiba-kōen, Minato-ku ☎ 03 3436 3028, ⓦ tmsc.jp. Mon–Fri 8.30am–5.30pm, Sat 8.30am–noon, by appointment only.

Insurance

It's essential to take out a good **travel insurance** policy (see box below), particularly one with comprehensive medical coverage, due to the high cost of hospital treatment in Japan.

Internet access

Many visitors soon realize that Japan doesn't quite live up to its tech-savvy reputation. A fair few local websites (including those of some expensive hotels and restaurants) are laughably bad; with italicized Times New Roman fonts and copious Clipart characters, many seem to have been imported directly from the mid-1990s.

However, things are finally starting to improve, and **wi-fi** access is becoming more widespread. Most big-city **cafés** offer it for free (though at some you have to register), and it's par for the course at privately run **hostels**, though at **hotels** you still can't be sure; at the top end, you may well have to pay a daily fee (typically ¥1000). Some hotels also offer free broadband in the rooms, and should be able to supply a cable if necessary. Others may provide at least one terminal for guests travelling without their own computer, generally also for free.

Wi-fi has now been rolled out in most **subway stations** and **convenience stores** – you have to register once, with a fake email address if necessary, then log in each time. At the time of writing,

Lawson stores were by far the easiest at which to get online, with 7-Eleven not far behind, and Family Mart at the bottom of the queue. Accommodation, restaurants and bars with wi-fi are indicated in the guide with the 🛜 symbol.

Laundry

All hotels provide either a laundry service or coin-operated machines. These typically cost ¥200–300 for a wash (powder ¥30–50) and ¥100–200 for ten minutes in the drier. Failing that, neighbourhood Laundromats are everywhere.

Left luggage

Most hotels will keep luggage for a few days. The baggage room (daily 7.30am–8.30pm) at Tokyo station can hold bags for the day for ¥600; the station information desks will point the way. Coin lockers can be found in many metro stations (¥300–800 depending on size), and can only be used for a maximum of three days.

Living and working in Tokyo

Employment opportunities for foreigners have shrunk since the Japanese economy took a nosedive, though finding employment is far from impossible, especially if you have the right qualifications (a degree is essential) and appropriate visa.

Unless you take part in the **working holiday visa** programme (see p.33), foreigners working in Japan must apply for a **work visa** *outside* the country, for which the proper sponsorship papers from your prospective employer will be necessary. Work visas do not need to be obtained in your home country, so if you get offered a job, it's possible to sort out the paperwork in South Korea, for example. A few employers may be willing to hire you before the proper papers are sorted, but you shouldn't rely on this, and if you arrive without a job make sure you have plenty of funds to live on until you find one. Anyone staying in Japan more than ninety days must also apply for residency status (see p.33).

The most common job available to foreigners is **teaching English**. Some of the smaller schools are far from professional operations (and even the big ones get lots of complaints), so before signing any contract it's a good idea to talk to other teachers and, if possible, attend a class and find out what will be expected of you. If you have a professional teaching qualification, plus experience, or if you also speak another language such as French or Italian, your chances of getting one of the better jobs will be higher.

Another option is to get a place on the government-run **Japan Exchange and Teaching Programme** (JET; 🌐 jetprogramme.org), aimed at improving foreign-language teaching in schools and promoting international understanding. The scheme is open to graduates aged 40 and under, preferably holding some sort of language-teaching qualification. Benefits include a generous salary, help with accommodation, return air travel to Japan and paid holidays. Applying for the JET programme is a lengthy process for which you need to be well prepared. Application forms for the following year's quota are available from late September, and the deadline for submission is early December. Interviews are held in January and February, with decisions made in March. After health checks and orientation meetings, JETs head off to their posts in late July on year-long contracts, which can be renewed for up to two more years by mutual consent.

Whatever work you're looking for – or if you're doing any sort of business in Japan – a smart set of clothes will give you an advantage, as will following other general rules of social etiquette (see p.27).

EMPLOYMENT RESOURCES

Apart from the websites listed below the main places to look for job adverts are the free magazines *Metropolis* and *Tokyo Notice Board* (see p.25).

Daijob 🌐 daijob.com. Japan's largest bilingual jobs website – and a great pun to boot (*daijobu* means "no problem").

GaijinPot 🌐 gaijinpot.com. Classifieds focused on English-language teaching.

Japan Association for Working Holiday Makers 🌐 jawhm.or.jp. Job referrals for people on working holiday visas.

Jobs in Japan 🌐 jobsinjapan.com. Broad range of classified ads.

Studying Japanese language and culture

Tokyo offers all sorts of opportunities to study Japanese language and culture. In order to get a student or **cultural visa**, you'll need various documents from the institution where you plan to study and proof that you have sufficient funds to support yourself, among other things. Full-time courses are expensive, but once you have your visa you may be allowed to undertake a minimal amount of paid work.

Japan's Ministry of Education, Culture, Sports, Science and Technology (MEXT; 🌐 www.mext.go.jp) offers various **scholarships** to foreign students wishing to further their knowledge of Japanese or Japanese studies, or to enrol at a Japanese university. You'll find further information on the informative Study in Japan website (Ⓦwww.study japan.go.jp), run by the Ministry of Foreign Affairs, or by contacting your nearest Japanese embassy or consulate.

Tokyo has numerous **Japanese language schools** offering intensive and part-time courses. Among the most established are Berlitz (Ⓦberlitz.co.jp), with over thirty schools in central Tokyo, and Tokyo Kogakuin Japanese Language School (5-30-16 Sendagaya, Shibuya-ku; ☎03 3352 3851, Ⓦtechnos-jpschool .ac.jp). The monthly bilingual magazine *Hiragana Times* (Ⓦhiraganatimes.com) and the magazines *Metropolis* and *Tokyo Journal* (see p.25) also carry adverts for schools, or check out the Association for the Promotion of Japanese Language Education (2F Ishiyama Bldg, 1-58-1 Yoyogi, Shinjuku-ku; ☎03 4304 7815, Ⓦwww.nisshinkyo.org), whose website lists accredited institutions.

Mail

Japan's **mail** service is highly efficient and fast, with thousands of post offices, easily identified by their red-and-white signs showing a T with a parallel bar across the top (the same symbol that you'll find on the red letterboxes) scattered across the capital. All post can be addressed in Western script (*rōmaji*), provided that it's clearly printed.

Major post offices that are open 24/7 include the **Central Post Office**, on the west side of Tokyo station, as well as ones in Shinjuku (see map, p.126), Shibuya (see map, p.122) and other city areas.

If you need to send bulkier items or **parcels** back home, you can buy reasonably priced special envelopes and boxes for packaging from any post office. The maximum weight for an overseas parcel is 30kg (less for some destinations). A good compromise between expensive air mail and slow sea mail is Surface Air Lifted (SAL) mail, which costs somewhere between the two, and takes around three weeks to reach most destinations. For English-language information about postal services, including postal fees, see the Post Office website (Ⓦpost.japanpost.jp).

Maps

Decent free **maps** of the city are available from any of the tourist information centres (see p.38). Bilingual maps on public notice boards outside the main exits to most subway and train stations are handy for getting your immediate bearings – these are usually oriented the way you are facing, so if you're facing southeast, for example, the top of the map will be southeast and the bottom northwest.

There are also decent maps **online**. Google's is typically excellent, while with a little hunting you'll be able to find apps offering offline-friendly maps of the city (Ⓦmaps.me is a good one). Perhaps equally useful are maps portraying the Tokyo subway network, since such maps are not visible anywhere once you're on the trains themselves – there is, of course, one in this guide (see map, pp.298–299).

Money

The **Japanese currency** is the **yen** (*en* in Japanese). Notes are available in denominations of ¥1000, ¥2000, ¥5000 and ¥10,000, while coins come in values of ¥1, ¥5, ¥10, ¥50, ¥100 and ¥500. Apart from the ¥5 piece, a copper-coloured coin with a hole in the centre, all other notes and coins indicate their value in Western numerals.

Though **credit and debit cards** are far more widely accepted than they were a few years ago, Japan is still very much a cash society. The most useful cards to carry are Visa and American Express, followed closely by MasterCard, then Diners Club; you should be able to use these in hotels, restaurants, shops and travel agencies accustomed to serving foreigners. However, many retailers only accept locally issued cards.

ATMs

The simplest way of obtaining cash in Japan is by making an **ATM** withdrawal on a credit or debit card. Both the **post office** and Seven Bank (whose machines are located in **7-Eleven** stores) operate ATMs that accept foreign-issued cards. Post office machines accept Visa, PLUS, MasterCard, Maestro, Cirrus and American Express, with instructions provided in English; 7-Eleven ATMs accept all of these, too, except overseas-issued MasterCard brand cash cards and credit cards (including Cirrus and Maestro cards). Withdrawal limits will depend

---

EXCHANGE RATES

Exchange rates at the time of writing are as follows:
£1 = ¥144
€1 = ¥123
US$1 = ¥117
Can$1 = ¥88
Aus$1 = ¥85
NZ$1 = ¥81

For current exchange rates see Ⓦxe.com.

CONSUMPTION TAX

A **consumption tax** (shōhizei) is levied on virtually all goods and services in Japan, including restaurant meals and accommodation. At the time of writing, the rate was eight percent, though it's set to rise to ten percent from October 2019. Tax is supposed to be included in the advertised price, though you'll come across plenty of shops, hotels, restaurants and bars which haven't quite got around to it; double-check to be on the safe side.

on the card issuer and your credit limit. If the machine doesn't allow you to withdraw money in the first instance, try again with a smaller amount.

Seven Bank ATMs are often accessible 24 hours. You'll also find post office ATMs not only in post offices, but also in stations, department stores and the like throughout the city – they're identified with a sticker saying "International ATM Service". Their ATMs have more **restricted hours** than the Seven Bank machines, but the ones in major post offices can be accessed at weekends and after the counters have closed, though none is open round the clock.

Changing money

You can change cash at the **exchange counters** (ryōgae-jo; 両替所) of main post offices and certain banks – the bigger branches of Tokyo-Mitsubishi UFJ (🕸 bk.mufg.jp/english) and SMBC (Sumitomo Mitsubishi Banking Corporation; 🕸 www.smbc group.com) are your best bet. The post office handles cash in six major currencies, including American, Canadian and Australian dollars, sterling and euros. **Hotels** are only supposed to change money for guests, but some might be persuaded to help in an emergency. Remember to take your passport along in case it's needed, and allow plenty

of time, since even a simple transaction can take twenty minutes or more.

Opening hours and public holidays

Business hours are generally Monday to Friday 9am to 5pm, though private companies often close much later in the evening and may also open on Saturday mornings. Department stores and bigger **shops** tend to open around 10am and shut at 7 or 8pm. Local shops, however, will generally stay open later, while most convenience stores stay open 24 hours. Most shops take one day off a week, not necessarily on a Sunday.

The majority of **museums** close on a Monday, but stay open on Sundays and national holidays; last entry is normally thirty minutes before closing. Most museums and department stores stay open on **national holidays** and take the following day off instead. However, during the New Year festival (January 1–3), Golden Week (April 29–May 5) and O-bon (the week around August 15), almost everything shuts down. Around these periods transport and accommodation can get booked out weeks in advance, and all major tourist spots get overrun.

Phones

You're rarely far from a payphone in Tokyo. The vast majority take both coins (¥10 and ¥100) and **phonecards**; they don't give change but do return unused coins, so for local calls use ¥10 rather than ¥100 coins.

Everywhere in Japan has an **area code** (Tokyo's is ☎ 030), which can be omitted if the call is a local one. All toll-free numbers begin with either ☎ 0120 or ☎ 0088. In a few cases you may come across codes such as ☎ 0570, which are not region-specific and thus should always be dialled wherever in Japan you're calling from. Numbers starting with ☎ 080 or ☎ 090 belong to mobiles.

PUBLIC HOLIDAYS

If one of the holidays listed below falls on a Sunday, then the Monday is also a holiday.

New Year's Day Jan 1
Coming-of-Age Day Second Mon in Jan
National Foundation Day Feb 11
Spring Equinox March 20/21
Shōwa Day April 29
Constitution Memorial Day May 3
Green Day May 4
Children's Day May 5
Mountain Day May 11

Marine Day Third Mon in July
Respect-the-Aged Day Third Mon in Sept
Autumn Equinox Sept 23/24
Health and Sports Day Second Mon in Oct
Culture Day Nov 3
Labour Thanksgiving Day Nov 23
Emperor's Birthday Dec 23 (date subject to change if there is a succession)

Mobile phones

Practically everyone in Japan has a **mobile phone** (*keitai-denwa*, sometimes shortened to *keitai*), many of which can be used like a prepaid travel card on trains, subways and in shops.

Most foreign **3G models** will work in Japan – contact your mobile phone service provider before leaving your home country. Another solution for short-term visitors is to **rent** a phone (buying a prepaid phone in Japan generally requires you to show proof of local residency) at the airport, in Tokyo or online; options include PuPuRu (Ⓦwww .pupuru.com/en) and B-Mobile (Ⓦwww.bmobile .ne.jp/english), who both also rent out data cards for internet access on your laptop. Other mobile phone operators include the predominant **DoCoMo** (Ⓦwww.nttdocomo.co.jp), and **Softbank** (Ⓦsoftbank.jp/en), both of which have rental booths at Narita Airport.

Alternatively, around all major stations (especially those on the Yamanote line) you'll be able to track down outlets selling pocket wi-fi "eggs"; plans with a decent amount of data tend to cost ¥750 per day, up to ¥10,000 for a month (check online at Ⓦen.wifi-rental-store.jp).

Phoning abroad from Japan

The main companies in Japan offering **international phone calls** are KDDI (☎001), Softbank Telecom (☎0041), Cable & Wireless IDC (☎0061) and NTT (☎0033). If you want to call abroad from Japan from any type of phone, choose a company (there's little difference between them all as far as rates are concerned) and dial the relevant access code, then the country code (UK ☎44; Ireland ☎353; US and Canada ☎01; Australia ☎61; New Zealand ☎64; South Africa ☎27), then the area code minus the initial zero, then the number. For operator assistance for overseas calls, dial ☎0051. You can make international operator-assisted calls by calling ☎0051 via KDDI.

Phoning Japan from abroad

To **call Japan** from abroad, dial your international access code (UK and Ireland ☎00; US ☎011; Canada ☎011; Australia ☎0011; New Zealand ☎00; South Africa ☎09), plus the country code ☎81, then the area code minus the initial zero, then the number.

Smoking

Smoking laws in Japan verge on the ridiculous – the practice is banned in public spaces but not inside bars and restaurants, so while you'll see smokers huddled together in dedicated zones on the street, you'll regularly find people lighting up next to you over your meal, coffee or beer. Tighter restrictions have been mooted, but in this conservative land these things take serious time – and, it has to be said, the Japanese are serious smokers.

Time

Tokyo is nine hours ahead of Greenwich Mean Time, fourteen hours ahead of New York, seventeen hours ahead of Los Angeles and two hours behind Sydney. There is no daylight saving time, so during British Summer Time, for example, the difference drops to eight hours.

Tourist information

Other than the resources below, **Goodwill Guides** (Ⓦwww.jnto.go.jp) can provide English-language information. These **volunteers** offer their services free – although you're expected to pay for their transport, entry tickets and any meals you have together. Their language abilities vary, but they do provide a great opportunity to learn more about Japanese culture and to visit local restaurants, shops and so forth with a Japanese-speaker. You can contact members through the JNTO and Asakusa information offices.

TOURIST INFORMATION RESOURCES

Asakusa Culture and Sightseeing Centre ☎ 03 3842 5566. Near Asakusa station, and housed in a highly distinctive building designed by Kengo Kuma. Daily 9am–8pm.

Japan National Tourism Organization Ⓦ jnto.go.jp. The JNTO maintains a number of overseas offices – see the website for a full list of locations. Their main Tokyo office (daily 9am–5pm; ☎ 03 3201 3331) is on the first floor of the Shin-Tokyo Building, near Yūrakuchō station; there are multilingual staff here, a desk for booking accommodation across Japan, and a notice board with information on upcoming events. There are also tourist information kiosks in the arrivals halls at Narita and Haneda airports.

Tokyo City i B1F Kitte Building, 2-7-2 Marunouchi Ⓦ en.tokyocity -i.jp; Tokyo station. The city's best tourist information centre, with multilingual staff, accommodation- and tour-booking facilities, and good general advice. Daily 8am–8pm.

Tokyo Tourist Information Centre 1F Tokyo Metropolitan Government No. 1 Building, 2-8-1 Nishi-Shinjuku ☎ 03 5321 3077, Ⓦ gotokyo.org; Tochōmae station. Another excellent tourist information centre (TIC), though it's a little bit out of the way unless you're visiting the Tokyo Metropolitan Government Building (see p.127). Daily 9.30am–6.30pm.

Travellers with disabilities

Disability has always been something of an uncomfortable topic in Japan, with disabled people generally hidden from public view. In recent years, however, there has been a certain shift in public opinion, particularly in the wake of the bestseller *No One's Perfect* by Ototake Hirotada, the upbeat, forthright autobiography of a 23-year-old student born without arms or legs. One can expect further attention during the approach to the 2020 Paralympics, which will be held in Tokyo.

The government is spearheading a drive to provide more accessible hotels and other facilities (referred to as "barrier-free" in Japan). All train and subway **stations** now have an extra-wide manned ticket gate and an increasing number have escalators or lifts. Some **trains**, such as the Narita Express, have spaces for wheelchair users, but you should reserve well in advance. For travelling short distances, **taxis** are an obvious solution, though they are not adapted to take wheelchairs, and few drivers will offer help getting in or out of the car.

Hotels are required to provide accessible facilities. Your best bet is one of the international chains or modern Western-style business hotels, which are most likely to provide fully adapted rooms, ramps and lifts; check ahead to ensure the facilities meet your requirements. Similarly, most modern shopping complexes, museums and other public buildings are equipped with ramps, wide doors and accessible toilets.

But while things are improving, Tokyo is not an easy place to get around for anyone using a wheelchair, or for those who find it difficult to negotiate stairs or walk long distances. Although it's usually possible to organize assistance at stations, you'll need a Japanese-speaker to phone ahead and make the arrangements. For further information and help, contact the **Japanese Red Cross Language Service Volunteers** (c/o Volunteers Division, Japanese Red Cross Society, 1-1-3 Shiba Daimon, Minato-ku, Tokyo 105-8521). You'll find useful information on their website (🅦accessible .jp.org).

The Imperial Palace and around

Wrapped round with moats and broad avenues, the enigmatic Imperial Palace lies at the city's geographical and spiritual heart. The palace itself – home to the emperor and his family since 1868 – is closed to the public, but the surrounding parks are a natural place to start any exploration of Tokyo. The most attractive is Higashi Gyoen, where remnants of the old Edo Castle still stand amid formal gardens; to its north lies Kitanomaru-kōen, a more natural park containing a collection of museums, including the excellent National Museum of Modern Art. Look east from the Imperial Palace area and you'll see that the flat parkland on its periphery is, almost immediately, punctuated by a wall of high-rise – this is Marunouchi (literally meaning "inside the circle"), whose crowded streets are transformed at dusk into neon-lit canyons, lined with many of Tokyo's swankiest places to eat, drink and sleep.

BEST OF THE IMPERIAL PALACE AREA

1

Higashi Gyoen Wonder "am I really in the middle of the world's biggest city?" in this peaceful palace park (see p.43)
Intermediatheque Explore one of the city's most popular new museums (see p.48)
Hoshinoya Check in at a five-star hotel with ryokan-like sensibilities – the perfect combination (see p.144)
The Oyster Shack Slurp down some molluscs beneath the train tracks (see p.156)
Old Imperial Bar Enjoy a "Mount Fuji" cocktail (see p.175)
Tamiya Plamodel Factory Relive your childhood at this model-kit emporium (see p.204)

Marunouchi has enjoyed a stylish reinvention of late, with the opening of several new shopping and restaurant complexes, and the recent redevelopment of **Tokyo station** and its environs. The adjoining **Yūrakuchō** district to the south is – like Marunouchi – home to theatres, airline offices, banks and corporate headquarters, as well as the dramatic modern architecture of the multipurpose **Tokyo International Forum**. Head south from Yūrakuchō and you'll soon be in the **Hibiya district**, highlight of which is its Western-style **park**, a refreshing oasis of greenery.

GETTING AROUND

Tours You can join free walking tours (Wed, Sat & Sun 1pm) of the area with English-speaking guides, starting from the JNTO tourist information office (see below).

Bike rental Every Sunday 150 bikes are made available for free rental (10am–3pm; ⟨w⟩jbpi.or.jp), at the police box by exit 2 of Nijūbashimae station – it's first come, first served, and you're only allowed to ride on the designated paths flanking the east side of the palace.

Underground tunnels The maze of tunnels in this

THE IMPERIAL PALACE AND AROUND

area is truly spectacular in scope: from Ōte-mon (the main gate to Higashi Gyoen) in the north, you'll be able to walk to Hibiya-kōen down south, without once popping your head above ground. The lattice of tunnels extends way past the rail tracks, linking the subway stations on both east and west sides of the tracks – very handy if it's rainy or too hot out, though getting from A to B can be a little confusing.

INFORMATION

Japan National Tourism Organization 2F Shin-Tokyo Building, 3-3-1 Marunouchi ☏03 3201 3331, ⟨w⟩jnto .go.jp; Yūrakuchō station. The main office of the national tourist organization is on the first floor of the Shin-Tokyo Building. Daily 9am–5pm.

Tokyo City i B1F Kitte Building, 2-7-2 Marunouchi ⟨w⟩en.tokyocity-i.jp; Tokyo station. Another excellent tourist information centre with English-speaking staff. Daily 8am–8pm.

The Imperial Palace

皇居, Kōkyo

The site of the **Imperial Palace** is as old as Tokyo itself. Edo Castle was built here by Tokugawa Ieyasu in 1497 (see p.253), and its boundaries fluctuated through the following centuries; at its greatest extent, the castle walls also surrounded what is now Tokyo station, as well as parts of present-day Marunouchi. The main citadel, however, lay in today's **Higashi Gyoen**, or East Garden, and this was surrounded by moats, watchtowers and ramparts spreading over several kilometres. Little remains today, save for three fortified towers and some massive stone walls.

The present-day incarnation of the palace is a long, sleek, 1960s structure, built to replace the nineteenth-century Meiji palace building, which burnt down in the 1945 bombing raids. The actual imperial **residences**, built in the early 1990s, are tucked away out of sight in the thickly wooded western section of the **palace grounds**, which cover 284 acres, surrounded by a protective moat. Further defence against attack was afforded in earlier times by the large, windswept island now known as the **Imperial Plaza**, where the shogunate's most trusted followers were allowed to build their

1

mansions; after 1899 these were razed to make way for today's austere expanse of spruce lawns and manicured pine trees.

The palace grounds

Entrance off Uchibori-dōri • Access by official tour only; apply online and bring your passport • Mon–Fri 10am & 1.30pm • 75min • Free • ☎ 03 3213 1111, ⚐ sankan.kunaicho.go.jp • Sakuradamon or Nijūbashimae stations

Except for the two days a year when Nijūbashi is open to the general public (see p.26), admission to the **palace grounds** is only on prearranged **official tours**, conducted in Japanese but with English-language brochures and audio-guides available. They are a bit of a hassle to get on, but there is a certain fascination in taking a peek inside this secret world, and the pre-tour video shows tantalizing glimpses of vast function rooms and esoteric court rituals.

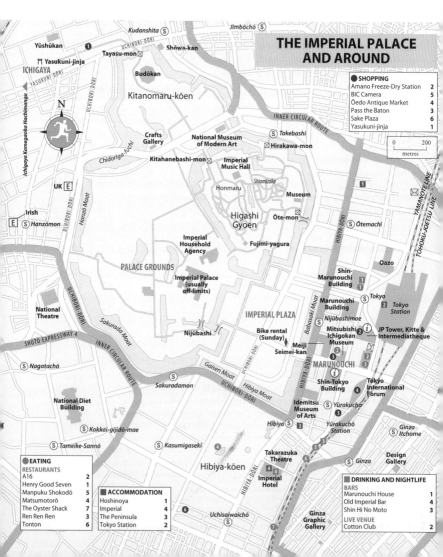

THE IMPERIAL PALACE AND AROUND

● SHOPPING
Amano Freeze-Dry Station	2
BIC Camera	5
Ōedo Antique Market	4
Pass the Baton	3
Sake Plaza	6
Yasukuni-jinja	1

● EATING
RESTAURANTS
A16	2
Henry Good Seven	1
Manpuku Shokodō	5
Matsumotorō	4
The Oyster Shack	7
Ren Ren Ren	3
Tonton	6

■ ACCOMMODATION
Hoshinoya	1
Imperial	4
The Peninsula	3
Tokyo Station	2

■ DRINKING AND NIGHTLIFE
BARS
Marunouchi House	1
Old Imperial Bar	4
Shin Hi No Moto	3

LIVE VENUE
Cotton Club	2

DESCENDANTS OF THE SUN GODDESS

Emperor Akihito, the 125th incumbent of the Chrysanthemum Throne, traces his ancestry back to 660 BC and Emperor Jimmu, great-great-grandson of the mythological Sun Goddess Amaterasu. Most scholars, however, acknowledge that the first emperor for whom there is any historical evidence is the fifth-century Emperor Ojin.

Until the twentieth century, emperors were regarded as living deities whom ordinary folk were forbidden to set eyes on, or even hear. Japan's defeat in World War II ended all that and today the emperor is a symbolic figure, a head of state with no governmental power. While he was crown prince, **Emperor Akihito** had an American tutor and studied at Tokyo's elite Gakushūin University, followed by a stint at Oxford University. In 1959 he broke further with tradition by marrying a commoner, **Shōda Michiko**.

Following in his father's footsteps, **Crown Prince Naruhito** married high-flying Harvard-educated diplomat Owada Masako in 1993. The intense press scrutiny the couple came under when they failed to produce a male heir (current laws prohibit a female succession) has been cited as one of the reasons for the princess's miscarriage in 1999. Two years later the crown princess gave birth to a baby girl, **Aiko**, but has barely been seen in public since, suffering from a variety of stress-related illnesses. One piece of good news for the royal succession is that Princess Kiko, wife of Naruhito's younger brother, gave birth to a boy, Hisahito, in 2006; the young prince is third in line for the throne after his uncle and father, though he may, in fact become second in line before too long – in August 2016, Akihito gave only his second-ever televised address, mentioning his health problems and advancing age, and hinting at an extremely rare Japanese abdication.

Nijūbashi

二重橋

The primary reason to follow the groups of tourists straggling across the broad avenues is to view one of the palace's most photogenic corners, **Nijūbashi**, where two bridges span the moat and a jaunty little watchtower perches on its grey stone pedestal beyond. Though this double bridge is a late nineteenth-century embellishment, the tower dates back to the seventeenth century and is one of the castle's few original structures. Twice a year (on Dec 23, the emperor's official birthday, and on Jan 2) thousands of well-wishers file across Nijūbashi to greet the royal family, lined up behind bulletproof glass, with a rousing cheer of "*Banzai!*" ("May you live 10,000 years!").

Higashi Gyoen

東御苑 • East entrance off Uchibori-dōri, north entrance opposite National Museum of Modern Art • Tues–Thurs, Sat & Sun 9am–4pm (closed occasionally for court functions) • Free token available at park entrance; hand back on exit • Ōtemachi or Takebashi stations

Hemmed in by moats, the **Higashi Gyoen**, or East Garden, was opened to the public in 1968 to commemorate the completion of the new Imperial Palace, and is a good place for a stroll. The towering granite walls, as well as several formidable gates, hint at the grandeur of the shogunate's Edo Castle, part of which stood here until being consumed by a catastrophic fire in the seventeenth century.

Ōte-mon

大手門 • Museum Tues–Thurs, Sat & Sun 9am–4pm • Free

The main gate to the former Edo Castle – and, today, to the garden – is **Ōte-mon**, an austere, moat-side construction whose bottom half is made up of charmingly wonky cubes of rock. Much of it was destroyed in 1945, but it has been lovingly restored since. The first building ahead on the right is a small **museum**, exhibiting a tiny fraction of the eight thousand artworks in the imperial collection, and worth a quick look.

Fujimi-yagura

富士見櫓

The finest of the fortress's remaining watchtowers is the three-tiered **Fujimi-yagura**, built in 1659 to protect the main citadel's southern flank. These days it rises above the

1

Higashi Gyoen like a miniature version of the old castle itself, standing clear above the trees to the north of the Imperial Plaza.

Shiomizaka and Honmaru

Retrace your steps from Fujimi-yagura and bank to the left; by following the gentle uphill path you'll soon be beneath the walls of the main Edo Castle citadel. The path then climbs more steeply towards **Shiomizaka**, the Tide-Viewing Slope, from where it was once possible to gaze out over Edo Bay rather than the concrete blocks of Ōtemachi. You emerge on a flat, grassy area which is a real rarity in Tokyo – somewhere in which it's tempting to walk barefoot. The stone foundations of **Honmaru** (the "inner citadel") rise from here, providing fine views from the top. Elsewhere are a scattering of modern edifices, among them the bizarre, mosaic-clad **Imperial Music Hall**; designed by Imai Kenji, the hall commemorates the sixtieth birthday of the then empress in 1963, and is used for occasional performances of court music.

Kitanomaru-kōen

北の丸公園 • North entrance off Yasukuni-dōri • 24hr • Free • Kudanshita or Takebashi stations

Edo Castle's old northern citadel is now occupied by the park of **Kitanomaru-kōen**. With its ninety-odd cherry trees, it's a popular viewing spot come *hanami* time, while rowing boats can be rented in warmer months on **Chidoriga-fuchi**, an ancient pond once incorporated into Edo Castle's moat. These natural pleasures aside, the park is also home to a couple of interesting museums: the **National Museum of Modern Art** to the south, and the **Crafts Gallery** to the west.

National Museum of Modern Art

国立近代美術館, Kokuritsu Kindai Bijutsukan • Tues–Sun 10am–5pm, Fri until 8pm • ¥1000; extra fees apply for special exhibitions • ☎ 03 5777 8600, ⓦ www.momat.go.jp

Located on the southern perimeter of the park is the **National Museum of Modern Art**. Strewn over three large levels, its excellent permanent collection showcases Japanese art since 1900, as well as a few pieces of work from overseas; the former includes Gyokudo Kawai's magnificent screen painting *Parting Spring* and works by Kishida Ryūsei, Fujita Tsuguharu and postwar artists such as Yoshihara Jiro. On the fourth floor you'll find the earliest works, as well as a resting area with fantastic views over the moat and palace grounds; the third floor contains perhaps the most interesting section, featuring art made either during wartime or its aftermath.

Crafts Gallery

工芸館, Kōgeikan • Daily 10am–5pm • ¥210; usually ¥550 for special exhibitions • ☎ 03 5777 8600, ⓦ www.momat.go.jp

Tucked away on the west side of Kitanomaru-kōen, the **Crafts Gallery** exhibits a selection of top-quality traditional Japanese craft works, many by modern masters. Erected in 1910 as the headquarters of the Imperial Guards, this neo-Gothic red-brick pile is one of very few Tokyo buildings dating from before the Great Earthquake of 1923 – it looks like the kind of place Harry Potter would have gone to school, had he been Japanese.

Budōkan

武道館

The **Budōkan** was built in 1964 to host Olympic judo events. The design, with its graceful, curving roof and gold topknot, pays homage to a famous octagonal hall at Hōryū-ji in Nara, near Kyoto, though the shape is also supposedly inspired by that of Mount Fuji. Today the huge arena is used for sports meetings, graduation ceremonies and, most famously, big-name rock concerts (the Beatles were first to play here); at the 2020 Olympics, it'll be the focus of the judo events (see box, p.120).

Ichigaya

1

市ヶ谷

When you're done with the regal gardens, the area around **Ichigaya** station – just northwest of the palace – has a few more sights, including two pertaining to World War II: a museum, and a shrine to the war dead.

Shōwa-kan

昭和館 • Off Yasukuni-dōri • Tues–Sun 10am–5.30pm • ¥300; English-language audio-guides free • ☎ 03 3222 2577, Ⓦ www.showakan.go.jp • Kudanshita station

There is something more than a little creepy about the **Shōwa-kan**, a museum devoted to life in Japan during and after World War II. It's almost as if the designers of this windowless corrugated building were acknowledging the secrecy that surrounds what really happened in those years – take a look at the exhibits and you'll see scarcely a mention of bombs or destruction. To be fair, the government originally wanted the museum to document the war's origins but ran into bitter opposition from pacifists, insistent on tackling the hot-potato issue of responsibility, and from a right-wing lobby opposed to any hint that Japan was an aggressor during the conflict. The resultant compromise sticks to a sanitized portrayal of the hardships suffered by wives and children left behind. However, there's some interesting material concerning life during the occupation in the sixth- and seventh-floor exhibition rooms, including empty hacky sacks from which starving children ate the dried beans used as stuffing.

Yasukuni-jinja

靖国神社 • Entrance off Yasukuni-dōri • Daily 6am–6pm • Free • Ⓦ www.yasukuni.or.jp • Kudanshita or Ichigaya stations

A monumental red steel *torii*, claimed to be Japan's tallest, marks the entrance to **Yasukuni-jinja**. This shrine, whose name means "for the repose of the country", was founded in 1869 to worship supporters of the emperor killed in the run-up to the Meiji Restoration. Since then it has expanded to include the legions sacrificed in subsequent wars, in total nearly 2.5 million souls, of whom some two million died in the Pacific War alone; the parting words of kamikaze pilots were said to be "see you at Yasukuni". Every year some eight million Japanese visit this shrine, which controversially includes several war criminals (see box below); security has been tight since a minor explosion here in late 2015.

Standing at the end of a long avenue lined with cherry and ginkgo trees and accessed through a simple wooden gate, the architecture is classic Shinto styling, solid and unadorned except for two gold imperial chrysanthemums embossed on the main doors. If this is all surprisingly unassuming, the same cannot be said for a couple of menacing metal lanterns near the entrance, whose distinctive Rising Sun-like patterns are most evident at dusk.

THE PROBLEM WITH YASUKUNI

Ever since its foundation as part of a Shinto revival promoting the new emperor, **Yasukuni-jinja** has been a place of high controversy. In its early years the shrine became a natural focus for the increasingly aggressive nationalism that ultimately took Japan to war in 1941. Then, in 1978, General Tōjō, prime minister during World War II, and thirteen other "Class A" war criminals were enshrined here, to be honoured along with all the other military dead. Japan's neighbours, still smarting from their treatment by the Japanese during the war, were outraged.

This has not stopped top politicians from visiting Yasukuni on the anniversary of Japan's defeat in World War II (August 15). Because Japan's postwar constitution requires the separation of state and religion, ministers have usually maintained that they attend as private individuals, but in 1985 Nakasone, in typically uncompromising mood, caused uproar when he signed the visitors' book as "Prime Minister". Recent PMs have continued to visit Yasukuni – always in an "unofficial" capacity – despite continued protests both at home and abroad.

1

Yūshūkan

遊就館 • Daily 9am–5pm • ¥800 • ☎ 03 3261 8326

To the right of the Inner Shrine you'll find the **Yūshūkan**, a military museum established in 1882. The displays are well presented, with plentiful information in English, but the problem is as much what is left out as what is included. Events such as the Nanking Massacre ("Incident" in Japanese) and other atrocities by Japanese troops are glossed over, while the Pacific War is presented as a war of liberation, freeing the peoples of Southeast Asia from Western colonialism. The most moving displays are the ranks of faded photographs and the "bride dolls" donated by the families of young soldiers who died before they were married. You exit through a hall full of military hardware, including a replica of the gliders used by kamikaze pilots on their suicide missions, its nose elongated to carry a 1200-kilo bomb, while a spine-chilling black *kaiten* (manned torpedo) lours to one side.

The garden

Before leaving the complex, walk through the little Japanese **garden** behind the shrine buildings. The sunken enclosure next door is the venue for a sumo tournament (not one of the official ones; see p.208) during the shrine's spring festival, when wrestlers perform under trees laden with cherry blossom. In early July the shrine also hosts a lively *matsuri*, when the precincts are illuminated by thousands of paper lanterns and there's dancing, parades and music nightly.

Ichigaya Kamegaoka Hachimangū

市谷亀岡八幡宮 • 15 Ichigaya Hachiman--chō, Shijuku-ku • Daily 24hr • Free • Ichigaya station

On the face of things, **Ichigaya Kamegaoka Hachimangū** is just another neighbourhood shrine. However, look a little harder at the statues and plaques and you'll notice many of them feature animals. This place is, in fact, a semiofficial shrine for locals to pray with their pets; this usually happens around New Year, but you'll still see the occasional dog, cat or tortoise getting into the Shinto spirit of things. Even if you're out of luck, you can take a look at the wooden *ema* plaques on which petitioners write their wishes, all of which feature some animal or other in picture form.

Marunouchi

丸の内

Squeezed between the Imperial Palace and Tokyo station, the business-focused **Marunouchi** district has been broadening its appeal with a raft of sleek, multistorey developments combining offices, hotels, shopping plazas and all manner of restaurants and cafés. Completed in 2002, the 36-storey **Marunouchi Building**, affectionately (or, perhaps, lazily) known as the "Maru Biru", was first off the blocks, followed by the **Oazo** complex, and the **Shin-Marunouchi Building**, with a seventh-floor upscale dining and drinking area (see p.175), and an outdoor terrace that offers terrific views. Then there's **Tokyo station** itself, whose red-brick entrance dates to the station's 1914 opening, and was inspired by the design of Amsterdam's Centraal station. The **Mitsubishi Ichigokan Museum**, meanwhile, fronts Marunouchi Brick Square, where shops and restaurants overlook a lovely landscaped garden.

Mitsubishi Ichigokan Museum

三菱一号館美術館 • 2-6-2 Marunouchi, Chiyoda-ku • Daily 10am–6pm, Fri until 8pm • Price depends on exhibition – usually ¥1600, with ¥200 discount to foreign tourists with ID • ☎ 03 5405 8686, ⓦ mimt.jp • Tokyo or Nijūbashimae stations

Worth a look for its design as much as its contents, the **Mitsubishi Ichigokan Museum** is housed in a meticulous reconstruction of a red-brick office block designed by British architect Josiah Conder (see box, p.61); the original was erected on the same site in

1

1894, only to be demolished in 1968. Exhibitions rotate every four months or so, and almost exclusively focus on nineteenth-century European art, usually of a pretty high calibre.

Meiji Seimei-kan

明治生命館 · 2-1-1 Marunouchi, Chiyoda-ku · Sat & Sun 11am–5pm · Free · Nijūbashimae or Yūrakuchō stations

A block west of Brick Square, the 1934 **Meiji Seimei-kan**, part of the newer My Plaza building, is home to the Meiji Yasuda life insurance company. On weekends you're allowed in to admire the highly polished marble floors and plaster detailing. Upstairs is a parquet-floored conference room, where the Allied Council of Japan met in the aftermath of World War II, and a dining room complete with dumbwaiters.

Intermediatheque

インターメディアテク · 2–3F Kitte Building, 2-7-2 Marunouchi, Chiyoda-ku · Mon–Thurs & Sun 11am–6pm, Fri & Sat 11am–8pm; closed a few days per month · Free · ☎ 03 5777 8600, ⊛ intermediatheque.jp · Tokyo station

The double-level **Intermediatheque** is, without doubt, one of the most intriguing museum spaces in the city, hosting exhibitions that are sharply curated and pieced together with a rare attention to aesthetic detail. The permanent exhibition is a well-presented mishmash of various objects of scientific and cultural heritage accumulated by the Tokyo University (see p.68); the animal skeletons are the most eye-catching exhibits, but poke around and you'll find everything from Central American headwear to objects damaged by the nuclear explosions in Nagasaki. There's a pleasing range to the temporary exhibitions, which can feature anything from photography to international objets d'art, via documentary work. Before you leave the building, check out the garden up on the roof.

Yūrakuchō

有楽町

South of Marunouchi lies **Yūrakuchō**, a high-rise district that's home to yet more giant pieces of urban furniture. Most notable is the arresting **Tokyo International Forum**, a stunning creation by American architect Rafael Viñoly, which hosts concerts and conventions, plus the Ōedo Antique Market (see box, p.195); in the 2020 Olympics (see box, p.120), it's due to host the weightlifting events. Its boat-shaped main hall consists of a 60m-high atrium sheathed in 2600 sheets of earthquake-resistant glass, with a ceiling ribbed like a ship's hull – it looks magical at night.

Idemitsu Museum of Arts

出光美術館, Idemitsu Bijutsukan · 9F Teigeki Building, 3-1-1 Marunouchi, Chiyoda-ku · Tues–Sun 10am–5pm, Fri until 7pm · ¥1000 · ☎ 03 5777 8600, ⊛ idemitsu.com/museum · Hibiya or Yūrakuchō stations

Sitting above the Imperial Theatre, the **Idemitsu Museum of Arts** houses a magnificent assortment of mostly Japanese art, though only a tiny proportion is on show at any one time. The collection includes many historically important pieces, ranging from fine examples of early Jōmon (10,000 BC–300 BC) pottery to Zen Buddhist calligraphy, hand-painted scrolls, richly gilded folding screens and elegant, late seventeenth-century *ukiyo-e* paintings. The museum also owns valuable collections of Chinese and Korean ceramics.

Hibiya

日比谷

The area south of where Edo Castle once stood was occupied by the Tokugawa shogunate's less favoured *daimyō*. The land was cleared after 1868, but was too waterlogged to support modern buildings, so in 1903 **Hibiya-kōen** (日比谷公園),

Tokyo's first European-style park, came into being. These days the tree-filled park is a popular lunchtime spot for office workers and courting couples, and makes a very pleasant escape from the bustle of the nearby skyscraper districts.

Imperial Hotel

1-1-1 Uchisaiwai-chō, Chiyoda-ku • Hibiya station

Across the road from Hibiya-kōen is the celebrated **Imperial Hotel**, Tokyo's first Western-style hotel when it opened in 1890 (see p.144). The original building was subsequently replaced by a stunning creation from American architect Frank Lloyd Wright: part Art Deco, part Aztec palace, it famously withstood both the Great Kantō Earthquake (which struck the city on September 1, 1923, the day after the hotel's formal opening) and World War II. After all this, Wright's building was replaced in the 1960s by the looming tower you see today. Still, a hint of Wright's style exists in the *Old Imperial Bar* (see p.175), which incorporates some of the original brickwork.

CHŪŌ-DŌRI, GINZA

Ginza and around

Ginza, the "place where silver is minted", took its name after Shogun Tokugawa Ieyasu started making coins here in the early 1600s. It turned into a happy association: one street, Chūō-dōri, soon grew to become Japan's most stylish shopping thoroughfare. Although now a couple of decades past its heyday, the glut of luxury malls and flagship stores here remains the envy of Tokyo, while various bars, restaurants and cafés still reverberate with distinct echoes of the "bubble period", a time in which Tokyo itself was the envy of the rest of the world. This slice of quintessential modern-day Japan is fascinating enough, but add a sprinkling of great museums and galleries, and you're set for the day, especially when you factor in the sights of the neighbouring districts of Nihombashi and Shiodome, which bookend Ginza to north and south.

2

Snaking above ground to the west of these areas is Tokyo's most important section of rail line: this carries the JR Yamanote line, with some tracks also designed to bear the famed Shinkansen bullet trains – you'll see these gleaming, high-speed beasts purring past every few minutes. There are some wonderfully atmospheric places to eat and drink lurking under the **railway arches**, also accessible from the western side of the tracks.

South of Ginza is **Shiodome**, where a clutch of sparkling skyscrapers harbour hotels, restaurants and a few bona fide tourist sights, the best of which is **ADMT**, a museum dedicated to advertising. North of Shiodome is **Ginza** itself; bar the revamped Kabukiza Theatre, there are no must-see sights here, but it's a compact area worth exploring, especially since even the most anonymous building can yield a speciality store or avant-garde gallery. North again you'll find the high-finance district of **Nihombashi**, once the heart of boisterous, low-town Edo but now the preserve of blue-suited bankers; it's home to the original **Mitsukoshi** department store, and a couple of fine art museums.

Shiodome

汐留

Shiodome was once most notable as the site of the Japan Railways freight terminal. While echoes of this history survive, most pertinently in the form of the **Railway History Exhibition Hall**, what now draws your gaze is a clutch of ultra-modern skyscrapers known collectively as **Shiodome Sio-Site** (汐留シオサイト); the towers are home to major companies, including Nippon TV and Kyodo News. The most interesting sight in this alienating concrete environment – one which can prove rather

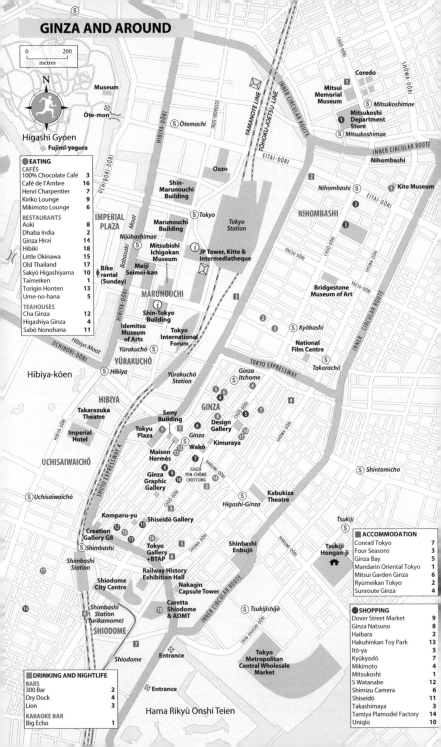

hard to traverse for newbie pedestrians – is the high-tech Advertising Museum Tokyo, or **ADMT**. From Shiodome, it's an easy walk to the **Hama Rikyū Onshi Teien** traditional garden or the Tsukiji fish market (see p.86); you can also pick up the monorail to Odaiba from here (see p.89).

Advertising Museum Tokyo (ADMT)

広告とマーケティングの資料館, Kōkoku to Māketingu no Shiryōkan • B1 Caretta Shiodome, Minato-ku • Tues–Fri 11am–6.30pm, Sat 11am–6pm • Free • ☎ 03 62182500, ⓦ admt.jp • Shiodome station

In the basement of the **Caretta Shiodome** skyscraper – the sleek headquarters of the Dentsu ad agency – you'll find **Advertising Museum Tokyo (ADMT)**, a small permanent exhibition providing a fascinating flick through some of the twentieth century's most arresting commercial images, including a decade-by-decade look at Japanese product design and advertising. Afterwards, zip up in the glass-fronted lifts to the restaurants on the 46th and 47th floors for a free panoramic view across Tokyo Bay and the Hama Rikyū Teien; *Hibiki* (see p.157) is the pick of several great restaurants occupying this lofty space.

Railway History Exhibition Hall

旧新橋停車場, Kyūshinbashi Teishajō • 1-5-3 Shiodome, Minato-ku • Tues–Sun 10am–5pm • Free • ☎ 03 3572 1872 • Shiodome or Shimbashi stations

Immediately west of Caretta Shiodome is Shiodome's second major tower complex, **Shiodome City Centre**. Back in 1872, this was the site of the original Shimbashi station, the terminus of Japan's first railway line. A faithful reproduction of the station building, designed by American architect R.P. Bridgens, now rests incongruously at the foot of the tower and contains the **Railway History Exhibition Hall**. Part of the foundations of the original building, uncovered during excavations on the site, have been preserved, and you can also see some engaging videos (in English) about Japan's early railways, as well as woodblock prints and old photos of how the area once looked.

Nakagin Capsule Tower

中銀カプセルタワー • 8-16-10 Ginza, Chūō-ku • Shiodome or Shimbashi stations

If you're in the area and have any interest in architecture, it's worth tracking down the **Nakagin Capsule Tower**, a true oddity brushing up against the expressway junction. Built in 1972, it's made up of 140 capsules, each a self-contained, ten-square-metre housing unit boasting a retro-futuristic circular window, and designed to be removable from the central body (though none ever have been). Initially constructed as a sort of architectural guinea pig, the concept never took off, and the building is falling into disrepair – at the time of writing, fewer than a quarter of the capsules were inhabited, with the rest either empty or used as storage space. You can occasionally find some listed as accommodation on Airbnb, though often at extortionate prices.

Hama Rikyū Onshi Teien

浜離宮恩賜庭園 • 1-1 Hamarikyūteien, Chūō-ku • Daily 9am–4.30pm • ¥300; tea ¥510 • Shiodome station

The beautifully designed traditional garden of **Hama Rikyū Onshi Teien** once belonged to the shogunate, who hunted ducks here. These days the ducks are protected inside the garden's nature reserve, and no longer used for target practice. Next to the entrance is a sprawling, 300-year-old pine tree and a manicured lawn dotted with sculpted, stunted trees. There are three ponds, the largest spanned by a trellis-covered bridge that leads to a floating teahouse, *Nakajima-no-Chaya*; in early spring lilac wisteria hangs in fluffy bunches from trellises around the central pond. From the Tokyo Bay side of the garden, there's a view across to the Rainbow Bridge (see p.93), and you can see the floodgate which regulates how much sea water flows in and out of the ponds with the tides.

By far the nicest way of approaching the gardens is to take a ferry from Asakusa, down the Sumida-gawa (see p.73); often the entry price is included with the ticket.

Ginza

銀座

Although cutting-edge fashion has moved elsewhere in Tokyo, **Ginza** retains much of its elegance and its undoubted snob appeal. Here you'll find the city's greatest concentration of exclusive shops and restaurants, the most theatres and cinemas, major department stores, and a fair number of art galleries (see box below).

The area is packed into a compact rectangular grid enclosed by the Shuto Expressway. Three broad avenues run from north to south, **Chūō-dōri** being the main shopping street, while **Harumi-dōri** cuts across the centre from the east. The two roads meet at a famed intersection known as **Ginza Yon-chōme crossing**, which marks the heart of Ginza: awesome at rush hour, this spot often features in films and documentaries as the epitome of this overcrowded yet totally efficient city.

One could argue, however, that it's in the smaller lanes where the "Ginza feel" is most palpable, in hidey-hole shops and restaurants – and a fair few "bubble-era" buildings which are now barely fit for habitation, and patiently awaiting the wrecking ball.

Kabukiza Theatre

歌舞伎座 • 4-12-15 Ginza, Chūō-ku • Gallery open daily 11am–7pm • Free • ⓦ kabuki-za.co.jp • Higashi-Ginza station

Tokyo rejoiced when the famed **Kabukiza Theatre**, one of Ginza's most iconic buildings, reopened its doors in early 2013. First opened in 1889, the theatre has been rebuilt several times, a victim of fires and war damage. The architect behind its most recent incarnation is Kengo Kuma (see box, p.266), who reinstated the elaborate facade of the original, which burned down in 1921; backed by a modern 29-storey office block, this is classic "city of contrasts" territory. Catch a play (see p.188) or simply check out the fifth-floor gallery, with its wonderful display of kabuki costumes.

Sony Building

ソニービル • 5-3-1 Ginza, Chūō-ku • Daily 11am–7pm • Free • ⓦ www.sonybuilding.jp • Ginza station

With four of its eleven storeys showcasing the latest Sony gadgets, and any number of products-in-development, the **Sony Building** is a must-see for techno-freaks. There's a

---

ON THE ART TRAIL IN GINZA

Though a little short on tourist sights, Ginza is the bastion of Tokyo's commercial galleries – there are enough of them here to keep you busy for a full day.

Design Gallery 3-6-1 Ginza, Chūō-ku ☎ 03 3571 5206; Ginza station. Hidden up on the seventh floor of the Matsuya Ginza department store, this gallery may be tiny, but shows are usually curated by Japan's top designers. The adjacent Design Collection retail area stocks the very best in product design. Mon & Tues 10am–7.30pm, Thurs–Sun 10am–8pm.

Ginza Graphic Gallery 7-7-2 Ginza, Chūō-ku ☎ 03 3571 5206, ⓦ www.dnp.co.jp/gallery/ggg; Ginza station. Single-room space hosting monthly exhibitions that cover – for the most part – graphic design work from the best of Japan's creators. Closes for a few days between shows. Mon–Fri 11am–7pm, Sat 11am–6pm.

Maison Hermès 8F 5-4-1 Ginza, Chūō-ku ☎ 03 3569 3611; Ginza station. Possibly the most charming gallery space in all Tokyo, set at the top of the Renzo Piano-designed "bubble-wrap" building that's home to Hermès' Tokyo boutique. Worth a look whatever the exhibit – the gallery usually hosts themed shows of Japanese and international art. Daily 11am–7pm.

Shiseidō Gallery B1F 8-8-3 Ginza, Chūō-ku ☎ 03 3572 3901, ⓦ group.shiseido.co.jp/gallery; Shimbashi or Ginza station. Located in the distinctive red showroom of the eponymous Japanese cosmetics giant, this small basement gallery hosts group and solo shows – some well worth a look, others merely so-so. Tues–Sat 11am–7pm, Sun 11am–6pm.

Tokyo Gallery + BTAP 7F 8-10-5 Ginza, Chūō-ku ☎ 03 3571 1808, ⓦ tokyo-gallery.com; Shimbashi station. Dating back to 1950, Tokyo Gallery shows cutting-edge work from the Chinese and Korean contemporary art scenes (they have a branch in Beijing). Tues–Fri 11am–7pm, Sat 11am–5pm.

HAMA RIKYŪ ONSHI TEIEN (P.53) >

tax-free shop on the fourth floor and restaurants on most levels, but even if you're a technophobe it's worth popping along to see just what all the fuss is about.

Komparu-yu

金春湯 • 8-7-5 Ginza, Chūō-ku • Daily 2–10pm • ¥460 • Ginza station

One of the most central bathhouses in Tokyo, **Komparu-yu** is a great little place to stop off for a scrub while touring Ginza. It's cheap, and suits the area nicely (as it should, having been here since 1863), with the decor featuring the near-obligatory Mount Fuji mural as well as other tiling depicting flowers, animals and the like. All in all, it's a lovely experience.

Nihombashi

日本橋

North of Ginza, **Nihombashi** (also Romanized as "Nihonbashi") was once the heart of Edo's teeming Shitamachi (see box, p.75), growing from a cluster of early seventeenth-century riverside markets to become the city's chief financial district; the early warehouses and moneylenders evolved into the banks, brokers and trading companies you'll see here today. The area takes its name from the **Nihombashi**, literally the "Bridge of Japan", which marks the point from which all distances from Tokyo are measured (look for the small disc in the middle of the road on the bridge). The original arched, red-lacquer-coated bridge was built in 1603, and was long a favourite of *ukiyo-e* artists; the current stone incarnation, erected in 1911 and now with the Shuto Expressway passing over it, hardly bears comparison. Recent years have seen whole chunks of the area ripped up for ambitious rebuilding projects, of which the most interesting to date is **Coredo**, a shopping, dining and office complex located opposite the Mitsui Memorial Museum.

Bridgestone Museum of Art

ブリヂストン美術館, Burijisuton Bijutsukan • 1-10-1 Kyōbashi, Chūō-ku • ☎ 03 3563 0241, ⓦ bridgestone-museum.gr.jp • Tokyo, Kyōbashi or Nihombashi stations

Closed for major renovation at the time of writing, and expected to reopen in 2019, the superb **Bridgestone Museum of Art** has an impressive collection of paintings by Van Gogh, Renoir, Degas, Monet, Manet, Miró, Picasso and other heavyweights, as well as Meiji-era Japanese paintings in Western style.

Kite Museum

凧の博物館, Tako-no Hakubutsukan • 5F 1-12-10 Nihombashi, Chūō-ku • Mon–Sat 11am–5pm • ¥200 • ☎ 03 3271 2465, ⓦ tako.gr.jp • Nihombashi station

There's no English sign for the cluttered little **Kite Museum**, but it's on the fifth floor above *Taimeiken* restaurant (see p.157). Since 1977 the restaurant's former owner has amassed over three hundred kites of every shape and size, from one no bigger than a postage stamp to a monster 18m square. If you have kids in tow, they can try making their own from bamboo and *washi* paper.

Mitsui Memorial Museum

三井記念美術館, Mitsui Kinen Bijutsukan • 7F Mitsui Main Building, 2-1-1 Nihombashi Muromachi, Chūō-ku • Tues–Sun 10am–5pm • ¥1000, or ¥1300 for special exhibitions • ☎ 03 5777 8600, ⓦ mitsui-museum.jp • Mitsukoshimae station

Just north of the main branch of the Mitsukoshi department store (see box, p.197), wood-panelled lifts rise to the seventh-floor **Mitsui Memorial Museum**, where a superb collection spanning three hundred years of Japanese and Asian art is on display. Put together by the Mitsui family (behind the eponymous, enormously successful trading dynasty), changing exhibitions follow a seasonal theme, and are mostly aimed at the connoisseur – you'll often see older Tokyoites purring with pleasure at the pottery, calligraphy, jades or jewellery before them.

EMA PRAYER TABLETS, YUSHIMA SEIDŌ

Akihabara and around

Up the tracks from the Ginza area, a blaze of adverts and a cacophony of competing audio systems announce Akihabara. "Akiba", as it's popularly known, is Tokyo's foremost discount shopping area for electrical and electronic goods of all kinds, but these days it has also become a hotspot for fans of anime and manga, and is famed as the spawning ground for the decidedly surreal "maid cafés" (see box, p.160). Though Akiba's buzzing, neon-lit streets are almost entirely dedicated to technological wizardry and pop culture, there are sights of a different nature to the west, including the lively Shinto shrine of Kanda Myōjin, and an austere monument to Confucius at Yushima Seidō.

BEST OF AKIHABARA

3331 Arts Chiyoda Check out cutting-edge contemporary art (see below)
Akiba 3D Theater Catch the latest anime flick (see box, p.60)
Super Potato Go all retro by pumping coins into some Nintendo arcade games (see box, p.60)
Origami Kaikan Purchase perfectly made origami souvenirs (see p.60 & p.195)
Yushima Seidō Savour the atmosphere at this peaceful shrine (see p.60)
Hachimaki Wolf down some of Tokyo's best *tendon* (tempura on rice) (see p.159)
Maid cafés Sup a coffee at *gaijin*-friendly *Maidreamin* or *Mai:lish* (see p.159 & p.160)
Tsukumo Robot Kingdom Sate your robot lust (see p.198)

There's yet more to see in the wide area south of the Kanda-gawa (神田川), a small river skirting the southern flank of Akihabara station. To the west, **Ochanomizu** has become rather trendy of late due to the opening of some stylish new shopping and eating complexes, while older sights such as the Nikolai Cathedral are also worthy of attention. To the east is **Bakurochō**, a notably artistic quarter.

Akihabara

秋葉原

The bulk of **Akihabara**'s attractions lie north of the small Kanda river, with Akihabara station the best starting point. The station's surroundings are excellent photo-fodder – an audiovisual cacophony of neon and teeming humanity, crisscrossed by elevated rail tracks. It's best to swing by on a Sunday, when much of the main drag, Chūō-dōri, is closed to traffic. Although the area can seem a little bewildering, it's surprisingly easy to get your fix of the anime, computer games and other facets of **contemporary culture** that Akihabara is known for (see box, p.60). For all this, Akihabara does actually have a few bona-fide sights: within easy walking distance you'll find the superb **3331 Arts Chiyoda** centre, the **Kanda Myōjin** Shinto shrine and the brooding **Yushima Seidō**.

3331 Arts Chiyoda

3331アーツ千代田 • 6-11-14 Sotokanda, Chiyoda-ku • Daily except Tues noon–7pm • Usually free, though charges apply for some special exhibitions • ☎ 03 6803 2441, ⊚ 3331.jp • Suehirochō station

Down a side street a little north of Suehirochō subway station is the landscaped entrance to the large **3331 Arts Chiyoda** complex. Based inside a renovated school, the centre hosts close to twenty galleries; although some spaces tend towards the twee, a handful of prominent artists have cut their teeth here, and all in all it usually makes for an absorbing look at the Japanese art scene. Stroll around and you'll find a revolving mix of exhibitions, interactive installations and workshops; there's also an on-site café-restaurant.

Kanda Myōjin

神田明神 • 2-16-2 Sotokanda, Shiyoda-ku • Daily 9am–4pm • Free • Ochanomizu station

A vermilion gate marks the entrance to **Kanda Myōjin**, one of the city's oldest shrines and host to one of its top three festivals, the **Kanda Matsuri** (see p.26). Founded in 730 AD, the shrine originally stood in front of Edo Castle, where it was dedicated to the gods of farming and fishing (Daikoku and Ebisu). Later, the tenth-century rebel Taira no Masakado – who was beheaded after declaring himself emperor – was also enshrined here. When Shogun Tokugawa Ieyasu was strengthening the castle's fortifications in 1616, he took the opportunity to move the shrine, but mollified Masakado's supporters by declaring him a guardian deity of the city. Poke around to the west of the main shrine, and you'll find charming *Imasa*, an almost otherworldly café (see p.159).

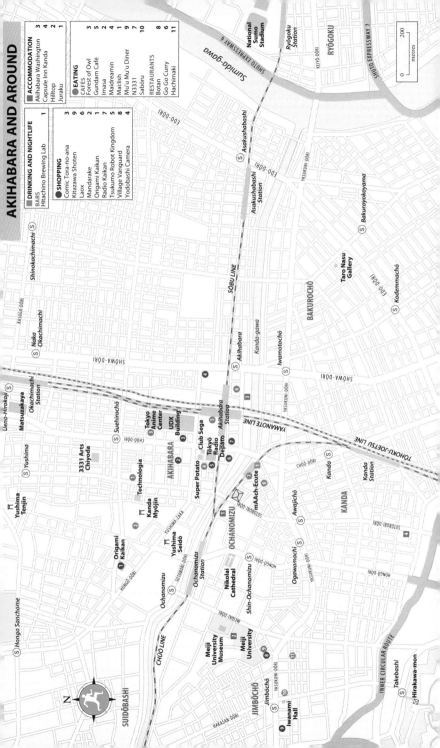

TAKING THE PULSE OF AKIHABARA

There are few other Tokyo districts in which so many travellers actually avoid the sights: instead, **contemporary culture** is Akihabara's main, or even exclusive, drawcard. Here are a few ways in which to enjoy the more modern delights of Akiba.

Anime Part of the UDX Building, a mainstay of the local IT industry, the **Tokyo Anime Center** (東京アニメセンター; 4F UDX Building, 4-14-1 Sotokanda; Tues–Sun 11am–7pm; ☎03 5298 1188, ⓦanimecenter.jp) features small displays on recent anime, and hosts regular events that can be a lot of fun. To nonbelievers, however, it might seem little more than a glorified shop selling anime-related goods – for which *Mandarake* (see p.194) is also a good bet. If you're here on a weekend, be sure to visit the ultra-high-tech **Akiba 3D Theater** in the same building, where some of the latest anime releases are on show.

Electronics Akihabara's electronic stores are descendants of a postwar black market in radios and radio parts that took place beneath the train tracks around Akihabara station. You can recapture some of the atmosphere in the **Tōkyō Radio Depāto** (東京ラジオデパート; 1-10-11 Sotokanda; daily 11am–7pm) – four floors stuffed with plugs, wires, boards and tools for making or repairing audiovisual equipment.

Maid cafés The whole area is riddled with maid cafés (see box, p.160), which come in many different guises: Cosplay maids, schoolgirl maids, sailor maids, OL maids (meaning "office lady", a Japanese porn staple), kimono maids, and many more. You'll see a bunch of cafés clamouring for custom on the road outside *Super Potato* (see below); two safe bets are *Mai-lish* (see p.160) and *Maidreamin* (see p.159) – the latter is on the second floor of the Zeniya Building, which boasts seven full levels of maid cafés, and nothing else.

Robots You'd have to bring quite a bit of cash to purchase the equipment necessary to put together a full robot at **Technologia** (テクノロジア; 4-12-9 Sotokanda; daily 10am–7pm), but this store carries a large amount of such goodies, and is well worth a peek even if you're not a roboteer. Smaller toys are available for purchase, as are DVDs of robot battles.

Video games Head on up to the fifth floor of **Super Potato** (スーパーポテト; 1-11-2 Sotokanda; daily 11am–8pm), which has a whole bunch of old-school arcade games including Bomberman, Mario (the NES version) and several iterations of Street Fighter II. If that sounds a little Nintendo-focused, try **Club Sega** (クラブセガ; 1-11-1 Sotokanda; daily 10am–11.30pm), which has two floors of arcade games and one of interactive music machines atop its six levels.

Origami Kaikan

おりがみ会館・1-7-14 Yushima, Bunkyō-ku・Mon–Sat 9.30am–6pm・☎03 3811 4025・Ochanomizu station

The six-storey **Origami Kaikan** is considered one of the "Six Cultural Treasures" of the Bunkyo Ward. This outpost for the production and dyeing of *washi* (Japanese paper) was founded in 1859, and to this day they continue to sell it on the premises (see p.195) – there's also an exhibition hall on the second floor. It's possible to take lessons (some free) in the art of paper folding here, although English instruction is unlikely.

Yushima Seidō

湯島聖堂・1-4-25 Yushima, Bunkyō-ku・Daily: May–Oct 9.30am–5pm; Nov–April 9.30am–4pm・Free・Ochanomizu station

A copse of woodland hides the distinctive shrine of **Yushima Seidō**, dedicated to the Chinese sage Confucius. The Seidō (Sacred Hall) was founded in 1632 as an academy for the study of the ancient classics at a time when the Tokugawa were promoting Confucianism as the state's ethical foundation. In 1691 the hall was moved to its present location, where it became an elite school for the sons of samurai and high-ranking officials, though most of these buildings were lost in the fires of 1923. Today, the quiet compound contains an eighteenth-century wooden gate and, at the top of broad steps, the imposing, black-lacquered Taisen-den, or "Hall of Accomplishments", where the shrine to Confucius is located. There are rarely many people here, and the place actually looks at its best in the rain or at dusk – darkness seems to show these brooding buildings in their best light.

Ochanomizu

御茶ノ水

The small Kanda-gawa runs between the JR and Tokyo Metro **Ochanomizu** stations. The name of the area (literally, "the water for the tea") dates back to the Edo period when water from the river was used to make the shogun's tea, though nowadays it's the stream itself that's usually tea-like in pigment; however, with trains appearing all over the place – crossing a bridge here, emerging from a tunnel there – it's all quite photogenic. The **rail arches** east of the JR station have also been subject to fairly major refurbishment of late, and around the confusingly-named mAAch-Ecute mini-mall you'll find the *Hitachino* brew-pub (see p.176) and *N3331* (see p.160), a café which pokes up between the tracks themselves.

Trains aside, the area boasts a relaxed air and a modest collection of interesting sights, including a pretty **cathedral** (wonderfully incongruous in its mid-Tokyo location), the city's prime **bookshop** area, and prestigious **Meiji University**, home to a diverting **museum**. In addition, just to the west, the lively student centre of **Jimbōchō** is home to dozens of secondhand **bookshops**, where racks of dog-eared novels and textbooks sit outside shops stacked high with dusty tomes; most are in Japanese, but some specialize in English-language books: try *Kitazawa Shoten* (see p.197).

3

Nikolai Cathedral

ニコライ堂, Nikorai-jō • 4-1-3 Kanda Surugadai, Chiyoda-ku • Tues–Sun: April–Sept 1–4pm; Oct–March 1–3.30pm • Suggested donation ¥300 • ☎ 03 3295 6879 • Shin-Ochanomizu station

If you're in the area in the afternoon, pay a visit to the Russian Orthodox **Nikolai Cathedral**. Founded by Archbishop Nikolai Kasatkin, who came to Japan in 1861 as chaplain to the Russian consulate in Hokkaidō, the cathedral took seven years to complete (1884–91). The plans were sent from Russia, but British architect Josiah Conder (see box below) gets most of the credit.

Meiji University Museum

明治大学博物館, Meiji Daigaku Hakubutsukan • 1-1 Kanda Surugadai, Chiyoda-ku • Daily 10am–5pm, sometimes closed weekends in summer • Free • ☎ 03 3296 4448, ⓦ www.meiji.ac.jp/museum • Jimbōchō station

The **Meiji University Museum** sits off Meidai-dōri in the basement of the university's Academy Common Building. The most interesting – and spine-chilling – exhibits are to be found in the "criminal zone", and come courtesy of the university's original 1881 incarnation as a law school. After breaking you in gently with examples of Edo-era laws and edicts, the displays move on to the tools used by police to arrest miscreants: goads, the U-shaped "military fork" and the delightfully named "sleeve entangler". Then it's a

---

JOSIAH CONDER

Of the many Western architects invited by the Meiji government to Japan to help it modernize, **Josiah Conder** had the greatest impact. When he arrived in 1877, a freshly graduated 25-year-old, his position was to teach architecture at what would become the Faculty of Engineering at Tokyo University. By the time he died in Tokyo in 1920 he had designed over fifty major buildings including the original **Imperial Museum** at Ueno, and the **Nikolai Cathedral** in Ochanomizu (see above). His crowning glory was generally considered to be the **Rokumeikan** reception hall in Hibiya, a synthesis of Japanese and Western architectural styles. This was torn down in 1940, but a model can be seen in the Edo-Tokyo Museum (see p.83). His students Tatsuno Kingo and Katayama Tōkuma went on, respectively, to design Tokyo station and the Akasaka Detached Palace.

In the West, Conder is perhaps best known for his study of Japanese **gardens** and his 1893 book *Landscape Gardens in Japan*. Kyū Iwasaki-tei in Ueno (see p.68) and Kyū Furukawa near Komagome (see p.140) are two houses he designed, with gardens which are open to the public. His Mitsubishi Ichigokan building (see p.46) has also been resurrected in recent years.

rapid descent into prints showing instruments of torture and methods of punishment, including some truly gruesome ways of carrying out the death penalty. The other two zones cover archeology and traditional crafts, and overall there's a fair amount of information in English.

Bakurochō

馬喰町

There are some quirky galleries east of Akihabara station in the district of **Bakurochō**, accessible via the subway station of the same name. The **Agata-Takezawa** building, a run-down office block which houses the **Taro Nasu Gallery**, is quickly becoming the hub of this up-and-coming arty neighbourhood: it also includes the nonprofit, university-funded **Alpha M** exhibition space and an interesting bunch of arts, crafts and fashion tenants.

Taro Nasu Gallery

タロウナスギャラリー, Taro Nasu Gyarerī • 1-2-11 Higashi-Kanda, Chiyoda-ku • Tues–Sat 11am–7pm • Free • ☎ 03 5856 5713, ⓦ taronasugallery.com • Bakurochō station

The respected **Taro Nasu Gallery** acts as an anchor of sorts to the trendy Agata-Takezawa building, having moved here in 2009 from their Ōsaka base. They have ten or so exhibitions per year, mainly of Japanese artists, mixed in with a few from Europe.

AMEYOKOCHŌ MARKET

Ueno and around

Directly north of Akihabara is Ueno, another of Tokyo's teeming mega-neighbourhoods. Around the area's main park, Ueno Kōen, you'll find a host of good museums, as well as a few relics from the vast temple complex at Kan'ei-ji, built on this hilltop in 1624 by the second shogun, Tokugawa Hidetada, to protect his castle's northeast quarter. The prestigious Tokyo National Museum alone could easily fill a day, but there's also the entertaining Museum of Nature and Science, the Museum of Western Art and the endearing Shitamachi Museum, which harks back to Ueno's proletarian past. Much of downtown Ueno, meanwhile, has a rough-and-ready feel, especially around the station and bustling Ameyokochō Market. Further west, there's a more sedate atmosphere in and around the ivory towers of Tokyo University.

BEST OF UENO AND AROUND

Shinobazu Pond Take a stroll along the causeway (see below)
Ueno Zoo Visit at feeding times to see the animals at their liveliest (see p.66)
National Museum of Nature and Science See Japan's hero mutt, Hachikō, in stuffed form (see p.67)
Tokyo University Mingle with Japan's future leaders (see p.68)
Sasa-no-yuki Purr over some of Tokyo's best tofu (see p.161)
Kayaba Bakery Stop for lunch in a charming wooden building (see p.161)
Jūsan-ya Pick up some wonderful wooden combs (see p.195)

North of the university campus are **Nezu** and **Yanaka**, two of Tokyo's most charmingly old-fashioned neighbourhoods and a world away from the usual hustle and bustle of the city. Along with **Sendagi** they form an area referred to as **Yanasen**, where you can experience a slower and more relaxed side of Tokyo. One draw is the historic and tranquil shrine of **Nezu-jinja**, but the whole area is strewn with small temples, craft shops and other attractions, such as the picturesque and historic **Yanaka Cemetery** and the old-style shopping street of **Yanaka Ginza**. There are also a couple of good traditional Japanese-style hotels around here (see p.148) for those who really want to soak up the atmosphere of Shitamachi (literally "low town") – the area's former incarnation (see box, p.75).

GETTING AROUND   **UENO AND AROUND**

Tours You can join free walking tours of the Ueno area (Wed, Fri & Sun 10.30am & 1.30pm), with English-speaking guides, starting from *Green Salon*, on the park-side exit of Ueno station (see map opposite).

Bike rental If you're planning to be in the Yanaka area for much of the day, consider renting a bike from the young team at Tokyobike (Wed–Sun 10am–7pm; ¥2500 for the day, ¥1500 for any subsequent days; ☏ 03 5809 0980, ⓦ tokyobike.com; see map opposite).

Ueno

上野

The **Ueno** district sprawls south and east of the eponymous **train station**, a real whopper that has the honour of hosting high-speed services – one of only three stations in Tokyo to do so. The atmosphere is completely different on the west side of the tracks, with much of the immediate area taken up by **Ueno Kōen**.

Ueno Kōen

上野公園 • Various entrances; information desk by east gate • Ueno station

Although it's far from being the city's most attractive park, all of Tokyo seems to flock to **Ueno Kōen** during spring's cherry blossom season. Outside this brief period, however, the park only really gets busy at weekends, and during the week it can be a pleasant place for a stroll, particularly around Shinobazu Pond. At the top of the steps leading up to the park from Ueno station you'll find a bronze statue of **Saigō Takamori**, the great leader of the Restoration army, which helped bring Emperor Meiji to power – his life story was the inspiration for the Tom Cruise movie *The Last Samurai*.

Shinobazu Pond

不忍池, Shinobazu-no Ike • Boat rental daily 10am–6pm • Rowboats ¥700, pedaloes ¥600–700 • Ueno station

Much of the park's southwest is taken up by **Shinobazu Pond**, whose western banks are lined with ancient cherry trees. Once an inlet of Tokyo Bay, the pond is now a wildlife protection area and hosts a permanent colony of wild black cormorants as well as temporary populations of migrating waterfowl. A causeway leads out across its reeds and lotus beds to a small, leafy island occupied by an octagonal-roofed temple, **Benten-dō**, dedicated to the goddess of good fortune, water and music (among other things). Inside the dimly lit worship hall you can just make out Benten's eight arms, each clutching a holy weapon, while the ceiling sports a snarling dragon.

Kiyomizu Kannon-dō

清水観音堂 • 24hr • Free

Built out over the hillside, the red-lacquered **Kiyomizu Kannon-dō** temple, dating from 1631, is a smaller, less impressive version of Kyoto's famous Kiyomizu temple, but it has the rare distinction of being one of the last parts of the Kan'ei-ji complex still

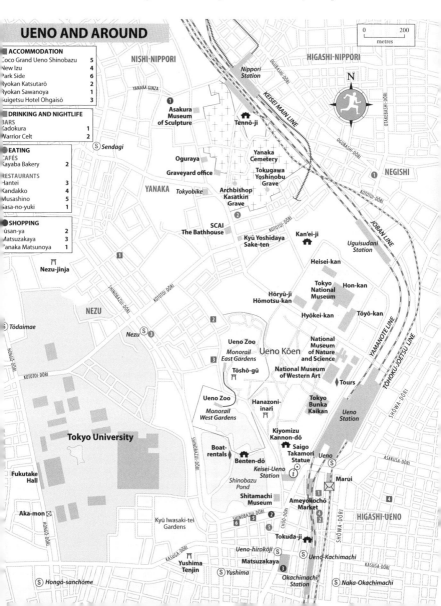

UENO AND AROUND

ACCOMMODATION

Coco Grand Ueno Shinobazu	5
New Izu	4
Park Side	6
Ryokan Katsutarō	2
Ryokan Sawanoya	1
Suigetsu Hotel Ohgaisō	3

DRINKING AND NIGHTLIFE

BARS	
Kadokura	1
Warrior Celt	2

EATING

CAFÉS	
Kayaba Bakery	2
RESTAURANTS	
Hantei	3
Kandakko	4
Musashino	5
Sasa-no-yuki	1

SHOPPING

Usan-ya	2
Matsuzakaya	3
Yanaka Matsunoya	1

standing. The temple is dedicated to **Senju Kannon** (the thousand-armed Kannon), whose image is displayed only in February, although the second-rank **Kosodate Kannon** receives more visitors as the Bodhisattva in charge of conception. Hopeful women leave dolls at the altar during the year, following which the dolls are all burnt at a rather sad memorial service on September 25.

Ueno Zoo

上野動物園, Ueno Dōbutsuen • 9-83 Ueno Kōen, Taitō-ku • Tues–Sun 9.30am–4pm • ¥600, free for children 12 and under; monorail ¥150 • ☎ 03 3828 5171, ⓦ www.tokyo-zoo.net

Considering the fact that **Ueno Zoo** is over a century old, it's less depressing than might be feared. In recent years the pens have been upgraded – though they're still small and concrete – and there's plenty of vegetation around, including some magnificent, corkscrewing lianas. Among the animals here are rare gorillas and pygmy hippos, as well as a couple of pandas – make a note of the feeding time when you enter the zoo, as they tend to spend the rest of the day doing very little at all. The macaques, particularly the younger ones, seem to have a whale of a time on the rocky crag they call home; the same cannot be said of the bears and big cats, who tend to pace around small corners of their pens. The east and west parts of the zoo are connected by monorail, though walking is just as pleasant.

Shitamachi Museum

下町風俗資料館, Shitamachi Fūzoku Shiryōkan • 2-1 Ueno Kōen, Taitō-ku • Tues–Sun 9.30am–5.30pm • ¥300 • ☎ 03 3823 7451, ⓦ www.taitocity.net/taito/shitamachi • Ueno or Ueno-Hirokōji stations

At the far southern end of the park, the interesting **Shitamachi Museum** is set in a distinctive, partly traditional-style building beside Shinobazu Pond. The museum opened in 1980 to preserve something of the working-class Shitamachi of old (see box, p.75), while it was still within living memory. The ground floor is made up of a reconstructed merchant's shophouse and a 1920s tenement row, complete with sweet shop and coppersmith's workroom. The upper floor is devoted to rotating exhibitions focusing on articles of daily life – old photos, toys, advertisements and artisans' tools, with all exhibits donated by local residents. There's plenty of information in English and it's possible to handle most items, but be sure to take off your shoes before exploring the shop interiors.

Tōshō-gū

東照宮 • 9-88 Ueno, Taitō-ku • Daily 9am–sunset • ¥200 • Ueno or Nezu stations

A tree-lined avenue marks the approach to Tokugawa Ieyasu's shrine, **Tōshō-gū**. Ieyasu died in 1616 and is buried in Nikkō, but this was his main shrine in Tokyo, founded in 1627 and rebuilt on a grander scale in 1651. For once it's possible to penetrate beyond the screened entrance and enclosing walls to take a closer look inside. A path leads from the ticket gate clockwise round the polychrome halls and into the worship hall, whose faded decorative work contrasts sharply with the burnished black and gold of Ieyasu's shrine room behind. Before leaving, take a look at the ornate, Chinese-style front gate, where two golden dragons carved in 1651 by Hidari Jingorō – he of Nikkō's sleeping cat fame (see p.213) – attract much attention. So realistic is the carving that, according to local tradition, the pair sneak off at midnight to drink in Shinobazu Pond. The seventeenth-century, five-storey pagoda rising above the trees to the north of Tōshō-gū is actually marooned inside Ueno Zoo (see above).

National Museum of Western Art

国立西洋美術館, Kokuritsu Seiyō Bijutsukan • 7-7 Ueno Kōen, Taitō-ku • Tues–Sun 9.30am–5.30pm, Fri until 8pm • ¥430, or more for special exhibitions • ☎ 03 3828 5131, ⓦ www.nmwa.go.jp • Ueno station

The **National Museum of Western Art** is instantly recognizable from the Rodin statues on the forecourt. The museum, designed by Le Corbusier, was erected in 1959 to house the mostly French Impressionist paintings left to the nation by Kawasaki shipping magnate Matsukata Kōjirō. Since then, works by Rubens, Tintoretto, Max Ernst and Jackson Pollock have broadened the scope of this impressive collection.

National Museum of Nature and Science

国立科学博物館, Kokuritsu Kagaku Hakubutsukan • 7-20 Ueno Kōen, Taitō-ku • Tues–Sun 9am–5pm, Fri until 8pm • ¥600 • ☎ 03 5777 8600, ⓦ www.kahaku.go.jp • Ueno station

The **National Museum of Nature and Science** offers lots of videos and interactive displays, and was recently expanded to include new, slightly fancier, wings on most floors. Six floors of displays cover natural history as well as science and technology. In the "exploration space" on the second floor, pendulums, magnets, mirrors and hand-powered generators provide entertainment for the mainly school-age audience, while down in the basement there's an aquarium and a dinosaur skeleton. One interesting highlight is on the second floor: sitting amid other stuffed animals, with surprisingly little fanfare, is Hachikō, Japan's canine hero (see box, p.121). Almost all visitors, even the locals, walk past without a second glance – a rather sad end for the country's most famous hound.

Tokyo National Museum

東京国立博物, Tokyo Kokuritsu Hakubutsukan • 13-9 Ueno Kōen, Taitō-ku • Tues–Sun 9.30am–5pm, though often later (see website) • ¥620 • ☎ 03 5405 8686, ⓦ www.tnm.jp • Ueno station

Dominating the northern reaches of Ueno Park is the **Tokyo National Museum**, containing the world's largest collection of Japanese art, plus an extensive collection of eastern antiquities. The museum style tends to old-fashioned reverential dryness, but among such a vast collection there's something to excite everyone's imagination. Displays are rotated every few months from a collection of around 110,000 pieces, and the special exhibitions are usually worth seeing if you can stand the crowds.

Hon-kan

It's best to start with the **Hon-kan**, the central building, which presents the sweep of Japanese art from Jōmon-period pottery (pre-fourth century BC) to paintings from the Edo period. On your way around you'll most likely spy theatrical costume for kabuki, nō and *bunraku*, as well as colourful Buddhist mandalas, *ukiyo-e* prints, samurai swords, exquisite lacquerware and even seventeenth-century Christian art from southern Japan. There's a decent shop in the basement – good for souvenirs.

Heisei-kan

In the building's northwest corner, look out for a passage leading to the **Heisei-kan** building, on the ground level of which is the splendid Japanese Archeology Gallery, containing important recent finds. Though some of the ground it covers is the same as at the Hon-kan, modern presentation really brings the objects to life – the best displays are refreshingly simple and burst with energy. Highlights are the chunky, flame-shaped Jōmon pots and a collection of super-heated Sue stoneware, made using a technique introduced from Korea in the fifth century. Look out, too, for the bug-eyed, curvaceous clay figures (*dogū*) of the Jōmon period, and the funerary *haniwa* from the fourth to sixth centuries AD – these terracotta representations of houses, animals, musicians and stocky little warriors were placed on burial mounds to protect the deceased lord in the afterlife. The upper level hosts special exhibitions – usually very well curated.

Hōryū-ji Hōmotsu-kan

In the southwest corner of the compound, behind the copper-domed Hyōkei-kan of 1908 (sadly closed off, but used for occasional talks and exhibitions), lurks the **Hōryū-ji Hōmotsu-kan**. This sleek newer gallery contains a selection of priceless treasures donated over the centuries to the Hōryū-ji in Nara, many dating back as far as the

AMEYOKOCHŌ

The bustling **market** area south of Ueno station, **Ameyokochō** (アメ横丁), extends nearly half a kilometre along the west side of the elevated JR train lines down to Okachimachi station. The name – an abbreviation of "Ameya Yokochō", or "Candy Sellers' Alley" – dates from the immediate postwar days when sweets were a luxury and the hundreds of stalls here mostly peddled sweet potatoes coated in sugar syrup (*daigakuimo*). Since **rationing** was in force, black marketeers joined the candy sellers, dealing in rice and other foodstuffs, household goods and personal items. Later, American imports found their way from army stores onto the streets here, especially during the Korean War in the early 1950s, which is also when the market was legalized. Ameyokochō still retains a flavour of those early days: stalls specializing in everything from bulk tea and coffee to jewellery and fish line the street, gruff men with sandpaper voices shout out their wares, and there's a clutch of *yakitori* bars under the arches.

seventh century. Exhibits are rotated occasionally, but keep your fingers crossed for an eye-catching display of gilt-bronze Buddhist statues. The upper level has separate rooms for wooden and lacquered material, metalwork and painting.

Tōyō-kan

Refurbished in 2013, the **Tōyō-kan** houses a delightful hotchpotch of antiquities, with Javanese textiles and nineteenth-century Indian prints rubbing shoulders with Egyptian mummies and a wonderful collection of Southeast Asian bronze Buddhas. The Chinese and, particularly, the Korean collections are also interesting for their obvious parallels with Japanese art.

Tokyo University and around

東京大学, Tōkyō Daigaku

The west side of central Ueno is dominated by seedy love hotels and dubious bars. Take a short walk past Yushima subway station, however, and you'll discover a remnant of a much more genteel past. Founded in 1869, **Tokyo University** – or Tōdai, as it's commonly known – is the nation's top-ranking establishment, and its graduates fill the corridors of power. The university occupies the former estate of the wealthy Maeda lords, though there's little sign of their mansion beyond a pond and the one-storey, red-lacquer gate, **Aka-mon**, which forms the front (west) entrance into the sleepy, pleasant campus. Passing through Aka-mon and immediately turning left brings you to **Fukutake Hall**, a concrete-lined piece of industrial chic designed by renowned architect Andō Tadao. In the area around the university, you'll find some sculpted **gardens** and a charming **shrine**.

Kyū Iwasaki-tei Gardens

旧岩崎邸庭園, Kyū Iwasaki-tei Teien • 1-3-45 Ikenohata, Taito-ku • Daily 9am–5pm • ¥400; tea ¥500 • ☎ 03 3823 8340 • Yushima station

Off the southeastern corner of Tokyo University, the **Kyū Iwasaki-tei Gardens** date from 1896 and surround an elegant **house**, designed by British architect Josiah Conder (see box, p.61), which combines a *café au lait*-painted, Western-style two-storey mansion with a traditional single-storey Japanese residence. The wooden Jacobean- and Moorish-influenced arabesque interiors of the mansion are in fantastic condition, in stark contrast to the severely faded screen paintings of the Japanese section. The lack of furniture in both houses makes them a little lifeless, but it's nonetheless an impressive artefact in a city where such buildings are increasingly rare. You can take **tea** in the Japanese section or sit outside and admire the gardens, which also combine Eastern and Western influences.

YANAKA GINZA (P.70) >

Yushima Tenjin

湯島天神 • 3-30-1 Yushima, Bunkyō-ku • 24hr • Free • Yushima station

Yushima Tenjin (also known as Yushima Tenmangū) is a shrine dedicated to Tenjin, the god of scholarship. The best time to visit is in late February when the plum trees are in blossom and candidates for university entrance exams leave mountains of *ema* (wooden votive tablets) inscribed with their requirements. At other times of year it's still worth a visit, with the tree-covered south end of the complex a lovely place to relax.

Nezu

根津

The old Tokyo district of **Nezu**, meaning "Water's Edge", is north of Tokyo University, a short walk west of Ueno Park. Its main sight is **Nezu-jinja**, a venerable, cedar-shaded shrine; while you're in the neighbourhood you may also want to visit *Hantei*, a traditional *kushiage* restaurant (see p.161).

Nezu-jinja

根津神社 • 1-28-9 Nezu, Bunkyō-ku • Daily 7am–sunset • Free • Nezu station

The cracking **Nezu** shrine dates from the early eighteenth century when it was built in honour of the sixth Tokugawa shogun, Ienobu. Ornate and colourfully decorated, it is notable for its corridor of vermilion *torii* (you may have to stoop to get under them) and a hillside bedecked with some three thousand azalea bushes which bloom in a profusion of pinks and reds during late April and early May, attracting throngs of camera-toting visitors. At other times the shrine is serene and peaceful.

Yanaka

谷中

After the Long Sleeves Fire of 1657 (see box, p.254), many temples relocated to the higher ground of **Yanaka**, where they remain today, alongside old wooden buildings that seem to have miraculously escaped the ensuing centuries' various calamities. It's a charming area to explore on foot, and you could spend many hours rambling through its narrow, quiet streets, discovering small temples, shrines and traditional craft shops.

Yanaka Ginza

谷中銀座 • Sendagi station

The focal point of Yanaka, for many, is the pedestrianized shopping street known as **Yanaka Ginza**, an appealing shopping promenade lined with small family businesses selling *geta* (wooden sandals), baskets, tea, *sembei* (rice crackers) and suchlike; recent years have seen it take a turn for the cheesy, but it's still worth a look.

Yanaka Cemetery

谷中霊園, Yanaka Reien • 24hr; graveyard offices daily 8.30am–5pm • Free • Nippori station

The Yanaka area is dominated by **Yanaka Cemetery**, one of Tokyo's oldest and largest graveyards. A couple of minutes' walk south of the Nippori entrance to the cemetery (there are several), you'll find one of the area's most attractive temples, **Tennō-ji** (天王寺), beside which stands a large copper Buddha dating from 1690. Head southwest down the cemetery's main avenue from here to reach the **graveyard offices**, opposite the public toilet, where you can pick up a Japanese map locating the graves of various notables, including the last Tokugawa shogun, Yoshinobu, who is buried in a large plot on the southern edge of the cemetery.

Asakura Museum of Sculpture

朝倉彫塑館, Asakura Chōsokan • 7-18-10 Yanaka, Taitō-ku • Tues–Thurs, Sat & Sun 9.30am–4.30pm • ¥500 • Nippori station

The **Asakura Museum of Sculpture**, the lovely former home, studio and gardens of sculptor Asakura Fumio (1883–1964), is one of Yanaka's many gems. It's filled with examples of his work, the largest of which are presented in airy rooms with soaring ceilings.

Oguraya

小倉屋 • 7-6-8 Yanaka, Taitō-ku • Thurs–Sun 10.30am–4.30pm • Free • ☎ 03 3828 0562 • Nippori station

Off the western flank of Yanaka cemetery, and sitting on an attractive residential street, is **Oguraya**, a pawnbroker's shop dating from 1847. It's now a gallery-cum-shop whose lofty interior is often filled with traditional paintings; also of interest is the black-painted, three-storey wooden *dozō* (storehouse), which is worth popping inside just to see this lovingly preserved and increasingly rare type of architecture.

Kyū Yoshidaya Sake-ten

旧吉田屋酒店 • 10-6 Ueno-Sakuragi 2-chōme, Taitō-ku • Tues–Sun 9.30am–4.30pm • Free • ☎ 03 3823 4408 • Nezu station

Just south of Yanaka cemetery, a five-minute walk from Nezu station along the major road Kototoi-dōri, is **Kyū Yoshidaya Sake-ten**, an early twentieth-century sake store which was moved here in 1987 and is an annexe of the Shitamachi Museum (see p.66). It is worth a quick glimpse to check out the giant glass bottles, china barrels and other accoutrements of the trade.

SCAI The Bathhouse

スカイザバスハウス • 6-1-23 Yanaka, Taitō-ku • Tues–Sat noon–6pm • Free • ☎ 03 3821 1144, Ⓦ scaithebathhouse.com • Nippori or Nezu stations

A bizarre little contemporary art gallery, **SCAI The Bathhouse** occupies a 200-year-old public bath west of Yanaka Cemetery. It's best known for bringing younger local artists greater international attention, though its own exhibits are often sourced from abroad – this successful East–West interplay resulted in both Anish Kapoor and Julian Opie finding Japanese inspiration. The gallery also hosts a range of lectures and performance art.

NAKAMISE-DŌRI AND SENSŌ-JI

Asakusa and around

Tokyo boasts many wonderful neighbourhoods, but few score as highly as
Asakusa for sheer charm. With its historic buildings, craft shops and ryokan,
the area wears its tradition gallantly, though it conceals a surprisingly seedy
heart – here you'll find vivid reminders of Edo's Shitamachi (see box, p.75),
and the popular culture it spawned. Asakusa is best known as the site of
Tokyo's most venerable Buddhist temple, Sensō-ji, whose towering worship
hall is filled with a continual throng of petitioners and tourists. Stalls before
the temple cater to the crowds, peddling trinkets and keepsakes as they have
done for centuries, while all around is the inevitable array of restaurants,
drinking places and fast-food stands. This infectious, carnival atmosphere
changes abruptly just to the west of the temple, where the Rokku area has
long been a byword for sleaze and vice.

BEST OF ASAKUSA

5

Himiko Float down the Sumida-gawa in style on a spaceship-like ferry (see below)
Sensō-ji Stroll along Nakamise-dōri to this wonderful temple (see p.75)
Jakotsu-yu Wallow in "black" hot-spring water (see p.76)
Tokyo Skytree Gaze down over the city from the world's second-tallest structure (see p.78)
Andon Ryokan Take in tradition with a twist at a friendly ryokan (see p.148)
Bunka Hostel Sup sake in the bar – or stay overnight – at this stylish hostel (see p.150)
Sometarō Stuff yourself with quality *okonomiyaki* (see p.162)

Though you can easily get to Asakusa by subway, it's more fun to arrive (or depart) by **ferry** along the Sumida-gawa (see below). The ferry station is beside the Azuma-bashi, a bridge that also makes a great viewing site for a couple of Tokyo's most striking pieces of modern architecture: dominating the horizon is the city's newest mega-structure, the soaring **Tokyo Skytree** telecommunications tower (see p.78); closer to the bridge is the Philippe Starck-designed Asahi Beer Hall, replete with what's supposed to be a stylized flame, but is known to all and sundry as the "Golden Turd" (金のうんこ, *kin-no-unko*).

ARRIVAL AND GETTING AROUND

By ferry Floating down the Sumida-gawa is by far the best way of getting to or from Asakusa. The Sumida-gawa service (see p.24) runs from Hinode Pier (every 30–50min, 10am–6.30pm; 40min; ¥780) to the jetty at Asakusa, by the bridge just east of the subway station. Alternatively, the space-age *Himoko* and *Hotaruna* ferries (see p.24) connect Odaiba with Asakusa, usually via Hinode (6 daily; ¥1560).

Tours You can join free walking tours (Sat & Sun 11am & 1.15pm) of the area with English-speaking guides, starting

ASAKUSA AND AROUND

from the tourist information office (see below).
Rickshaw rides You'll see plenty of *jin-riki-sha* (the Japanese term which begat the bastardized English one) hawking for business outside the tourist office; some speak English. Figure on ¥2000 for a ten-minute ride, up to ¥10,000 for an hour.
Bike rental Sumida-kōen bicycle park is underground beside the bridge (daily 6am–8pm; ¥200 for 4hr, ¥300 for a day, ¥1200 for the week; ☎ 03 5246 1305), although they only have a limited number of bikes available.

INFORMATION

Tourist information The Asakusa Culture and Sightseeing Centre is in front of Sensō-ji's main gate, Kaminari-mon (daily 9am–8pm; ☎ 03 3842 5566), and provides English-language information on local festivals, tours and so on; staff here give better ferry information than the staff in the ferry terminal itself, and can also advise on places to eat. The office almost counts as a sight in itself – designed by Kengo Kuma (see p.266), the interior is rather striking, and it's also possible to take the lift up to the eighth floor for spectacular views out over the Asakusa area.

Asakusa

浅草

Most of Tokyo's backpackers call **Asakusa** home during their stay in the capital, and they're in the right place: it's full of pep and vigour, great things to see, and suitably

ASAKUSA, KING OF FESTIVALS

Taking place annually on the third weekend in May, and centred on Asakusa, the **Sanja Matsuri** is Tokyo's biggest festival, attracting up to two million spectators. The climax comes on the second day, when over one hundred *mikoshi* (portable shrines) are paraded through the seething crowds, among them the three *mikoshi* of Asakusa-jinja, each weighing around 1000kg and carried by at least seventy men.

There are numerous other festivals held in Asakusa throughout the year, including the **Samba Carnival** at the end of August. East of the Amuse Museum, alongside narrow **Sumida-kōen** (隅田公園) park, the river provides the stage for one of the city's great summer **firework displays** (*hanabi taikai*), held on the last Saturday in July.

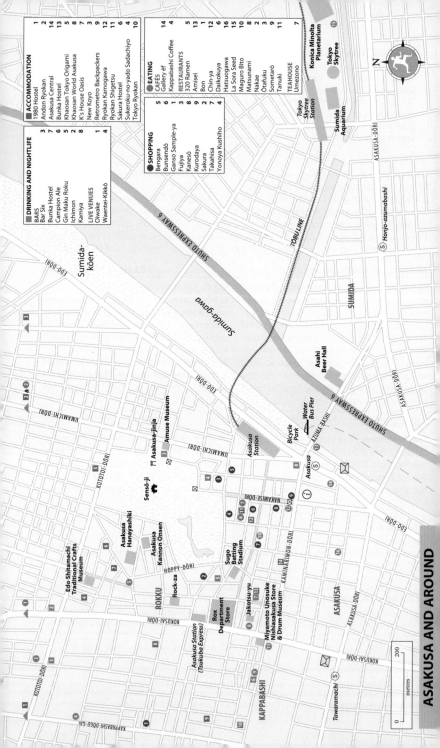

ASAKUSA AND AROUND

ACCOMMODATION

1980 Hostel	1
Andon Ryokan	2
Asakusa Central	14
Bunka Hostel	13
Khaosan Tokyo Origami	5
Khaosan World Asakusa	7
K's House Oasis	8
New Koyo	3
Retrometro Backpackers	9
Ryokan Kamogawa	12
Ryokan Shigetsu	11
Sakura Hostel	6
Sukeroku-no-yado Sadachiyo	4
Tokyo Ryokan	10

DRINKING AND NIGHTLIFE

BARS
Bar Six	3
Bunka Hostel	7
Campion Ale	6
Gin Maku Roku	5
Ichimon	2
Kamiya	8

LIVE VENUES
Oiwake	1
Waentei-Kikkō	4

SHOPPING
Bengara	5
Bunsendō	6
Ganso Sample-ya	1
Fujiya	3
Kanesō	8
Kurodaya	9
Sakura	2
Takahisa	7
Yonoya Kushiho	4

EATING

CAFÉS
Gallery ef	14
Kappabashi Coffee	4

RESTAURANTS
320 Ramen	5
Amisei	13
Bon	1
Chin-ya	12
Daikokuya	6
Hatsuogawa	16
La Sora Seed	15
Maguro Bito	10
Matsunami	8
Nakae	2
Otafuku	3
Sometarō	9
Tanuki	11

TEAHOUSE
Umezono	7

SHITAMACHI

Although the Tokyo of today is a city made up of umpteen mega-districts, under Tokugawa rule (1603–1867) things were a little different. Edo, as Tokyo was known in those times, was essentially divided by caste: the *daimyō* (feudal lords) and samurai resided in the high city, known as **Yamanote** ("the hand of the mountains"), while merchants, artesans and other elements of the working class lived down in cramped **Shitamachi** ("under-town"), an area which resembled a shantytown, its wooden buildings often going up in flames.

While Yamanote is today best-known as the name of the JR line that encircles central Tokyo, elements of Shitamachi have survived through the intervening centuries, especially in the areas around Ueno and Asakusa (and, indeed, all the way up to Kita-Senju). Some original wooden buildings still stand, and the packed layout of yore is evident in countless meandering alleyways. Many elements of culture now thought of as quintessentially Japanese can trace their lineage back to Shitamachi, too – sumo, kabuki and all manner of arts and crafts started life as subcultures spawned by Shitamachi's unique combination of deprivation and artistic creation.

earthy places in which to eat, drink and be merry. South of Sensō-ji are hundreds of small shops and stands, some of which have been around for centuries; west of the temple things take a turn for the seedier, and many a traveller has got sozzled along a small lane known as "**Hoppy-dōri**" (named after Hoppy, a beer-like drink).

When kabuki and *bunraku* were banished from central Edo in the 1840s, they settled in the area known as **Rokku** ("Block 6"), between Sensō-ji and today's Kokusai-dōri. Over the next century almost every fad and fashion in Japanese popular entertainment started life here, from cinema to cabaret and striptease. Today a handful of the old venues survive, most famously **Rock-za**, with its daily strip shows, and there are loads of cinemas, pachinko parlours (see box, p.128), gambling halls and drinking dives. It's not all lowbrow, though: several small theatres in the area, such as Asakusa Engei Hall, still stage *rakugo*, a centuries-old form of comic monologue in which familiar jokes and stories are mixed with modern satire.

Sensō-ji

浅草寺 • North end of Nakamise-dōri • 24hr • Free • Asakusa station

Walking west from the river or Asakusa subway station, you can't miss the solid red-lacquer Kaminari-mon gate, with its enormous paper lantern, that marks the southern entrance to **Sensō-ji**. This magnificent temple, also known as Asakusa Kannon, was founded in the mid-seventh century to enshrine a tiny golden image of Kannon, the goddess of mercy, which had turned up in the nets of two local fishermen. Most of the present buildings are postwar concrete reconstructions, and recent renovation work has seen the roof of the main structure completely covered in titanium tiles, to improve earthquake resistance.

Kaminari-mon

The main temple approach starts under **Kaminari-mon**, or "Thunder Gate", which shelters statues of the guardian gods of Thunder and Wind (named Raijin and Fūjin). More notable, and photogenic, is the gate's gigantic red paper lantern – four metres in height, it weighs in at a whopping 670kg. On your way to the temple you'll proceed along **Nakamise-dōri**, a colourful parade of small shops packed with gaudy souvenirs, tiny traditional dolls, kimono accessories and sweet-scented piles of *sembei* rice crackers.

Hōzō-mon

A double-storeyed treasure gate, **Hōzō-mon** stands astride the entrance to the main temple complex. The treasures themselves, fourteenth-century Chinese sutras, are locked away on the upper floor. The gate's two protective Niō – the traditional

5

guardians of Buddhist temples – are even more imposing than those at Kaminari-mon; look out for their enormous rice-straw sandals slung on the gate's rear wall.

The main hall

Beyond Hōzō-mon there's a constant crowd clustered around a large, bronze incense bowl where people waft the pungent smoke over themselves: considered the breath of the gods, it is supposed to have curative powers. There's nothing much to see inside the temple itself, since the little Kannon – said to be just 7.5cm tall – is a *hibutsu* or hidden image, considered too holy to be put on view. The hall, however, is full of life, with the rattle of coins being tossed into a huge wooden coffer, the swirling plumes of incense smoke and the constant bustle of people coming to pray, buy charms and fortune papers or to attend a service. Three times a day – at 6.30am, 10am and 2pm – drums echo through the hall into the courtyard as priests chant sutras beneath the altar's gilded canopy.

Asakusa-jinja

浅草神社 • Ⓦ asakusajinja.jp

Like many Buddhist temples, Sensō-ji accommodates Shinto shrines in its grounds, the most important being **Asakusa-jinja**, dedicated to the two fishermen brothers who netted the Kannon image, and their overlord. The shrine was founded in the mid-seventeenth century by Tokugawa Iemitsu and the original building still survives, though it's hard to tell under all the restored paintwork. More popularly known as Sanja-sama, "Shrine of the Three Guardians", this is the focus of the tumultuous **Sanja Matsuri** (see box, p.73).

Niten-mon

Sensō-ji's eastern entrance is guarded by the attractively aged **Niten-mon**. Originally built in 1618, this gate is all that remains of a shrine honouring Tokugawa Ieyasu, which was relocated to Ueno in 1651 after a series of fires. Niten-mon has since been rededicated and now houses two seventeenth-century Buddhist guardians of the south and east.

Asakusa Hanayashiki

浅草花やしき • 2-28-1 Asakusa, Taitō-ku • Daily 10am–6pm • Adult ¥1000, child aged 7–12 ¥500, under-7s free; ride tickets ¥100; free pass adults ¥2300, children ¥2000 • ☎ 03 3842 8780, Ⓦ hanayashiki.net • Asakusa station

Japan's oldest amusement park, dating back to 1853, **Asakusa Hanayashiki** seems a little incongruous in the refined Asakusa area – it's really more in keeping with the hedonistic Rokku district to the west. The park features rickety roller-coasters (rickety but safe – this *is* Japan) and vintage funfair rides and attractions, including a haunted house.

Jakotsu-yu

蛇骨湯 • 1-11-11 Asakusa, Taitō-ku • Daily except Tues 1pm–midnight • ¥460, plus extra for towels • Asakusa station

"Black", mineral-rich, hot-spring water is the thing at the **Jakotsu-yu** bathhouse, located down a back alley just south of Rox department store. One bath is designed to give you a mild but stimulating electric shock, and another provides a water-jet experience, while outside is a tiny pond filled with carp and a slightly larger open-air bath (*rotemburo*) and cold-pool.

Asakusa Kannon Onsen

浅草観音温泉 • 2-7-26 Asakusa, Taitō-ku • Asakusa station

Dating back to 1957, this ivy-covered bathhouse closed permanently in 2016 on account of a broken boiler, but it's such a part of the fabric of Asakusa that locals are trying to raise funds for its reopening – check with the local tourist office for the latest information (see p.73).

PLAYING DRESS-UP

Asakusa has plenty of shops selling kimono, both new and used, and these can make for fantastic souvenirs (see p.203). However, if you're not sure that you'll ever need one again, you can make use of the many **kimono rental spots** dotted around the area – there seems to be one on almost every street (there are also a few in Harajuku, Shibuya and other areas). Figure on ¥3000 for the day, and ¥1500 to have your hair done.

If you really want to go the whole hog, there's also the **Studio Geisha Café** over the river in the Ryōgoku area (2-21-4 Morishita, Koto-ku; Ⓣ 03 3846 7616, Ⓦ www.geishacafe.jp; see map, p.82), where they'll doll you up with immaculate make-up for a photo shoot; it'll cost around ¥15,000. Gentlemen are also welcome to go geisha here, though many might prefer the swashbuckling costume stylings on offer at the **Samurai Museum** over in Shinjuku (see p.130).

Amuse Museum

アミューズミュージアム • 2-34-3 Asakusa, Taitō-ku • Tues–Sun 10am–6pm • ¥1080 • Ⓣ 03 5806 1181, Ⓦ amusemuseum.com • Asakusa station

Just outside the east gate of Sensō-ji is the **Amuse Museum**, a six-storey complex incorporating a café, shop and bar, bridging the gap between old and new with a few quirky exhibition spaces dedicated to Japan's cultural past. It's mostly filled by a rotating showcase of items from private collector Tanaka Chuzaburo's collection of more than 30,000 items, displayed with stylish panache – the permanent display of traditional patched clothing (*boro*) looks more like the interior of a trendy boutique. The building's rooftop terrace, home to *Bar Six* (see p.176), offers amazing views of Sensō-ji and the Tokyo Skytree.

Edo Shitamachi Traditional Crafts Museum

江戸下町伝統工芸館, Edo Shitamachi Dentō-kōgei-kan • 2F 2-22-13 Asakusa, Taitō-ku • Daily 10am–8pm • Free • Ⓣ 03 3842 1990 • Asakusa station

At the top end of Hisago-dōri, a covered arcade stretching north of Rokku, is the **Edo Shitamachi Traditional Crafts Museum**, whose modest collection of traditional implements won't detain you for more than ten minutes, though it's still worth popping by. At weekends a variety of artisans can be seen at work, and there are occasional video presentations about crafts production. There's also a selection of crafts on sale in the ground-floor lobby.

Miyamoto Unosuke Nishi-Asakusa Store and Drum Museum

宮本卯之助西浅草店, 2-1-1 Nishi-Asakusa • Wed–Sun 10am–5pm; shop daily 9am–6pm • ¥500 • Ⓣ 03 3842 5622, Ⓦ miyamoto-unosuke.co.jp • Asakusa station

Easily identifiable from the elaborate *mikoshi* (portable shrines) in the window, the **Miyamoto Unosuke Nishi-Asakusa Store** is an Aladdin's cave of traditional Japanese percussion instruments and festival paraphernalia: masks, shortened kimono-style *happi* coats, flutes, cymbals and, of course, all kinds of *mikoshi*, the largest with a price tag of over ¥3 million. Since 1861, however, the family passion has been drums, resulting in an impressive collection from around the world – one that now fills the fourth-floor **Drum Museum**. There's every type imaginable here and, best of all, you're allowed to have a go on some. A red dot on the name card indicates those not to be touched; blue dots mean you can tap lightly, just with your hands; and the rest have the appropriate drumsticks ready and waiting.

Kitchenware Town

かっぱ橋道具街, Kappabashi Dōgu-gai • Many shops closed on Sun • Ⓦ kappabashi.or.jp • Asakusa station

Just west of the Rokku area is the main road of **Kappabashi Dōgu-gai**, flanked with covered walkways and signs from the "bubble period". Locally known as **Kappabashi**,

5

or "Kitchenware Town", the surrounding area is essentially a wholesale market where you can kit out a whole restaurant. You don't have to be a bulk buyer, however, and this is a great place to pick up unusual souvenirs, such as the **plastic food** displayed outside restaurants to tempt the customer. This practice, which originally used wax instead of plastic, dates from the nineteenth century but came into its own about forty years ago when foreign foods were being introduced to a puzzled Japanese market.

Sumida

墨田

On the opposite side of the Sumida-gawa from Asakusa, the district of **Sumida** is utterly dominated by the **Tokyo Skytree**, a whopper built to replace the comparatively puny Tokyo Tower (see p.102) as the city's digital broadcasting beacon. The sightseeing potential of the Skytree has been fully exploited, with the city's highest public **observatory** – a dizzying 450m above the ground – as the main draw, as well as an **aquarium** and **planetarium** at the tower's base, plus tourist shops, restaurants and landscaped public spaces.

Tokyo Skytree

東京スカイツリー • 1-1-2 Oshiage, Sumida-ku • ☎ 03 6658 8012, ⓦ tokyo-skytree.jp • Oshiage or Tokyo Skytree stations

At 634m, the **Tokyo Skytree** is, for now, the world's second-tallest structure after Dubai's mighty Burj Khalifa (830m). Popular though it is as a tourist attraction, the tower divides opinion. Sited close to Asakusa, one of Tokyo's most proudly traditional areas, attempts were made to give the Skytree an appropriate feel – note the Japanese design motifs in the lobby and lifts. Yet some of it comes across as rather forced – it's hard, after all, to paint ancient tradition over something shaped like a gigantic hypodermic needle. Though the shape isn't terribly pleasing, it's now part and parcel of the Tokyo skyline.

Triangular at the base, its pale-blue, latticed sides gently morph towards a circular shape before hitting the lower observation deck; the second deck is another 100m up, with the super-skinny transmitting antenna protruding another 184m beyond.

The observation decks

Daily 8am–10pm • 350m deck ¥2060, or ¥2570 booked online (currently in Japanese only) with time assigned; 450m deck ¥1030 extra, no advance purchase possible • Foreign visitors with ID can also purchase a special "Fast Skytree" ticket, which beats the queues: 350m deck ¥3000, both decks ¥4000

There's a certain tingly excitement to be had in watching the numbers on the lift panel getting higher and higher – even the **lower deck** is marked as "Floor 350". The views from here are, predictably, fantastic: giant touch-screen displays show precisely what you're looking at, and also let you see how the view would appear at night (or by day, if you're visiting in the evening). Mount Fuji is, in theory, within visible range, but the unfortunate reality is that mist often blocks the view even in sunny weather, and it's usually only visible a couple of times each month.

Those who choose to head on to the **upper deck** will see more or less the same thing, although its space-age interior design is rather lovely – the inclined walkway wraps around the building, giving you the impression that you're climbing to the top. There's a pricey **restaurant** on the upper deck, and a cheaper **café** on the lower one, though there's far more choice on the 30th and 31st floors of the adjacent Solamachi building, from where you can actually see the tower.

Note that there's a lot of queuing involved, especially on weekends and holidays – first to buy the ticket, then for the lift up, and again for the lift to the upper level. Foreign visitors with valid ID can beat the queues for a small premium, and most find it worth the extra investment.

Sumida aquarium

すみだ水族館, Sumida Suizokukan • 5F and 6F Tokyo Solamachi West Yard • Daily 9am–9pm • ¥2050 • ☎ 03 5619 1821,
Ⓦ sumida-aquarium.com

Every major tower in Tokyo seems to have an aquarium attached, and the Skytree is no exception. The **Sumida aquarium** is a pretty good one, though, with a 350,000-litre tank (the largest in Japan) at its centre; clever design of the glass walls mean that you can see the whole tank from almost any angle. Most visitors make a beeline for the seals and penguins, but the jellyfish display is worth tracking down too.

Konica Minolta planetarium

コニカミノルタプラネタリウム • 7F Tokyo Solamachi East Yard • Hourly shows daily 11am–9pm • ¥1200 • ☎ 03 5610 3043

At the **Konica Minolta planetarium** – part planetarium, part 4D cinema – the delights of the cosmos are relayed, for the sake of superfluous technology, in glorious smell-o-vision. Science has yet to capture the true scent of the stars, and though it's probably fair to assume that Finnish forests and Asian aromatherapy oils might be a bit wide of the mark, it's a fun experience nonetheless.

Ryōgoku and Kiyosumi

There's a surprise in store just down the Sumida-gawa from touristy Asakusa: Ryōgoku is a sort of sumo town, where shops sell outsize clothes and restaurants serve flavourful tureens of *chanko-nabe*, the wrestlers' traditional body-building hotpot. The area is also home to the absorbing, ultra-modern Edo-Tokyo Museum. A short train ride south, and all within walking distance of each other in the Kiyosumi area, are Kiyosumi Teien, a pleasant Meiji-era garden; the delightful Fukagawa Edo Museum, an atmospheric re-creation of a mid-nineteenth-century Shitamachi neighbourhood; and the Museum of Contemporary Art, gathering together the best of post-1945 Japanese art in one spacious, top-class venue.

BEST OF RYŌGOKU AND KIYOSUMI

National Sumo Stadium Watch gargantuan fighters in action (see below)
Edo-Tokyo Museum Spend a day exploring this huge collection (see p.83)
Kiyosumi Teien Stroll through some enchanting gardens (see p.83)
Tomioka Hachiman-gū Visit the birthplace of sumo (see p.84)
Tomoegata Eat like a sumo wrestler (see p.163)

Ryōgoku

6

両国

The **Ryōgoku** area has just two sights, and one of those is only accessible for a few weeks of the year. But even if your visit doesn't coincide with a tournament at the **National Sumo Stadium**, it's still worth coming along to visit a sumo training "**stable**" (see p.209) or to see the fantastic **Edo-Tokyo Museum** – or even just to take a stroll down the banks of the Sumida-gawa.

National Sumo Stadium

両国国技館, Ryōgoku Kokugikan • 1-3-28 Yokoami, Sumida-ku • See p.208 for details of tickets for tournaments • Ryōgoku station

For a fortnight each January, May and September, major sumo tournaments fill the **National Sumo Stadium** with a pageant of thigh-slapping, foot-stamping and arcane ritual (see p.208 and box below). The streets south of the stadium were, until recently, home to many of the major "**stables**" where wrestlers lived and trained. Though rising land prices have forced most of them out, a fair few remain, and there's still a good chance of bumping into some junior wrestlers, with slicked-back hair, wearing *yukata* (loose dressing gowns) and *geta* (wooden sandals), popping out for a quick snack of *chanko-nabe*. If you're feeling peckish yourself, try either

SUMO: WHO'S WHO AND WHAT'S WHAT

Japan's national sport, **sumo**, developed out of the divination rites performed at Shinto shrines, and its religious roots are still apparent in the various rituals which form an integral part of a *basho*, or **tournament**. These take place in odd-numbered months: Tokyo's are in January, May and September (see p.208), with other tournaments taking place in Ōsaka, Nagoya and Fukuoka. Starting on the second Sunday of the month, and lasting for fifteen days, the fights run from 9am to 6pm, although the top competitors only appear after 4pm or so. The bouts involve two huge wrestlers, each weighing 170 kilos on average and wearing nothing but a hefty loincloth, facing off in a small ring of hard-packed clay. The loser is the first to step outside the rope or touch the ground with any part of the body except the feet – the contest is often over in seconds, but the **pageantry** and ritual make for a wonderfully absorbing spectacle. The top two divisions of wrestlers fight every day, and the top-division fighter with the most wins out of fifteen is declared champion.

In recent years, champions have been almost exclusively **Mongolian** in origin. The Japanese veteran **Kotoshogiku**'s victory in January 2016 came ten long years after the previous win by a Japanese-born wrestler, with Mongolian fighters scooping an incredible 57 of the 59 intervening tournaments (the other two were won by Kotooshu from Bulgaria, and Estonia's Baruto). The Mongolian run started in 2002 with the great **Asashōryū** who, in 2005, became the first wrestler in history to win all six tournaments in a calendar year. "Asa" was something of a pantomime villain, stirring up controversy on a regular basis before being ushered out of the sport in 2010. By then he had developed a tremendous rivalry with his closest challenger, fellow-Mongolian **Hakuhō**, who had broken his most-wins-in-a-year record by winning 86 out of 90 bouts in 2009. These two great fighters both became *yokozuna*; the very top level of wrestler, this is a lifelong rank and does not necessarily signify the most recent champion. Shortly after Asashōryū's retirement, Hakuhō was joined as *yokozuna* by **Harumafuji** and **Kakuryū**, two fellow Mongolians; at the time of writing, all three were still going strong, and Hakuhō had become the most decorated wrestler in centuries of sumo history.

the *Yoshiba* or *Tomoegata* restaurants (see p.163), two of the best places to sample the hearty stew.

In the 2020 Olympics (see box, p.120), the National Sumo Stadium will host the boxing events.

Edo-Tokyo Museum

江戸東京博物館, Edo-Tōkyō Hakubutsukan • 1-4-1 Yokoami, Sumida-ku • Tues–Fri & Sun 9.30am–5.30pm, Sat 9.30am–7.30pm • ¥600 • ☎ 03 3626 9974, ⓦ edo-tokyo-museum.or.jp • Ryōgoku station

You'll need plenty of stamina for the extensive **Edo-Tokyo Museum**, housed in a colossal building (supposedly modelled on a *geta*) behind the Sumo Stadium, although the ticket lasts a whole day so you can come and go. With plenty of information in English, including a free audio-guide, the museum tells the history of Tokyo from the days of the Tokugawa shogunate to postwar reconstruction, using life-size replicas, models and holograms, as well as more conventional screen paintings, ancient maps and documents.

The museum starts on the sixth floor, where a bridge (a replica of the original Nihombashi; see p.56) takes you over the roofs of some typical Edo landmarks – a kabuki theatre, *daimyō* residence and Western-style office – on the main exhibition floor below. The displays then run roughly chronologically, with a particularly strong treatment of life in Edo's Shitamachi, with its pleasure quarters, festivals and vibrant popular culture, and on the giddy days after 1868, when Japan opened up to the outside world.

Kiyosumi

The district of **Kiyosumi** gets even fewer travellers than Ryōgoku, but there's actually more to see, with the beautiful **Kiyosumi Teien**, the excellent **Fukagawa Edo Museum** and the **Tokyo Museum of Contemporary Art** all vying for your attention. Getting here from Ryōgoku is easy by subway, though it's more pleasurable to walk down the pedestrianized banks of the Sumida-gawa, then cut east along the banks of a tributary which runs just to the north of the sights listed here. The Kiyosumi area also has more temples than you could count – whichever one you pop into, you're likely to see no other visitors. This is unlikely to be the case at pyromaniacal **Fukagawa Fudō-dō**, located a short way south, near the shrine where sumo was born.

Kiyosumi Teien

清澄庭園 • 3-9 Kiyosumi, Kōtō-ku • Daily 9am–5pm • ¥150 • ☎ 03 3641 5892 • Kiyosumi-shirakawa station

A beautiful Edo-era garden surrounding a large pond, **Kiyosumi Teien** counts as a must-see if you're in the area. Originally the property of a merchant, the gardens were landscaped to within an inch of their life upon their acquisition by a local feudal lord; the stones that you'll see around the grounds come from all over Japan. The gardens are particularly worth visiting in spring for their cherry blossom and azaleas.

Fukagawa Edo Museum

深川江戸資料館, Fukagawa Edo Shiryōkan • 1-3-28 Shirakawa, Kōtō-ku • Daily 9.30am–5pm, closed second & fourth Mon of the month • ¥400; guidebook ¥500 • ☎ 03 3630 8625 • Kiyosumi-shirakawa station

Located down a charming neighbourhood shopping street is the captivating **Fukagawa Edo Museum**, which re-creates a Shitamachi neighbourhood (see box, p.75). The museum's one-room exhibition hall could be a film set for nineteenth-century Edo and contains seven complete buildings: the homes of various artisans and labourers, a watchtower and storehouses. As you walk through the rooms furnished with the clutter of daily life, you're accompanied by the cries of street vendors and birdsong, while the lighting shifts from dawn through to a soft dusk. It's worth investing in the English-language guidebook before going in.

6

Tokyo Museum of Contemporary Art

東京都現代美術館, Tōkyō-to Gendai Bijutsukan • 4-1-1 Miyoshi, Kōtō-ku • ☎ 03 5245 4111, ⓦ mot-art-museum.jp • 15min walk north of Kiba station

A severe glass-and-grey-steel building houses Tokyo's premier modern art venue, the **Tokyo Museum of Contemporary Art**. The vast white spaces inside provide the perfect setting for a fine collection of works by Japanese and Western artists (notably Roy Lichtenstein) from the post-1945 avant-garde through the 1950s abstract revolution to pop art, minimalism and beyond. At the time of writing the museum was closed for major renovation, most likely until early 2019, but check the website for the latest developments.

Fukagawa Fudō-dō

深川不動堂 • 1-17-3 Tomioka, Kōtō-ku • ☎ 03 3641 8288 • Fire rituals 9am, 11am, 1pm, 3pm & 5pm • Monzennakachō station

Just south of the main Kiyosumi sights, and reached via an unusually blocky *torii*, the **Fukagawa Fudō-dō** is certainly up there with Tokyo's most interesting temples. It belongs to the Shingon sect, also known as the "Japanese Esoteric" offshoot; however, the casual observer is more likely to be interested in the temple's liberal use of fire – rituals involving objects being passed over flames take place at least five times daily, with drums and sutra-chanting providing atmospheric backing tracks. Don't miss the stunning prayer corridor, in which almost 10,000 crystal Buddha statues glow in the dark.

Tomioka Hachiman-gū

富岡八幡宮 • 1-20-3 Tomioka, Kōtō-ku • ☎ 03 3642 1315 • Monzennakachō station

It may look like just another shrine, but **Tomioka Hachiman-gū** has an interesting claim to fame: less than six decades after its founding in 1627, it became the birthplace of the style of sumo used today. Around the back of the main hall you'll find the *yokozuna* stone, onto which the names of those who've reached the eponymous level of grand champion (see box, p.81) are engraved; at the time of writing these numbered 71 (plus an ancient fighter known as Raiden, who was never promoted to *yokozuna*, but was considered pretty good anyway). *Yokozuna* promotions are rare events (every two or three years, on average), but the official unveilings always take place at this shrine – you'd have to be very, very lucky to see one.

FUJI TV BUILDING, ODAIBA

Bayside Tokyo

So thoroughly urban is Tokyo that it can seem surprising to discover that
the city is actually beside the sea. Yet many of the *ukiyo-e* masterpieces of
Hokusai and Hiroshige depict waterside scenes around Tokyo Bay, and
several of the city's prime attractions are to be found here, not least the vast
Tsukiji fish market, whose proposed relocation has been a major controversy
of late. Across the bay to the south lies Odaiba, built on vast islands of
reclaimed land; its principal sights are a couple of excellent museums and
a raucous onsen complex, as well as some of Tokyo's most striking and
distinctive architecture.

BEST OF BAYSIDE TOKYO

Tsujiki Watch the world-famous tuna auctions (see below)
Panasonic Center Tokyo Try out Nintendo's latest gadgets (see p.89)
Mega Web Take a brand-new Toyota for a spin (see p.90)
Tokyo Leisureland Hone your Dance Dance Revolution moves (see p.90)
Ramen Kokugikan Enjoy twinkly night-time bay views and some of Tokyo's best noodles (see p.163)
Sushi Bun Indulge in some of the finest sushi on the planet (see p.163)
Ageha Throw some shapes at one of Asia's biggest nightclubs (see p.182)

Tsukiji

築地

A dawn visit to the vast **Tokyo Metropolitan Central Wholesale Market**, more popularly referred to by the name of its surrounding area, **Tsukiji**, has long been one of Tokyo's undisputed highlights. The site on which the market is located dates back to 1657, when Tokugawa Ieyasu (see p.253) had the debris from the Furisode (Long Sleeves) Fire shovelled into the marshes at the edge of Ginza, thus creating "reclaimed land", or "*tsukiji*". Proposals have long been afoot to shift the market east to Toyosu, though progress on the move has been anything but smooth (see box below) and at the time of writing the market remains at its original site – contact one of the city's tourist offices (see p.38) for the latest developments.

Jōnai-shijō

場内市場 • Mon–Sat 4am–2pm; check website for occasional holidays • ⓦ tsukiji-market.or.jp • Tsukiji or Tsukijishijō stations

While the future of the market is up in the air, it's still possible that nothing at all will change. For now, Tsukiji's main action is centred on its **jōnai-shijō** (main market), lying closest to the water in a crescent-shaped hangar. Eels from Taiwan, salmon from Santiago and tuna from Tasmania are among the 480 different types of seafood – two thousand tonnes of it – that come under the hammer here daily.

The headline **tuna auctions** happen between 5.25am and 6.15am. Though viewing tours had been suspended at the time of writing, they'll hopefully recommence whether the market stays here or moves to Toyosu – many a traveller has ended up waxing lyrical about getting up before dawn to witness sales of these rock-solid frozen fish, looking like steel torpedoes, all labelled with yellow stickers indicating their weight and country of origin.

TSUKIJI TROUBLES

It's been dubbed the "fish market at the centre of the world" for its influence on world seafood prices. Generating almost **¥2 billion** (£14m/US$17.5m) in sales daily, Tsukiji is undoubtedly big business, but during recent years the market's volume of trade has been dropping, along with the number of wholesalers and middlemen who work there.

Uppermost on merchants' minds is the Tokyo Metropolitan Government's plan to shift the market to **Toyosu**, 2km across the bay. The site was previously used by Tokyo Gas, and the highly toxic ground was cleaned up before construction started on the new complex, which cost around ¥590bn (£4.2bn/US$5.2bn) to build. The stalls were all supposed to move out to Toyosu in November 2016, but surveys conducted in the months before showed that the new site's levels of mercury, benzene, arsenic and cyanide – slightly worrying substances, even away from raw fish – were all above government standards. Because of these concerns over **toxins**, ones echoed by many of the marketfolk themselves, Tokyo governor Yuriko Koike brought a sudden halt to proceedings just before the move.

At the time of writing, everything remained up in the air, with market life going on as normal at the old site, and the new building sat waiting for tenants who may never arrive.

BAYSIDE TOKYO

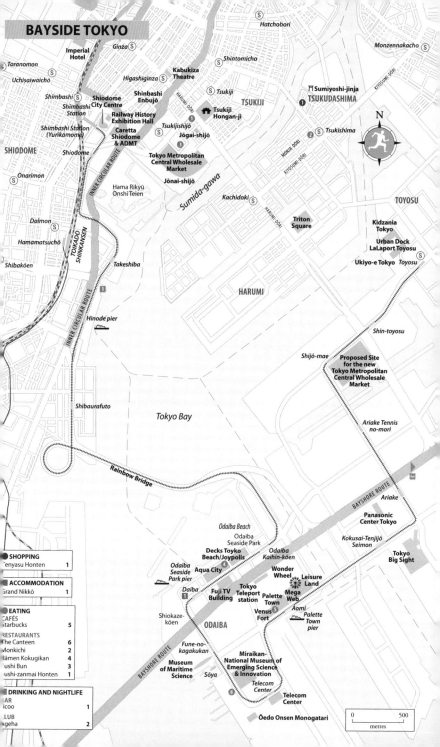

N

Toranomon Ⓢ
Uchisaiwaichō

Ginza Ⓢ

Imperial
Hotel

Higashiginza Ⓢ

Kabukiza
Theatre

Hatchobori Ⓢ

Shintomicho

Monzennakacho Ⓢ

Shimbashi Ⓢ
Shimbashi
Station

Shinbashi
Enbujō

Ⓢ Tsukiji

Shiodome
City Centre

Ⓢ

Railway History
Exhibition Hall

Tsukiji
Hongan-ji

TSUKIJI

Sumiyoshi-jinja
TSUKUDASHIMA

Shimbashi Station
(Yurikamome)

Caretta
Shiodome
& ADMT

Tsukijishijō Ⓢ
Jōgai-shijō Ⓢ

Ⓢ

Tsukishima

SHIODOME

Shiodome

Onarimon

Ⓢ

Tokyo Metropolitan
Central Wholesale
Market

Ⓢ Tsukishima

Jōnai-shijō

Daimon
Hamamatsuchō

Hama Rikyū
Onshi Teien

Sumida-gawa

Kachidoki Ⓢ

TOYOSU

Triton
Square

Kidzania
Tokyo

Urban Dock
LaLaport Toyosu

Shibakōen

Takeshiba

Ⓢ

HARUMI

Ukiyo-e Tokyo Toyosu

Hinode pier

Shin-toyosu

Shijō-mae

Proposed Site
for the new
Tokyo Metropolitan
Central Wholesale
Market

Shibaurafuto

Tokyo Bay

Ariake Tennis
no-mori

Rainbow Bridge

BAYSHORE ROUTE

Ariake

Panasonic
Center Tokyo

Odaiba Beach

Odaiba
Seaside Park

Kokusai-Tenjijō
Seimon

Tokyo
Big Sight

SHOPPING
Tenyasu Honten   1

ACCOMMODATION
Grand Nikkō   1

EATING
CAFÉS
Starbucks   5
RESTAURANTS
The Canteen   6
Monkichi   2
Rāmen Kokugikan   4
Sushi Bun   3
Sushi-zanmai Honten   1

DRINKING AND NIGHTLIFE
BAR
icoo   1
CLUB
ageha   2

Decks Toyko
Beach/Joypolis

Odaiba
Kaihin-kōen

Odaiba
Seaside
Park pier

Aqua City

Wonder
Wheel

Leisure
Land

Daiba

Fuji TV
Building

Tokyo
Teleport
station

Mega
Web

Palette
Town

Shiokaze-
kōen

ODAIBA

Venus
Fort

Aomi

Palette
Town pier

Fune-no-
kagakukan

Miraikan-
National Museum of
Emerging Science
& Innovation

Museum
of Maritime
Science

Sōya

Telecom
Center

Telecom
Center

Ōedo Onsen Monogatari

0   500
metres

At the time of writing, it was still possible to eat at the many, many **sushi restaurants** flanking the market; *Sushi Bun* (see p.163) is recommended.

Jōgai-shijō and around
場外市場 · Tsukiji or Tsukijishijō stations

The **jōgai-shijō** (outer market) is arrayed around a dense grid of streets immediately to the northeast of the main fish market. It's heaving with fishmongers, grocers, pottery merchants and kitchenware sellers, and many of these are likely to stay put even if or when the main market moves out to Toyosu.

Tsukiji Hongan-ji
築地本願寺 · 3-15-1 Tsukiji · Free · Ⓦ tsukijihonwanji.jp · Tsukiji station

If you're in the area, it's worth a quick visit to **Tsukiji Hongan-ji**, one of the largest and most Indian-looking of Tokyo's Buddhist temples. From the outside, it looks a little like a European bank topped with a South Asian roof; inside it's more traditional, with an intricately carved golden altar and cavernous interior, and room for a thousand worshippers.

Tsukudashima
佃島

Across the Sumida-gawa from Tsukiji is **Tsukudashima** (meaning "island of rice fields"), a tiny enclave of wooden houses and shops clustered around a backwater spanned by a dinky red bridge. Sheltering in the shadow of the modern River City 21 residential tower blocks, the area has a history stretching back to 1613, when a group of Ōsaka fishermen were settled on the island by the shogun.

Tsukudashima is famous for several types of **food**: *tsukudani*, preserved seaweed and fish best bought at *Tenyasu Honten* (see p.202); and the savoury pancakes known as *okonomiyaki* and *monjayaki* (see box, p.155), served in restaurants lining Monja-dōri, a colourful shopping street a short walk southwest from Tsukishima station – try *Monkichi* (see p.163).

Sumiyoshi-jinja
住吉神社

In addition to providing food for the castle, the island's founding fishermen were expected to report on any suspicious comings and goings in the bay. For their spiritual protection, they built themselves the delightful **Sumiyoshi-jinja**, a shrine dedicated to the god of the sea. The roof of the well beside the shrine's *torii* has eaves decorated with exquisite carvings of scenes from the fishermen's lives. Every three years, on the first weekend in August, the shrine hosts the Sumiyoshi Matsuri, during which a special *mikoshi* (portable shrine) is doused in water as it is paraded through the streets; this is symbolic of the real dunking it would once have had in the river.

Toyosu
豊洲

Just over 2km down the bay from Tsukiji, **Toyosu** is likely to become the venue of the new wholesale **fish market** – the building is there already, but environmental concerns (see box, p.86) have seen the issue become a political hot-potato, and it's possible that the move will never take place. Should the market relocate, it's likely that its tuna auctions will once again become the most prominent feature. Unlike in Tsukiji, tourists will probably be kept at arm's length from the action, restricted to walkways overlooking the wholesale fish section; this would help solve the problems caused at the old site by increasingly large groups of tourists disrupting the key tuna auctions.

KidZania Tokyo

キッザニア東京 • Urban Dock LaLaport Toyosu, 2-4-9 Toyosu, Kōtō-ku • Daily 9am–3pm & 4–9pm • Adults ¥1850, children ¥2850–4850 depending upon age and visiting time • ☎ 0120 924901, ⊛ www.kidzania.jp • Toyosu station or monorail

Set inside a giant shopping mall, **KidZania Tokyo** is an imaginative mini theme-park where kids run all the various shops and services. It's designed for children aged 2 to 12, and although everything is in Japanese it's possible for non-Japanese-speaking children to join in the fun. Prices vary depending upon the day of the week, what time you arrive and so on – see the website for details.

Odaiba

お台場

Odaiba is an island of reclaimed land, sitting pretty in Tokyo Bay. The name means "cannon emplacements", referring to the defences set up in the bay by the shogun in 1853 to protect the city from Commodore Perry's threatening Black Ships (see p.254). The remains of the two cannon emplacements, one now a public park, are these days dwarfed by the huge landfill site Rinkai Fukutoshin, of which Odaiba is a part. Here the Metropolitan Government set about constructing a brand-new urban development, fit for the twenty-first century, in 1988. The subsequent economic slump and spiralling development costs slowed the project down and, when the **Rainbow Bridge** linking Odaiba to the city opened in 1993, the area was still a series of empty lots.

7

More than two decades on, Odaiba has blossomed into one of the most popular spots in the city for locals, who love its seaside location and sense of space – so rare in Tokyo. At night, the illuminated Rainbow Bridge, giant technicolour Ferris wheel and twinkling towers of the Tokyo skyline make Odaiba a romantic spot – you'll see plenty of canoodling couples staring wistfully at the glittering panorama.

ARRIVAL AND GETTING AROUND   ODAIBA

By monorail The simplest way of getting to Odaiba is to hop on the Yurikamome monorail (⊛ yurikamome.co.jp), which starts at Shimbashi station and arcs up to the Rainbow Bridge on a splendid circular line, stopping at all the area's major sites before terminating at Toyosu, also a subway stop; single tickets here from the "mainland" are around ¥320.

By train Trains on the Rinkai line, linked to the JR Saikyō line and the Yūrakuchō subway line, run to the central Tokyo-Teleport station on Odaiba; if you're coming to the area on JR trains, this usually works out cheaper than the monorail, and there are direct services from Ikebukuro, Shinjuku, Shibuya and Ebisu, among other places.

By bus Buses from Shinagawa station, southwest of the bay, cross the Rainbow Bridge and run as far as the Maritime Museum, stopping at Odaiba Kaihin-kōen on the way. Once you're on Odaiba, you can make use of the free Tokyo Bay Shuttle bus services, which depart on a loop every 20min or so.

By ferry Ferries shuttle from the pier at Hinode (日の出) to either Odaiba Seaside Park or Palette Town; some also stop next to Tokyo Big Sight. The journey costs from just ¥480 and doubles as a Tokyo Bay cruise. The space-age *Himoko* and *Hotaruna* ferries (see p.24) also connect Odaiba with Asakusa, sometimes via Hinode (6 daily; ¥1560), and there are also ferries to Kasai Rinkai-kōen, 7km east, home to an excellent aquarium (see p.93).

Panasonic Center Tokyo

パナソニックセンター東京 • 3-5-1 Ariake, Kōtō-ku • Tues–Sun 10am–6pm • Free; RiSuPia ¥500 • ☎ 03 3599 2600, ⊛ panasonic.net /center/tokyo • Ariake or Kokusai Tenjijō Seimon monorail stations

Less than a minute's walk from Ariake station is **Panasonic Center Tokyo**, the electronics group's showcase. Here you can try out the latest Nintendo games on a large-screen plasma display or high-resolution projector, as well as check out the company's technologies of tomorrow. The centre includes the fun "digital network museum" **RiSuPia**, at which you're issued with an electronic tag upon entering; as you learn about science and mathematics from the computer games and simulations within the high-tech display hall, the tag keeps track of how well you're doing.

Tokyo Big Sight

東京ビッグサイト • 3-11-1 Ariake, Kōtō-ku • ☎ 03 5530 1111, ⓦ bigsight.jp • Kokusai Tenjijō Seimon monorail station

Outside Kokusai Tenjijō Seimon station, you can't fail to see the Tokyo International Exhibition Centre, better known as the **Tokyo Big Sight**. This is one of Japan's largest venues for business fairs and exhibitions, with an entrance composed of four huge inverted pyramids; also look out for a 15.5m-high sculpture of a saw, sticking out of the ground as if left behind by some absent-minded giant. Events held here include vast antique fairs, the twice-yearly Design Festa (see p.26) and Comiket manga events, as well as the Tokyo Anime Fair in March.

Palette Town

パレットタウン • 1-3-15 Aomi, Kōtō-ku • Aomi monorail station

Aomi station is the stop for the vast **Palette Town** shopping and entertainment complex, which offers something for almost everyone: test-drive a Toyota, go for a spin on a giant Ferris wheel, see Tokyo at its wackiest in Tokyo Leisureland, or sip coffee on a faux Italian piazza at Venus Fort. Outside Harajuku and Akihabara, this is the most popular place in Tokyo for *cosplay* costume-wearing youngsters.

Mega Web

メガウェブ • Daily 11am–9pm • Entry and simulations free, vehicle rental at Ride Studio ¥200–300 • ☎ 03 3599 0808, ⓦ megaweb.gr.jp

On Palette Town's east side, **Mega Web** is a design showcase for Toyota's range of cars. For the casual visitor, it's most interesting as a glimpse into the future of the company, and by extension the automotive industry in general. It's often possible to pilot some kind of futuristic electric vehicle along the pleasing blue track that swoops around the building; consult the website for information, and note that you'll probably need to show an international driving licence. Kids (and adults with zero shame) can take an extremely slow spin around the Ride Studio, housed in a separate building just to the east.

Wonder Wheel

ワンダーウィール • Daily 10am–10pm • ¥920

Just behind the Mega Web showroom are some more high-tech diversions, the best of which is the **Wonder Wheel**, a candy-coloured, 115m-diameter Ferris wheel, which takes sixteen minutes to make a full circuit. If heights hold no fear then plump for one of the wheel's four fully transparent gondolas, which enable you to see down through the floor; they cost no extra, though you may have to queue.

Tokyo Leisureland

東京レジャーランド • Site open 24hr; Game Corner daily 10am–midnight • Entry free, charges for all activities

Just in from the base of the Ferris wheel is the shrine to entertainment that is **Tokyo Leisureland** – if you want to see "crazy" Japan, this is a pretty good place to start. The complex features a bowling alley, a baseball-batting centre (see box, p.206) and karaoke rooms, but best of all is the **Game Corner** on the first floor. In this extremely noisy area you'll see Tokyoites – and not just the young ones – perfecting their moves on the dance machines, thrashing the hell out of computerized drum kits, playing all sorts of screen-whacking games, and using grabbing cranes to pluck teddies for their dates.

Venus Fort

ヴィナスフォート • Daily 11am–9pm • ⓦ www.venusfort.co.jp

The west side of Palette Town is dominated by **Venus Fort**, one of Tokyo's most original shopping and factory outlet malls. It's partly designed as a mock Italian city, complete with piazza, fountains and Roman-style statues – even the ceiling is painted and lit to resemble a perfect Mediterranean sky from dawn to dusk – and is worth swinging

TSUKIJI FISH MARKET (P.86) >

through if only to gawk at the sheer lunacy of it all. The on-site *Starbucks* (see p.164) is located on a particularly charming "piazza".

Ōedo Onsen Monogatari

大江戸温泉物語 • 2-6-3 Aomi, Kōtō-ku • Daily 11am–9am (next day) • Mon–Fri ¥2610 (¥2070 after 6pm), Sat & Sun ¥2830 (¥2290 after 6pm), ¥2160 surcharge 1am–6am • ⓦ daiba.ooedoonsen.jp • Telecom Center monorail station, or free shuttle buses from Shinagawa, Tokyo and Tokyo Teleport stations

More of a theme park than a bathhouse, the giant **Ōedo Onsen Monogatari** goes in for nostalgic kitsch in a big way. Extra fees are charged for massages, hot sand and stone baths and a separate footbath in which tiny fish nibble the dead skin from your feet – more pleasant than it sounds. Free shuttle buses head here, so if you're planning to hit the onsen you can save some money on your trip to Odaiba.

Miraikan

日本科学未来館, Nihon Kakagu Miraikan • 2-3-6 Aomi, Kōtō-ku • Daily except Tues 10am–5pm • ¥620, Dome Theater ¥300 • ⓣ 03 3570 9151, ⓦ www.miraikan.jst.go.jp • Telecom Center monorail station

West of Palette Town is Tokyo's best science museum, the **National Museum of Emerging Science and Innovation**, also known as the **Miraikan**. Here you can learn about the latest in robot technology, superconductivity (including Maglev trains), space exploration, earthquakes and much more, as well as check out the weather around the world by looking up at a giant sphere covered with one million light-emitting diodes showing the globe as it appears from space that day. For an extra fee you can catch a science flick in the spherical Dome Theater.

Museum of Maritime Science

船の科学館, Fune-no Kagakukan • 3-1 Higashiyashio, Shinagawa-ku • *Sōya* daily 10am–5pm • Free • ⓦ funenokagakukan.or.jp • Fune-no-kagakukan monorail station

The **Museum of Maritime Science**, housed in a concrete reproduction of a cruise ship, was undergoing substantial renovation at the time of writing, with no real completion deadline; check the website for the latest developments. For now you'll have to be content with poking around a real boat instead: the *Sōya*, which undertook scientific missions to the South Pole, is moored outside.

Shiokaze-kōen

潮風公園 • 2 Higashiyashio, Shinagawa-ku • 24hr • Daiba monorail station

Over on the western side of Odaiba island is **Shiokaze-kōen**, a pleasant park where families come to use the outdoor barbecue pits in good weather. It provides a ringside seat to watch the action across the bay at the container port, where lines of red cranes look like giraffes at feeding time. You may notice an odd triangular tower on your way in: this is an air vent for the road tunnel that goes under Tokyo Bay.

Odaiba beach

お台場浜, Odaiba-hama • Daiba monorail station

On the north side of the island, Odaiba's man-made **beach** – part of **Odaiba Seaside Park** – boasts a fantastic view of the Rainbow Bridge (see opposite), as well as an unexpected scale copy of the Statue of Liberty. It's a wonderful place to be in the evening, looking at the bridge and twinkly lights beyond, especially if you take off your shoes and dip your feet into the water.

Joypolis

ジョイポリス • 1-6-1 Daiba, Minato-ku • Daily 10am–10pm • Adult ¥800, child aged 7–17 ¥500; passsport for unlimited rides (day/evening) adult ¥4300/3300, child ¥3300/2300 • ⓣ 03 5500 1801, ⓦ tokyo-joypolis.com • Odaiba-Kaihin-kōen monorail station

Fronting the beach are a couple of linked shopping malls, **Aqua City** and **Decks Tokyo Beach**. Apart from plenty of shops and restaurants, the former includes the Mediage multiplex cinema, while the latter has **Joypolis**, a three-floor, high-tech amusement park packed with the latest in Sega's arcade video and computer games, as well as extreme thrill rides such as a spinning roller-coaster.

Fuji TV Building

富士テレビビル, Fuji Terebi Biru · 2-4-8 Daiba, Minato-ku · Viewing platform Tues–Sun 10am–6pm · ¥550 · Daiba monorail

A surreal, sci-fi aura hangs over Tange Kenzō's **Fuji TV Building** – with a huge metal sphere suspended in its middle, it looks as if it's been made from a giant Meccano set. You can head up to the free rooftop garden on the seventh floor, or pay to visit the 25th-floor **viewing platform**; alternatively, save the cash for a drink in the *Sky Lounge* at the top of the neighbouring *Grand Pacific Le Daiba* hotel, where spectacular views are thrown in for free.

Rainbow Bridge

レインボーブリッジ · Observation rooms and promenade daily: Jan–March, Nov & Dec 10am–6pm; April–Oct 9am–9pm · Free · Shibaura Futō monorail station

From Odaiba you can cross back to mainland Tokyo along the **Rainbow Bridge**, a 918m-long, single-span suspension bridge in two levels: the lower bears the waterfront road and the monorail, the upper the Metropolitan Expressway. On both sides is a pedestrian **promenade** linking the **observation rooms** in the anchorages at either end of the bridge. The walk along the bridge takes about half an hour and provides good views across the bay, even as far as Mount Fuji if the sky is clear.

7

East of Odaiba

An enjoyable way to experience Tokyo Bay is to head out to **Kasai Rinkai-kōen** (葛西臨海公園), some 7km east of Odaiba. The park's biggest draw is its superb aquarium, the **Tokyo Sea Life Park**, but it's also a favourite weekend spot for many families who visit to picnic, cycle or paddle off its small, crescent-shaped beach. Bird enthusiasts also come to ogle water birds and waders in the well-designed sanctuary. Just to the east is Tokyo's own take on the **Disney** mega-park theme.

Tokyo Sea Life Park

葛西臨海水族館, Kasai Rinkai Suizokukan · 6-2-3 Rinkai-chō, Edogawa-ku · Daily except Wed 9.30am–5pm, last entry 4pm · ¥700, children free · ☎ 03 3869 5152, ⓦ www.tokyo-zoo.net · Ferry from Odaiba Seaside Park; 50min; ¥1130 one way, ¥1650 return; last boat back around 5pm · Kasai Rinkai-kōen station; from Odaiba, take the Rinkai line and transfer to JR Keiyo line at Shin-Kiba

The highlight of the **Tokyo Sea Life Park**, set under a glass-and-steel dome overlooking the sea, is a pair of vast tanks filled with tuna and sharks, where silver shoals race round you at dizzying speeds. Smaller tanks elsewhere showcase sea life from around the world, from flashy tropical butterfly fish and paper-thin seahorses to the lumpy mudskippers of Tokyo Bay.

Tokyo Disney Resort

東京ディズニーリゾート · 1-1 Maihama, Urayasu-shi, Chiba · Generally open 8/9am–10pm; call to check times beforehand · One-day passport for Tokyo Disneyland or Tokyo DisneySea adult ¥7400, child aged 12–17 ¥6400, child aged 4–11 ¥4800; two-day passport for both parks ¥13,200/11,600/8600 respectively; discount passports available from 3pm · ☎ 0570-008632, ⓦ www.tokyodisneyresort.co.jp · Maihama station

This big daddy of Tokyo's theme parks, **Tokyo Disney Resort**, is made up of two main sections: **Tokyo Disneyland**, a close copy of the Californian original; and **Tokyo DisneySea**, a water- and world travel-themed area. With an average of over 30,000 visitors per day (many more over weekends and holidays), expect queues.

TOKYO CITY VIEW OBSERVATION DECK

Akasaka and Roppongi

At one time, Akasaka and Roppongi were pretty much all about nightlife – the former a nocturnal playground for bureaucrats and politicians, the latter popular with younger Japanese and *gaijin*. In recent years, with the opening of complexes such as Tokyo Midtown, the emphasis has shifted to daytime activity. Roppongi is styling itself as Tokyo's arts hub, home to the National Art Center, Suntory Museum of Art and Mori Art Museum, the last of which sits atop the area's other mega-development, Roppongi Hills. Both districts have old-established attractions, too, such as Akasaka's premier shrine, Hie-jinja; Zōjō-ji, near Roppongi, once the temple of the Tokugawa clan; and some pretty Japanese gardens. And while Tokyo Tower is no longer the city's most elevated viewing spot, it remains an iconic landmark.

BEST OF AKASAKA AND ROPPONGI

Hie-jinja Explore one of the city's finest Shinto shrines (see below)
Tokyo Midtown and Roppongi Hills Take the pulse of modern Tokyo at these huge developments (see p.100 & p.102)
Mori Art Museum and Tokyo City View See some top-notch art, then head one floor up for a killer view (see p.102)
Gonpachi Get your *Kill Bill* fix (see p.164)
Kurosawa Satisfy your *Yojimbo* cravings over a bowl of soba (see p.164)
Cask Strength Savour some rare Japanese whiskies (see p.177)
Art & Design Store Stock up on products from some of Japan's most famous designers (see p.196)

Akasaka

赤坂

Lying southwest of the Imperial Palace, **Akasaka** was once an agricultural area where plants producing a red dye were farmed – hence the locality's name, which means "red slope". Akasaka developed as an entertainment district in the late nineteenth century, when *ryōtei* restaurants, staffed with performing geisha, began to cater for the modern breed of politicians and bureaucrats. The area still has its fair share of exclusive establishments, shielded from the hoi polloi by high walls and even higher prices, and their presence lends Akasaka a certain cachet.

Hie-jinja

8

日枝神社 • 2-10-15 Nagatachō, Chiyoda-ku • 24hr • Free • Akasaka, Akasaka-mitsuke or Tameike-sannō stations

At the southern end of Akasaka's main thoroughfare, Sotobori-dōri, stands a huge stone *torii*, beyond which is a picturesque avenue of red *torii* leading up the hill to **Hie-jinja**, a Shinto shrine dedicated to the god Ōyamakui-no-kami, who is believed to protect against evil. Hie-jinja's history stretches back to 830 AD, when it was first established on the outskirts of what would become Edo. The shrine's location shifted a couple more times before Shogun Tokugawa Ietsuna placed it here in the seventeenth century as a source of protection for his castle (now the site of the Imperial Palace); the current buildings date from the 1950s.

From the main entrance through the large stone *torii* on the east side of the hill, 51 steps lead up to a spacious enclosed courtyard. To the left of the main shrine, look for the carving of a female monkey cradling her baby, a symbol that has come to signify protection for pregnant women. In June, Hie-jinja hosts one of Tokyo's most important festivals, the **Sannō Matsuri** (see p.27).

National Diet Building

国会議事堂, Kokkai Gijidō • 1-7-1 Nagatachō, Chiyoda-ku • Tours of House of Councillors Mon–Fri 9am–4pm unless in session • Free • ☎ 03 5521 7445, ⓦ www.sangiin.go.jp • Kokkai-gijidō-mae station

The squat, three-storey **National Diet Building** is dominated by a central tower block decorated with pillars and a pyramid-shaped roof. On the left stands the House of Representatives, the main body of government; on the right is the House of Councillors, which is similar to Britain's House of Lords and open for hour-long **tours**.

There's an Edwardian-style grandeur to the Diet's interior, especially in the carved-wood debating chamber and the central reception hall, which is decorated with paintings reflecting the seasons, and bronze statues of significant statesmen. The room the emperor uses when he visits the Diet is predictably ornate, with detailing picked out in real gold. The tour finishes at the Diet's front garden, planted with native trees and plants from all of Japan's 47 prefectures.

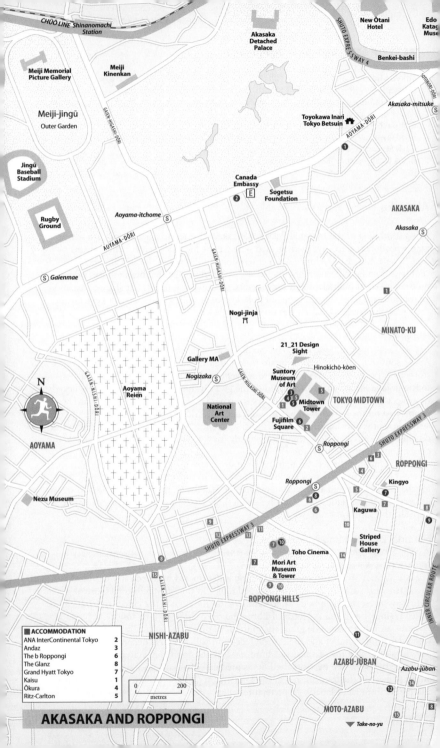

CHŪŌ LINE Shinanomachi Station

New Ōtani Hotel

Edo Katac Muse

Meiji Memorial Picture Gallery

Meiji Kinenkan

Akasaka Detached Palace

Benkei-bashi

Meiji-jingū
Outer Garden

Toyokawa Inari Tokyo Betsuin

Akasaka-mitsuke

AKASAKA

Jingū Baseball Stadium

Canada Embassy

Sogetsu Foundation

Akasaka

Ⓢ Akasaka

Rugby Ground

Aoyama-itchome **Ⓢ**

AOYAMA-DŌRI

Ⓢ Gaienmae

Nogi-jinja

MINATO-KU

21_21 Design Sight

Gallery MA

Hinokichō-kōen

Nogizaka **Ⓢ**

Suntory Museum of Art

TOKYO MIDTOWN

N

Aoyama Reien

National Art Center

Midtown Tower

Fujifilm Square

Ⓢ Roppongi

ROPPONGI

AOYAMA

Roppongi **Ⓢ**

Kingyo

Nezu Museum

Roppongi

Kaguwa

Striped House Gallery

Toho Cinema

Mori Art Museum & Tower

ROPPONGI HILLS

NISHI-AZABU

AZABU-JŪBAN

Azabu-jūban

0   200
metres

MOTO-AZABU

▼ Take-no-yu

AKASAKA AND ROPPONGI

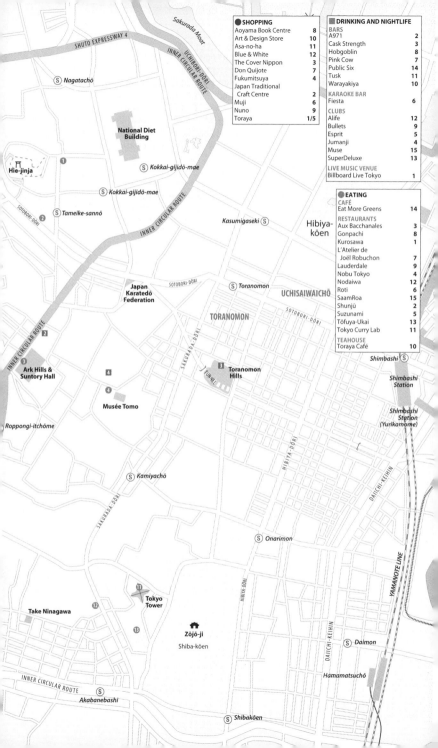

● SHOPPING

Aoyama Book Centre	8
Art & Design Store	10
Asa-no-ha	11
Blue & White	12
The Cover Nippon	3
Don Quijote	7
Fukumitsuya	4
Japan Traditional Craft Centre	2
Muji	6
Nuno	9
Toraya	1/5

■ DRINKING AND NIGHTLIFE

BARS

A971	2
Cask Strength	3
Hobgoblin	8
Pink Cow	7
Public Six	14
Tusk	11
Warayakiya	10

KARAOKE BAR

Fiesta	6

CLUBS

Alife	12
Bullets	9
Esprit	5
Jumanji	4
Muse	15
SuperDeluxe	13

LIVE MUSIC VENUE

Billboard Live Tokyo	1

● EATING

CAFÉ

Eat More Greens	14

RESTAURANTS

Aux Bacchanales	3
Gonpachi	8
Kurosawa	1
L'Atelier de Joël Robuchon	7
Lauderdale	9
Nobu Tokyo	4
Nodaiwa	12
Roti	6
SaamRoa	15
Shunjū	2
Suzunami	5
Tōfuya-Ukai	13
Tokyo Curry Lab	11

TEAHOUSE

Toraya Café	10

Edo Ise Katagami Museum

江戸伊勢型紙美術館, Edo Ise Katagami Bijutsukan • 3-32 Kioichō, Chiyoda-ku • Tues & Thurs–Sun 11am–5.30pm • ¥1000; tea ceremonies ¥1000 • ☎ 03 3265 4001 • Akasaka-mitsuke or Nagatachō stations

The delightful **Edo Ise Katagami Museum** is tucked away in an apartment building behind the *Akasaka Prince Hotel*. The light-flooded museum and gallery display a dazzling collection of intricately carved stencils used for making patterns on kimono. Some of the stencils are used for original gifts in the museum shop, and the curator, who speaks good English, is happy to explain the collection. Call ahead – especially if you want to book a tea ceremony here – as they do keep erratic hours.

New Ōtani hotel garden

4-1 Kiyoichō, Chiyoda-ku • Daily 6am–10pm • Free • Kojimachi, Akasaka-mitsuke or Nagatachō stations

Near Benkei-bashi, the bridge that spans what was once the outer moat of the shogun's castle, you'll find the **New Ōtani hotel** – you may recognize the place from Bond film *You Only Live Twice*, where it functioned as Blofeld's Tokyo base. Within its grounds is a traditional Japanese **garden**, originally designed for the *daimyō* Katō Kiyomasa, lord of Kumamoto in Kyūshū over four hundred years ago. It's actually one of the most spectacular in the whole city, with a vermillion bridge overlooking a miniature waterfall. Those visiting in the shoulder seasons may get to see cheery pink flowers or fiery autumnal leaves, though it's a pretty place at any time of the year.

Toyokawa Inari Tokyo Betsuin

豊川稲荷東京別院 • 1-4-7 Motoakasaka, Minato-ku • 24hr • Free • Akasaka-mitsuke station

The colourful **Toyokawa Inari Tokyo Betsuin**, also known as Toyokawa Inari, is a combined temple and shrine. Such holy places were much more common across Japan before the Meiji government forcibly separated Shinto and Buddhist places of worship. The temple's compact precincts are decked with red lanterns and banners, while the main hall is guarded by statues of pointy-eared foxes wearing red bibs: messengers of the Shinto god Inari, they are found at all Inari shrines.

Akasaka Detached Palace

迎賓館, Geihinkan • 2-1-1 Motoakasaka, Minato-ku • Entry by lottery, usually in Sept • ⓦ www8.cao.go.jp/geihinkan • Yotsuya station

Sitting amid extensive grounds, the grand, European-style **Akasaka Detached Palace** serves as the official State Guesthouse. When it was completed in 1909, this vast building, modelled on Buckingham Palace on the outside and Versailles on the inside, had only one bathroom in the basement, and the empress's apartments were in a separate wing from her husband's (an arrangement that suited the emperor fine, since he was in the habit of taking his nightly pick from the ladies-in-waiting). The palace is only open to the public for a few weeks each year, usually around September, with entry limited to 2000 people per day, chosen by lottery from postcard applications – the process is detailed in Japanese on the website. It's sometimes possible to gain entry on the spot on these days; even if you're out of luck, the front gardens are free to enter on the days the palace is open, and count as a consolation prize. At other times of year you can peek through the main gates, close to Yotsuya station.

Sōgetsu Foundation

草月会館, Sōgetsu Kaikan • 7-2-21 Akasaka, Minato-ku • Hour-long trial classes ¥3240; reserve online • ☎ 03 3408 1209, ⓦ sogetsu.or.jp • Aoyama-itchōme station

Founded in 1927, the **Sōgetsu Foundation** is a famous school of *ikebana* – traditional Japanese flower-arranging – and holds classes in English. It is housed in a glass-fronted building designed by influential architect Tange Kenzō (see box, p.266), and the lobby features strikingly contemporary *ikebana* displays, as well as sculptures by the renowned American-Japanese artist Isamu Noguchi.

Toranomon

虎ノ門

As with Roppongi before it, **Toranomon** has seen its stock rise in recent years with the opening of a mammoth new development: **Toranomon Hills**. While not as flashy or as interesting to the casual tourist as its near namesake, Roppongi Hills, it's still worth an amble around if you're in the area; it's topped by the fancy *Andaz Tokyo* hotel (see p.146), and tailed by a rather predictable clutch of shops and restaurants. It will be interesting to see what effect this development has on the rest of the area, but for now Toranomon's only real draw is the excellent **Musée Tomo** gallery.

Musée Tomo

智美術館, Tomo Bijutsukan · 4-1-35 Toranomon, Minato-ku · Tues–Sun 11am–6pm · Most exhibitions ¥1000 · ☎ 03 5733 5131, ⓦ musee-tomo.or.jp · Roppongi-itchōme, Kamiyachō or Toranomon stations

Home to the outstanding contemporary Japanese ceramics collection of Tomo Kikuchi, the classy **Musée Tomo** gallery is as elegant as its exhibits – fifty-odd pieces carefully spotlit as objets d'art. Inside is a stunning stairwell with a barley-sugar-like banister and slivers of *washi* paper decorating the walls, while out the front is the old Kikuchi family home, an incongruous Taishō-era villa. From the museum's fancy French café and restaurant, *Voie Lactée*, there's a lovely view on to the old home's tranquil garden.

Roppongi

六本木

Its name meaning "six trees", **Roppongi** was once reputed to be home to six *daimyō*, all of whom coincidentally had the Chinese character for "tree" in their names. From the Meiji era onwards, the area was a military stamping ground, first for the imperial troops and then, during the American Occupation, for US forces. Thus the *gaijin* community started hanging out here, and today's entertainment district was born. Roppongi is still principally a party town, but three major developments – Roppongi Hills, the National Art Center and Tokyo Midtown – have recast the area in a more refined light, and today it's increasingly known for its galleries and arts scene (see box below). Roppongi subway station is the principal access point for the area, although you can also use Nogizaka for the National Art Center and Kamiyachō for Tokyo Tower.

8

ROPPONGI GALLERIES

Those bumping and grinding in Roppongi's clubs would likely scoff at you for suggesting so, but the area is now almost as notable for its excellent **art scene** as it is for drinking – there are **galleries** dotted all over the place, all the way south to Azabu-Jūban. As well as those listed here, there's excellent art on display at Musée Tomo in Toranomon (see above), the Suntory Museum of Art (see p.100) and 21_21 Design Sight (see p.100) in Tokyo Midtown, the lofty Mori Art Museum atop Roppongi Hills (see p.102) and the National Art Center (see p.100).

Gallery MA 8-11-27 Akasaka, Minato-ku ☎ 03 3402 1010; Nogizaka station. Across the road from the Nogi-jinja (see p.100), there's often an interesting exhibition at Gallery MA, on the third floor of the TOTO Nogizaka building (which belongs to Japan's largest manufacturer of toilets). The gallery specializes in interior design and architecture, both from Japan and overseas, and has an excellent bookstore. Tues–Thurs & Sat 11am–6pm, Fri 11am–7pm.

Striped House Gallery 5-10-33 Roppongi, Minato-ku ☎ 03 3405 8108, ⓦ striped-house.com;

Roppongi station. Taking its name from the striped brick building in which it's based, this gallery has an eclectic range of exhibitions, almost all of which focus on young, adventurous local artists. Daily 11am–6.30pm.

Take Ninagawa 2-12-4 Higashi-Azabu, Minato-ku ☎ 03 5571 5844, ⓦ takeninagawa.com; Azabu-Jūban station. Representing mixed media artists such as Ohtake Shinrō and Misaki Kawai, it's worth swinging by to see what's on at this space for up-and-coming local artists. Wed–Sun 11am–7pm.

Tokyo Midtown

東京ミッドタウン • 9-7-1 Akasaka, Minato-ku • ⓦ www.tokyo-midtown.com • Roppongi or Nogizaka station

Tokyo Midtown is an enormous mixed-use complex of offices, shops, apartments, a convention centre, two museums and other public facilities, plus the small park Hinokichō-kōen, all revolving around the 248m-high **Midtown Tower**. Completed in 2007, this was Tokyo's tallest building until the Skytree came along; oddly, there's no viewing deck. With its slightly bulbous middle, the tower's design was inspired by an Isamu Noguchi sculpture; in keeping with a general theme of traditional motifs, the pattern of the tower's windows is reminiscent of a woven bamboo fence.

Suntory Museum of Art

サントリー美術館, Santorii Bijutsukan • 3F Galleria, Tokyo Midtown • Mon & Sun 10am–6pm, Wed–Sat 10am–8pm • Entry price varies by exhibition, usually around ¥1000 • ☎ 03 3470 1073, ⓦ www.suntory.co.jp/sma

Landscaped gardens planted with 140 trees nestle behind and along the west side of the Tokyo Midtown complex, where you'll find the **Suntory Museum of Art**. This elegant Kuma Kengo-designed building hosts changing exhibitions of ceramics, lacquerware, paintings and textiles. There's also an on-site café serving tasty nibbles from Kanazawa, the capital of Ishikawa prefecture.

21_21 Design Sight

9-7-6 Akasaka, Minato-ku • Daily 10am–7pm • ¥1100 • ☎ 03 3475 2121, ⓦ 2121designsight.jp

Two giant triangular planes of steel, concrete and glass peeking out of a green lawn are part of the **21_21 Design Sight**, a fascinating collaboration between architect Andō Tadao and fashion designer Issey Miyake. The building's seamless shape was inspired by Miyake's A-POC ("A Piece Of Cloth") line, and the main gallery digs one floor into the ground to provide an elevated, airy space in which to view the various design exhibitions.

Fujifilm Square

フジフイルムスクエア • 1F Midtown West, Tokyo Midtown • Daily 10am–7pm • Free • ⓦ fujifilmsquare.jp

At the front of the Midtown complex, facing Gaien-Higashi-dōri, is **Fujifilm Square**, with photography exhibitions changing on a monthly basis, and a permanent display showcasing the history of cameras, from the relatively ancient to the modern day. There's also a shop selling fine photographic prints.

National Art Center

国立新美術館, Kokuritsu Shin Bijutsukan • 7-22-2 Roppongi, Minato-ku • Daily except Tues 10am–6pm, Fri 10am–8pm • Entrance fee varies with exhibition • ☎ 03 6812 9900, ⓦ www.nact.jp • Nogizaka or Roppongi station

The stunning **National Art Center** is one of the three principal points on the **Roppongi Art Triangle**, which also includes the Suntory Museum of Art (see above) and Mori Art Museum (see p.102). A billowing wave of pale green glass ripples across the facade of the Kurokawa Kisha-designed building which, at 48,000 square metres, is Japan's largest such museum, the huge halls allowing for some very ambitious works to be displayed. Of the twelve exhibition rooms, two are devoted to shows curated by the museum (the centre has no collection of its own); the rest of the rooms are organized by various art associations from across Japan, with the sum total making for a very eclectic mix. While you are here, linger in the main atrium to admire the conical pods that soar up three storeys, and explore the excellent museum shop.

Nogi-jinja

乃木神社 • 8-11-27 Akasaka, Minato-ku • 24hr • Free • Nogizaka station

The small shrine and terraced garden of **Nogi-jinja** honour the Meiji-era **General Nogi Maresuke**, a hero in both the Sino-Japanese and Russo-Japanese wars. When the

Emperor Meiji died, Nogi and his wife followed the samurai tradition and committed suicide in his house within the shrine grounds.

There's a good **antique flea market** here, while the interesting Gallery MA (see box, p.99) sits just on the other side of the main road.

Roppongi Hills

六本木ヒルズ • 8-11-27 Akasaka, Minato-ku • ⓦ roppongihills.com • Roppongi station

Originally billed as an "Urban New Deal" for Tokyo, **Roppongi Hills** is the development that spearheaded Roppongi's partial evolution from sleaze to sophistication. The overhead utility cables that plague the rest of Tokyo have been banished here, and there's a good dose of open space and greenery, so unusual in this land-starved city. A Japanese garden and pond, a liberal sprinkling of funky street sculptures, an open-air arena for free performances, several roof gardens and even a rice paddy on the roof above the multiplex cinema are all part of the mix. Louise Bourgeois' **Maman**, a giant bronze, stainless steel and marble spider, squats at the base of the 54-storey, Kohn Pedersen Fox-designed **Mori Tower**, home to the Mori Art Museum and the Tokyo City View observation deck.

Mori Art Museum

森美術館, Mori Bijutsukan • 53F Mori Tower, Roppongi Hills • Daily 10am–10pm, Tues closes 5pm • ¥1600 • ⓣ 03 6406 6100, ⓦ mori.art.museum

The "Museum Cone", a glass structure enclosing a swirling staircase, forms the entrance to the **Mori Art Museum**, more than fifty storeys overhead. This large gallery space, which occupies the prime top floors of the Mori Tower, puts on large and adventurous exhibitions, with a particular focus on Asian artists – they're generally extremely well-curated affairs, even down to themed menu items at the on-site café.

Tokyo City View

東京シティビュー • 54F Mori Tower, Roppongi Hills • Daily 9am–1am, last entry midnight • ¥1800; Skydeck ¥500 extra • ⓦ www.roppongihills.com/tcv/en

In the same tower as the Mori Art Museum, one floor up, the **Tokyo City View** observation deck is one of the best viewpoints in the city. If the weather is fine, it's possible to get out on to the rooftop **Skydeck** for an alfresco view that's particularly enchanting during and after sunset.

Azabu-Jūban and around

麻布十番

Of the many expats and moneyed Japanese you'll see traipsing their kids around Roppongi's various shops and cafés, a fairly high proportion actually live just to the southeast in **Azabu-Jūban**. There's little of note for the traveller in this rather grey area, bar the giant **matsuri** which takes place in August – up there with the busiest summer festivals in Tokyo – when most streets become absolutely rammed with food stalls and beer-toting visitors. However, just to the east of Azabu-Jūban is one of the city's most prominent sights: **Tokyo Tower**, flanked on its eastern side by a large park, **Shiba-kōen**, and **Zōjō-ji**.

Tokyo Tower

東京タワー • 4-2-8 Shiba-kōen • Daily 9am–11pm • Main observatory ¥900, top observatory ¥700 extra • ⓣ 03 3433 5111, ⓦ tokyotower.co.jp • Akabanebashi or Kamiyachō stations

You can't miss **Tokyo Tower**, a distinctive red-and-white structure rising high above the wider Roppongi area. Built during an era when Japan was becoming famous for producing cheap copies of foreign goods, this 333m-high replica of the Eiffel Tower, opened in 1958, manages to top its Parisian role model by several metres. At the tower's base a plethora of the usual souvenir shops, restaurants and other minor attractions have been added over the years, most incurring additional fees and none really worth seeing in their own right. There are good views of Tokyo Bay from the uppermost observation deck but, at 250m, it's no longer the city's highest viewpoint – you can get 20m higher at the nearby Tokyo City View (see opposite), while the Tokyo Skytree (see p.78) rises to a vertiginous 450m.

Zōjō-ji

増上寺 • 4-7-35 Shiba-kōen • 24hr • Free • Akabanebashi, Onarimon or Shiba-kōen stations

The main point of interest at **Shiba-kōen** (芝公園) is **Zōjō-ji**, the family temple of the Tokugawa clan. Dating from 1393, Zōjō-ji was moved to this site in 1598 by Tokugawa Ieyasu (the first Tokugawa shogun) in order to protect southeast Edo spiritually and provide a waystation for pilgrims approaching the capital from the Tōkaidō road. This was once the city's largest holy site, with 48 sub-temples and over a hundred other buildings. Since the fall of the Tokugawa, however, Zōjō-ji has been razed to the ground by fire three times, and virtually all the current buildings date from the mid-1970s; some find it all rather lacking in charm.

San-gadatsu-mon

One ancient element still standing at the temple is its imposing **San-gadatsu-mon**, a 21m-high gateway dating from 1612 – it is the oldest wooden structure in Tokyo and designated one of Japan's Important Cultural Properties. The name translates as "Three Deliverances Gate" (Buddhism is supposed to save believers from the evils of anger, greed and stupidity). As you pass through, look out for the tower with a large bell, said to have been made from melted metal hairpins donated by the ladies of the shogun's court, and for the pair of Himalayan cedar trees, one planted by US President Grant when he visited the temple in 1879 and the other by the then Vice President George Bush in 1982. Ahead lies the **Taiden** (Great Main Hall), while to the right are ranks of *jizō* statues, capped with red bonnets and decorated with plastic flowers and colourful windmills that twirl in the breeze. Amid this army of mini-guardians lie the remains of six shogun, behind a wrought-iron gate decorated with dragons.

Take-no-yu

竹の湯 • 1-15-12 Minami-Azabu, Minato-ku • Tues–Thurs, Sat & Sun 3.30–11.30pm • ¥460 • Azabu-Jūban station

A short walk south of Azabu-Jūban, the **Take-no-yu** baths are somewhat different to most other Tokyo establishments for one major reason: the water in these parts comes out brown, and is so prized for its medical properties that locals pay to take it away by the litre. The experience of bathing here is a little like being steeped in tea – or being a dirty plate in a sink full of dirty dishwater.

Ebisu and the south

The area immediately to the south of Shibuya has, of late, become one of the most fashionable in the city – a maze of chic cafés, tiny clothing boutiques, and lunchtime specials of foreign and fusion cuisine. Like Shibuya, Ebisu is best visited at night, when its many bars and restaurants are at their liveliest. The district is also home to the former Yebisu brewery (the old transliteration of Ebisu lives on in the name of the beer), now developed into the Yebisu Garden Place complex, where you'll find the excellent Tokyo Photographic Art Museum. Head uphill to the west of Ebisu and you'll hit Daikanyama, one of Tokyo's most upscale districts and a great place to chill out at a pavement café or browse boutiques. Dip downhill again to explore a rather more down-to-earth version of the same in Nakameguro, whose cherry tree-lined river banks are prime strolling territory.

BEST OF EBISU AND THE SOUTH

Tokyo Photographic Art Museum Ogle world-class images (see below)
Nakameguro Stroll the river banks or have a *hanami* party in this delightful district (see p.108)
Hillside Terrace Take your pick of one of the countless cafés (see p.108)
Hokkaido Enjoy good seafood and a 38th-floor view (see p.166)
Iroha Scoff a super-cheap, yet very high quality sushi set (see p.166)
Nakameguro Taproom Sample some of Tokyo's best draught beer (see p.178)
Meguro Cinema Go retro with an old film (see p.192)

South along the Meguro River from here is **Meguro**, site of the tranquil **National Park for Nature Study** and the serene gardens of **Happōen**. Near the transport and hotel hub of **Shinagawa**, east of Meguro, you'll find the historic temple **Sengaku-ji**, a key location in Tokyo's bloodiest true-life samurai saga, and the **Hara Museum of Contemporary Art**, which houses an interesting collection of modern art and a lovely café.

Ebisu

恵比寿

The main focus of **Ebisu** (named after the Shinto god of good fortune) is **Yebisu Garden Place**, a sprawling shopping, office and entertainment development, built on the site of the nineteenth-century brewery that was once the source of the area's fortunes. The brewery is now a small **museum** dedicated to Yebisu beer, while the worthy **Tokyo Photographic Art Museum** also lies within the wider complex. The excellent **Yamatane Museum of Art**, due northeast of Ebisu station, is another artsy sight to tick off in the area.

Yebisu Garden Place

恵比寿ガーデンプレイス • 4-20 Ebisu, Shibuya-ku • Ebisu station

Slated as an architectural cock-up, the **Yebisu Garden Place** complex – connected to Ebisu station by a series of moving walkways – includes the glitzy *Westin Hotel*, a cinema, a performance hall and a mock French château housing a Joël Robuchon restaurant. Rising up above it all is the 39-storey **Yebisu Tower**, from the top floor of which you can take in some spectacular free city views; there are plenty of restaurants taking advantage of these lofty surroundings, with *Hokkaido* (see p.166) recommended for its cheap-ish seafood.

Tokyo Photographic Art Museum

東京都写真美術館, Tōkyō-to Shashin Bijutsukan • Yebisu Garden Place • Tues–Sun 10am–6pm, Thurs & Fri until 8pm • Admission charges vary • ☎ 03 3280 0031, ⓦ topmuseum.jp

The best sight in the Ebisu area is the **Tokyo Photographic Museum** – also known as the **TOP Museum** – which was fully remodelled in 2016 and hosts excellent exhibitions by major Japanese and Western photographers. There are three full floors of exhibitions (two above ground, one below), with a café on the entrance floor; exhibitions can last anything from two weeks to three months, but there's usually a good spread of themes at any one time.

Museum of Yebisu Beer

エビスビール記念館, Yebisu Biiru Kinenkan • B1 west side of Yebisu Garden Place complex, best accessed through Mitsukoshi mall • Tues–Sun 11am–7pm • Free; beer samples ¥400 • ☎ 03 5423 7255, ⓦ sapporobeer.jp/yebisu/museum

Beer drinkers may care to visit the **Museum of Yebisu Beer** to find out about the history of the Yebisu brand – now owned by the Sapporo Brewery, though still sold under its old label – and of the brewery that used to be here. There's not all that much to see, bar

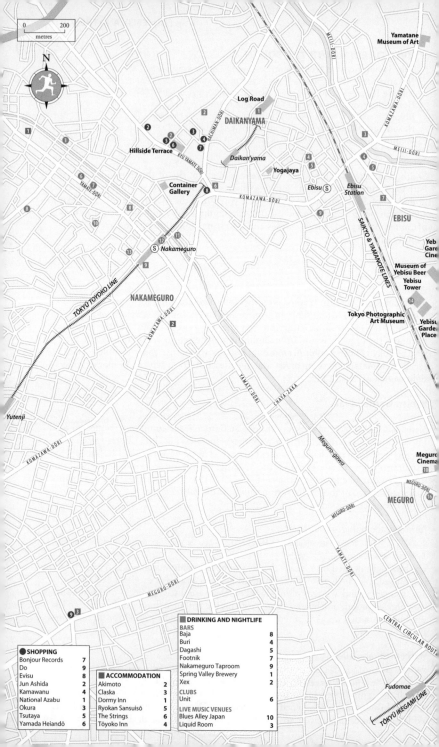

Yamatane
Museum of Art

MEIJI-DŌRI

Log Road

DAIKANYAMA

Hillside Terrace

Daikan'yama

Yogajaya

Container
Gallery

KOMAZAWA-DŌRI

Ebisu Ⓢ

Ebisu
Station

EBISU

Nakameguro Ⓢ

Yeb
Gare
Cine

Museum of
Yebisu Beer

Yebisu
Tower

NAKAMEGURO

Tokyo Photographic
Art Museum

Yebisu
Garde
Place

TŌKYŪ TŌYOKO LINE

Yutenji

KOMAZAWA-DŌRI

YAMATE-DŌRI

CHAYA-ZAKA

Meguro-gawa

Meguro
Cinema

MEGURO-DŌRI

MEGURO

YAMATE-DŌRI

MEGURO-DŌRI

CENTRAL CIRCULAR ROUTE

Fudomae

TŌKYŪ IKEGAMI LINE

● SHOPPING

Bonjour Records	7
Do	9
Evisu	8
Jun Ashida	2
Kamawanu	4
National Azabu	1
Okura	3
Tsutaya	5
Yamada Heiandō	6

■ ACCOMMODATION

Akimoto	2
Claska	3
Dormy Inn	1
Ryokan Sansuisō	5
The Strings	6
Tōyoko Inn	4

■ DRINKING AND NIGHTLIFE

BARS

Baja	8
Buri	4
Dagashi	5
Footnik	7
Nakameguro Taproom	9
Spring Valley Brewery	1
Xex	2

CLUBS

| Unit | 6 |

LIVE MUSIC VENUES

| Blues Alley Japan | 10 |
| Liquid Room | 3 |

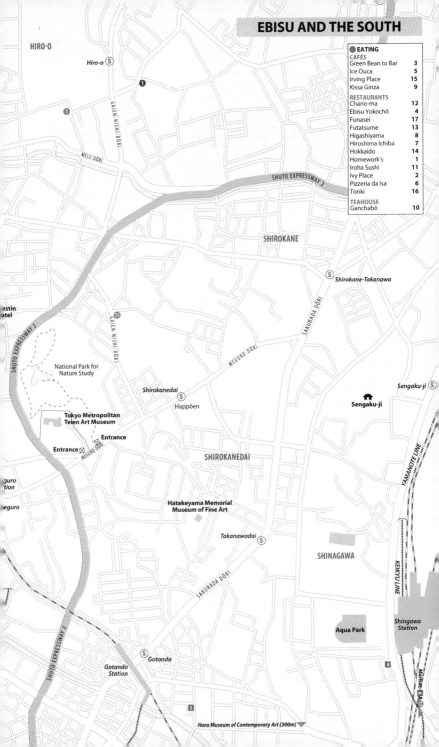

EBISU AND THE SOUTH

HIRO-O

Hiro-o Ⓢ

MEIJI-DŌRI

GAIEN-NISHI-DŌRI

SHUTO EXPRESSWAY 2

SHIROKANE

Shirokane-Takanawa Ⓢ

SHUTO EXPRESSWAY 2

estin otel

GAIEN-NISHI-DŌRI

SAKURADA-DŌRI

MEGURO-DŌRI

National Park for Nature Study

Sengaku-ji Ⓢ

Shirokanedai Ⓢ

Happōen

Sengaku-ji

Tokyo Metropolitan Teien Art Museum

Entrance

Entrance

guro tion

eguro

MEGURO-DŌRI

SHIROKANEDAI

Hatakeyama Memorial Museum of Fine Art

Takanawadai Ⓢ

SHINAGAWA

YAMANOTE LINE

KEIKYU LINE

SAKURADA-DŌRI

Shingawa Station

Aqua Park

Ⓢ Gotanda

SHUTO EXPRESSWAY 2

Gotanda Station

Hara Museum of Contemporary Art (300m) ▼

9

a display of how the company's beer bottles have become progressively uglier over the years, but thanks to relatively late opening hours, the tasting room is a great place to sample some of Sapporo's beers.

Yamatane Museum of Art

山種美術館, Yamatane Bijutsukan · 3-12-36 Hiro-o, Shibuya-ku · Tues–Sun 10am–5pm · ¥1200 · ☎ 03 5777 8600,
ⓦ www.yamatane-museum.or.jp · 10min walk northeast of Ebisu station

Art lovers should consider dropping by the refined **Yamatane Museum of Art**. The museum's focus is Japanese paintings from the Meiji Era, of which it has an impressive collection – over 1800 works. There are usually six or seven different exhibitions a year, all arranged around a particular genre, era or artist.

Daikanyama

代官山

The classy residential suburb of **Daikanyama** has a village-like atmosphere that provides a refreshing break from the frenzy of nearby Shibuya, just one stop away on the Tōkyū Tōyoko line (or a nice half-hour walk). It's also possible to get here from Ebisu station, by taking a ten-minute stroll uphill heading west along Komazawa-dōri. The area is most notable for its many boutiques (see map, pp.106–107) and cafés (see map, pp.106–107), but even if you're not in the market for clothing or caffeine it's worth visiting for the relaxed air. Major developments here include **Hillside Terrace**, a one-stop area for drinking, dining and shopping; and the even newer **Log Road** complex, a relatively small affair bookended by craft-beer pubs.

Hillside Terrace

Off Kyū-yamate-dōri · ⓦ www.hillsideterrace.com · Daikanyama station

Daikanyama's contemporary style has been defined by the **Hillside Terrace** shopping and dining complex, designed by Maki Fumihiko, recipient of the 1993 Pritzker Prize for architecture. Strung along leafy Kyū-yamate-dōri, the various stages of Hillside Terrace were developed over nearly a quarter-century, its courtyards and vistas paying homage to ancient Japanese and Buddhist concepts of space. Poke around and you'll find plenty of appealing boutiques and ritzy restaurants and cafés. It's impossible to miss the huge Tsutaya book store (see p.197), while the **Hillside Gallery** (Tues–Sun 10am–5pm; free), opposite the Danish Embassy, has interesting modern art exhibitions.

Nakameguro

中目黒

Immediately to the southwest of Daikanyama is **Nakameguro**, one of Tokyo's trendiest areas, with a laidback, boho feel and a liberal sprinkling of eclectic boutiques (see map, pp.106–107), restaurants (see map, pp.106–107) and bars (see map, pp.106–107). The district hugs the banks of the Meguro-gawa and is a particularly lovely spot to head during *hanami* season, thanks to its generous number of cherry trees. This is also one of the less sweltering places in Tokyo come high summer, with evaporation from the languid waterway providing some natural air conditioning. Another thing in Nakameguro's favour is convenience: as people from all over Tokyo will attest with envy, the area is directly accessible from almost all major parts of the city.

The Container Gallery

ザコンテナギャラリー · 1F Hills Daikanyama, 1-8-30 Kamimeguro, Meguro-ku · Mon & Wed–Fri 11am–9pm, Sat & Sun 10am–8pm ·
Free · ⓦ the-container.com · Nakameguro station

One of the smallest galleries in the city – the clue's in the name – the **Container Gallery** is set inside a shipping container, itself set inside a hair salon; exhibitions change every couple of months, and showcase a mix of young Japanese and international talent.

Meguro

目黒

Within walking distance of Nakameguro and Ebisu, **Meguro** is decidedly less appealing than its neighbouring areas – the atmosphere here is rather more city than village. Nevertheless, there are a few interesting things to see, even if they're frustratingly spread out.

Tokyo Metropolitan Teien Art Museum

東京都庭園美術館, Tōkyō-to Teien Bijutsukan • 5-21-9 Shirokanedai, Meguro-ku • **Museum** Daily 10am–6pm, closed second & fourth Wed of the month • Entry varies by exhibitions, usually ¥1000 • **Garden** Daily 10am–9pm • Entry included with museum ticket, otherwise ¥100 • ☎ 03 3443 0201, ⓦ www.teien-art-museum.ne.jp • Meguro or Shirokanedai stations

The Art Deco building housing the elegant **Tokyo Metropolitan Teien Art Museum** is the former home of Prince Asaka Yasuhiko, Emperor Hirohito's uncle, who lived in Paris for three years during the 1920s, where he developed a taste for the European style. It's worth popping in to admire the gorgeous interior decoration (particularly in the octagonal study room upstairs) and tranquil surrounding Japanese gardens; the exhibitions themselves tend to be curated along similarly genteel lines.

National Park for Nature Study

自然教育園, Shizen Kyōiku-en • 5-21-5 Shirokanedai, Meguro-ku • Tues–Sun 9am–4.30pm, May–Aug until 5pm • ¥310 • ⓦ www.ins.kahaku.go.jp • Meguro or Shirokanedai station

The spacious **National Park for Nature Study** is a worthy attempt to preserve the original natural features of the countryside before Edo was settled and developed into Tokyo. Among the eight thousand trees in the park are some that have been growing for five hundred years, while frogs can be heard croaking amid the grass beside the marshy ponds. The whole place is a bird-spotter's paradise, and it's also one of the few areas in Tokyo where you can really escape the crowds; the entrance is a stone's throw to the east of the Teien Art Museum (see above).

Happōen

八芳園 • 1-1-1 Shirokanedai, Meguro-ku • **Garden** Daily 10am–5pm • Free • **Teahouse** Daily 11am–5pm • ¥800 • Shirokanedai station

Shirokanedai subway station is the handiest jumping-off point for the lovely **Happōen**. The garden's name means "beautiful from any angle" and, despite the addition of a modern wedding hall on one side, this is still true. A renowned adviser to the shogunate, Hikozaemon Okubo, lived here during the early seventeenth century, but most of the garden's design dates from the early twentieth century, when a business tycoon bought up the land, built a classical Japanese villa (still standing by the garden's entrance) and gave the garden its present name. Take a turn through its twisting pathways and you'll pass two bonsai trees, each more than a hundred years old, a stone lantern said to have been carved eight hundred years ago by the Heike warrior Taira-no Munekiyo, and a central pond. Nestling amid the trees is the delightful **teahouse**, where ladies in kimono will serve you *matcha* and *okashi*. At weekends many smartly dressed wedding parties line up for group photos against the verdant backdrop.

Hatakeyama Memorial Museum of Fine Art

畠山記念館, Hatakeyama Kinenkan • 2-20-12 Shirokanedai, Meguro-ku • Tues–Sun: April–Sept 10am–5pm; Oct–March 10am–4.30pm • ¥700; tea ¥500 • ☎ 03 3447 5787, ⓦ www.ebara.co.jp/csr/hatakeyama • Takanawadai station

Devoted to the art of the tea ceremony, the **Hatakeyama Memorial Museum of Fine Art** is situated in the midst of a quiet residential area, overlooking a pretty Japanese garden.

9

This compact but appealing museum houses the collection of business magnate Hatakeyama Issei, who made his fortune manufacturing waste incinerators and pumps. Hatakeyama had exquisite taste and his collection contains many lovely works of art; he also designed the building, which reflects the structure of a traditional teahouse, albeit on a much larger scale. Tea is served in the exhibition hall.

Shinagawa

品川

The transport and hotel hub of **Shinagawa** was once the location of one of the original checkpoints on the Tōkaidō, the major highway into Edo during the reign of the shoguns. These days, most travellers who find themselves in Shinagawa are merely changing trains or passing through on one of the many train lines snaking through the area, but those with a little time to spare have a few sights to choose from, including the eclectic **Hara Museum of Contemporary Art**.

Aqua Park

アクアパーク • 4-30-10 Takanawa, Shinagawa-ku • Daily 10am–10pm • Adult ¥2200, child aged 7–15 ¥1200, child under 7 ¥700 • ☎ 03 5421 1111, ⓦ aqua-park.jp • Shinagawa station

There are some three hundred different species of marine life on display at the aquarium in the large **Aqua Park** entertainment complex, sitting behind the *Shinagawa Prince* hotel. It also offers dolphin and sea lion shows, amusement rides and a range of themed restaurants.

Hara Museum of Contemporary Art

原美術館, Hara Bijutsukan • 4-7-25 Kitashinagawa, Shinagawa-ku • Tues–Sun 11am–5pm, Wed until 8pm • ¥1100 • ☎ 03 3445 0651, ⓦ www.haramuseum.or.jp • Shinagawa station

In a quiet residential area around 800m south of Shinagawa station, the **Hara Museum of Contemporary Art** has a small permanent collection including quirky installations, such as *Rondo*, by Morimura Yasumasa, whose self-portrait occupies the downstairs toilet. The building itself, a 1938 Bauhaus-style house designed by Watanabe Jin, the architect responsible for Ueno's Tokyo National Museum and the Wakō department store in Ginza, is worth a look, as are the tranquil sculpture gardens overlooked by the museum's pleasant café.

Sengaku-ji

泉岳寺 • 2-11-1 Akanawa, Minato-ku • **Temple** Daily: April–Sept 7am–6pm; Oct–March 7am–5pm • Free • ☎ 03 3441 5560, ⓦ sengakuji.or.jp • **Museum** Daily: April–Sept 9am–4.30pm; Oct–March 9am–4pm • ¥500 • Sengaku-ji station

Around a kilometre north of Shinagawa is **Sengaku-ji**, home to the graves of **Asano Takumi** and his **47 rōnin** (see box opposite). Most of what you see now was rebuilt after World War II, but a striking gate decorated with a metalwork dragon dates back to 1836.

REAL-LIFE MARIO KART

If you're in Tokyo for any length of time, you may well see Mario, Luigi, Toad, Yoshi and other characters from classic game **Super Mario Kart** dashing around the city streets in tiny go-karts. This is no mere marketing stunt, but an activity that you can actually take part in yourself. Whizzing about in a costume, and most likely unable to remove the cartoonish grin from your face, this is about the best fun you can have in Tokyo, whether you're a fan of the game or not.

The **Maricar** team (☎ 03 6712 8275, ⓦ maricar.com) run three separate courses from their office in Shinagawa; all of them take in Tokyo Tower and Roppongi, with Shibuya and Odaiba also options, and prices start at ¥8000. You'll need to be in possession of a foreign or international driving licence (full details are on the website). Note that you'll be driving on real roads, and unlike in the game, you only have one life.

THE 47 RŌNIN

Celebrated in kabuki and *bunraku* plays, as well as on film, **Chūshingura** is a true story of honour, revenge and loyalty. In 1701, a young *daimyō*, Asano Takumi, became embroiled in a fatal argument in the shogun's court with his teacher and fellow lord Kira Yoshinaka. Asano had lost face in his performance of court rituals and, blaming his mentor for his lax tuition, drew his sword within the castle walls and attacked Kira. Although Kira survived, the shogun, on hearing of this breach of etiquette, ordered Asano to commit *seppuku*, the traditional form of suicide, which he did.

Their lord having been disgraced, Asano's loyal retainers, the **rōnin** – or masterless samurai – vowed revenge. On December 14, 1702, the 47 *rōnin*, lead by **Oishi Kuranosuke**, stormed Kira's villa, cut off his head and paraded it through Edo in triumph before placing it on Asano's grave in Sengaku-ji. The shogun ordered the *rōnin*'s deaths, but instead all 47 committed *seppuku* on February 14, 1703, including Oishi's 15-year-old son. They were buried with Asano in Sengaku-ji, and today their graves are still wreathed in the smoke from the bundles of incense placed by their gravestones.

The graves of the 47 *rōnin* are in the temple grounds (it's hard to resist the temptation to count them all), as well as the statue and grave of **Oishi Kuranosuke**, their avenging leader; a **museum** to the left of the main building contains their personal belongings, as well as a receipt for the severed head of Kira. The entrance is on the eastern side of the complex, which is a little tricky to track down.

STREET STYLE, HARAJUKU

Harajuku, Aoyama and Shibuya

If it's "wacky" Japan you're after, Harajuku should be neighbourhood number one on your list – indeed, in terms of human traffic, there can be few more fascinating districts on the whole planet. Much of Tokyo's youth culture starts here, on streets which often resemble densely-populated catwalks, complete with zany clothing, hairstyles and accessories; in the surrounding soup of quirky boutiques and cafés, you'll be able to kit yourself out and dine in much the same manner as the local fashionistas. Shibuya, just south of Harajuku, is almost absurdly busy – a neon-drenched, *kanji*-splattered, high-rise jungle second only to Shinjuku for sheer eye-popping madness. East of Harajuku, those with gilt-edged credit cards will feel more at home among the antique shops of Aoyama and the big brand boutiques along Omotesandō, the area's key tree-lined boulevard, often referred to as Tokyo's Champs-Elysées.

BEST OF HARAJUKU, AOYAMA AND SHIBUYA

Harajuku station Gawp at some of Japan's craziest fashion (see box below)
Meiji-jingū Wander the paths of the richly forested Inner Garden (see p.116)
Nezu Museum Enjoy the captivating gardens at this superbly designed museum (see p.118)
Caravan Tokyo Bed down for the night in a caravan (see p.147)
Ramen Nagi Slurp down a true rarity – pesto and cheese ramen (see p.169)
L'Occitane Sip a coffee and gaze down over teeming Shibuya Crossing (see p.170)
Karaoke-kan Do your very best Lady Gaga or Bill Murray impression (see box, p.181)
Omotesandō Check out the fashion flagships (see below)

10

Traditional sights take a bit of a back seat in these areas, and yet there is plenty to take in, the best being the verdant grounds of the city's most venerable shrine, **Meiji-jingū**, which merge into the greenery of **Yoyogi-kōen** to the south, one of the most pleasant parks in Tokyo, and often full of picnickers on sunny afternoons. Just off Omotesandō are several interesting **galleries**, including the **Nezu Museum** with its beautiful garden; the **Ōta Memorial Museum of Art**, dedicated to *ukiyo-e* prints; and the anarchic **Design Festa Gallery**.

Harajuku

原宿

Crammed with places to eat, drink and shop, the **Harajuku** area is bisected by **Omotesandō** (表参道), an elegant, ginkgo-tree-lined boulevard which leads from the main entrance of **Meiji-jingū** to the cluster of contemporary designer boutiques on the other side of Aoyama-dōri. On either side are dense networks of streets, packed with funky little boutiques, restaurants and bars.

The hungry mouth of the **Takeshita-dōri** (竹下通り) shopping alley gobbles up teenage fashion victims as they swarm out of the north exit of Harajuku station, and spits them out the other end on Meiji-dōri, minus their cash. Selling every kind of tat imaginable, the shops here are hugely enjoyable to root around in and provide an intriguing window on Japanese teen fashion.

The hip, independent Harajuku style is very much in evidence south of Omotesandō on **Cat Street**, a curvy pathway lined with cafés, small restaurants and eclectic emporia. Shadowing the course of the old Shibuya river (now built over), it provides a far more pleasant walking route to Shibuya than the busy main roads.

HARAJUKU STYLE

With its name immortalized in several Western songs, Harajuku is better known abroad for its zany **youth culture** than it is for shopping, and with very good reason. Swing by the Harajuku station area on a weekend and you'll see crowds of youngsters, mainly female, dressed up to the nines in a series of bizarre costumes; the epicentre is Jingū-bashi, a small bridge heading towards Meiji-jingū (see p.116) from Harajuku station.

Of the styles to look out for, **Cosplay** is probably the most familiar to outsiders: it involves dressing up as an anime, manga or game character, with occasionally startling results. Also easy to spot is **Gothic Lolita**, a mix of the gothic and the girlie; this itself is split into subgenres including punk, black, white (as in the hues) and country style. There are plenty more, including a whole host of smaller genres: **Visual Kei** adherents go for crazy make-up and hairstyles; **Decora** is a bright, flamboyant style often featuring myriad toys, pieces of jewellery and other accessories; **Kawaii**, which means "cute" in Japanese, usually involves clothing more appropriate to children. More styles are born every year, of course.

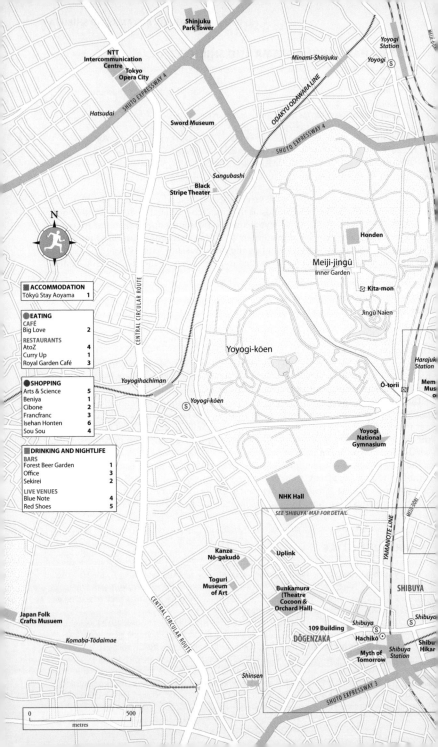

N

ACCOMMODATION
Tōkyū Stay Aoyama   1

EATING
CAFÉ
Big Love   2
RESTAURANTS
AtoZ   4
Curry Up   1
Royal Garden Café   3

SHOPPING
Arts & Science   5
Beniya   1
Cibone   2
Francfranc   3
Isehan Honten   6
Sou Sou   4

DRINKING AND NIGHTLIFE
BARS
Forest Beer Garden   1
Office   3
Sekirei   2
LIVE VENUES
Blue Note   4
Red Shoes   5

Shinjuku
Park Tower

NTT
Intercommunication
Centre
Tokyo
Opera City

Minami-Shinjuku

Yoyogi
Station

Yoyogi

Hatsudai

ODAKYU ODAWARA LINE

SHUTO EXPRESSWAY 4

Sword Museum

SHUTO EXPRESSWAY 4

Sangubashi

Black
Stripe Theater

Honden

Meiji-jingū
Inner Garden

⊠ Kita-mon

Jingū Naien

CENTRAL CIRCULAR ROUTE

Yoyogi-kōen

Yoyogihachiman

Harajuku
Station

Yoyogi-kōen Ⓢ

Ō-torii

Mem
Mus

Yoyogi
National
Gymnasium

NHK Hall

SEE 'SHIBUYA' MAP FOR DETAIL

Kanze
Nō-gakudō

Uplink

Toguri
Museum
of Art

Bunkamura
(Theatre
Cocoon &
Orchard Hall)

YAMANOTE LINE

MEIJI-DŌRI

SHIBUYA

Japan Folk
Crafts Musuem

CENTRAL CIRCULAR ROUTE

109 Building

Shibuya

Shibuya Ⓢ

Ⓢ Shibuya

Komaba-Tōdaimae

DŌGENZAKA

Hachikō

Shibu
Hikar

Myth of
Tomorrow

Shibuya
Station

Shinsen

SHUTO EXPRESSWAY 3

0   500
metres

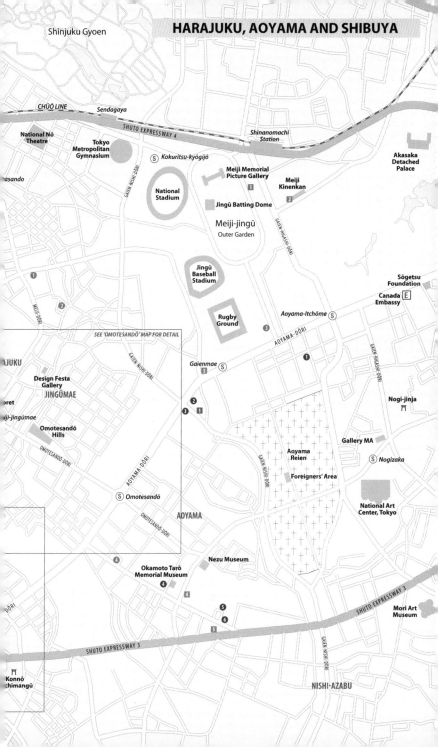

HARAJUKU, AOYAMA AND SHIBUYA

Shinjuku Gyoen

CHŪŌ LINE   *Sendagaya*

National Nō
Theatre

SHUTO EXPRESSWAY 4

Tokyo
Metropolitan
Gymnasium

*Shinanomachi
Station*

Akasaka
Detached
Palace

Ⓢ *Kokuritsu-kyōgijō*

Meiji Memorial
Picture Gallery

1

Meiji
Kinenkan

2

National
Stadium

Jingū Batting Dome

Meiji-jingū
Outer Garden

Sōgetsu
Foundation

Canada Ⓔ
Embassy

Jingū
Baseball
Stadium

asando

0

2

Rugby
Ground

3

Aoyama-Itchōme Ⓢ

AOYAMA-DŌRI

MEIJI-DŌRI

SEE 'OMOTESANDŌ' MAP FOR DETAIL

GATEN-NISHI-DŌRI

Gaienmae Ⓢ

3

1

JUKU

Design Festa
Gallery

JINGŪMAE

oret

iji-jingūmae

Omotesandō
Hills

2

3 1

OMOTESANDŌ-DŌRI

AOYAMA-DŌRI

Ⓢ *Omotesandō*

OMOTESANDŌ-DŌRI

AOYAMA

4

Okamoto Tarō
Memorial Museum

4

4

Nezu Museum

Aoyama
Reien

Foreigners' Area

Nogi-jinja ⛩

Gallery MA

Ⓢ *Nogizaka*

National Art
Center, Tokyo

GATEN-HIGASHI-DŌRI

GATEN-HIGASHI-DŌRI

GATEN-NISHI-DŌRI

GATEN-NISHI-DŌRI

5

6

5

SHUTO EXPRESSWAY 3

Mori Art
Museum

SHUTO EXPRESSWAY 3

DŌRI

⛩
Konnō
chimangū

NISHI-AZABU

Meiji-jingū

明治神宮 • Daily sunrise–sunset • Free • ⓦ meijijingu.or.jp

Covering parts of both Aoyama and Harajuku are the grounds of **Meiji-jingū**, Tokyo's premier Shinto shrine, a memorial to Emperor Meiji and his empress Shōken. Together with the neighbouring shrines to General Nogi and Admiral Tōgō, Meiji-jingū was created as a symbol of imperial power and Japanese racial superiority. Rebuilt in 1958 after being destroyed during World War II, the shrine is the focus of several annual **festivals** (see box opposite). Apart from the festivals, Meiji-jingū is best visited midweek, when its calm serenity can be appreciated without the crowds.

The **Inner Garden**, beside Harajuku station, includes the emperor's shrine, the empress's iris gardens, the Treasure House and extensive wooded grounds. The less important **Outer Garden** (see p.120), 1km east, south of Sendagaya and Shinanomachi stations, contains the Meiji Memorial Picture Gallery and several sporting arenas.

10

Inner Garden

御苑 • Daily sunrise–sunset • Free • Harajuku or Meiji-jingumae stations

The best approach to the **Inner Garden** is through the southern gate next to Jingū-bashi, the bridge that crosses over from Harajuku's toytown-like station, complete with mock-Tudor clock tower. From the gateway, a wide gravel path runs through densely forested grounds to the 12m-high **Ō-torii**, the largest Myōjin-style gate in Japan, made from 1500-year-old Taiwanese cypress pine trees.

OMOTESANDŌ

●EATING	
CAFÉS	
Bunbōgu	4
Crisscross	14
Tokyo Snake Center	6
RESTAURANTS	
Bepokah	2
Commune 246	9
Harajuku Gyōzaro	7
Hiroba	10
La Fée Délice	8
Las Chicas	12
Maisen	5
Sakuratei	3
Solomons	1
Two Rooms	13
TEAROOM	
Aoyama Flower Market	11

●SHOPPING	
6% Dokidoki	6
Bapexclusive	20
Bedrock	9
Billionaire Boys Club	3
Chicago	4
Comme des Garçons	16
Dresscamp	18
Gallery Kawano	11
Hakusan	24
Hysterics	19
Inhabitant	13
Issey Miyake	15
Kiddyland	
Kura Chika Yoshida	14
Laforet	4
Musubi	
Onitsuka Tiger	
Oriental Bazaar	1
Prada	1
Ragtag	1
Tsumori Chisato	2
Undercover	2
United Arrows	
Yohji Yamamoto	2

■DRINKING AND NIGHTLIFE	
BARS	
Hasegawa-Saketen	2
Montoak	1
LIVE VENUE	
Crocodile	3

■ACCOMMODATION	
Caravan Tokyo	1

0   100
metres

FESTIVALS AT MEIJI-JINGŪ

The most popular of the many festivals held at Meiji-jingū is **Hatsu-mōde** (literally, "first shrine visit of the year"), held on January 1 and attracting three million visitors – traffic lights are set up within the shrine grounds to control the crowds on the day.

On **Seijin-no-hi** (Adults' Day), the second Monday in January, 20-year-olds attend the shrine to celebrate their coming of age and to seek blessings from the gods; the women often dress in elaborate long-sleeved kimono, with fur stoles wrapped around their necks, while Meiji-jingū's gravel approach is lined with ice sculptures and there's a colourful display of traditional *momoteshiki* archery by costumed archers.

From April 29 to May 3 and November 1 to 3, **bugaku** (court music and dances) are performed on a stage erected in the shrine's main courtyard, while **Shichi-go-san-no-hi** (Seven-Five-Three Day), on November 15, provides an opportunity to see children of these ages dressed in mini-kimono.

10

Signed paths make it simple to push on a little further to the picturesque **Jingū Naien** (see below). From here, the gravel path turns right and passes through a second wooden *torii*, **Kita-mon** (north gate), leading to the impressive **Honden** (central hall). With their Japanese cypress wood and green copper roofs, the Honden and its surrounding buildings are a fine example of how Shinto architecture can blend seamlessly with nature. There are exits from the courtyard in front of the central hall; alternatively, follow either of the paths northwards through the woods to arrive at pleasant grassy slopes and a pond.

Jingū Naien

神宮内苑 • Daily 8.30am–5pm • ¥500

To the left of the Ō-torii is one entrance to the **Jingū Naien**, a traditional garden said to have been designed by the Emperor Meiji for his wife; if this entrance is closed then use the one a further ten minutes up the path. The garden is at its most beautiful in June, when over one hundred varieties of **iris**, the empress's favourite flower, pepper the greenery with their purple and white blooms.

Yoyogi-kōen

代々木公園 • Daily 24hr • Free • Tandem bike rental: Daily except Mon 9am–4.30pm • ¥210 for first hour, then ¥100 for each 30min • Harajuku, Yoyogi-kōen or Meiji-jingumae stations

Tokyo's largest park, **Yoyogi-kōen**, is a favourite spot for joggers and bonneted groups of kindergarten kids with their minders. Once an imperial army training ground, the park was dubbed "Washington Heights" after World War II, when it housed US military personnel. In 1964 the land was given over to the Olympic athletes' village, after which it became Yoyogi-kōen. Two of the stadia, built for those Olympics and also due to host events in the 2020 Olympics (see box, p.120), remain the area's most famous architectural features: the boat-shaped steel suspension roof of Tange Kenzō's **Yoyogi National Gymnasium** was a structural engineering marvel at the time; the smaller stadium, in the shape of a giant swirling seashell, is used for basketball.

Ōta Memorial Museum of Art

太田記念美術館, Ōta Kinen Bijutsukan • 1-10-10 Jingūmae, Shibuya-ku • Daily except Mon 10.30am–5.30pm • Usually ¥700 for regular exhibitions, ¥1000 for special exhibitions • ☎ 03 3403 0880, ⓦ ukiyoe-ota-muse.jp • Harajuku or Meiji-jingumae stations

Just off Omotesandō, behind the trendy boutique complex **Laforet**, is the excellent **Ōta Memorial Museum of Art**. Put on slippers to wander the small galleries on two levels, which feature *ukiyo-e* paintings and prints from the private collection of the late Ōta Seizō, an insurance tycoon. The art displayed comes from a collection of twelve thousand pieces, including masterpieces by Utamaro, Hokusai and Hiroshige.

Design Festa Gallery

デザイン・フェスタ・ギャラリー・3-20-18 Jingūmae, Shibuya-ku・Daily 11am–8pm・Free・☎ 03 3479 1442, ⓦ designfesta.com・Harajuku or Meiji-jingumae stations

An anything-goes arts space sprouting out of Harajuku's backstreets, the **Design Festa Gallery** is an offshoot of the Design Festa, Japan's biggest art and design event (see p.26). Behind the day-glo paintings, graffiti, sculptures and red scaffolding swarming over the building's front like some alien metal creeper, the interior features eclectic displays ranging from quirky sculpture to video installations – even the toilet is plastered from floor to ceiling with artwork. Many spaces are rented by the week – or even the day – and they are often presided over by the artists themselves.

Omotesandō Hills

4-12-10 Jingūmae, Shibuya-ku・Meiji-jingūmae or Omotesandō stations

The Andō Tadao-designed **Omotesandō Hills** is a glitzy complex of upmarket designer shops, restaurants and residences. At the southeastern corner Andō re-created part of the Dojunkai Aoyama Apartments, as an homage to the much-loved housing block that once stood on the site. In their later years, the crumbling apartments were occupied by artists and small boutiques, and many felt that something of the district's bohemian spirit had been lost when they were destroyed to make way for Omotesandō Hills.

Aoyama

青山

Harajuku's chaotic creativity finally gives way to Aoyama's sleek sophistication, as Omotesandō crosses Aoyama-dōri and narrows to a two-lane street lined with the boutiques of many of Japan's top designers (see map, p.116). The most striking building of all is the glass bubble designed by Herzog & de Meuron for Prada (see p.201), though others come close, notably the main shrine to Issey Miyake (see p.201).

Okamoto Tarō Memorial Museum

岡本太郎記念館, Okamoto Tarō Kinenkan・6-1-19 Minami-aoyama, Minato-ku・Daily except Tues 10am–5.30pm・¥600・ⓦ taro-okamoto.or.jp・Omotesandō station

The quirky **Okamoto Tarō Memorial Museum** once functioned as the studio of the avant-garde artist (see box below); it now houses examples of his intriguing, often whimsical work, as well as a pleasant café. If this has whetted your appetite, you might consider heading to the far larger Okamoto Tarō Museum of Art in Kawasaki, between Tokyo and Yokohama (ⓦ www.taromuseum.jp).

Nezu Museum

根津美術館・6-5-1 Minami-aoyama, Minato-ku・Daily except Mon 10am–5pm・¥1100・☎ 03 3400 2536, ⓦ www.nezu-muse.or.jp・Omotesandō or Nogizaka stations

The prestigious **Nezu Museum** sits at the far eastern end of Omotesandō, in an elegant building designed by Kengo Kuma (see box, p.266). The museum houses

---

ART IS AN EXPLOSION

One of Japan's most famous post-World War II artists, **Okamoto Tarō** (1911–96) was born in Kawasaki and worked for part of his career in Aoyama, where his old studio is now a museum (see above). His *Tower of the Sun* sculpture was the symbol of Ōsaka's Expo in 1970. In Tokyo, Okamoto's bizarre, cartoon-like sculptures can be seen outside Shibuya's National Children's Castle (see p.30) and next to the Toshiba Building in Ginza. Together with his enormous mural *Myth of Tomorrow* in Shibuya station (see p.121), his sculptures neatly encapsulate the artist's dictum that "art is an explosion".

FROM TOP SHIBUYA (P.121); KITA-MON, MEIJI-JINGŪ (P.117) >

a classy collection of Oriental treasures, including the celebrated *Irises* screens, traditionally displayed for a month from the end of each April – expect big crowds for this popular exhibition. The museum's best feature, enjoyable any time of year and fully justifying the entrance fee, is its extensive garden, which slopes gently away around an ornamental pond. Dotted through it are several traditional teahouses, and mossy stone and bronze sculptures.

Aoyama Reien

青山霊園 • 2-32-2 Minami-aoyama, Minato-ku • Aoyama-itchōme, Gaienmae or Nogizaka stations

Tokyo's most important graveyard is officially entitled **Aoyama Reien**, but most know it as **Aoyama Bochi**. Everyone who was anyone is buried here, and the graves, many decorated with elaborate calligraphy, are interesting to browse – hunt around and you may find the grave of Ueno Hidesaburō, the scientist who found posthumous fame through his faithful hound, Hachikō (see box opposite). Easier to spot is the section where foreigners are buried: their tombstones provide a history of early *gaijin* involvement in Japan. One quirk of this cemetery is that locals enjoy partying here during the *hanami* season, under the candyfloss bunches of pink cherry blossoms.

Meiji-jingū Outer Garden

外苑, Gaien • Ⓦ www.meijijingugaien.jp • Shinanomachi, Aoyama-itchōme or Kokuritsu-kyōgijō stations

A pretty, ginkgo-tree-lined approach road heads to the south entrance of the **Outer Garden** – a dazzling, golden sight in the autumn. You'll spy the the wedding hall complex **Meiji Kinenkan** to your right, and several sporting stadiums and grounds on your left, including one of Japan's most famous sporting arenas, the **National Stadium**, which at the time of writing was being rebuilt ready for the 2020 Olympic Games (see box below).

THE 2020 OLYMPICS

In 2020 Tokyo will host the **Olympic and Paralympic Games** (Ⓦtokyo2020.jp), becoming the first Asian city to host the Games twice. The opening ceremony will get underway on 24 July, 2020, at the **National Stadium** in Meiji-jingū Outer Garden. The original stadium, built for the 1964 Olympics, was demolished in 2015 as part of preparations for the Games, and it's safe to say that even clockwork-efficient Japan has failed to escape the Olympic curses of funding and planning. In late 2012, it was announced that a design by the late British-Iraqi architect **Zaha Hadid** had been selected by the Sport Council, but her plans drew a raft of criticism, notably from Japanese architects ("turtle-like" and "rather vaginal" were among the most cutting descriptions), and city politicians worried about the cost. Said costs started to spiral, with Hadid's team blaming a lack of competition among contractors; by the time her plans were finally ditched in 2015, the estimates had risen to ¥252 billion (£1.82bn/$2.43bn). A cheaper design by **Kengo Kuma** (see box, p.266) was selected as the alternative, and is set to be completed by November 2019. All being well, the stadium will host the opening ceremony, the athletics events and the football final.

Mercifully, two of Tokyo's most iconic venues are due to change little for the 2020 Games: the superlative **Tokyo Metropolitan Gymnasium** (see opposite) and the **Yoyogi National Gymnasium** (see p.117), each a design classic built for the 1964 event, and respectively set to host the table tennis and handball. Other notable venues will include the **Budōkan** (see p.44), to be used for judo; the **Tokyo International Forum** (see p.48), scheduled to host the weightlifting; and the **National Sumo Stadium** (see p.81), which for sixteen days will have to put up with boxers' punches instead of sumo slaps. In addition, the **Imperial Palace gardens** (see p.41) will form an incredibly photogenic backdrop to the road cycling events. The rest of the action will take place around Tokyo Bay, or in arenas outside the city centre. Knowing Tokyo, and following Prime Minister Shinzō Abe's humble-yet-hilarious Super Mario impression at the closing ceremony of the Rio Games in 2016, it's going to be quite a party.

Meiji Memorial Picture Gallery

聖徳記念絵画館, Seitoku Kinen Kaigakan • 1-1 Kasumigaokamachi, Shinjuku-ku • Daily 9am–5pm • ¥500

At the northern end of the Outer Garden's ginkgo-lined entrance road is the **Meiji Memorial Picture Gallery**, built in a similar Western style to the National Diet Building (see p.95) with a marble-clad entrance hall that soars up to a central dome. Inside are forty paintings depicting the life story of Emperor Meiji, of interest more for their scenes of Japan emerging from its feudal past than for their artistic merits.

Tokyo Metropolitan Gymnasium

ⓦ www.tef.or.jp

10

On the western side of the National Stadium – and best viewed from outside Sendagaya station – is the Outer Garden's most striking feature, the **Tokyo Metropolitan Gymnasium**, designed by Pritzker Prize-winning architect Maki Fumihiko. At first the building looks like a giant spacecraft, though on closer examination it becomes obvious that the inspiration is a traditional samurai helmet. The corrugated stainless-steel-roofed building houses the main arena, while to the right, crowned with a glass pyramid roof, are public swimming pools and a subterranean gym. Unlike the National Stadium, this venue is not expected to change too greatly before it is employed during the 2020 Olympic Games (see box opposite).

Shibuya

渋谷

As a mind-blowing introduction to contemporary Tokyo, it's hard to beat **Shibuya**, birthplace of a million-and-one consumer crazes, and best visited at night when the neon signs of restaurants, bars and cinemas battle it out with five-storey TV screens for the attention of passers-by. This blaze of lights doesn't get much brighter than around the plaza on the northwest side of Shibuya station, where you'll also find one of the most famous **pedestrian crossings** in the world outside London's Abbey Road – its stock only rose further following its depiction in the film *Lost in Translation*. One perch from which to view the crowds of people swarming across is the bridge corridor linking the JR station with Shibuya Mark City complex. This space has been put to excellent use as the gallery for Okamoto Tarō's fourteen-panel painting **Myth of Tomorrow** (*Asu-no-shinwa*), a 30m-long mural depicting the moment the atomic bomb exploded in Hiroshima. Originally created in 1969 for a luxury hotel in Mexico, then lost for decades, this powerful work seldom seems to stop the rushing commuters in their tracks.

East of Shibuya station you'll spy the tall **Shibuya Hikarie** building, while immediately west of the crossing, the **109 Building** stands at the apex of Bunkamura-dōri and Dōgenzaka, the latter leading up to **Dōgenzaka** (道玄坂), one of Tokyo's most famous love-hotel districts. This area is named after Owada Dōgen, a thirteenth-century highwayman who robbed travellers on their way through the then-isolated valley.

HACHIKŌ

A statue outside Shibuya station marks the waiting spot of **Hachikō** (1923–35), an Akita dog who would come to greet his master every day as he returned home from work – a practice that continued for almost a decade after the professor's death, with the dog arriving on time every day to greet the train. Locals were so touched by Hachikō's devotion that a **bronze statue** was cast of the dog. During World War II, the original Hachikō statue was melted down for weapons, but a replacement was reinstated beside the station in 1948 – it remains one of Tokyo's most famous rendezvous spots. You can see the real Hachikō in the National Science Museum, where he lives on in stuffed form (see p.67), and there's a memorial by his master's grave in Aoyama Cemetery (see opposite).

Running parallel to the north of Bunkamura-dōri is the pedestrianized **Centre Gai** (センター街), always packed with trend-obsessed Tokyoites gathering to create or spot the latest look.

Shibuya Hikarie building

渋谷ヒカリエ • 2-21-1 Shibuya, Shibuya-ku • Creative Space 8 daily 11am–8pm • ⓦ hikarie.jp • Shibuya station

A 34-storey tower just east of Shibuya station, **Shibuya Hikarie** is one of the city's more inventive recent constructions. Designed like a stack of mismatching building blocks, this complex contains offices, shops, restaurants and various cultural facilities, including a 2000-seat theatre whose lobby provides a sweeping view of the skyline. The prime attraction is **Creative Space 8** on the eighth floor, a quirky mix of gallery and shops.

Konnō Hachimangū

金王八幡宮 • 3-5-12 Shibuya, Shibuya-ku • Daily 24hr; buildings open 6am–5pm; ceremony daily 9am • Free • Shibuya station

One of the few bona fide sights in the Shibuya station area, the modest **Konnō Hachimangū** is of major importance. First established in 1092, though rebuilt many times since, the shrine was used as a place of worship by the Shibuya clan, who gave the area its present name. Their castle was once adjacent to the shrine, though only a couple of pieces of fortress stone are preserved on the site. Nevertheless, it's a pleasant escape from the noise of modern-day Shibuya; pop by for the morning ceremonies, if possible.

Toguri Museum of Art

戸栗美術館, Toguri Bijutsukan • 1-11-3 Shōto, Shibuya-ku • Tues–Sun 10am–5pm; English-language tours 2pm • ¥1000 including tours; check website for discount admission coupons • ☏ 03 3465 0070, ⓦ www.toguri-museum.or.jp • Shibuya station

A little to the west of central Shibuya, the superb **Toguri Museum of Art** displays Edo-era and Chinese Ming-dynasty (1368–1644) ceramics. The small but exquisitely

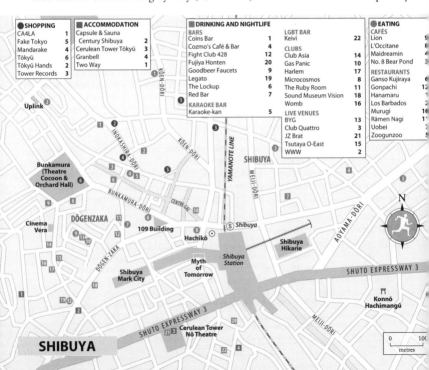

● SHOPPING	
CA4LA	1
Fake Tokyo	5
Mandarake	4
Tōkyū	6
Tōkyū Hands	2
Tower Records	3

■ ACCOMMODATION	
Capsule & Sauna	
Century Shibuya	2
Cerulean Tower Tōkyū	3
Granbell	4
Two Way	1

■ DRINKING AND NIGHTLIFE	
BARS	
Coins Bar	1
Cozmo's Café & Bar	4
Fight Club 428	12
Fujiya Honten	20
Goodbeer Faucets	9
Legato	19
The Lockup	6
Red Bar	7
KARAOKE BAR	
Karaoke-kan	5

LGBT BAR	
Keivi	22
CLUBS	
Club Asia	14
Gas Panic	10
Harlem	17
Microcosmos	8
The Ruby Room	11
Sound Museum Vision	18
Womb	16
LIVE VENUES	
BYG	13
Club Quattro	3
JZ Brat	21
Tsutaya O-East	15
WWW	2

● EATING	
CAFÉS	
Lion	9
L'Occitane	8
Maidreamin	8
No. 8 Bear Pond	6
RESTAURANTS	
Ganso Kujiraya	
Gonpachi	12
Hanamaru	
Los Barbados	
Murugi	10
Rāmen Nagi	1
Uobei	
Zoogunzoo	5

KŌEN-DŌRI

Uplink

INOKASHIRA-DŌRI

KŌEN-DŌRI

YAMANOTE LINE

MEIJI-DŌRI

SHIBUYA

Bunkamura
(Theatre
Cocoon &
Orchard Hall)

BUNKAMURA-DŌRI

CENTRE GAI

Cinema
Vera

DŌGENZAKA

DŌGEN-ZAKA

109 Building

Hachikō

Ⓢ Shibuya

Shibuya
Hikarie

AOYAMA-DŌRI

N

Shibuya
Mark City

Myth
of
Tomorrow

Shibuya
Station

SHUTO EXPRESSWAY 3

SHUTO EXPRESSWAY 3

Cerulean Tower
Nō Theatre

Konnō
Hachimangū

MEIJI-DŌRI

SHIBUYA

0   100
metres

displayed exhibition, comprising selections from a collection of some 6000 pieces, is a must for those interested in pottery. Carefully positioned mirrors enable you to inspect the fine detail of work on the underside of displayed plates and bowls, and there's a pretty garden beside the lobby. At the time of writing the museum was set to undergo fairly substantial renovations; it should have reopened by the time you read this.

Japan Folk Crafts Museum

日本民芸館, Nihon Mingeikan • Tues–Sun 10am–5pm • ¥1100 • ☎ 03 3467 4527, Ⓦ mingeikan.or.jp • Komaba-Tōdaimae station

Two stops down the Keiō Inokashira line from Shibuya station is the outstanding **Japan Folk Crafts Museum**. Set in a handsome stone-and-stucco building five minutes' walk northwest of the station, the museum is a must-see for Japanese-craft fans, with an excellent collection of pottery, textiles and lacquerware. The gift shop is a fine source of souvenirs, and an annual competition and sale of new works is held every December.

Opposite the museum stands a nineteenth-century **nagayamon** (long gate house), brought here from Tochigi-ken prefecture in northern Honshū by the museum's founder, Yanagi Soetsu, father of the famous designer Yanagi Sori; it's opened up for a couple of days each month (see website for details).

OMOIDE YOKOCHŌ, SHINJUKU

Shinjuku and the west

No Tokyo neighbourhood has as evocative a name as Shinjuku, the very mention of which will conjure images of buzzing neon, teeming masses and drunken debauchery to anybody with more than a superficial knowledge of the city. Only 4km due west of the leafy tranquillity of the Imperial Palace, Shinjuku has a long and illustrious history of pandering to the more basic of human desires. This action-packed district has it all, from the love hotels and hostess bars of Kabukichō to shop-till-you-drop department stores and dazzlingly designed skyscrapers. Throw in robot performances, two-hour all-you-can-drink specials, Tokyo's main gay bar stretch and teeming covered arcades, and you've still only just scratched the surface.

BEST OF SHINJUKU AND THE WEST

Shinjuku station Take in the mind-boggling madness at rush hour (see box, p.127)
Tokyo Metropolitan Government Building Catch a spectacular sunset from the observation decks (see p.127)
Omoide Yokochō Grab a pre-drink bite in crowded "Piss Alley" (see p.128)
Kabukichō Sneak a peek at the red lights and *yakuza* (see p.130)
Golden Gai Head for this cluster of minuscule bars (see p.130)
Shinjuku Gyoen Escape the area's neon insanity in a beautifully landscaped garden (see p.131)
Shimokitazawa Hang out with hipsters in this boho enclave (see p.132)
Suginami Animation Museum & Ghibli Museum Get a handle on anime culture (see p.132)
Robot Restaurant Go goggle-eyed over a jaw-dropping performance (see box, p.190)
Shinjuku Nichōme See Japanese gay culture in full swing (see p.186)

Shinjuku is split in two by a thick band of train tracks. The western half, **Nishi-Shinjuku**, with its soaring towers, including the monumental **Tokyo Metropolitan Government Building**, is a showcase for contemporary architecture; the raunchier eastern side, **Higashi-Shinjuku**, is a nonstop red-light and shopping district – though it's also home to one of Tokyo's most attractive parks, **Shinjuku Gyoen**. As you head west from the station, the JR Chūō line will transport you to two must-see sights for anime fans: the **Suginami Animation Museum** and the **Ghibli Museum** at Mitaka. Also out this way is **Shimokitazawa**, dubbed one of the world's coolest neighbourhoods by *Vogue* in 2014.

Brief history

The district takes its name from the "new lodgings" (*shin juku*) which were set up here in the seventeenth century for travellers en route to Edo. It eventually evolved into one of the city's six **licensed quarters**, catering mainly to the lower classes. By the late nineteenth century, Shinjuku – nicknamed "Tokyo's anus", due to the transportation of human waste through its streets to the countryside – had the most prostitutes of any area in the city.

A turning point came in 1885 when the opening of the railway encouraged people to move out of the city into the western suburbs. The commuters made Shinjuku the ideal location for the department stores which sprang up here during the early twentieth century. In the immediate postwar decades Shinjuku's seediness attracted a bohemian population of writers, students and radical intellectuals, who hung out in its jazz bars and coffee shops.

The area's first **skyscraper**, the 47-storey *Keiō Plaza Hotel*, opened in 1971 and was swiftly followed by several more earthquake-defying towers, while Tange Kenzō's **Tokyo Metropolitan Government Building** set the modernist seal on the area two decades later.

INFORMATION   SHINJUKU

Tourist information The excellent Tokyo Tourist Information Centre is on the ground floor of the Tokyo Metropolitan Government Building No. 1 (daily 9.30am–6.30pm; ☎ 03 5321 3077).

Nishi-Shinjuku

西新宿

West of the station, **Nishi-Shinjuku** is dominated by skyscrapers; the biggest of these is the futuristic Tokyo Metropolitan Government Building complex, from which the city is administered. Several skyscrapers have free observation rooms on their upper floors, along with a wide selection of restaurants and bars with good views. Collectively, their impact is striking, mainly because their scale, coupled with the spaciousness of the surroundings, is so unusual for Tokyo – despite the recent boom of high-rise buildings across Asia, this remains predominantly a low-rise city.

MAKING SENSE OF SHINJUKU STATION

Shinjuku station is the busiest in the world, with an average of around 3.7 million people (more than the population of Uruguay) passing through its gates every single day. Many visitors to Tokyo erroneously assume that rail staff are employed to squeeze people onto crowded train carriages – in fact, this only happens at rush-hour in very few stations, but Shinjuku is certainly one of them. The station also features 36 platforms, and more than two hundred exits, so if you find yourself lost and a little bewildered, nobody would blame you – unless you happen to be in their way.

The station is, in fact, comprised of three overland terminals (the main **JR station**, plus the **Keiō** and **Odakyū** stations beside their respective department stores on the area's west side) and three connecting subway lines. There's also the separate **Seibu-Shinjuku station**, northeast of the JR station. The rivers of people constantly flowing along the many underground passages only add to the confusion. It's easy to get lost; if this happens, head immediately for street level and get your bearings from the skyscrapers to the west. If you're good with maps you will also be able to work out your location from the ones located next to most exits.

11

Tokyo Metropolitan Government Building

東京都庁, Tōkyō Tochō • 2-8-1 Nishi-shinjuku, Shinjuku-ku; both observation rooms 45F • South observation room daily 9.30am–5.30pm; north observation room daily 9am–11pm; each observation room is closed a couple of days per month • Free • Free tours Mon–Fri 10am–3pm • Tochōmae station

Some 13,000 city bureaucrats clock in each day at the Gotham City-like **Tokyo Metropolitan Government Building** (TMGB), a 400,000-square-metre complex designed by Tange Kenzō. The complex includes twin 48-storey towers, an adjacent tower block, the Metropolitan Assembly Hall (where the city's councillors meet) and a sweeping, statue-lined and colonnaded plaza. Kenzō's inspiration was Paris's Notre Dame, and there's certainly something of that cathedral's design in the shape of the twin towers. But the building is also unmistakeably Japanese, with the dense crisscross pattern of its glass and granite facade reminiscent of both traditional architecture and the circuitry of an enormous computer chip.

Free **tours** of the complex depart from the tourist office on the ground floor (see p.125). Both the towers have **observation rooms**: the southern one is quieter, more open and has a pleasant café, while the northern one is open later, and features a shopping area and overpriced restaurant. It's worth timing your visit for dusk, so you can see Shinjuku's multicoloured lights spark into action.

Shinjuku Park Tower

新宿パークタワー • 3-7-1 Nishi-shinjuku, Shinjuku-ku • Tochōmae or Hatsudai stations; free shuttle bus from opposite Odakyū department store to south side of tower

On the south side of Shinjuku Chūō-kōen, a dusty park, lies **Shinjuku Park Tower**, another building that bears Kenzō's confident modernist signature. Comprising three linked towers, all topped with glass pyramids, the style credentials of this complex are vouched for by the presence of the luxurious *Park Hyatt* hotel, which occupies the building's loftiest floors (see p.148).

NTT Intercommunication Centre (ICC)

NTT インターコミュニケーションセンター • 3-20-2 Nishi-Shinjuku, Shinjuku-ku • Tues–Sun 11am–6pm • Free, although usually ¥500 for special exhibitions • ☎ 03 5353 0900, ⓦ www.ntticc.or.jp • Hatsudai station

A ten-minute walk west of the Shinjuku Park Tower is **Tokyo Opera City** (東京オペラシティ) with 54 floors of offices, shops, restaurants and a major concert hall (see p.191). On the fourth floor you'll find the invariably fascinating **NTT Intercommunication Centre** (better known as the ICC), an innovative interactive exhibition space that seeks to encourage a dialogue between technology and the arts: past displays of high-tech art have included a soundproof room where you listen to your own heartbeat, and light-sensitive robots you can control with your brain waves. The free regular exhibitions change annually;

the special exhibitions usually rotate monthly. On your way up, check out the Antony Gormley-designed statue, standing alone on the second floor.

Sword Museum

刀剣博物館, Tōken Hakubutsukan • 2F 4-25-10 Yoyogi, Shibuya-ku • Tues–Sun 10am–4.30pm • ¥800 • ☎ 03 3379 1386, ⓦ touken.or.jp • Hatsudai station

In the backstreets east of Hatsudai station is the small **Sword Museum**. Fans of swashbuckling samurai dramas will love this place, and even if you're determinedly anti-violence it's hard not to admire the incredible decorative detail on the blades, handles and sheaths of the lethal weapons displayed. However, some find it a long way to go to see one room of fairly samey material – for a bit more variety, try the Samurai Museum east of Shinjuku station (see p.130).

Seiji Tōgō Memorial Sompo Japan Museum of Art

損保ジャパン東郷青児美術館, Sompo Japan Tōgō Seiji Bijutsukan • 42F Sompo Japan Building, 1-26-1 Nishi-Shinjuku, Shinjuku-ku • Tues–Sun 10am–6pm • Fee varies by exhibition • ⓦ www.sjnk-museum.org • Shinjuku, Nishi-Shinjuku or Shinjuku-nishiguchi stations

On the 42nd floor of the Sompo Japan Building you'll find the **Seiji Tōgō Memorial Sompo Japan Museum of Art**, home to one in the series of *Sunflowers* paintings by Vincent van Gogh, flanked by other top-drawer Impressionist pieces by Cézanne and Gauguin. The *Sunflowers* canvas, dating from 1888, was bought for the astronomical sum of ¥5 billion (a shade under $40m) during the height of Japan's "bubble economy" years. More interesting and unusual is the collection of over two hundred pieces by Tōgō Seiji, a popular Japanese artist best known for his soft, contoured depictions of women.

The dazzling 50-storey crosshatched structure next to the Sompo Japan Building is known as **Mode Gakuen Cocoon Tower**, home to a fashion and computer studies college. Sadly, none of the cafés or restaurants in the lower levels give any real feel for the building's striking design.

Omoide Yokochō

思い出横丁

Squashed up against the train tracks running north from the Odakyū department store is **Omoide Yokochō**, commonly known as Memories Alley. Lit by hundreds of

---

THE BIG BUSINESS OF PACHINKO

Japan's economy may have been going through tough times for a couple of decades, but one industry that continues to rake it in – to the tune of ¥19 trillion (£138bn/$185bn) a year – is **pachinko**. This pinball gambling game is one of Japan's top pastimes, and Tokyo has thousands of pachinko parlours, plenty of them in Shinjuku. They're easy to spot since they look like mini Las Vegas casinos on steroids, all flashing lights and big neon signs. Inside, the atmosphere is no less in-your-face, and the inevitable smoke considerably more so. The noise of thousands of steel balls clattering through the upright electronic bagatelles is deafening, yet rows of players sit mesmerized as they control the speed with which balls fall through the machine – though the game requires only limited skill and a fair amount of luck.

The aim is to make the balls drop into the right holes so that more balls can be won. These are traded in for tokens, or **prizes** such as cigarette lighters and calculators; although it's illegal for the parlours to pay out cash, there's always a cubby-hole close by where prizes can be exchanged for money, a charade that the authorities have long turned a blind eye to. For all the noise, pachinko is a mind-numbingly tedious pastime; the most fun visitors can have is to simply open the parlour doors and allow the exhilarating cascade of noise and smoke to pour out into the street. If you'd like to indulge in the mechanized mayhem yourself, the initial cost can be as little as ¥100 for 25 ball bearings – just remember to take your earplugs.

akachochin (red lanterns), it's also known as Shomben Yokochō (しょんべん横丁, Piss Alley), a reference to the time when patrons of the area's many cramped *yakitori* joints and bars relieved themselves in the street, for want of other facilities. Don't be put off: the alley remains a cheap and atmospheric place to eat and drink (and there are toilets these days). Enjoy it while you can, too, as there's regular talk of redeveloping the area. A pedestrian tunnel at the southern end of the alleys, just to the right of the cheap clothes outlets, provides a short cut to the east side of Shinjuku station.

Higashi-Shinjuku

東新宿

Some days it seems as if all of Tokyo is waiting at Shinjuku's favourite meeting spot, beneath the huge TV screen on the **Studio Alta** building on the east side of the JR station. This area and neighbouring Kabukichō is best visited in the evening when the neon sparks into action and legions of Tokyoites descend to shop and party.

Kabukichō

歌舞伎町

The lively red-light district of **Kabukichō** was named after a never-built kabuki theatre that was planned for the area in the aftermath of World War II. Although there have been plans for redevelopment, the myriad host and hostess bars, girly shows, sex venues and love hotels are well entrenched. For casual strollers it's all pretty safe, thanks to street security cameras. Take a wander in the grid of streets around Hanamichi-dōri and you can't miss the peacock-preening young Japanese male touts who hook women into the male host bars, and the notably less primped gents, often immigrants from Africa, who do likewise for hostess bars – the *yakuza* who run the show are there, too, though generally keeping a much lower profile.

Samurai Museum

サムライミュージアム・2-25-6 Kabukichō, Shinjuku-ku・Daily 10.30am–9pm・¥1800, plus ¥500 to dress up in samurai clothing・
Ⓦ samuraimuseum.jp・Shinjuku or Seibu-Shinjuku stations

The **Samurai Museum** is a funky new addition to the Shinjuku area, and one likely to please a different type of visitor to the more refined displays on the other side of the tracks at the Sword Museum (see p.128). Here you can check out displays of samurai costumes and helmets, and if you're willing to shell out more on top of the already-hefty ticket price you can don similar togs yourself. If you time it right, there are four daily "shows" in which a genuine samurai actor comes by to show off his sword-wielding prowess.

Hanazono-jinja

花園神社・5-17-3 Shinjuku, Shinjuku-ku・24hr・Free・Shinjuku, Seibu-shinjuku, Higashi-shinjuku or Shinjuku-sanchōme stations

Set in grounds studded with vermillion *torii*, the attractive **Hanazono-jinja** predates the founding of Edo by the Tokugawa, but the current granite buildings are modern re-creations – the shrine was originally sited where the department store Isetan now is. At night spotlights give the shrine a special ambience and every Sunday there's a flea market in its grounds (see box, p.195).

Golden Gai

ゴールデン街

Just west of the Hanazono-jinja is **Golden Gai**, one of Tokyo's most atmospheric (and seedy) bar quarters. Since just after World War II, intellectuals and artists have rubbed shoulders with Kabukichō's demimonde in the tiny bars here. For decades this hugely atmospheric warren of around 150 drinking dens was teetering on the brink of oblivion, the cinderblock buildings under threat from both property developers and from their own shoddy construction. However, Golden Gai has since undergone a mini-renaissance, with a younger generation of bar masters and mistresses taking over – or at least presiding over – some of the shoebox establishments. Many bars continue to welcome regulars only (and charge exorbitant prices to newcomers), but *gaijin* visitors no longer risk being fleeced rotten, since most places now post their table and drink charges outside the door (see p.181 for a few recommendations).

Shinjuku Gyoen

新宿御苑 • 11 Naitomachi, Shinjuku-ku • **Garden** Tues–Sun 9am–4.30pm, last entry 4pm; villa second & fourth Sat of month 10am–3pm • ¥200 • **Rakū-tei** Tues–Sun 10am–4pm • Tea ¥700 • Main entrance Shinjuku-gyoenmae station; west gate Sendagaya station

The largest garden in Tokyo, and arguably the most beautiful, is **Shinjuku Gyoen**. Its grounds, which once held the mansion of Lord Naitō, the *daimyō* of Tsuruga on the Sea of Japan coast, became the property of the Imperial Household in 1868, and the garden was opened to the public after World War II.

Apart from spaciousness, the garden's most notable feature is the variety of design. The southern half is traditionally Japanese, with winding paths, stone lanterns, artificial hills and islands in ponds linked by zigzag bridges, and is home to *Rakū-tei*, a pleasant **teahouse**. At the northern end are formal, French-style gardens, with neat rows of tall birch trees and hedge-lined flowerbeds. Clipped, broad lawns dominate the middle of the grounds, modelled on English landscape design. On the eastern flank, next to the large greenhouse, there's a replica of an imperial wooden **villa** from 1869. In spring, the garden bursts with pink and white cherry blossoms, while in early November kaleidoscopic chrysanthemum displays and golden autumn leaves are the main attractions.

There are several **cafés** within the garden where you can grab a reasonable lunch for around ¥1000, but it's much nicer to bring a picnic and relax in the tranquil surroundings.

Western Tokyo

Tokyo sprawls for quite some way west of Shinjuku, and there are some very fashionable neighbourhoods dotted around this densely populated but relatively low-level jigsaw of suburbs. By far the most interesting for shorter-term visitors to Japan is **Shimokitazawa**, Tokyo's own little hipster paradise. Heading even further out, but still easily accessible by train, the **Suginami** area has long been associated with the animation industry; it's the location for several production houses, and home to many

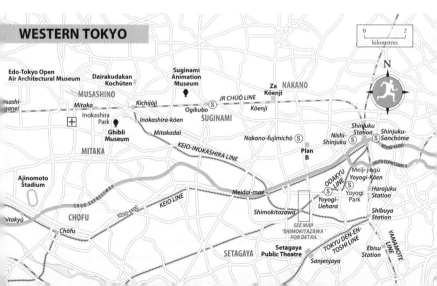

key artists; but of more interest to the traveller is the immensely popular **Ghibli Museum**. Even further out, there's another great draw at the **Edo-Tokyo Open Air Architectural Museum**, which inspired at least one anime "set".

Shimokitazawa

下北沢 • Shimokitazawa station, 4 stops west of Shibuya on the Keio-Inokashira line, or 6 stops southwest of Shinjuku on the Odakyū line

Small, cute and quirky, **Shimokitazawa** – known as **Shimokita** for short – is a prime draw for young, bohemian sorts, and a nice escape from "regular" Tokyo; gone are the high-rise blocks and incessant noise of Shinjuku, just 5km to the east, replaced here with narrow, relatively traffic-free lanes, and a general air of calm. The charms of Shimokita are essentially the same as most hipster areas around the world: vintage clothing stores, record shops, galleries, live music bars, and independent cafés serving flat whites to people writing blogs on their Macs. However, here they come overlaid with a double-thick slice of Japan (both the regular and the quirky), and the resultant cocktail is quite potent. There's not all that much in the way of sights here, bar a couple of tucked-away shrines, but you'll find plenty of shops, cafés and bars (see map below) at which to while away the time.

Suginami Animation Museum

杉並アニメーションミュージアム • 3-29-5 Kamiogi, Suginami-ku • Tues–Sun 10am–6pm • Free • ⓦ sam.or.jp • 20min walk or 5min bus ride (platform 0 or 1; ¥220) from Ogikubo station on the JR lines or Marunouchi subway line

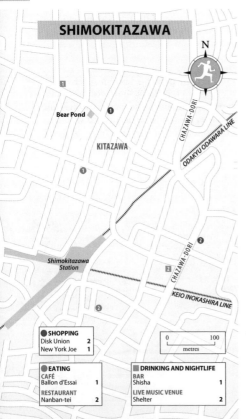

Astroboy, Gundam and many other anime characters are all present and correct at the well-organized **Suginami Animation Museum**, situated atop a retro-looking function hall. Colourful displays trace the development of animation in Japan, from the simple black-and-white 1917 feature *Genkanban-no-maki* (The Gatekeepers) to digital escapades such as *Blood: The Last Vampire*. Videos with English subtitles explain how anime are made, while interactive computer games allow you to create your own animations. You can watch anime screenings in the small theatre, and there's also a library packed with manga and DVDs (some with English subtitles).

Ghibli Museum

ジブリ美術館, Jiburi Bijutsukan • 1-1-83 Shimorenjaku, Mitaka-ku • Daily except Tues 10am–6pm • ¥1000; advance bookings only (museum can be booked out for weeks at a time); 2400 tickets per day are available and can be bought online or from Lawson convenience stores • ☎ 0570 055777, ⓦ ghibli-museum.jp • Short walk (follow signs) or bus ride (¥210) from south exit of Mitaka station, on JR Chūō line; or walkable from Kichijōji station, also on JR Chūō line

A few stops west of the Suginami Animation Museum is the utterly beguiling **Ghibli Museum**, one of Tokyo's top draws for international visitors – and an essential one for those interested in anime. It's very popular, so reserve tickets well ahead of time. Though it needs little introduction, the Ghibli animation studio was responsible for blockbuster movies including *My Neighbour Totoro*, *Princess Mononoke* and the Oscar-winning *Spirited Away*. Visiting the museum is a little like climbing inside the mind of famed Ghibli director Hayao Miyazaki: walls are plastered with initial sketches of the characters that would eventually garner worldwide fame; a giant clock is bisected by a winding staircase; and – of course – there's the grinning cat-bus from *Totoro*. There's also a small movie theatre where original short animated features, exclusive to the museum, are screened. All in all, it's a guaranteed fun day out for all, that will probably have you scurrying to watch the films later.

Ghibli Museum sits inside pretty **Inokashira Park** (井の頭公園, Inokashira Kōen); from Kichijoji station, it's a pleasant fifteen-minute stroll through the park's tree-shaded walks to the museum, past a pleasant carp-filled lake and a small zoo. A favourite haunt of courting couples, the park is mobbed by everyone during *hanami* season, when it explodes in a profusion of pink blossoms.

Edo-Tokyo Open Air Architectural Museum

江戸東京たてもの園, Edo-Tōkyō Tatemono-en • 3-7-8 Sakura-chō, Koganei • Tues–Sun: April–Sept 9.30am–5.30pm; Oct–March 9.30am–4.30pm • ¥400 • ⓦ tatemonoen.jp • 5min bus ride (¥200) from Musashi-Koganei station, on JR Chūō line

A kind of retirement home for old Japanese buildings, the **Edo-Tokyo Open Air Architectural Museum** was the inspiration for the abandoned theme park in Studio Ghibli's *Spirited Away*. Some 35 buildings of varying degrees of interest are gathered within the parkland of Koganei-kōen, plus an exhibition hall with archeological artefacts and folk crafts.

On the west side of the sprawling complex, check out the grand **Mitsue Residence**, an 1852 mansion moved from Kyoto and furnished with painted screens, lacquered shrines and chandeliers. There are also several thatched farmhouses. On the east side, there's a reconstructed **Shitamachi** street (see box, p.75), including a tailor's shop and stationer's, plus kitchenware and flower stores. The **public bathhouse** here is a veritable palace of ablutions, with magnificent Chinese-style gables and a lakeside view of Fuji painted on the tiled wall inside. Also look out for the **Uemura-tei**, a 1927 shophouse, its copper cladding pocked by shrapnel from World War II bombings.

11

BASEBALL GAME, TOKYO DOME

Ikebukuro and the north

Little more than marshland until the dawn of the twentieth century, Ikebukuro
is a real product of the train age; eight lines now connect the area with central
Tokyo and the low-cost dormitory suburbs to the north and east, meaning that
its primary function is as a sort of commuter gateway to the city. It's not as
trendy or hip as Shinjuku or Shibuya, and the area is also something of a
byword for Tokyo sleaze, with its glut of "soaplands" (brothels). However, stick
around long enough and you'll find some of the city's best noodles, classic
gardens to stroll in, a handful of butler cafés (see box, p.160) and some truly
fascinating pieces of architecture. All in all, Ikebukuro and its environs provide
a good window in which to see Tokyo simply being Tokyo.

BEST OF IKEBUKURO AND THE NORTH

Ding-ding train Ride Tokyo's last remaining tramline (see box, p.139)
St Mary's Cathedral Check out the stunning interior of this retro-futurist cathedral (see p.139)
Gardens Take it easy at Rikugi-en, Kyū Furukawa or Koishikawa-Kōrakuen (see p.140, p.140 & p.141)
Tokyo Dome Get a handle on the Japanese baseball obsession (see p.140)
Spa LaQua Dip into the exquisite onsen waters (see p.141)
Mutekiya Join the queues for tasty ramen (see p.172)
Assist Wig Try on a colourful wig or two (see p.202)

Garden lovers should head to **Komagome** to visit **Rikugi-en**, one of the city's most attractive Edo-period gardens, as well as the nearby and equally lovely **Kyū Furukawa Gardens**, combining Western and Japanese styles of horticulture. Follow this with a stop in **Mejirodai** for **Chinzan-so**, a classic garden; **Suidōbashi**, home to the Tokyo Dome and yet more gardens; and **Kagurazaka**, a trendy, Frenchified area still home to a clutch of geisha.

Ikebukuro

池袋

Around one million passengers pass through **Ikebukuro station** every day – it's second only to Shinjuku (see box, p.127) in numbers – and its warren of connecting passages, shopping arcades and countless exits is notoriously difficult to negotiate. Two of the largest department stores in Japan, Tōbu and Seibu, square off against each other from opposite sides of the tracks.

The area to the west, **Nishi-Ikebukuro**, is the more interesting to explore, and is surprisingly nice to stroll around, particularly the wedge of streets spreading out towards the attractive **Rikkyō University** campus, which boasts a plethora of bars, restaurants and good, old-fashioned sleaze. Over on the east side of Ikebukuro station is **Higashi-Ikebukuro**, the main shopping area, which has even more going on – all the way to Sunshine City, a complex featuring the area's tallest tower. Pressing on east again, you can hop on Tokyo's last **tramway**, the Toden-Arakawa Line (see box, p.139).

12

Myonichi-kan

明日館 • 2-31-3 Nishi-Ikebukuro, Toshima-ku • Tues–Sun 10am–4pm, closed during functions • ¥400, or ¥600 including coffee or Japanese tea and sweets • ☏ 03 3971 7535, ⦿ jiyu.jp • Ikebukuro station

Fans of the American architect Frank Lloyd Wright should track down one of his lesser-known but still very distinctive buildings, the **Myonichi-kan**, or "House of Tomorrow". While working on the *Imperial Hotel* (see p.144), Wright and his assistant Endo Arata also designed this complex to house the Jiyū Gakuen school. The geometric windows and low-slung roofs are trademark Wright features, but the buildings are best appreciated from inside, where you get the full effect of the clean, bold lines, echoed in the hexagonal chairs, light fittings and other original furnishings.

Rikkyō University

立教大学 • Nishi-Ikebukuro, Toshima-ku • Ikebukuro station

Fronted by a square, red-brick gateway, **Rikkyō University** was founded as St Paul's School in 1874 by an American Episcopalian missionary. Through the gateway, the old university courtyard has an incongruous Ivy League touch in its vine-covered halls, white windows and grassy quadrangle, making it a favourite venue for film crews. Originally located in Tsukiji, the university moved to Ikebukuro in 1918 and weathered the 1923 earthquake with minimal damage except for one toppled gate tower. The lopsided look was retained, so it's said, as a memorial to those who died, but a deciding factor was perhaps the sheer lack of bricks.

IKEBUKURO AND THE NORTH

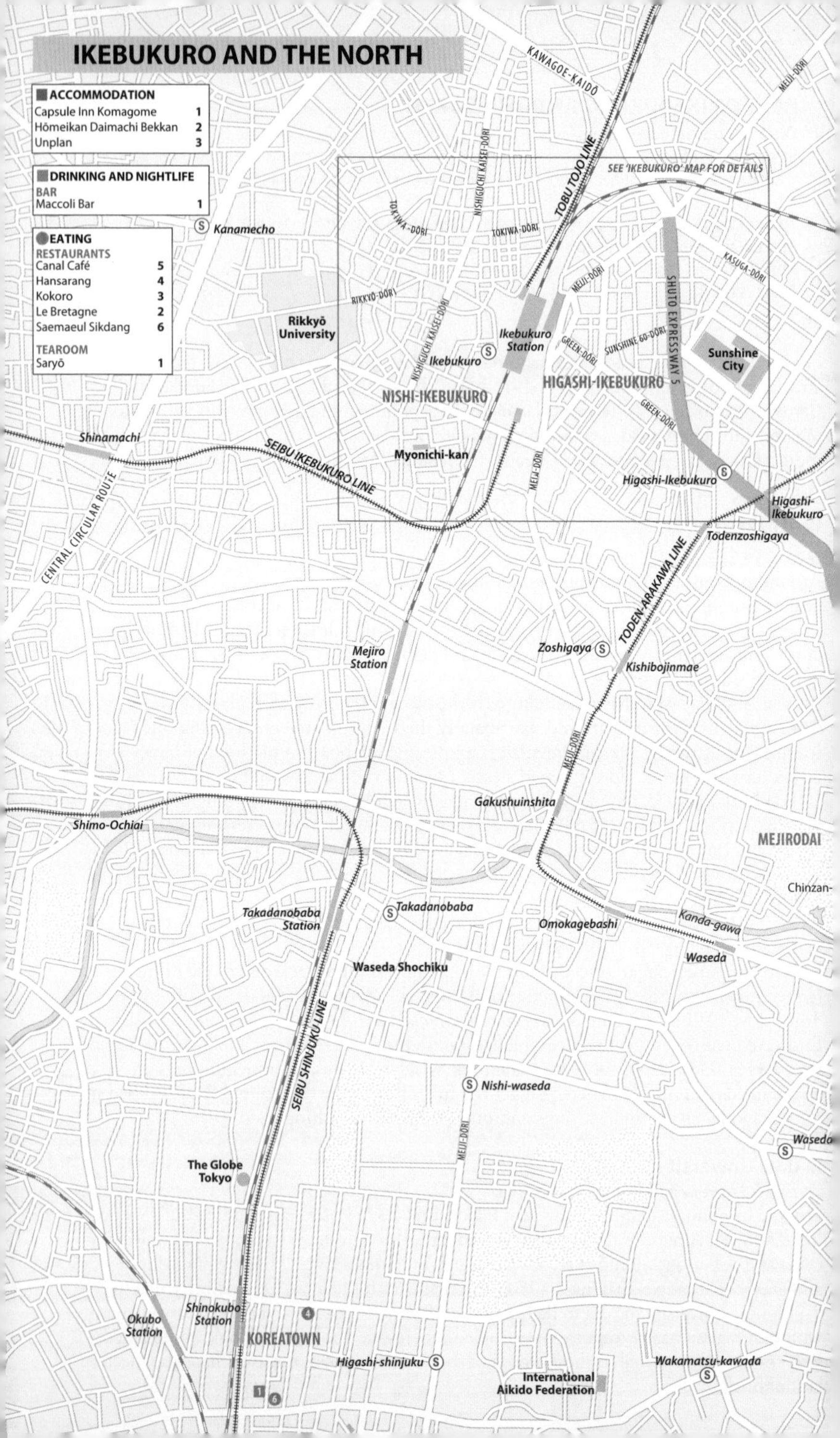

ACCOMMODATION
Capsule Inn Komagome	1
Hōmeikan Daimachi Bekkan	2
Unplan	3

DRINKING AND NIGHTLIFE
BAR	
Maccoli Bar	1

EATING
RESTAURANTS	
Canal Café	5
Hansarang	4
Kokoro	3
Le Bretagne	2
Saemaeul Sikdang	6
TEAROOM	
Saryō	1

KAWAGOE-KAIDŌ

MEIJI-DŌRI

TOBU TOJO LINE

SEE 'IKEBUKURO' MAP FOR DETAILS

NISHIGUCHI KAISEI-DŌRI

TOKIWA-DŌRI

TOKIWA-DŌRI

KASUGA-DŌRI

(S) Kanamecho

RIKKYŌ-DŌRI

MEIJI-DŌRI

GREEN-DŌRI

SHUTO EXPRESSWAY 5

SUNSHINE 60-DŌRI

Sunshine
City

Rikkyō
University

NISHIGUCHI KAISEI-DŌRI

Ikebukuro
(S) Ikebukuro
Station

HIGASHI-IKEBUKURO

NISHI-IKEBUKURO

GREEN-DŌRI

Shinamachi

SEIBU IKEBUKURO LINE

Myonichi-kan

MEIJI-DŌRI

Higashi-Ikebukuro (S)

Higashi-
Ikebukuro

CENTRAL CIRCULAR ROUTE

Todenzoshigaya

Mejiro
Station

Zoshigaya (S)

TODEN-ARAKAWA LINE

Kishibojinmae

Shimo-Ochiai

MEIJI-DŌRI

Gakushuinshita

MEJIRODAI

Chinzan-

Takadanobaba
Station

(S) Takadanobaba

Omokagebashi

Kanda-gawa

Waseda Shochiku

Waseda

SEIBU SHINJUKU LINE

(S) Nishi-waseda

MEIJI-DŌRI

Waseda
(S)

The Globe
Tokyo

Shinokubo
Station

Okubo
Station

(4)

KOREATOWN

Higashi-shinjuku (S)

International
Aikido Federation

Wakamatsu-kawada
(S)

[1] [6]

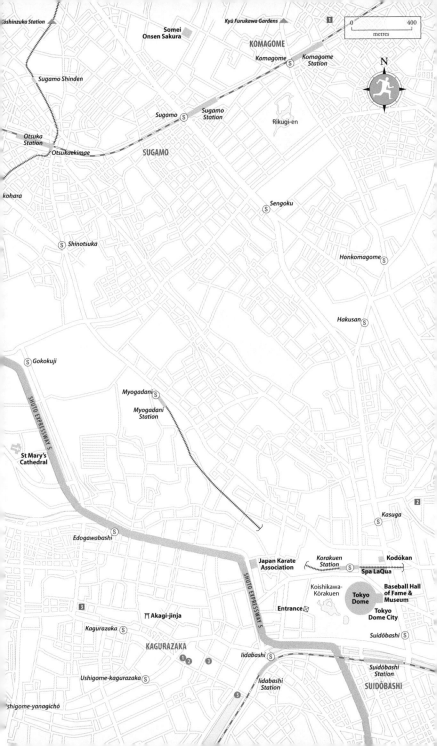

Sunshine City

サンシャインシティ・3-1 Higashi-Ikebukuro, Toshima-ku・Observation deck daily 10am–10pm・¥1800・☎ 03 3989 3455, ⓦwww
.sunshinecity.co.jp・Higashi-Ikebukuro station

Heading east from Ikebukuro station, you can't miss the monstrous sixty storeys of the
Sunshine 60 Tower, which at 240m was Japan's tallest building until it was pipped by
Yokohama's Landmark Tower in 1993. An underground passage at the end of Sunshine
60-dōri leads into the tower, just one of four buildings comprising the **Sunshine City**
complex of shops, offices, a hotel and various cultural centres. Compared to the city's
newer developments it all looks rather dowdy, bar the freshly renovated (and overpriced)
observation deck on the top floor, and the excellent aquarium (see below).

Sunshine Aquarium

サンシャイン水族館, Sanshain Suizokukan・Daily: April–Oct 10am–8pm; Nov–March 10am–6pm・Adult ¥2000, child ¥1000・
☎ 03 5950 0765, ⓦ www.sunshinecity.co.jp/aquarium

The wonderful **Sunshine Aquarium** is by far the best in Tokyo, with its rather high
ticket price justified by inventive attractions, best of which are the "Sunshine Aqua
Ring", where you'll be able to see sea-lions torpedoing around above your head, and
the magical "Jellyfish Tunnel". Performances take place through the day.

Namco Namja Town

ナムコナンジャタウン・Daily 10am–10pm・Adult ¥500, child ¥300; passport adult ¥3300, child ¥2600・☎ 03 5950 0765, ⓦ namco.co.jp

Part of the Sunshine City complex, **Namco Namja Town** is a noisy indoor amusement
centre based around a couple of cat characters. It's notable for its various themed eating

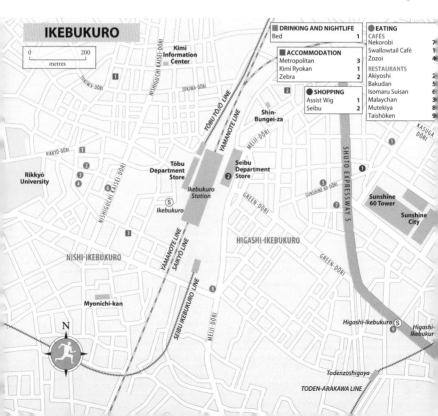

IKEBUKURO

◼ DRINKING AND NIGHTLIFE	
Bed	1

◼ ACCOMMODATION	
Metropolitan	3
Kimi Ryokan	1
Zebra	2

◼ SHOPPING	
Assist Wig	1
Seibu	2

● EATING	
CAFÉS	
Nekorobi	7
Swallowtail Café	1
Zozoi	4
RESTAURANTS	
Akiyoshi	2
Bakudan	5
Isomaru Suisan	6
Malaychan	3
Mutekiya	8
Taishōken	9

TOKYO'S LAST TRAMLINE

Early twentieth-century Tokyo boasted a number of tramlines, or *chin chin densha* ("ding ding trains", from the sound of the trams' bells), of which only the 12km-long **Toden-Arakawa Line** (都電荒川線) remains, running north from Waseda to Minowa-bashi. The most interesting section lies along a short stretch from **Kōshinzuka station**, a 15min walk northwest of Sugamo station, from where the line heads southwest towards Higashi-Ikebukuro, rocking and rolling along narrow streets and through Tokyo backyards.

Most of the original tramlines were private enterprises and have gradually been replaced with subways. The Toden-Arakawa Line, built purely to take people to the spring blossoms in Asukayama Park, will probably survive for its nostalgia value if nothing else, and recent replacements of all the cars have some sporting a retro look.

Prepaid cards can be used on the system, as can Toei day-tickets (see box, p.22). Ordinary tickets cost ¥170, however far you travel; pay as you enter. Note that station signs and announcements are in Japanese and English.

---

areas, including sections specializing in *gyoza* (Chinese-style fried and steamed dumplings), ice cream (flavours have, in the past, included squid and shark), and desserts from around Japan. The passport allows unlimited access to fourteen of the attractions, which include a mosquito-zapping gun game, a fishing challenge and a zombie-hunting video game.

Mejirodai

目白台

12

Riding the Toden-Arakawa line (see box above) to Waseda station will bring you to the edge of the hilly **Mejirodai** area. The top attraction here is a stroll along the **Kanda River** (神田川), where the pathways explode in cherry blossom pink at the end of March and early April.

Chinzan-sō

椿山荘 · 2-10-8 Sekiguchi, Bunkyō-ku · Daily 9am–8pm · Free · Ⓦ www.chinzanso.com · Waseda station (Toden-Arakawa line)

The area's prime sight is the **Chinzan-sō**, a beautiful, expansive nineteenth-century garden set around a small pond. Though sandwiched between a wedding hall complex and the *Hotel Chinzansō*, it's surprisingly easy to ignore those two ugly buildings, and concentrate on the greener delights of the garden. If you swing by the entrance after lunch, you may get to see a giant horned tortoise out for a walk.

St Mary's Cathedral

東京カテドラル聖マリア大聖堂, Tōkyō Katedoraru Sei Maria Daiseidō · 3-16-15 Sekiguchi, Bunkyō-ku · Ⓦ tokyo.catholic.jp · Waseda station (Toden-Arakawa line) or Gokokuji station

St Mary's Cathedral has been the centre of Tokyo's Catholic community for well over a century, with congregations a mix of foreigners and Japanese. The original Gothic structure was built in 1899, but burned down in the World War II air raids; the present building, designed by Tange Kenzō (see box, p.266), was completed in 1964. Steel-clad and shaped like a giant cross, it's rather iconic, almost enough to count as a Tokyo must-see. Be sure to take a peek at the dramatic interior; dominated by a massive pipe organ at one end and a retro-futurist cross at the other, it brings to mind scenes from Fritz Lang's *Metropolis*.

Komagome

駒込

There are a couple of wonderful natural spots in the Komagome area, easily accessible from Ikebukuro station, just three stops to the west. The top sight here is **Rikugi-en**, a sculpted garden redolent of old Edo; just to the north, you'll find more of the same at the gorgeous **Kyū Furukawa Gardens**.

Rikugi-en

六義園 • 6 Honkomagome, Bunkyō-ku • Daily 9am–5pm • ¥300 • Entrance on Hongō-dōri, 5min south of Komagome station

Komagome's most appealing sight is **Rikugi-en**, Tokyo's best surviving example of a classical Edo-period stroll garden. In 1695 the fifth shogun granted one of his high-ranking feudal lords, Yanagisawa Yoshiyasu, a tract of farmland to the north of Edo. Yanagisawa was both a perfectionist and a literary scholar: he took seven years to design his celebrated garden – with its 88 allusions to famous scenes, real or imaginary, from ancient Japanese poetry – and then named it Rikugi-en, "garden of the six principles of poetry", in reference to the rules for composing *waka* (poems of 31 syllables). After Yanagisawa's death, Rikugi-en fell into disrepair until Iwasaki Yatarō, founder of Mitsubishi, bought the land in 1877 and restored it as part of his luxury villa. The family donated the garden to the Tokyo city authorities in 1938, since when it has been a public park.

Unsurprisingly, few of the 88 landscapes have survived – the guide map issued at the entrance identifies a mere eighteen. Nevertheless, Rikugi-en still retains its beauty, and is large enough to be relatively undisturbed by surrounding buildings and traffic noise.

Kyū Furukawa Gardens

旧古河庭園, Kyū Furukawa Teien • 1-27-39 Nishigahara, Kita-ku • Daily 9am–5pm • ¥150; tea ¥500 • Entrance 5min uphill from Komagome station

Designed by Ogawa Jihei, a famed gardener from Kyoto, the **Kyū Furukawa Gardens** combine delightful Japanese-style grounds with an Italian-style terrace of rose beds and artfully shaped azalea bushes. The gardens cascade down the hill from the mansion designed in 1914 by British architect Josiah Conder (see box, p.61), who was also responsible for the similar Kyū Iwasaki-tei house and gardens in Ueno (see p.68). It's possible to take tea and cake in the mansion and to go on a tour of the empty (and frankly boring) rooms, but it's much more enjoyable to sample *matcha* and traditional Japanese sweets in the teahouse in the Japanese part of the garden. The best times to visit are in late April, when the azaleas bloom, and in mid-May, when the roses are out in full force.

Somei Onsen Sakura

染井温泉桜 • 5-4-24 Komagome, Toshima-ku • Daily 10am–11pm • ¥1300 • Komagome station

Most of Tokyo's bathhouses are either small, bare-bones establishments costing next to nothing, or over-the-top mega-complexes costing way too much and giving little in the way of a traditional feel. Hooray, then, for the **Somei Onsen Sakura**, which strikes a nice halfway-house vibe: pleasantly "regular" in feel, it's a great example of the Japanese onsen experience. As you may have inferred from the name, it's best visited during cherry-blossom (*sakura*) season, when the on-site trees are cloaked with fluffy pink petals; however, it's a pretty enough place at any time of the year.

Suidōbashi

水道橋

Some way southeast of Ikebukuro, on the way back towards the Imperial Palace, the district of **Suidōbashi** has a handful of minor attractions including an upmarket spa complex, an amusement park and a classic seventeenth-century garden, all revolving around **Tokyo Dome City**, one of the city's most important sports complexes. The centrepiece here is the plump, white-roofed **Tokyo Dome** (東京ドーム), Tokyo's major baseball venue, popularly known as the "Big Egg".

Tokyo Dome City Attractions

東京ドームシティ アトラクションズ • 1-3-61 Kōraku, Bunkyō-ku • Daily 10am–10pm • Passport with unlimited rides adult ¥4200, child aged 13–17 ¥3700, child aged 3–12 ¥3100; after 5pm ¥3000/2700/2500 respectively • ☏ 03 5800 9999, ⓦ at-raku.com • Suidōbashi or Kōrakuen station

The best rides at the large **Tokyo Dome City Attractions** amusement park, part of the Tokyo Dome complex, are those in the LaQua section, where the highlight is Thunder

Dolphin, a high-speed roller coaster guaranteed to get you screaming (for ages 8 and older). If you haven't got the stomach for that, try the Big O, the world's first hub-less and spoke-less Ferris wheel (it's spun by the two supports below), which provides a gentler ride and plenty of time to take a photo of the passing view. Tiny tots will enjoy Toys Kingdom, a space packed with playthings.

Spa LaQua

6F 1-1-1 Kasuga, Bunkyō-ku • Daily 11am–9am (next day) • Mon–Fri ¥2630, Sat & Sun ¥2960; ¥1940 surcharge 1am–6am; access to Healing Baden set of special therapeutic saunas ¥525 extra • Ⓦ www.laqua.jp • Suidōbashi or Kōrakuen stations

Spread over five floors, and part of the Dome City complex, **Spa LaQua** is by far the most sophisticated of Tokyo's bathing establishments (not to mention one of the most expensive), and is fed by onsen water pumped from 1700m underground.

Baseball Hall of Fame and Museum

Gate 21, Tokyo Dome • Tues–Sun: March–Sept 10am–6pm; Oct–Feb 10am–5pm • ¥600 • ☎ 03 3811 3600, Ⓦ baseball-museum.or.jp • Suidōbashi or Kōrakuen stations

Tokyo Dome is most famed for being the home of the Yomiuri Giants baseball team (see p.206). Its **Baseball Hall of Fame and Museum** is really for die-hard fans only; as well as footage of early games, there's all sorts of baseball memorabilia here, including one of Babe Ruth's jackets.

Koishikawa-Kōrakuen

小石川後楽園 • 1-6-6 Kōraku, Bunkyō-ku; entrance in southwest corner of garden • Daily 9am–5pm; English-language tours Sat 10am & 1pm • ¥300 • ☎ 03 3811 3015, Ⓦ tokyo-park.or.jp • Iidabashi station

12

Immediately to the west of Tokyo Dome is **Koishikawa-Kōrakuen**, a fine, early seventeenth-century stroll garden. Winding paths take you past waterfalls, ponds and stone lanterns, down to the shores of a small lake draped with gnarled pines and over daintily humped bridges, where each view replicates a famous beauty spot. Zhu Shun Shui, a refugee scholar from Ming China, advised on the design, so Chinese as well as Japanese landscapes feature, the most obvious being the Full Moon Bridge, echoing the ancient stone bridges of western China, and Seiko Lake, modelled on the famed West Lake in Hangzhou, a major city near China's eastern seaboard. The garden attracts few visitors, though occasional squeals and rattles from the Tokyo Dome fairground rides, peeking up over the trees, mean it's not always totally peaceful.

Kagurazaka

神楽坂

Just west of Iidabashi station, the district of **Kagurazaka** has become a popular spot of late with Tokyoites young and old. Chic restaurants, cafés and shops line Kagarazaka-dōri, the area's main drag, and there are plenty more dotting the genteel alleyways to the north. If you're in luck, you'll spot a geisha or two tripping along the lanes – some still work hereabouts, remnants of the area's history as an entertainment quarter.

Akagi-jinja

赤城神社 • 1-10 Akagi-Motomachi, Shinjuku-ku • Daily 24hr • Free • Iidabashi station

For something a little out of the ordinary, take a trip to **Akagi-jinja**, a shrine remodelled in 2010 by star architect Kengo Kuma (see box, p.266). Most Japanese shrines come across as somewhat brooding and secretive, but this one is effectively ensconced in a sort of giant glass box, approached by a small run of steps and flanked by a modern apartment block. It's perhaps more interesting than truly beautiful, but most find it worth the effort to get here.

Accommodation

Japan's reputation for being an extremely expensive place to visit is a little outdated in most fields, but it's certainly justified as far as accommodation goes. However, the quality of accommodation in Tokyo is generally very high at all levels, from luxury hotels to budget dorms; security and cleanliness are top-notch; and except at the bottom end of the scale, you'll usually find someone who speaks at least a smattering of English. While there are few bargains, if you look hard you'll find plenty of affordable places. You'll often find the best value – along with plenty of atmosphere – at a traditional ryokan or a family-run minshuku, the Japanese equivalent of a B&B. The cheapest beds are provided by privately run hostels, mainly in the city's northern districts. Capsule hotels are a little more expensive but certainly worth trying once, if only for the experience.

WHICH AREA?

With Tokyo the size it is, and with each district boasting its own character, it's important to consider which part of the city to use as your base.

Imperial Palace and around There are a fair few high-end establishments dotted between the palace and the train tracks.

Ginza Highly central area with plenty to see and shopping opportunities galore. Most hotels here are, however, rather expensive.

Akihabara Tokyo's electro-capital makes a great base for those in the mood to see maid cafés, robot shops and other quirky facets of the city. There are plenty of cheap business hotels here.

Ueno Way up north and not terribly convenient, though there are lots of sights in and around the area. There are a few good places to stay south of the large park, and a cluster of love hotels further south again.

Asakusa One of Tokyo's most characterful areas, and the de facto choice for backpackers thanks to its large concentration of hostels. There are also some great ryokan choices here.

Ryōgoku and Kiyosumi A few of the hostels in the wider Asakusa area fall under the extent of this chapter in our guide.

Bayside Tokyo The city's bayside area is

quite beautiful, especially when seen from the upper floors of one of its upscale hotels.

Akasaka and Roppongi Roppongi is famed for its nightlife, and boasts some of Tokyo's best hotels. Neighbouring Akasaka is somewhat earthier, and correspondingly cheaper.

Ebisu, Meguro and the south Few choose to stay way down south in Ebisu, though nearby neighbourhoods such as charming Nakameguro are surprisingly convenient for the city's sights.

Harajuku, Aoyama and Shibuya There's so much to see in this wide area, both historical and contemporary, that you're unlikely to get bored. Most places are rather expensive, bar the huge cluster of love hotels in Shibuya.

Shinjuku For many visitors, Shinjuku represents the *real* Tokyo, though there are precious few budget places in this neon paradise.

Ikebukuro Not terribly convenient, or all that interesting, few visitors use Ikebukuro as a base, though it has some good cheap options, including several ryokan.

Whatever your budget, it's wise to **reserve** your first few nights' accommodation before arrival. This is especially true of the cheaper places, which tend to fill up quickly, particularly over national holidays and in late February, when thousands of students head to Tokyo for the university entrance exams. Rooms are also in short supply during holiday periods, as well as during the cherry-blossom season in late March and early April. Good deals can be found **online** via hotel websites and general booking engines (see below), and it's always worth asking if there are any promotions on offer.

ESSENTIALS

Prices Staying in Tokyo will cost you from around ¥2500 for a hostel dorm bed or ¥4000 for the very cheapest private rooms. You'll be looking at upwards of ¥10,000 for a more comfortable en-suite double in a business hotel. Mid-range hotels start in the region of ¥15,000, while top-end hotels charge at least twice that and often many times more. Rates in the text are given for high season (see box, p.144).

Taxes All hotel rates include an 8 percent consumption tax, on top of which top-end hotels levy a service charge, typically 10 percent. If your room costs over ¥10,000 per person per night, there's also a Tokyo Metropolitan Government tax of ¥100 per person per night (¥200 if the room costs over ¥15,000).

Reservations The international standbys have plenty of Tokyo options: try ⓦ trivago.com or ⓦ booking.com for hotels, or ⓦ hostelworld.com for hostels. Locals usually use ⓦ travel.rakuten.com, which has an English site (though

you'll need to register). Also worth checking out is ⓦ ryokan .or.jp/English, which lists good places to stay, mostly ryokan, in Tokyo and beyond, though it has no booking mechanism.

Internet Connectivity has certainly improved in Tokyo's hotels and ryokan in recent years. Free wi-fi is almost always provided for free in the latter, though in hotels and ryokan you may be charged for the service; in addition, some places still have LAN cables rather than wi-fi. Accommodation with wi-fi is indicated in the guide with a 🛜 symbol.

Breakfast Breakfast tends to come as standard in ryokan (though you can usually forgo it to get a cheaper rate) but rarely features in hostels. At hotels it usually costs extra, from ¥700–3000 per person, essentially depending upon room price; usually you can add or forgo breakfast when booking. Establishments offering free breakfast have been noted in the listings.

13

ROOM RATES

Unless otherwise stated, the rates listed are for the cheapest **double or twin room** (inclusive of taxes) in high season (summer); typically these rates rise during peak holiday periods, in particular around Christmas and New Year, the Golden Week (April 29–May 5) and O-bon (the week around August 15). Single rates are typically a third less than for doubles; at **ryokan** the difference can show greater variation, so both single and double prices have been given in our reviews. For **dormitory** accommodation and **capsule hotels**, the price per person is listed.

HOTELS

There are a few discrete stripes of **hotel** in Tokyo. Running the gamut from budget to luxury, they all feature Western-style rooms with en-suite bathrooms, TV, phone and a/c as standard; a few of the larger ones also offer tatami (traditional straw mat flooring) rooms, which tend to be a little more expensive. Many fit into the category of **business hotels**: cheap, functional places aimed at salarymen, with rooms that may be super-small but are always clean, and feature everything needed for a night's rest. Lastly, there are **love hotels**, which cater for couples seeking the privacy often not available in a small Japanese apartment (see box, p.147).

THE IMPERIAL PALACE AND AROUND

★**Hoshinoya** 星のや 1-9-1 Ōtemachi, Chiyoda-ku ☎050 3786 1144, ⊛hoshinoyatokyo.com; Ōtemachi station; map p.42. Tokyo has been crying out for a place like this, and finally it's here: a top-end hotel with ryokan-like elements to its decor and service. As such, despite being seventeen floors high, it all feels rather intimate; the scent of flowers and incense waft through the common areas, and rooms manage to exude a traditional yet contemporary air. The private *ochamoma* lounge is a grand place for tea or even sake. 🛜 **¥72,000**

Imperial Hotel 帝国ホテル 1-1-1 Uchisaiwai-chō, Chiyoda-ku ☎03 3504 1111, ⊛www.imperialhotel .co.jp; Hibiya station; map p.42. Facing the Imperial Palace, this is still one of Tokyo's most prestigious addresses, despite increasingly stiff competition. Best are the three exclusive "Imperial" floors, with butler service and the latest technological wizardry. You'll find no fewer than thirteen top-class restaurants, as well as three bars (see p.175 for the best). 🛜 **¥45,000**

The Peninsula ザ ペニンシュラ東京 1-8-1 Yūrakuchō, Chiyoda-ku ☎03 6270 2288, ⊛peninsula.com; Tokyo or Yurakuchō stations, Hibiya station; map p.42. Elegantly designed luxury hotel with an unbeatable location – offering views right across to the emperor's pad – and some of the city's most spacious rooms; pleasingly decorated along earth-tone lines, they almost feel more like a home than a hotel. There's also an opulent spa, and a chic rooftop restaurant and bar. 🛜 **¥67,000**

Tokyo Station 東京ステーションホテル 1-9-1 Marunouchi, Chiyoda-ku ☎03 5220 1111, ⊛www .thetokyostationhotel.jp; Tokyo station; map p.42. It has been great to see this grand old dame back in business – this hotel, set within Tokyo station itself, first opened for business in 1915, but was closed throughout the station's mammoth refurb. Following the template set by the hotel renovations at London's St Pancras, designers have plumped for dainty Euro-chic in the rooms, and set chandeliers all over the place. 🛜 **¥47,000**

GINZA AND AROUND

★**Conrad Tokyo** コンラッド東京 1-9-1 Higashi-Shinbashi, Minato-ku ☎03 6388 8000, ⊛conradtokyo .co.jp; Shiodome station; map p.52. This luxury hotel easily holds its own when it comes to cutting-edge contemporary design and five-star facilities. But it's the views that really steal the show – from the lobby and bayside rooms feast your eyes on what are arguably the best vistas in Tokyo, taking in Hama Rikyū Teien, Odaiba and the Rainbow Bridge. It's absolutely magical at night. 🛜 **¥60,000**

Four Seasons フォーシーズンズホテル丸の内 Pacific Century Place, 1-11-1 Marunouchi, Chiyoda-ku ☎03 5222 7222, ⊛fourseasons.com/tokyo; Tokyo station; map p.52. Chic interior design and superb service are two pluses for this luxury hotel. With only 57 rooms, there's a personal touch – let them know your arrival time and someone will be there on the platform to greet you at nearby Tokyo station. Facilities include a spa, fitness centre, and a stylish bar and French restaurant. 🛜 **¥65,000**

Mandarin Oriental Tokyo マンダリンオリエンタル東京 2-1-1 Nihombashi-Muromachi, Chūō-ku ☎03 3270 8800, ⊛mandarinoriental.com/tokyo; Mitsukoshi-mae station; map p.52. No expense has been spared here, from the dramatic 37th-floor lobby to some of the biggest standard-size rooms in Tokyo, where picture windows make the most of the stunning cityscapes. There's no pool, but guests can take advantage of a fabulous (and very pricey) spa, a fitness centre and seven restaurants. 🛜 **¥52,000**

★**Mitsui Garden Ginza** 三井ガーデンホテル銀座 8-13-1 Ginza, Chūō-ku ☎03 3543 1131, ⊛www .gardenhotels.co.jp; Shimbashi station; map p.52. Italian designer Piero Rissoni's chic design for Mitsui's flagship hotel helps it stand out from the crowd. Rooms are decorated in earthy tones with great attention to detail, but it's the bird's-eye views of the city and bay that grab the attention – quite spectacular from each and every room. 🛜 **¥25,000**

Ryūmeikan Tokyo ホテル龍名館東京 1-3-22 Yaesu, Chūō-ku ☎ 03 3271 0971, Ⓦ ryumeikan-tokyo.jp; Tokyo station; map p.52. This long-standing traditional inn has transformed into a stylish hotel, each room mixing Western comfort with attractive Japanese touches, accented in Edo-period purple (*edomurasaki*). Big discounts on offer for those who book in advance, and usually a free breakfast too. 🛜 **¥37,000**

★Sunroute Ginza ホテルサンルート銀座 1-15-11 Ginza, Chūō-ku ☎ 03 5579 9733, Ⓦ sunroute.jp; Ginza-itchōme station; map p.52. This business hotel is one of the cheaper options in fancy Ginza (especially if you book online), and just a few minutes' walk from several metro stations. Rooms are stylish and well equipped, and surprisingly large for the price and location. 🛜 **¥15,000**

AKIHABARA AND AROUND

Akihabara Washington ワシントンホテル秋葉原 1-8-3 Kanda-Sakumachō, Chiyoda-ku ☎ 03 3255 3311, Ⓦ akihabara.washington-hotels.jp; Akihabara station; map p.59. A branch of the Washington chain of business hotels, with simple, clean rooms – including one single room that comes with its own train track – and a handy location right next to Akihabara station. Solo travellers often get big discounts (with the exception of the train room). The hotel also includes a nice café that opens for breakfast and turns into a bar at night. 🛜 **¥17,000**

Hilltop 山の上ホテル 1-1 Kanda-Surugadai, Chiyoda-ku ☎ 03 3293 2311, Ⓦ yamanoue-hotel.co.jp; Ochanomizu station; map p.59. Perched on a small rise above Meiji University, this small 1930s hotel was formerly the commissioned officers' quarters during the Occupation, and then became the haunt of famous writers, notably Mishima (see p.260). Its rooms are far from Tokyo's grandest, but there are Art Deco touches and a friendly welcome; oxygen and supposedly refreshing negative ions are pumped around the premises. Note that you can often lop up to 50 percent off the inflated rack rate. 🛜 **¥24,000**

Juraku ホテルジュラク 2-9 Kanda-Awajichō, Chiyoda-ku ☎ 03 3271 7222, Ⓦ hotel-juraku.co.jp/ocha; Ochanomizu or Akihabara stations; map p.59. Now, this is a super little

place. On entry, it comes across as something like a four-star, with a quirky, faux-industrial facade and a smart, honey-toned lobby. The rooms (some female-only) are superbly designed too. Throw in a convenient location and cheery staff, and you can't really go wrong. 🛜 **¥17,000**

UENO AND AROUND

Coco Grand Ueno Shinobazu ココグラン上野不忍 ホテル 2-12-14 Ueno, Taitō-ku ☎ 03 3834 6221, Ⓦ coco grand.co.jp/uenoshinobazu; Yushima station; map p.65. Reliable hotel with friendly staff and a choice of Western- or Japanese-style accommodation, the latter quite spacious but a bit more expensive. Many rooms have great views across Shinobazu pond. 🛜 **¥19,000**

New Izu 伊豆ホテル 3-13-1 Higashi-Ueno, Taitō-ku ☎ 03 3831 8666, Ⓦ izuhotel.co.jp; Ueno station; map p.65. This friendly, business-style hotel has few frills, though it's great if you simply want a cheap, well-located place to stay. They have a handful of Japanese-style rooms for slightly higher prices, and it's worth splashing out a little extra (¥860) on a traditional breakfast. 🛜 **¥9800**

Park Side ホテルパークサイド 2-11-18 Ueno, Taitō-ku ☎ 03 3836 5711, Ⓦ parkside.co.jp; Yushima station; map p.65. One of the few non-sleazy hotels in the Ueno area where the room prices are still in the ¥10,000–15,000 range – indeed, they don't cost much more than the love hotels just to the west. Although there are few services, the rooms are kept in good nick, and some have lovely park views; a couple also have heavenly open-air baths. 🛜 **¥12,500**

Suigetsu Hotel Ohgaisō 水月ホテル鷗外荘 3-3-21 Ikenohata, Taitō-ku ☎ 03 3822 4611, Ⓦ ohgai.co.jp; Nezu station; map p.65. A rare example of a mid-range hotel with a Japanese flavour, this place is built around the Meiji-period house and traditional garden of novelist Mori Ōgai. The three wings contain a mix of Western and tatami rooms; the latter offer more atmosphere, but at double the price. Rates with or without meals available. 🛜 **¥15,000**

ASAKUSA

Asakusa Central 浅草セントラルホテル 1-5-3 Asakusa, Taitō-ku ☎ 03 3847 2222, Ⓦ pelican.co.jp/asakusacentral hotel; Asakusa station; map p.74. Modest business hotel which, despite a recent price hike, still rises above the

---

TOKYO'S BEST PLACES TO STAY

Best for views *Conrad Tokyo* (see opposite)
Best for glamping *Caravan Tokyo* (see p.147)
Best modern-style ryokan *Andon Ryokan* (see p.148)
Best for cocktails *Imperial Hotel* (see opposite)
Best for Godzilla fans *Gracery Shinjuku* (see p.148)

Best for luxury *Hoshinoya* (see opposite)
Best old-school ryokan *Sukeroku-no-yado Sadachiyo* (see p.149)
Best love hotel *Two Way* (see box, p.147)
Best hostel *Bunka Hostel* (see p.150)
Best for weirdness Capsule hotels (see box, p.150) or all-night internet cafés (see box, p.151)

13

competition thanks to the winning combination of English-speaking staff, a convenient location on Asakusa's main street, and small but well-appointed rooms, all of which come with TV and telephone. 🛜 **¥13,000**

BAYSIDE TOKYO

Grand Nikkō ホテルグランドニッコー 2-6-1 Daiba, Minato-ku ☎03 5500 6711, 🌐tokyo.grand-nikko.com; Daiba monorail; map p.87. Rising up over the bay, the most luxurious of Odaiba's hotels has a light-filled lobby, walls peppered with contemporary art and, from all but the lower levels, great views of the Rainbow Bridge and the city across Tokyo Bay. Rooms are spacious (you'll pay a bit more for bridge views), and staff helpful to a tee. 🛜 **¥47,500**

AKASAKA AND ROPPONGI

ANA InterContinental Tokyo ANAインターコンチネンタルホテル 1-12-33 Akasaka, Minato-ku ☎03 3505 1111, 🌐anaintercontinental-tokyo.jp; Tameike-sannō station; map pp.96–97. Offering great views across to Tokyo Midtown and the National Diet Building, this stylish hotel has contemporary decoration, attentive staff, a swimming pool, scores of restaurants (including the Tokyo home of French super-chef Pierre Gagnaire) and attractive public areas. 🛜 **¥42,000**

Andaz アンダズ 1-23-4 Toranomon, Minato-ku ☎03 6830 1234, 🌐tokyo.andaz.hyatt.com; Toranomon station; map pp.96–97. Japan's first branch of Hyatt's luxury Andaz offshoot has touched down in Tokyo, taking up the upper section of the new Toranomon Hills complex. No attention to detail has been spared, from the perfumed lobby to the immaculate rooms, all decorated with Japanese-style flourishes from award-winning interior designers. 🛜 **¥45,000**

The b Roppongi ザb六本木 3-9-8 Roppongi, Minato-ku ☎03 5412 0451, 🌐roppongi.theb-hotels.com; Roppongi station; map pp.96–97. A boutique-style hotel that won't break the bank or offend the eyes, even if uninspiring plastic-unit bathrooms are the norm throughout. 🛜 **¥16,000**

The Glanz ホテルザグランツ 2-21-3 Azabu-Jūban, Minato-ku ☎03 3455 7770, 🌐theglanz.jp; Azabu-Jūban station; map pp.96–97. Highly appealing option with sleek, designer-style rooms including spa-style bathrooms and glimpses of Tokyo Tower. There are reduced rates if you check in after 10pm, and all rates include breakfast. 🛜 **¥15,000**

★Grand Hyatt Tokyo グランドハイアットホテル東京 6-10-3 Roppongi, Minato-ku ☎03 4333 1234, 🌐tokyo.grand.hyatt.jp; Roppongi station; map pp.96–97. Glamour is the order of the day at the *Grand Hyatt*. The rooms' appealing design uses wood and earthy-toned fabrics, and restaurants and bars are all very chic, particularly *The Oak Door* and the slick sushi bar *Roku Roku*. 🛜 **¥59,000**

Ōkura ホテルオークラ 2-10-4 Toranomon, Minato-ku ☎03 3582 0111, 🌐www.hotelokura.co.jp/tokyo; Kamiyachō station; map p.96–97. Although only one wing remains of the iconic *Ōkura* (a new one is being built at the time of writing), it remains a Tokyo classic with its 1970s time-warp lobby and beguiling garden view. The rooms are more contemporary, but really it's the retro ambience of the public areas that's the sell here. 🛜 **¥47,000**

The Ritz-Carlton リッツカールトン東京 Tokyo Midtown, 9-7-1 Akasaka, Minato-ku ☎03 6434 8100, 🌐ritzcarlton .com; Roppongi station; map pp.96–97. Occupying the top nine floors of the 53-floor Midtown Tower, this ultra-luxury hotel has a more contemporary look than usual for a Ritz-Carlton. The choice is between deluxe rooms or suites – both offering the height of comfort. 🛜 **¥81,000**

EBISU, MEGURO AND THE SOUTH

★Claska クラスカホテル 1-3-18 Chūō-chō, Meguro-ku ☎03 3719 8121, 🌐claska.com; Meguro station; map pp.106–107. This oversized Rubik's Cube is a real hipster's choice. A 10min bus or taxi ride from Meguro station, it makes up for a relatively remote location with an abundance of contemporary Tokyo style. Some rooms have been individually decorated by different local artists – worth considering, although they're not the largest or most practical in the hotel. There's also a stylish lobby café/bar and very classy gift shop, Do (see p.203). Cheaper rates for weekly stays are available. 🛜 **¥30,000**

Dormy Inn ドーミーイン目黒青葉台 3-21-8 Aobadai, Meguro-ku ☎03 3760 2211; Nakameguro station; map pp.106–107. Within walking distance of trendy Nakameguro and a stone's throw from the banks of the delightful Meguro-gawa (see p.108), this functional business hotel is a good deal. Each room has a hotplate and small fridge, so it's feasible to self-cater. There's also a large communal bathroom and sauna, plus free bike rental. 🛜 **¥13,000**

The Strings ストリングスインターコンチネンタル Shinagawa East One Tower, 2-16-1 Konan, Minato-ku ☎03 4562 1111, 🌐intercontinental-strings.jp; Shinagawa station; map pp.106–107. Watch the Shinkansen come and go from this chic eyrie, part of the Intercontinental chain, located 26 floors up in one of the brace of towers next to Shinagawa station. The airy atrium lobby, with its combination of water, wood and stone, evokes traditional Japanese design in a contemporary way. 🛜 **¥50,500**

Tōyoko Inn Shinagawa-eki Takanawaguchi 東横 品川駅高輪口 4-23-2 Takanawa ☎03 3280 1045, 🌐toyoko-inn.com; Shinagawa station; map pp.106–107. A handy branch of this bargain business hotel chain that doesn't stint on facilities (including trouser press), although rooms are tiny. Rates include a continental breakfast. 🛜 **¥9000**

LOVE HOTELS

13

Generally clustered in entertainment districts such as Shibuya, Shinjuku, Ueno and Ikebukuro, **love hotels** are places where you can rent rooms by the hour. Often sporting ornate exteriors and a sign quoting prices for "rest" or "stay", they're not as sleazy as they might sound, and the main market is young people or married couples taking a break from crowded apartments. For the bold, they can be a cheaper and far more interesting place to stay than a bland business hotel.

All kinds of tastes are indulged at love hotels, with rotating beds in mirror-lined rooms being almost passé in comparison to some of the fantasy creations on offer. You usually choose your room from a backlit display indicating those available, and then pay a cashier lurking behind a tiny window (eye-to-eye contact is avoided to preserve privacy). Rest **rates** start at about ¥3000 for two hours in the evening or night-time, and are around the same for a "day-pack", which usually gives you from noon to about 6pm. The price of an **overnight stay** can cost the same as a basic business hotel (¥7800 is the general rate), though you usually can't check in until around 10pm. Double these rates for fancier love hotels, with rooms featuring four-poster beds, jacuzzi pools, swings and the like.

Colourful P&A ホテルカラフルP&A 2-45-10 Kabukichō, Shinjuku-ku ☏03 5155 5544, ⓦ paplaza. com; Seibu-Shinjuku station; map p.126. Quirky Shinjuku love hotel with colour-coded floors – take your pick from the pink rooms of the second floor to the purple of the seventh. The "VIP" eighth floor has pricier themed rooms, including "Aqua Fantasy", "Oriental World" and the zebra-print-infested "Designer Home". ⏦ "Rest" from **¥5500**, "stay" from **¥9900**

Two Way ホテルツーウェイ 15-2 Maruyama-chō, Shibuya-ku ☏03 3476 2020, ⓦ hote-twoway.jp; Shibuya station; map p.122. Of Tokyo's hundreds upon hundreds of love hotels, this place in Shibuya, with decor that veers towards Southeast Asian in style, is one of the best value. There's even a "group" room,

the infamous #405: goodness only knows what might occasionally go on in here, but on more innocent evenings it's home to groups of uni students having a boozy party, or even bunches of local lads watching a Premier League football game. ⏦ "Rest" from **¥3600**, "stay" from **¥5700**

Zebra ホテルゼブラ 1-37-1 Higashi-Ikebukuro, Toshima-ku ☏03 3986 5015, ⓦ hotel-zebra.net; Ikebukuro station; map p.138. Even amidst the "soaplands" of Ikebukuro, it's hard to miss this love hotel, which is adorned not only with the stripes hinted at in the name, but also all sorts of buttons, spikes and glowing panels. Considering the fact that there are costumes to borrow in the lobby, the rooms come across as surprisingly functional. ⏦ "Rest" from **¥4800**, "stay" from **¥7800**

HARAJUKU, AOYAMA AND SHIBUYA

Caravan Tokyo キャラバントウキョウ 3-13 Minami-Aoyama, Minato-ku ☏080 4145 3422, ⓦ caravantokyo .com; Omotesandō station; map p.116. Glamping in Tokyo? Yep, it's quite possible, at this custom-built caravan located in the *Commune 246* snack-courtyard complex (see p.168); mod-cons include a/c, heating, a shower and a real bed. Not quite the great outdoors, but pretty great nonetheless. Book on Airbnb. ⏦ **¥20,000**

Cerulean Tower Tōkyū Hotel セルリアンタワー東急ホテル 26-1 Sakuragaoka-chō, Shibuya-ku ☏03 3476 3000, ⓦ ceruleantower-hotel.com; Shibuya station; map p.122. Shibuya's ritziest accommodation, with a range of intriguingly designed rooms, some featuring bathrooms with glittering views of the city. Also on site are a pool and gym (free to guests on the executive floor), several restaurants, a jazz club (see p.185) and even a nō theatre in the basement (see p.188). ⏦ **¥55,000**

Granbell Hotel グランベルホテル 15-17 Sakuragaoka-chō, Shibuya-ku ☏03 5457 2681, ⓦ granbellhotel.jp; Shibuya station; map p.122. This boutique hotel has a

hip feel, courtesy of curtains with Lichtenstein-style prints, kettles and TVs from the trendy local electronics range Plus Minus Zero, and a neutral palette of greys, crisp whites and natural colours. ⏦ **¥22,000**

★ **Tōkyū Stay Aoyama** 東急ステイホテル青山 2-27-18 Minami-Aoyama, Shibuya-ku ☏03 3497 0109, ⓦ tokyustay.co.jp; Gaienmae station; map pp.114–115. Designed for long-staying guests, but open to short-stay visitors too, this high-rise hotel and apartment complex scores for facilities, location and slick decor. There's a women-only floor and wonderful views, and rates include breakfast. There are thirteen other Tokyū Stays around the city. ⏦ **¥32,400**

SHINJUKU AND THE WEST

Century Southern Tower ホテルセンチュリーサザンタワー 2-2-1 Yoyogi, Shibuya-ku ☏03 5354 0111, ⓦ southerntower.co.jp; Shinjuku station; map p.126. Smart, stylish place that's better value than similar options in Nishi-Shinjuku. Come evening time, the views overlooking the station lend the place a *Blade Runner*-ish feel. ⏦ **¥25,000**

13

★**Gracery Shinjuku** ホテルグレイスリー新宿 1-19-1 Kabukichō, Shinjuku-ku 🕿03 6833 2489, 🌐shinjuku .gracery.com; Seibu-Shinjuku station; map p.126. Yes, this is the "Godzilla hotel" that you may have spotted on your walk around Shinjuku. Despite the presence of the hulking beast by the upper-level lobby (he looks particularly fine when guarding you over breakfast), and the stylish rooms, it's not all that expensive a place to stay. 📶 **¥19,000**

Kadoya かどやホテル 1-23-1 Nishi-Shinjuku, Shinjuku-ku 🕿03 3346 2561, 🌐kadoya-hotel.co.jp; Shinjuku station; map p.126. This efficient business hotel is a little charmer. Single rooms (from ¥9980) are a bargain for such a handy location, and the doubles won't break the bank either. A major plus is the lively *izakaya* in the basement. 📶 **¥15,800**

Keiō Plaza 京王プラザホテル 2-2-1 Nishi-Shinjuku, Shinjuku-ku 🕿03 3344 0111, 🌐keioplaza.co.jp; Tochōmae station; map p.126. Though it's long since been knocked off its perch as the tallest, most glamorous hotel in Shinjuku, this enormous place nevertheless retains some of its original cachet. The premier rooms, in grey and brown tones, are very stylish, and those on the west side have sweeping views across to the Tokyo Metropolitan Government Building; there are also garish Hello Kitty rooms available. An outdoor pool opens up in summer. 📶 **¥32,500**

★**Park Hyatt Tokyo** パークハイアット東京 3-7-1-2 Nishi-Shinjuku, Shinjuku-ku 🕿03 5322 1234, 🌐tokyo .park.hyatt.jp; Tochōmae station; map p.126. Occupying the upper section of Tange Kenzō's Shinjuku Park Tower (see p.127), this is the epitome of sophistication and holding up very well to newer rivals. All the huge rooms have breathtaking views, as do the restaurants and spa, pool and fitness centre at the pinnacle of the tower. 📶 **¥64,000**

Super Hotel Kabukichō スーパーホテル歌舞伎町 2-39-9 Kabukichō, Shinjuku-ku 🕿03 6855 9000, 🌐superhoteljapan.co.jp; Higashi-Shinjuku station; map p.126. A budget treat, with small but comfortable en-suite rooms, rather beautiful communal bathing areas, well-trained staff, and a surprisingly generous free breakfast. Rates for a double room occasionally drop below ¥10,000. 📶 **¥12,000**

IKEBUKURO AND THE NORTH

Metropolitan ホテルメトロポリタン 1-6-1 Nishi-Ikebukuro, Toshima-ku 🕿03 3980 1111, 🌐www .metropolitan.jp; Ikebukuro station; map p.138. Part of the *Crowne Plaza* group, Ikebukuro's plushest hotel offers all the facilities you'd expect, including several restaurants, a fitness club (¥2400) and limousine bus connections to Narita airport. The rooms are comfortable and well priced, and the hotel is located on the more interesting west side of Ikebukuro. 📶 **¥25,000**

RYOKAN AND MINSHUKU

One of the highlights of a visit to Tokyo is staying in a **ryokan**, a traditional inn (see box opposite). **Minshuku**, the Japanese equivalent of a bed-and-breakfast, are generally cheaper and more informal, but the same basic rules apply. The more expensive ryokan usually include two traditional meals – dinner and breakfast – as part of the price; it's usually possible to forgo them for a cheaper rate, but the meals are usually excellent and form part of the experience.

UENO AND AROUND

Ryokan Katsutarō 旅館勝太郎 4-16-8 Ikenohata, Taitō-ku 🕿03 3821 9808, 🌐katsutaro.com; Nezu station; map p.65. Handily located within walking distance of Ueno Park, this homely place has just seven slightly faded tatami rooms, plus coin laundry and complimentary coffee. They also run a newer annexe in Yanaka (see website for details). No meals. 📶 Singles **¥5500**, doubles **¥9900**

★**Ryokan Sawanoya** 旅館澤の屋 2-3-11 Yanaka, Taitō-ku 🕿03 3822 2251, 🌐sawanoya.com; Nezu station, map p.65. This welcoming family-run inn is a real home from home in a very convivial neighbourhood within walking distance of Ueno Park. Though nothing fancy, it offers good-value tatami rooms, all with washbasin, TV, telephone and a/c. Few are en suite, but the two lovely Japanese-style baths more than compensate. Facilities also include bike hire (¥300 per day), coin laundry and complimentary tea and coffee. No meals. 📶 Singles **¥5400**, doubles **¥10,200**

ASAKUSA AND AROUND

★**Andon Ryokan** 行燈旅館 2-34-10 Nihonzutsumi, Taitō-ku 🕿03 3873 8611, 🌐andon.co.jp; Minowa station; map p.74. At this architectural gem, fusing traditional ryokan design with modern materials, the owner's fantastic antique collection is displayed alongside kitsch toys – and somehow it works. The dimly lit tatami rooms share bathrooms and are tiny, but sport DVD players and very comfortable futons. Other plusses include a top-floor jacuzzi spa you can book for private dips, free internet access, regular events such as sake tastings and tea ceremonies (see p.162) and super-friendly, English-speaking staff. Breakfast included. 📶 Singles **¥6500**, doubles **¥8100**

New Koyo ホテルニュー紅陽 2-26-13 Nihonzutsumi, Taitō-ku 🕿03 3873 0343, 🌐newkoyo.com; Minowa station; map p.74. Tiny little place with tatami rooms that's about as cheap as you can get for a private room in Tokyo; there are also Western-style rooms available for the same price. It's a bit out of the way, but still within walking distance of Asakusa, and bike hire is available.

STAYING AT A RYOKAN

Staying at a traditional Japanese inn, known as a **ryokan** or **minshuku**, is one of the best experiences that a trip to Tokyo can throw at you. However, as exotic as these stays may be, many components can be utterly unfamiliar to Westerners – there are countless ways in which you may find yourself losing face, and as such it's essential to know what you're getting into before taking the plunge. However, most Japanese are pretty forgiving, and in many establishments you'll be handed an English-language printed list of dos and don'ts.

Upon entry, there'll be a row of **slippers** ready for you to change into – wear these at all times, since bare feet are a no-no in common areas. You'll be ushered to your bedroom, which will have **tatami** (rice-straw matting) on the floor, and little else beyond a low table, dresser and a few cushions. At almost all places, you'll be sleeping on futons on the floor – this may seem alien at first, but most people find them just as comfortable as a bed. The bedding is stored behind sliding doors during the day, and laid out in the evening. In most establishments, this is done for you, usually when you're having dinner.

All ryokan provide a **yukata**, a loose cotton robe tied with a belt, and a short jacket in cold weather. Always wrap the left side of the *yukata* over the right; the opposite way is used to dress bodies for a funeral. You may wear this to your evening **meal**; these tend to be served early, at 6 or 7pm, and you may be asked to stipulate a set time on check-in. Smarter ryokan generally serve meals in your room, while communal dining is the norm in cheaper places. At night, some ryokan **lock their doors** pretty early, so check before going out – they may let you have a key.

Lastly, all ryokan and most minshuku feature a **traditional Japanese bath** (*furo*), a luxurious experience with its own set of rules (see p.29). Note that ryokan usually have separate bathrooms for men and women, while minshuku may only have one bathroom, in which case there'll either be designated times for males and females, or guests take it in turn. It's perfectly acceptable for couples and families to bathe together, though there's not usually a lot of space.

No meals. ☞ Singles ¥2900, doubles ¥5200

Ryokan Kamogawa 旅館加茂川 1-30-10 Asakusa, Taitō-ku ☎ 03 3843 2681, ⓦ f-kamogawa.jp; Asakusa station; map p.74. Simple but well-maintained tatami rooms, with or without bath, in a welcoming minshuku one block west of Nakamise-dōri. Breakfast and dinner extra. ☞ Singles ¥8700, doubles ¥15,400

Ryokan Shigetsu 旅館指月 1-31-11 Asakusa, Taitō-ku ☎ 03 3843 2345, ⓦ shigetsu.com; Asakusa station; map p.74. Just off bustling Nakamise-dōri, this smart little ryokan is a haven of kimono-clad receptionists and tinkling *shamisen* (Japanese lute) music, with a choice of small rooms, all en suite. There's a Japanese bath on the top floor, with views over temple roofs. Breakfast included. ☞ Western singles ¥8000, tatami twins ¥17,000

★**Sukeroku-no-yado Sadachiyo** 助六の宿 貞千代 2-20-1 Asakusa, Taitō-ku ☎ 03 3842 6431, ⓦ sadachiyo .co.jp; Asakusa or Tawaramachi stations; map p.74. Step back into Edo-era Asakusa in this delightful old inn marked by a willow tree and stone lanterns, northwest of Sensō-ji. The elegant tatami rooms are all en suite, though you can also use the traditional Japanese-style baths. Dinner and breakfast are included, and they can also arrange performances of traditional arts, including geisha dances. ☞ ¥21,600

★**Tokyo Ryokan** 東京旅館 2-4-8 Nishi-Asakusa, Taitō-ku ☎ 090 8879 3599, ⓦ www.tokyoryokan.com; Tawaramachi station; map p.74. Beautifully rendered traditional design elements and attention to detail make this modern establishment stand out from the crowd. With just three tatami rooms (including one triple; ¥10,500) above a communal lounge area and a shared bathroom, it feels like you're staying in someone's home. No meals. ☞ ¥7000

EBISU, MEGURO AND THE SOUTH

Akimoto 旅荘秋元 3-2-8 Nakameguro, Meguro-ku ☎ 03 3711 4553; Nakameguro station; map pp.106–107. This minshuku is a super little find in fashionable Nakameguro, an area which is pricey at the best of times. There are a few floors of small tatami rooms (not en-suite), a general air of calm and an extremely relaxed manager. No wi-fi; no meals. Singles ¥2800, doubles ¥4000

Ryokan Sansuisō 旅館山水荘 2-9-5 Higashi-Gotanda, Shinagawa-ku ☎ 03 3441 7475, ⓦ sansuiso.net; Gotanda station; map pp.106–107. This modest ryokan is beautifully maintained and run by friendly people. Only a few of the simple tatami rooms have en-suite bath. It's a 5min walk from the station, near the Meguro-gawa – quite convenient, despite the out-of-the-way location, thanks to its location on the Yamanote line. No meals. ☞ Singles ¥5500, doubles ¥9400

IKEBUKURO AND THE NORTH

★**Hōmeikan Daimachi Bekkan** 鳳明館台町別館 5-12-9 Hongō, Bunkyō-ku ☎ 03 3811 1187,

13

ⓦhomeikan.com; Hongō San-chōme or Kasuga station; map pp.136–137. Of the three ryokan under the *Hōmeikan* name, this one is the real looker, with its ancient carpentry and traditional design. There are no en-suite bathrooms, but all rooms have tatami mats and look out on an exquisite little Japanese garden. Service is impeccable, too. The sister establishment across the road, the Meiji-era *Honkan*, is the only inn in the city that's a listed cultural property. No meals. ⓦ **¥12,000**

Kimi Ryokan 貴美旅館 2-36-8 Ikebukuro, Toshima-ku ☏ 03 3971 3766, ⓦkimi-ryokan.jp; Ikebukuro station; map p.138. A great-value institution on Tokyo's budget scene, and a good place to meet fellow travellers – make sure you book well ahead. Rooms are compact but clean, access to a kitchen helps keep eating costs down and staff are friendly and speak English. There is a 1am curfew, and the place is a bit tricky to find, in the backstreets of west Ikebukuro. ⓦ Singles **¥4900**, doubles **¥7200**

HOSTELS

Until fairly recently, hostelling in Tokyo meant staying in one of the few municipal-run youth hostels. Now, however, you can forget about evening curfews and three-night maximum stays, since a glut of excellent privately run hostels have come on the scene, driving prices down and standards up. The majority are in, or near, the Asakusa area – another plus. Dormitories tend to be cramped but are kept clean; free wi-fi and 24hr hot water are a given; and most places have common areas which make good places to socialize.

ASAKUSA AND AROUND

1980 Hostel 1泊1980円ホテル 3-10-10 Shitaya, Taitō-ku ☏ 03 6240 6027, ⓦ1980stay.com; Inya station; map p.74. The numbers in the name are the price, not the year – this is basically the cheapest hostel in Tokyo, and its capsule-like beds are just fine. ⓦ Dorms **¥1980**

★Bunka Hostel ブンカホステル 1-13-5 Asakusa, Taitō-ku ☏ 03 5806 3444, ⓦbunkahostel.jp; Asakusa station; map p.74. A remarkably stylish addition to the Asakusa hostel scene, with comfy, curtained-off berths

---

CAPSULE HOTELS

Catering mainly to drunken salarymen who have missed their trains home, **capsule hotels** are made up of floors lined with two levels of tiny rooms, each containing a thin mattress, a comfy blanket, and (in most) a TV and radio built into the plastic surrounds. A metre wide, a metre high and two metres long, the rooms are just about big enough to stand in, but not much else. However, the clichéd description of them as being "coffin-like" is rather wide of the mark: while claustrophobics and anyone over 2m tall should give them a miss, most actually find these minuscule rooms surprisingly comfortable. Capsule hotels are generally clustered around major train stations, and cost ¥3000–4000. The majority are for men only, but some are female-friendly.

9 Hours ナインアワーズ Narita Airport, Terminal 2 ☏ 0476 335109, ⓦninehours.co.jp. If you've a late arrival or early departure, this aiport capsule hotel can save you heaps on a cab ride. ⓦ Overnight **¥4900**, "nap" **¥1500** for first 2hr then **¥500** for each 1hr

Capsule & Sauna Century Shibuya カプセル&サウナセンチュリー渋谷 1-19-14 Dōgenzaka, Shibuya-ku ☏ 03 3464 1777; Shibuya or Shinsen stations; map p.122. Right in the heart of Shibuya's prime sleaze quarter, this is a decent enough capsule hotel to use if you're too tired to wait for the first train of the morning; rates for daytime use are also reasonable at just ¥1200. Male only. ⓦ **¥3700**

Capsule Inn Kanda カプセルイン神田 1-8-9 Uchikanda, Chiyoda-ku ☏ 03 3295 9000, ⓦcapsule inn.com; Kanda station; map p.59. Just two minutes' walk from the west exit of the Kanda JR station, this ten-storey inn features 144 rooms, with separate levels for women and men. ⓦ **¥4200**

Capsule Inn Komagome カプセルイン駒込 2-4-8 Nakazato, Kita-ku ☏ 03 3915 6670; Komagome station; map pp.136–137. A little way out in Komagome, this is one of the cheapest capsule hotels in Tokyo, and it has a dedicated female-only floor. The communal hot tubs are a nice touch. ⓦ **¥3000**

Ginza Bay Hotel 銀座ベイホテル 7-13-15 Ginza, Chūō-ku ☏ 03 6226 1078, ⓦbay-hotel.jp; Higashi-Ginza station; map p.52. More expensive than most capsule hotels, but designed with far more care too, with little flourishes such as gorgeous pine fittings in the bathing areas, and USB ports in the pods. It's also the cheapest place to stay in the Ginza area, and has a female-only floor. ⓦ **¥5000**

Green Plaza Shinjuku グリーンプラザ新宿 1-29-2 Kabukichō, Shinjuku-ku ☏ 03 3207 4923, ⓦhgpshinjuku.jp; Shinjuku station; map p.126. Giant capsule hotel with 630 rooms (making it the largest such facility in Japan), friendly staff and a good fitness and sauna area; the rooftop spa baths cost extra, as do rooms with wi-fi. Male only. ⓦ **¥4500**

13

TOKYO'S CHEAPEST SLEEPS

The cheapest places to stay in Tokyo are not sleazy love hotels (from around ¥8000). They're not even capsule hotel pods (from ¥3000) or hostel dormitories (from ¥2000). No, to really hit the bottom of the barrel in Tokyo you have to head to an **internet café**, where you can get a night's sleep for under ¥1700. Those thinking that such places cannot count as accommodation would be wrong – while most have "regular" computer terminals lining open corridors, many have terminals in tiny walled-off cubicles, often with a choice between a soft, reclining chair and a cushioned floor (the latter being particularly comfortable). Many also have shower facilities (usually ¥100, if not free), snack counters and free soft-drink vending machines. Indeed, many Tokyoites actually live semi-permanently in these places if they can't afford rent elsewhere (known locally as "cyber-homeless"). Drawbacks include occasional loud snorers and neighbouring couples making the most of some rare privacy. The main companies, **Popeye** (ポパイ), **Bagus** (バガス) and **Manboo** (マンブー), have cafés sprinkled all over Tokyo; you'll often need to pay a one-off membership fee of around ¥300.

adding some rare privacy to the dorm experience – a true bargain, as far as Tokyo accommodation goes. The lobby bar is a real winner, too (see p.176). 🛜 Dorms **¥3000**

★**Khaosan Tokyo Origami** カオサン東京オリガミ 3-4-12 Asakusa, Taitō-ku ☎03 3871 6678, ⓦkhaosan-tokyo .com; Asakusa station; map p.74. Part of the *Khaosan* chain, but a far more appealing option than the unfriendly original – rooms have been given Japanese stylings, and you'll see a fair few paper cranes around the place. There are grand views of Asakusa from the lounge, and the location can't be sniffed at. 🛜 Dorms **¥3200**, doubles **¥7200**

Khaosan World Asakusa カオサンワールド浅草 3-15-1 Nishi-Asakusa, Taitō-ku ☎03 3843 0153, ⓦkhaosan -tokyo.com; Asakusa station; map p.74. The latest addition to the *Khaosan* empire is a real winner, with superbly stylish rooms – some are modern twists on the ryokan concept, others look almost space-age, and the "party" maisonettes suit groups with energy to burn. Staff are friendly and informative, and the dorms are up there with Tokyo's cheapest sleeps. 🛜 Dorms **¥2800**, doubles **¥12,000**

★**K's House Oasis** ケイズハウスオアシス 2-14-10 Asakusa-Nichōme, Taitō-ku ☎03 3844 4447, ⓦkshouse .jp/tokyo-oasis-e; Asakusa station; map p.74. Not wanting to be outdone by *Khaosan* in the hostel empire-building stakes, *K's House* (see below) have opened up a second branch in Asakusa. It's a real winner, too, with Zen-like stylings, facilities galore, charming common areas, comfy dorm beds and en-suite private rooms. 🛜 Dorms **¥2950**, twins **¥9200**

★**Retrometro Backpackers** レトロメトロバックパッカーズ 2-19-1 Nishi-Asakusa, Taitō-ku ☎03 6322 7447, ⓦretrometrobackpackers.com; Asakusa or Tawaramachi stations; map p.74. As far as backpackers go, it takes one to know one, and the owner of this tiny, two-dorm hostel (one dorm is female-only) certainly knows her stuff. Balinese and Thai stylings betray her favourite former travel destinations, and there's a sense of cosiness here absent from some of Tokyo's larger hostels. 🛜 Dorms **¥2600**

Sakura Hostel サクラホステル 2-24-2 Asakusa, Taitō-ku ☎03 3847 8111, ⓦsakura-hostel.co.jp; Asakusa station; map p.74. This friendly, well-run hostel occupies a cherry-pink building a couple of minutes' walk northwest of Sensō-ji. Each floor has its own shower and toilet area and there's a good kitchen and TV lounge. They also operate a hotel near Jimbōchō station, with similar prices. 🛜 Dorms **¥3000**, twins **¥8500**

RYŌGOKU AND KIYOSUMI

Anne Hostel 庵ホステル 2-21-14 Yanagibashi, Taitō-ku ☎03 5829 9090, ⓦj-hostel.com; Asakusabashi or Kuramae station; map p.82. A lovely little place: part hostel, part traditional minshuku (see p.148), it's tremendously popular with international guests. Most rooms, even a couple of the dorms, boast tatami flooring, and prices include a decent little breakfast. 🛜 Dorms **¥2600**, twins **¥6800**

K's House Tokyo ケイズハウス東京 3-20-10 Kuramae, Taitō-ku ☎03 5833 0555, ⓦkshouse.jp/tokyo-e; Kuramae station; map p.82. This spick-and-span hostel, just south of Asakusa, gets lots of accolades. There's no shortage of showers and toilets, plus an attractive lounge area with a well-equipped kitchen and a roof terrace. 🛜 Dorms **¥2900**, twins **¥7000**

Nui Hostel & Bar Lounge ヌイホステルバーラウンジ 2-14-13 Kuramae, Taitō-ku ☎03 6240 9854, ⓦbackpackersjapan.co.jp/nui; Kuramae station; map p.82. Just 15min on foot from Asakusa, this hostel is an excellent choice. The funky common area features a bar that's hugely popular with locals, and a great mingling spot; the pine beds in the dorms aren't quite as fancy, but they do the job. 🛜 Dorms **¥3000**, doubles **¥7400**

AKASAKA AND ROPPONGI

★**Kaisu** カイス 6-13-5 Akasaka, Minato-ku ☎03 5797 7711, ⓦkaisu.jp; Akasaka station; map pp.96–97. Think you might prefer Akasaka to Asakusa? This is one of the only hostels in the club-heavy Roppongi area – it's not

13

TO BE, OR NOT TO AIRBNB?

The world's largest city it may be, but Tokyo suffers from something of a **dearth of accommodation** at more or less all budget levels – a problem sure to raise its head during the 2020 Olympic Games. A combination of high occupancy rates and high accommodation prices have led many travellers to give **Airbnb** (airbnb.com) a go; the bulk of apartments go for ¥10,000–20,000 per night, and private rooms ¥3000–12,000. Tokyo duly became the site's fastest-growing market worldwide in early 2016, bringing the government under pressure from a hotel industry haemorrhaging revenue. Fears of a total crackdown on non-licensed guesthouses, known as *minpaku* (民泊) in Japan, were allayed in August of that year, when restrictions were lowered, rather than raised – a two-night stay is now the minimum. However, with the situation still somewhat up in the air, you're advised to check the site for updates far in advance of your visit.

cheap, but being able to stagger home at 4am certainly saves money over a long cab ride. This is no party hostel, however, but a beautiful place set into an old geisha house. Dorms ¥4300

IKEBUKURO AND AROUND

Unplan アンプラン 23-1 Tenjinchō, Shinjuku-ku 03 6457 5171, unplan.jp; Kagurazaka station; map pp.136–137. One of the new wave of flashpacker hostels offering capsule-like dorm "rooms"; set in pine frames and concealed by curtains, they're quite cosy. The bar downstairs can get quite rocking, especially if you take advantage of their all-you-can-drink deals. Dorms ¥4500, family room ¥19,800

NARITA

See also the review of *9 Hours* capsule hotel in Narita Airport (see box, p.150).

★**Azure Guesthouse** ゲストハウスアズール 2-6-4 Hiyoshidai, Tomisato-shi, 10min walk southwest of the train stations 0476 915708, azure-guesthouse.com. A friendly, surprisingly stylish place with English-speaking staff and good facilities. Book online for the best rates. Dorms ¥2900, doubles ¥7900

LONG-TERM ACCOMMODATION

Gaijin houses Those on a budget usually start off in what's known as a *gaijin* house – a privately owned house or apartment consisting of shared or private rooms with communal kitchen and bathroom. They're usually rented by the month, though if there's space, weekly or even nightly rates may be available. Monthly rates start at ¥35,000–45,000 per person for a shared room and ¥60,000–70,000 for a single; a deposit may also be required. Try looking at *Metropolis* (see p.25) for listings.

Private apartments Private apartments are usually rented out by real-estate companies, although agencies recommended here (see below) have apartments on their books. Apart from the first month's rent, be prepared to pay a deposit of 1–2 months' rent in addition to key money (usually 1–2 months' non-refundable rent when you move in), and a month's rent in commission to the agent. You may also be asked to provide information about your financial situation and find someone – generally a Japanese national – to act as a guarantor. Rentals in Tokyo start at ¥60,000 per month for a one-room box, or ¥100,000 for somewhere with a separate kitchen and bathroom. For serviced apartments, figure on daily rates of ¥13,000 and up, and minimum terms of one month.

GAIJIN HOUSE AGENCIES

★**Freshroom** 03 3851 6707, freshroom.jp. Growing year by year, this excellent agency often houses *gaijin* in slightly larger buildings than others – great for students or businessfolk who'd like to make a few friends, especially since many guests are Japanese.

Kimi Information Center 8F Oscar Building, 2-42-3 Ikebukuro 03 3986 1604, kimiwillbe.com. Runs a useful letting agency, with plenty of budget choices; they can also help with shorter-term arrangements.

Sakura House 2F K-1 Building, 7-2-6 Nishi-Shinjuku, Shinjuku-ku 03 5330 5250, sakura-house.com. One of the biggest and best-known agencies for *gaijin* houses, with a tremendous range of places to stay across the city and helpful, well-informed staff.

APARTMENT RENTALS

Hikari Tokyo Apartment tokyoapartment81.com. Agency used to dealing with foreign clients, with a wide range of affordable options.

Mori Living www.moriliving.com. Excellent upper-end choice, mostly serviced apartments; a good option for those in Tokyo on business, or with a family.

Tōkyū Stay tokyustay.co.jp. Good range of upmarket serviced apartments, many of which are in highly convenient locations.

Eating

Get ready for the gastronomic experience of a lifetime: when it comes to eating and drinking, few places in the world can compare to Tokyo. The number, range and quality of places is outstanding, with practically any world cuisine you can think of available alongside all the usual – and many unusual – Japanese dishes. The city's range of places to dine runs the gamut from simple noodle bars up to high temples of gastronomy where the eye-popping beauty of the food on the plate is matched by an equally creative approach to interior design. This being Japan, there are also scores of novelty theme restaurants, where the food plays second fiddle to the wacky atmosphere.

14

There's no need to panic about prices. Practically everywhere, including Michelin-starred restaurants, offers bargain **set-meal specials** for lunch, and there's a plethora of **fast-food** options, including stand-up noodle bars and conveyor-belt sushi restaurants, many clustered around and inside train stations. If you'd rather eat well and party at the same time, then **izakaya** (bars that serve food) are the way to go; a few with especially good food are reviewed here, others in the "Drinking and nightlife" chapter. There are also a great number of local **chain restaurants** (see box, p.158), where prices are at a minimum, and English-language menus are guaranteed; the quality of food at these places is often surprisingly good.

You can hardly walk a block of central Tokyo without passing a chain **café** – as often as not a *Starbucks*, although local operations such as *Doutor*, *Tully's* and *Caffe Veloce* are also common. Despite the convenience of these places, one of Tokyo's great joys is whiling away time in non-chain cafés (sometimes called *kissaten*), where the emphasis is on service and creating an interesting, relaxing, highly individual space. Recently, a glut of hipster-style coffee joints has sprung up around the country – to Western travellers, they'll feel a lot more familiar than the *kissaten*. Apart from drinks, many of the cafés listed in this chapter also serve wonderful pastries and a fine selection of more substantial foods which means they're good places for snacks and light meals. Some offer alcohol, too, making for a more relaxed alternative to bars. Do note, however, that many of Tokyo's cafés have no dedicated nonsmoking areas.

Traditional **teahouses** (*sabō*) are thinner on the ground than cafés; track one down and you can sample Japanese sweets made from compounded sugar or pounded rice cake (*mochi*) and red bean paste, the sweetness of which balances the bitterness of the tea. It's worth noting that while cafés often keep late hours, teahouses are generally a daytime affair.

ESSENTIALS

INFORMATION

Listings For up-to-date information on Tokyo's restaurant scene, check out *Metropolis* (Ⓦ metropolis.co.jp), *Time Out* (Ⓦ timeout.com/tokyo), Bento.com (Ⓦ bento.com), and the rather more homespun Tokyo Belly (Ⓦ tokyobelly.com) and Tokyo Cheapo (Ⓦ tokyocheapo.com).

PRACTICALITIES

Breakfast The traditional Japanese breakfast features miso soup, fish, pickles and rice, washed down with green tea, though many Japanese now prefer a quick *kōhii* and *tōsuto* (coffee and toast), served at most cafés on the "morning service" menu (from ¥500 up). If you really want to jump into local culture, eat a tray of *nattō*: part-fermented soya beans served with soy sauce and mustard – it'll certainly wake you up. Many ryokan and top hotels offer a choice between a Western- or Japanese-style breakfast, which is sometimes included in the rates (see box, p.144).

Meal times Hardly any locals linger over lunch (usually taken from noon to 2pm) but that's no reason why you should follow suit. Dinner can be eaten as early as 6pm (with many places taking last orders around 9pm), although Tokyo is not short of options for late-night dining. Opening times are given throughout this chapter, though note that last orders tend to fall either 30min or an hour before the stipulated closing time; this goes for lunch too. These timings are just like the Shinkansen – arrive a minute late, and you've missed it.

Set meals Many restaurants offer set menus (*teishoku*), usually at around ¥1000 for a couple of courses plus a drink, and only rarely topping ¥3000 per person. At both lunch and dinner you may also come across what is described as a "course menu" (*kōsu menyū*), which is in fact a set menu of several courses and more expensive than the *teishoku*.

Reservations are advisable for many places, especially on Friday, Saturday and Sunday nights. At some popular venues you may have to queue at lunch- and dinnertime, even if a reservation system is in place.

Wi-fi Eating places with wi-fi are indicated in the guide with a 🛜 symbol.

ETIQUETTE

Reading the menu These days more places are providing menus translated into English, and it's always worth asking for one (*Eigo no menyū ga arimasu ka?*) if it's not automatically presented. To assist with ordering, consult our Food and drink glossary (see p.274).

Table manners Before you start eating you'll usually be handed an *oshibori*, a damp, folded hand towel, usually steamed hot, to clean your hands. When the food arrives, wish your companions bon appétit by saying *itadakimasu*. Don't stick chopsticks (*hashi*) upright in your rice – this is an allusion to death (relatives traditionally pass pieces of bone from the cremation pot to the funeral urn with long chopsticks). Never cross your chopsticks when you put them on the table, and don't point at things with them.

JAPANESE STAPLE DISHES

With Japanese food now popular across the globe, most visitors will, before even setting foot in the country, have sampled at least a couple of its main staple dishes. However, any national cuisine is best tasted in its homeland, and chances are that it'll be cheaper here, too. **Sushi** is perhaps the country's most famous food; go to a good restaurant and you'll never want to eat it outside Japan again.

SUSHI

Unless you're totally disgusted by the thought of raw fish, you absolutely have to give sushi a go during your time here. The name refers not to the fish, but to the vinegared rice it (or other ingredients) are laid upon; simple raw fish is actually known as **sashimi**. At a traditional *sushi-ya*, each plate is freshly made by a team of chefs working in full view of the customers. Choices include tuna (*maguro*), salmon (*sâmon*), shrimp (*ebi*), eel (*unagi*), scallop (*hotate*) and egg (*tamago*); order by pointing, or going for a set (*mori-awase*; usually served at lunch). **Kaiten-zushi** shops, where you pluck your selections from a conveyor belt, are an inexpensive, convenient way of sampling the cuisine; plates are colour-coded according to price, and the total number of plates is totted up at the end. You'll be served green tea with your meal, and expected to pour your own soy sauce, into which some stir *wasabi* (already included beneath the fish in some sushi); note that it's the fish, not the rice, which is supposed to be dipped into the soy, though this is only possible if you have good chopstick skills.

NOODLES AND RAMEN

There are three main types of noodle to try in Tokyo. The first two usually go side by side in simple noodle restaurants (see box, p.158): **soba**, a thin, grey noodle made from buckwheat powder; and **udon**, a fatter, white noodle made from wheat flour. These come with all sorts of toppings, and in either a hot or a cold broth (the latter usually a bit more expensive). King of the noodles, however, is **ramen**, a Chinese-style yellow noodle served in dedicated, often atmospherically steamy establishments; this can come in a soy or miso-based broth, and the additional ingredients vary. It's not unusual for long lines to form outside hit ramen stalls and there are scores of blogs devoted to the quest for the best bowl – English ones include Ⓦ www.ramenadventures.com and Ⓦ ramentokyo.com. Lastly, **tsukemen** is a sort of ramen in which the broth is served separately – often lukewarm, and with less liquid to slurp, many prefer it in the summertime, when it can be tough to pluck up the courage to fill oneself with boiling soup.

OKONOMIYAKI, MONJAYAKI AND ODEN

Savoury **okonomiyaki** are fast gaining currency outside Japan. Restaurants specializing in this pancake-like batter dish have tables featuring hot plates; usually the batter and ingredients are brought out for you to cook yourself. Fillings can vary, but seafood, noodles and veggies are popular choices. Tokyo has its own variant, known as **monjayaki**; with a far looser consistency than *okonomiyaki*, this is always a DIY job, though staff will do the necessaries for you if you ask.

A popular winter dish (though available all year round) is **oden**, large chunks of simmered tofu, *daikon (*radish), root-vegetable jelly, seaweed, hard-boiled eggs and fishcakes, traditionally eaten with a smear of mustard; *oden* is best eaten in *izakaya*, though convenience stores also sell it.

GRILLED MEATS, CUTLETS AND TEMPURA

Yakitori are delicious skewers of grilled chicken (or sometimes other meats, offal and vegetables). Traditionally seen as something of a non-gourmet, working-class meal, it has recently undergone a popularity explosion; inexpensive places to enjoy it include the atmospheric stalls under the tracks at Shimbashi and Yurakuchō. Similar to *yakitori* are **kushiage**: skewers of meat, seafood and vegetables, coated in breadcrumbs and deep-fried.

If your tastes turn to pork, then you'll not want to miss out on **tonkatsu**, larger cuts of meat also coated in breadcrumbs and usually served on shredded cabbage with a brown, semisweet sauce. This forms part of the king of comfort foods – **katsu-karē**, a breaded cutlet (usually pork) served with Japanese-style curry, sometimes served on a bed of rice.

Lastly, there's **tempura**, a series of battered, deep-fried comestibles including okra, shrimp (particularly tasty) and sweet potato; some restaurants serve a few varieties on a bed of rice (*tendon*).

14

When eating soupy noodles it's considered good manners to slurp them noisily from the bowl.

Service, taxes, tipping and the bill When you want the bill, say *o-kanjō o kudasai* ("bill please"); the usual form is to pay at the till on the way out. Consumption tax (8 percent) will push up the total cost if not included in the prices. Some restaurants and bars serving food, especially those in hotels, add on a service charge (typically 10 percent). Tipping is not expected, but it's polite to say *gochisō-sama deshita* ("that was delicious") to the waiter or chef. Payment by credit card is becoming more common, but having enough cash to cover your tab is still a good idea.

THE IMPERIAL PALACE AND AROUND

RESTAURANTS

A16 Brick Square, 2-6-1 Marunouchi, Chiyoda-ku ☎ 03 3212 5215, ⊛ www.giraud.co.jp/a16; Tokyo station; map p.42. One of the most pleasantly located restaurants in the boutique-heavy Marunouchi area, serving Californian-Italian cuisine at indoor and outdoor tables facing the lovely garden at Brick Square – a great place to chill over a glass of wine and a crisp pizza (try the *funghi*; ¥2050). Mon–Sat 11am–11pm, Sun 11am–10pm.

Henry Good Seven ヘンリーグッドセブン 7F Shin-Marunouchi Building, 1-5-1 Marunouchi, Chiyoda-ku ☎ 03 5220 0267, ⊛ heads-west; Tokyo station; map p.42. Sitting pretty on the seventh floor of the Shin-Marunouchi Building, with fantastic views over Tokyo station, this swanky café-restaurant serves surprisingly affordable lunch sets (from ¥1000); the menu changes seasonally, but mackerel and eel often make an appearance. It's also a great coffee or cocktail spot. 🛜 Daily 11am–midnight.

Matsumotorō 松本楼 1-2 Hibiya-kōen, Chiyoda-ku ☎ 03 3503 1451, ⊛ matsumotoro.co.jp; Hibiya station; map p.42. On a sunny day it's a pleasure to sit on the terrace of this venerable restaurant, which is as old as the park – Hibiya-kōen, Tokyo's first Western-style park – in which it's located. The food is pretty standard, along the lines of *omuraisu* (rice-filled omelette; ¥1200), hamburgers and other Western "favourites". Daily 10am–9pm.

The Oyster Shack かき小屋 1-6-1 Uchisaiwai-chō, Chiyoda-ku ☎ 03 6205 4328, ⊛ kakigoya.jimdo.com; Shimbashi station; map p.42. One of the city's most atmospheric oyster bars, snuggled under the train track arches north of Shimbashi station. Oysters cost from ¥300 (with occasional all-you-can-eat specials for ¥3000); alternatively, there's a whole aquarium's worth of scallops, turban shells, garlic calamari and other stuff to slurp down. Mon–Fri 4–11.30pm, Sat & Sun noon–11pm.

Ren Ren Ren 人人人 1F Tokia Tokyo Building, 2-7-3 Marunouchi, Chiyoda-ku ☎ 03 5252 7361; Tokyo station; map p.42. Cheap-but-attractive Chinese lunch option in the Tokyo station area. Sets of chilli shrimp, *mapo tofu* (chunks of tofu with minced meat in an oily, spicy sauce) or fried rice go for just ¥1000, and you can wash it down with some Shaoxing rice wine (¥650), which is something of an acquired taste. 🛜 Mon–Fri 11am–4am, Sat & Sun 11am–10pm.

Tonton 登運とん 2-1-10 Yurakuchō, Chiyoda-ku ☎ 03 3508 9454; Hibiya station; map p.42. One of the most famous under-the-tracks restaurants in all Tokyo – not entirely on account of its food, most of which is served in grilled-skewer form (offal being the speciality), but more due to its superb location, and an atmospheric, ever-present cloud of smoke which can make the chefs hard to see. Daily 11.30am–10.30pm.

GINZA AND AROUND

RESTAURANTS

Aoki 寿司屋青木 3-4-16 Ginza, Chūō-ku ☎ 03 6228 6436; Ginza station; map p.52. This may look like a conventional sushi spot, but one look at the menu will prove otherwise: additions such as avocado, camembert and foie gras may offend the purists, but they taste rather good. Daily 11.30am–3pm & 5–11pm.

★ Dhaba India ダバインディア 2-7-9 Yaesu, Chūō-ku ☎ 03 3272 7160, ⊛ dhabaindia.com; Kyōbashi station; map p.52. Give your taste buds a workout at this bustling South Indian restaurant, one of the best of its kind in Tokyo. The colourful decor avoids the usual clichés, and the specialities include a prawn and fish curry (¥1530), and a range of *dosa* (from ¥1200). Mon–Fri 11.15am–3pm &

TOKYO'S BEST RESTAURANTS

Best budget chain *Yoshinoya* (see box, p.158)

Best okonomiyaki *Sometarō* (see p.162) or *Sakuratei* (see p.169)

Best rāmen *Ramen Nagi* (see p.169) or *Ramen Kokugikan* (see p.163)

Best views *Hibiki* (see p.157)

Best soba *Kurosawa* (see p.164)

Best sushi *Sushi Bun* (see p.163) or *Iroha* (see p.166)

Best tempura *Hachimaki* (see p.159) or *Suzuya* (see p.171)

Best tonkatsu *Tonki* (see p.166)

Best tofu *Sasa-no-yuki* (see p.161) or *Ume-no-hana* (see opposite)

Best yakitori *Omoide Yokochō* (see p.171)

5–11pm, Sat & Sun noon–3pm & 5–10pm.

Ginza Hirai 銀座ひらい 5-9-5 Ginza, Chūō-ku ☎03 6280 6933; Higashi-Ginza station; map p.52. About as old-school Ginza as you can get: mustard-yellow walls and dark-wood furnishings make it an atmospheric venue to tuck into conger eel on rice – ¥1800 will get you a bowl of the stuff, plus pickles and miso soup. Daily 11.30am–2.30pm & 5.30–10pm.

Hibiki 響 46F Caretta Shiodome Building, 1-8-1 Higashi-Shinbashi, Minato-ku ☎03 6215 8051, ⓦwww .dynac-japan.com/hibiki; Shiodome station; map p.52. This modern *izakaya* boasts some of Tokyo's best views, high up on the 46th floor with large windows facing out over Tokyo Bay. The cuisine is contemporary Japanese, and lunch sets (¥1300 for the daily special, ¥1200 for a fried fish set) are particularly good value; count on around ¥6000 a head in the evening. Mon–Fri 11am–3pm & 5–11.30pm, Sat & Sun 11am–4pm & 5–11pm.

★**Little Okinawa** リトル沖縄 8-7-10 Ginza, Chūō-ku ☎03 3572 2930; Shimbashi station; map p.52. The welcome at this cosy Okinawan restaurant is as warm as it would be in the southern islands. Try Ryūkyū dishes such as *goya champurū* (noodles with stir-fried bitter melon; ¥950), washed down with the strong rice liquor *awamori*. Mon–Fri 5pm–3am, Sat & Sun 4pm–midnight.

Manpuku Shokodō まんぷく食堂 2-4-1 Yurakuchō, Chiyoda-ku ☎03 3211 6001; Yurakuchō station; map p.52. Squashed under the train tracks, this place is something like an American diner (with the music to match) gaudily decorated with Japanese *matsuri* scenes and a yellowing bunch of movie posters. The food is a mix of spaghetti, curry and *tonkatsu* cutlets (most ¥980); if you're feeling brave, you can have them all on one plate. Open daily 24hr.

Old Thailand オールドタイランド 2-15-3 Shimbashi, Minato-ku ☎03 6206 1532; Shimbashi station; map p.52. Lively Thai restaurant whose menu eschews the regular rundown, instead offering unusual creations such as specialities from the northeastern Isaan region, and delectable Chiang Mai curry noodles (¥1100). Mon–Sat 11.30am–3pm & 5pm–11pm.

Sakyō Higashiyama 左京ひがしやま B1F Oak Ginza, 3-7-2 Ginza Chūō-ku ☎03 3535 3577, ⓦsakyo higashiyama.com; Ginza station; map p.52. Refined *kyō-ryōri* (Kyoto-style cuisine) is served at this rustic basement space, decorated with bamboo and with an open kitchen that feels a million miles from Ginza's bustle. The lunch set (¥2200) includes six delicious, seasonal courses. Mon–Sat 11.30am–3pm & 5.30–11pm.

Taimeiken たいめいけん 1-12-10 Nihombashi, Chūō-ku ☎03 3271 2463, ⓦtaimeiken.co.jp; Nihombashi station; map p.52. Tokyoites love the nostalgia of one of Tokyo's original Western-style restaurants, whose *omu-raisu* (fried rice wrapped in an omelette; ¥1950) featured in the cult

movie *Tampopo*. Staff bustle about the cheap and cheerful downstairs section, serving large portions of curry rice, *tonkatsu* and noodles. Upstairs is a more formal restaurant serving the same menu at slightly higher prices. Mon–Sat 11am–9pm, Sun 11am–8.30pm.

★**Torigin Honten** 鳥ぎん本店 5-5-7 Ginza, Chūō-ku ☎03 3571 3333, ⓦtorigin-ginza.co.jp; Ginza station; map p.52. Bright, popular restaurant hidden away on a side street – look for the red sign. They serve snacks like *yakitori* (from ¥170 per stick) and *kamameshi* (kettle-cooked rice with a choice of toppings; from ¥880). Their ¥750 weekday *toridon* (chicken on rice) lunch sets are a real bargain. Daily 11.30am–10pm.

Ume-no-hana 梅の花 5F 2-3-6 Ginza, Chūō-ku ☎03 3538 2226, ⓦwww.umenohana.co.jp; Ginza-itchōme station; map p.52. Trickling streams and bamboo screens set the mood in this elegant restaurant specializing in melt-in-the-mouth tofu creations. The tofu comes natural, deep-fried, boiled, grilled or sweetened for dessert; sets change by the season, but lunch courses generally go from ¥2100, while dinner sets start at ¥3560. Daily 11am–4pm & 5–10pm.

CAFÉS

100% Chocolate Café 100%チョコレートカフェー 2-4-16 Kyōbashi, Chūō-ku ☎03 3273 3184, ⓦchoco -cafe.jp; Kyōbashi station; map p.52. You've got to admire the sheer style of this place: its chocolate-bar-styled ceiling, as well as the "chocolate library" lining one wall, were dreamed up by Masamichi Katayama, one of Tokyo's hottest designers. While you can just pop in to buy a selection of small chocolates (¥440 for two, from a selection of 56), it would be a sin not to indulge in a hot chocolate (¥430), or their wonderful range of slurp-worthy desserts. Mon–Fri 8am–8pm, Sat & Sun 11am–7pm.

Café de l'Ambre カフェドランブル 8-10-15 Ginza, Chūō-ku ☎03 3571 1551; Shimbashi station; map p.52. One of Tokyo's best coffee venues – at least for those who don't mind the semi-permanent cloud of cigarette smoke. This old-school Ginza *kissaten* has been roasting up 300g batches of beans since the 1950s, achieving something approaching coffee perfection in the intervening years. Most cups (from ¥700) are made with a cotton-felt filter – the process is quite mesmerizing. Daily noon–9.30pm.

Henri Charpentier アンリシャルペンティエール 2-8-20 Ginza, Chūō-ku ☎03 3562 2721, ⓦhenri-charpentier .com; Ginza-itchōme station; map p.52. This deep-pink boutique offers the ultimate in Tokyo patisseries on the ground floor and a *salon de thé* below. Here you can enjoy crêpe suzette (¥1725), flambéed at your table, as well as a range of gold-flecked chocolate morsels and seasonal specialities, to go with a choice of coffees, teas and infusions (¥860 or so). Don't leave before checking out the cleverly hidden toilets. Daily 11am–9pm.

14

14

DINING ON THE CHEAP

Tokyo isn't exactly paradise for budget travellers, but as far as food goes there are some very good ways to stretch your yen. Most head straight to the city's chain **convenience stores** such as 7-Eleven, AM/PM and Lawson (see box, p.202), which sell snacks and meals round the clock; these include sandwiches and pastries, plus more intrinsically Japanese sustenance such as *oden* (see box, p.155) and *onigiri* (rice wrapped in lavered seaweed, with various fillings). Not quite as numerous, but still found in all parts of town, **supermarkets** sell sandwich fodder and other regular backpacker staples, as well as bentō sets (rice with all manner of other ingredients, in a plastic tray) and super-cheap fresh noodles; note that in the hours before closing (9–11pm) they tend to lop up to half of the price off sushi and other bentō.

If you want to eat out, try a **standing noodle bar**; these are usually referred to as a *soba-ya* or *udon-ya*, though in practice the vast majority sell both. A bowl of soba or udon will cost from ¥250, though it can be tricky to operate the Japanese-only ticket machines used to transact cash in a hygienic fashion. However, the best value is to be had at Tokyo's **fast-food** chains, almost all of which supply English-language menus. All of the following can be found in every single part of town; just ask around.

FAST-FOOD CHAINS

Caffé Veloce カフェベローチェ. In a city where a simple mug of Joe can easily set you back ¥600, this budget café chain is a great fallback option: in cheap but pleasing Italianate environs, coffee costs from just ¥200, and doesn't taste bad at all. Typically daily 8am–7pm.

CoCo Ichiban-ya ココ壱番屋 Ⓦ ichibanya.co.jp. A quirky curry chain which allows you to piece together your meal. First, choose the type of stock you desire, then the amount of rice you want (up to a mighty 900g), then your desired level of spice (level one barely registers a hit; level ten provides a veritable spice-gasm). Then comes the fun add-your-ingredients bit: choices include beef, okra, scrambled egg, cheese, *tonkatsu*, *nattō* and a whole lot more. It'll end up costing ¥600–1100. Daily 8am–midnight, often later.

Fuji Soba 富士そば. Sometimes you just want something quick, cheap and easy. This simple, round-the-clock chain (not as ubiquitous as others on this list, but there's at least one in most major areas) certainly scratches those particular itches, with ramen from ¥410, *curry katsudon* for ¥530 and a range of similarly

priced local staples – all surprisingly tasty. Daily 24hr.

Matsuya 松屋 Ⓦ www.matsuyafoods.co.jp. Fronted by yellow, Japanese-only signs with red and blue blobs on them, this chain specializes in cheap curry (from ¥330) and *gyūdon* (beef on rice; ¥380). They chuck in a steaming-hot bowl of miso soup with whatever you order. Daily 24hr.

Saizeriya サイゼリヤ屋 Ⓦ www.saizeriya.co.jp. Budget Italian food, often surprisingly good; their tasty *doria* (meaty rice gratin) will fill a hole for ¥299, pasta dishes and small pizzas can be had from ¥399, or have a fried burger-and-egg set for ¥399. The wine prices are also ridiculous – ¥100 per glass, or an astonishingly cheap ¥1080 for a 1.5-litre bottle. Daily 8am–midnight, often later.

★**Yoshinoya** 吉野屋 Ⓦ www.yoshinoya.com. You can't miss the bright orange signs marking branches of the nation's favourite fast-food chain, famed for its cheap, tasty bowls of *gyūdon* (beef on rice) from just ¥380. When they started reselling this dish after sales were choked off by a BSE scare there was a 1.5km-long line outside their main Shinjuku branch. Daily 24hr.

Kiriko Lounge キリコラウンジ 6F Tokyo Tokyu Plaza 5-2-1 Ginza, Chūō-ku ☎ 03 6264 5590; Ginza station; map p.52. Set in Tokyu Plaza, one of central Tokyo's newest large developments, this swanky place allows you to drain coffee (from ¥650) with a superlative view of Ginza's high-rises, through some truly gigantic windows. You can save a few hundred yen by taking it in a paper cup, and sitting in the common area. Mon–Sat 11am–11pm, Sun 11am–9pm.

Mikimoto Lounge 御木本ラウンジ 3F Mikimoto Ginza 2, 2-4-12 Ginza, Chūō-ku ☎ 03 3562 3134; Ginza station; map p.52. The Toyo Ito-designed boutique for pearl jewellery company Mikimoto (see p.200) has a café

with drinks (from ¥650) and very appealing Western-style desserts and cakes on the menu (¥1300 or so). Mon–Sat 11am–7.30pm, Sun 11am–7pm.

TEAHOUSES

Cha Ginza 茶銀座 5-5-6 Ginza, Chiyoda-ku ☎ 03 3571 1211; Ginza station; map p.52. This teahouse, run by a tea wholesaler, offers a modern take on the business of sipping *sencha*. Iron walls add a contemporary touch, and the rooftop area, where they serve *matcha*, is the place to hang out with those Tokyo ladies who make shopping a career. ¥800 gets you two different cups of the refreshing green stuff, plus a traditional sweet. Tues–Sun 11am–6pm.

Higashiya Ginza 東家銀座 2F Pola Ginza, 1-7-7 Ginza, Chūō-ku 03 3538 3230; Ginza station; map p.52. This tearoom and shop is known for its relaxing atmosphere and delicious assortments of seasonal Japanese sweets (from ¥600). Daily 11am–9pm.

Sabō Nonohana 茶房 野の花 3-7-21 Ginza, Chūō-ku 03 5250 9025; Ginza station; map p.52. Lovely tearoom on the second floor of Nonohana Tsukasa, a shop that specializes in traditional flower arrangements and crafts. The *teishoku* (set meal) lunches – starting at ¥1000 – are beautifully presented, and the green-tea ice cream (¥750) is hard to turn down. Mon–Sat 11am–7pm, Sun 11.30am–6pm.

14

AKIHABARA AND AROUND

RESTAURANTS

Botan ぼたん 1-15 Kanda-Sudachō, Chiyoda-ku 03 3251 0577; Awajichō station; map p.59. Chicken *sukiyaki* (a stew-like dish served in a hotpot) is the order of the day at this atmospheric old restaurant, tucked into the backstreets of Kanda. At around ¥7000 a head it's not cheap, but this is the genuine article, where the chicken, vegetables and tofu simmer gently over individual braziers in small rooms. Mon–Sat 11.30am–9pm.

Go Go Curry ゴーゴーカレー 1-16-1 Kanda-Sakumachō, Chiyoda-ku 03 5256 5525, www.gogocurry.com; Akihabara station; map p.59. No doubt about it, the official meal of Akihabara regulars is *tonkatsu* curry (fried pork cutlet on rice, smothered in curry sauce), and one of the heartiest you'll find is at this chain, whose main branch – complete with gorilla logo – is in Akihabara. Plates start at ¥700, and in keeping with the rather odd opening hours ("go" is Japanese for the number five), you get ¥100 off before 5.55pm. Daily 9.55am–9.55pm.

★ **Hachimaki** はちまき 1-19 Kanda-Jimbōchō, Chiyoda-ku 03 3291 6222; Jimbōchō station; map p.59. Dating back to 1931, this tempura specialist is one of Tokyo's best time-warp restaurants: black-and-white photos abound, yellowing wallpaper makes it feel like the whole place has been dunked in tea, and there's nary a sign that you're in the twenty-first century. Have a crack at their delectable *tendon*, which gets you four freshly made tempura on rice (¥1000). Daily 11am–9pm.

CAFÉS

★ **Forest of Owl** アウルの森5F 4-5-8 Soto-Kanda, Chiyoda-ku 03 3254 6366, 2960.tokyo; Akihabara station; map p.59. One of the newest additions to Akiba's swarm of quirky cafés – and Tokyo's ever-increasing roster of animal-related ones (see box, p.160) – this place allows you to sip a vending-machine beverage (included in the ¥890 entrance fee) amidst a "forest" featuring a few dozen owls. You're likely to see one flashing past your face or feet quite regularly, and can even pop one onto your hand (staff will assist and give you a kitchen glove for protection). Mon & Tues, Thurs–Sun noon–10pm, Wed noon–4pm.

Gundam Café ガンダムカフェー 1-1 Kanda-Hanaokachō, Chiyoda-ku 03 3251 0078, g-cafe.jp; Akihabara station; map p.59. In the suitably sci-fi interior of this café you can experience what a pilot from the incredibly popular anime series *Mobile Suit Gundam* would eat – or at least our terrestrial equivalent. Café time and bar time (from 5pm) have different menus. Coffee from ¥400. Mon–Fri 10am–10pm, Sat 8.30am–11pm, Sun 8.30am–9.20pm.

★ **Imasa** 井政 2-16-9 Sotokanda, Chiyoda-ku 03 3258 0059; Ochanomizu station; map p.59. This café is something of a treat: essentially forming part of the Kanda Myojin complex (see p.58), it's set in a wooden building dating from the 1920s, fringed with gardens and boasting a mix of traditional and modern fittings. The coffee's great, too (from ¥600) – though even if it were awful this place would still be worth a visit. Mon–Fri 11am–4.30pm.

Maidreamin メイドリーミング 2F 1-8-10 Soto-Kanda, Chiyoda-ku 03 6252 3263, maidreamin.com; Akihabara station; map p.59. The spangly, anime-like Akiba branch of the *Maidreamin* maid café chain (see box, p.160) draws a small stream of foreigners thanks to English-speaking staff – they'll let you know exactly which cute poses to make, which cute sounds to mimic and so on. It's all rather fun, and charged at ¥500 per person per hour,

TOKYO'S TOP CAFÉS AND TEAHOUSES

Best for chocoholics *100% Chocolate Café* (see p.157)
Best for Japanese desserts *Umezono* (see p.163)
Best for tea *Cha Ginza* (see opposite)
Best for music fans *Big Love* (see p.169)
Best for weirdness value *Maidreamin* (see above & p.170) and *Swallowtail Café* (see p.173)
Best for artsy folk *Gallery éf* (see p.162)
Best for aromas *Aoyama Flower Market* (see p.170)
Best animal cafés *Calico* (see p.172) and *Forest of Owl* (see above)
Best for a 1970s Tokyo vibe *Café de l'Ambre* (see p.157)
Best for views *L'Occitane* (see p.170)

14

MAIDS, BUTLERS AND CATS: TOKYO'S QUIRKY CAFÉS

Japan is famed for appropriating Western cultural standards, and Tokyo's various quirky takes on the humble café are all worth sampling – some would say that you haven't really visited Tokyo if you haven't tried at least one.

MAID AND BUTLER CAFÉS

The weird and wonderful **maid cafés** range in style from seedy to sci-fi via the unashamedly kitsch. Some visitors assume a link exists with the sex industry, but the majority of venues are actually rather tame, with nothing bar the weirdness to worry about. Most maid cafés are clustered among the electronics outlets to the west of Akihabara station; head there after sunset and you'll see lines of girls clamouring for custom. The deal is usually the same: costumed girls (and sometimes guys) serve up food and drink in an excruciatingly "cute" manner, their voices screeching a full two octaves above their natural pitch. There's usually an hourly fee, and you're also expected to order some food or drink from the menu. Keep an eye on the other customers, too: the mix of office groups, courting couples, old sleazebags and lonely young men can be a fascinating window onto contemporary Japanese culture, though remember that you're not usually allowed to take pictures. Recommended places to try include *Mai:lish* (see below), and the *Maidreamin* branches in Akihabara (see p.159) and Shibuya (see p.170).

The success of maid cafés spawned a male equivalent: the equally interesting **butler cafés**, where handsome, dressed-up young chaps (often Westerners) serve coffee, cake and wine to an exclusively female clientele. Though the format is essentially the same as that for the maid café, butler cafés tend to be fancier and are often rather more expensive. A good one to try is *Swallowtail Café* in Ikebukuro (see p.173).

ANIMAL CAFÉS

The current hit formula in Tokyo's polymorphous *kissaten* culture is the **animal café**. The craze started relatively tamely with cat cafés; offering quality time with pedigree cats, these cafés have long been popular with young women and dating couples, and the concept has since been extended to China, South Korea and even Europe. In recent years, cafés have popped up offering experiences with other animals – rabbits, hedgehogs, snakes, owls and even penguins. However, some establishments are clearly putting profit over animal welfare. Recommended establishments listed in this guide include the *Calico* (see p.172) and *Nekorobi* (see p.173) cat cafés, *Tokyo Snake Center* (see p.170) and *Forest of Owl* (see p.159), all of which treat their animals well. If you are visiting an animal café, things to bear in mind are whether or not the animals are kept in cages, if they are allowed "off-time" away from visitors, and whether they have enough space to wander.

with an order from the menu mandatory: drinks cost ¥600–1000, with meals a little more expensive. Each of the seven levels of this building also host maid cafés, and there's another good branch of *Maidreamin* in Shibuya (see p.170). Daily 10am–11pm.

Mai:lish マイリシ 2F FH Kowa Square, 3-6-2 Soto-Kanda, Chiyoda-ku ☎03 5289 7310, ⓦmailish.jp; Suehirochō station; map p.59. Akiba's famed maid cafés (see box above) come in all sorts of shapes, sizes and styles; this is one of the originals, a relaxed venue in which costumed girls pander to their customers' every whim. It's ¥500 per hour, and you're obliged to order something from the menu: drinks cost from ¥550. Daily 11am–10pm.

Mu'u Mu'u Diner ムームーダイナー 3-14-3 Kanda-Ogawamachi, Chiyoda-ku ☎03 3518 6787; Jimbōchō station; map p.59. There's a sunny Hawaiian vibe at this café-restaurant, decked out with surfboards and hibiscus garlands. Besides Hawaiian Kona coffee, it also serves Kona beer as well as a few dishes, such as *kimchi*-octopus (¥820),

hamburgers and *loco moco* (a Hawaiian dish of white rice topped with a burger, fried egg and gravy; ¥1080). Daily 11am–11pm.

N3331 mAAch-Ecute Building, 1-25-4 Kanda-Sudachō, Chiyoda-ku ☎03 5295 2788, ⓦn3331.com; Akihabara station; map p.59. Fun even if you're not a trainspotter, this inventively-located café pokes up over the rails near Akihabara – there'll be a JR service whizzing past the floor-to-ceiling windows every minute or two. As well as passable coffee (from ¥480), they serve a range of alcoholic drinks. Mon–Sat 11am–11pm, Sun 11am–9pm.

Saböru さぼーる 1-11 Kanda-Jimbōchō, Chiyoda-ku ☎03 3291 8404; Jimbōchō station; map p.59. Appealingly rustic, tree-house-like *kissaten* tucked away on the alley running parallel to Yasukuni-dōri. Once a popular hideaway for school kids skipping lessons (the nearby bookshops presumably functioned as an excuse), this three-level establishment now attracts an older, more cosmopolitan clientele. Coffee from ¥400. Mon–Sat 9am–11pm.

UENO AND AROUND

RESTAURANTS

Hantei はん亭 2-12-15 Nezu, Bunkyō-ku ☎ 03 3828 1440, ⓦhantei.co.jp; Nezu station; map p.65. Stylish dining in a beautiful, three-storey wooden house. There's only one dish, *kushiage* (deep-fried pieces of meat, fish and vegetables skewered on sticks), served in combination plates, six at a time: ¥3000 for the first plate (plus two appetisers); ¥1500 thereafter, until you say stop. Tues–Sat noon–2.30pm & 5–10pm, Sun 11.30am–2.30pm & 4–9.30pm.

Kandakko 神田っ子 6-9-20 Ueno, Taitō-ku ☎ 03 3834 3662; Ueno station; map p.65. A decent spot for seafood, including clams, *maguro* on rice and grilled squid (all around ¥500). Bustling and boozy, it suits Ueno down to the ground. Daily 11am–11pm.

Musashino 武蔵野 2-8-1 Ueno, Taitō-ku ☎ 03 3831 1672; Ueno-Hirokōji station; map p.65. One of Ueno's few remaining old-style restaurants serving *tonkatsu*, for which the area was once famed. They come in big, thick, melt-in-the-mouth slabs; choose between standard *rōsu* (fatty belly meat) and the leaner *hire* (loin fillet), both costing ¥1000 including soup, rice

and pickles. Daily 11.30am–9pm.

★**Sasa-no-yuki** 笹乃雪 2-15-10 Negishi, Taitō-ku ☎ 03 3873 1145, ⓦsasanoyuki.com; Uguisudani station; map p.65. Three centuries ago, the chef here was said to make tofu like "snow lying on bamboo leaves", and both the name and the quality have survived, though the old wooden house is now marooned among flyovers. Calm prevails over the tatami mats as you feast on delicately flavoured silk-strained tofu. Prices are reasonable, with most tofu plates priced at around ¥750, and full courses starting at ¥5000 (or ¥2200 for lunch). Tues–Sun 11.30am–9pm.

CAFÉS

Kayaba Bakery カヤバベーカリー 2-15-6 Uenosakuragi, Taitō-ku ☎ 03 5809 0789, ⓦkayaba-bakery.com; Nezu station; map p.65. This small, charming bakery in the Yanaka area, tucked into a complex of wooden buildings, offers inventive pastries and breads such as cod roe *fougasse*. Coffee is available from the window by the outdoor seats. Daily except Mon 9am–7pm.

14

ASAKUSA

RESTAURANTS

320 Ramen 320ラーメン 2-15-1 Asakusa, Taitō-ku, no phone; Asakusa station; map p.74. Don't expect any culinary fireworks at this spit-and-sawdust ramen bar, but the bowls – at just ¥320 – are excellent backpacker fare, and they don't taste too bad at all. Daily except Sat 10am–7.30pm.

★**Bon** 梵 1-2-11 Ryusen, Taitō-ku ☎ 03 3872 0375, ⓦfuchabon.co.jp; Iriya station; map p.74. A rare chance to sample *fucha ryōri*, a distinctive style of Zen Buddhist cuisine in which each of the ornately presented vegetable dishes is traditionally served from one large bowl, and the meal begins and ends with tea. The setting, a charming old Japanese house, and the calm service, make it an experience not to be missed. Reservations essential, with courses starting at ¥5400. Mon & Tues, Thurs & Fri noon–1.30pm & 5–7pm, Sat noon–7pm, Sun noon–6pm.

Chin-ya ちんや 1-3-4 Asakusa, Taitō-ku ☎ 03 3841 0010, ⓦwww.chinya.co.jp; Asakusa station; map p.74. Founded in 1880, this famous *shabu-shabu* and *sukiyaki* (styles of Japanese hotpots) restaurant offers sets from ¥4500. The place occupies seven floors, with more casual dining in the basement, where you can go for steak instead (¥2000). Mon & Wed–Fri noon–3.30pm & 4.30–9.30pm, Sat & Sun 11.30am–9pm.

Daikokuya 大黒家 1-38-10 Asakusa, Taitō-ku ☎ 03 3844 1111 and 1-31-9 Asakusa ☎ 03 3844 2222, ⓦtempura.co.jp; Asakusa station; map p.74. There's always a lunchtime queue at this venerable tempura restaurant, set in an attractive old building. The speciality is

tendon – shrimp, fish and prawn fritters on a bowl of rice (from ¥1550). If the main branch is too busy, head for the annexe around the corner. Mon–Fri & Sun 11.10am–8.30pm, Sat 11.10am–9pm.

Hatsuogawa 初小川 2-8-4 Kaminarimon, Taitō-ku ☎ 03 3844 2723; Asakusa station; map p.74. Look for the profusion of potted plants outside this tiny, rustic eel restaurant. It's very foreigner-friendly and a lovely place to experience one of Japan's most delectable fish dishes (eel sets from ¥1500). Mon–Sat noon–1.30pm & 5–7.30pm, Sun 5–7.30pm.

La Sora Seed ラソラシド 31F Solamachi, 1-1-2 Oshiage, Sumida-ku ☎ 03 5414 0581, ⓦkurkku.jp; Oshiage station; map p.74. Ecologically sound operation boasting one of the best possible views of the huge Skytree tower (see p.78). It leans on European flavours, including great meatballs made with organic pork. Lunch sets go from ¥3100, dinner for almost three times that. Daily 11am–4pm & 6–11pm.

Maguro Bito まぐろ人 1-21-8 Asakusa, Taitō-ku ☎ 03 3844 8736, ⓦmagurobito.com; Asakusa station; map p.74. Fuji TV viewers once voted this the top *kaiten-zushiya* in Japan, and it's easy to see why: the quality of fish and other ingredients is excellent, the turnover fast and the decor on the ritzy side. Expect a queue (but it moves fast). Electronically price-coded plates range from ¥170 to ¥530. Mon–Fri 11.30am–9.30pm, Sat & Sun 11am–10pm.

Matsunami ステーキハウス松波 1-11-6 Asakusa, Taitō-ku ☎ 03 3844 3737, ⓦwww.matsunami.net;

14

THE WAY OF TEA

Tea was introduced to Japan from China in the ninth century and was popularized by Zen Buddhist monks, who appreciated its caffeine kick during their long meditation sessions. Gradually, tea drinking developed into a formal ritual known as *cha-no-yu*, the **tea ceremony**, whose purpose is to heighten the senses within a contemplative atmosphere.

In its simplest form the ceremony takes place in a tatami room, undecorated save for a hanging scroll or display of *ikebana* (traditional flower arrangement). Using beautifully crafted utensils of bamboo, iron and rustic pottery, your host will whisk **matcha** – the strong powdered form of green tea – into a thick, frothy brew and present it to each guest in turn. First eat the accompanying sweet (*wagashi*), then take the bowl in both hands, turn it clockwise a couple of inches and drink it down in three slow sips.

The *Imperial* (see p.144) and *Ōkura* hotels (see p.146) all have traditional rooms in which tea ceremonies are regularly held; the cost will be around ¥1000. Some of the most appealing places to take tea are the city's **parks**, where small tearooms charge around ¥500 for a cup, often served with a small sweet treat. The best are located in Hama Rikyū Teien (see p.53), Shinjuku Gyoen (see p.131), Happōen (see p.109), Kyū Iwasaki-tei Gardens (see p.68) and Kyū Furukawa Gardens (see p.140).

Japan's tea culture embraces many **types of tea**. **Bancha**, the cheapest grade of tea is for everyday drinking and, in its roasted form, is used to make the smoky **hōjicha**, or mixed with popped brown rice for the nutty **genmaicha**. Medium-grade **sencha** is commonly served in upmarket restaurants, while top-ranking, slightly sweet **gyokuro** (dewdrop) is reserved for special occasions. Although usually reserved for tea ceremonies, thick and strong **matcha** is often available in regular teahouses, and is a great local alternative to an espresso.

Asakusa or Tawaramachi stations; map p.74. If you want to try some of Japan's melt-in-the-mouth beef, head to this traditional steakhouse, where the chef cooks the meat in front of you. Lunchtime sets start at ¥4200, so won't break the bank. At night, prices begin at ¥1575 per portion, and quickly go up: you'll spend at least ¥7000 per head. Daily 11.30am–2pm & 5–11pm, Sun closes 10pm.

Nakae 中江 1-9-2 Nihonzutsumi, Taitō-ku ☎03 3872 5398, ⓦsakuranabe.com; Minowa station; map p.74. This venerable restaurant specializes in dishes made with horse meat, including *sukiyaki* (hotpot). The interior, decorated with beautiful ink paintings of horses, looks pretty much like it did a century ago when the whole area was a thriving red-light district. Small one-pot dishes start at ¥1700, and full courses will run you close to ¥10,000. Tues–Fri 5–10pm, Sat & Sun 11.30am–9pm.

Ōtafuku 大多福 1-6-2 Senzoku, Taitō-ku ☎03 3871 2521, ⓦotafuku.ne.jp; Iriya station; map p.74. Customers have been coming to this charming restaurant for over eighty years to sample its delicious selection of *oden* boiled in a soy and *dashi* broth. Wash it all down with a glass of pine-scented *tarozake* (sake). There's a picture menu (individual pieces ¥130–600) or you can sit at the counter and point at what you want in the bubbling brass vats. Mon–Sat 5–11pm, Sun 5–10pm.

★Sometarō 染太郎 2-2-2 Nishi-Asakusa, Taitō-ku ☎03 3844 9502; Tawaramachi station; map p.74. This rambling, wooden restaurant specializing in *okonomiyaki*, but also offers some quirky house creations such as *osomeyaki* (a variation of *okonomiyaki*, made with Worcester

sauce), all costing from ¥800. There are English instructions on the menu, and staff are pleased to help out with your on-the-table creations. Daily noon–10.30pm.

Tanuki たぬき 1-8-9 Asakusa, Taitō-ku ☎03 3845 1785; Tawaramachi station; map p.74. Old-fashioned restaurant whose exterior is presided over by a couple of the eponymous animals (you'll see *tanuki* – Japanese racoon dogs – all over Japan). The food is a mix of grills (veggies, shellfish and seafood) and sashimi. Daily 1–11pm.

CAFÉS

★Gallery éf ガラリーエフ 2-19-18 Kaminarimon, Taitō-ku ☎03 3841 0442, ⓦgallery-ef.com; Asakusa station; map p.74. The *kura* (traditional storehouse) at the back of this appealing café provides an intimate venue for an eclectic mix of concerts, performance art, and exhibitions that cover most of the space – the rest is taken up by the café's collection of retro goods. Drinks, meals (mostly Western-style, like chilli beans and spaghetti), and desserts are served using vintage tableware, and they carry a few import beers as well. Choose from four different types of blended coffee (¥550), or plump for a tasty fruit juice (¥630). Daily except Tues: café and gallery 11am–7pm, bar 6pm–midnight.

Kappabashi Coffee 合羽橋コーヒー 3-25-11 Nishi-Asakusa, Taitō-ku ☎03 5828 0308; Iriya or Tawaramachi stations; map p.74. A little way west of central Asakusa, this place has a completely different vibe, eschewing the area's traditional leanings for chunky wooden furniture, dapper waiters and a sophisticated air – the place looks great at night. They serve a wide range of coffees (from ¥450), teas (from ¥600), infusions and juices, as well as cakes and light meals. Mon–Fri 8am–9pm, Sat & Sun 8am–8pm.

TEAHOUSE

Umezono 梅園 1-31-12 Asakusa, Taitō-ku ☏ 03 3841 7580; Asakusa station; map p.74. This traditional tearoom in the heart of Asakusa is famous for its *awa-zenzai*, millet flour cakes wrapped in sweet azuki bean paste, served with seeds of Japanese basil for contrast. Alternatively, choose a bowl of *anmitsu* from the window display: a colourful concoction of agar jelly, azuki beans and sticky rice topped with a variety of fruits (and, if you're really hungry, whipped cream or ice cream; from ¥800). Daily except Wed 10am–8pm.

RYŌGOKU AND KIYOSUMI

RESTAURANTS

Tomoegata 巴潟 2-17-6 Ryōgoku, Sumida-ku ☏ 03 3632 5600, ⓦ tomoegata.com; Ryōgoku station; map p.82. In the heart of sumo territory, and a grand place to head if you're off to a tournament, this is a good place to sample *chanko-nabe*, the wrestlers' protein-packed meat, seafood and vegetable stew. Their sets (¥860–4860) come in sizes named after the various levels of sumo – the *yokozuna* course would fill a whale, but even the cheapest one is pretty hearty. Daily 11.30am–2pm & 5–11pm.

Yoshiba 吉葉 2-14-5 Yokoami, Sumida-ku ☏ 03 3623 4480, ⓦ kapou-yoshiba.jp; Ryōgoku station; map p.82. Set in an old sumo *dōjō* (practice hall; book ahead for the prime tables around the ring), this is a richly atmospheric place to come for *chanko-nabe* (from ¥3000; minimum two persons); cheaper sets with sushi, *tendon* and the like are also available for lunch. On Mon, Wed and Fri there's live singing of traditional songs. Mon–Sat 11.30am–1.30pm & 5–10pm.

CAFÉS

Cielo y Rio シエロイリオ 2-15-5 Kuramae, Taitō-ku ☏ 03 5820 8121, ⓦ cieloyrio.com; Kuramae station; map p.82. Precious few places make use of the Sumida-gawa's visual appeal, but this cool little café does just that. Espresso is cheap (¥300), there are plenty of types of tea available and they also serve good Western-style lunch specials. Daily 11am–11pm.

BAYSIDE TOKYO

RESTAURANTS

The Canteen ザキャンティーン 1F The Soho, 2-7-4 Aomi, Koto-ku ☏ 03 5530 0261; Fune-no-Kagakukan monorail; map p.87. Cosy up in the booths and flip through the glossy mags with creative types at this hip office complex near the Odaiba waterfront. Expect to pay around ¥1000 for Japanese home cooking such as fried chicken and rice, or just grab a coffee or fruit juice. 🛜 Mon–Fri 9am–10pm, Sat 10am–6pm.

Monkichi もん吉 3-8-10 Tsukushima, Chūō-ku ☏ 03 3531 2380; Tsukishima station; map p.87. As patronized by no less a luminary than Brad Pitt (whose photo is on the wall), this friendly place is a classic *monjayaki* restaurant on an alley just off Monja-dōri. Try their speciality, *omu-raisu monja*, for ¥1080. Daily 11am–10pm.

★Ramen Kokugikan ラーメン国技館 5F Aqua City, 1-7-1 Daiba, Minato-ku ☏ 03 3599 4700; Odaiba Kaihin-kōen monorail; map p.87. Six top ramen noodle chefs from around Japan square off against each other in this section of Aqua City's restaurant floor. A bowl will cost you from ¥800 (the Hakata variety, from Fukuoka city, is well worth trying). The outdoor balcony, when it's open, boasts fantastic views across the bay towards Tokyo's twinkling lights. 🛜 Daily 11am–11pm.

★Sushi Bun 鮨文 5 Tsukiji, Chūō-ku ☏ 03 3541 3860; Tsukijishijō station; map p.87. One of the most *gaijin*-friendly options among the rows of sushi stalls within the old Tsukiji fish market. They have an English menu with sets

---

DINING ON THE WATER

Lunch and dinner cruises on **yakatabune**, low-slung traditional boats lit up with paper lanterns, are a charming Tokyo eating institution, dating back to the Edo period. The boats accommodate anything from sixteen to a hundred people on trips along the Sumida-gawa and out on Tokyo Bay. For a bar-like alternative, see *Jicoo* (see p.177).

Amisei あみ清 ☏ 3 3844 1869, ⓦ amisei.com; map p.74. *Amisei* set off from the southwest side of the bridge of Azumabashi, Asakusa. Two-hour evening cruises cost ¥8640, including all the tempura you can eat. More lavish menus can be ordered and, naturally, prices skyrocket for cruises on the night when Asakusa holds its annual fireworks extravaganza in July.

Funasei 船清 ☏ 03 5479 2731, ⓦ www.funasei .com; map pp.106–107. Bay cruises, lasting two and a half hours, run out of Shinagawa and offer a choice of Japanese- and Western-style menus, with unlimited bar access, for around ¥10,800 per person.

14

at ¥2800, though you won't regret spending ¥1000 more for their top-quality ten-piece selection including creamy *uni* (sea urchin). Mon–Sat 6am–2.30pm, but closed during occasional market holidays.

Sushi-zanmai Honten すしざんまい本店 4-11-9 Tsukiji Chūō-ku ☎03 3541 1117; Tsukiji station; map p.87. This pleasantly noisy place is the main, and best, branch of a popular chain of sushi restaurants run by Kimura Kiyoshi, the self-proclaimed "King of Tuna". Filling sushi sets go from ¥1620. Daily 24hr.

CAFÉ

Starbucks スターバックス Venus Fort, Kōtō-ku ☎03 5500 5090; Aomi station; map p.87. Recommending a *Starbucks* might be terribly uncool, but while the coffee here's the same old same old, this Venus Fort branch is nestled into a faux-Italian piazza, sitting under a permanently twilit "sky" like something out of *The Truman Show* – twee, but somehow rather satisfying, especially on a rainy day. ☎ Daily 9.30am–9pm.

AKASAKA AND ROPPONGI

RESTAURANTS

Aux Bacchanales オーバッカナル 2F Ark Mori Building, 1-12-32 Akasaka, Minato-ku ☎03 3582 2225; ⓦauxbacchanales.com; Roppongi-itchōme station; map pp.96–97. Tucked away in the Ark Hills complex, this is one of Tokyo's most authentic Parisian-style brasseries – their steak frites (¥2580) is the real thing – and it's a pleasant spot to hang out sipping coffee or red wine. Pastries start at ¥210, while daily lunch specials of both meat and fish dishes go for under ¥1300. Daily 10am–midnight.

Gonpachi 権八 1-13-11 Nishi-Azabu, Minato-ku ☎03 5771 0170; ⓦgonpachi.jp; Roppongi station; map pp.96–97. A faux-Edo-period storehouse is home to this atmospheric Japanese restaurant. Take your pick between reasonably priced soba (from ¥800) and grilled items (from ¥180) on the ground and second floors, or sushi on the third floor – a full meal will set you back around ¥3000. There's a wonderful samurai drama atmosphere, and it's easy to see how the place inspired the climactic scenes of Quentin Tarantino's *Kill Bill Vol. 1*. Daily 11.30am–3.30am.

★**Kurosawa** 黒澤 2-7-9 Nagatachō, Chiyoda-ku ☎03 3580 9638, ⓦ9638.net/nagata; Tameike-sannō station; map pp.96–97. The design of this atmospheric restaurant was inspired by the sets from Akira Kurosawa's movies *Yojimbo* and *Red Beard*, and a meal here is a superb experience. Given the quality, the lunch prices are a real steal. On entry you'll be asked whether you want to sit in the downstairs soba section (bowls from under ¥800), or head on to the refined upstairs rooms, where you'll have to remove your shoes, for juicy *tonkatsu* cutlet (sets around ¥1300). ☎ Mon–Fri 11.30am–3pm & 5–10pm, Sat noon–9pm.

L'Atelier de Joël Robuchon 2F Roppongi Hills Hillside, 6-10-1 Roppongi, Minato-ku ☎03 5772 7500, ⓦrobuchon.jp; Roppongi station; map pp.96–97. The French master chef has six Tokyo outposts; this one in Roppongi Hills is the best, offering tasting menus starting at ¥3520 for lunch, ¥5720 for dinner. There's a no-bookings policy, so you may have to wait to get a seat at the long counter, facing the open kitchen where black-garbed chefs create culinary mini-masterpieces before your very eyes. ☎ Daily 11.30am–2.30pm & 6–10pm.

Lauderdale ローダデール 6-15-1 Roppongi, Minato-ku ☎03 3405 5533, ⓦlauderdale.co.jp; Roppongi station; map pp.96–97. Top hotels aside, there aren't too many places in Tokyo where you can get as good a Western-style gourmet breakfast as at this super-casual place, which successfully conjures up the stylish South Beach vibe in the midst of Roppongi Hills; try the eggs Benedict for (¥1800) or buttermilk pancakes (¥1400). ☎ Daily 7am–10pm.

Nobu Tokyo 東京 Toranomon Towers Office, 4-1-28 Toranomon, Minato-ku ☎03 5733 0070, ⓦnobu restaurants.com; Kamiyachō station; map pp.96–97. There's a dramatic Japanese-style design for Nobu Matsuhisa's Tokyo operation, where you can sample the famous black-cod dinner (Robert de Niro's favourite) for around ¥4600. For something a bit different, try *tiradito*, *Nobu*'s South American twist on sashimi. Mon–Fri 11.30am–2pm & 6–10.30pm, Sat & Sun 6–10.30pm.

★**Nodaiwa** 野田岩 1-5-4 Higashi-Azabu, Minato-ku ☎03 3583 7852, ⓦnodaiwa.co.jp; Kamiyachō station; map pp.96–97. Kimono-clad waitresses shuffle around this 160-year-old *kura* (storehouse), converted into one of Tokyo's best eel restaurants; a set meal will cost around ¥5000. The private rooms upstairs can only be booked by parties of four or more; if it's busy, they may guide you to the annexe around the corner, which has an almost identical interior. Mon–Sat 11am–1.30pm & 5–8pm.

Roti 1F Piramide Building, 6-6-9 Roppongi, Minato-ku ☎03 5785 3671, ⓦroti.jp; Roppongi station; map pp.96–97. You'd better be hungry before dining at this modern American brasserie, as portions are huge. Their speciality is rotisserie chicken (a half-bird is ¥1900), while many of their other grilled meat dishes could easily feed two. Microbrew beers and a tempting range of desserts are also available. ☎ Mon–Fri 11.30am–3pm & 6–11pm, Sat noon–5pm & 6–11pm, Sun 10am–3pm & 6–10pm

SaamRoa サムロア 2-12-9 Azabu-Jūban, Minato-ku ☎03 5484 3388, ⓦsaamroa.com; Azabu-Jūban station; map pp.96–97. A fine and tempting range of authentic Thai dishes are served at this casual place bedecked with colourful ethnic trinkets. The set lunches are great value (around ¥1000), though also consider the *laa* (a dryish curry made with pork, basil and water spinach; ¥1490). Daily 11.30am–2pm & 5–11pm.

Shunjū 春秋 27F Sannō Park Tower, 2-11-1 Nagatachō, Chiyoda-ku ☎03 3592 5288, ⓦshunju.com; Tameike-sannō station; map pp.96–97. The modern Japanese dining experience *par excellence*, matching stylish interior design with food made from the freshest seasonal ingredients. The ¥1200 lunch deals are good (although the place gets busy with office workers); ¥400 extra gets you a go at the veggie buffet. In the evening it's overpriced, as you can easily spend ¥6000 on a set. Mon–Sat 11.30am–2.30pm & 5–11pm.

Suzunami 鈴波 B1F Galleria, Tokyo Midtown, 9-7-4 Akasaka, Minato-ku ☎03 5413 0335, ⓦsuzunami .co.jp; Roppongi station; map pp.96–97. Try the house speciality at this restaurant, hidden behind a shop in Tokyo Midtown's basement level – silver cod marinated in what's left of the rice mash after it's been used to make sake. Their filling set meals, rounded off with a glass of plum wine, are great value, starting at ¥1300. ⓦ Daily 11am–10pm.

★Tōfuya-Ukai とうふ屋うかい 4-4-13 Shiba-kōen, Minato-ku ☎03 3436 1028, ⓦukai.co.jp; Akabanebashi station; map pp.96–97. At the foot of Tokyo Tower, this stunning re-creation of an Edo-era mansion, incorporating huge beams from an old sake brewery, serves unforgettable tofu-based *kaiseki*-style cuisine. Book well ahead, especially for dinner (at least a month in advance). Set meals only, with lunch from ¥5940 on weekdays, and dinner from ¥10,800. Daily 11am–10pm.

Tokyo Curry Lab 東京カレーラボ 4-2-8 Shiba-kōen, Minato-ku ☎03 5425 2900, ⓦtokyocurrylab.jp; Kamiyachō station; map pp.96–97. Whether you choose to go up Tokyo Tower or not, this super-slick operation at its base is worth checking out for a taste of *tonkatsu* curry, the quintessential local comfort food. Most curries clock in at ¥1100–1500. Plates are shaped so that you can easily get every last grain of rice. ⓦ Daily 11am–10pm.

CAFÉ

Eat More Greens イートモアグリーンズ 2-2-5 Azabu-Jūban, Minato-ku ☎03 3798 3191, ⓦeatmoregreens.jp; Azabu-Jūban station; map pp.96–97. Taking its inspiration from urban US vegetarian cafés and bakeries, this appealing place mixes random pieces of wood furniture, good organic food (¥1000 for a set meal) and a street-side terrace, along with seriously good doughnuts (from ¥220). Quality has dropped slightly since a change of ownership, however, and there are fewer vegan-friendly choices on the menu. Mon–Fri 11am–11pm, Sat & Sun 9am–11pm.

TEAHOUSE

Toraya Café トラヤカフェ Keyakizaka-dōri, 6-12-2 Roppongi, Minato-ku ☎03 5789 9811; Roppongi station; map pp.96–97. Stylish café specializing in Japanese teas and sweets made from azuki beans; figure on over ¥1000 for both the former and the latter. It's usually busy with ladies lunching or sipping tea between boutique visits. Daily 10am–10pm.

14

EBISU, MEGURO AND THE SOUTH

RESTAURANTS

Chano-ma チャノマ 6F Nakameguro Kangyō Building, 1-22-4 Kami-Meguro, Meguro-ku ☎03 3792 9898; Nakameguro station; map pp.106–107. Dining while seated on the floor is not exactly uncommon in Tokyo, but at this casual eatery the dining space is actually a padded, bed-like platform – this is true lounging. (They do also have regular tables.) Overlooking the river in swanky Nakameguro, they serve some very tasty rustic-style Japanese fusion dishes (lunch sets from ¥1000), as well as a great selection of teas and flavoured lattes. Mon–Thurs & Sun noon–2am, Fri & Sat noon–4am.

Ebisu Yokochō 千恵比寿横丁 Ebisu, Minato-ku; Ebisu station; map pp.106–107. Not a restaurant, but a whole clutch of them, crammed into a hugely atmospheric covered arcade east of Ebisu station. Come in the evening and take your pick – there's a curry stand, several noodle joints, places specializing in seafood, and even a miniature karaoke bar. In addition, the venues and the tables in them are arranged in a way that lends itself to mingling. Daily 5pm–late.

Futatsume ふたつめ 3-9-5 Kami-Meguro, Meguro-ku ☎03 3712 2022; Nakameguro station; map pp.106–107. Grand little *kushiage* (deep-fried sticks) place, selling skewered snacks from just ¥100; choices include breaded

BEAUTIFUL BANQUETS

Gourmands will not want to miss the opportunity to sample Japan's finest style of cooking, **kaiseki-ryōri**, while in Tokyo. A *kaiseki* meal consists of a series of small, carefully balanced and beautifully presented dishes, the ingredients reflecting the seasons, served by a waitress in kimono on exquisite china and lacquerware. It began as an accompaniment to the tea ceremony and still retains the meticulous design of that elegant ritual. While a *kaiseki* dinner can easily run to ¥10,000 or more, a *kaiseki* bentō (boxed lunch) is a more affordable option. Apart from recommended restaurants such as *Kakiden* (see p.171) and *Tōfuya-Ukai* (see above), top hotels are the best places for enjoying this style of cuisine.

14

camembert, shiitake and salmon, and they're all best washed down with a gigantic highball (¥980). Mon–Sat 6pm–3am.

Higashiyama 東山 1-21-25 Higashiyama, Meguro-ku ☏ 03 5720 1300, ⓦ higashiyama-tokyo.jp; Nakameguro station; map pp.106–107. An elegant restaurant and bar that's the epitome of Tokyo cool. The multilevel space has an open kitchen that allows you to watch the delicious range of dishes being prepared. The lunchtime "course menus" (see p.154) are just about affordable at ¥3500 (dinner's more like ¥6000), and they have a fine selection of sake and *shōchū* to match. Mon–Sat 11.30am–3pm & 6pm–midnight.

★ Hiroshima Ichiba 広島市場 1-29-12 Aobadai, Meguro-ku ☏ 03 3760 7147; Nakameguro station; map pp.106–107. This chain sells the best *tantan-men* (ramen with a spicy, oily sauce and minced pork; ¥850) in the city, and their delectable *gyoza* (¥310) aren't far off. The attractive Nakameguro branch basically does the simple things really, really well, and every customer walks out rubbing their belly. Daily 11am–2am.

★ Hokkaido 北海道 39F Ebisu Garden Place Tower, 4-20-3 Ebisu, Shibuya-ku ☏ 03 5448 9521; Ebisu station; map pp.106–107. One of the best views in Tokyo, looking out west from the highest tower in Ebisu – Fuji is visible on a clear day. The food is cheap, considering, with the seafood *yakisoba* a steal at ¥890, and rice dishes blanketed with roe for a little more. The ¥500 cocktails make this a surprisingly romantic sunset spot. Daily 11.30am–2.30pm & 4.30–9.30pm.

Homework's 5-1-20 Hiro-o, Shibuya-ku ☏ 03 3444 4560, ⓦ homeworks-1.com; Hiro-o station; map pp.106–107. This popular pit stop at the end of Hiro-o's main shopping street does good, chunky, home-made burgers (from ¥1050) – and the French fries are well up to scratch, too. Mon–Sat 11am–8.30pm, Sun 11am–5.30pm.

★ Iroha Sushi いろは寿司 1-5-13 Kami-Meguro, Meguro-ku ☏ 03 5722 3560, ⓦ irohasushi.com; Nakameguro station; map pp.106–107. Relaxed sushi den that's the diametric opposite of most diners in this fancy part of town – you won't see any hipsters or bohos here, just salary-folk and older locals. Every single piece is freshly made, yet the place remains cheaper than any *kaiten-zushiya*, especially at lunchtime, when huge sets go from just ¥680; the largest is just ¥1050, and will fill almost any belly. Daily 11.30am–2.30pm & 5–10.30pm.

Ivy Place アイヴィプレイス 16-15 Sarugakuchō, Shibuya-ku ☏ 03 6415 3232, ⓦ tysons.jp; Daikanyama station; map pp.106–107. This large, attractive venue is *so* Daikanyama – always full at brunchtime with shopping-bag-toting folk, tucking into buttermilk pancakes (¥1300), eggs with chorizo and potatoes (¥1400) and more. Good coffee, too. Daily 7am–11pm.

Pizzeria da Isa ピッツェリアダイーサ 1-28-9 Aobadai, Minato-ku ☏ 03 5768 3739, ⓦ da-isa.jp; Nakameguro station; map pp.106–107. The Japanese head chef at this authentically Italian-style pizzeria scooped a clutch of awards in Napoli – if he made his mark in the very home of pizza, you can be sure that this is the best you'll find in all Japan. Pizzas go from ¥1500, though note that every diner needs to order one dish and a drink; service is also notoriously uppity. Tues–Sun 11.30am–2pm & 5.30–11pm.

★ Tonki とんき 1-1-2 Shimo-Meguro, Meguro-ku ☏ 03 3491 9928; Meguro station; map pp.106–107. This minimalist, sharp-looking, family-run restaurant – where a seemingly telepathic team create order out of chaos – is the most famous place in town for *tonkatsu*. Expect to have to queue up for a seat at mealtimes. Sets cost from ¥1800, cutlet alone ¥1250. Daily except Tues 4–10.45pm.

CAFÉS

Green Bean to Bar グリーン ビーン トゥ バー 2-16-11 Aobadai, Meguro-ku ☏ 03 5728 6420, ⓦ greenchocolate .jp; Nakameguro station; map pp.106–107. Perhaps the nicest café in the Nakameguro area is this industrial, mint-coloured, streamside affair, which sells delectable hot chocolate (¥600) and extremely expensive bars of single-estate chocolate. Daily except Wed 11am–9pm.

Ice Ouca アイス桜花 1-6-6 Ebisu, Shibuya-ku ☏ 03 5449 0037, ⓦ ice-ouca.com; Ebisu station; map pp.106–107. Small ice-cream café serving delicious scoops (three for ¥400), with interesting flavours ranging from tomato sorbet to pumpkin. Daily noon–11pm.

Irving Place アービングプレイス Adam et Rope Biotop, 4-6-44 Shirokanedai, Minato-ku ☏ 03 5449 7720, ⓦ www.biotop.jp/irvingplace; Shirokanedai station; map pp.106–107. It's worth the trek to visit this out-of-the-way, rustic-chic café-bar, whose lofty location includes a sunny terrace surrounded by greenery, and a charming tree house. As well as good coffee (from ¥600), the lunch sets can be quite inventive – think swordfish and guacamole, or steak and pineapple. Daily 11am–11pm.

Kissa Ginza 喫茶銀座 1-3-9 Ebisu-Minami, Shibuya-ku ☏ 03 3710 7320; Ebisu station; map pp.106–107. The main draw of this place is the retro-cool 1960s-style decor. By day it's a café, serving standard café dishes and drinks (coffees from ¥450), and popular with a slightly older crowd, but in the evening it morphs into a DJ bar complete with glitter ball. Daily 10am–late.

TEAROOM

Ganchabō 岩茶房 3-15-5 Kami-Meguro, Meguro-ku ☏ 03 3714 7425; Nakameguro station; map pp.106–107. Housed in a lovely residential-style building in the backstreets off Yamate-dōri, this place specializes in Chinese teas (¥800–1600), and has some good Chinese food too. Tues–Sun 11am–7pm.

TOKYO FOR VEGETARIANS

It may be the capital of a historically Buddhist nation, but Tokyo is a surprisingly bad place in which to be **vegetarian**. The problem stems from the fact that, although the average Japanese eats far less meat than the average Westerner, vegetarianism is extremely rare here: you might ask for a vegetarian (*saishoku*) dish in a restaurant, and still be served something with meat or fish in it. For example, the popular tofu dish *hiya yakko* (a small slab of chilled tofu topped with grated ginger, spring onions and soy sauce) is usually sprinkled with flakes of *bonito* (dried tuna). If you're a committed vegetarian, things to watch out for include *dashi* stock, which contains *bonito*; breads and cakes, as these can contain lard; and omelettes, which can contain chicken stock.

The good news is that places specializing in vegetarian and vegan food in Tokyo are on the rise. In this chapter, see the reviews for *Bon* (see p.161), *Eat More Greens* (see p.165) and *Hiroba* (see below); in addition, **Vege-Navi** (Ⓦvege-navi.jp) lists many vegetarian, vegan and macrobiotic options.

HARAJUKU, AOYAMA AND SHIBUYA

RESTAURANTS

AtoZ 5F 5-8-3 Minami Aoyama, Shibuya-ku Ⓣ03 5464 0281; Omotesandō station; map pp.114–115. Enter the offbeat world of artist Yoshitomo Nara, whose pieces decorate this impressive café – part art installation, part kindergarten for the art-school set. The food includes tasty salads, noodle and rice dishes – all the things a Japanese mum might cook up – for around ¥1000 a meal. Try the green-tea coconut parfait for dessert. Daily 11.30am–11.30pm.

Bepokah ベポカ 2-17-6 Jingūmae, Shibuya-ku Ⓣ03 6804 1377, Ⓦbepocah.com; Meiji-jingūmae station; map p.116. Given their mutual adoration of raw fish, you'd think that Peruvian cuisine would have a bigger impact in Japan. This is one of the only places in Tokyo in which you'll find quality *ceviche* (dishes from ¥1800), as well as Andean staples such as *lomo saltado* (stir-fried beef on rice; ¥1600) and *aji de gallina* (chicken in an almost curry-like yellow cream; ¥1600). Pricey, but just about worth it. Mon–Fri 6pm–1am, Sat 5pm–midnight.

Commune 246 コミューン２４６ 3-13 Minami-Aoyama, Minato-ku; no phone, Ⓦcommune246.com; Omotesandō station; map p.116. This open-air courtyard space is almost like a boho slice of London, San Francisco or Melbourne – a clutch of small snack shacks selling all sorts, from gourmet hot dogs and burgers to Thai food and ramen. It's also a good drinking spot. Daily 11am–10pm; closed Dec–Feb.

Curry Up 2-35-9 Jingūmae, Shibuya-ku Ⓣ03 5775 5446, Ⓦcurryup.jp; Meiji-jingūmae station; map pp.114–115. Punning name aside, there's not much to dislike about this small but stylish curry canteen where they keep the menu simple and the food hot and spicy. Try their butter chicken (¥800–1200 depending on the size of the portion). Daily 11.30am–9pm (Sun until 8pm).

Ganso Kujiraya 元祖くじら屋 2-9-22 Dōgenzaka, Shibuya-ku Ⓣ03 3461 9145, Ⓦwww.kujiraya.co.jp; Shibuya station; map p.122. Like it or not, the Japanese have eaten whale meat for centuries, and this smart, surprisingly cheap venue is a good option if you'd like to see – and taste – what the fuss is about; if you're curious, it tastes a bit like liver. You may not be able to make head or tail of the menu (though it does feature pictures of the latter), so take a Japanese-speaker along if possible; most dishes are ¥780–980, but it's best visited at lunch when you'll get a hearty set from ¥1000. Mon–Fri 11am–2pm & 5–10.30pm, Sat & Sun 11.30am–11.30pm.

Gonpachi 権八 14F E-Space Tower, 3-6 Maruyama-chō, Shibuya-ku Ⓣ03 5784 2011, Ⓦgonpachi.jp; Shibuya station; map p.122. A sister restaurant to the famous one in Roppongi (see p.164), this fourteenth-floor spot is great for a meal with a view – even Bill Clinton came along once. Under an elegant grid of dangling lamps, sushi dishes go for ¥250 and up; interesting veggie options include okra, ginger and seaweed. Daily 11.30am–2am.

Hanamaru はなまる B1, 2-1 Udagawa-chō, Shibuya-ku Ⓣ03 5428 0870, Ⓦhanamaruudon.com; Shibuya station; map p.122. Simple noodle restaurant which is a touch classier than the bigger chains, and certainly makes tastier food. Their cheapest udon is ¥280, and though nothing's in English, picture menus help out somewhat. Daily 9am–10pm.

Harajuku Gyōzaro 原宿餃子楼 6-2-4 Jingūmae, Shibuya-ku Ⓣ03 3406 4743; Meiji-jingūmae station; map p.116. Though there are few Japanese customers at this atmospheric dumpling spot, the fare on offer is cheap and tasty – just ¥290 for a round of succulent *gyoza*, and ¥250 for cucumber in miso paste (mix some chilli oil into the latter and you'll draw some funny looks, but it tastes great). Daily 11.30am–4am (Sun until 11pm).

Hiroba 広場 B1 3-8-15 Kita-Aoyama, Minato-ku Ⓣ03 3406 6409; Omotesandō station; map p.116. Hearty lunch buffets with plenty of veggie options for ¥1500 are served at this casual operation, attached to the Crayon House natural food shop just off Omotesandō. Daily 11am–10pm.

La Fée Délice ラフェデリース 5-11-13 Jingūmae, Shibuya-ku ☎03 5766 4084, ⓦlafeedelice.com; Meiji-jingūmae station; map p.116. The best of Harajuku's many crêperies – most just plonk a mini Fuji of whipped cream on their creations, but the chefs here have actually trained in France. Sweet and savoury crêpes go for ¥1000 and up. Mon–Sat 11.30am–11pm, Sun 11am–10pm.

Las Chicas ラスチカス 5-47-6 Jingūmae, Shibuya-ku ☎03 3407 6865, ⓦlaschicas.jp; Omotesandō station; map p.116. A green oasis in the backstreets of Harajuku that's always been a winner for its fairy-lit, relaxed ambience. Safest are the burgers and chunky sandwiches (around ¥1400) or eggs Benedict (¥1400); more interesting choices include *feijoada*, a black-bean stew originating in Rio de Janeiro. Daily 11.30am–11pm (Fri & Sat until 11.30pm).

★**Los Barbados** ロスバルバドス 41-26 Udagawachō, Shibuya-ku ☎03 3496 7157; Shibuya station; map p.122. This little *izakaya* is, well, a little different from the norm. Under a large map of the Congo, the Africa-phile owner whips up great food from across the African continent, including Tunisian *brik* (an eggy, flash-fried pastry; ¥850) and Senegambian rice-and-meat staples such as *maafe* and *yassa*. Wash it all down with some Kenya Cane. Mon–Sat noon–11pm.

Maisen まい泉 4-8-5 Jingūmae, Shibuya-ku ☎03 3470 0071, ⓦmai-sen.com; Omotesandō station; map p.116. Located in an old bathhouse, this long-running *tonkatsu* restaurant serves up great-value set meals from ¥1580; prices dip under ¥1000 for lunch. The actual bathhouse bit is the smoking section of the restaurant. Daily 11am–10pm.

Murugi ムルギ 2-29-1 Dōgenzaka, Shibuya-ku ☎03 3462 0241; Shibuya station; map p.122. In the heart of Shibuya's sleazeland, this curry restaurant has been going for decades – since 1951, in fact – perhaps thanks to their distinctive Fuji-shaped rice mounds (actually more like the Matterhorn, but whatever). The curries will set you back ¥1000, and taste just fine; the only problem is that the restaurant is only open for lunch. Daily except Fri 11.30am–3pm.

★**Ramen Nagi** ラーメン凪 1-3-1 Higashi, Shibuya-ku ☎03 3499 0390, ⓦn-nagi.com; Shibuya station; map p.122. At this crazy-busy gourmet ramen joint, the waiter will give you a choice of how soft or hard you'd like your (superb) noodles cooked. There are a few interesting selections available on the fun cross-section menu, including the "Midorio", made with basil and cheese – weird, but it works. More regular varieties are served in a rich broth, topped with delicious pork slices and a heap of chopped spring onions – a bargain at ¥890 a bowl. Mon–Sat 11.30am–4pm & 5pm–4am, Sun noon–2am.

Royal Garden Café 2-1-19 Kita-Aoyama, Minato-ku ☎03 5414 6170, ⓦroyal-gardencafe.com; Gaienmae station; map pp.114–115. With its spacious reclaimed-wood interior, on-site bakery and wraparound terrace

sheltered by an umbrella of ginkgo trees (which look amazing in the autumn), this organic food café at the entrance to Meiji-jingū Outer Garden strikes all the right notes. Good set lunches, including pasta or salad as a main, are ¥1000 during the week; it's around ¥2000 for weekend brunch. Daily 11am–11pm.

★**Sakuratei** さくら亭 3-20-1 Jingūmae, Shibuya-ku ☎03 3479 0039, ⓦsakuratei.co.jp/en; Meiji-jingūmae station; map p.116. Funky, cook-your-own *okonomiyaki*, *monjayaki* and *yakisoba* joint behind the weird and wonderful Design Festa gallery (see p.118). Dishes start at ¥950, and feature some quirky options such as curry or Okinawan ingredients. A good drinks selection means it's a fun place at night. 📶 Daily 11am–11pm.

Solomons ソロモンズ B1F Accorder Jingūmae, 2-31-20 Jingūmae, Shibuya-ku ☎03 6434 9201; Meiji-jingūmae station; map pp.114–115. This stylish basement space is a great lunch spot: ¥1000 will buy you a main (options include pasta, Korean spicy chicken and Okinawan taco-rice), plus a go at the large salad and drink bar. Daily 11.30am–3pm & 6pm–midnight.

Two Rooms 5F AO Building, 3-11-7 Kita-Aoyama, Minato-ku ☎03 3498 0002, ⓦtworooms.jp; Omotesandō station; map p.116. Sophisticated, high-end restaurant featuring a relaxed bar, and a spacious outdoor terrace that provides striking views. Perfectly cooked European food using top-quality Japanese ingredients is enhanced by wonderfully polite service. On Sunday they do a brunch for ¥2950; otherwise lunch sets start at ¥2000, and dinner mains from ¥4000. Restaurant 11.30am–2.30pm & 6–10pm; bar 11.30am–2am (Sun till 10pm).

Uobei 魚べい 2-29-1 Dōgenzaka, Shibuya-ku ☎03 3462 0241; Shibuya station; map p.122. Searingly bright restaurant in which your sushi is ordered by touch screen, then delivered by rail on automated plates – the only humans you see are those who point you to your table and take your cash. Gimmicky, yes, but it's a lot of fun – not to mention cheap, since most plates are ¥108 for two sushi. Daily 11am–midnight.

Zoogunzoo ズーガンズー B1 Aoyama City Building, 2-9-11 Shibuya, Shibuya-ku ☎03 3400 1496, ⓦzoogunzoo.com; Shibuya station; map p.122. The earthy tones and baked mud walls of this narrow basement space conjure up the outback, while the menu also reflects the tastes of Down Under, with Pacific Rim fusion cuisine and an extensive selection of Australian wines. Try dishes such as grilled crocodile, Gorgonzola crostini or kangaroo steak; most are priced in the ¥2000 region. Restaurant Mon–Sat 6–11pm; bar Mon–Sat 6pm–2am.

CAFÉS

★**Big Love** ビッグラヴ 3F Houei Bldg, 2-31-3 Jingūmae, Shibuya-ku ☎03 5775 1315; Harajuku or Meiji-jingūmae stations; map pp.114–115. One of

14

JAPANESE COOKERY COURSES

Learning to cook is currently very popular in Tokyo, with cooking schools setting up shop in big shopping malls. You'll usually need to book well in advance.

ABC Cooking Studio In the basement of Tokyo Midtown ☎03 5413 3476, ⓦwww.abc-cooking .co.jp. Though this school focuses on Japanese students baking Western-style treats such as bread and cake, they have English-speaking instructors on hand to guide you through the basics of Japanese and other Asian cuisines.

Arigato Japan ☎090 6484 9577, ⓦarigatojapan .co.jp. Highly popular dining tours around Japanese markets, helping you to identify all those weird and wonderful Japanese products.

Buddha Bellies ☎03 5716 5751, ⓦbuddha belliestokyo.jimdo.com. Cultivate your own Buddha belly after lessons in making sushi, bentō, udon or even *washoku* (traditional meals) at this foreigner-friendly school.

Mayuko's Little Kitchen ☎080 3502 2005, ⓦmayukoslittlekitchen.com. Learn Japanese home-cooking skills at the home of the eponymous Mayuko, a highly personable local. Options include sushi, bentō and "everyday meals", and guests get a printed recipe sheet and apron to take home.

Tokyo's quirkier cafés, set at the back of a small record store selling a fab collection of indie LPs, CDs and cassette tapes (remember them?) from around the world. They also offer home-baked goods, light meals and a craft beer selection. Mon–Fri noon–10pm, Sat & Sun 1pm–7pm.

Bunbōgu ブンボーグ B1 4-8-1 Jingūmae, Shibuya-ku ☎03 3470 6420; Omotesandō station; map p.116. This quirky space is part-café, part-library and part-stationery store. Those who like to doodle while they sup should note that for a one-off membership fee of ¥700, you'll be given a key that opens the stationery drawers tucked under the tables. Daily 10am–11.30am.

Crisscross クリスクロス 5-7-28 Minami-Aoyama, Minato-ku ☎03 6434 1266; Omotesandō station; map p.116. One of Aoyama's "it" places at the time of writing, selling good coffee (from ¥600) and dessert dishes such as buttermilk pancakes (¥1600). For cheaper eats, pick up something from the adjoining Breadworks bakery. Daily 8am–10pm.

★**Lion** ライオン 2-19-13 Dōgenzaka, Shibuya-ku ☎03 3461 6858; Shibuya station; map p.122. Not the place for animated conversations, this *Addams Family*-style institution set amid the love hotels of Dōgenzaka is where businessmen bunking off work come to appreciate classical music with their coffee (¥500 and up). Seats are arranged to face a pair of enormous speakers. Daily 11am–10.30pm.

L'Occitane 2F Likes Bldg, 2-3-1 Dōgenzaka, Shibuya-ku ☎03 5428 1564; Shibuya station; map p.122. This café above the eponymous cosmetics store has one huge draw – it's a prime viewing spot for Shibuya crossing. Thankfully, the coffee's fine. Daily 10am–9pm.

★**Maidreamin** メイドリーミング B1 30-1 Udagawachō, Shibuya-ku ☎03 6427 8938, ⓦmaidreamin.com; Shibuya station; map p.122. This sci-fi-style maid café (see box, p.160) is an all-out cuteness assault, its glammed-up staff sporting inch-long fake eyelashes and umpteen petticoat layers. The food follows suit – think curry served in heart-shaped rice mounds and burgers cut up to look like teddy bears – and there's also a range of soft and alcoholic drinks. Entry ¥500 per hour, plus you have to make one order from the menu. Mon–Thurs & Sun 1–11pm, Fri & Sat 1pm–5am.

No. 8 Bear Pond No8ベアボンド 1-17-1 Shibuya, Shibuya-ku ☎03 6427 7273; Shibuya station; map p.122. Also known as the "On the Corner" café, this industrial-chic venue is hugely popular with local youth. Coffee costs from ¥500, or a little less if you sit in the entrance and drink from a paper cup. Daily 11.30am–midnight.

Tokyo Snake Center 東京スネークセンター 8F Sanpo-Sogo Building, 6-5-6 Jingūmae, Shibuya-ku ☎03 6427 9912, ⓦsnakecenter.jp; Meiji-jingūmae station; map p.116. One of the better "weird-animal" cafés in Tokyo, and decently priced at ¥1000 entry, including a drink; it's ¥540 more to pet a small snake. Daily except Tues 11am–8pm.

TEAROOM

★**Aoyama Flower Market** 青山フラワーマーケット B1 5-1-2 Aoyama, Minato-ku ☎03 3400 0887, ⓦafm -teahouse; Omotesandō station; map p.116. Yes, it's a flower shop – but one whose heady aromas also permeate a fantastic tea-space, tucked away through a door at the back. They've a good range of herbal and green-tea concoctions on offer in the ¥750 range, though prepare for a half-hour queue on weekends. Daily 11am–8pm.

SHINJUKU AND THE WEST

RESTAURANTS

Asia Yokochō アジア横丁 1-21-1 Kabukichō, Shinjuku-ku, no phone; Seibu-Shinjuku station; map p.126. Chefs and customers from all over Asia gather at this quirky open-air spot, on the rooftop of the Maruhan Building. The atmosphere can be as raucous as at any *yokochō* (see box below), and a poke around the various stalls will reveal everything from Korean meat to Indian curries, via Filipino food and Turkish shishas. Daily noon–late.

J.S. Burgers Café 3F 4-1-7 Shinjuku, Shinjuku-ku ☎ 03 5367 0185, ⓦburgers.journal-standard.jp; Shinjuku station; map p.126. A fab range of home-made chunky burgers, hot dogs and sandwiches are served at this retro-styled café – it's ¥1210 for a bacon-and-egg burger, and ¥1620 for the three-patty monster. ☎ Mon–Fri 11.30am–10pm, Sat 10.30am–10.30pm, Sun 10.30am–9pm.

Kakiden 柿傳 8F Yasuyo Building, 3-37-11 Shinjuku, Shinjuku-ku ☎ 03 3352 5121, ⓦkakiden.com; Shinjuku station; map p.126. One of the best places in Tokyo to sample *kaiseki-ryōri* (see box, p.165). There's a lunch set for ¥4320, but you won't regret investing in the eighteen-course dinner for ¥8640. They also conduct *kaiseki* appreciation classes. Daily 11am–9pm.

Mita-Seimen 三田製麺 1-13-3 Nishi-Shinjuku, Shinjuku-ku ☎ 03 5909 3832; Shinjuku station; map p.126. Illuminated by faux-paper-windows, this attractive joint sells cheap, tasty *tsukemen* (¥730) from its winning location in Nishi-Shinjuku. Daily 11am–2am.

Nakajima 中嶋 3-32-5 Shinjuku, Shinjuku-ku ☎ 03 3356 4534, ⓦshinjyuku-nakajima.com; Shinjuku station; map p.126. At lunch all the delicious dishes served here are made with sardines – they're a bargain at around ¥1000 a set, though not all that filling. For dinner it's worth the expense (over ¥8000 per person) to sample the chef's Kansai *kapo* style of cooking, similar to *kaiseki-ryōri*; after all, it's earned him a Michelin star. Mon–Sat 11.30am–1.45pm & 5.30–8.30pm.

Nanban-tei なんばん亭 2F 2-12-3 Kitazawa, Setagaya-ku ☎ 03 3419 6938, ⓦnanbantei.net; Shimokitazawa station; map p.132. Highly atmospheric *okonomiyaki* restaurant (mains from ¥900) in Shimokitazawa, with lampshades that seem vaguely medieval, latticed windows looking down onto the street, and staff who amble around with cooking utensils in their holsters, like culinary cowboys. Daily 5pm–1am.

New York Grill 52F Park Hyatt Tower, 3-7-1-2 Nishi-Shinjuku ☎ 03 5323 3458, ⓦtokyo.park.hyatt.jp;

Tōchōmae station; map p.126. Sitting pretty on the 52nd floor of the *Park Hyatt*, the *New York Grill* offers great views and Stateside-sized portions – after the ¥6200 buffet lunch you won't need to eat much else all day. Bookings essential. Daily 11.30am–2.30pm & 5.30–10.30pm.

★**Omoide Yokochō** 思い出横丁 1-2-7 Nishi-Shinjuku, Shinjuku-ku; Shinjuku station; map p.126. It's almost pointless recommending specific establishments on this hugely atmospheric *yokochō* alley (see box below) – just stroll along a few times, until you've spied both the food you desire, and a free seat. Most places daily 4pm–midnight.

Suzuya すずや Kabukichō Ichibangai-iriguchi, Shinjuku-ku ☎ 03 3209 4408; Shinjuku station; map p.126. Famous *tonkatsu* restaurant, which first opened just after World War II. Their twist on the breaded pork cutlet dish is to serve it *ochazuke* style (¥1530) – you pour green tea over the meat and rice to make a kind of savoury porridge. Daily 11am–10.30pm.

★**Tsunahachi** つな八 3-31-8 Shinjuku, Shinjuku-ku ☎ 03 3352 1012, ⓦtunahachi.co.jp; Shinjuku station; map p.126. The main branch of the famous tempura restaurant almost always has a queue outside, though you're likely to get seated quickly if you settle for the upstairs rooms away from the frying action (or ask for the nonsmoking section). Everything is freshly made, and even the smallest set (¥1500, including soup, rice and pickles) will fill you up. Daily 11am–10pm.

CAFÉS

Ballon d'Essai バロンデッセ 2-30-11 Kitazawa, Setagaya-ku ☎ 03 6407 0511, ⓦballondessai.com; Shimokitazawa station; map p.132. Most caffeine-hunters in Shimokitazawa make a bee-line to *Bear Pond*, a café that can take up to an hour to enter. Those without the Japanese love of queuing should head instead to this little hipster hidey-hole, which makes equally good coffee, purportedly from a blend of five types of bean – at least take a photo of the artwork before downing your flat white (¥360). ☎ Mon–Fri 11.30am–9pm, Sat & Sun 10.30am–9pm.

YOKOCHŌ

A trip to Tokyo is not complete without a night out at one of the city's many **yokochō**. These market-style areas often focus on food and drink, and many are packed with dozens upon dozens of minuscule eateries. With smoke and steam rising from the open-air "kitchens" (often nothing more than a small grill), they can be hugely photogenic. English-language menus and signage are rare at these places, but many places specialize in a particular type of food, making selection and ordering a simple exercise in walking around and pointing. Almost all stalls will sell beer, as well as sake.

The most famous *yokochō* in Tokyo is Shinjuku's *Omoide Yokochō* (see above); a short distance away, *Asia Yokochō* (see opposite) is an attempt to cram other Asian cuisines into a similar space. However, there are atmospheric *yokochō* all around town – just ask around for the nearest one.

14

Café Comme Ça カフェーコッムサ 5F Five Foxes Building, 3-26-6 Shinjuku, Shinjuku-ku ☏ 03 5367 5551; Shinjuku station; map p.126. On an upper floor of the trendy Five Foxes store, this ideal Shinjuku pit-stop serves delicious cakes (from ¥750, and mostly topped with fruit) against a background of stark concrete surfaces enlivened by paintings of Buddhist deities. Daily noon–8pm.

Calico きゃりこ 6F, 1-16-2 Kabukichō, Shinjuku-ku, ☏ 03 6457 6387, ⊚ catcafe.jp; Shinjuku station; map p.126. A great place to experience the cat café phenomenon (see box, p.160); ¥600 gets you thirty minutes of quality time with some fifty gorgeous kitties. With instructions and menu in English, it's very foreigner friendly, and offers inexpensive drinks and food. No kids under 12 are allowed. Daily 11am–10pm.

Tajimaya 但馬屋 Omoide Yokochō, Shinjuku-ku ☏ 03 3342 0881; Shinjuku station; map p.126. Surprisingly genteel for this ragged area of dining and drinking alleys (see *Omoide Yokochō*, p.171), this elegant café serves quality drinks and cakes on a pretty assortment of china. Coffees from ¥600. Daily 10am–10.30pm.

IKEBUKURO AND THE NORTH

RESTAURANTS

Akiyoshi 秋吉 3-30-4 Nishi-Ikebukuro, Toshima-ku ☏ 03 3982 0601, ⊚ akiyoshi.co.jp; Ikebukuro station; map p.138. Unusually large *yakitori* bar with a good atmosphere and a helpful picture menu. You might have to queue at peak times for the tables, but there's generally space at the counter. Most dishes are around ¥400 for five skewers. Daily 5pm–midnight (Sun until 11pm).

Bakudan ばくだん 1-21-1 Higashi-Ikebukuro, Toshima-ku, no phone; Ikebukuro station; map p.138. Most *takoyaki* booths are much of a muchness, but the name of this place – "bomb" – hints at its super-sized servings. One of its *takoyaki* (octopus balls – ball-shaped snacks of batter filled with minced or diced octopus; from ¥370) is as large as a whole tray of normal-sized octopus balls. A long queue is inevitable, giving you time to choose from toppings such as *yakitori* sauce, *kimchi* and lavered seaweed. Daily 10am–11pm.

Canal Café カナルカフェー 1-9 Kagurazaka, Shinjuku-ku ☏ 03 3260 8068, ⊚ canalcafe.jp; Iidabashi station; map pp.136–137. This is a surprisingly tranquil and appealing waterside spot, particularly romantic at night when the old clapperboard boathouses sparkle with fairy lights, or during the blossom-heavy *sakura* season. The café-restaurant has decent-value pasta and pizza meals (sets from ¥1300); for coffee alone, you can head to the outdoor section, though annoyingly they only serve in paper cups. Tues–Fri 11.30am–11pm, Sat & Sun 11.30am–9.30pm.

Hansarang ハンサラン 2F 1-16-15 Ōkubo, Shinjuku-ku ☏ 03 5292 1161; Shin-Ōkubo station; map pp.136–137. Designed like a Korean farmhouse with wooden beams and intimate booths, this restaurant is a good place to get acquainted with the diversity of Korean cuisine. Various set courses, served with multiple side-dishes (*banchan*) start at ¥1500. Daily 11am–midnight.

★**Isomaru Suisan** 磯丸水産 3-25-10 Nishi-Ikebukuro, Toshima-ku ☏ 03 5953 2585; Ikebukuro station; map p.138. This fantastic seafood *izakaya* is heaving all evening, every evening – in fact, it's so popular that it never shuts. There's no English menu, but there are plenty of pictures and live sea creatures to point at – try their colossal *sazae* (sea snails), or the splendid-value eel on rice (*unadon*; ¥980). Daily 24hr.

Kokoro 心 3-1 Kagurazaka, Shinjuku-ku ☏ 03 3269 4495; Iidabashi station; map pp.136–137. This unassuming restaurant in the popular Kagurazaka area exudes proper style in its retro second-floor dining area. Lunch is cheap (¥890 will get you some sashimi, tempura and six other small dishes), while at dinnertime the sashimi-and-oyster set is insanely affordable at ¥790. Daily 11.30am–2pm & 5–11pm.

Le Bretagne 4-2 Kagurazaka, Shinjuku-ku ☏ 03 3235 3500, ⊚ le-bretagne.com; Iidabashi station; map pp.136–137. Attractive French-run restaurant down a little side-street in Kagurazaka, offering authentic crepes (both sweet and savoury) and buckwheat *galettes* from ¥1080, as well as home-made Breton-style cider. Also serves good coffee. Tues–Sat 11.30am–10.30pm, Sun 11.30am–9pm.

Malaychan 3-22-6 Nishi-Ikebukuro, Toshima-ku ☏ 03 5391 7638, ⊚ www.malaychan-satu.jp; Ikebukuro station; map p.138. Tiny, unpretentious Malay restaurant dishing up decent food, from grilled fish on a banana leaf and *mee goreng* (fried noodles) to winter steamboats (the Malay equivalent of *sukiyaki*). Weekday lunch menus start at ¥850, and in general you'll eat well for under ¥2000. Mon 5–11pm, Tues–Sat 11am–2.30pm & 5–11pm, Sun 11am–11pm.

★**Mutekiya** 無敵家 1-7-1 Minami-Ikebukuro, Toshima-ku ☏ 03 3982 7656, ⊚ mutekiya.com; Ikebukuro station; map p.138. Ramen fans should head straight to this joint, where the queue often stretches a full 40m from the door – don't worry, since it moves along fairly quickly. While you wait you can decide on the size of your helping – bowls start at ¥700 or so – its flavour, and whether you want extra toppings and so forth. It's all delicious. Daily 10.30am–4am.

★**Saemaeul Sikdang** セマウル食堂 1-1-4 Hyakuninchō, Shinjuku-ku ☏ 03 6205 6226; Shin-Ōkubo station; map pp.136–137. This outpost of an authentic Korean chain is by far the best *yakiniku* restaurant in Koreatown. Order some *yeoltan bulgogi* (the meat from

KOREATOWN EATS

There's a point as you walk north from Kabukichō where you'll notice that the Japanese characters on shop signs are matched or replaced by *hangul* – Korean script. Welcome to Tokyo's **Koreatown**, where you can not only pick up the latest CD of hit K-pop boy bands or poster of soap star Bae Yong-joon, but also tuck into excellent Korean cuisine. Apart from *yakiniku* (beef or pork strips sizzled atop a grill at your table), *bibimbap* (rice topped with vegetables, egg and meat) and *kimchi* (the fiery fermented cabbage pickle) there's a vast range of other Korean dishes to sample, including *bindaeddeok* (pancakes made with yellow mung beans); *sundubu* (tofu stews); and *samgyetang* (chicken in a herb and ginseng soup).

For tasty Korean staples, try *Han Sarang* (see opposite); for barbecued meat, *Saemaeul Sikdang* (see opposite) is your best bet. If you fancy sampling Korean rice beer, head to *Maccoli Bar* (see p.182). All of these are near Shin-Ōkubo station, within walking distance of Shinjuku.

14

shabu-shabu without the soup, mixed with spicy paste; ¥880 per portion), and a boiling *doenjang jjigae* (a spicier, chunkier miso soup served with rice; a ¥780 portion will feed two), and watch as the ethnic-Korean staff nonchalantly blanket the rest of your table with free side-dishes. To make things feel even more like Seoul, order a bottle of flavoured *soju* to wash everything down with. Daily 11.30am–2am.

Taishōken 大勝軒 2-42-8 Minami-Ikebukuro, Toshima-ku ☎03 3981 9360; Higashi-Ikebukuro station; map p.138. Diners at this noodle restaurant are arranged almost as if they're praying to the chefs at work in the centre – and, in a sense, they are here to worship. This is the *honten* (head branch) of the eponymous noodle behemoth, and the very birthplace of *tsukemen* – try a bowl here (from ¥700) and you'll notice that the original taste is somewhat more subtle than the fatty broths in vogue these days. Daily except Wed 11am–10pm.

CAFÉS

Nekorobi ねころび 3F Tact TO Bldg, 1-28-1 Higashi-Ikebukuro, Toshima-ku ☎03 6228 0646, ⓦnekorobi.jp; Ikebukuro station; map p.138. This cat café (see box, p.160) has a minimum ¥1100 cover charge for the first hour (¥1300 on weekends), which gets you unlimited drinks and use of internet, Wii or DVD terminals – though most go straight for the cat toys, and a play with their favourite

felines. Daily 11am–10pm.

Swallowtail Café スワロウテイル B1F 3-12-12 Higashi-Ikebukuro, Toshima-ku ⓦbutlers-cafe.jp; Ikebukuro station; map p.138. A "butler café" (see box, p.160) where young guys dressed like Jeeves are the solicitous waiters in a room hung with chandeliers and antique-style furniture. Booking through the (mostly Japanese) website is essential. Expect to spend at least ¥2500 per head. Daily 10.30am–9pm.

Zozoi ゾゾイ 3-22-6 Nishi-Ikebukuro, Toshima-ku ☎03 5396 6676; Ikebukuro station; map p.138. Sheepskin-covered stools and a Beefeater statue are part of the eclectic decor at this small, amiable café offering good coffee (from ¥450), home-made cakes and biscuits, and a pleasant view onto a small park. Daily except Tues noon–8pm.

TEAROOM

Saryō 茶寮 5-9 Kagurazaka, Shinjuku-ku ☎03 3266 0880, ⓦsaryo.jp; Iidabashi station; map pp.136–137. This is the head branch of an ever-growing tearoom chain, of which there are now more than a dozen nationwide; this one has a charming, backstreet setting in Kagurazaka, with outdoor seating on a wooden veranda. As well as good tea (from ¥650), they have yummy strawberry fondue (¥1000) and a variety of ice creams. Mon–Sat 11.30am–11pm, Sun 11.30am–10pm.

STREET-SIDE *IZAKAYA*

Drinking and nightlife

If you thought that Tokyo had more than enough restaurants to last several lifetimes, then take a deep breath before diving into its equally vast and inventive bar scene. Take your pick from a myriad of cocktail bars, pubs and *izakaya* (traditional bars serving food), offering practically any brand of booze from around the world as well as local tipples such as sake and *shōchū* (two clear local spirits), as well as award-winning Japanese whisky. Tokyo is a key destination on the international clubbing scene, too, with big-name overseas DJs regularly jetting in to play alongside talented local mix masters. If you prefer live music, then you'll be happy to hear the city has an incredibly varied appetite for music from all corners of the globe.

Tokyo's drinking establishments range from shoebox-sized bars for regular patrons only to sophisticated cocktail lounges in hotels. The most common type are **izakaya**, which are generally quite large, serve a good range of drinks and food and often have a lively atmosphere. **Chains** include *Kirin City*, Sapporo's *Lions Beer Hall*, identikit Irish bar *The Dubliners* and the faux-Victorian British pub the *Rose & Crown*.

Typically being smoky, cramped, exclusively male and expensive, the appeal of **nomiya** is not immediately apparent. However, the close quarters means you can't help but start chatting with fellow drinking companions and you're sure to be looked after by the bar keeper – usually a genial woman called a *mama-san* (a male owner is called a master). *Nomiya* act like private clubs where regular customers keep a bottle of their favourite tipple behind the counter with their name on it. Many *nomiya* can be found under the tracks at Yūrakuchō (see p.48), along Shinjuku's Omoide Yokochō (see p.171) and Golden Gai (see p.130), and on Nonbei Yokochō, the alley running alongside the train tracks just north of Shibuya station; *gaijin*-friendly ones are listed in this chapter.

Tachinomiya (bars without seats) continue to be popular, with venues serving not just beer and nibbles but also specialist sake, *shōchū* and wines. Café-bars are covered in the "Eating" chapter.

There's a healthy **clubbing** scene in Tokyo, with high-profile international DJs regularly roped in for a spin (and an ever-increasing number of Japanese doing likewise abroad). While Tokyo still plays second fiddle to Ōsaka for **live music**, there's still a fair bit of variety here, while the city's **gay and lesbian scene** is by far the best developed in East Asia.

15

BARS

Tokyo's bars can be a little confusing to the first-time visitor, but you should be able to work things out before too long. One common source of confusion is the **table charge** levied at some places, including almost all *izakaya*; it'll be anything from ¥200 to ¥1000. The small snack you may be served with your first drink is the official justification for the charge, though some places levy one without providing anything extra. If there's live music, you'll often pay for it through a cover charge or higher drink prices.
Opening hours are long, generally from 5pm (often much earlier) until around midnight Sunday to Thursday, extended to 4am on Friday and Saturday. Bars with **wi-fi** are indicated in the guide with a 🛜 symbol. If you're socializing with Japanese it's polite to pour your companions' drinks, and let them pour yours. You can make a **toast** by lifting your glass and saying "*kampai*".

THE IMPERIAL PALACE AND AROUND

Marunouchi House 丸の内ハウス 7F Shin-Marunouchi Bldg, 1-5-1 Maranouchi, Chiyoda-ku ☎03 5218 5100; Tokyo station; map p.42. The best thing about the open-plan space here, with its seven different restaurants and bars, is that you can take your drinks out on to the broad wraparound terrace for great views of Tokyo station and towards the Imperial Palace. Cover charges may apply at night. Daily 11am–4am (Sun until 11pm).

Old Imperial Bar Imperial Hotel, 1-1-1 Uchisaiwaichō, Chiyoda-ku ☎03 3539 8088, ⓦ www.imperialhotel .co.jp; Hibiya station; map p.42. All that remains in Tokyo of Frank Lloyd Wright's Art Deco *Imperial Hotel* (see p.144) is this re-created bar. Try its signature Mount Fuji cocktail (¥1630), a wickedly sweet blend of gin, cream, egg white and sugar syrup with a cherry on top, which was invented here in 1924. While you sip it, ask to see the photo albums of how the hotel once looked. Smart attire recommended. 🛜 Daily 11.30am–midnight.

★**Shin Hi No Moto** 新日の基 2-4-4 Yūrakuchō, Chiyoda-ku ☎03 3214 8021; Yūrakuchō or Hibiya stations; map p.42. Known to all and sundry as "Andy's", this is a lively English-owned *izakaya* under the tracks

just south of Yūrakuchō station. Reservations essential. Mon–Sat 5pm–midnight.

GINZA AND AROUND

300 Bar 300円バー B1 Fazenda Building, 5-9-11 Ginza, Chūō-ku ☎03 3572 6300; Ginza station; map p.52. The bargain-basement face of Ginza is this unusually large standing-only bar, where all food and drinks are ¥315; although you have to buy two food/drink tickets to enter, it'd be cheap by the standards of rural Japan, let alone Ginza. Daily 5pm–2am (Sun until 11pm).

Dry Dock ドライドック 3-25-10 Shimbashi, Minato-ku ☎03 5777 4755; Shimbashi station; map p.52. Cosy craft-beer bar with a nautical theme nestling beneath the train tracks. Its no-smoking policy is a welcome change, and patrons often spill outside to enjoy the regularly changing menu of Japanese and overseas microbrews. Note there's no food served on Saturday. Mon–Fri 5pm–midnight, Sat 5pm–10pm.

Lion ライオン 7-9-20 Ginza, Chūō-ku ☎03 3571 2590; Ginza station; map p.52. Opened in 1934, this flagship beer hall of the Sapporo chain is a rather baronial place, with dark tiles and mock wood panelling. As well as good

TOKYO'S TOP PLACES TO DRINK

Best for cheapskates 300 Bar, Coins Bar
and Gas Panic (see p.175, p.178 & p.183)

Best for Art Deco stylings Old Imperial Bar
(see p.175)

Best for a sake education Bunka Hostel
(see below) and Buri (see p.178)

Best for views Bar Six (see below)

Best for events Pink Cow (see opposite)

Best for microbrewed beer Nakameguro
Taproom (see p.178) and Campion Ale
(see below)

Best for Japanese whisky Cask Strength
(see opposite)

Best for weirdness value The Lockup
(see p.180)

Best club Ageha (see p.182)

Best gay venue Arty Farty (see p.186)

15

draught beer (giant ones ¥1080), there are sausages, sauerkraut and other German snacks on offer alongside international pub grub, and a restaurant upstairs. You'll find other branches scattered around Tokyo, all using the same formula. 🛜 Daily 11.30am–11pm (Sun until 10.30pm).

AKIHABARA AND AROUND

Hitachino Brewing Lab 常陸野ブルーイングラボ mAAch-Ecute Building, 1-25-4 Kanda-Sudachō, Chiyoda-ku ☎ 03 3254 3434, 🌐 hitachino.cc; Akihabara station; map p.59. One of Tokyo's most attractive microbreweries, serving Hitachino's famous Nest ale and another eight varieties on tap, as displayed in a beer-rainbow array of test tubes. Try a taster set for ¥880. Mon–Sat 11am–11pm, Sun 11am–9pm.

UENO AND AROUND

★Kadokura カドクラ 6-13-1 Ueno, Taitō-ku ☎ 03 3832 5335; Ueno station; map p.65. Bustling tachinomiya that usually gets boisterous even before office kicking-out time – a great place to make new friends over a freezing beer or highball (from ¥400). Daily 10am–11pm.

Warrior Celt ウォリアーケルト 3F Ito Building, 6-9-22 Ueno ☎ 03 3836 8588, 🌐 warriorcelt.jp; Ueno station; map p.65. Occasionally wild bar whose regulars are led on by a veritable United Nations of bar staff. Key ingredients include a fine range of beers, good food, a nightly happy hour (5–7pm), live bands and, last but not least, "Ladies Night" on Thursdays (cocktails ¥500 for female customers). 🛜 Mon–Thurs 5pm–midnight, Fri & Sat 5pm–5am.

ASAKUSA

Bar Six バー6 6F 2-34-3 Asakusa, Taitō-ku ☎ 03 5806 5106; Asakusa station; map p.74. Sophisticated watering hole on the sixth floor of the Amuse Museum complex (see p.77), surrounded by a standing-only outdoor terrace. The Asakusa views are amazing, especially of Sensō-ji, which is illuminated at night. Give the "Asakusa" mojitos a whizz. Tues–Sun 6pm–2am.

★Bunka Hostel ブンカホステル 1-13-5 Asakusa,

Taitō-ku ☎ 03 5806 3444, 🌐 bunkahostel.jp; Asakusa station; map p.74. The lobby of this excellent hostel (see p.150) doubles as a bar, as stylish as any in the area – the wall of Bunka-labelled sake jars behind the bar is extremely photogenic. They've more than thirty varieties of sake on offer, with the type (dry, sweet, strong, etc) explained on the English-language menu – a perfect place in which to get acquainted with Japan's most traditional drink. 🛜 Tues–Sun 6pm–2am.

★Campion Ale カンピオンエール 2-2-2 Nishi-Asakusa, Taitō-ku ☎ 03 6231 6554, 🌐 campionale.com; Tawaramachi station; map p.74. Brew-pubs are ten-a-penny in Tokyo these days, but this one stands out from the pack: not only is it ideally located for the Asakusa backpacker and tourist crowds, it's British-owned, and serves suitably authentic ales (usually 15 on tap) and hearty pub dishes. Mon–Fri 5–11.30pm, Sat & Sun noon–11.30pm.

Gin Maku Roku 銀幕ロック 2F 1-41-5 Asakusa ☎ 03 5828 6969; Asakusa or Tawaramachi stations; map p.74. The Asakusa spirit is alive and kicking in this intimate, backstreet bar, festooned with homely bric-a-brac and full of colourful characters. A stage is squeezed in for the occasional gig (around ¥1000), which could feature anything from rockabilly to Balkan gypsy music. Daily 9pm–5am.

Ichimon 一文 3-12-6 Asakusa, Taitō-ku ☎ 03 3875 6800; Tawaramachi station; map p.74. Traditional izakaya with a cosy atmosphere, specializing in various types of sake and dishes made with a range of unusual meats, including ostrich, turtle, crocodile and (ethics alert) whale. Payment is by wooden tokens, which you purchase on entering. Tues–Sun 3pm–2am.

Kamiya 神谷 1-1-1 Asakusa, Taitō-ku ☎ 03 3841 5400; Asakusa station; map p.74. Established in 1880, this was Tokyo's first Western-style bar. It's famous for its Denki Bran ("electric brandy" – a mix of gin, wine, Curaçao and brandy), invented in 1883. It's a potent tipple (and just ¥270 a shot), though they also make a "weaker" version. It's a restaurant of sorts, so choose the lively ground floor if you're only after a drink; pay for your first round as you enter. Daily except Tues 11.30am–10pm.

BAYSIDE TOKYO

Jicoo ジコー **☎**0120 049490, **ⓦ**jicoofloatingbar.com; Hinode station; map p.87. This night-time persona of the futuristic ferry *Himiko* (see p.24) shuttles between Hinode, under the Rainbow Bridge, and Odaiba. To board costs ¥2600 (it takes half an hour from point to point, but you can stay on as long as you like), drinks run from ¥700 and there's a DJ playing so you can take to the illuminated dancefloor and show off your best John Travolta moves. Daily 8am–11pm.

AKASAKA AND ROPPONGI

A971 Tokyo Midtown, 9-7-3 Akasaka, Minato-ku **☎**03 5413 3210; Roppongi station; map pp.96–97. This relaxed café-bar and restaurant at the front of the Midtown complex, with mid-twentieth-century modernist furnishings, has proved itself a popular hangout with the area's many expats. **⌁** Mon–Thurs 10am–2am, Fri & Sat 10am–5am, Sun 10am–midnight.

★Cask Strength B1 3-9-11 Roppongi, Minato-ku **☎**03 6432 9772, **ⓦ**cask-s.com; Roppongi station; map pp.96–97. Attractive basement venue with one of Tokyo's best selections of whisky, including some rare Japanese choices – those with a nose for Karuizawa or Yamazaki Single Malt will be in paradise. Daily 6pm–late.

Hobgoblin ホップゴブリン Aoba Roppongi Building, 3-16-33 Roppongi, Minato-ku **☎**03 3568 1280, **ⓦ**hobgoblin.jp; Roppongi station; map pp.96–97. British microbrewery Wychwood serves up its fine ales at this spacious bar where you'll be part of a very boozy, noisy crowd of *gaijin* at weekends and on nights when sport

events are shown on the big-screen TVs. A plus is the very comforting English pub-style food, including shepherd's pie (¥1200) and fish and chips (¥1500). **⌁** Mon–Fri 5pm–late, Sat & Sun noon–late.

Pink Cow ピンクカーウ B1 5-5-1 Roppongi, Minato-ku **☎**03 6434 5773, **ⓦ**thepinkcow.com; Roppongi station; map pp.96–97. There's always something interesting going on – book readings, art classes, comedy improv nights – at this funky haven for local artists and writers. It stocks a good range of imported wines and has tasty Tex-Mex-style food; mains start at ¥1180. Daily 5pm–late.

Public Six 6-8-22 Roppongi, Minato-ku **☎**03 5413 3182, **ⓦ**bagus-99.com; Roppongi station; map pp.96–97. This new gastropub boasts a truly zany exterior, and has become popular as a place to watch sports over some good food and drink. Food is generally Western in nature, though often with Japanese flourishes; drinks-wise, they have at least six craft beers on tap, as well as house cocktails, and plenty of varieties of sake. Mon–Sat 5pm–5am, Sun 5pm–3am.

Tusk タスク 1F Roppongi Hills West Walk, 6-10-1 Roppongi, Minato-ku **☎**03 3478 9991, **ⓦ**tuskbar.jp; Roppongi station; map pp.96–97. One of Roppongi's most popular hangout spots, this swanky DJ bar isn't all that pricey, considering the location. Order your cocktail or tequila (all around ¥1500) from the 10m-long bar, and throw it back under the gaze of two whopping paintings. **⌁** Daily 5pm–5am (Sun to midnight).

Warayakiya わらやき屋 6-8-8 Roppongi, Minato-ku **☎**03 5410 5560; Roppongi station; map pp.96–97. Appealingly gloomy *izakaya* that looks like it was pieced

15

JAPANESE BEER

American brewer William Copeland set up Japan's first brewery in Yokohama in 1870 to serve fellow expats streaming into the country in the wake of the Meiji Restoration. Back then the Japanese had to be bribed to drink beer, but these days they need no such encouragement, knocking back a whopping **5.5 billion litres** of the stuff a year – almost 60 litres per adult.

Copeland's brewery eventually became **Kirin**, now one of Japan's big four brewers along with **Asahi**, **Sapporo** and **Suntory**. All turn out a range of lagers and dark beers, as well as low-malt beers called *happōshu*, and no-malt varieties called *dai-san-no-biiru*, which are popular because of their lower price (the higher the malt content, the higher the government tax), even if they generally taste insipid. Some of the standard cans and bottles are **design classics**, among them Kirin Ichiban, Asahi Super Dry and a couple of the Sapporo beers; beautiful seasonal additions to the cans and bottles feature the likes of snowflakes, red leaves or *sakura* flowers.

Standard-size **cans** of beer cost around ¥150 from convenience stores, while **bottles** (*bin-biiru*) usually start at ¥500 in restaurants and bars. **Draught beer** (*nama-biiru*) is sometimes available and, in beer halls, will be served in a *jokki*, a mug-like glass which comes in three sizes: *dai* (big), *chū* (medium) and *shō* (small).

An increasing number of Tokyo bars – try *Campion Ale* (see see opposite), *Dry Dock* (see p.175), *Nakameguro Taproom* (see p.178) and the *Hitachino Brewing Lab* (see opposite) for starters – serve **microbrew craft beers** from around Japan (sometimes called *ji-biiru* – "regional beer"). Most of these ales have way more character than the products of the big four, though prices are not cheap – figure on ¥1000 for a half-litre at most establishments. For more information on the craft-beer scene there's the bilingual free magazine *The Japan Beer Times* (**ⓦ**japanbeertimes.com) and the blog *Beer in Japan* (**ⓦ**beerinjapan.com).

SUMMER BEER GARDENS

Helping to mitigate Tokyo's sticky summers are the **outdoor beer gardens** that sprout around the city from late May through to early September, typically on the roofs of department stores such as Tobu in Ikebukuro, or in street-level gardens and plazas. A couple of the best beer gardens can be found in Meiji-Jingū's Outer Garden close to Shinanomachi station; try the *Forest Beer Garden* (see below) or *Sekirei* (see p.181). **Rooftop bars** are also very pleasing places to drink in warm months; *Xex* (see below) is a good option.

together from a fallen-down temple. As well as reasonable fish and meat dishes, it serves a full range of drinks, including some rare chestnut *shōchū*. Daily 5pm–5am (Sun until 11pm).

EBISU, MEGURO AND THE SOUTH

★ **Baja** バハ 1-16-12 Kami-Meguro, Meguro-ku, no phone; Nakameguro station; map pp.106–107. Seemingly decorated with everything the owner could find in his garage, this is one of the most entertaining bars in the Nakameguro area, with a good mix of foreigners and oddball Japanese. Drinks (including cocktails) cost ¥500; no tax, no table charge, cool music, and they also whip up yummy tacos – a winner. Daily 5pm–5am.

★ **Buri** ぶり 1-14-1 Ebisu-nishi, Shibuya-ku ☎ 03 3496 7744; Ebisu station; map pp.106–107. A great range of chilled "one-cup sake" (a sealed glass, the size of a small can, ready filled with sake that you just pull the top off; ¥800) is the speciality at this trendy *tachinomiya* that's one of the best in town. Good *yakitori*, too, and just wait until you see the toilet door. Daily 3pm–midnight.

Dagashi 駄菓子 1-13-7 Ebisu-Nishi, Shibuya-ku ☎ 03 5458 5150; Ebisu station; map pp.106–107. Sweet-toothed customers will be in heaven at this fun *izakaya*, which is festooned with baskets of all-you-can-eat candies which patrons can dip into for free. It's trying its best to be old school, right down to the antique bus sign sitting outside – it works, too, as do the reasonable prices. Daily 5pm–2am.

Footnik フットニック 1F Asahi Building, 1-11-2 Ebisu, Shibuya-ku ☎ 03 5795 0144, ⊛ footnik.net; Ebisu station; map pp.106–107. A bar devoted to soccer, with a game or two on the big screen every night, pints of imported beer for ¥1000 or so, and reasonable food. For popular matches you'll have to pay an entry charge. 📶 Daily 3pm–1am, later at weekends.

★ **Nakameguro Taproom** 中目黒タップルーム GT Plaza C-Block 2F, 2-1-3 Kami-Meguro, Meguro-ku ☎ 03 5768 3025, ⊛ bairdbeer.com; Nakameguro station; map pp.106–107. This sleek real-ale nirvana serves beers (¥1000) from Baird Brewing Company, which started life out west in Numazu, on the Izu Peninsula (see map, p.212). It also serves good food, and gets nice and busy on weekends. 📶 Mon–Fri 5pm–midnight, Sat & Sun noon–midnight.

Spring Valley Brewery スプリングバレーブルワリー 13-1 Daikanyama, Shibuya-ku ☎ 03 6416 4960; Daikanyama station; map pp.106–107. Owned by Kirin, one of the most famous beer names in Japan, this large brew-pub – part of the new Log Road development – produces ales far better than the cans of Kirin Ichiban you'll find at the 7-Eleven. You can try samples of six ales for ¥1000, then go for a large glass of your favourite. Mon–Sat 8am–midnight, Sun 8am–10pm.

Xex 3F La Fuente, 11-1 Sarugaku-chō, Shibuya-ku ☎ 03 3476 065, ⊛ xexgroup.jp; Daikanyama station; map pp.106–107. This sleek rooftop bar is more like something you'd expect to find in Southeast Asia than Tokyo, with loungey seating dotted around a small pool. Pizza and sushi are on offer to augment the wine selection, and there's occasional live jazz. Mon–Fri 5.30pm–4am, Sat & Sun 5.30pm–midnight.

HARAJUKU, AOYAMA AND SHIBUYA

Coins Bar コインズバー B1 Noa Shibuya Building, 36-2 Udagawa-chō, Shibuya-ku ☎ 03 3463 3039; Shibuya station; map p.122. This cool little basement bar offers most drinks for ¥320, making it a top choice if you're on a budget. Music is usually hip-hop and r'n'b, despite the soul vinyl covers dotting the place; they also bring in DJs most weekends, when there's a ¥300 entry fee. Daily 4pm–12.30am, later at weekends.

Cozmo's Café & Bar コスモス 1-6-3 Shibuya, Shibuya-ku ☎ 03 3407 5166, http://bit.ly/2gE190x; Shibuya station; map p.122. Gloomy in a way that's actually rather appealing, this café-bar hosts an interesting series of events, detailed on their Facebook page. Tues–Sun 5pm–midnight, often later on weekends.

★ **Fight Club 428** ファイトクラブ428 2-27-2 Dōgenzaka, Shibuya-ku ☎ 03 3464 1799; Shibuya station; map p.122. Of Shibuya's array of weird bars, this is one of the oddest – part of a fitness centre, the bar itself is set right next to a functional kickboxing cage. You can spar there yourself for ¥1000, though staff will only allow you to do this before your drink (most priced at ¥500). Mon–Thurs 6pm–midnight, Fri & Sat 6pm–5am, Sun noon–6pm.

Forest Beer Garden 森のビアガーデン 14-13 Kasumigaoka-Machi, Minato-ku ☎ 03 5411 3715; Shinanomachi station; map pp.114–115. This open-air beer garden, fronting the Meiji Kinenkan wedding hall,

offers an eat-and-drink-all-you-can deal (*tabi-nomi-hōdai*) for men (¥4200) and women (¥3900). June–Sept only: Mon–Fri 5pm–10pm, Sat & Sun noon–10pm.

Fujiya Honten 富士屋本店 2-3 Sakuragaoka-chō, Shibuya-ku ☎03 3461 2128; Shibuya station; map p.122. No-frills, good-value standing bar with some fifty different wines on offer from as little as ¥1600 a bottle, and a dozen by the glass at ¥500. Daily noon–midnight.

★**Goodbeer Faucets** グッドビアフォーセツ 2F 1-29-1 Shoto, Shibuya-ku ☎03 3770 5544, ⓦgoodbeerfaucets .jp; Shibuya station; map p.122. An excellent place for craft beer, selling over forty varieties on draught – some made by the Goodbeer brewery, others from across Japan and abroad. Large glasses of the good stuff cost ¥750–1300, with ¥200 off during happy hour (Mon–Thurs 5–8pm, Sun 1–7pm). 📶 Mon–Thurs 5pm–midnight, Fri 5pm–3am, Sat & Sun 1pm–midnight.

Hasegawa-Saketen はせがわ酒店 3F Omotesandō Hills, 4-12-10 Jingūmae Shibuya-ku ☎03 5785 0833, ⓦhasegawasaketen.com; Omotesandō station; map p.116. The standing bar at this classy retail sake shop allows you to sample various rice wines from boutique breweries around the country before buying a bottle. Daily 11am–10pm.

Legato レガート 15F E-Space Tower, 3-6 Maruyama-chō, Shibuya-ku ☎03 5784 2121, ⓦlegato-tokyo.jp; Shibuya station; map p.122. This fancy Italian restaurant offers a memorable floor-to-ceiling view over Shibuya from fifteen floors up. Wines from ¥1000 a glass. Daily 11.30am–2pm & 5.30pm–midnight (Fri & Sat until 4am).

★**The Lockup** ザロックアップ B1 33-1 Udagawachō, Shibuya-ku ☎03 5728 7731; Shibuya station; map p.122. The house-of-horrors-style entrance is so dark it's a trip merely walking into this bar, the best of a small chain of prison-themed establishments. Make it through and you'll be handcuffed then led to a cell-like room where you can take your pick of weird cocktails: some arrive in test tubes; others have fake eyeballs inside. Periodically, the lights dim and staff try their best to terrify customers – brilliant fun, believe it or not. Mon–Thurs 5pm–1am, Fri & Sat 5pm–5am, Sun 5pm–midnight.

Montoak モントオーク 6-1-9 Jingūmae, Shibuya-ku ☎03 5468 5928; Meiji-jingūmae station; map p.116. Stylish but rather snooty café-bar which faces Harajuku's famous shopping street, with no sign whatsoever – look for the large glass facade. DJs create a suitable loungey vibe, and there's live music sometimes at weekends. Daily 11am–3am.

SAKE AND SHŌCHŪ

It's said that Japan's ancient deities brewed **sake** from the first rice of the new year. Over ten thousand different brands of the clean-tasting rice wine (also known as *nihonshu*) are now produced across Japan by some two thousand breweries. Pronounced more like "sah-kay" than the "sah-kee" Westerners usually go for, sake primarily comes in sweet (*amakuchi*) and dry (*karakuchi*) varieties. Some types are cloudier and less refined than others, while a few are aged. If you're after the best quality, take a look at bottles labelled *ginjō-zukuri* (or *ginjō-zō*), the most expensive and rare of the *junmai-shu* pure rice sake.

In restaurants and *izakaya* you'll have the choice of drinking sake warm (*atsukan*), with water (*mizu*), iced (*rokku*) or cold (*reishu*). Drinking it cold will enable you to properly taste the wine's complex flavours; you should never drink fine premium sake warm. Warm sake is always served in a small flask (*tokkuri*), but cold sake is sometimes poured directly from a large bottle into a small wooden box (*masu*), with a smidgen of salt on the rim to counter the slightly sweet taste. Glasses are traditionally filled right to the brim and often placed on a saucer to catch any overflow; they're generally small because, with an alcohol content of fifteen percent or more, sake is a strong drink – note that it goes to your head even more quickly if drunk warm. For more on sake, check out the books and informative website (ⓦsake-world.com) of long-time resident expert John Gautner.

Shōchū is another clear spirit that is generally stronger and more flavoursome than sake – with an alcohol content of anything from twenty to fifty percent, it's no surprise that some call it "white lightning". Served in the same variety of ways as sake, it can be made from many different ingredients, all with their own particular taste: ask your bartender for sweet potato (*imo*), brown sugar (*kurozatō*), rice (*kome*), barley (*mugi*) or the nettle-like perilla leaf (*shiso*). The best is said to come from Kagoshima and Miyazaki prefectures, both in the far south of Japan on the island of Kyūshū; non-purists mix it with lemon sour, or even oolong tea.

Glasses of sake and *shōchū* tend to **cost** from ¥350 at cheaper **bars and restaurants**, though they can easily start at double that at regular bars; at places selling premium varieties, the prices rise higher still. If you want to drink on the cheap, try a **convenience store**, which all sell large (and usually extremely beautiful) bottles of both sake and *shōchū* from around ¥900; sake also comes in jar-like "cups" from ¥200, and even in carton form from ¥100.

KARAOKE BARS AND BOXES

Legend has it that **karaoke**, literally translated as "empty orchestra", was invented by an Ōsaka record-store manager in the early 1970s. Today the mainstay of this ¥1 trillion-a-year business are **karaoke boxes** – buildings packed with comfy booths kitted out with a karaoke system. Rental of these boxes is by the hour and they have proved particularly popular with youngsters, women and families, who prefer them to the smoky bars frequented by salarymen that were the original preserve of karaoke.

You'll find branches of the biggest chains – *Karaoke-kan*, *Shidax* and *Big Echo* – all over the city; the charge is typically ¥800 per person per hour, but some independent bars are cheaper. There are always plenty of English-language songs to butcher, although it certainly helps to have a Japanese-speaker on hand to operate the karaoke system. Almost all venues serve alcohol, and many have drink-all-you-can (*nomi-hōdai*) specials; two hours of booze costs ¥3000 or so, plus the actual singing fee, and as a rule of thumb these deals usually work out cheaper if you're planning to have four or more drinks. If you're a first-timer, alcohol certainly helps to ease things along – those who are too shy to sing at the beginning of a session often end up hogging the microphone all night long.

15

Big Echo ビッグエコー 4-2-14 Ginza, Chūō-ku ☎ 03 3563 5100; Ginza station; map p.52. The most appealing branch of this major chain, with a few interesting themed rooms, including a Hello Kitty one. From ¥850 per person, with a minimum order of one drink. Daily 24hr.

Fiesta フィエスタ B1 6-2-35 Roppongi, Minato-ku ☎ 03 5410 3008, ⓦ fiesta-roppongi.com; Roppongi station; map pp.96–97. A particularly good karaoke bar for newbie *gaijin*, offering thousands of songs in English, as well as several other languages – 26,000

hits, in all. ¥3500 including three drinks. Mon 7pm–midnight, Tues–Sat until 5am.

Karaoke-kan カラオケ館 30-8 Udagawachō, Shibuya-ku ☎ 03 3462 0785; Shibuya station; map p.122. Japan's premier karaoke-box operator has branches liberally peppered across the capital. Rooms 601 and 602 in their Udagawachō branch were featured in the movie *Lost in Translation*. An hour of karaoke here costs from ¥900 per person, with a minimum order of one drink. Daily 24hr.

Office オフィス 5F 2-7-18 Kita-Aoyama, Minato-ku ☎ 03 5788 1052; Gaienmae station; map pp.114–115. A bar for those who don't really want to leave work: here you can huddle round the photocopier and knock back the booze (beers ¥800) without your boss raising their eyebrows. At ground level in the same building is its sister café-bar *Sign*, where a DJ keeps punters grooving along nicely. Mon–Sat 7pm–3am.

Red Bar レッドバー 1-12-22 Shibuya, Shibuya-ku; Shibuya station; map p.122. Tucked around the corner from Shibuya's main post office is this tiny Ali Baba's cave, hung with chandeliers and lamps. It can be cliquey, but at 3am, when it hits its stride, that hardly seems to matter. Most drinks ¥700. Daily 8pm–late.

Sekirei 鶺鴒 2-2-23 Moto-Akasaka, Minato-ku ☎ 03 3403 1171, ⓦ meijikinenkan.gr.jp; Shinanomachi station; map pp.114–115. Inside the Meiji Kinenkan wedding hall complex, this swanky bar overlooks a floodlit garden where classical Japanese dance (Nihon Buyō) is performed nightly at around 8pm. June–Sept only: Mon–Sat 4.30–10.30pm, Sun 5.30–10.30pm.

SHINJUKU AND THE WEST

Brooklyn Parlour ブルックリンパーラー B1 Shinjuku Marui Annex, 3-1-26 Shinjuku ☎ 03 6457 7763, ⓦ brooklynparlor.co.jp; Shinjuku-sanchōme station;

map p.126. Pleasant New York-themed bar and jazz basement venue, serving amber ales from Brooklyn Brewery, original *chai* cocktails, and deli-style sandwiches and burgers. Daily 11.30am–11.30pm.

Champion チャンピオン Golden Gai, off Shiki-no-michi; Shinjuku-sanchōme station; map p.126. At the western entrance to the Golden Gai stretch (see p.130), this is the largest bar in the area. There's no cover charge and most drinks are a bargain ¥500 – some even less. The catch? You have to endure tone-deaf patrons crooning karaoke for ¥100 a song. Mon–Sat 6pm–6am.

Hair of the Dogs ヘアオヴザドッグ 1st Street, Golden Gai; Shinjuku-sanchōme station; map p.126. Punk rockers will get a kick from this tiny bar, whose location in Golden Gai (see p.130) is indicated by a Sex Pistols poster on the door and a thudding soundtrack of rebellious music inside. Cover charge ¥800. Mon–Sat 6pm–4am.

Kushikatsu Dengana 串かつでんがな 1-11-1 Kabukichō, Shinjuku-ku ☎ 03 3209 011; Seibu-Shinjuku station; map p.126. A good, unpretentious place for cheap fried *kushiage* sticks, a beer or three, and a chat with whoever's sat next to you. Daily 6pm–3am.

★Shisha シーシャ 3-30-3 Kitazawa, Setagaya-ku ☎ 03 3468 0601; Shimokitazawa station; map p.132. This tiny, loungey Shimokitazawa bar has perhaps the city's cheapest shisha (from ¥800 per person), with a wide range of flavours to choose from. Drop by before 5pm and you can have a drink for an extra ¥100 – they're usually affordable at ¥400, in any case. Daily 2pm–3am or so.

Square スクエーア 2F 3rd Street, Golden Gai; Shinjuku-sanchōme station; map p.126. Cute, squashed little upper-floor bar in Golden Gai (see p.130) with cheery staff, cheery customers, decent drinks, and some dangerous-looking bras on the wall. Look out for the blue sign, which is, ironically, a circle. Cover charge ¥500. Mon–Sat 6pm–4am.

Vagabond ヴァガボンド 1-4-20 Nishi-Shinjuku, Shinjuku-ku ☎03 3348 9109; Shinjuku station; map p.126. A local institution, with jazz pianists who tinkle the ivories every night and colourful art plastered on the walls. There's a ¥500 cover charge. Also has a downstairs bar, without live music. Daily 5–11.30pm.

Zoetrope ゾートロープ 7-10-14 Nishi-Shinjuku, Shinjuku-ku ☎03 3363 0162; Seibu-Shinjuku station; map p.126. The most vaunted whisky bar in the Shinjuku area, with umpteen varieties of foreign and Japanese scotch and single malts (if rather unfriendly management). Mon–Sat Sun 7pm–4am.

IKEBUKURO AND THE NORTH

Maccoli Bar マコリバー 1-5-24 Hyakunin-chō, Shinjuku-ku ☎03 6380 3487; Shin-Ōkubo station; map pp.136–137. *Makgeolli* (incorrectly Romanized in this bar's name) is a milky-coloured Korean rice beer with a growing following in Japan – it tastes like drinking yoghurt with a mild alcoholic kick. At this tiny, but stylish, Koreatown bar, you can sample it straight (it's only 6 percent ABV), or mixed with various fruits (around ¥2000 per bottle). Daily 6pm–late.

CLUBS

The Tokyo **clubbing** scene took a turn for the better in 2016, when a *Footloose*-like law forbidding dancing was finally repealed; the law, on the books since 1948, banned dancing in licensed premises after midnight (and in unlicensed premises at all), though in practice it was ignored for much of the twentieth century and only enforced occasionally since 2001, so not all that much has changed, especially in the main clubbing regions, **Roppongi** and **Shibuya**. Local **DJs** to look out for are Satoshi Tomiie, a house legend since the early '90s; Ken Ishii, well known for his techno sets; the hard-house-loving Ko Kimura; and rising star Xonora, a ball of energy who has spun her smooth beats at most of Tokyo's top clubs.

ESSENTIALS

Prices and times Cover charges are typically ¥2500–3500, usually including your first drink; the majority of venues don't really get going until after 11pm, especially at weekends, with most staying open until around 4am.

ID At many clubs you'll have to show some ID to get in – national ID cards or a driving licence should be fine (though some clubs also insist on proof of your profession!), otherwise you may need to risk losing your precious passport.

Information Check listings magazines and online resources to see what's on before heading out; most major clubs post their schedules online. The ⓦ iflyer.jp website provides a good overview of the clubbing scene, and offers discounts from the cover charge at some venues.

BAYSIDE TOKYO

Ageha アゲハ Studio Coast, 2-2-10 Shin-Kiba, Kōtō-ku ☎03 5534 2525, ⓦ ageha.com; Shin-Kiba station; map p.87. Ultra-cool mega-club with an outdoor pool, body-trembling sound system and roster of high-profile events. It's out by Tokyo Bay, but there's a free shuttle bus here from Shibuya – check the website for details and make sure you turn up at least half an hour before you want to depart to get a ticket to board the bus. Entry usually ¥3000. Usually Fri & Sat only.

AKASAKA AND ROPPONGI

Alife 1-7-2 Nishi-Azabu, Minato-ku ☎03 5785 2531, ⓦ e-alife.net; Roppongi station; map pp.96–97. Closed

for a while, this famed venue reopened in 2016, and is setting about reclaiming its mantle as one of Roppongi's top spots. As with the earlier incarnations, the second-floor lounge area is a good place to chill out after you've worked up a sweat to the house and techno being spun on the large dancefloor below. The cost of entry varies, but expect to pay more on weekends, even more after 11pm, and yet more again if you're a guy. Events most nights except Sun.

Bullets ブレツ B1F Kasumi Bldg, 1-7-11 Nishi-Azabu, Minato-ku ☎03 3401 4844, ⓦ bul-lets.com; Roppongi station; map pp.96–97. This small, cosy club hosts DJs who veer towards breakbeats. Electronica, ambient and abstract tracks can be heard on other nights as well as good old rock and pop. Entry around ¥2000, sometimes free on weekdays. Events most nights.

Esprit エスプリ 2/3F B&V Bldg, 5-1-6 Roppongi, Minato-ku ☎03 3470 1371, ⓦ esprit-tokyo.net; Roppongi station; map pp.96–97. Mega-club with state-of-the-art sound and lighting systems, and a roster of high-end local and international DJs. Entry around ¥3500 for guys, ¥2000 for girls. Events most nights.

Jumanji ジュマンジ Marina Building 3-10-5 Roppongi, Minato-ku ☎03 5410 5455, ⓦ jumanji55.com; Roppongi station; map pp.96–97. Aptly, considering its name, *Jumanji* can be a bit of a zoo: with the ¥1000 early-entry fee often including a couple of drinks (and sometimes, particularly for women, unlimited trips to the bar within a certain time window), there's essentially no

PECHAKUCHA NIGHT

It started in 2003 as an idea to bring people to a new "creative art" basement venue called *SuperDeluxe* in the then pre-Roppongi Art Triangle days, but in a few short years **PechaKucha Night** (⨎pechakucha.org) became a worldwide **phenomenon** – it has now spread to over 700 cities and counting. Co-created by Tokyo-based architects Astrid Klein and Mark Dytham (KDa), the presentation format – 20 images shown for 20 seconds each, with the exhibitor talking along in time – keeps participants on their toes, often forcing funny ad-lib moments due to the high pace. More importantly it acts as a platform for these creators to share their ideas. PechaKucha ("chit-chat") has ended up being the perfect platform for Tokyo's **young, up-and-coming creators** who would never previously have had a place to share their works in front of a large audience.

PechaKucha usually takes place at *SuperDeluxe* (see below) once a month, and there are occasional events held at Shibuya's Hikarie Building (see p.122).

entry charge, meaning that on weekends there's barely any wiggle-room. Great fun, though, and a hugely popular pick-up spot. Open most nights.

Muse ミューズ B1 4-1-1 Nishi-Azabu, Minato-ku ☎03 5467 1188, ⨎muse-web.com; Roppongi station; map pp.96–97. A pick-up joint, but an imaginatively designed one, with lots of interesting little rooms to explore or canoodle in. The dancefloor at the back gets packed at weekends (there's room for 1200 people, in theory), when they mostly play r'n'b. Free entry weekdays, weekends ¥3000; women usually free. Closed Mon.

★**SuperDeluxe** スーパーデラックス B1F 3-1-25 Nishi-Azabu, Minato-ku ☎03 5412 0515, ⨎super-deluxe .com; Roppongi station; map pp.96–97. Billing itself as a place for "thinking, drinking people", this club hosts a brilliant range of arty events – anything from live music performances and album launches to the monthly PechaKucha nights (see box above), a showcase for Tokyo's creative community. Events most nights.

EBISU, MEGURO AND THE SOUTH

★**Unit** ユーニット Za-House Bldg, 1-34-17 Ebisu-Nishi, Shibuya-ku ☎03 5459 8630, ⨎unit-tokyo.com; Ebisu or Daikanyama stations; map pp.106–107. DJ events and gigs from an interesting mix of artists and bands at this cool three-floor club, café and lounge bar. Events most nights.

HARAJUKU, AOYAMA AND SHIBUYA

Club Asia クラブアジア 1-8 Maruyamachō, Shibuya-ku ☎03 5458 2551, ⨎clubasia.co.jp; Shibuya station; map p.122. A mainstay of the clubbing scene, with the emphasis on techno and trance nights, though they occasionally wander into other territories such as reggae and new wave. It's in the heart of the Dōgenzaka love hotel district, and a popular place for one-off gigs by visiting DJs. Entry usually ¥3000 plus a drink. Open Fri & Sat, and sometimes Sun & Thurs.

Gas Panic ガスパニック B1 21-7 Udagawachō, Shibuya-ku ☎03 3462 9099, ⨎gaspanic.co.jp; Shibuya

station; map p.122. For many a year, the various *Gas Panic* clubs have, between them, constituted Tokyo's meat markets, with this one now the biggie. Free entry, cheap drinks, and lots of youngsters (both Japanese and foreign) doing things their parents wouldn't be proud of. Free entry. Daily 6pm–late.

★**Harlem** ハーレム 2-4 Maruyama-chō, Shibuya-ku ☎03 3461 8806, ⨎www.harlem.co.jp; Shibuya station; map p.122. The city's prime hip-hop venue for two full decades, keeping abreast of the genre's undulations with a roster of young, energetic DJs. The crowd are almost all dressed to the nines – do likewise or you might as well not be here. Usually ¥3000 with a drink. Events most nights; sometimes closed Sun or Mon.

Microcosmos ミックロコスモス 2-23-12 Dōgenzaka, Shibuya-ku ☎03 5784 5496, ⨎microcosmos-tokyo.com; Shibuya station; map p.122. A good example of the new breed of Tokyo club, this chic dance space has a relaxed vibe, and tends to draw a sophisticated crowd. Music ranges across the spectrum from reggae and hip-hop to electro and techno. Usually ¥2500 with a drink. Events Fri & Sat.

The Ruby Room ルビールーム 2-25-17 Dōgenzaka, Shibuya-ku ☎03 3780 3022, ⨎rubyroomtokyo.com; Shibuya station; map p.122. Cosy, unpretentious cocktail bar/club with frequent live music. Their open-mic night on Tuesdays (from 7pm) is a long-running affair that attracts a diverse crowd and throws up some talented performers. Events most nights.

Sound Museum Vision サウンドミュージアムヴィジョン B1F 2-10-7 Dōgenzaka, Shibuya-ku ☎03 5728 2824, ⨎vision-tokyo.com; Shibuya station; map p.122. Even before Daikanyama club *Air* closed its doors forever, its owners were far more focused on their new venue – a 1500-capacity club in Shibuya. Four giant rooms, a bunch of regular club nights, and some seriously heavy sound systems; their EDM events are best of all. Usually ¥2500 with a drink. Events Fri & Sat.

★**Womb** ウーム 2-16 Maruyama-chō, Shibuya-ku ☎03 5459 0039, ⨎womb.co.jp; Shibuya station; map p.122.

15

Mega-club with a spacious dancefloor, enormous glitter ball (reputedly the largest in Asia) and a pleasant chill-out space. Top DJs work the decks, but be warned that at big events it can get ridiculously crowded. Usually ¥3000 with a drink; discount before midnight. Events most nights.

SHINJUKU AND THE WEST

Garam ガラム 7F Dai-Roku Polestar Bldg, 1-16-6 Kabukichō, Shinjuku-ku ☎03 3205 8668; Shinjuku station; map p.126. This tiny, Jamaican-style dancehall is very friendly, and the place to head if you're into reggae.

The cover charge is unusually reasonable, and includes one drink. Entry ¥1000–1500. Daily 9pm–6am.

IKEBUKURO AND THE NORTH

Bed ベッド B1F Fukuri Building, 3-29-9 Nishi-Ikebukuro ☎03 3981 5300, ⓦikebukurobed.com; Ikebukuro sftation; map p.138. Ikebukuro isn't known for its hip nightlife, but this place is hugely popular with local students. DJs keep things jumping with a mix of hip-hop, reggae, jungle, r'n'b and occasional drum'n'bass. Also stages live music performances. Entry ¥2000. Events most nights until 5am.

LIVE MUSIC VENUES

Pop and **rock** acts usually play in **"live houses"**, many of which are little more than a pub with a small stage, although some clubs such as *SuperDeluxe* (see p.183) and *Unit* (see p.183) also have live music events. **Jazz** and **blues** are also incredibly popular in Tokyo, with scores of clubs across the city. There are several **larger venues** where top local and international acts do their thing, most notably the cavernous Tokyo Dome (see p.140), and the Nippon Budōkan (see p.44). **Tickets** for concerts can be bought through ticket agencies (see box, p.188).

ROCK AND POP

Billboard Live Tokyo ビルボードライブ東京 4F Tokyo Midtown 9-7-4 Akasaka, Minato-ku ☎03 3405 1133, ⓦbillboard-live.com; Roppongi station; map pp.96–97. A relatively intimate space at which everyone on the three levels gets a great view of the stage. Acts tend to appeal to an older crowd, with everything from jazz to bossa nova (Sergio Mendes has performed here a few times), and R&B to funk. Tickets usually from ¥5800, but can be much higher for the big names. Events most nights.

BYG 2-19-14 Dōgenzaka, Shibuya-ku, ⓦwww.byg .co.jp; Shibuya station; map p.122. Tiny rock venue which has been around since the late 1960s – the acts often play music of a similar vintage. Tickets ¥1500–3500. Usually a few events each week, 5.30pm–2am.

Club Citta クラブチッタ 4-1-26 Ogawachō, Kawasaki ☎044 246 8888, ⓦclubcitta.co.jp; Kawasaki station. A major live-music venue in Kawasaki, around 20min from central Tokyo (see map, p.212), hosting a variety of local and international rock bands. It's part of an entertainment and shopping complex called La Cittadella. Tickets ¥2000–3000. Events most nights.

Club Quattro クラブクアットロ 5F Quattro Building, 32-13 Udagawa-chō, Shibuya-ku ☎03 3477 8750, ⓦclub-quattro.com; Shibuya station; map p.122. Intimate rock music venue which tends to showcase up-and-coming bands and artists, though it also plays host to well-known local and international acts. Tickets ¥2000–4500. Events most nights.

Crocodile クロコダイル 6-18-8 Jingūmae, Shibuya-ku ☎03 3499 5205, ⓦcrocodile-live.jp; Meiji-jingūmae or Shibuya stations; map p.116. You'll find everything from samba to blues and reggae at this long-running basement space on Meiji-dōri, between Harajuku and Shibuya. Tickets ¥3000–4000. Events most nights.

Liquid Room リキッドルーム 3-16-6 Higashi, Shibuya-ku ☎03 5464 0800, ⓦliquidroom.net; Ebisu station; map pp.106–107. Live-music venue hosting some pretty prominent bands; they also throw DJ events from time to time in their *Liquid Loft* space. Tickets ¥2800–5800. Events most nights.

Red Shoes レッドシューズ B1F Chigau Aoyama Building, 6-7-14 Minami-Aoyama, Minato-ku ☎03 3486 1169, ⓦredshoes.jp; Omotesandō station; map pp.114–115. Fledgling bands try out their stuff at this place south of Omotesandō station – worth a look. Tickets range from free to ¥3000. Events most weekends.

Shelter シェルター 2-6-10 Kitazawa, Setagaya-ku ☎03 3466 7430, ⓦloft-prj.co.jp; Shimokitazawa station; map p.132. This is the most reliable of the many live-music venues in Shimokitazawa, and one of the oldest, too. Acts are usually young four-piece guitar bands with stars in their eyes. Tickets ¥2000–3000. Shows most days from 7pm, and sometimes also at noon.

Tsutaya O-East 2-14-8 Dōgenzaka, Shibuya-ku ☎03 5458 4681, ⓦshibuya-o.com; Shibuya station; map p.122. This complex has several venues, all hosting live-music events, ranging from J-pop to hard rock. International bands also play here. Tickets from ¥2500. Events most nights.

★WWW B1F Rise Building, 13-17 Udagawachō, Shibuya-ku ☎03 5458 7685, ⓦwww-shibuya.jp; Shibuya station; map p.122. The closure of arthouse Cinema Rise was a real loss to Tokyo movie-lovers, but its replacement has been an even bigger hit with fans of live music – and not just because the extant tiered cinema hall works so well as a place to stand and tap your feet. Acts are a mixed bag of genres, from shoegaze to electronica, but they're all pretty high quality; all-night events sometimes take place in the upper level, and they sell out fast. Tickets from ¥2500. Events most nights.

MUSIC FESTIVALS

Music fans visiting in the summer can get their teeth into a few excellent **music festivals**. Fuji Rock is still the biggest such event in Asia, and Summer Sonic quite possibly the second-largest.

Fuji Rock Three days at the end of July; Naeba Ski Resort, Niigata prefecture ⓦfujirock-eng.com. The most established event, as far as foreign bands go, hosting a wide range of top-name acts covering musical genres from dance and electronica to jazz and blues on multiple stages. It takes place at Naeba Ski Resort in Niigata prefecture, easily accessible from Tokyo by train (around 1hr 25min from Tokyo station to Echigoyuzawa by Shinkansen, then a short shuttle-bus ride). It's possible to visit for the day, camp, or stay in the hotels that, in winter, cater to the ski crowd.

Summer Sonic Two days in early August; Chiba, Chiba prefecture ⓦsummersonic.com. A two-day event split between Ōsaka and Chiba, the latter a 30min train ride east of central Tokyo. An audience of well over 100,000 line up to see a terrific mix of both local and overseas bands over nine stages – Muse, Jay-Z, Metallica and local rock legend Eikichi Yazawa are among the many star acts to have performed here.

Rock in Japan Two weekends in August; Hitachi Seaside Park, Ibaraki-ken ⓦrijfes.jp. Held north of Tokyo, and accessible from Ueno station, this smaller event focuses on home-grown bands.

15

JAZZ AND BLUES

Blue Note ブルーノート 6-3-16 Minami-Aoyama, Minato-ku ☏03 5485 0088, ⓦbluenote.co.jp; Omotesandō station; map pp.114–115. Tokyo's premier jazz venue, part of the international chain, attracts world-class performers. Entry for shows is ¥6000–10,000 (including one drink) depending on the acts, though prices hit the stratosphere for the global stars. Events most evenings.

Blues Alley Japan ブルーズアリー B1F Hotel Leon, 1-3-14 Meguro, Meguro-ku ☏03 5740 6041, ⓦbluesalley.co.jp; Meguro station; map pp.106–107. This offshoot of the Washington DC blues and jazz club occupies a small basement space near the station. Apart from blues, you can expect to hear jazz, soul and various Latin sounds. Ticket prices average ¥4500. Performances usually daily 6pm & 7.30pm.

Cotton Club コットンクラブ 2F Tokia Building, 2-7-3 Marunouchi ☏03 3215 1555, ⓦcottonclubjapan.co.jp; Tokyo station; map p.42. Ritzy jazz club with top-class performers, from the same stable as the Blue Note (see above). It's run as a supper club with two shows a night; ticket prices vary (¥5000–12,000) depending on where you sit and who's on. Two shows per evening.

JZ Brat 2F Cerulean Tower Tōkyū Hotel, 26-1 Sakuragaoka-chō, Shibuya-ku ☏03 5728 0168, ⓦjzbrat.com; Shibuya station; map p.122. Swanky jazz club and restaurant in a top Shibuya hotel, with a spacious contemporary design and a respectable line-up of artists. Cover charge from ¥3000. Daily 3–9pm.

New York Bar Park Hyatt Hotel, 3-7-1-2 Nishi-Shinjuku, Shinjuku-ku ☏03 5322 1234, ⓦtokyo.park.hyatt.jp; Tochōmae station; map p.126. Top-class live jazz plus a glittering night view of Shinjuku are the attractions of this sophisticated bar attached to the Park Hyatt's New York Grill (see p.171); the cover charge (¥2600) is waived if you eat there. Smart attire recommended. Evening shows start 8pm (7pm Sun).

Shinjuku Pit Inn 新宿ピットイン B1F Accord Shinjuku Building, 2-12-4 Shinjuku, Shinjuku-ku ☏03 3354 2024, ⓦpit-inn.com; Shinjuku station; map p.126. Serious, long-standing jazz club which has been the launch platform for many top Japanese performers. Tickets ¥3000. Shows most evenings from 7.30pm.

TRADITIONAL JAPANESE MUSIC

★**Oiwake** 追分 3-28-11 Nishi-Asakusa, Taitō-ku ☏03 3844 6283, ⓦoiwake.info; Iriya station; map p.74. A fantastic izakaya, especially if you're into traditional Japanese music: three times a night, a clutch of musicians appear armed with shamisen (Japanese lutes), shakuhachi (flute) and the like, and pour their wonderful tunes out while visitors down their sake. Music charge ¥2000, plus one food-and-drink order per customer. Tues–Sat Mon 6pm–midnight.

Waentei-Kikkō 和えん亭吉幸 2-2-13 Asakusa, Taitō-ku ☏03 5828 8833, ⓦwaentei-kikko.com; Asakusa station; map p.74. A rare chance to see an excellent live performance of the shamisen (Japanese lute) in a delightful wooden house transported to Asakusa from Takayama. The lunch bentō is beautifully presented kaiseki-style food (see box, p.165) and costs ¥2500; dinner starts at ¥6800. There are five performances daily; see the website for the schedule. Daily except Wed 11.30am–1.30pm & 5–9.30pm.

LGBT BARS

With over 150 bars and clubs, **Shinjuku-Nichōme** is the most densely packed area of gay and lesbian venues in Japan, but clubbing events are held around the city. Check websites for regular monthly standbys such as Shangri-la at Ageha

GAY FESTIVALS

Out-and-proud gay life in Tokyo is still somewhat coming out of its shell, and until recently there were no concrete annual events. However, there are now at least a couple of established fixtures on the calendar.

Rainbow Reel Late July ⓦrainbowreeltokyo.com. This annual film festival is now a permanent fixture of Tokyo's gay calendar, showing films from around the world with English subtitles. A dance party typically rounds things off.

Tokyo Pride Parade Two days in May ⓦtokyo

rainbowpride.com. The city's Pride Parade failed, for years, to establish itself as a regular "thing". Now it seems to be here to stay, acting as the hub of a full-on Rainbow Week. However, the dates have been in flux – check the website for details.

15

(see p.182), Goldfinger (ⓦgoldfingerparty.com) and Diamond Cutter (ⓦdiamondcutter.jp), all of which will have a cover charge of around ¥3000. The "Basics" section of this book has more general advice on Tokyo's gay and lesbian scene (see p.29).

HARAJUKU, AOYAMA AND SHIBUYA

★**Keivi** ケイヴィ 4F Yoshino Building, 17-10 Sakuragaoka-chō, Shibuya-ku ☎03 3462 9200, ⓦkeivi.com; map p.122. They've packed an awful lot into this friendly bar, with barely an inch of empty space – the extraordinary decor includes animal skulls, fairy lights, Japanese dolls and tropical fish. Drinks are reasonably priced, too. Daily 6pm–late.

SHINJUKU AND THE WEST

★**Aiiro Café** アイイロカフェ Tenka Building 7, 2-18-1 Shinjuku, Shinjuku-ku ☎03 3358 3988, ⓦaliving.net; Shinjuku-sanchōme station; map p.126. Many a night in Nichōme starts with a drink at this place, and quite a few finish here too. The bar itself is tiny, which is why scores of patrons hang out on the street corner outside, creating a block party atmosphere on weekends. Daily 6pm–4am (Sun until 1am).

★**Arty Farty** アーティファーティ 2F Dai 33 Kyutei Building, 2-11-7 Shinjuku, Shinjuku-ku ☎03 5362 9720, ⓦarty-farty.net; Shinjuku-sanchōme station; map p.126. As the night draws on, this pumping bar with a small dancefloor gets packed with an up-for-fun crowd. Their annexe bar, within staggering distance, hits its stride later in the evening and draws a younger clientele. Daily 6pm–1am.

A-Un 阿吽 3F 2-14-16 Shinjuku, Shinjuku-ku ☎070 6612 9014; Shinjuku-sanchōme station; map p.126. A quirky bar in many ways: it's lesbian-friendly but doesn't mind fellas coming in; the sound system is unusually good; and you can bring your own booze for ¥500. Entry is usually ¥1000 including a free drink. The bar's name represents the first and last letters of the Sanskrit alphabet. Daily 6pm–2am, Fri & Sat until 4am.

Campy! カンピー 2-13-10 Shinjuku, Shinjuku-ku ☎03 6273 2154; Shinjuku-sanchōme station; map p.126. This highly colourful venue is perhaps the tiniest of the

area's many minuscule gay bars, but what it lacks in size it makes up for in pizzaz – the drag queen staff sure help. One of the better local venues for straight folk. Daily 6pm–2am (Fri & Sat until 4am).

Dragon Men ドラゴンメン 2-11-4 Shinjuku, Shinjuku-ku ☎03 3341 0606; Shinjuku-sanchōme station; map p.126. The average Nichōme bar is pretty tiny, but this is a relative whopper – big enough for a proper dancefloor. Good music, a street-side terrace, daily happy-hour specials and strong drinks served by tattooed *gaijin* waiters clad only in underpants also account for its popularity. Daily 6pm–3am (Fri & Sat until 5am).

Goldfinger ゴールドフィンガー 2-12-11 Shinjuku, Shinjuku-ku ☎03 6383 4649; Shinjuku-sanchōme station; map p.126. This fun, female-only bar is famed for the regular wild parties it runs (ⓦgoldfingerparty.com), and though these are actually held elsewhere, the bar itself is a fun drinking hole, styled something like an old motel and presided over by glamourpuss DJs. Daily 6pm–2am (Fri & Sat until 4am).

Kinsmen キンズメン 2F 2-18-5 Shinjuku, Shinjuku-ku ☎03 3354 4949; Shinjuku-sanchōme station; map p.126. Long-running and unpretentious bar – you're as likely to be carousing with a mixed group of office workers here as with a drag queen. Check out their famous *ikebana* – traditional flower displays. Tues–Sun 8pm–1am (Fri & Sat until 3am).

★**Paddy's Junction** パッディーズジャンクション 2-13-16, Shinjuku, Shinjuku-ku ☎03 3355 7833, ⓦpaddys -junction.com; Shinjuku-sanchōme station; map p.126. With its foreign and English-speaking staff, this Irish-style pub offers the area something a wee bit different. They've cheap food (including excellent fish and chips), lots of imported beers, and cocktails are just ¥300 during the 5–7pm happy hour – a great starting or meet-up point for a night on the tiles. Daily 5pm–1am.

ROBOT RESTAURANT, KABUKICHŌ

Entertainment and the arts

When it comes to exploring Tokyo's diverse theatre scene, it's easy to enjoy colourful extravaganzas like Takarazuka or the more traditional kabuki even if you don't understand the language. The notoriously difficult nō and *butō* are also worth trying at least once. Tokyo can be a good place for English-language drama too, with international theatre groups often passing through on foreign tours, while opera is slowly gaining currency. Moving from the highbrow to slightly lower ground, there are numerous multiplex and independent cinemas, as well as a handful of fun, glitzy shows featuring drag queens, robots and more. Tokyo does a fine line in fun theme-parks, too, which are great if you are travelling with children.

TICKET AGENCIES

To buy tickets for theatre performances, concerts and sporting events, it's simplest to head to the venue in advance. However, using one of the ticket agencies listed below may save a lot of time. In addition, major events sell out quickly; don't expect to be able to buy tickets at the venue door unless you get them some time beforehand. All of the online ticketing agencies below have Japanese-only websites, and English is rarely spoken at their ticket booths – the best plan is to get a Japanese-speaker to assist you.

CN Playguide ⓦwww.cnplayguide.com. Japanese-only website covering almost all major events.
HMV ⓦl-tike.com. Connected to Lawson, a convenience-store chain with thousands of branches across the country, and hundreds in Tokyo alone. Tickets can be purchased

online, or from in-branch machines.
Ticket Pia ⓦt.pia.co.jp. Branches can be found in shopping malls and department stores in main city areas such as Ginza, Shinjuku and Shibuya.

TRADITIONAL THEATRE

The easiest of Japan's traditional performance arts for foreigners to enjoy are **kabuki** and the puppet theatre of **bunraku**. If you don't want to sit through a full performance, which can last up to four hours, single-act tickets are often available. **Nō**, the country's oldest form of theatre, isn't as appealing, though some find the rarefied style incredibly powerful; **kyōgen**, short satirical plays with simple plots, liven up the intervals. Take advantage of hiring recorded commentaries in English at the theatre to gain a better understanding of what's happening on stage. Subtitles displayed on a screen beside the performers (or, at some venues, on the back of each seat) are also sometimes used. Apart from the lines being spoken, information on the background of the story and the characters is also provided. For more on traditional theatre, see p.264.

16

Cerulean Tower Nō Theatre セルリアンタワー能楽堂 26-1 Sakuragaoka-chō, Shibuya-ku ☎03 3477 6412, ⓦwww.ceruleantower-noh.com; Shibuya station; map p.122. In the basement of the luxury *Cerulean Tower* hotel (see p.147), this theatre provides an elegant setting for both professional and amateur nō and *kyōgen* performances (tickets typically ¥3500 and up).
★**Kabukiza** 歌舞伎座 6-18-2 Ginza, Chūō-ku ☎03 3541 2600, ⓦkabuki-bito.jp; Higashi-Ginza station; map p.52. Tokyo's oldest and largest kabuki theatre, this is the best place to head if you're at all interested in catching a performance. Getting a ticket (¥4000–22,000), on the other hand, can be tricky; they usually become easier to buy after the fifteenth of each month. Single-act tickets (¥800–2000) are available on the door for those who don't want to commit to a whole performance.
Kanze-Nō-Gakudō 観世能楽堂 1-16-4 Shōtō, Shibuya-ku ☎03 3469 5241, ⓦkanze.net; Shibuya station; map pp.114–115. The home theatre of Kanze, the best-known of Tokyo's several nō troupes, and one of the city's most traditional nō theatres. Tickets from ¥3000.

National Nō Theatre 国立能楽堂 4-18-1 Sendagaya, Shibuya-ku ☎03 3230 3000, ⓦwww.ntj.jac.go.jp; Sendagaya station; map p.126. Hosts nō performances several times a month, with tickets starting at around ¥2700. Printed English explanations of the plot help make some sense of what's going on.
National Theatre 国立劇場 4-1 Hayabusachō, Chiyoda-ku ☎03 3230 3000, ⓦwww.ntj.jac.go.jp; Hanzōmon station; map p.42. In its two auditoria, Tokyo's National Theatre puts on a varied programme of traditional theatre and music, including kabuki, *bunraku*, court music and dance. English-language earphones and programmes are available. Tickets start at around ¥1500 for kabuki and ¥4500 for *bunraku*.
Shimbashi Embujō 新橋演舞場 6-18-2 Ginza, Chūō-ku ☎03 3541 2600, ⓦshinbashi-enbujo.co.jp; Higashi-Ginza station; map p.52. This large theatre stages a range of traditional dance, music and theatre, including the "Super-kabuki" (kabuki with all the bells and whistles of modern musical theatre). Single-act tickets for regular kabuki performances range from ¥800 to ¥1500 depending on the length of the act.

CONTEMPORARY AND INTERNATIONAL THEATRE

Camp as a row of tents, the most unique theatrical experience you can have in Tokyo is **Takarazuka** (see box opposite), the all-singing, all-dancing, all-female revue which appears occasionally at the Takarazuka Theatre (see opposite). If your Japanese is up to it, you'll find plenty of modern **Japanese dramas** to enjoy: look out for productions by chelfitsch (see opposite), or anything by the director Ninagawa Yukio, famous for his reinterpretations of Shakespeare. **Overseas theatre companies** often appear at the Tokyo Globe or Shinjuku's New National Theatre, though seats sell out months in advance for the bigger names.

Black Stripe Theater B1 Sangubashi Guesthouse, 4-50-8 Yoyogi, Shibuya-ku ☎080 4184 0848, ⓦblackstripetheater.com; Sangubashi station; map pp.96–97. A relatively recent addition to the expat theatre scene, this company has staged plays by Harold Pinter and David Mamet. Tickets ¥4000.

chelfitsch ⓦchelfitsch.net. Founded by award-winning writer Okada Toshiki, this internationally acclaimed group put on excellent shows in Tokyo when they're not busy touring the globe (which is most of the time). They can usually be relied on for one new performance each year, although the venues and prices vary.

★**The Globe Tokyo** 東京グローブ座 3-1-2 Hyakunin-chō, Shinjuku-ku ☎03 3366 4020, ⓦwww.tglobe.net; Shin-Ōkubo station; map pp.136–137. A variety of works, including Shakespearean plays and Western-style operas, are performed in this modern-day replica of the famous Elizabethan stage in London. Tickets from ¥4500.

New National Theatre 新国立劇場 1-20 Honmachi, Shinjuku-ku ☎03 5352 9999, ⓦnntt.jac.go.jp; Hatsudai station; map p.126. Just behind Tokyo Opera City, the New National Theatre comprises three stages specially designed for Western performing arts, including opera, ballet, dance and drama. Discount tickets (under ¥2000) for restricted-view seats are sold from 10am on the day; you'll otherwise pay at least double that

★**PUK** 2-12-3 Yoyogi, Shibuya-ku ☎03 3370 5128, ⓦpuppettheatrepuk.wordpress.com; Shinjuku station; map p.126. This charming puppet theatre was founded in 1929 as La Pupa Klubo, and survived a government witch-hunt during the war. It's home to a resident group of puppeteers, as well as visiting troupes, and puts on shows that both young and old can enjoy.

Setagaya Public Theatre 世田谷パブリックシアター 4-1-1 Taishido, Setagaya-ku ☎03 5432 1526, ⓦsetagaya-pt.jp; Sangenjaya station; map p.131. One of Tokyo's most watchable contemporary theatre companies, spread across two auditoria and specializing in contemporary drama and dance.

★**Takarazuka Theatre** 宝塚劇場 1-1-1 Yūrakuchō, Chūō-ku ☎03 5251 2001, ⓦkageki.hankyu.co.jp; Hibiya station; map p.42. Mostly stages musicals, punched out by a huge cast in fabulous costumes. The theatre, immediately north of the *Imperial Hotel* (see p.144), also stages regular Takarazuka performances (see box below). Tickets start at ¥3500; performances run most days except Wed at either 11am or 1pm, and at 3pm.

Theatre Cocoon シアターコクーン 2-24-1 Dōgenzaka, Shibuya-ku ☎03 3477 9999, ⓦwww.bunkamura.co.jp; Shibuya station; map p.122. Part of Shibuya's Bunkamura arts centre, this modern theatre hosts some of Tokyo's more accessible fringe productions.

Tokyo International Players ⓦtokyoplayers.org. Tokyo International Players has been going since 1896 (in other words, exactly as long as the modern Olympics), feeding off the ever-changing cast of foreign acting talent that passes through the city. Their website lists their productions, mounted four or five times a year at venues across the city (though their Facebook site is kept more up-to-date); details can also be found in the English-language press.

Za Kōenji 座高円寺 2-1-2 Kōenji-Kita, Suginami-ku ☎03 3223 7300, ⓦza-koenji.jp; Kōenji station; map p.131. Managed by the nonprofit Creative Theater Network, and set in a suitably dramatic building designed by leading architect Itō Toyō, this venue presents a high-quality programme of drama, dance and music performances.

16

TAKARAZUKA

There's a long tradition of men performing female roles in Japanese theatre, acting out a male fantasy of how women are supposed to behave. It's not so strange, then, that actresses playing idealized men have struck such a chord with contemporary female audiences. Along with glitzy productions, this has been the successful formula of the all-female **Takarazuka Review Company** (ⓦkageki.hankyu.co.jp), founded in 1914 in Takarazuka, a town 20km northwest of Ōsaka.

The company's founder, Kobayashi Ichizō, was mightily impressed by performances of Western operas he'd seen in Tokyo. He sensed that Japanese audiences were ripe for lively Western musical dramas, but he wanted to preserve something of Japan's traditional theatre, too. So, as well as performing dance reviews and musicals, Takarazuka act out classical Japanese plays and have developed shows from Western novels, including *Gone With the Wind* and *War and Peace*.

Thousands of young girls apply annually to join the troupe at the age of 16, and devote themselves to a punishing routine of classes that will enable them to embody the "modesty, fairness and grace" (the company's motto) expected of a Takarazuka member. They must also forsake boyfriends, but in return are guaranteed the slavish adoration of an almost exclusively female audience, who go particularly crazy for the male impersonators or *otoko-yaku*.

TOKYO'S RARE GEISHA

Less than a century ago, **geisha** – female performers of traditional music and dance – were a common sight around certain areas of Tokyo. The capital had certain geisha quarters – the so-called *roku kagai* (meaning "six flower districts") – where geisha lived and entertained clients in teahouses and *ryōtei* (banqueting houses): Akasaka, Asakusa, Kagurazaka, Mukōjima and Yoshi-chō were the most prominent. Today, however, even in **Mukōjima**, once the largest of these districts, the number of *ryōtei* is down from 400 to fewer than 20 and it's thought that there are only around 120 geisha practising their arts.

As a result of this rarity, an audience with a geisha is far from being a cheap affair, costing in the region of ¥50,000. There are, however, occasional chances to see geisha in their finery for much less, and even for free. The main opportunity is when geisha **parade** during the Sanja Matsuri (see p.27). Special **performances** by geisha of Japanese dancing at theatres such as the Shimbashi Embujō (see p.188) or at top hotels, often during the cherry blossom season, are also affordable, often ¥10,000 or under.

DANCE

The highly expressive avant-garde dance form of **butō** (also Romanized as "butoh"), which originates from Japan, shouldn't be missed if you're interested in modern dance. It can be minimalist, introspective, and often violent or sexually explicit. *Butō* aside, there's a vast range of other types of dance shows staged in Tokyo, including **ballet**, **tap** and **tango**. It's also possible to sometimes see **geisha** perform their beautiful dances (see box above).

Dairakudakan Kochūten 大駱駝艦壺中天 B1 2-1-18 Kichijōji-Kitamachi, Musashinoshi, ☎0422 214982, ⓦdairakudakan.com; Kichijōji station; map p.131. The studio of legendary *butō* troupe Dairakudakan; sometimes there are joint productions here with visiting foreign dancers.

Plan B B1F Monark Nakano Building, 4-26-20 Yayoi-chō, Nakano-ku ☎03 3384 2051, ⓦi10x.com/planb; Nakano-Fujimichō station; map p.131. Apart from dance or musical performances, you might also catch documentary film screenings or experimental music nights here.

COMEDY

Punchline Comedy Club 3F Pizza Express, 4-30-3 Jingūmae, Shibuya-ku ☎03 5775 3894, ⓦpunchline comedy.com. This international organization occasionally brings top foreign talent to the city, with an event every month or so; see website for details. Tickets ¥6500, or ¥8500 with dinner buffet and two drinks.

Tokyo Comedy Store ⓦtokyocomedy.com. For comedy in English, this team hosts well-attended shows at several venues across the city; there are usually two or three performances per week, and sometimes they also venture into musical or sketch shows. See website for details. Tickets ¥500–1500.

CABARET BARS

A couple of **cabaret bars** host glitzy shows with drag queen performers in fabulous costumes. They usually open up around an hour before the performance – plenty of time to get in the mood with a drink or three.

DINING WITH ROBOTS

Opened in 2012, the **Robot Restaurant** (ロボットレストラン; 1-7-1 Kabukichō, Shinjuku-ku ☎03 3200 5500, ⓦshinjuku-robot.com; Shinjuku station) is perhaps Tokyo's zaniest attraction, and provides a little trip back to the wild days before Japan's financial bubble burst. It all starts at the entrance foyer, where there's nary an inch of regular, boring space – everything glistens, shines, flashes or reflects. There's far more of the same heading down the stairs to the trippy, video-screen-lined hall where you'll be sat with other excited tourists and locals. Though the website, and plenty of YouTube clips, will give you a great idea of what to expect, the performances are far more fun if you have no idea what's coming – for now, it should suffice to say that dozens of robots, scantily dressed girls, more LEDs than anyone could ever count, and a wall of roaring music are on the cards. Most visitors enjoy it, but a fair few leave grumbling about the price – a recent hike raised tickets to ¥8000 per head (plus ¥1000 for a light bentō meal). Performances run daily at 5.55pm, 7.50pm & 9.45pm, and sometimes also 4pm.

16

Kaguwa 香和 5-4-2 Roppongi, Minato-ku ☎03 5414 8818, ⓦkaguwa-roppongi.com; Roppongi station; map pp.96–97. Hidden away in the Roppongi back alleys, and concealed with an unassuming facade of lanterns and lacquer, this is Tokyo's prime cabaret venue, putting on a couple of performances most nights, plus afternoon shows on weekends. Tickets ¥4200.

Kingyo 金魚 3-14-17 Roppongi, Minato-ku ☎03 3478 3000, ⓦkingyo.co.jp; Roppongi station; map pp.96–97. Snazzy place putting on extremely energetic "New Half" (transsexual) shows. Entry ends up costing just under ¥6000, after tax and the obligatory food and drink orders. Nightly shows at 7.30pm & 10pm. Closed Mon.

CLASSICAL MUSIC AND OPERA

The city is well stocked with Western **classical music** venues, and there are usually one or two concerts every week, either by one of Tokyo's several resident symphony orchestras or by a visiting group, as well as occasional performances of **opera**. Concerts of **traditional Japanese music**, played on instruments such as the *shakuhachi* (flute), the *shamisen* (a kind of lute that is laid on the ground), and the *taiko* (drum), are much rarer; two Asakusa venues hosting excellent *shamisen* performances are *Waentei-Kikkō* restaurant (see p.185) and *Oiwake izakaya* (see p.185).

NHK Hall NHKホール 2-2-1 Jinnan, Shibuya-ku ☎03 3465 1751, ⓦwww.nhk-sc.or.jp/nhk_hall; Harajuku or Shibuya stations; map pp.114–115. One of Tokyo's older auditoria for classical concerts, but still well thought of and home to the highly rated NHK Symphony Orchestra. It's next to the NHK Broadcasting Centre, south of Yoyogi-kōen. Tickets cost from ¥2000 to ¥10,000, depending upon the performance.

Orchard Hall オーチャードホール 2-24-1 Dōgenzaka, Shibuya-ku ☎03 3477 9111, ⓦwww.bunkamura.co.jp; Shibuya station; map p.122. Part of the Bunkamura arts centre, this large concert hall hosts a wide range of classical music performances throughout the year, and has very good acoustics.

★**Suntory Hall** Ark Hills サントリーホール 1-13-1 Akasaka, Minato-ku ☎03 3505 1001, ⓦwww.suntory .co.jp/suntoryhall; Roppongi-itchōme station; map pp.96–97. Reputed to have the best acoustics in the city, this elegant concert hall has one of the world's largest pipe organs, which is sometimes used for free lunchtime recitals; check the website for details of this and other events. Prices vary by performance.

Tokyo Bunka Kaikan 東京文化会館 5-45 Ueno, Taitō-ku ☎03 3828 2111, ⓦt-bunka.jp; Ueno station; map p.65. Tokyo's largest classical music venue, with an extravagantly-designed main hall that seats over 2300. It has a busy and varied schedule of performances and a marvellous interior dating back to the 1960s, while ticket prices tend to be cheap.

Tokyo International Forum 東京国際フォーラム 3-5-1 Marunouchi, Chiyoda-ku ☎03 5221 9000, ⓦwww.t-i-forum.co.jp; Yūrakuchō station; map p.42. The Forum's four multipurpose halls (including one of the world's largest auditoria, with over five thousand seats) host an eclectic mix of performing arts, including classical music and opera.

Tokyo Opera City 東京オペラシティ 3-20-2 Nishi-Shinjuku, Shinjuku-ku ☎03 5353 9999, ⓦoperacity.jp; Hatsudai station; map p.126. This stunningly designed concert hall, with a giant pipe organ, seats over 1600 and has excellent acoustics – though despite its name it hosts only music concerts, not full-blown opera. There's a more intimate recital hall too.

CINEMA

There are numerous multiscreen **cinemas** that show Hollywood blockbusters – usually with Japanese subtitles – while a decent number of smaller venues specialize in independent and art-house releases. On "First Day" (in other words the first day of the month, though some chains have their own monthly "Cinema Day" on different dates), **tickets** cost ¥1100, as opposed to the regular price of around ¥1800, or ¥2500 for a reserved seat (*shitei-seki*). Women can also get discounted tickets (¥1000) on Ladies Day, usually Wednesday. Otherwise, you can buy slightly reduced tickets in advance from a ticket

---

AMUSEMENT AND THEME PARKS

Amusement and **theme parks** are huge business in Japan, and they can certainly come in handy if you're dragging around kids – or if you simply want to bring out the kid in yourself.

Aqua Park (see p.110).
Asakusa Hanayashiki (see p.76).
Joypolis (see p.92).
KidZania Tokyo (see p.89).

Namco Namja Town (see p.138).
Tokyo Disney Resort (see p.93).
Tokyo Dome City (see p.140).

16

TOKYO FILM AND THEATRE FESTIVALS

The biggest of the city's several **film festivals** is the **Tokyo International Film Festival** (Ⓦtiff-jp.net), held each autumn at Roppongi Hills (see p.102) and other venues around Tokyo. It's one of the few opportunities to catch Japanese and world cinema with English subtitles, not to mention seeing some films that would never get a general release, although it's increasingly becoming a vehicle for promoting major releases from the US. Also worth catching is the annual gay-and-lesbian **Rainbow Reel Festival** (see p.27).

The city's major **theatre** event is **Festival/Tokyo** (Ⓦfestival-tokyo.jp), held annually from October through to December. It showcases a diverse range of productions, with performances both from Japanese and visiting international troupes.

agency (see box, p.188). Note that the last screening of the day can be as early as 7 or 8pm. **Listings** are published on Friday in *The Japan Times*, and can also be found on online sources such as *Metropolis* (Ⓦmetropolisjapan.com) and *Time Out* (Ⓦtimeout.com/tokyo). Apart from cinemas listed here, which tend to specialize in independent films, there are many more **multiplexes** in Ginza, Ikebukuro, Shibuya and Shinjuku, mostly showing the latest Hollywood releases.

★**Cinema Vera** シネマヴェーラ 4F Kinohaus, 1-5 Maruyama-chō, Shibuya-ku ☎03 3461 7703, Ⓦcinema vera.com; Shibuya station; map p.122. The vast majority of films here are Japanese-language only; however, they're mainly black-and-white or Technicolor classics dating from the 1950s to the 1970s, and the location in the heart of Shibuya's raucous love-motel district makes this a good date spot.

Iwanami Hall 岩波ホール 10F, 2-1 Kanda-Jimbōchō, Chiyoda-ku ☎03 3262 5252, Ⓦiwanami-hall.com; Jimbōchō station; map p.59. Long-established venue showing non-commercial European films from places as diverse as Greece and Poland, as well as quirky Japanese movies, often from female directors.

★**Meguro Cinema** 目黒シネマ B1F Meguro Nishiguchi Buidling, 2-24-15 Kamiosaki, Shinagawa-ku ☎03 3491 2557; Meguro station; map pp.106–107. With just one screen and a ten-by-ten seat formation, seeing a film here is a bit like taking a trip back through time to the dawn of cinema. Staff sometimes wear dickie-bows, or costumes related to the films on show – a mix of genres, and very cheap too, with double-bill tickets just ¥1500.

National Film Centre 東京国立近代美術館フィルムセンター 3-7-6 Kyōbashi, Chūō-ku ☎03 3272 8600, Ⓦwww.momat.go.jp; Kyōbashi station; map p.52. A treasure-trove for cinephiles, with a small gallery on the seventh floor for film-related exhibitions and two small cinemas screening retrospectives from their vast movie archive. Most are Japanese classics, though they occasionally dust off their collection of foreign films.

Shin-Bungei-za 新文芸坐 3F Maruhan-Ikebukuro Building, 1-43-5 Higashi-Ikebukuro, Toshima-ku ☎03 3971 9422, Ⓦshin-bungeiza.com; Ikebukuro station; map p.138. Amid the game parlours and sex venues ("soaplands") of Ikebukuro is this theatre specializing in classic reruns and art-house movies. All-night screenings on Sat.

Toho Cinemas Roppongi Hills TOHOシネマズ六本木ヒルズ Roppongi Hills, Roppongi, Minato-ku ☎03 5775 6090; Roppongi station; map pp.96–97. Ultra-modern multiplex cinema with bookable seats, late-night screenings and popular Japanese films with English subtitles.

Uplink アップリンク 37-18 Udagawachō, Shibuya-ku ☎03 6825 5502, Ⓦuplink.co.jp; Shibuya station; map p.122. World cinema is a staple at this arts centre, which combines a couple of cinemas with a gallery, live music, bar and various workshops.

Waseda Shōchiku 早稲田松竹 1-5-16 Takadanobaba, Shinjuku-ku ☎03 3200 8968, Ⓦwasedashochiku.co.jp; Takadanobaba station; map pp.136–137. Popular with students from the nearby university, this cinema is cheaper (¥1300 for a double bill) and less fancy than others in town, but still shows a decent selection of mainstream and non-commercial releases.

Yebisu Garden Cinema 恵比寿ガーデンシネマ Yebisu Garden Place, 4-20 Ebisu, Shibuya-ku ☎03 5420 6161; Ebisu station; map pp.106–107. There are two screens at this modern cinema, with numbered seating, showing an interesting range of non-mainstream US and British releases.

16

AKIHABARA

Shopping

Cruising the boutiques while toting a couple of designer-label carrier bags is such a part of Tokyo life that it's hard not to get caught up in the general enthusiasm. There are shops to suit every taste and budget, including some great crafts shops and wonderfully quirky souvenir and novelty stores. Antique and bargain hunters shouldn't miss out on a visit to one of the city's flea markets, which if nothing else can turn up some unusual curios. Always at the cutting edge of consumerism, the city is also a prime hunting ground for the latest electronic gadgets, as well as fashions in both what to wear and how to style your home.

17

> ## DUTY-FREE SHOPPING
>
> Foreigners can make purchases **duty-free** – that is, without the eight percent consumption tax, due to rise to ten percent in 2017 (see box, p.37) – in a whole bunch of shops around the country. Participating outlets usually have a Duty Free sticker in the window by the entrance (look for a Rising Sun-style red circle with white flower petals).
>
> To take advantage of the scheme, you'll need a **minimum total spend** of ¥5000 at a single store; there's an upper limit of ¥500,000 on **perishable goods** such as food, drinks, tobacco, cosmetics and film, which have to be taken out of the country within 30 days. Your passport will be required on purchase, and it must have an **entry stamp** from customs; if you manage to enter Japan without one (such as by using the automatic gates at the airport), ask for a stamp from an immigration officer. The shop will attach a copy of the **customs document** (*wariin*) to your passport, which will be removed by customs officers when you leave Japan.

Ginza, stacked with department stores and brand shops, is still regarded as Tokyo's traditional shopping centre, although **Shinjuku** has long put up a strong challenge. Young and funky, **Shibuya** and **Harajuku** are probably the most enjoyable places to shop: even if you don't want to buy, the passing fashion parade doesn't get much better. **Asakusa** is home to a plethora of small, traditional crafts shops, particularly on and around Nakamise-dōri. **Akihabara** has long been known as "electric town" thanks to its myriad high-tech emporia, but is also now the go-to location for manga and anime goods. **Ueno** is famous for the lively Ameyokochō market (see box, p.68), while **Ikebukuro** is home to two mammoth department stores and many discount outlets. Also worth a look are the shopping malls out at **Odaiba**, such as Venus Fort (see p.90).

Chic **Daikanyama** has an appealing village atmosphere and is a good place to check out up-and-coming Japanese designers; nearby **Nakameguro** is better for "multi-shops" (which contain several brands in one space) than individual labels, with a host of small, funky stores lining the streets beside the Meguro-gawa. **Shimokitazawa** has a studenty, bohemian air with shops selling secondhand clothes, where you can scoop big-name labels at bargain prices – and keep an eye open too for fashion and art creations by local students.

ANIME AND MANGA

Manga (see p.264) are available just about everywhere, from train station kiosks to bookshops – at the latter and in CD shops (see p.197) you'll also find **anime** DVDs. **Akihabara** is the key shopping area for anime, manga and associated character goods, though with some time on your hands you could also give Ikebukuro or Nakano a try. Apart from the places listed below, devoted fans should schedule time at the shops in the **Ghibli Museum** (see p.132).

AKIHABARA AND AROUND

Comic Tora-no-ana コミックとらのあな 4-3-1 Soto-Kanda, Chiyoda-ku ☎ 03 3526 5330; Akihabara station; map p.59. Seven floors of manga- and anime-related products, including self-published works and secondhand comics on the top floor. There are several other branches across the city. Daily 10am–10pm.

Radio Kaikan ラジオ会館 1-15-16 Soto-Kanda, Taitō-ku; Akihabara station; map p.59. This complex is a real nirvana for *otaku* (obsessive fans). Originally an electronics specialist, this huge store now caters to a rich and varied set of anime and manga tastes – everything from lifelike dolls, figurines and model kits to fantasy

and sexually charged items. Mon–Sat 10.30am–8pm, Sun 10.30am–7.30pm.

HARAJUKU, AOYAMA AND SHIBUYA

Mandarake まんだらけ 31-2 Udagawachō, Shibuya-ku ☎ 03 3477 0777, ⓦ mandarake.co.jp; Shibuya station; map p.122. If you're into character dolls and plastic figures based on anime and manga, this subterranean operation is the place to head. They also have a wide range of second-hand manga as well as posters, cards and even costumes. There's another branch in Akihabara (see map, p.59). Daily noon–8pm.

ARTS AND CRAFTS

Tokyo has a wealth of specialist arts and crafts shops, with the largest concentration in and around **Asakusa**. All the following outlets are good places to hunt for souvenirs, including **paper** products, satin-smooth **lacquerware** ansumptuous **textiles**. Also check out the splendid gift shop at the Japan Folk Crafts Musem (see p.123) for folk craft items, and the ones in the basement of the National Art Center (see p.100) for great contemporary gifts.

GINZA AND AROUND

★**Ginza Natsuno** 銀座夏野 6-7-4 Ginza, Chūō-ku ☎ 03 3569 0952, ⓦ www.e-ohashi.com; Ginza station; map p.52. Stuffed to the rafters with an incredible collection of over 1000 types of chopstick, plus chopstick rests and rice bowls. Prices range from ¥200 up. Several other branches around the city. Mon–Sat 10am–8pm, Sun 10am–7pm.

Haibara はいばら 2-7-1 Nihombashi, Chūō-ku ☎ 03 3272 3801, ⓦ haibara.co.jp; Nihombashi station; map p.52. This shop has been selling traditional *washi* paper – and everything made from it – since 1806. They've moved a couple of times since, and are now located in more modern-looking environs, but their products are just as great. Mon–Fri 10am–6.30pm, Sat & Sun 10am–5.30pm.

★**Itō-ya** 伊東屋 2-7-15 Ginza, Chūō-ku ☎ 03 3561 8311, ⓦ ito-ya.co.jp; Shibuya station; map p.52. This fabulous stationery store comprising 11 floors and two annexes (Itō-ya 2 & 3), is a treasure-trove full of packable souvenirs such as traditional *washi* paper, calligraphy brushes, inks and so on. There are several other branches around the city, including one in Ginza station. Mon–Sat 10.30am–8pm, Sun 10.30am–7pm.

★**Kyūkyodō** 鳩居堂 5-7-4 Ginza, Chūō-ku ☎ 03 3571 4429; Ginza station; map p.52. Filled with the dusty smell of *sumi-e* ink, this venerable shop has been selling traditional paper, calligraphy brushes and inkstones since 1800. During Edo times, they provided incense to the emperor but the shop's history actually goes back even further – it was first founded in Kyoto in 1663 and,

amazingly, the same family still runs it. Daily 10am–7pm.

S Watanabe 渡邊木版美術画舖 8-6-19 Ginza, Chūō-ku ☎ 03 3571 4684; Shimbashi station; map p.52. Small shop specializing in woodblock prints at a range of prices, with designs both modern and traditional in nature. You'll spy original *ukiyo-e* as well as reproductions of works by famous artists. Mon–Sat 9.30am–8pm.

AKIHABARA AND AROUND

★**Origami Kaikan** おりがみ会館 1-7-14 Yushima, Bunkyo-ku ☎ 03 3811 4025, ⓦ origamikaikan.co.jp; Ochanomizu station; map p.59. This outpost for the production and dyeing of *washi* (Japanese paper) was founded in 1858, and to this day they continue to sell it on the premises – there's also an exhibition hall on the second floor. It's possible to take lessons (some free) in the art of paper folding here. Mon–Sat 9.30am–6pm.

UENO AND AROUND

★**Jūsan-ya** 十三や 2-12-21 Ueno, Taitō-ku ☎ 03 3831 3238; Ueno-Hirokōji station; map p.65. Tiny shop across the road from Shinobazu Pond, where a craftsman sits making beautiful boxwood combs – just as successive generations have done since 1736. A truly beautiful place to visit, even if you're not buying. Mon–Sat 10am–6.30pm.

Yanaka Matsunoya 谷中松野屋 3-14-14 Yanaka, Taitō-ku ☎ 03 3823 7441; Nippori station; map p.65. Appealing hand-crafted everyday items such as shopping bags, baskets, brooms and stools are the stock-in-trade of

ANTIQUE AND FLEA MARKETS

There's at least one **flea market** in Tokyo every weekend, though you'll need to arrive early for any bargains; see below for a roundup of the main venues and ask at a tourist information office (see p.38) for the current schedule. Note that **outdoor markets** are cancelled if the weather is bad. Alternatively, head for the permanent **antique halls**, which gather various dealers under one roof.

Hanazono-jinja 花園神社 5-17-3 Shinjuku, Shinjuku-ku; Shinjuku-sanchōme station; map p.126. You're more likely to find junk than real antiques at this market, but its setting in the grounds of a shrine, on the east side of Shinjuku (see p.130), is highly attractive. Most Sundays 6am–3pm.

Heiwajima Zenkoku Komingu Kottō Matsuri 平和島全国古民具骨董祭り Ryūtsū Center, 6-1-1 Heiwajima, Ōta-ku ☎ 03 3980 8228, ⓦ kottouichi .com; Ryūtsū Center monorail. One of the biggest antique fairs, this three-day event takes place about five times a year at the Ryūtsū Center, one stop on the monorail from Hamamatsuchō to Haneda. Usually Feb/March, May, June, Sept & Dec.

★**Ōedo Antique Market** 大江戸骨董市 Tokyo International Forum, 3-5-1 Marunouchi, Chiyoda-ku ⓦ antique-market.jp; Yūrakuchō station; map p.42. One of the largest regular flea markets in Tokyo, with some 250 vendors offering real antiques and interesting curios. Don't expect any bargains, though. Usually first and third Sun of month 9am–4pm.

Yasukuni-jinja 靖国神社 3-1-1 Kudankita, Chiyoda-ku; Kudanshita or Ichigaya stations; map p.42. One of the few temple flea markets which actually takes place every week, the goods on offer here aren't always particularly impressive, but the dramatic setting (see p.45) makes it a great visit anyway. Sun dawn–dusk.

17

this artfully rustic shop, at the top of the steps linking Nippori station with Yanaka Ginza. Daily except Tues 11am–7pm.

ASAKUSA AND AROUND

Bengara べんがら 1-35-6 Asakusa, Taitō-ku ☏ 03 3841 6613; Asakusa station; map p.74. This tiny store is crammed with a wide variety of *noren*, the split curtain seen hanging outside every traditional shop or restaurant. Even if you don't own a shop or restaurant, there'll be somewhere suitable in your own home for one of these. Daily 10am–6pm; closed third Sun of month.

Bunsendō 文扇堂 1-30-1 Asakusa, Taitō-ku ☏ 03 3841 0088; Asakusa station; map p.74. Shops selling paper fans are ten-a-penny in Asakusa, but this is one of the higher-grade offerings. They have two stores here, almost side by side. Daily 10.30am–6pm.

Fujiya ふじ屋 2-2-15 Asakusa, Taitō-ku ☏ 03 3841 2283; Asakusa station; map p.74. Hand-printed cotton towels (*tenugui*) designed by the Kawakami family; some end up becoming collectors' items, so choose carefully. Daily except Thurs 10am–6pm.

Kanesō かね惣 1-18-12 Asakusa, Taitō-ku ☏ 03 3844 1379; Asakusa station; map p.74. A mind-boggling array of knives, scissors, shears and files, crafted by the Hirano family over five generations. Daily 11am–7pm.

Kurodaya 黒田屋 1-2-5 Asakusa, Taitō-ku ☏ 03 3844 7511; Asakusa station; map p.74. Kurodaya has been selling woodblock prints and items made of traditional *washi* paper since 1856. Tues–Sun 11am–7pm.

Takahisa 高久 1-21-7 Asakusa, Taitō-ku ☏ 03 3844 1257; Asakusa station; map p.74. Shop selling row upon row of richly decorated *hagoita*: battledores which are traditionally used by young girls playing shuttlecock at New Year. You wouldn't want to be playing sport with these fancy, lacquered versions, but they make great souvenirs. Daily 10am–8pm.

Yonoya Kushiho よのや櫛舗 1-37-10 Asakusa, Taitō-ku ☏ 03 3844 1755; Asakusa station; map p.74. Tokyo's finest hand-crafted boxwood combs and hair decorations; much of the wood used here is sourced from forest land south of Kagoshima, and it's reputed to be particularly suitable for hair. Daily except Wed 10.30am–6pm.

AKASAKA AND ROPPONGI

Art & Design Store 3F Roppongi Hills Mori Tower, 6-10-1 Roppongi, Minato-ku ☏ 03 6406 6654; Roppongi station; map pp.96–97. A wonderful store near the entrance to Roppongi Hills' City View. The selection is ever-changing, but often features products from some of Japan's most famous contemporary designers; look out for the polka-dot-splashed produce of Yayoi Kusama. There's also a small gallery space here. Daily 11am–9pm.

Asa-no-ha 麻の葉 1-5-24 Azabu-Jūban, Minato-ku ☏ 03 3405 0161, ⓦ www.artsou.co.jp; Azabu-Jūban station; map pp.96–97. Small shop selling some

wonderful handkerchiefs, fans and other implements. All designs feature, or at least reference, traditional Japanese styles and patterns. Daily 10.30am–7pm.

★ **Blue & White** ブルー＆ワイと 2-9-2 Azabu-Jūban, Minato-ku ☏ 03 3451 0537; Azabu-Jūban station; map pp.96–97. Small store that sells exclusively blue-and-white-coloured products made in Japan including *yukata*, *furoshiki* (textile wrapping cloths), quilts, pottery and traditional decorations. Mon–Sat 10am–6pm, Sun 11am–6pm.

Japan Traditional Craft Centre 伝統工芸青山スクエア 1F Akasaka Ouji Building, 8-1-22 Akasaka, Minato-ku ☏ 03 5785 1001, ⓦ kougeihin.jp; Aoyama-itchōme station; map pp.96–97. This centre showcases the works of craft associations across the nation – everything from finely crafted chopsticks to elegant lacquerware and metalwork. Daily 10am–7pm.

EBISU, MEGURO AND THE SOUTH

Kamawanu かまわぬ 1-19-23 Sarugaku-chō, Shibuya-ku ☏ 03 3797 4788; Daikanyama station; map pp.106–107. Small shop selling excellent *tenugui* cloths in a variety of styles which, although modern, also make use of Japanese motifs. They also have a very nice looking range of traditional fans. Daily 11am–7pm.

Yamada Heiandō 山田平安堂 2F Hillside Terrace, 18-12 Sarugaku-chō, Shibuya-ku ☏ 03 3464 5541, ⓦ heiando.com; Daikanyama station; map pp.106–107. Hunt down this store for lacquerware – both traditional and contemporary – found on tables no less distinguished than those of the imperial household and Japan's embassies. Mon–Sat 10.30am–7pm, Sun 10.30am–6.30pm.

HARAJUKU, AOYAMA AND SHIBUYA

Beniya べにや民芸店 2-7-1 Minami-Aoyama, Minato-ku ☏ 03 5875 3261, ⓦ beniya.m78.com; Aoyama-itchōme station; map pp.114–115. It's a bit out of the way, but this place stocks one of Tokyo's best ranges of folk crafts (*mingei*). They also stage craft exhibitions at which you may get to meet the artist. Daily except Thurs 10am–7pm.

Musubi むす美 2-31-8 Jingūmae, Shibuya-ku ☏ 03 5414 5678; Meiji-jingūmae station; map pp.114–115. Pick up beautifully printed fabric *furoshiki* here to use instead of wrapping paper – they're also great gifts in themselves. Their origami design prints are particularly unusual. Note that there's no obvious sign on the shop – look for the dangling handbags on the ground level of a silver building. Daily except Wed 11am–7pm.

Oriental Bazaar オリエンタルバザール 5-9-13 Jingūmae, Shibuya-ku ☏ 03 3400 3933, ⓦ orientalbazaar.co.jp; Meiji-jingūmae station; map p.116. Although it may seem like a tourist trap, this very popular, one-stop souvenir emporium, selling everything from secondhand kimono to origami paper and top-class antiques, offers great deals and an almost unbeatable selection. Daily except Thurs 10am–7pm.

BOOKS AND MUSIC

Despite high prices, it can be enjoyable to browse the city's many **bookshops**, and bookworms should also rummage around the secondhand outlets of Jimbōchō (see p.61). Most big hotels have a shop stocking English-language books on Japan, as well as imported newspapers and magazines. In an age of digital downloads, Tokyo bucks the trend by sustaining many **CD and record shops**. The range of music on offer is impressively eclectic, with a huge range of foreign imports boosting an already mammoth local output of cheesy J-pop. Shibuya has the city's highest concentration of recorded music shops: head to the Udagawachō district near Tōkyū Hands to find scores of outlets specializing in hip-hop, house and techno. The music stores of Shimokitazawa are another good place to root around.

AKIHABARA AND AROUND

Kitazawa Shoten 北沢書店 2F 2-5 Jimbōchō, Chiyoda-ku ☎03 3263 0011; Jimbōchō station; map p.59. The stately granite- and brick-fronted building houses one of the best selections of English-language titles among the dozens of secondhand stores in Jimbōchō. It's on Yasukuni-dōri, just west of the junction with Hakusan-dōri, on the second floor of the Bookhouse store. Mon–Fri 11am–6.30pm, Sat noon–5.30pm.

AKASAKA AND ROPPONGI

Aoyama Book Center 青山本屋 6-1-20 Roppongi, Minato-ku ☎03 5485 5511, ⍟aoyamabc.jp; Roppongi station; map pp.96–97. Innovative bookshop with a fine collection of titles related to design, architecture and photography. Also carries lots of foreign magazines. Daily 10am–10pm.

EBISU, MEGURO AND THE SOUTH

★**Bonjour Records** 24-1 Sarugaku-chō, Shibuya-ku ☎03 5458 6020, ⍟www.bonjour.co.jp; Daikanyama station; map pp.106–107. It may not be the biggest CD store in Tokyo, but it's certainly the trendiest (they sell their own designer T-shirts) and has an über-cool curated selection. Daily 11am–7pm.

★**Tsutaya** 蔦屋 17-5 Sarugaku-chō, Shibuya-ku ☎03 3770 2525, ⍟tsite.jp; Daikanyama station; map pp.106–107. The design of this bookshop, whose exterior weaves together a lattice of white letter Ts, has scooped architects Klein Dytham a bunch of awards. Filled all day, every day with a preening young crowd, it's now the fulcrum

---

DEPARTMENT STORES

Although they're not as popular as they once were, Tokyo's massive **department stores** are likely to have almost anything you're looking for. They're also more likely to have English-speaking staff and a duty-free service than smaller shops, though prices tend to be slightly above average. Seasonal sales can offer great bargains.

★**Isetan** 伊勢丹 3-14-1 Shinjuku, Shinjuku-ku ☎03 3352 1111, ⍟isetan.co.jp; Shinjuku-sanchōme station; map p.126. One of the city's best department stores, with an emphasis on well-designed local goods and a reputation for promoting up-and-coming fashion designers. Their annexe, housing men's clothing and accessories, is particularly chic. The daily opening ceremony, with all staff bowing as you walk through the store, is worth attending. Daily 10am–8pm.

Matsuzakaya 松坂屋 3-29-5 Ueno, Taitō-ku ☎03 3832 1111, ⍟www.matsuzakaya.co.jp/ueno; Ueno-Hirokōji station; map p.65. This 300-year-old store is based in Ueno, where its main outlet barely shows its age thanks to an updated look. Daily 10am–8pm.

Mitsukoshi 三越 1-4-1 Nihombashi-Muromachi, Chūō-ku ☎03 3241 3311; Mitsukoshimae station; map p.52. Tokyo's most prestigious and oldest department store – dating back to 1673 – is elegant, spacious and renowned for its high-quality merchandise. Designer boutiques and more contemporary fashions are concentrated in the southerly *shin-kan* ("new building").

Daily 10.30am–7.30pm.

Seibu 西武 1-28-1 Minami-Ikebukuro, Toshima-ku ☎03 3981 0111; Ikebukuro station; map p.138. Sprawling department store with a reputation for innovation, especially in its homeware store Loft, and its clothing and lifestyle offshoot Parco. There's a great chill-out area on the rooftop. Mon–Sat 10am–9pm, Sun 10am–8pm.

Takashimaya 高島屋 2-4-1 Nihombashi, Chūō-ku ☎03 3211 4111; Nihombashi station; map p.52. Like Mitsukoshi, Takashimaya has a long and illustrious past, a great food hall and a very broad range of goods, though it appeals to decidedly conservative tastes. There's a huge branch in Shinjuku at Takashimaya Times Square (see map, p.126). Daily 10am–8pm.

Tōkyū 東急 2-24-1 Dōgenzaka, Shibuya-ku ☎03 3477 3111; Shibuya station; map p.122. Top dog in the Shibuya department store stakes, with branches all over the area, particularly around the train station. This main store specializes in designer fashions and interior goods. Daily 11am–7pm.

17

of the whole Daikanyama area. They've a tremendous selection of English-language books, as well as a *Starbucks* (good luck finding a seat) and lounge bar. Daily 7am–2am.

HARAJUKU, AOYAMA AND SHIBUYA

Tower Records タワーレコード 1-22-14 Jinnan, Shibuya-ku ☎03 3496 3661; Shibuya station; map p.122. An entertainment superstore, with six floors of CDs, DVDs, books, magazines, videos and games. Other branches across the city. Daily 10am–10pm.

SHINJUKU AND THE WEST

Disk Union ディスクユニオン 1-40-7 Kitazawa, Setagaya-ku ☎03 3467 3231; Shimokitazawa station; map p.132. Of the twenty-odd Disk Union branches scattered around Tokyo, the Shimokitazawa one is by far the most notable – a huge venue with pretty much every major genre and subgenre covered, and one of Tokyo's best vinyl collections. Daily 11.30am–9pm.

★Kinokuniya 紀伊國屋 Takashimaya Times Square, Annex Building, 5-24-2 Sendagaya, Shinjuku-ku ☎03 5361 3301; Shinjuku station; map p.126. The sixth floor of Kinokuniya's seven-storey Shinjuku outlet offers Tokyo's widest selection of foreign-language books and magazines, including loads of Rough Guides. Daily 10am–8pm; closed one Wed each month.

CAMERAS AND ELECTRONIC GOODS

Akihabara boasts Tokyo's biggest concentration of stores selling **electronic goods**. **Shinjuku** is Tokyo's prime area for **cameras** and photographic equipment, though Ikebukuro also has a solid reputation for new and secondhand deals at reasonable prices. There are also plenty of **discount outlets** in Shinjuku and Shibuya. Compare prices – many shops are open to bargaining – and make sure there's the appropriate voltage switch (the Japanese power supply is 100V). It's also important to check that whatever you buy will be compatible with equipment you have at home. For English-language instructions, after-sales service and guarantees, stick to export models, which you'll find mostly in the stores' duty-free sections. Some of the larger Akihabara stores offering export models are listed below and at ⊚e-akihabara.jp.

IMPERIAL PALACE AND AROUND

BIC Camera ビックカメラ 1-11-1 Yūrakuchō, Chiyoda-ku ☎03 5221 1111; Yūrakuchō station; map p.42. The main branch of BIC offers hard-to-beat prices for cameras and audio and electronic goods – practically any gizmo you want can be found here. You'll find other branches scattered around Tokyo's main shopping centres, including several in Ikebukuro, Shinjuku and Shibuya. Daily 10am–10pm.

GINZA AND AROUND

Shimizu Camera 清水カメラ 4-3-2 Ginza, Chūō-ku ☎03 3564 1008; Ginza station; map p.52. Reputable used-camera specialist in the backstreets of Ginza, still going strong despite the decline of the industry. Mon–Sat 10.30am–8pm, Sun 11am–7pm.

AKIHABARA AND AROUND

Laox ラオクス 1-2-9 Soto-Kanda, Chiyoda-ku ☎03 3255 9041; Akihabara station; map p.59. One of the most prominent names in Akiba and probably the best place to start browsing: they have a well-established duty-free section with English-speaking staff, and nine stores where you can buy everything from pocket calculators to plasma screen TVs. Mon–Fri 10am–8pm, Fri & Sat 10am–9pm.

Tsukumo Robot Kingdom 九十九 1-9-9 Soto-Kanda, Chiyoda-ku ☎03 3253 5599; Akihabara station; map p.59. Tsukumo is a general electrical store with three outlets – look for the one with the sign "Robot". Upstairs you'll find a floor aimed at model enthusiasts building their very own androids, but there are also a few demonstration models of working robots. The videos are fun to watch, too. Daily 10am–10pm.

Yodobashi Camera ヨドバシカメラ 1-1 Kanda-Hanaokachō, Chiyoda-ku; Akihabara station; map p.59, 1-11-1 Nishi-Shinjuku, Shinjuku-ku ☎03 3346 1010; Shinjuku station; map p.59. Vast electronics store selling everything from PCs to exercise bikes, by way of cameras. There are other branches throughout the city; the Shinjuku outlet (see map, p.126) claims to be the world's largest camera shop, and offers decent reductions. Daily 9.30am–10pm.

FASHION AND COSMETICS

The city's epicentre of clothing chic is **Omotesandō**, where dazzlingly designed **boutiques** for famed brands such as Chanel, Ralph Lauren and Louis Vuitton vie to outdo each other in extravagance. Alongside you'll also find top **Japanese labels** such as Issey Miyake and Comme des Garçons, while the area's backstreets are prime hunting grounds for fashionistas searching for up-and-coming designers. **Daikanyama, Nakameguro** and **Shimokitazawa** are also worth browsing around – shops in the last two areas tend to be slightly cheaper. Finding clothes that fit is still a challenge (especially, it has to be said, for many foreign females), but is becoming easier as young Japanese are, on average, substantially bigger than their parents; **shoes** remain more of a problem, with the range of larger sizes still pretty limited. Along with department stores (see box, p.197), the ubiquitous ABC-Mart and Ginza's Washington shoe

FROM TOP CIBONE, AOYAMA (P.203); PRADA, OMOTESANDŌ (P.201) >

17

shop are usually your best bet. Good places to hunt for bargain footwear are Shinjuku, especially around Studio Alta, and Ueno's Ameyokochō market.

GINZA AND AROUND

★**Dover Street Market** 6-9-6 Ginza, Chūō-ku ☏03 6228 5080, ⓦginza.doverstreetmarket.com; Ginza station; map p.52. This large new complex has started to draw fashionistas back to Ginza from the west, and with good reason – the several floors here feature clothing from almost every major Japanese designer, plus a few of the Antwerp Six, without the department-store atmosphere that usually goes with such choice. Mon–Sat 11am–8pm.

Mikimoto 三木本 4-5-5 Ginza, Chūō-ku ☏03 3535 4611, ⓦwww.mikimoto.co.jp; Ginza station; map p.52. The famous purveyor of cultured pearls has branched out into diamonds and other jewellery lines, all shown off to perfection in its dramatic main store in the heart of Ginza. An annexe aound the corner focuses on high-fashion clothes, accessories and beauty products – look for the pale, pearly pink building with holes punched in it, the work of architect Itō Toyō. Daily 11am–7pm.

Shiseidō 資生堂 8-8-3 Ginza, Chūō-ku ☏03 3572 3913, ⓦshiseido.co.jp; Ginza or Shimbashi stations; map p.52. One of the oldest cosmetics companies in the world, and the fourth largest globally, Shiseidō was established in Tokyo in 1872. Their main branch occupies a distinctive red building that also features a gallery (see p.54) and several places to eat and drink. Mon–Sat 11.30am–7.30pm, Sun 11.30am–7pm.

Uniqlo ユニクロ 5-7-7 Ginza, Chūō-ku ☏03 3569 6781 ⓦwww.uniqlo.co.jp; Ginza station; map p.52. Inexpensive but still cool, this local brand has found mammoth success overseas. This is their flagship Tokyo store, designed by Klein Dytham, also responsible for the Tsutaya bookshop in Daikanyama (see p.197). Other branches all over the city. Daily 11am–9pm.

EBISU, MEGURO AND THE SOUTH

Evisu エヴィス 1-1-5 Kami-Meguro, Meguro-ku ☏03 3710 1999, ⓦevisu.com; Nakameguro station; map pp.106–107. Main branch of the ultra-trendy – and ultra-pricey – Japanese jeans designer. Stock up here on shirts, T-shirts, sweatshirts and a full range of accessories. Daily noon–8pm.

Jun Ashida ジュン　アシダ 17-16 Sarugakuchō, Shibuya-ku ☏03 3462 5811, ⓦjun-ashida.co.jp; Daikanyama station; map pp.106–107. The headquarters of Jun Ashida, one of Japan's top designers of womenswear, as well as his daughter Tae, who recently achieved fame by becoming the first ever designer of luxury spacewear. Daily 11am–7pm.

★**Okura** オクラ 20-11 Sarugaku-chō, Shibuya-ku ☏03 3461 8511; map pp.106–107. Daikanyama station. Youthful boutique specializing in indigo-dyed traditional and contemporary Japanese fashions, from jeans and

T-shirts to kimono and *tabi* socks. No English sign – look for a low, wooden-style building, usually with some form of indigo fabric hanging outside. Daily 11am–8pm.

HARAJUKU, AOYAMA AND SHIBUYA

6% Dokidoki ロクパーセントドキドキ 2F 4-28-16 Jingūmae, Shibuya-ku ☏03 3479 6116, ⓦdokidoki6 .com; Meiji-jingūmae station; map p.116. Focusing on the "Kawaii" clothing genre (see box, p.113), this second-floor store is as loud as it gets: loud clothing, loud decor, loud music. Daily noon–8pm.

Arts & Science 6-6-20 Minami-Aoyama, Minato-ku ☏03 3498 1091, ⓦarts-science.com; Omotesandō station; map pp.114–115. Sonya Park, the Korean-born, Hawaii-raised owner of this boutique, has a great eye for what works in fashion. Her collection includes original pieces alongside such things as sheepskin Scandinavian army coats and French perfumes. Daily noon–8pm.

★**Bapexclusive** 5-5-8 Minami-Aoyama, Minato-ku ☏03 3407 2145, ⓦbape.com; Omotesandō station; map p.116. A Bathing Ape, the streetwear brand of designer Nigo, has a string of boutiques all over Aoyama and Harajuku, of which this is the main showroom. One of their T-shirts will set you back at least ¥6000. Daily 11am–8pm.

Bedrock ベッドロック B1 Omotesandō Hills West Wing, 4-12-10 Jingūmae, Shibuya-ku ☏03 3423 6969; Omotesandō station; map p.116. Enter Omotesandō Hills at street level and take the stairs down to this darkly glamorous shop stocking hip Harajuku fashions. Daily 11am–8pm.

Billionaire Boys Club ビリオネールボイズクラブ 4-5-21 Jingūmae, Shibuya-ku ☏03 5775 2633, ⓦbbcicecream.com; Meiji-jingūmae station; map p.116. Boutique selling the hip-hop-inspired clothes of Pharrell Williams and the tutti-frutti-coloured sneaker line Ice Cream (his collaboration with Japanese designer Nigo, of A Bathing Ape fame). Daily 11am–7pm.

CA4LA 1-18-2 Kaminami, Shibuya-ku ☏03 3770 5051, ⓦca4la.com; Shibuya station; map p.116. Hat shop to the eternally trendy, with everything from foppish fedoras and broad-brimmed sun hats to hip-hop beanies and designer baseball caps. The name is pronounced "Ka-shi-ra", by the way. Daily 11am–8pm.

Comme des Garçons 5-2-1 Minami-Aoyama, Minato-ku ☏03 3406 3951, ⓦcomme-des-garcons .com; Omotesandō station; map p.116. More like an art gallery than a clothes shop, this beautiful store is a suitable setting for the high-fashion menswear and womenswear by renowned designer Kawakubo Rei. Daily 11am–8pm.

Dresscamp ドレスキャンプ 5-5-1 Minami-Aoyama, Minato-ku ☏03 5778 3717, ⓦdresscamp.jp; Omotesandō station; map p.116. Indulge your inner rock god or goddess at this glitzy boutique. The styles on display are very wacky, and more than a little pricey, though undeniably fashion-show-friendly. Daily noon–9pm.

Fake Tokyo フェーク東京 18-4 Udagawa-chō, Shibuya-ku ☎03 5456 9892, ⓦwww.faketokyo.com; Shibuya station; map p.122. Hidden away on a back street near the Loft mall, this two-level store is great for contemporary female fashion. Candy, on the ground level, caters to younger tastes, while Sister up above is a fair bit more elegant. Daily noon–2am.

★**Hysterics** 5-5-3 Minami-Aoyama, Minato-ku ☎03 6419 3899, ⓦhystericglamour.jp; Omotesandō station; map p.116. The premier outlet for Hysteric Glamour, a fun, retro-kitsch Americana label which is one of Japan's leading youth brands. Daily noon–8pm.

Inhabitant インハビタント 6-7-10 Jingūmae, Shibuya-ku ☎03 5778 4006, ⓦinhabitant.jp; Meiji-jingūmae station; map p.116. Stylish skaters, cyclists and snowboarders kit up at this shop, in a great location on Harajuku's famous "Cat Street". Daily 11am–8pm.

Isehan Honten 伊勢半本店 6-6-20 Minami-Aoyama, Minato-ku ☎03 5467 3735, ⓦisehanhonten.co.jp; Omotesandō station; map pp.114–115. Traditional cosmetics are the speciality of Isehan Honten. Their key product is *beni*, a safflower-based lip colour with a lustrous green glow in its concentrated form, though it paints on red; only one percent of the yellow flower's pigment is red, making it expensive. It's sold in lovely china pots, and you can learn about its history in the attached small museum. Tues–Sun 11am–7pm.

★**Issey Miyake** 三宅一生 3-18-11 Minami-Aoyama, Minato-ku ☎03 3423 1407, ⓦisseymiyake.co.jp; Omotesandō station; map p.116. One of the top names in world fashion, famous for his elegant, eminently wearable designs. This flagship store, a pink building with Art Deco touches, is suitably fancy. Daily 11am–8pm.

★**Kura Chika Yoshida** クラチカヨシダ 5-6-8 Jingūmae, Shibuya-ku ☎03 5464 1766, ⓦwww.yoshidakaban .com; Omotesandō station; map p.116. Access the full range of bags, wallets and luggage at this shrine to the hip Japanese brand Porter. It's just off Omotesandō, behind Tokyo Union Church. Daily except Wed noon–8pm.

Laforet ラフォーレ 1-11-6 Jingūmae, Shibuya-ku ☎03 3475 0411, ⓦlaforet.ne.jp; Meiji-jingūmae station; map p.116. This pioneering "fashion building" is packed with boutiques catering to the fickle tastes of Harajuku's teenage shopping mavens. Wander through and catch the zeitgeist. Daily 11am–8pm.

Onitsuka Tiger おにつかタイガー 4-24-14 Jingūmae, Shibuya-ku ☎03 3405 6671, ⓦonitsukatiger.com; Meiji-jingūmae station; map p.116. Selling trainers as seen on the most fashionable feet, this Japanese brand started business back in 1949. Other branches across the city. Daily 11am–8pm.

Prada プラダ 5-2-6 Minami-Aoyama, Shibuya-ku ☎03 6418 0400, ⓦprada.com; Omotesandō station; map p.116. Without doubt the most attractive shop in Aoyama – which is saying something. Walk in like you own the place, head up to the top floor, and walk down the spiral stairs feeling like a superstar. Mon–Thurs 11am–8pm, Fri–Sun 11am–9pm.

★**Ragtag** ラグタグ 6-14-2 Jingūmae, Shibuya-ku ☎03 6419 3770, ⓦragtag.jp; Meiji-jingūmae station; map p.116. A great place selling secondhand goods from selected designers, including local über-brands Comme des Garçons, Yohji Yamamoto and United Arrows. Daily 11am–8pm.

★**Sou Sou** そうそう 5-4-24 Minami-Aoyama, Minato-ku ☎03 3407 7877, ⓦsousou.co.jp; Omotesandō station; map pp.114–115. After the Japanese saying "sō sō", meaning "I agree with you", this range of modern design shoes and clothes based on traditional forms, such as split-toe *tabi* (socks), is eminently agreeable. Their plimsolls are an ideal match for jeans. There's also an outlet in Venus Fort (see p.90). Daily 11am–8pm.

★**Tsumori Chisato** 津森千里 4-21-25 Minami-Aoyama, Minato-ku ☎03 3423 5170; Omotesandō station; map p.116. Girlish streetwear that captures the Harajuku look, but with better tailoring, materials and attention to detail. Daily 11am–8pm.

UnderCover アンダーカバー 5-3 Minami-Aoyama, Minato-ku ☎03 3407 1232; Omotesandō station; map p.116. Jun Takahashi's UnderCover brand of clothing isn't so underground any more, but remains youthful and eclectic. Daily 10am–8.30pm.

United Arrows ユナイテッドアローズ 3-28-1 Jingūmae, Shibuya-ku ☎03 3479 8180, ⓦunited-arrows.co.jp; Meiji-jingūmae station; map p.116. Main store of the upmarket fashion chain, famous for its clean-cut men's shirts and suits. Head to the top floor to have your measurements taken for a custom-made kimono or cotton shirt. Also look out for their Beauty & Youth (ⓦbeauty andyouth.jp) stores in all major shopping areas. Mon–Fri noon–8pm, Sat & Sun 11am–8pm.

Yohji Yamamoto 山本耀司 5-3-6 Minami-Aoyama, Shibuya-ku ☎03 3409 6006, ⓦyohjiyamamoto.co.jp; Omotesandō station; map p.116. Flagship store of Japanese fashion icon Yohji Yamamoto, famed for his edgy, single-colour designs. Daily 11am–8pm.

SHINJUKU AND THE WEST

Comme Ça Store 3-26-6 Shinjuku, Shinjuku-ku ☎03 5367 5551; Shinjuku station; map p.126. Stylish, multi-level showcase for Comme Ça du Mode, a bright and affordable unisex clothing brand; also has a good café up top (see p.172). Mon–Sat 11am–11pm, Sun 11am–8pm.

New York Joe ニューヨークジョー 3-26-4 Kitazawa, Setagaya-ku ☎03 5738 2077; Shimokitazawa station; map p.132. Set in what was once a bathhouse, this is the

17

best of the area's many vintage clothing stores, selling a wide range of first-rate secondhand goods. All items are under ¥10,000, and you can get a big discount if taking suitable goods to swap. Daily noon–8pm.

IKEBUKURO AND THE NORTH

Assist Wig アシストウイッグ 3-4-1 Higashi-Ikebukuro, Toshima-ku ☎079 228 9625, ⓦassistcosplay.com; Ikebukuro station; map p.138. Ape the wild Harajuku hairstyles with a cartoonish wig from this store, which claims to have more colours on offer than any other wig-shop in the world; at 500 and counting, perhaps they're right. Daily 11.30am–9pm.

FOOD AND DRINK

The best one-stop places to find unusual and souvenir food and drink items – such as beautifully boxed biscuits, cakes and traditional sweets (*wagashi*), and sake from across the country – are the department store **food halls** (see box, p.197). There are also some highly regarded food and drink shops in Tokyo, some of which have been around for centuries. Premium **teas** are sold at Cha Ginza and Higashiya Ginza teahouses (see p.158 & p.159). General foodstuffs and snacks are easily bought from 24-hour **convenience stores** (see box below).

IMPERIAL PALACE AND AROUND

Amano Freeze-Dry Station アマノフリーズドライステーション B1F Kitte Building, 2-7-2 Marunouchi, Chiyoda-ku ☎03 6256 0911; Tokyo station; map p.42. A fun little shop where everything for sale is freeze-dried – take some soups, curries or risotto home, boil some water, and dine like a Japanese astronaut. Daily 10am–8pm.

Sake Plaza 酒プラザー 1-1-21 Nishi-Shinbashi, Minato-ku ☎03 3519 2091; Toranomon or Uchisai-wachō stations; map p.42. Run by the Japan Sake Brewers Association, this shop and tasting room has an excellent range of sake from all over the country, and they often offer cheap sample tastings. It promotes a different region each season, and the sakes on offer change daily. Mon–Fri 10am–6pm.

BAYSIDE TOKYO

Tenyasu Honten 天安本店 1-3-14 Tsukuda, Chūo-ku ☎03 3532 3457; Tsukishima station; map p.87. This ancient shop specializes in *tsukudani*, delicious morsels of seaweed and fish preserved in a mixture of soy sauce, salt and sugar – a speciality of the local area. A wooden box of six different types from their selection of eighteen costs ¥2050; the preserves last for three weeks. Daily 9am–6pm.

AKASAKA AND ROPPONGI

Fukumitsuya 福光屋 B1 Tokyo Midtown Galleria, 9-7-4 Akasaka, Minato-ku ☎03 6804 5341, ⓦfukumitsuya .co.jp; Roppongi station; map pp.96–97. Tucked away in the basement level of Tokyo Midtown, this boutique sake shop represents the oldest brewery in Kanazawa (founded 1625), in north central Japan. There are fifty different sakes on offer, from which you can taste a selection of three for ¥1100. Otherwise, prices start at ¥400 a shot. Daily 11am–9pm.

★**Toraya** とらや 4-9-22 Akasaka, Minato-ku ☎03 3408 4121, ⓦtoraya-group.co.jp; Akasaka-Mitsuke station; map pp.96–97. Makers of *wagashi* (traditional confectionery often used in tea ceremonies) for the imperial family. Everything is beautifully packaged and products vary with the season. Sample the products, along with green tea, in the café downstairs. This flagship branch will be closed for reconstruction until 2018; until then you can visit the branch at Tokyo Midtown. Mon–Fri 11am–7pm, Sat & Sun 11am–5.30pm.

EBISU, MEGURO AND THE SOUTH

National Azabu ナショナル麻布 4-5-2 Minami-Azabu, Minato-ku ☎03 3442 3181, ⓦnational-azabu.com; Hiro-o station; map pp.106–107. Supermarket firmly geared towards the tastes of the expat community, with a great selection of international foods as well as fresh veggies, fruits, meat and fish. Daily 9.30am–8pm.

CONVENIENCE STORES

It's fair to say that Tokyo has a fair few convenience stores: some estimates clock a figure approaching ten thousand. Wherever you are in the city, there are always a dozen or so within easy walking distance, selling food, soft drinks and alcohol (and often spare underwear) at every hour of the day, every day of the year. Locals use them for tasks such as bill paying and booking concert tickets. The largest chains of **kombini**, as locals usually call them, are **7-Eleven**, **Lawson**, **Family Mart** and **Mini Stop**. Most offer fried snacks from ¥85, cup noodles from ¥120, cartons of sake from ¥100, and cans of beer for ¥150 and up. Indeed, with liberal public drinking laws, and the price of a beer running to over ¥500 in most Tokyo bars (plus sit-down charge), it's no surprise that students, backpackers and others on tight budgets often end up racing to their nearest store for a "*kombini* martini".

HOMEWARE AND INTERIOR DESIGN

17

Japan is justly famous for the delicate beauty and practicality of its **interior design**, particularly the ingenious way it makes the most of limited space, and for its *wabi-sabi* sensibility, which finds beauty in imperfection. In Tokyo's top interior design shops you can find products by legendary designers such as Isamu Noguchi and Yanagi Sori, as well as up-and-coming and overseas talents.

IMPERIAL PALACE AND AROUND

Pass the Baton Brick Square, 2-6-1 Marunouchi, Chiyoda-ku ☎ 03 6269 9555; Tokyo station; map p.42. Styling itself a "personal culture marketplace", this curate's egg of a shop is like a boutique recycling store with carefully chosen new and old decorative objects as well as a few fashion items. Mon–Sat 11am–9pm, Sun until 8pm.

AKASAKA AND ROPPONGI

★**The Cover Nippon** 3F Galleria, Tokyo Midtown, 9-7-3 Akasaka, Minato-ku ☎ 03 5413 0658, ⓦ thecover nippon.jp; Roppongi station; map pp.96–97. The most interesting shop on Tokyo Midtown's interior design floor, with a fantastic selection of Japanese designer goods made by small, quality manufacturers – everything from cotton fabric and furniture to lacquerware. Daily 11am–9pm.

★**Nuno** ぬの B1 Axis, 5-17-1 Roppongi ☎ 03 3582 7997, ⓦ nuno.com; Roppongi station; map pp.96–97. In the basement of the Axis Building (which has several other good interior design shops), Nuno stocks its own range of exquisite original fabrics made in Japan, either sold on their own by the metre or made into clothes, cushions and other items. Mon–Sat 11am–7pm.

EBISU, MEGURO AND THE SOUTH

Do Claska, 1-3-18 Chūō-chō, Meguro-ku ☎ 03 3719 8124, ⓦ claskashop.com; Meguro station, then bus or taxi; map pp.106–107. The shop and gallery of the fab *Claska* hotel (see p.146) is packed with beautiful pieces of Japanese contemporary design – everything from straw hats and fish-shaped soaps to woven lacquerware boxes and sleek wooden chopsticks. There's also an online store. Daily 11am–7pm.

HARAJUKU, AOYAMA AND SHIBUYA

Cibone B1F Aoyama Bell Commons, 2-27-25 Minami-Aoyama, Minato-ku ☎ 03 3475 8017, ⓦ cibone.com; Gaienmae station; map pp.114–115. All kinds of furniture and interior design goods can be purchased at this stylish store, which has a strong representation of local designers, as well as good books and CD sections. Daily 11am–9pm.

Francfranc フランフラン 3-1-3 Minami-Aoyama, Minato-ku ☎ 03 5413 2511, ⓦ francfranc.com; Omotesandō station; map pp.114–115. You can get an idea of how free-spending young and on-trend Japanese like to decorate their homes at this fun interior design store which offers an appealing range of colourful, affordable items that wouldn't look out of place at Ikea. Daily 11am–10pm.

Hakusan 白山 Floor G, From First Bldg, 5-3-10 Minami-Aoyama, Minato-ku ☎ 03 5774 8850; Omotesandō station; map pp.114–115. Sophisticated, award-winning porcelain produced at the Kyūshū town of Hasami, near Nagasaki. Daily 11am–8pm.

★**Tōkyū Hands** 東急ハンズ 12-10 Udagawachō, Shibuya-ku ☎ 03 5489 5111; Shibuya station; map p.122. This offshoot of the Tōkyū department store is the place to head if you're planning home improvements or have practically any hobby – they stock everything you could possibly need, from paper, paints and pencils to backpacks and kayaks. It's also a great place to look for quirky souvenirs. Other branches across the city. Daily 10am–8pm, except second and third Wed of the month.

SHINJUKU AND THE WEST

★**Muji** 無印良品 B1-2F Shinjuku Piccadilly, 3-15-15 Shinjuku, Shinjuku-ku ☎ 03 5367 2710; Shinjuku station; map p.126. One of the newest and biggest branches of this homeware, lifestyle and fashion chain, a "no-brand" concept whose logo is now, ironically, seen across the world. Carries a wide range of their goods, including the classy Muji Labo fashion range, which you'll also find at their store in Tokyo Midtown (see map, pp.96–97). Daily 10am–9pm.

KIMONO AND YUKATA

Japan's national costume, the kimono, is still worn by both sexes for special occasions, such as weddings and festival visits to a shrine. Ready-made kimono can easily cost ¥100,000, while ¥1 million is not uncommon for the best made-to-measure garments. Secondhand or **antique kimono**, with prices as low as ¥1000, can be found at tourist shops, flea markets or in the kimono sales held by department stores, usually in spring and autumn; Oriental Bazaar (see p.196) also offers a good selection of pre-loved kimono. You'll pay more for the highly decorated **wedding kimono** (they make striking wall hangings), as well as for the most beautifully patterned *obi*, the broad, silk sash worn with a kimono. Light cotton **yukata** are popular with both sexes as dressing gowns; you'll find them in all department stores and many speciality stores, along with *happi* coats – the loose jackets that just cover the upper body. To complete the outfit, pick up a pair of traditional wooden sandals (*geta*).

17

NEO-KIMONO

Demand for new kimono has dipped in recent years, a trend that has gone hand in hand with Japan's declining birth rate and the antipathy of the younger generation to this style of clothing. A bright spot for the industry is the trend to adapt old kimono to **new uses**: young women sometimes wear kimono like a coat over Western clothes, or coordinate it with coloured rather than white *tabi* (traditional split-toed socks). At the same time, **fashion designers** are turning to kimono fabrics and styles for contemporary creations. **Do Justice** (🌐 www.dojustice.jp) uses antique kimono and *obi* fabric to decorate jeans and create ties, shirts and other fashion items (available online); it's not cheap but each one-off item is utterly original.

ASAKUSA AND AROUND

Sakura 桜 2-41-8 Asakusa, Taitō-ku ☎ 03 5826 5622; Asakusa station; map p.74. Not your regular kimono shop – this tiny store sells Gothic-style clothing made with patches of old kimono fabric (see box above). Their pantaloons, which morph from skirt to trousers by way of hidden buttons, are fantastic. Daily 12.30–9.30pm.

HARAJUKU, AOYAMA AND SHIBUYA

Chicago シカゴ 4-26-26 Jingūmae, Shibuya-ku ☎ 03 5414 5107, 🌐 www.chicago.co.jp; Meiji-jingūmae station; map p.116. There's a fine selection of kimono, *obi* and so on at this Harajuku thrift store, as well as rack upon rack of good used clothes. Daily 11am–8pm.

Gallery Kawano ギャラリー 川野 102 Flats-Omotesandō, 4-4-9 Jingūmae, Shibuya-ku ☎ 03 3470 3305; Omotesandō station; map p.116. Excellent selection of vintage kimono, *yukata* and *obi*, with swatches of gorgeous kimono fabric available too. Daily 11am–6pm.

TOYS, GAMES AND NOVELTIES

The land that gave the world Super Mario Brothers, Hello Kitty and Pokemon is forever throwing up new **must-have toys**, games and novelties – Tokyo's top stores are prime hunting grounds for the next big craze before it hits the world market. For more traditional playthings, poke around the **craft stalls** of Asakusa's Nakamise-dōri. Also keep an eye out for the ubiquitous "**¥100 Shops**" (everything's actually ¥108, including tax), which can yield a crop of bargain souvenirs.

GINZA AND AROUND

Hakuhinkan Toy Park 博品館 8-8-11 Ginza, Chūō-ku ☎ 03 3571 8008, 🌐 hakuhinkan.co.jp; Shimbashi station; map p.52. This huge toy shop also houses a theatre, staging Japanese-language shows which might entertain little ones – or at least distract them from spending up a storm on your behalf. Daily 11am–8pm.

Tamiya Plamodel Factory タミヤプラモデルファクトリー 6 Toyokaiji Building, 4-7-2 Shimbashi, Minato-ku ☎ 03 3719 8124, 🌐 tamiya-plamodel factory.co.jp; Shimbashi station; map p.52. Model-kit enthusiasts rejoice – the Japanese manufacturer's entire range is available in this three-level emporium, showcasing thousands of scale and radio-controlled models of automobiles, planes, boats and military hardware. Mon–Fri noon–10pm, Sat & Sun noon–6pm.

AKIHABARA AND AROUND

Village Vanguard ヴィレッジヴァンガード B1F 3-14 Kanda-Ogawamachi, Chiyoda-ku ☎ 03 5281 5535; Jimbōchō or Ogawamachi stations; map p.59. This "exciting bookstore" stocks an amazing hotchpotch of toys and novelties, from inflatable bananas to Batman accessories – and a few fun books and CDs. You'll find quite a few branches around the city. Daily 10am–11pm.

ASAKUSA

Ganso Sample-ya 元祖サンプル屋 3-7-6 Nishi-Asakusa, Taitō-ku ☎ 0120 171839, 🌐 ganso-sample.com; Tawaramachi station; map p.74. The most traveller-friendly shop in "Kitchenware Town" (see p.77), selling fun items such as sushi key-fobs and fake bowls of miso soup – great souvenir fodder. Daily 10am–5.30pm.

AKASAKA AND ROPPONGI

Don Quijote ドンキホーテ 3-14-10 Roppongi, Minato-ku ☎ 03 578 6811, 🌐 donki.com; Roppongi station; map pp.96–97. Fancy some sushi-print socks? A mind-boggling array of stuff is piled high and sold cheap here – everything from liquor to sex toys, as well as gadgets galore. A national institution, it's worth visiting just for the gawp factor. Several branches around the city. Daily 24hr.

HARAJUKU, AOYAMA AND SHIBUYA

Kiddyland キッディランド 6-1-9 Jingūmae, Shibuya-ku ☎ 03 3409 3431, 🌐 www.kiddyland.co.jp; Meiji-jingūmae station; map p.116. Flagship store boasting six full floors of toys, stationery, sweets and other souvenirs. Daily 10am–8pm, closed every third Tues.

MEN PRACTISING KENDO

Sport and health

In 1964, Tokyo became the first Asian city to host the Olympic Games; in 2020, it will become the first to do so twice (see box, p.120). Together with the World Cup that Japan co-hosted in 2002, these events hint at a surprisingly sporty scene in a country that most outsiders might associate more closely with academic performance than with athletic endeavour. It's not uncommon for parts of Tokyo to come to a complete standstill during crucial baseball games as fans gather around television screens in homes, offices, bars and even on the street. Baseball is the city's premier sporting obsession, but hot on its heels is football (soccer), with the Japanese national team improving every decade.

Although its popularity has slipped in recent decades, **sumo wrestling** also has a high profile, with big tournaments (*basho*) televised nationwide and wrestlers enjoying celebrity status. Tokyo also has numerous *dōjō* (practice halls) where it's possible to watch **martial arts** such as aikido, judo and karate, and learn about these ancient fighting methods.

Check local media for details of events. For tickets, approach one of the major **ticket agencies** (see box, p.188).

18 BASEBALL

The baseball season runs from April–Oct and watching a **professional match** is great fun; even if you're not a fan, the audience enthusiasm can be infectious. Tickets start at under ¥2000, and go on sale on the Friday two weeks prior to a game. It's rare to find anyone who doesn't support one of Tokyo's two main baseball (*yakyū*) teams, the **Yomiuri Giants** and the **Yakult Swallows**; Yokohama has the Yokohama Baystars. As well as the two professional leagues (Central and Pacific), there's the equally popular All-Japan High School Baseball Championship, and you might be able to catch one of the local play-offs before the main tournament held each summer in Ōsaka; check with the tourist office for details.

Jingū Baseball Stadium 神宮球場 13 Kasumigaoka, Shinjuku-ku ☎ 03 3404 8999, ⓦ www.jingu-stadium .com; Gaienmae station; map pp.114–115. One of the stadia grouped in Meiji-jingū's Outer Gardens, this is the base of the Yakult Swallows and hosts the college baseball Tokyo Big Six league.

Tokyo Dome 東京ドーム 1-3 Koraku, Bunkyō-ku ☎ 03 5800 9999, ⓦ www.tokyo-dome.co.jp; Suidōbashi station; map pp.136–137. This huge covered arena, affectionately nicknamed the "Big Egg", is home to the Yomiuri Giants, and is a great place to take in a night game.

FOOTBALL

The national "sakaa" team didn't qualify for the FIFA World Cup until 1998, but have made every finals since – they even co-hosted the 2002 edition with South Korea. This has helped make the game a huge crowd-puller here; professional **J-League** (ⓦ jleague. jp) games are held from March to October, with a break in August. Eighteen clubs play in the top J1 division, and together with teams from lower leagues, they also participate in the **Emperor's Cup**, primarily a winter event, its final takes place on New Year's Day (oddly meaning that the cup of any given year is actually won the day after that year ends). At an **amateur level**, there's the Tokyo Metropolis League (ⓦ footyjapancompetitions.com); check the website for games, or if you're interested in taking part. Other than the clubs mentioned below, look out for Kawasaki Frontale (ⓦ frontale.co.jp) and Yokohama F Marinos (ⓦ www .f-marinos.com), both based in the wider Tokyo area.

BATTING STATIONS

If you fancy practising to be the next baseball superstar, or just want to let off some steam, then a trip to one of Tokyo's **batting stations** is what's called for. You'll pay around ¥400 for 20 balls; machines fire these your way one by one, and you're sometimes able to adjust the speed of their flight.

Leisure Land 東京レジャーランド Palette Town; Aomi station; map p.87. A series of cages hidden away in the game centre behind the giant Ferris wheel. Daily 10am–11.50pm.

★**Meiji-jingū Gaien** 明治神宮外苑 ⓦ meijijingu gaien.jp/english/batting.html; Gaienmae station; map pp.114–115. Set of practice cages abutting the Yakult Swallows stadium in the Outer Gardens area of Meiji-jingū. This place is special, since the balls come from the hands of actual pitchers – okay, clever projections of actual pitchers, but the effect is surprisingly realistic. Daily 9am–8.30pm; Nov–Feb until 7.30pm.

Shinjuku Batting Center 新宿バッティングセ ンター 2-21-14 Kabukichō, Shinjuku-ku; Shinjuku-nishiguchi station; map p.126. In the heart of Kabukichō, the Shinjuku Batting Center allows you to choose between balls pitched at a leisurely 70kph or super-fast 130kph. Daily 10am–4am.

Sugō Batting Stadium スゴーバッティングスタ ジアム 1-27 Asakusa, Taitō-ku; Asakusa station; map p.74. Just what you need in the centre of Tokyo's most traditional area – a complex featuring several batting cages, as well as a whole clutch of zany arcade games. Daily 10am–2am.

A TRIP TO THE HOT SPRINGS

Until a few decades ago life in Tokyo's residential neighbourhoods focused round the **sentō**, the public bath. A surprising number of *sentō* survive; those with at least one bath fed by natural spring water are usually referred to as onsen (the term that is more familiar to the Western world), though there are few such places in Tokyo. Then there are the larger **hot-spring resorts** – good fun, though in terms of traditional atmosphere they're not a patch on the smaller *sentō* facilities found elsewhere in the city. Wherever you head, note that it's hugely important to observe local bathing etiquette (see p.29).

Establishments listed in the Guide include the large **Ōedo Onsen Monogatari** (see p.92) and **Spa LaQua** (see p.141) complexes, as well as the smaller **Komparu-yu** (see p.56) in Ginza, **Jakotsu-yu** (see p.76) in Asakusa, **Take-no-yu** (see p.103) near Roppongi and **Somei Onsen Sakura** (see p.140) near Ikebukuro.

18

STADIA

Ajinomoto Stadium 味の素スタジアム 376-3 Nishimachi, Chōfu ☎0424 400555; Tobitakyū station. Head west on the Keiō line to reach this stadium, home to FC Tokyo (ⓦfctokyo.co.jp) and Tokyo Verdy (ⓦwww.verdy.co.jp).

National Stadium 国立競技場 10 Kasumigaoka-chō, Shinjuku-ku ☎03 3403 1151; Sendagaya station; map pp.114–115. Big Japanese and international games have long been held here, though at the time of writing the stadium was being reconstructed for the 2020 Olympics (see box, p.120).

Saitama Stadium 埼玉スタジアム 2002 500 Nakanoda, Saitama ☎048 812 2002; Urawa Misono station. The home of the Urawa Red Diamonds (ⓦwww.urawa-reds .co.jp), this is Japan's largest soccer-only stadium, seating 63,700.

MARTIAL ARTS

Japan has a pleasing selection of indigenous **martial arts**, and it's fairly easy to see events at any time of year. Studying is a different matter, however; martial arts require time and patience, meaning that it's only really going to be worth your while taking **classes** if you're in Tokyo for an extended period. Even then, the best first step is usually the relevant federation in your home country.

AIKIDO

Blending elements of judo, karate and kendo is aikido, which translates as "the way of harmonious spirit". Created in Japan in the 1940s, it is a form of self-defence performed without weapons. For a painfully enlightening and humorous take on the rigours of aikido training, read Robert Twigger's *Angry White Pyjamas* (see p.260).

International Aikido Federation 全日本合気道連盟 17-18 Wakamatsuchō, Shinjuku-ku ☎03 3203 9236, ⓦaikikai.or.jp; Wakamatsu-Kawada station; map pp.136–137. You can learn more about the sport by heading here – if you like what you see and are in Tokyo for a while, it's quite possible to participate in their classes.

JUDO

Probably the martial art most closely associated with Japan, judo is a self-defence technique that developed out of the Edo-era style of fighting called *jujutsu*.

All-Japan Judo Federation 全日本柔道連盟 ☎03 3818 4199, ⓦjudo.or.jp. Federation controlling judo activities throughout Japan.

Kōdōkan 講道館 1-16-30 Kasuga, Bunkyō-ku ☎03 3818 4172, ⓦkodokan.org; Kasuga or Kōrakuen stations; map pp.136–137. This *dōjō* has an upper-floor spectators' gallery open to visitors free of charge, with classes held most evenings. There's also a hostel here where you can stay if you have an introduction from an authorized judo body or an approved Japanese sponsor. Classes Mon–Fri 5–8pm, Sat 5–7.30pm.

Nippon Budōkan 日本武道館 2-3 Kitanomaru-kōen, Chiyoda-ku ☎03 3216 5143, ⓦnipponbudokan.or.jp; Kudanshita station; map p.42. Around fifty free martial-arts exhibition matches are held annually at this large, octagonal arena, an important centre for all martial arts, as well as judo.

K-1

K-1 isn't exactly an ancient fighting form, and as far as mixed modern martial arts go its global standing has taken a bit of a kicking with the rise of the rival UFC (Ultimate Fighting Championship). However, the upside of its declining global popularity is that Tokyo now gets to host the vast majority of K-1 events (see ⓦk-1wg.com), since the form remains popular in Japan; these take place at the Yoyogi International Gymnasium (see p.117) every couple of months.

18

STAYING FIT IN TOKYO

The success of the Tokyo Marathon, held in February, has prompted a **running boom** in the city. Many people make circuits of Yoyogi-kōen, or jog around the 5km course encircling the Imperial Palace (don't dare to go clockwise, lest you flaunt one of Japan's litany of silent, unwritten laws). There are also running clubs such as Namban Rengo and several Hash House Harrier groups. **Gyms** are liberally sprinkled around the city, with private chains including Tipness (ⓦ tipness.co.jp) and Gold's Gym (ⓦ goldsgym.jp) – if you're a member overseas you can use their facilities here. At some gyms you can take **yoga** classes.

Hash House Harriers ⓦ tokyohash.org. Tokyo's own branch of the international "drinkers with a running problem" society.

Namban Rengo ⓦ namban.org. Long-established running club that's highly popular with local expats.

Tokyo Marathon ⓦ marathon.tokyo. One of Asia's biggest marathons, with more than thirty thousand runners padding the Tokyo streets each February.

Tokyo Metropolitan Gymnasium 1-17-1 Senda-gaya, Shibuya-ku; Sendagaya station; map pp.114–115. Includes 25m and 50m pools, as well as a gym.

Yogajaya 1-25-11 Ebisu-nishi, Shibuya-ku ☎ 03 5784 3622, ⓦ yogajaya.com; Daikanyama station; map pp.106–107. Yoga classes in Daikanyama.

KARATE

Karate has its roots in Okinawa and China, and only hit mainland Japan in 1922. Since then the sport has developed into many different styles, with several major governing bodies and federations based in Tokyo.

Japan Karate Association 日本空手協会 2-23-15 Kōraku, Bunkyō-ku ☎ 03 5800 3091, ⓦ jka.or.jp; Iidabashi or Kōrakuen stations; map pp.136–137. Home of the world's largest karate association teaching the Shokotan tradition. You can apply to train here, but it's best to call or email first.

Japan Karatedō Federation 全日本空手道連盟 6F, 2 Nippon Zaidan Building, 1-11-2 Toranomon, Minato-ku ☎ 03 3503 6640, ⓦ karatedo.co.jp; Toranomon station; map pp.96–97. This umbrella-organization can fill you in on the main styles of karate, and advise on the best places to see practice sessions or take lessons.

KENDO

Kendo ("the way of the sword") is Japanese fencing using a long bamboo weapon (the *shinai*) or the metal *katana* blade. This is the oldest fighting skill in Japan, dating from the Muromachi period (1392–1573). It was developed as a sport in the Edo period and is now watched over by the All-Japan Kendo Federation.

All-Japan Kendo Federation 全日本剣道連盟 Nippon Budōkan, 2-3 Kitanomaru-kōen, Chiyoda-ku ☎ 03 3211 5804; Kudanshita station; map p.42. The Budōkan is the venue for the All-Japan Championships each autumn, and the children's kendo competition in the summer.

RUGBY

Rugby has been something of a niche sport in Japan. The national team was famously obliterated 145–17 by New Zealand in the 1995 World Cup (a record defeat), but the game in Japan has since come on leaps and bounds: Japan even provided the shock of the 2015 tournament – some would say the entire history of rugby – with a last-second win over South Africa. Partly as a result of said improvement, Japan is due to host the **2019 World Cup** tournament; Tokyo will host some games in the Ajinomoto Stadium out west, and some will also be held in Yokohama. On the **domestic** front, several teams from around Tokyo compete in the national Top League, which runs from August to January (check ⓦ en.rugby-japan.jp for schedule and venue information).

SUMO

Japan's national sport, sumo, has declined substantially in popularity since the turn of the millennium – successive **scandals** and a wave of **non-Japanese wrestlers** (see box, p.81) have damaged the sport's reputation. However, it's currently undergoing something of a renaissance, and if you're in Tokyo at **tournament** (*basho*) time, it's certainly worth popping along – relatively devoid of the commercialism entwined with Western sports, and dripping with mesmerizing ritual, this is Japanese sporting culture at its finest.

TOURNAMENTS

National Sumo Stadium 国技館 1-3-28 Yokoami, Kōtō-ku ☎ 03 3622 1100, ⓦ sumo.or.jp; Ryōgoku station; map p.82. The National Sumo Stadium in Ryōgoku is the venue for Tokyo's three *basho* during the middle fortnights of January, May and September, with tickets going on sale a month before each tournament. They're available from ticket agencies (see box, p.188), but the cheapest ones (up in the gods) are only sold on the day (¥2200); come before midday and you should be fine, but tickets sometimes sell out on the first and last days of the 15-day tournament. For further information, consult the website.

PRACTICE SESSIONS

It's possible to watch practice sessions (*keiko*) at the stables (*heya*) where the wrestlers live and train. These take place in the early morning (usually from 5 or 6am to 10.30am) except during and immediately after a *basho* or when the wrestlers are out of town. A few stables accept visitors without an appointment, but double-check first at a tourist information office (see p.38) to make sure they're actually training that day. Visitors are expected to watch in silence, and women must wear trousers. Some recommended stables include Dewanoumi-beya at 2-3-15 Ryōgoku, Sumida-ku (出羽海部屋; ☎03 3632 4920; Ryōgoku station); Kasugano-beya at 1-7-11 Ryōgoku, Sumida-ku (春日野部屋; ☎03 3631 1871; Ryōgoku station); and Tokitsukaze-beya at 3-15-4 Ryōgoku, Sumida-ku (時津風部屋; ☎03 5600 2561; Ryōgoku station).

VOLLEYBALL

Tokyo hosts the FIVB World Cup, volleyball's **top international tournament**, every single time it's held. It's on a four-year loop, with the next tournaments set to take place in 2019 and 2023; they take place at the Tokyo Metropolitan Gymnasium (see box opposite), usually in late August and early September, though dates can vary. Tickets are pretty easy to buy on the door, and the arena hosts many other smaller events in addition to the World Cup.

MOUNT FUJI FROM KAWAGUCHI-KO

Around Tokyo

Tokyo functions as a giant magnet to visitors from abroad – there's simply so much to see, eat and do in the capital that many never make it beyond the city centre, let alone the city limits. However, there's plenty to see within day-trip range, and many places fully deserve a night or two of their own. If you make one trip from Tokyo, it should be to the pilgrim town of Nikkō, famed for its World Heritage-listed, mountain-based shrine complex. Out west there is the scenic Fuji Five Lakes area, from which you'll be able to attack Japan's highest and most majestic peak; and Hakone, a mix of sulphur-seeping moonscapes, thrilling cable-car rides and hot springs. Closer to Tokyo are Yokohama, a huge city with plenty to see, and Kamakura, home to a famed giant Buddha statue.

Nikkō and around

日光

"NIKKŌ is Nippon", goes the town's slogan. It's only half-correct, though: visitors to Japan come prepared to take the ancient with the modern, but this town, 128km north of the capital, is up there with the most traditional in the country. It certainly lives up to its billing better than Kyoto, the vaunted dynastic capital way out west.

Most visit Nikkō to see the World Heritage-listed shrine complex of **Tōshō-gū**, which sits at the base of mountains crisscrossed by the outstanding hiking trails of **Nikkō National Park**. It's also worth investigating the far less crowded **Tōshō-gū Museum of Art**, and the **Tamozawa Imperial Villa Memorial Park**, before crossing the Daiya-gawa to explore the dramatically named **Ganman-ga-fuchi abyss**, which is in fact a modest gorge flanked by a tranquil walking path. The most beautiful parts of the aforementioned national park are around **Chūzenji-ko** lake, some 17km west of Nikkō, and the quieter resort of **Yumoto**, higher up in the mountains.

Despite its popularity as a tourist destination today, barely a century ago, in the wake of the Meiji Restoration, Nikkō was running to seed. It was foreign diplomats and businesspeople who began to favour it as a highland retreat from the heat of summer in Tokyo; grand villas such as the Meiji-no-Yakata (see p.215) were built and the *Kanaya Inn* – now the *Nikkō Kanaya Hotel* – was founded by Kanaya Zen'ichirō in 1873.

Outside the peak summer and autumn reasons, and with a very early start, it's possible to see both Tōshō-gū and Chūzenji-ko in a long day-trip from Tokyo, but to get the most out of the journey it's best to stay **overnight**. In contrast to most Japanese urban areas, the town is refreshingly quiet after dark: very little is open after 8pm, bar a couple of renegade bars and two convenience stores, allowing you to wander the town's lanes unmolested by traffic or flashing lights, drinking in the fresh air which remains clement all through the summer.

19

Shin-kyō

神橋 • Off Nihon Romantic Highway • Daily: April–Sept 8am–5pm; Oct to mid-Nov 8am–4pm; mid-Nov to March 9am–4pm • ¥300

At the top of Nikkō's main street is the red-lacquered **Shin-kyō**, a bridge that is one of the town's most famous landmarks. Legend has it that when the Buddhist priest Shōdō Shōnin visited Nikkō in the eighth century, he was helped across the Daiya-gawa at this very spot by the timely appearance of two snakes, which formed a bridge and then vanished. The original arched wooden structure first went up in 1636, but has been reconstructed many times since, most recently in 2005. There's no need to pay the entrance fee, since the structure is clearly visible (and more photogenic) from the road.

Rinnō-ji

輪王寺 • Daily: April–Oct 8am–5pm; Nov–March 8am–4pm • ¥400, or ¥900 including Taiyūin Reibyō (see p.214); Treasure House ¥300

North of Shin-kyō, an uphill pedestrian path works through gorgeous woodland; follow it up and you'll soon emerge in front of the main compound of **Rinnō-ji**, a Tendai Buddhist temple founded in 766 by Shōdō Shōnin, whose statue stands on a rock at the entrance. The large, red-painted hall, **Sanbutsu-dō**, houses three giant gilded statues: the

---

NIKKŌ IN WINTER

The one time of year when the crowds taper off at Nikkō is winter. Be sure to pack warm clothes, as there are **cross-country ski trails** and downhill slopes to be discovered; for those who haven't packed snowshoes, skis or a snowboard, the tourist offices (see p.217) will be able to advise on equipment hire. Winter is also the perfect time to enjoy Nikkō's **onsen** (see p.216); most ryokan have bathing facilities on site, though there are a few other pools around town. More temptations to get you up here in winter include discounted rates at practically all accommodation, and half-price bus passes (see box, p.216) if you're staying at either Chūzenji or Yumoto.

AROUND TOKYO

thousand-handed Kannon, the Amida Buddha and the fearsome horse-headed Kannon. It's worth the entry fee to view these awe-inspiring figures from directly beneath their lotus-flower perches. Note that this hall will remain under protective housing until 2020, as part of a mammoth restoration programme. Rinnō-ji's **Treasure House** (宝物殿, Hōmotsuden), opposite the Sanbutsu-dō, has some interesting items on display, but its nicest feature is the attached Shōyō-en, an elegant garden with a strolling route around a small pond.

Tōshō-gū

東照宮 • Daily: April–Oct 8am–5pm; Nov–March 8am–4pm • ¥1300

Although Nikkō has been a holy place in the Buddhist and Shinto religions for over a thousand years (a hermitage was built here in the eighth century), its fortunes only took off with the death of **Tokugawa Ieyasu** in 1616. In his will, the shogun requested that a shrine be built here in his honour. However, the complex, completed in 1617, was deemed not nearly impressive enough by Ieyasu's grandson, **Tokugawa Iemitsu**, who ordered work to begin on the elaborate mausoleum seen today. Iemitsu's dazzling vision was driven by practical as well as aesthetic considerations: he wanted to stop rival lords amassing money of their own, so he ordered the *daimyō* to supply the materials for the shrine, and to pay the thousands of craftsmen.

The mausoleum was completed in 1634, and ever since the jury has been out on its over-the-top design, the antithesis of the usually austere Shinto shrines, and often considered overbearingly gaudy. Whatever you make of it, **Tōshō-gū** (the name means "sunlight") certainly conveys the immense power and wealth of the Tokugawa dynasty.

The shrine complex

A broad, tree-lined lane leads up to the main **entrance** to Tōshō-gū, just to the northwest of Rinnō-ji. You'll pass under a giant stone *torii* (one of the few remaining features of the original 1617 shrine), while on the left is an impressive red and green five-storey pagoda, an 1819 reconstruction of a 1650 original, which burned down. Ahead is the Omote-mon gate, the entrance to the main shrine precincts. Once inside, turn left to reach the **Three Sacred Storehouses** (Sanjinko) on the right and the **Sacred Stables** (Shinkyūsha) on the left, where you'll spot some of Tōshō-gū's many famous painted woodcarvings – the "hear no evil, see no evil, speak no evil" **monkeys**, which represent the three major principles of Tendai Buddhism. The route leads to the steps up to the dazzling **Yōmei-mon** (Sun Blaze Gate), with its wildly ornate carvings, gilt and intricate decoration. A belfry and drum tower stand alone in front of the gate. Behind the drum tower is the **Honji-dō**; this small hall is part of Rinnō-ji and contains a ceiling painting of a "roaring dragon"; a priest will demonstrate how to make the dragon roar by standing beneath its head and clapping to create an echo.

Beyond the Yōmei-mon, just above the Sakashita-mon gate to the right of the inner precinct, the temple's famed **sleeping cat** (*nemuri neko*) is usually accompanied by gawping crowds – you'd otherwise easily miss this minute, underwhelming carving. Two hundred stone steps lead uphill from the gate to the surprisingly unostentatious **tomb of Ieyasu**, amid a glade of pines, and about the only corner of the shrine where tourists are generally absent.

NIKKŌ FESTIVALS

Every year, on May 18, the **Grand Festival** restages the spectacular burial of Ieyasu at Tōshō-gū, with a cast of over one thousand costumed priests and warriors taking part in a colourful procession through the shrine grounds, topped off with horseback archery. It's well worth attending, as is the smaller-scale festival on October 17, which doesn't have the archery and only lasts half a day. This is followed by **"Light Up Nikkō"** (end of Oct/beginning of Nov), during which the major temple buildings are illuminated at night to great effect.

Directly in front of the Yōmei-mon is the serene white and gold gate of **Kara-mon**, beyond which is the **Haiden**, or hall of worship. The side entrance to the hall is to the right of the gate; you'll need to remove your shoes and stop taking photographs. Inside, you can walk down into the Honden, the shrine's central hall, still decorated with its beautiful original paintwork.

Futarasan-jinja

二荒山神社 • Daily: April–Oct 8am–4.30pm; Nov–March 9am–3.30pm • Free; garden ¥200

A short tramp west of Tōshō-gū is the fantastic **Futarasan-jinja**, whose simple red colour scheme comes as a relief to the senses after the gaudiness of Tōshō-gū. This shrine, originally established by the priest Shōdō Shōnin in 782, is the main one dedicated to the deity of Mount Nantai, the volcano whose eruption created nearby Chūzenji-ko. There are some good paintings of animals and birds on votive plaques in the shrine's main hall, while the attached garden offers a quiet retreat, with a small teahouse serving *matcha* green tea and sweets. You can also inspect the *bakemono tōrō*, a "phantom lantern" made of bronze in 1292 and said to be possessed by demons.

Taiyūin Reibyō

大猷院霊廟 • Daily: April–Oct 8am–5pm; Nov–March 8am–4pm • ¥550, or ¥900 including Rinnō-ji (see p.211)

The charming **Taiyūin Reibyō** contains the mausoleum of the third shogun, Tokugawa Iemitsu, who died in 1651. This complex, hidden away on a hillside and surrounded

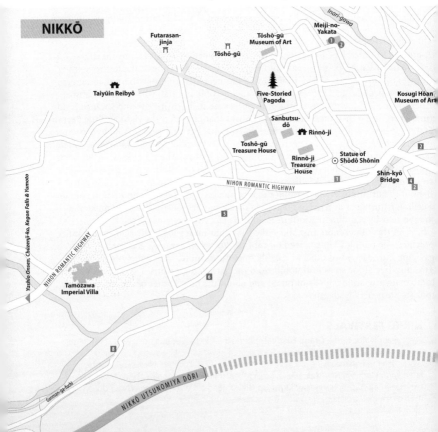

by lofty pines, was deliberately designed to be less ostentatious than Tōshō-gū. Look out for the green god of wind and the red god of thunder in the alcoves behind the Futatsuten-no-mon gate, and the beautiful Kara-mon (Chinese-style gate) and fence surrounding the gold-and-black-lacquer inner precincts – extremely photogenic, especially when dusk begins to encroach.

Tōshō-gū Museum of Art

東照宮美術館, Tōshō-gū Bijutsukan • Daily: April–Oct 8am–5pm; Nov–March 8am–4pm • ¥800

Tucked away behind Tōshō-gū, the **Tōshō-gū Museum of Art** – the former head office of the shrine – is set in a huge, traditional, wooden mansion dating from 1928. Inside, the collection features little bar an array of sliding doors and screens decorated by the top Japanese painters of the early twentieth century; together, they constitute one of Japan's most beautiful collections of such art.

Meiji-no-Yakata

明治の館 • Daily 24hr • Free

The pretty gardens of **Meiji-no-Yakata** were formerly the grounds of American trade representative F.W. Horne's early twentieth-century holiday home. The various houses amid the trees are now fancy restaurants (see p.217), but even if you don't eat here, it's worth wandering around to take in the sylvan setting.

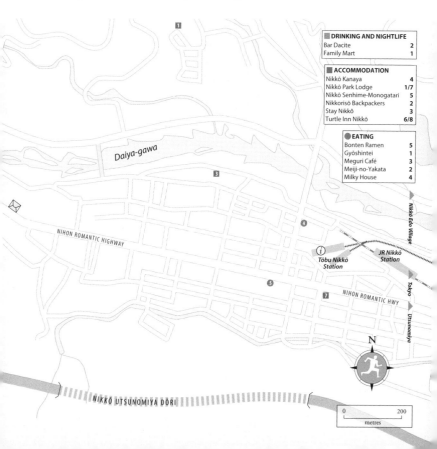

DRINKING AND NIGHTLIFE
| Bar Dacite | 2 |
| Family Mart | 1 |

ACCOMMODATION
Nikkō Kanaya	4
Nikkō Park Lodge	1/7
Nikkō Senhime-Monogatari	5
Nikkōrisō Backpackers	2
Stay Nikkō	3
Turtle Inn Nikkō	6/8

EATING
Bonten Ramen	5
Gyōshintei	1
Meguri Café	3
Meiji-no-Yakata	2
Milky House	4

Daiya-gawa

NIHON ROMANTIC HIGHWAY

Nikkō Edo Village

Tōbu Nikkō Station

JR Nikkō Station

Tokyo

Utsunomiya

NIHON ROMANTIC HWY

NIKKŌ UTSUNOMIYA DŌRI

N

0   200
metres

Tamozawa Imperial Villa

日光田母沢御用邸記念公園, Tamozawa Goyōtei Kinen Kōen • Off Nihon Romantic Highway • Daily except Tues 9am–4.30pm • ¥500

In stark contrast to Nikkō's temples and shrines is the Zen-like simplicity of the beautifully restored **Tamozawa Imperial Villa**, a ten-minute walk west of the Shin-kyō bridge along the main road. This 106-room residence, surrounded by manicured gardens (including a 400-year-old weeping cherry tree), combines buildings of widely different heritage, some parts dating back to 1632. Three emperors have lived in it, including Akihito, who was evacuated here during World War II. As you stroll the corridors, take time to appreciate the intricate details and the gorgeous screen paintings.

Ganman-ga-fuchi abyss

含満ヶ淵 • Daily 24hr • Free

The wonderfully named **Ganman-ga-fuchi abyss** is a rocky little gorge cut through by a river that, while crystal-clear, can be a roaring beast after the rains. Accessed via a small path from the road, a delightful, easy-to-walk **trail** hugs the south side of the rocky river valley. Part of the walk is lined by the **Narabi-jizō**, a few dozen decaying stone statues of Jizō, the Buddhist saint of travellers and children. Sporting scarlet bibs and woven caps, and backed by forest, they make for an absolutely enchanting sight; all in all, it's a place bound to remind you of just how special Japan is.

Yashio Onsen

やしおの湯, Yashio-no-Yu • 1726-4 Kiyotakiwanoshiro-machi • Daily except Thurs 10am–9pm • ¥300 • ☎ 0288 53 6611

Nikkō's municipal onsen, **Yashio**, is set a little way west of the town, and offers large communal baths and *rotemburo* (outdoor baths). It's quite possible to walk here from central Nikkō if you have an hour or so to spare; the most pleasant route is via the Ganman-ga-fuchi abyss (see above), after which you turn right onto the main road, then look for the signs.

ARRIVAL AND DEPARTURE   **NIKKŌ**

Nikkō is accessible on two lines from Tokyo, which serve stations sitting almost side-by-side in the east of the town. The JR station is a real beauty, a historic wooden building designed by Frank Lloyd Wright; however, unless you've got a JR Pass, the Tōbu line will generally be more convenient.

Tōbu train The Tōbu-Nikkō line (ⓦ www.tobu.co.jp) runs from Tōbu-Asakusa station, connected by tunnel to Asakusa subway station; an alternative access point for this line is Kita-Senju station, at the end of the Hibiya line. Note that on some trains you'll need to change at Shimo-Imaichi, while some direct trains split on the way, so be sure to board the right carriage. There are two types of train to choose from: the regular "Kaisoku" ones (2hr 20min; ¥1360), or the fancier limited express "Spacia" (1hr 50min;

¥2700); most people end up travelling with a travel pass (see box below).

JR train You can also reach Nikkō on JR trains but the fares are far higher (¥5380 each way if travelling with Shinkansen), so travelling this way only makes sense if you have a JR pass (see p.23). The fastest route (around 2hr total) is by Shinkansen from either Tokyo or Ueno to Utsunomiya (宇都宮), where you change to the JR Nikkō line for a local train to the JR Nikkō terminus, just east of the Tōbu station.

NIKKŌ TRAVEL PASSES

Tōbu offers **travel passes** to foreigners, covering the return trip from Tokyo and transport around the Nikkō area. These tickets, which can only be bought at Tōbu stations, include the fare from Asakusa to Nikkō (express train surcharges of ¥830–1160 for the Spacia still apply), unlimited use of local buses, and discounts on entrance charges at many of the area's attractions. If you're planning a trip out to Chūzenji-ko (see p.218), the most useful ticket is the **four-day All Nikkō Pass** (¥4520 April–Nov, ¥4150 Dec–March). The **two-day pass** (¥2670) is a similar price to the standard return train fare from Tokyo to Nikkō, so basically only saves you the local bus fares around Nikkō.

INFORMATION AND SERVICES

Tourist information The main tourist office, the Nikkō Kyōdo Centre, is on the main road from the station to the Tōshō-gū complex (daily 9am–5pm; ☎0288 542496, ⌨nikko-jp.org). If you're planning on walking in the area, you can pick up the free *Tourist Guide of Nikkō*, which shows you all the hiking trails found within Nikkō National Park. There's also an excellent information desk at the Tōbu-

Nikkō station (daily 8.30am–5pm; ☎0288 53 4511).

Services The main post office (Mon–Thurs 8.45am–6pm, Fri 8.45am–7pm, Sat & Sun 9am–5pm) on the approach road to Tōshō-gū has an ATM which accepts foreign-issued cards, as do the ones in the post offices opposite Tōbu station and up at Chūzenji; otherwise, it's near impossible to use credit cards in the town.

ACCOMMODATION

Nikkō has plenty of accommodation, and is the best base for the area. If you want to be closer to nature or are looking for a quieter environment, consider staying up at Chūzenji-ko or Yumoto (see p.218). Rates at virtually all places are slightly higher in the **peak seasons**: August, from October to early November, and during major holidays. During these periods reservations are essential.

Nikkō Kanaya 日光金谷ホテル 1300 Kami-hatsuishimachi ☎0288 54 0001, ⌨kanayahotel.co.jp. This charming heritage property, practically a museum piece, remains Nikkō's top Western-style hotel, harking back to the glamorous days of early twentieth-century travel. There are some cheaper rooms with en-suite shower or just a toilet (the hotel has a communal bath) but for the full effect, splash out on the deluxe grade. Note that there's another *Kanaya* up in Chūzenji-ko (see p.220). ⌨ **¥17,820**

Nikkō Park Lodge 日光パークロッジ 11-6 Matsubara-chō & 2828-5 Tokorono ☎0288 53 1201, ⌨nikkopark lodge.com. This hostel has two locations in town: one right by the Tōbu station, and the other in a lovely spot high up on the north bank of the river – not terribly convenient, but it makes for a memorable stay. Vegan dinners are available. ⌨ Dorms **¥2800**, doubles **¥8980**

Nikkō Senhime-Monogatari 日光千姫物語 6-48 Yasukawa-chō ☎0288 54 1010, ⌨senhime.co.jp. Large, highly comfortable option in the calm western side of town, boasting a mix of tatami and Western-style rooms, and charming bathing facilities. Their meals are also quite superb. ⌨ **¥18,360**

★**Nikkorisō Backpackers** にっこり荘バックパカーズ 1107 Naka-hatsuishimachi ☎0288 54 0535, ⌨nikkorisou .com. Housed in a building which looks like a giant school

carpentry experiment, this amiable hostel has a delightful location near the river, and small but cosy rooms. Discounts kick in if you're staying more than one night. ⌨ Dorms **¥3000**, twins **¥6900**

★**Stay Nikkō** ステイ日光ゲストハウス 2-360-13 Inarimachi ☎0288 25 5303, ⌨staynikko.com. A relatively recent addition to the town's accommodation scene, this place is a real winner – presided over by a super-friendly (and English-speaking) Japanese–Thai couple, it only has four rooms, all with shared facilities, making for an atmosphere halfway between a guesthouse and a homestay. The breakfasts (¥800) go down very well, and the peaceful riverside location is another bonus. ⌨ **¥7900**

Turtle Inn Nikkō タートル・イン日光 2-16 Takumi-chō ☎0288 53 3168, ⌨turtle-nikko.com. Popular pension run by an English-speaking family, in a quiet location next to the river. There are small, plain tatami rooms with common bathrooms, and en-suite Western-style rooms, plus a cosy lounge. Add ¥1080 for breakfast, and ¥2160 for the evening meal. They also run a fancier, slightly more expensive annexe, the *Hotori-an*, down the road beside the path to the Ganman-ga-fuchi abyss; it boasts a pottery shop on site, as well as a bath with forest views, and meals are taken at the *Turtle Inn*. ⌨ **¥9600**

EATING

The Nikkō area's culinary speciality is **yuba-ryōri** – milky, thin strips of tofu, usually rolled into tubes and cooked in various stews; this can be enjoyed at many local restaurants, but you may well be served it as part of meals at your accommodation. Note that most **restaurants** in town shut at around 8pm.

★**Bonten Ramen** 梵天ラーメン 264-1 Matsubara-chō ☎0288 53 6095. This ramen bar is one of very few places in Nikkō open for a late-ish dinner. You'll find miso, burnt soy and salt soup varieties on the English-language menu (all ¥500–960); they're all pretty darn good, but those made with springy thicker noodles tend to be best. Daily 11am–9.30pm.

Gyōshintei 堯心亭 2339-1 Sannai ☎0288 53 3751.

Sample exquisitely prepared *shōjin-ryōri* (Buddhist vegetarian cuisine) in a traditional tatami room, served by kimono-clad waitresses: bentō lunches cost from ¥2200, dinner from ¥4500, and some sets include fish. It's part of the charming *Meiji-no-Yakata* complex (see p.215), so you can gaze out on a lovely garden as you eat, then walk off the calories in and around the surrounding sights. Daily except Thurs 11.30am–7pm.

19

Meguri Café Café 廻 909-1 Naka-hatsuishimachi ☎ 0288 25 3122. Run by a husband-and-wife team, this true vegan café has a great laidback atmosphere. Meals use vegetables grown in their own garden, as well as local organic produce. You'll also find some yummy dessert choices, mostly Western style (such as cakes), and plenty of fresh fruits. Daily 11.30am–6pm.

★**Meiji-no-Yakata** 明治の館 2339-1 Sannai ☎ 0288 53 3751. If you get to this charmingly nostalgic stone villa (once a Meiji-era holiday home) at around 10am, you can make a table reservation, then go sightseeing; come back when it opens at 11am, and treat yourself to the best coffee this side of Tokyo, plus some cheesecake (¥1080 will get you both), possibly after some clam chowder (¥700).

With everything served by starched-shirted sorts, with fancy bowls and utensils, it's a small price to pay for some luxury. Otherwise, go the whole hog with their mix of Japanese and Western staples – mains start at ¥1500. 📶 Daily 11am–7.30pm.

Milky House みるきーはうす 2-2-3 Inarimachi ☎ 0288 53 4166. A short walk from the train stations, this friendly local spot is a good place to sample *yuba-ryōri*; sets including it as a main cost ¥1650, but better for most people are the small "sampler sets" featuring the tofu (which is particularly fresh here) and some mushroom tempura for just ¥500. They've also a full roster of tasty soba and udon bowls. Daily except Wed 11am–3pm.

DRINKING

Bar Dacite バーデイサイト 1300 Kami-hatsuishimachi ☎ 0288 54 0001, ⓦ kanayahotel.co.jp. The dark and cosy hotel bar at the swanky *Nikkō Kanaya* (see p.217) is the town's best spot for a nightcap – not that there's much competition. Cocktails suit the elegant atmosphere best, and the menu features some house specials. Daily 6–10.30pm.

Family Mart ファミリーマート 1-16 Yasukawa-chō, no phone. This convenience store may be a left-field drinking

recommendation, but there are a few sound reasons behind it: first, its location – from the outdoor tables you'll be able to hear the rushing river, and see the dark mountains behind; secondly, it has a splendid selection of boutique cup sake, including an exceedingly tasty local brown-glass number, long served by appointment to Tōshō-gū; and finally, after a certain hour, it's the only place in Nikkō you can go for a drink. 📶 Daily 24hr.

Around Nikkō: Chūzenji-ko and Yumoto

The tranquil lake of **Chūzenji-ko** (中禅寺湖) lies some 10km west of Nikkō, and is most famed for the dramatic **Kegon Falls** that flow from it. Local buses run east along Route 120 and up the twisting, one-way road to reach **CHŪZENJI**, the lakeside resort. Both the lake and waterfalls were created thousands of years ago, when nearby **Mount Nantai** (Nantai-san; 男体山; 2486m) erupted, its lava plugging the valley.

Many buses from Nikkō continue northwest of Chūzenji to terminate 45 minutes later at the onsen village of **YUMOTO**, which nestles cosily at the base of the mountains on the northern shore of lake **Yuno-ko**.

Kegon Falls

華厳の滝 Kegon-no-taki • Daily: Jan, Feb & Dec 9am–4.30pm; March, April & Nov 8am–5pm; May–Sept 7.30am–6pm; Oct 7.30am–5pm • Lift ¥550 • ⓦ kegon.jp

The best view of the **Kegon Falls** can be had from the viewing platform at their base. The lift to this vantage point lies east across the car park behind the Chūzenji bus station; don't be put off by the queues of tour groups – a shorter line is reserved for independent travellers. The lift drops 100m through the rock to the base of the falls, from where you can see over a tonne of water per second cascading from the Ojiri River, which flows from the Chūzenji-ko lake.

Italian Embassy Villa Memorial Park

イタリア大使館別荘記念公園本邸, Itaria Taishikan Bessō Kinen Kōen Hontei • 2482 Chigushi • Daily: April–June & Sept–Nov 9am–4pm; July & Aug 9am–5pm • Free • ☎ 0288 55 0388

Head 3km south along the lakeshore from Chūzenji, past several of the compounds still reserved for diplomatic retreats, and on the southeastern fringe of the lake you'll find the **Italian Embassy Villa Memorial Park**. The handsome lakeside villa here, designed by Antonin Raymond and built in 1928, was used by the Italian ambassador up until 1997. Standing here, it's easy to imagine the languid atmosphere of summer house parties and yacht races.

Futarasan-jinja

二荒山神社 • Off Nihon Romantic Highway • 24hr • Free; Mount Nantai ¥500

This colourful shrine, around 1km west of the Kegon Falls along the shore of Chūzenji-ko, is the second **Futarasan-jinja** of the Nikkō area (the first is in Nikkō itself). The shrine, which once bore the name Chūzenji, has a pretty view of the lake, but is nothing extraordinary. There's also a third Futarasan-jinja, on the actual summit of Mount Nantai; to reach it you'll have to pay to climb the volcanic peak, which is owned by the shrine. The hike up is beautiful but takes around four hours, and should only be attempted in good weather; the tourist offices in Nikkō (see p.217) can provide you with maps.

Ryūzu Falls

竜頭の滝, Ryūzu no Taki • Daily 24hr • Free • ☎ 0288 55 0388

Heading 6km west around Chūzenji-ko from Futarasan-jinja, on a gorgeous lakeside path, you'll eventually spot the spectacular, 60m-high **Ryūzu Falls**, which boast clear views of the lake. At the base of the falls are several gift shops and noodle bars, one of which has a superb location overlooking the water as it gushes into the lake. Note that there's also a great hiking route from here to Yumoto (see below).

Yumoto

湯元

The village of **YUMOTO** nestles cosily at the base of the mountains on the northern shore of lake **Yuno-ko**, 15km northwest of Chūzenji-ko. A lovely way to take in the scenery is to rent a rowing boat at the lakeside *Yumoto Rest House* (¥1000 for 50min; May–Oct only). Alternatively, you could walk around the lake in about an hour.

Five minutes' walk from the bus terminal at the back of the village is **Onsen-ji** (温泉寺; April–Nov daily 10am–2pm; ¥500), a small temple notable for its onsen bath, which you can use. Nearby is **Yu-no-daira**, a field where bubbling water breaks through the ground – this is the source of the sulphur smell that hangs so pungently in the air. There's a free footbath, great for soaking weary feet, near the *Yumoto Hillside Inn* (see p.220).

Senjōgahara marshland plateau

戦場ヶ原

If you're feeling energetic, it's worth embarking on the easy and enjoyable 10km **hike** from Yumoto across the **Senjōgahara marshland plateau**, past two spectacular waterfalls and back to Chūzenji-ko. First, follow the west bank of Yuno-ko around to the steps down to the picturesque Yudaki Falls (湯滝), where you can stop off at the lodge serving delicious grilled fish and rice cakes (*mochi*) dipped in sweet miso paste. The trail continues along the Yu-gawa through shady woods before emerging beside the Izumiyado, a large pond and the start of a two-hour tramp across the raised walkways above the Senjōgahara marshland, which blooms with many wild flowers during the summer. Roughly one hour further on, at the Akanuma junction, you can branch off back to the main road, or continue along the riverside path for thirty minutes to the main road and bridge overlooking the **Ryūzu Falls** (see above).

ARRIVAL AND DEPARTURE

CHŪZENJI-KO AND YUMOTO

By bus Buses up to Chūzenji-ko lake (¥1100 one-way) and on to Yumoto (¥1700) run at fairly frequent intervals from outside both of Nikkō's train stations between 6am and 6pm, and usually take 45min, though travelling times can easily double – or even triple – during *kōyō* in mid-October, the prime time for viewing the changing autumn leaves,

when traffic is bumper-to-bumper. If you haven't bought a Tōbu pass (see box, p.216), it's still possible to save money on transport by buying a two-day bus pass at either train station; for unlimited return trips to Chūzenji-ko the cost is ¥2000, while to Yumoto it's ¥3000.

MINAKAMI AND ADVENTURE SPORTS

The sprawling township of **MINAKAMI** (水上), buried deep in the mountains of Gunma-ken, about 65km west of Nikkō, has become one of the hottest spots in Japan for adventure sports. No fewer than ten whitewater rafting companies, including **Canyons** (☎0278 722811, ⓦcanyons.jp), offer trips down the Tone-gawa. Other activities include paragliding, canyoning, abseiling, rock-climbing and a wide variety of treks, including the ascent to the summit of **Tanigawa-dake** (谷川岳; 1977m). To relax after all this, you can head to **Takaragawa onsen** (宝川温泉; daily 9am–5pm; ¥1500 before 4pm, ¥1000 after 4pm; ⓦtakaragawa.com), famous for its mixed-sex bathing (though it also has separated baths) and its four huge *rotemburo*.

To reach Minakami, take the Shinkansen to **Jōmō-Kōgen** (上毛高原), from where the town is a 20min bus ride. The **tourist office** (daily 9am–5.15pm; ☎0278 72 2611, ⓦenjoy-minakami .com) is opposite the station. **Places to stay** include the Canyons-run *Alpine Lodge* (from ¥4000 per person), which offers private rooms and tatami dorms, plus a lively bar; and the aforementioned **Takaragawa onsen** (from ¥21,600 per person).

19

ACCOMMODATION

Chūzenji Kanaya Hotel 中禅寺金谷ホテル 2482 Chugushi ☎0288 51 0001, ⓦkanayahotel.co.jp. The most luxurious place to stay on the lake, and affiliated to the eponymous hotel in Nikkō (see p.217). It's a couple of kilometres away from the tourist village, en route to the Ryūzu Falls, and has been especially designed to blend in with the woodland surroundings. 🛜 **¥24,000**

Yumoto Hillside Inn 湯元ヒルサイドイン 2536 Yumoto ☎0288 62 2434, ⓦhillsideinn.jp. A Western-style hotel in a wooden chalet with an outdoor deck, English-speaking owners, a small heated swimming pool and indoor and outdoor onsen. Rates include two meals. 🛜 **¥20,000**

Fuji Five Lakes

The best reason for heading 100km west from Tokyo towards the area known as **FUJI FIVE LAKES** is to climb **Mount Fuji** (富士山), Japan's most sacred volcano and, at 3776m, its highest mountain. Fuji-san, as it's respectfully known by the Japanese, has long been worshipped for its latent power (it last erupted in 1707) and near-perfect symmetry; it is most beautiful from October to May, when the summit is crowned with snow. The climbing season is basically July and August; even if you don't fancy the rather daunting ascent, just getting up close to Japan's most famous national symbol is a memorable experience. Apart from Mount Fuji, don't miss the wonderfully atmospheric shrine **Fuji Sengen-jinja**, in the area's transport hub of **Fuji-Yoshida**.

During the summer, the **five lakes** in the area are packed with urbanites fleeing the city. **Kawaguchi-ko** is not only a popular starting point for climbing Mount Fuji, but also features a kimono museum and the easily climbable Mount Tenjō, which has outstanding views of Mount Fuji and the surrounding lakes. The smallest of the other four lakes, horseshoe-shaped **Shōji-ko** (精進湖), 2km west of Kawaguchi-ko, is by far the prettiest. The largest lake, **Yamanaka-ko** (山中湖), southeast of Fuji-Yoshida, is just as developed as Kawaguchi-ko and has fewer attractions, while **Motosu-ko** (本栖湖) and **Sai-ko** (西湖) – both good for swimming and camping – are fine, but not so extraordinary that they're worth the trouble of visiting if you're on a short trip.

Fuji-Yoshida

富士吉田

FUJI-YOSHIDA, some 100km west of Tokyo, lies so close to Mount Fuji that when the dormant volcano eventually blows her top the local residents will be toast. For the time being, however, this small, friendly town acts as an efficient transport hub for the area, as well as the traditional departure point for journeys up the volcano, with frequent buses leaving for Mount Fuji's fifth station (see p.223) from outside the train station.

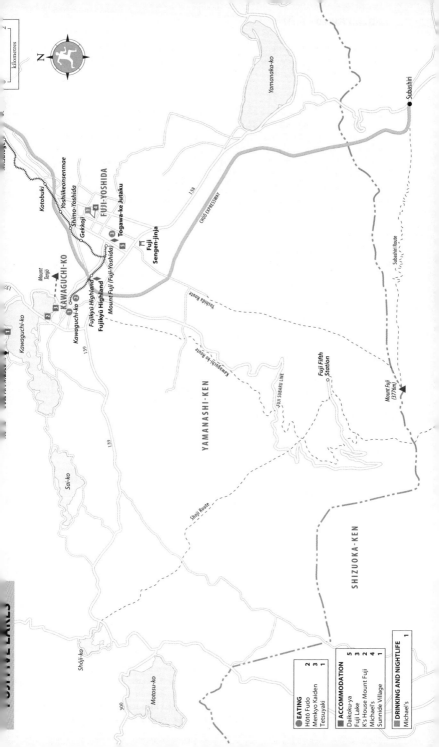

N
kilometres

Subashiri

Yamanaka-ko

Kotobuki

Yoshiikeonsenmae

Shimo-Yoshida

Gekkoji

FUJI-YOSHIDA

Togawa-ke Jutaku

Fuji
Sengen-jinja

CHŪŌ EXPRESSWAY

138

Subashiri Route

Mount
Tenjō

KAWAGUCHI-KO

Fujikyū Highland

Fujikyū Highland

Mount Fuji (Fuji-Yoshida)

Kawaguchi-ko

Yoshida Route

Kawaguchi-ko

Kawaguchi-ko Route

139

Sai-ko

FUJI SUBARU LINE

Fuji Fifth
Station

YAMANASHI-KEN

139

Shoji Route

Mount Fuji
(3776m)

SHIZUOKA-KEN

Shoji-ko

Motosu-ko

300

● EATING
Hōtō Fudo   2
Menkyo Kaiden   3
Tetsuyaki   1

■ ACCOMMODATION
Daikoku-ya   5
Fuji Lake   3
K's House Mount Fuji 2
Michael's   4
Sunnide Village   1

■ DRINKING AND NIGHTLIFE
Michael's   1

If you're in town in late August, you'll find the main thoroughfare illuminated spectacularly, when seventy bonfires are lit along its length at night-time during the **Yoshida Fire Festival** (August 26 & 27).

Fuji Sengen-jinja

富士浅間神社 • Off Fuji Panorama Line road • 24hr • Free • Head uphill from the train station along the main street towards Mount Fuji; turn left where the road hits a junction and walk 200m

The volcano aside, Fuji-Yoshida's main attraction is its large, colourful Shinto shrine, **Fuji Sengen-jinja**, set in a small patch of forest. Sengen shrines, dedicated to the worship of volcanoes, encircle Fuji, and this is the most important, dating right back to 788. The beautiful main shrine was built in 1615. Look around the back for the jolly, brightly painted wooden carvings of the deities Ebisu the fisherman and Daikoku, the god of wealth, good humour and happiness, who appears content to let a rat nibble at the bales of rice he squats upon.

Togawa-ke Jutaku

19

戸川家受託 • Off Fuji-michi • Daily 9.30am–5pm • ¥100

Between the Fuji Sengen-jinja and the train station you'll likely spot a few old **pilgrims' inns** (*oshi-no-ie*) set back from the road, their entrances marked by narrow stone pillars. Some of these old lodging houses, where pilgrims used to stay before climbing Mount Fuji, still operate as minshuku today, and one, **Togawa-ke Jutaku**, has been opened up as a tourist attraction; its various tatami halls are worth pottering around, though the staff will want to explain every single thing to you in Japanese.

Fujikyū Highland

富士急ハイランド • Mon–Fri 9am–5pm, Sat & Sun 9am–6pm; closed second Tues of month • Entry ¥1500; one-day ride pass including entry ¥5700 • ⓦ www.fujiq.jp • One train stop west of Mount Fuji station

An appealingly ramshackle amusement park, **Fujikyū Highland** features a handful of hair-raising roller coasters, including the Takabisha, which claims to have the world's steepest drop – 121 degrees of terror. Avoid coming at weekends or holidays unless you enjoy standing in long queues.

Kawaguchi-ko

河口湖

The small lakeside resort of **KAWAGUCHI-KO** lies a couple of kilometres west of Fuji-Yoshida, and makes a more appealing place to stay. With its cruise boats and crass souvenir shops, it's the tourist hub of the area, and is often choked with traffic during the holiday season. However, the lake is placid and strikingly beautiful, especially at night, when the various visitors are clip-clopping around its southern fringes in their wooden *geta* sandals (said footwear being de rigueur for those staying at ryokan).

Tenjō-zan

天上山 • Off Misaka-michi • **Cable car** Daily 9am–5pm • ¥450 one-way, ¥800 return

The fabulous view of Mount Fuji from the top of **Tenjō-zan** is probably the highlight of a trip to Kawaguchi-ko; of course, you'll also get a great view of the lake from here, since it's right next door. You can either take a three-minute cable-car ride up to the lookout, or get some exercise by hiking up, which takes around 45 minutes.

Itchiku Kubota Art Museum

久保田一竹美術館 Kubota Itchiku Bijutsukan • 2255 Guchiko, 4km northwest of Kawaguchi-ko • April–Nov daily 9.30am–5.30pm; Dec–March daily except Wed 10am–4.30pm • ¥1300 • ☎ 0555 76 8811, ⓦ itchiku-museum.com • Bus from Kawaguchi-ko station (25min)

One of the highlights of Kawaguchi-ko is the **Itchiku Kubota Art Museum**, on the northern shore of the lake. This small museum, housed in a Gaudí-esque building, showcases the work of Itchiku Kubota, who refined the traditional *tsujigahana* textile-patterning technique and applied it to kimono. Inside the pyramid-shaped building are pieces from the artist's *Symphony of Light* series, a continuous mountain landscape through the seasons, formed when the kimono are placed side by side.

Mount Fuji

富士山

"A wise man climbs Fuji once. A fool climbs it twice", says the Japanese proverb. Don't let the sight of children and grannies trudging up lull you into a false sense of security: at 3776m in height – more than enough for altitude sickness to take hold – this is a tough climb. There are several **routes** up the volcano, with the ascent on each divided into sections known as **stations**; the summit is the tenth station. Most people take a bus to the fifth station (*go-gōme*) on the **Kawaguchi-ko route**, about halfway up the volcano, where a Swiss-chalet-style gift shop marks the end of the road; for most people, it's four or five hours from here to the summit. The traditional hike, though, begins down at Fuji-Yoshida and ascends via the **Yoshida route**; it takes around five hours to walk up to this route's fifth station, and another six hours to reach the summit. The shortest route (around four hours from the fifth station) is the **Fujinomiya-guchi** to the south, accessible by bus from Shin-Fuji station, on the Shinkansen route; these buses also pass Fujinomiya JR station en route. Many climbers choose to ascend the mountain at **night** in order to reach the summit by dawn; during the season, the lights of climbers' torches resemble a line of fireflies trailing up the volcanic scree.

19

Essential items to carry include at least one litre of water and some food, a torch and batteries, a raincoat and extra clothes. However hot it might be at the start of the climb, the closer you get to the summit the colder it becomes, with temperatures dropping to well below freezing. Sudden rain and lightning strikes are not uncommon.

Mount Fuji's official **climbing season**, when all the facilities on the mountain are open, including lodging huts (see box below) and phones at the summit, runs from July 1 to the end of August. You can climb outside these dates, but don't expect all, or indeed any, of the facilities to be in operation, and be prepared for snow and extreme cold towards the summit. Once you're at the summit, it will take around an hour to make a circuit of the crater.

ARRIVAL AND DEPARTURE   FUJI FIVE LAKES

By bus The easiest way to reach the Fuji Five Lakes area is to take the bus (¥1800; 1hr 45min in good traffic) from the Shinjuku bus terminal in Tokyo, on the west side of the train station; there are also services from Tokyo station and Shibuya. During the climbing season there are frequent services, including at least three a day that run directly to the fifth station on the Kawaguchi-ko route, halfway up Mount Fuji (¥1540 one-way, ¥2100 return; 1hr 15min). If you're planning on visiting the Hakone area, the regular bus to Gotemba costs ¥1510 (hourly; 2hr); alternatively,

the Fuji Hakone Pass allows you to combine the Fuji Five Lakes area with a trip around Hakone (see box, p.231).
By train The train journey from Shinjuku station involves transferring from the JR Chūō line to the Fuji Kyūkō line at Ōtsuki, from where local trains (some with Thomas the Tank Engine decoration) chug first to Mount Fuji station (the old name, Fuji-Yoshida, is still commonly used) and then on to Kawaguchi-ko; the whole process will take at least 2hr (¥4310).

ACCOMMODATION ON MOUNT FUJI

There are seventeen **huts** on Fuji, most of which provide dorm accommodation from around ¥5300 per night (add ¥1000 on weekends) for just a bed (no need for a sleeping bag), with an option to add meals for ¥1000 each. It's essential to book in advance during the official climbing season (July & Aug). The huts also sell snacks and stamina-building dishes, such as curry rice. For a full list of the huts, with contact numbers, see the Fuji-Yoshida city website (ⓦ www.city.fujiyoshida.yamanashi.jp).

GETTING AROUND

By bus A comprehensive system of buses will help you get around once you've arrived at either Fuji-Yoshida or Kawaguchi-ko. The two-day Retrobus pass (¥1200 or ¥1500, depending on the route) allows travel around the Fuji Five Lakes area.

On foot It's easy enough to walk from Kawaguchi-ko station down to the lake in 15min or so, and those without too much luggage can access most of its surrounding hotels on foot.

By bicycle You'll see plenty of tourists pedalling around the Kawaguchi-ko area. Most rent bikes from their accommodation, though there are plenty of other rental outlets around, including one just opposite the train station, on the left (¥500/hr, ¥1500/day).

INFORMATION

Fuji-Yoshida tourist office On the left as you exit Mount Fuji station (daily 9am–5pm; ☎0555 22 7000, ⓦwww.city.fujiyoshida.yamanashi.jp), with tonnes of information in English. If you're here to climb Fuji, pick up a free copy of the various maps on offer (also available at the Kawaguchi-ko tourist office – see below); there's similar information on the tourist office website.

Kawaguchi-ko tourist office Outside Kawaguchi-ko station, this branch (daily 8.30am–5.30pm; ☎0555 72 6700) is just as useful as its counterpart in Fuji-Yoshida.

19

ACCOMMODATION

Fuji-Yoshida and Kawaguchi-ko have plenty of good places to stay, including youth hostels and hotels. Fuji **climbers** could consider overnighting in one of the mountain huts (see box, p.223), but the claustrophobic might prefer to stick to the roomier accommodation at the base of the mountain. There are also several **campsites** around the lakes.

FUJI-YOSHIDA

Daikoku-ya 大国屋 Honchō-dōri, Fuji-Yoshida ☎0555 22 3778. This original pilgrims' inn on the main road still takes guests in its very traditional and beautifully decorated tatami rooms (though the owner prefers guests who can speak some Japanese). Rate includes two meals. Closed Oct–April. **¥14,000**

Michael's マイケルズ 3-21-37 Shimo-yoshida ☎0555 72 9139, ⓦmtfujihostel.com. American-run hostel with spick-and-span rooms, a quiet backstreet location – though one very close to the train station – and a lively bar (see opposite). Private rooms are a particularly good deal for single travellers. ☞ Dorms **¥3000**, private rooms (per person) **¥3600**

KAWAGUCHI-KO

★**Fuji Lake** 富士レークホテル 1 Funatsu, Kawaguchi-ko-machi ☎0555 72 2209, ⓦfujilake.co.jp. Large lakeside hotel that dates back to the 1930s, making it one of Japan's oldest such facilities. Its rooms are all large and very stylish, and feature charming wash-rooms into which onsen water is piped. There's another fantastic onsen downstairs. ☞ **¥14,700**

★**K's House Mount Fuji** ケイズハウス富士山 6713-108 Funatsu, Kawaguchi-ko-machi ☎0555 83 5556, ⓦkshouse.jp. Super-friendly hostel with a choice of either bunk-bed dorms or private tatami-style rooms, some en suite. Also on offer are a well-equipped kitchen, comfy lounge, internet access, laundry and bike rental, as well as a small bar. They'll even pick up from the station for free (8am–7.30pm). Their new hostel, *Fuji View*, further up the slopes, is a similar operation. ☞ Dorms **¥2500**, doubles **¥7200**

Sunnide Village サンイデヴィレッジ Kawaguchi-ko ☎0555 76 6004, ⓦwww.sunnide.com. This attractive complex of hotel and holiday cottages offers spectacular views across the lake towards Mount Fuji, and has lovely public baths, too. It's on the north side of the lake, towards the Itchiku Kubota Art Museum. ☞ Doubles **¥12,600**, cottages **¥16,000**

EATING

FUJI-YOSHIDA

★**Menkyo Kaiden** 麺許皆伝 849-1 Kami-Yoshida ☎0555 23 8806. This is the undisputed udon favourite with lunching locals; you may have to wait for a seat. The menu can be a little confusing, but staff recommend the *yokubari*, which comes in a miso-base soup (¥550). Mon–Sat 11am–2pm.

KAWAGUCHI-KO

★**Hōtō Fudo** ほうとう不動 Train station plaza ☎0120 41 0457. Right in front of the train station in a building with a wood-panelled exterior, this small restaurant serves decent *hōtō* (see box opposite) for ¥1080, as well as *basashi* (raw horse meat; ¥1080) and a range of other tasty Japanese food. Daily 11am–9pm.

Tetsuyaki 鉄焼き 3486-5 Kawaguchiko-chō, no phone. This teppanyaki spot is frequently the only place in town open after 8pm. Mains go from ¥800, and include steak, *okonomiyaki* (pancake-like batter dish with various fillings) and rice dishes; mercifully, since few bars around the lake stay open too long after sundown, they also sell alcoholic drinks. Daily noon–10pm.

FUJI-NOODLES

Both Fuji-Yoshida and Kawaguchi-ko are renowned for their thick *teuchi* (handmade) **udon noodles**. Fuji-Yoshida udon comes topped with shredded cabbage and carrot, and is usually prepared and served in people's homes at lunchtime only; the tourist offices can provide a Japanese list and map of the best places serving it. Most of these will serve just three types of dish: *yumori*, noodles in a soup; *zaru*, cold noodles; and *sara*, warm noodles dipped in hot soup. In Kawaguchi-ko, be sure to try **hōtō**, a hearty broth served piping hot; ingredients vary, and some places serve it with exotic meats such as venison and bear, but sweet pumpkin is the local favourite.

DRINKING

Michael's マイケルズ 3-21-37 Shimo-yoshida ☎0555 72 9139, ⓦ mtfujihostel.com. Even if you're not staying overnight at this Fuji-Yoshida hostel (see opposite), it's worth swinging by the bar if you're in the area – the atmosphere can be surprisingly raucous for provincial Japan. Simple pub snacks are on offer alongside a modest range of drinks. 🛜 Daily except Thurs 7pm–2am; lunch served daily except Sat 11.30am–4pm.

Hakone

箱根

South of Mount Fuji and 90km west of Tokyo is the lakeland, mountain and onsen area known as **HAKONE**, always busy at weekends and holidays. Most visitors follow the well-established day-trip route, which is good fun and combines rides on several trains or buses, a funicular, a cable car and a sightseeing ship, styled as a seventeenth-century galleon, across Ashino lake. However, the scenery is so pretty, and there's so much else to do – such as seeing great **art** at the Hakone Open-Air Museum and the Pola Museum of Art, not to mention soaking in numerous **onsen** – that an overnight stay is encouraged. Weather permitting, you'll also get great views of nearby Mount Fuji.

The traditional day-trip itinerary, described below, runs anticlockwise from **Hakone-Yumoto**, gateway to the **Fuji-Hakone-Izu National Park**, then over the peaks of **Sōun-zan**, across the length of **Ashino-ko** to **Moto-Hakone**, and back to the start. Approaching Hakone from the west, you can follow a similar route clockwise from Hakone-machi, on the southern shore of Ashino-ko, to Hakone-Yumoto.

Hakone-Yumoto

箱根湯元

HAKONE-YUMOTO, the small town nestling in the valley at the gateway to the national park, is marred by scores of concrete-block hotels and *bessō*, vacation villas for company workers – not to mention the usual cacophony of souvenir shops. It does, however, have some good **onsen** (see box, p.227) which are ideal for unwinding after a day's sightseeing around the park.

Miyanoshita

宮ノ下

Rising up into the mountains, the Hakone-Tozan **switchback railway** zigzags for nearly 9km alongside a ravine from Hakone-Yumoto to the village of Gōra. There are small traditional inns and temples at several of the stations along the way, but the single best place to alight is the village onsen resort of **MIYANOSHITA**. Interesting antique and craft shops are dotted along its main road, and there are several hiking routes up **Mount Sengen** (804m) on the eastern flank of the railway – one path begins just beside the station. At the top (an hour's walk or so) you'll get a great view of the gorge below. After the walk you can relax in the appealing day-onsen **Tenoyu** (see box, p.227). Miyanoshita's real draw, however, is its handful of splendid **hotels**, the most historic of which is the *Fujiya* (see p.232), which opened for business in 1878; it's well worth a look even if you're not staying, and its *Orchid Lounge* is great for afternoon tea.

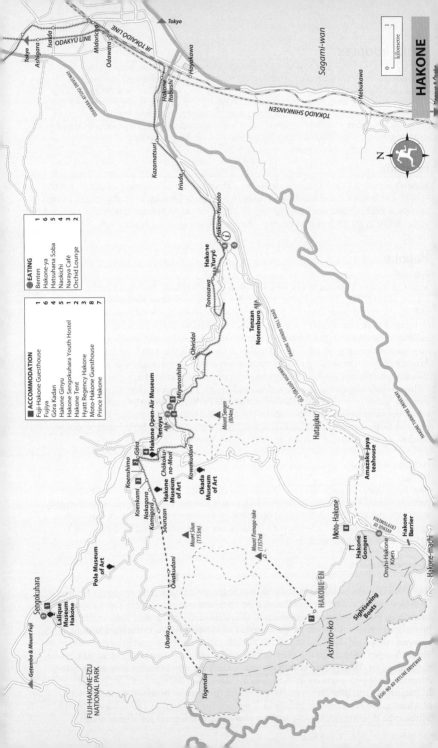

HAKONE

■ ACCOMMODATION	
Fuji-Hakone Guesthouse	1
Fujiya	6
Gôra Kadan	4
Hakone Ginyu	5
Hakone Sengokuhara Youth Hostel	1
Hakone Tent	2
Hyatt Regency Hakone	3
Moto-Hakone Guesthouse	8
Prince Hakone	7

● EATING	
Benten	1
Hakone-ya	6
Hatsuhana Soba	5
Naokichi	4
Naraya Café	3
Orchid Lounge	2

Sagami-wan

Tokyo

Tokyo

Isehara

ODAKYU LINE

Midorichô

Odawara

JR TOKAIDO LINE

Hakone-Itabashi

Hayakawa

TÔKAIDÔ SHINKANSEN

Nebukawa

ODAWARA-ATSUGI DRIVEWAY

Kazamatsuri

Iriuda

Hakone-Yumoto

Hakone Yuryô

Tonosawa

Ohiradai

Miyanoshita

Tenzan Notemburo

HAKONE SHINDÔ TOLL ROAD

Kowakudani

Mount Sengen (804m)

Hatajuku

Kô Tôkaido Highway

Chôkoku-no-Mori

Hakone Open-Air Museum

Tenyu

Gôra

Koenshimo

Hakone Museum of Art

Okada Museum of Art

Amazake-jaya teahouse

HAKONE TÔGE DRIVEWAY

Koenkami

Nakagora

Kamigora

Sôunzan

Pola Museum of Art

Mount Sôun (1153m)

Ôwakudani

Ubako

Mount Komaga-take (1357m)

Moto-Hakone

Hakone Gongen

Onshi-Hakone Kôen

AVENUE OF CRYPTOMERIA

Hakone Barrier

Hakone-machi

HAKONE-EN

Sightseeing Boats

Ashino-ko

Tôgendai

Sengokuhara

Lalique Museum Hakone

Gotemba & Mount Fuji

FUJI-HAKONE-IZU NATIONAL PARK

HAKONE ASHINOKO SKYLINE DRIVEWAY

N

0 1 kilometre

Hakone Open-Air Museum

彫刻の森美術館, Chōkoku-no-Mori Bijutsukan • 1121 Ninotaira • Daily 9am–5pm • ¥1600 • ⓦ hakone-oam.or.jp

Travelling two stops uphill from Miyanoshita on the Hakone-Tozan railway brings you to Chōkoku no Mori (彫刻の森), where you should alight if you want to visit the nearby **Hakone Open-Air Museum**. This worthwhile museum is packed with sculptures, ranging from works by Rodin and Giacometti to Michelangelo reproductions and bizarre modern formations scattered across the landscaped grounds, which have lovely views across the mountains to the sea. There's an enclave of 26 pieces by Henry Moore; a "Picasso Pavilion", which houses over three hundred paintings, lithographs, ceramics and sculptures by the Spanish artist; and four galleries featuring works by Chagall, Miró and Renoir, plus work by modern Japanese artists such as Umehara Ryūzaburō and Hayashi Takeshi. You can rest between the various galleries at several restaurants or cafés, and there's also a traditional Japanese teahouse here.

Okada Museum of Art

岡田美術館, Okada Bijutsukan • 493-1 Kowakudani • Daily 9am–5pm • ¥2800 • ⓦ okada-museum.com

A little bit out of the way, and more than a little pricey, the **Okada Museum of Art** is a bit of a connoisseur's choice. The items on display here are almost exclusively East Asian – not only Japanese but Korean and Chinese ceramics, metalwork, folding screens and the like, dating back to umpteen notable dynastic periods.

Gōra to Ashino-ko

Funicular tram Every 10–15min • ¥420 one-way • **Cable car** Every 1–2min • ¥1370 one-way to Ashino-ko

The Hakone-Tozan railway terminates at **GŌRA** (強羅), where you can stop for lunch, or overnight. Continuing west on the day-trip route, you'll transfer to a **funicular tram**, which takes ten minutes to cover the short but steep distance to **Sōunzan**, the start of the cable-car ride. From here, the **cable car** floats like a balloon on its thirty-minute journey high above the mountain to the Tōgendai terminal beside Ashino-ko, stopping at a couple of points along the way.

Hakone Museum of Art

箱根美術館, Hakone Bijutsukan • 1300 Gōra • Daily except Thurs 9am–4pm • ¥900 • ⓦ moaart.or.jp/hakone

En route to Sōunzan, you might want to stop at Kōen-kami (公園上), a couple of stops on the funicular tram from Gōra, for the **Hakone Museum of Art**. Its collection of ancient ceramics – some of which date back as far as the Jōmon period – is likely to appeal to experts only, but the delicate moss gardens and the view from the traditional teahouse across the verdant hills are captivating.

TAKING AN ONSEN DIP IN HAKONE

The sulphuric steam rising from the mountain of Sōun-zan makes it clear that something is going on beneath the surface of Hakone. As with any such place in Japan, this volcanic activity also makes it a prime spot for a soak in mineral-heavy **onsen** water.

Hakone Yuryō 箱根湯寮 ⓦ hakoneyuryo.jp. Set back in the forest near Hakone-Yumoto, this onsen is a good option; bathing out by the trees is quite delightful, even if the weather's chilly. Free shuttle buses from Hakone-Yumoto station. Daily 10am–8pm; ¥1400.

Tenoyu てのゆ Attractive onsen with *rotemburo* (outdoor hot springs), a short walk out of Miyanoshita along the main road to Gōra. Mon–Fri 11am–7pm, Sat & Sun 11am–8pm; ¥1600 Mon–Fri, ¥2100 Sat & Sun.

Tenzan Notemburo 天山野天風呂. The most stylish bathhouse in the area is this luxurious riverside complex close to Hakone-Yumoto station, and connected to it by free shuttle buses. There are outdoor baths for men and women, including waterfalls and jacuzzis in a series of rocky pools, plus a clay-hut sauna for men. For an extra charge both men and women can use the wooden baths in the building across the car park. Rarely for Japan, visible tattoos are allowed. Daily 9am–11pm; ¥1300.

Ōwakudani

大涌谷

If the weather is playing ball, you should get a good glimpse of Mount Fuji in the distance as you pop over the hill at the first cable-car stop, **ŌWAKUDANI**. This is the site of a constantly bubbling and steaming valley formed by a volcanic eruption three thousand years ago. A series of tectonic belches in recent years saw the cable-car station and surrounding area fully closed down, with visitors unable to get off and explore; however, the station and many of its surrounding paths were reopened in 2016. Should the remainder of Ōwakudani be opened up, you'll be able to hike through the lava formations to bubbling pools where eggs are traditionally boiled until they are black and scoffed religiously by every tourist, for no better reason than it has long been the done thing when visiting Ōwakudani.

North from Gōra

North of Gōra are a couple of excellent museums, both worthy of a detour: the splendid **Pola Museum of Art** and the quirky **Lalique Museum Hakone**. The latter is in the pleasant village of **SENGOKUHARA** (仙石原), a good place to stay the night.

Pola Museum of Art

ポーラ美術館, Pōra Bijutsukan • 1285 Sengokuhara • Daily 9am–5pm • ¥1800 • ⓦ polamuseum.or.jp • Bus from Gōra station (15min; ¥300)

The superb **Pola Museum of Art** boasts a diverse and eclectic collection of Western art, predominantly from French Impressionists and École de Paris artists. When you've had your fill of checking out pieces by the likes of Renoir, Monet, Picasso, Van Gogh, Cezanne and Gallé, hunt down the glasswork section, and the Japanese paintings and ceramics. The artworks are all displayed in modern galleries in a stunning building that blends beautifully with the surrounding forest, and there's a café and restaurant on site too.

Lalique Museum Hakone

箱根ラリック美術館, Hakone Rarikku Bijutsukan • 186-1 Sengokuhara • Daily 9am–5pm • ¥1500, or ¥2100 including train carriage with drinks and dessert (reservation necessary) • ☏ 0406 84 2225, ⓦ lalique-museum.com • Bus from Gōra station (25min; ¥420)

Perhaps the most interesting – and certainly the most beautifully situated – of Sengokuhara's museums is the **Lalique Museum Hakone**, dedicated to the delicate glass pieces of the French artist René Lalique. At the entrance is a parked *Orient Express* Pullman train carriage, kitted out with Lalique glass panels, which is a great place for tea.

Ashino-ko and around

Sightseeing boats Tōgendai to Moto-Hakone or Hakone-machi ¥1000 • Daily 9.30am–5pm, every 30–40min • ⓦ hakone-kankosen.co.jp • **Komaga-take cable car** ¥1080

From **Tōgendai** (桃原台) – the westernmost point of the cable-car route from Gōra – a shoreline trail winds along the western side of **Ashino-ko** (芦ノ湖) to the small resort of **HAKONE-MACHI** (箱根町) some 8km south, taking around three hours to cover. This western lakeshore is not covered by the Hakone Free Pass (see box, p.231) and is thus somewhat marginalized – and all the more peaceful for it. Most visitors, however, hop straight from the cable car on to one of the colourful **sightseeing ships**, modelled after the seventeenth-century man-o'-war *The Sovereign of the Seas*, that regularly sail the length of the lake in around thirty minutes; you can see Fuji's peak reflected in the waters from the northern end of Ashino-ko. A cluster of upmarket hotels and ryokan can be found at Hakone-machi, where the sightseeing boats dock before or after hitting Moto-Hakone.

Boats also run from Tōgendai to the *Prince* hotel resort at **Hakone-en** (箱根園), midway down the east side of the lake. A cable car here glides up the 1357m **Komaga-take** (駒ヶ岳), from where there's a fabulous view.

THE HAKONE BARRIER

In 1618 the second shogun, Tokugawa Hidetada, put up the **Hakone Barrier** (Sekisho) – actually more of a large compound than a single gate – which stood at Hakone-machi until 1869. The shogun decreed that all his lords' wives and their families live in Edo (now Tokyo) and that the lords themselves make expensive formal visits to the capital every other year, a strategy designed to ensure no one attempted a rebellion. The Tōkaidō, on which the barrier stands, was one of the major routes in and out of the capital, and it was here that travellers were carefully checked to see how many guns they were taking into the Edo area; the barrier also ensured that the lords' families were prevented from escaping. Any man caught trying to dodge the barrier was crucified and then beheaded, while accompanying women had their heads shaved and were, according to contemporary statute, "given to anyone who wants them".

Hakone Barrier

箱根関所, Hakone Sekisho • Daily: March–Nov 9am–5pm; Dec–Feb 9am–4.30pm • ¥500

The southern end of the lake is the location of the **Hakone Barrier**, a gateway through which all traffic on the **Tōkaidō**, the ancient road linking Kyoto and Edo, once had to pass (see box above). What stands here today is a reproduction, enlivened by waxwork displays which provide the historical background, and there's nothing much to keep you.

Onshi-Hakone Kōen

恩賜箱根公園 • Daily 9am–4.30pm • Free

North of the Hakone Barrier, the wooded promontory between Hakone and Moto-Hakone, **Onshi-Hakone Kōen**, is an easily accessible Fuji-viewing spot. After panting your way up 200-odd steps, you'll come to a garden area and an observation point; despite the hordes of tourists pouring off the ferries to the south, and padding their way through Moto-Hakone to the north, this place is usually pretty quiet.

Moto-Hakone

元箱根

Part of the Tōkaidō ancient road – shaded by 420 lofty cryptomeria trees planted in 1618 and now designated "Natural Treasures" – runs for around 1km beside the road leading from the Hakone Barrier to the lakeside **MOTO-HAKONE** tourist village. The prettiest spot around here is the vermilion *torii*, standing in the water just north of Moto-Hakone – a scene celebrated in many an *ukiyo-e* print and modern postcard. The gate belongs to the **Hakone Gongen** (箱根権現) and is the highlight of this small Shinto shrine, where samurai once came to pray.

Ashino-ko to Hakone-Yumoto

From either Hakone-machi or Moto-Hakone you can take a **bus** back to Hakone-Yumoto or Odawara. Far more rewarding, however, is the 11km **hike** along part of the Tōkaidō ancient road, which begins five minutes up the hill from the Hakone-Tozan bus station in Moto-Hakone; to find the start of the route, keep an eye out for a spot where large paving stones are laid through the shady forests. After the first 2km the route is all downhill and takes around four hours.

When the path comes out of the trees and hits the main road, you'll see the Amazake-jaya teahouse. From here, the path shadows the main road to the small village of **HATAJUKU** (畑宿), where since the ninth century craftsmen have perfected the art of *yosegi-zaiku*, or marquetry. The wooden boxes, toys and other objects inlaid with elaborate mosaic patterns make great souvenirs; there are workshops throughout the village, including one right where the path emerges onto the main road. Hatajuku is a good place to pick up the bus the rest of the way to Hakone-Yumoto if you don't fancy hiking any further.

ARRIVAL AND INFORMATION

By train Most people visit Hakone aboard the Odakyū-line train from Shinjuku, using one of the company's excellent-value travel passes (see box below). To get to Hakone-Yumoto – at the end of the line – on the basic trains (2hr; ¥1190), you may have to change in Odawara (小田原); for an extra fee you can take the more comfortable "Romance Car" (hourly; 1hr 30min; ¥2080) all the way. If you're using a JR Pass (see p.23), the fastest route is to take a Shinkansen to Odawara, from where you can transfer to an Odakyū train or bus into the national park area.

By bus The Odakyū express bus (hourly; ¥1950) from Shinjuku bus terminal will get you to Hakone in a couple of hours. Buses stop first at Hakone-Yumoto, followed by Moto-Hakone, the *Prince* hotel at Hakone-en (see below) and finally Tōgendai. It's also possible to visit by bus from the Fuji Five Lakes area, in which case you'll enter Hakone through Sengokuhara to the north, passing through the major town of Gotemba; passes will save you money (see box below), as well as hassle on the local buses, which don't give any change.

Tourist information You can pick up a map of the area and plenty of other information at the very friendly Hakone tourist office (daily 9am–5.45pm; ☎ 0460 85 5700, ⓦ hakone.or.jp), situated in the buildings at the bus terminal, across the street from Hakone-Yumoto station.

ACCOMMODATION

Excellent transportation links mean you can stay pretty much anywhere in the national park and get everywhere else easily. There's a good range of budget options and some top-grade ryokan; a profusion of offerings on Airbnb has seen prices decrease slightly at the lower end of the spectrum.

19

ASHINO-KO

Moto-Hakone Guesthouse 元箱根ゲストハウス 103 Moto-Hakone ☎0460 83 7880, ⓦmotohakone.com. Simple guesthouse a short bus ride (get off at Ōshiba) or stiff 10min walk uphill from Moto-Hakone village. The reward for the journey is spotless Japanese-style rooms and extremely friendly service – a cup of coffee will be plonked in front of you in no time at all. Surcharge of ¥1000 at weekends. ☞ **¥4860** per person

Prince Hakone プリンス箱根 144 Moto-hakone ☎0460 83 1111, ⓦprincehotels.com. This hotel boasts a prime location on the eastern shore of Ashino-ko and a multitude of facilities, including access to an outdoor hot bath with a view of the lake. ☞ **¥20,000**

GORA

Gōra Kadan 強羅花壇 1300 Gōra ☎0460 82 3331, ⓦgorakadan.com. One of Hakone's most exclusive ryokans is the stuff of legend, which means you might have to wait an eternity to secure a reservation. Expect beautiful tatami rooms, antiques, exquisite meals and a serene atmosphere. Rates include two meals. ☞ **¥54,000**

★**Hakone Tent** 箱根テント 1320-257 Gōra ☎0460 83 8021, ⓦhakonetent.com. Created from an old ryokan, this striking, modern guesthouse has been a fantastic recent budget addition to the area. The on-site onsen is a delight, and travellers usually end up having a natter over sake or beer at the welcoming bar before collapsing onto their futons. The single room is great

---

HAKONE TRAVEL PASSES

Touring the Hakone area is great fun, but the various train, funicular, cable car and boat tickets can add up quickly. One way to prevent this, and save a bundle of cash, is to invest in one of the many **travel passes** covering the area. As well as covering almost all transport, they can be used to lop a little off entry prices to some sights. You can buy passes at the **Odakyū Sightseeing Service Centre** at the west exit of Shinjuku station (daily 8am–6pm; ☎03 5321 7887, ⓦ www.odakyu.jp/english); the English-speaking staff here can also make reservations for tours and hotels.

Hakone Freepass If you plan to follow the traditional Hakone route, invest in this pass, which comes in either two- or three-day versions; from Shinjuku, it costs ¥5140/¥5640 (2/3 days); from Odawara or Gotemba it costs ¥4000/¥4500 (2/3 days). The pass covers a return journey on the Odakyū line from Shinjuku to Odawara, and unlimited use of the Hakone-Tozan line, Hakone-Tozan funicular railway, cable car, boats across the lake and most local buses.

Hakone One-day Pass If you're already in Odawara or

Gotemba you can buy a special one-day pass for ¥2000. It doesn't cover the journeys to or from Tokyo, nor the cable car and boat.

Fuji Hakone Pass If you're going directly from Hakone to the neighbouring Fuji Five Lakes area (or vice versa) then the three-day Fuji Hakone Pass (¥8000 from Shinjuku, ¥5650 from Odawara) is the way to go. This offers the same deal as a Hakone Freepass but also covers a one-way express bus trip between the Hakone area and Kawaguchi-ko.

value at ¥4000. 🛜 Dorms **¥3500**, doubles **¥9000**

Hyatt Regency Hakone ハイアット リージェンシー箱根 1320 Gōra 📞 0460 82 2000, 🌐 hakone.regency.hyatt .com. This slickly designed hotel is a treat, offering some of the largest rooms in Hakone and elegant facilities, including a lounge, two restaurants and the Izumi onsen spa. For those who can't bear to be parted from their pooch, there are even dog-friendly stone-floored rooms. 🛜 **¥30,000**

MIYANOSHITA

Fujiya 富士屋ホテル 359 Miyanoshita 📞 0460 82 2211, 🌐 fujiyahotel.jp. The first Western-style hotel in Japan, this place is a living monument to a more glamorous era of travel, and boasts lots of Japanese touches, including traditional gardens and decorative gables like those found in temples. The plush 1950s-style decor is retro-chic, the rooms are good value, and there are a couple of great on-site places to eat and drink. 🛜 **¥14,000**

Hakone Ginyu 箱根吟遊 100-1 Miyanoshita 📞 0460 82 3355, 🌐 hakoneginyu.co.jp. Outstanding luxury ryokan, where guests are assured maximum comfort.

The views across the valley are stunning and the interiors are a tasteful blend of old and new. Huge *hinoki* wood tubs on private verandas are a major plus. Rates include two meals. 🛜 **¥68,000**

SENGOKUHARA

Fuji-Hakone Guesthouse 富士箱根ゲストハウス 912 Sengokuhara 📞 0460 84 6577, 🌐 fujihakone.com. Tucked into a pleasingly secluded spot, this convivial guesthouse – run by the friendly, English-speaking Takahashi-san and his family – has comfortable tatami rooms, though the defining feature is the onsen water piped into no fewer than four separate baths. Breakfast available. 🛜 **¥10,800**

Hakone Sengokuhara Youth Hostel 箱根仙石原ユー スホステル 912 Sengokuhara 📞 0460 84 8966, 🌐 jyh.or.jp. Directly behind the *Fuji-Hakone Guesthouse*, and run by the same family, this hostel offers good dorm accommodation in a lovely wooden building. The on-site hot spring is a nice bonus if you've been hiking. 🛜 Dorms **¥3550**

EATING

ASHINO-KO

Hakone-ya 箱根家 45 Moto-Hakone 📞 0460 83 6107. This is the best of the rather motley bunch of tourist restaurants in Moto-Hakone, serving dishes such as extremely filling *katsu-don* (¥1080) and cheaper bowls of soba or udon, with pretty views out over the lake. Daily 10am–7pm.

HAKONE-YUMOTO

Hakone-Yumoto is stacked with good places to eat. There are also three good-value restaurants at the nearby Tenzan Notemburo bathhouse (see box, p.227) serving rice, *shabu-shabu* (hotpot) and *yakiniku* (grilled meat) dishes.

Hatsuhana Soba はつ花そば 635 Hakone-Yumoto 📞 0460 85 8287. The Hakone area is famed for its soba, on account of purity of the local water, and this restaurant is the best place to try it. Several options are available,

including tempura and curry bowls, but you can't go wrong with the *teijo soba*, served with grated yam and raw egg (¥1000). To get here from the station, follow the riverbank into town, then turn left at the first bridge – it's right on the other side, overlooking the river. Daily 10am–7pm.

★**Naokichi** 直吉 696 Hakone-Yumoto 📞 0460 85 5148. Excellent, elegant restaurant serving the scrumptious local speciality, *yubadon* – soy milk skin in fish broth served on rice (¥980). Not sold yet? There's also a free onsen footbath just outside. To find it, head up the river path from the station; you'll soon spot the place on your right. Daily except Tues 11am–6pm.

MIYANOSHITA

★**Naraya Café** ならやカフェー 404-13 Miyanoshita. There's one major draw at this lovely café, just down the

---

MOUNT TAKAO

An hour west of Shinjuku, **Mount Takao** (高尾山; 600m; 🌐 takaotozan.co.jp), also referred to as Takao-san, is a particularly pleasant place for a quick escape from Tokyo, and is a starting point for longer trails into the mountains in the **Chichibu-Tama National Park** (秩父多摩国立公園). The Keiō line from Shinjuku provides the simplest and cheapest way of reaching the terminus of Takao-san-guchi (1hr; ¥370). After a hike up or a ride on the cable car or chairlifts (both ¥470 one-way, ¥900 return), you'll get to **Yakuo-in** (薬王院; 🌐 takaosan.or.jp/index.html), a temple founded in the eighth century and notable for the ornate polychromatic carvings that decorate its main hall. It hosts the spectacular **Hiwatarisai** fire ritual on the second Sunday in March back in Takao-san-guchi, where you can watch priests and pilgrims march across hot coals – and even follow them yourself. From the temple, it's a relatively short walk to Takao's summit.

road from Miyanoshita station – a footbath that runs under the table in the outdoor section, making it possible to bathe your toes while sipping a latte (¥400), or perhaps even a cocktail. Hot dogs and other snacks are available, and there's a gallery on the top level. 🛜 Daily except Wed 10.30am–6pm.

Orchid Lounge 359 Miyanoshita ☎0460 82 2211, 🖲 fujiyahotel.co.jp. The tea lounge at the wonderful *Fujiya* hotel (see opposite) is a grand spot for coffee (¥1500 with cake) or afternoon tea (¥1000); it's a pleasure to sit down and relax with a view over the garden and carp-filled pond. Daily 9am–9pm.

SENGOKUHARA

Benten 弁天 226 Sengokuhara. If you're staying in the Sengokuhara area, this simple *izakaya* is a good bet for dinner and a drink – it's one of the few places around in which the majority of customers are locals. It serves simple bowls of ramen from ¥450, plus fried seafood, and a range of local drinks. Daily 2–9pm.

Kamakura and around

鎌倉

The small, relaxed town of **KAMAKURA** lies an hour's train ride south of Tokyo, trapped between the sea and a circle of wooded hills. The town is steeped in history, and many of its 65 temples and 19 shrines date back some eight centuries, when, for a brief and tumultuous period, it was Japan's political and military centre. Its most famous sight is the **Daibutsu**, a glorious bronze Buddha surrounded by trees, but its ancient **Zen temples** are equally compelling. Kamakura's prime sights can be covered on a day-trip from Tokyo, but the town more than justifies a two-day visit, allowing you time to explore the enchanting temples of **east Kamakura** and follow one of the gentle "hiking courses" up into the hills, or head out west to **Enoshima** and its own clutch of appealing sights.

19

Brief history

In 1185 the warlord **Minamoto Yoritomo** became the first permanent shogun and the effective ruler of Japan. Seven years later he established his military government – known as the Bakufu, or "tent government" – in Kamakura. Over the next century, dozens of grand monuments were built here, notably the great Zen temples founded by monks fleeing Song-dynasty China. Zen Buddhism flourished under the patronage of a warrior class who shared similar ideals of single-minded devotion to duty and rigorous self-discipline. The Minamoto rule was brief and violent. Almost immediately, Yoritomo turned against his valiant younger brother, Yoshitsune, who had led the clan's armies, and hounded him until Yoshitsune committed ritual suicide (*seppuku*) – a favourite tale of kabuki theatre. Both the second and third Minamoto shoguns were murdered, and in 1219 power passed to the Hōjō clan, who ruled as fairly able regents behind puppet shoguns. Their downfall followed the Mongol invasions in the late thirteenth century, and in 1333 Emperor Go-Daigo wrested power back to Kyoto; as the imperial armies approached Kamakura, the last Hōjō regent and an estimated eight hundred retainers committed *seppuku*. Kamakura remained an important military centre before fading into obscurity in the late fifteenth century. Its temples, however, continued to attract religious pilgrims until Kamakura was "rediscovered" in the last century as a tourist destination and a desirable residential area within commuting distance of Tokyo.

KAMAKURA THROUGH THE YEAR

The town's biggest **festivals** take place in early April (second Sun to third or fourth Sun) and mid-September, including displays of horseback archery and costume parades, though the summer fireworks display (second Tues in Aug) over Sugami Bay is the most spectacular event.

Kamakura is also well known for its **spring blossoms** and **autumn colours**, while many temple gardens are famous for a particular flower – for example, Japanese apricot at Zuisen-ji and Tōkei-ji (Feb) and hydrangea at Meigetsu-in (mid-June).

Kita-Kamakura

As the Tokyo train nears the station at **Kita-Kamakura**, the town's northern suburb, urban sprawl gradually gives way to gentle, forested hills which provide the backdrop for some of Kamakura's greatest Zen temples. Chief among these are **Kenchō-ji** and the wonderfully atmospheric **Engaku-ji**. It takes over an hour to cover the prime sights, walking south along the main road, the Kamakura-kaidō, to the edge of central Kamakura. If you have more time, follow the Daibutsu Hiking Course (see box, p.236) up into the western hills.

Engaku-ji

円覚寺 • 409 Yama-no-uchi • Daily: April–Oct 8am–5pm; Nov–March 8am–4pm • ¥300; Butsunichi-an ¥100, or ¥500 including tea

The second most important – but most satisfying – of Kamakura's major Zen temples, **Engaku-ji** lies buried among ancient cedars just two minutes' walk east of Kita-Kamakura station. It was founded in 1282 to honour victims (on both sides) of the ultimately unsuccessful Mongolian invasions in 1274 and 1281. The layout follows a traditional Chinese Zen formula – a pond and bridge (now cut off by the train tracks), followed by a succession of somewhat austere buildings – but the encroaching trees and secretive gardens add a gentler touch.

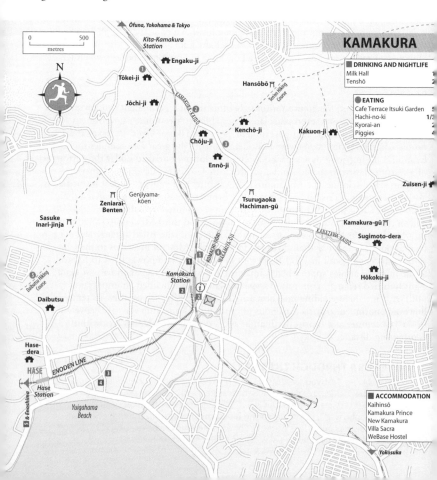

ZAZEN

Zazen, or sitting meditation, is a crucial aspect of Zen Buddhist training, particularly among followers of the Rinzai sect. Several temples in Kamakura hold public *zazen* sessions at various levels, of which the most accessible are those at Engaku-ji (April–Oct daily 5.30am; Nov–March daily 6am; plus second and fourth Sun of month at 10am; ☎ 0467 22 0478) and Kenchō-ji (Fri & Sat 5pm in the Hōjō; ☎ 0467 22 0981). These hour-long sessions are free and no reservations are required, though it's best to check the current schedule with the temple or Kamakura tourist office (see p.242) before setting out, and you should get there at least fifteen minutes early. Though non-Japanese-speakers are welcome, you'll get much more out of it if you have someone with you who can translate.

The first building inside the compound is Engaku-ji's two-storey main gate, **San-mon**, a magnificent structure rebuilt in 1783; beneath it the well-worn flagstones bear witness to generations of pilgrims. Beyond, the modern **Butsu-den** (Buddha Hall) houses the temple's primary Buddha image, haloed in soft light, while behind it lies the charming **Shari-den**, tucked off to the left past an oblong pond. This small reliquary hall, usually closed to visitors, is said to contain a tooth of the Buddha brought here from China in the early thirteenth century. It's also considered Japan's finest example of Song-dynasty Zen architecture, albeit a sixteenth-century replica. The main path continues gently uphill to another pretty thatched building, **Butsunichi-an**, where regent Hōjō Tokimune was buried in 1284; in fine weather green tea is served in its attractive garden. Finally, you'll come to tiny **Ōbai-in**, which enshrines a pale-yellow Kannon statue, although its best attribute is a nicely informal garden with a grove of Japanese apricot.

19

On the way out, follow signs up a steep flight of steps to the left of San-mon to find Kamakura's biggest bell, **Ōgane**, forged in 1301 and an impressive 2.5m tall; the adjacent teahouse, *Bentendō*, is a great place to relax.

Tōkei-ji

東慶寺 • 1367 Yama-no-uchi • Daily: March–Oct 8.30am–5pm; Nov–Feb 8.30am–4pm • ¥100 • **Treasure House** Tues–Sun 9.30am–3.30pm • ¥300 • ⦿ tokeiji.com

A short walk along the main road from Engaku-ji, **Tōkei-ji** was founded as a nunnery in 1285 by the young widow of Hōjō Tokimune. It's an intimate temple, with a pleasing cluster of buildings and a profusion of flowers at almost any time of year: Japanese apricot in February, magnolia and peach in late March, followed by peonies and then irises in early June; September is the season for cascades of bush clover. At the back of the temple, take a walk round the peaceful, mossy cemetery hidden among stately cryptomeria trees, where many famous and forgotten nuns lie buried.

Tōkei-ji is more popularly known as the **"Divorce Temple"**. Up until the mid-nineteenth century, when women were given the legal right to seek divorce, this was one of the few places where wives could escape domestic ill-treatment. If they reached the sanctuary, which many didn't, they automatically received a divorce after three years according to traditional temple law. Husbands could be summoned to resolve the dispute or, ultimately, sign the divorce papers. Some of these documents are preserved, along with other temple treasures, in the **Treasure House**, including two books detailing the women's reasons for seeking sanctuary – unfortunately, not translated.

Jōchi-ji

浄智寺 • 1402 Yama-no-uchi • Daily 9am–4.30pm • ¥200

Almost immediately to the south of Tōkei-ji, a sign to the right indicates Jōchi-ji, the fourth most important of Kamakura's great Zen temples, and the start of the wonderful

Daibutsu Hiking Course (see box below). Founded by the nephew of Hōjō Tokimune in 1283, Jōchi-ji was almost completely levelled by the 1923 earthquake. Nevertheless, it's worth walking up the lane to see its beautifully proportioned Chinese-style gate which doubles as a bell tower. The small worship hall contains a trinity of Buddhas while, at the back, there's a graveyard, sheltered by a bamboo grove.

Kenchō-ji

建長寺 • 8 Yama-no-uchi • Daily 8.30am–4.30pm • ¥300 • ⓦ kenchoji.com

The greatest of Kamakura's Zen temples is **Kenchō-ji**, headquarters of the Rinzai sect and Japan's oldest Zen training monastery. More formal than Engaku-ji and a lot less peaceful, largely because of the neighbouring high school, Kenchō-ji contains several important buildings, most of which have been relocated here from Tokyo and Kyoto to replace those lost since the temple's foundation in 1253. Again, the design of the layout

KAMAKURA HIKING COURSES

There are two extremely pleasant **hiking courses** to tackle in central Kamakura, both giving you the chance to enjoy some lovely wooded scenery. The hikes, while a decent workout, are both pretty straightforward and quite possible to do in flip-flops (though trickier if it has been raining).

DAIBUTSU HIKING COURSE

Beside the temple of Jōchi-ji (see p.235) you'll find the steps that mark the start of the **Daibutsu Hiking Course** (大仏ハイキングコース), a meandering 2.2km-long ridgetop path which makes an enjoyable approach to the **Daibutsu**, Hase's Great Buddha (see p.240). Even if you're not walking the whole route it's well worth going as far as the captivating cave-shrine dedicated to the goddess **Zeniarai Benten** (銭洗弁天), the "Money-Washing Benten", an incarnation of the goddess of good fortune, music and water. To find it, follow the somewhat erratic signs from **Genjiyama-kōen** (源氏山公園), a pleasant park, which lead you along a trail heading vaguely south through the park to a road junction where the main trail turns right; here, you'll pick up signs pointing steeply downhill to where a *torii* and banners mark the Zeniarai Benten shrine entrance. Duck under the tunnel to emerge in a natural amphitheatre filled with a forest of *torii* wreathed in incense and candle smoke. According to tradition, money washed in the spring, which gushes out of a cave on the opposite side from the entrance, is guaranteed to double at the very least, though not immediately.

If you're following the Daibutsu Hiking Course all the way to Hase, then rather than retracing your steps, take the path heading south under a tunnel of tightly packed *torii*, zigzagging down to the valley bottom. Turn right at a T-junction to find another avenue of vermilion *torii* leading uphill deep into the cryptomeria forest. At the end lies a simple shrine, **Sasuke Inari-jinja** (佐助稲荷神社), which dates from before the twelfth century and is dedicated to the god of harvests, whose messenger is the fox; as you head up the steep path behind, to the left of the shrine buildings, climbing over tangled roots, you'll find fox statues of all shapes and sizes peering out of the surrounding gloom. At the top, turn right and then left at a white signboard to pick up the hiking course for the final 1.5km to the Daibutsu (see p.240).

TEN'EN HIKING COURSE

The **Ten'en Hiking Course** (天園ハイキングコース) begins just behind the Hōjō in Kenchō-ji (see above). It takes roughly one and a half hours to complete the 5km trail, which loops round the town's northeast outskirts to Zuisen-ji (see p.240); for a shorter walk (2.5km), you can cut down earlier to Kamakura-gū (see p.238). This trail is less trafficked than the Daibutsu course, and even on a sunny weekend, it's quite possible to find yourself alone in the forest for decent periods of time; you'll likely find a few trekkers having a snack or vending-machine coffee at a curious pit-stop, hidden in the bamboo thickets just after the golf course as you approach from Kenchō-ji.

shows a strong Chinese influence; the founding abbot was another Song Chinese émigré, in this case working under the patronage of Hōjō Tokiyori, the devout fifth regent and father of Engaku-ji's Tokumine.

The main complex begins with the towering, copper-roofed **San-mon**, an eighteenth-century reconstruction, to the right of which hangs the original temple **bell**, cast in 1255 and considered one of Japan's most beautiful. Beyond San-mon, a grove of gnarled and twisted juniper trees hides the dainty, nicely dilapidated **Butsu-den**. The main image is, unusually, of Jizō (the guardian deity of children) seated on a lotus throne, his bright, half-closed eyes piercing the gloom. Behind is the **Hattō**, or lecture hall, one of Japan's largest wooden Buddhist buildings. The curvaceous Chinese-style gate, **Kara-mon**, and the **Hōjō** hall beyond are much more attractive structures. Walk round the latter's balcony to find a **pond-garden** generally attributed to a thirteenth-century monk, making it Japan's oldest-surviving Zen garden, though it's been spruced up considerably. Behind the Hōjō entrance, a path heads up the steep steps past **Hansōbō**, a shrine guarded by statues of long-nosed, mythical *tengu*; this is the start of the **Ten'en Hiking Course** (see box opposite).

Ennō-ji

円応寺 • 1543 Yama-no-uchi • Daily 9am–3.30pm • ¥200

On the other side of the road to Kenchō-ji, **Ennō-ji** looks fairly insignificant, but inside its hall reside the red-faced King of Hell, Enma, and his ten cohorts. This ferocious crew are charged with deciding the appropriate level of reincarnation in your next life and their wonderfully realistic expressions are meant to scare you into better ways. From Ennō-ji it's only another five minutes through the tunnel and downhill to the side entrance of Tsurugaoka Hachiman-gū (see below).

Central Kamakura

Modern Kamakura revolves around the central **Kamakura station** and a couple of touristy streets leading to the town's most important shrine, **Tsurugaoka Hachiman-gū**. The traditional approach to this grand edifice lies along **Wakamiya-ōji**, which runs straight from the sea to the shrine entrance. Shops along here peddle a motley collection of souvenirs and crafts, the most famous of which is *kamakura-bori*, an 800-year-old method of laying lacquer over carved wood. More popular, however, is *hato*, a pigeon-shaped French-style biscuit first made by Toshimaya bakers a century ago. Shadowing Wakamiya-ōji to the west is **Komachi-dōri**, a narrow, pedestrian-only shopping street, packed with more souvenir shops, restaurants and, increasingly, trendy boutiques.

Tsurugaoka Hachiman-gū

鶴岡八幡宮 • 2-1-31 Yuki-no-shita • Daily 6am–8.30pm • Free

A majestic, vermilion-lacquered *torii* marks the south-facing front entrance to **Tsurugaoka Hachiman-gū**, the Minamoto clan's guardian shrine since 1063. Hachiman-gū, as it's popularly known, was moved to its present site in 1191, since when it has witnessed some of the more unsavoury episodes of Kamakura history. Most of the present buildings date from the early nineteenth century, and their striking red paintwork, combined with the parade of souvenir stalls and the constant bustle of people, create a festive atmosphere in sharp contrast to that of Kamakura's more secluded Zen temples.

Three humpback bridges lead into the shrine compound between two connected ponds known as **Genpei-ike**. These were designed by Minamoto Yoritomo's wife, Hōjō Masako, and are full of heavy, complicated symbolism, anticipating the longed-for victory of her husband's clan over their bitter enemies, the Taira; strangely, the bloodthirsty Masako was of Taira stock. The **Mai-den**, an open-sided stage at the end of a broad avenue, was the scene of another unhappy event in 1186, when Yoritomo forced his brother's mistress, Shizuka, to dance for the assembled samurai. Yoritomo wanted his popular brother,

Yoshitsune, killed and was holding Shizuka prisoner in the hope of discovering his whereabouts; instead, she made a defiant declaration of love and only narrowly escaped death herself, though her newborn son was murdered soon after. Her bravery is commemorated with classical dances and nō plays during the shrine **festival** (Sept 14–16), which also features demonstrations of horseback archery on the final day.

Beyond the Mai-den, a long flight of steps leads up beside a knobbly, ancient ginkgo tree – reputedly a thousand years old and scene of the third shogun's murder by his vengeful nephew – to the **main shrine**. This is an attractive collection of buildings set among trees, though, as with all Shinto shrines, you can only peer in. Appropriately, the principal deity, Hachiman, is the God of War.

Near the front of the Tsurugaoka Hachiman-gū complex, you'll find the beautifully restrained, black-lacquered **Shirahata-jinja**, dedicated to the first and third Kamakura shoguns.

East Kamakura

19 The eastern side of Kamakura contains a scattering of less-visited shrines and temples, including two of the town's most enchanting corners. It's possible to cover the area on foot in a half-day, or less if you hop on a bus for the return journey.

Hōkoku-ji

報国寺 • 2-7-4 Jomyoji • Daily 9am–4pm • Bamboo gardens ¥200

The well-tended gardens and simple wooden buildings of **Hōkoku-ji**, or Take-dera, the "Bamboo Temple", are accessed via a small bridge off Kanazawa-kaidō. The temple is best known for a grove of evergreen bamboo protected by the encircling cliffs. This dappled forest of thick, gently curved stems, where tinkling water spouts and the soft creaking of the wind-rocked canes muffle the outside world, would seem the perfect place for the monks' meditation. Too soon, though, the path emerges beside the manicured rear garden, which was created by the temple's founding priest in the thirteenth century.

Sugimoto-dera

杉本寺 • 903 Nikaido • Daily 8am–4.30pm • ¥200

One of Kamakura's oldest temples, **Sugimoto-dera** is set at the top of a steep, foot-worn staircase lined with fluttering white flags, overlooking the main road. Standing in a woodland clearing, the small, thatched temple, founded in 734, exudes a real sense of history. Inside its smoke-blackened hall, spattered with pilgrims' prayer stickers, you can slip off your shoes and take a look behind the altar at the three wooden statues of Jūichimen Kannon, the eleven-faced Goddess of Mercy. The images were carved at different times by famous monks, but all three are at least a thousand years old. According to legend, they survived a devastating fire in 1189 by taking shelter – all by themselves – behind a giant tree; since then the temple has been known as Sugimoto ("Under the Cedar").

Kamakura-gū

鎌倉宮 • 154 Nikaido • Daily 9am–4pm • ¥300

Mainly of interest for its history and torchlight nō dramas in early October, **Kamakura-gū** was founded by Emperor Meiji in 1869 to encourage support for his new imperial regime. The shrine is dedicated to Prince Morinaga, a forgotten fourteenth-century hero who helped restore his father, Emperor Go-Daigo, briefly to the throne. The prince was soon denounced, however, by power-hungry rivals and held for nine months in a Kamakura cave before being executed. The small cave and a desultory treasure house lie to the rear of the classically styled shrine, but don't really justify the entry fee.

THE DAIBUTSU, KAMAKURA (P.240) >

A road heading north from Kamakura-gū marks the beginning – or end – of the shortcut to the Ten'en Hiking Course (see box, p.236).

Zuisen-ji

瑞泉寺 • 710 Nikaido • Daily 9am–4.30pm • ¥200

Starting point of the main trail of the Ten'en Hiking Course (see box, p.236), **Zuisen-ji**'s quiet, wooded location and luxuriant gardens make it an attractive spot, though the temple's fourteenth-century Zen garden, to the rear of the main building, is rather dilapidated.

Hase

長谷

The west side of Kamakura, an area known as **Hase**, is home to the town's most famous sight, the **Daibutsu** (Great Buddha), cast in bronze nearly 750 years ago. On the way, it's worth visiting **Hase-dera** to see an image of Kannon, the Goddess of Mercy, which is said to be Japan's largest wooden statue. These sights are within walking distance of Hase station, three stops from Kamakura station on the private Enoden line.

Hase-dera

長谷寺 • Daily: March–Sept 8am–5pm; Oct–Feb 8am–4.30pm • ¥300 • ⓦ hasedera.jp • Hase station

Hase-dera stands high on the hillside a few minutes' walk north of Hase station, with good views of Kamakura and across Yuigahama beach to the Miura peninsula beyond. Though the temple's present layout dates from the mid-thirteenth century, according to legend it was founded in 736, when a wooden eleven-faced Kannon was washed ashore nearby. The statue is supposedly one of a pair carved from a single camphor tree in 721 by a monk in the original Hase, near Nara; he placed one Kannon in a local temple and pushed the other out to sea.

Nowadays the **Kamakura Kannon** – just over 9m tall and gleaming with gold leaf (a fourteenth-century embellishment) – resides in an attractive, chocolate-brown and cream building at the top of the temple steps. This central hall is flanked by two smaller buildings: the right hall houses a large Amidha Buddha carved in 1189 for Minamoto Yoritomo's 42nd birthday to ward off the bad luck traditionally associated with that age; the hall on the left shelters a copy of an early fifteenth-century statue of Daikoku-ten, the cheerful God of Wealth. The real statue is in the small **treasure hall** immediately behind, alongside the original temple bell, cast in 1264. The next building along is the **Sutra Repository**, where a revolving drum contains a complete set of Buddhist scriptures – one turn of the wheel is equivalent to reading the whole lot. In the far northern corner of the complex, a **cave** contains statues of the goddess Benten and her sixteen children, or disciples, though it can't compete with the atmospheric setting of the Zeniarai Benten cave-shrine (see box, p.236).

Ranks of **jizō statues** are a common sight in Hase-dera, some clutching sweets or "windmills" and wrapped in tiny woollen mufflers; these sad little figures commemorate stillborn or aborted children.

The Daibutsu

大仏 • 4-2-28 Hase • Daily: April–Sept 7am–6pm; Oct–March 7am–5.30pm • ¥200 • **Entering statue** Daily 8am–4.30pm • ¥20

After all the hype, the **Daibutsu**, in the grounds of Kōtoku-in temple, can seem a little disappointing at first sight. But as you approach, and the Great Buddha's serene, rather aloof face comes more clearly into view, the magic begins to take hold. He sits on a stone pedestal, a broad-shouldered figure lost in deep meditation, with his head slightly bowed, his face and robes streaked grey-green by centuries of sun, wind and rain. The 13m-tall image represents Amida Nyorai, the future Buddha who receives souls into the Western Paradise, and was built under the orders of Minamoto Yoritomo to rival the larger Nara Buddha, near Kyoto. Completed in 1252, the statue is constructed of bronze plates bolted together around a hollow frame – you can climb inside for a fee – and evidence suggests that, at some time, it was covered in gold leaf. Amazingly, it has withstood fires, typhoons, the tsunami of 1495 which washed away its surrounding hall, and even the Great Earthquake of 1923.

Enoshima

江の島

Tied to the mainland by a 600m-long bridge, and easily reached from Kamakura, the tiny, sacred island of **Enoshima** has a few sights – some shrines, a botanical garden and a couple of caves – but its prime attraction is as a pleasant place to walk, away from motor traffic. Enoshima's eastern side shelters a yacht harbour and car parks, but otherwise the knuckle of rock – less than 1km from end to end – is largely covered with woods and a network of well-marked paths.

The private Enoden-line train rattles from Kamakura to Enoshima station, from where it's roughly a fifteen-minute walk southwest to the island, via a bridge constructed over the original sand spit. Once over the bridge, walk straight ahead under the bronze *torii* and uphill past restaurants and souvenir shops to where the steps to the main shrine begin; though the climb's easy enough, there are three **escalators** tunnelled through the hillside (¥350 for all three).

Enoshima-jinja

江の島神社 • Daily 9am–4.30pm • ¥150, or Eno-pass (see box below)

The island features a wide-ranging shrine area. Most make a beeline for Hatsu-no-miya, inside which sits Enoshima's most famous relic – a naked **statue of Benten**, housed in an octagonal hall halfway up the hill. The statue has been here since the days of Minamoto Yoritomo (1147–99) of the Kamakura Shogunate, who prayed to it for victory over the contemporary Fujiwara clan. Although ranked among Japan's top three Benten images, it's a little hard to see what all the fuss is about.

Samuel Cocking Park

サムエル・コッキング苑, Samyueru Cokkingu-en • April–June, Sept & Oct Mon–Fri 9am–6pm; Sat & Sun 9am–8pm; July & Aug daily 9am–8pm; Nov–March Mon–Fri 9am–5pm, Sat & Sun 9am–8pm • Park ¥200, lighthouse ¥300; both are included in the Eno-pass (see box below)

This nicely laid-out botanical garden is known as the **Samuel Cocking Park** after the English merchant and horticulturalist who built Japan's first greenhouse here in 1880. If it's a clear day, you'll get good views south to Ōshima's (occasionally smoking) volcano, and west to Fuji from the lighthouse inside the garden.

Iwaya

岩屋 • Daily: March–Oct 9am–5pm; Nov–Feb 9am–4pm • ¥500, or Eno-pass (see box below)

From the botanical garden, the path drops down steeply past restaurant-bars perched over the cliff – great for a sunset beer in fine weather – to the island's rocky west shore and two caves known as **Iwaya**. The caves themselves aren't all that special; more enjoyable is the walk along the wave-side boardwalk that runs between them.

ENOSHIMA PASS

The sights of Enoshima are covered by the one-day **Eno-pass**, which allows entry to Enoshima-jinja, Samuel Cocking Park and lighthouse, and the Iwaya caves, as well as unlimited rides of the escalators. The pass costs ¥1000 and is available from Enoshima's tourist office (see p.242), as well as the ticket booth at the first section of the escalators.

19

ARRIVAL AND DEPARTURE

KAMAKURA

By train You can take either the JR Yokosuka line from Tokyo station via Yokohama, or the JR Shōnan-Shinjuku line from Shinjuku via Shibuya and Yokohama (both 1hr; ¥920); from Tokyo station, make sure you board a Yokosuka- or Kurihama-bound train to avoid changing at Ōfuna. Trains stop at Kita-Kamakura station before pulling into the main Kamakura station a few minutes later.

ENOSHIMA

By train If you're visiting Enoshima after Kamakura, you can hop onto the Enoden line (ⓦenoden.co.jp) at Kamakura station (every 12min; 25min; ¥260); trains pull in to Enoshima station, from where it's roughly a

15min walk southwest to the island, over the bridge. Alternatively, if you're heading straight to Enoshima from Tokyo, the most straightforward route is the Odakyū-Enoshima line direct from Shinjuku to Katase-Enoshima station (片瀬江ノ島駅), which lies just north of the bridge, on the western side of the river; a helpful travel pass (see p.241) is available for this route.

Travel pass If you're planning to visit Enoshima, it's worth considering the Odakyū Enoshima-Kamakura Freepass, a one-day discount ticket (¥1470) covering a return trip to Katase-Enoshima station on the Odakyū line from Shinjuku, and unlimited travel on the Enoden line; it means that you'll have to hit Enoshima first and last, while visiting Kamakura on a loop trip, but it's feasible.

19

GETTING AROUND

By train Given the narrow roads and amount of traffic, it's usually quickest to use the trains as far as possible and then walk. On the west side of Kamakura station are ticket machines and platforms for the private Enoden line (ⓦenoden.co.jp) to Hase and Enoshima (every 12min; daily 6am–11pm). If you plan to hop on and off the Enoden line a lot and haven't got any other form of discount ticket, it's worth investing in the Kamakura-Enoshima Pass (¥700), which entitles you to unlimited travel on this line, plus JR services.

By bus The only time a bus might come in handy is for the more far-flung restaurants or the eastern shrines and temples. Local buses depart from the main station concourse; for the eastern shrines you want stand 4 for Kamakura-gū and stand 5 for Sugimoto-dera (¥200 minimum fare). To make three or more journeys by bus, you'll save money by buying a Kamakura Free Kippu day pass (¥550), which is available from the JR ticket office. The pass also covers JR trains from Kamakura to Kita-Kamakura and Enoden line services as far as Hase.

INFORMATION

Kamakura tourist office Outside the main, eastern exit of Kamakura station, immediately to the right, there's a small tourist information window (daily: April–Sept 9am–5.30pm; Oct–March 9am–5pm; ☎0467 23 3050), with English-speaking staff.

Enoshima tourist office You can pick up an

English-language map of the island at the small tourist office, which is on your left as you come off the bridge (daily 10am–5pm; ☎0466 26 9544, ⓦfujisawa-kanko.jp).

Services There's an international ATM (Mon–Fri 8am–9pm, Sat & Sun 8am–7pm) at the post office on Wakamiya-ōji.

ACCOMMODATION

Most people visit Kamakura on a day-trip from Tokyo, but if you do want to stay over note that many places charge more at weekends and during peak holiday periods, when it can be tough to get a room. Central Kamakura offers little budget accommodation, but has a fair choice of mid-range hotels.

Kaihinsō かいひん荘 4-8-14 Yuigahama ☎0467 22 0960, ⓦkaihinso.jp. Nestled by the beach, this hotel is one for the romantics: the surrounding area is sleepy, and the interior furnishings are elegant and beautiful. The building went up in 1924 as a private residence; though added to since, the Western-style section is now protected property. You can stay in one of the two rooms here, or in tatami rooms in the newer Japanese section; some of the latter have views onto the garden. ⊚ **¥26,000**

★**Kamakura Prince** 鎌倉プリンスホテル 1-2-18 Shichirigahama-higashi ☎0467 32 1111, ⓦprince

hotels.com/kamakura. Located by the beach, just a couple of stops west of Hase station on the Enoden line, this hotel is a real winner, and great value at this price range. Guest rooms surround a delightful pool, while floor-to-ceiling windows offer generous ocean views (from some rooms you can see Mt Fuji, too); a golf range and excellent teppanyaki restaurant round things off. ⊚ **¥12,500**

New Kamakura ホテルニューカマクラ 13-2 Onarimachi ☎0467 22 2230, ⓦnewkamakura.com. One of the best-value places to stay in Kamakura is this early twentieth-century, Western-style building, a minute's walk north of Kamakura station. It's a little bit worn, but in a way which many would find pleasant; most rooms are light and airy, with a choice of Western or Japanese style. ☞ **¥7000**

★**Villa Sacra** ヴィラサクラ 13-29 Onarimachi ☎ 0467 22 5311, ⓦ villasacra.com. For something a bit different, give this modern ryokan a whirl. It's situated in an old Japanese house, renovated with funky artistic flourishes. Staff are switched on, and the common room is a nice place to hang out with other guests. No meals; breakfast available for an extra fee. ☞ **¥8500**

★**WeBase Hostel** ウィーベースホステル 4-10-7 Yuigahama ☎ 0467 22 1221, ⓦ we-base.jp. Superbly convenient hostel, just over 15min on foot from Kamakura station, and 2min from the beach. Brand new at the time of writing, it's a large place which feels rather more modern than you'd expect in Kamakura – features include a couple of outdoor showers, a large veranda for coffee and chit-chat, and even a yoga studio. ☞ Dorms **¥3800**, doubles **¥9600**

EATING

Kamakura is famous for its beautifully presented **Buddhist vegetarian cuisine**, known as *shōjin-ryōri*, though there's plenty more casual dining on offer at local restaurants. You can have a stab at creating some Japanese food yourself with the **cooking classes** on offer from Mariko, a friendly local (from ¥7000 for 2–3hr; various options available, in English; ⓦ japanese-cooking-class-kamakura.com).

19

KAMAKURA

Cafe Terrace Itsuki Garden カフェテラス樹ガーデン On Daibutsu Hiking Course. A fantastic place to get your breath back if you're panting your way along the Daibutsu Hiking Course (see box, p.236). There are seats inside, but in warmer months everyone's out on the steeply arrayed outdoor terraces. Coffees and teas cost around ¥600, alcoholic drinks a little more. Daily 10am–7pm.

Hachi-no-ki 鉢の木 7 Yamanouchi ☎ 0467 22 8719; Kita-Kamakura branch ☎ 046 723 3722. Reservations are recommended for this famous *shōjin-ryōri* restaurant beside the entrance to Kenchō-ji, though it's easier to get a table at their newer Kita-Kamakura branches. Whichever you opt for, prices start at around ¥3500. Kenchō-ji branch Tues–Fri 11.30am–2.30pm, Sat & Sun 11am–3pm; main Kita-Kamakura branch daily except Wed 11am–2.30pm & 5–7pm.

Kyorai-an 去来庵 157 Yamanouchi ☎ 0467 24 9835. Beef stew prepared in a demi-glacé sauce has a long history in Japan, and *Kyorai-an* has one of the tastiest around; the set (¥2800) served with toast or rice, salad and coffee is the best value. The restaurant itself is inside a traditional Shōwa-era Japanese house. Mon–Thurs 11am–3pm, Sat & Sun 11am–5pm.

★**Piggies** ピギーズ 1-6-28 Yuki-no-shita ☎ 0467 95 9063. This small Peruvian-run place certainly stands out from the tourist-trap restaurants in central Kamakura. The Andean soul-food includes hearty meat sandwiches (¥800) and *choripapas* (a plate of fries and chunks of chorizo, smothered in sauce; ¥600), plus Peruvian drinks such as luminous-yellow Inca Cola (¥300) and a full range of Cusqueña beer (¥600; the red one's best). At the time of writing, they were also set to introduce ceviche to the menu. Mon–Fri 11am–6pm, Sat & Sun 10am–8pm.

ENOSHIMA

Kinokuniya 紀伊国屋 1-3-16 Tasegaikan ☎ 0466 22 4247; Enoshima station. Heading towards Enoshima from the station, you'll pass this simple ryokan-cum-restaurant on your right. It's highly popular with locals on account of the cheap sets; try the *kin-me-dai* (a delicious local red fish, served in soy) set, which goes for ¥1000, including coffee. Daily 11am–4pm.

Shonan Burger 湘南バーガー Enoshima ☎ 0466 29 0688. Fun little burger bar, just over the Enoshima bridge on the right. Their eponymous burger (¥400) is a real treat: a fishcake patty served with ground radish, perilla leaf and a miniature shoal of tiny sardines – look inside before you bite. Daily 11am–7pm.

DRINKING

In summer, wooden **bars** line the beaches from Kamakura to Enoshima. The nightlife in Kamakura town itself won't exactly remind you of Shibuya, but for a small place there's still a fair bit of activity until the last trains zoom off.

Milk Hall ミルクホール 2-3-8 Komachi ☎ 0467 22 1179, ⓦ milkhall.co.jp. Dimly lit, jazz-playing coffee-house-cum-antique-shop buried in the backstreets west of Komachi-dōri. Best for an evening beer, wine or cocktail (all from ¥700), rather than as a place to eat. Occasional live music. Daily 11am–10.30pm.

★**Tenshō** 天昇 1-3-4 Komachi ☎ 0467 22 6099. Get away from the tourists and down with the locals at this *tachinomiya*, whose raucous nature is the very antithesis of the regular genteel Kamakura atmosphere. *Yakitori* sticks go from ¥130, and sets of Hoppy (a type of fake beer with added alcohol) from ¥400. Daily except Mon 3–10pm.

Yokohama

横浜

On its southern borders Tokyo merges with **YOKOHAMA**, Japan's second most populous city (home to 3.6 million people) and a major international port. Though essentially part of the same mega-conurbation, central Yokohama feels far more spacious and airy than central Tokyo, thanks to its open harbour frontage and generally low-rise skyline, and though it can't claim any outstanding sights, the place has enough of interest to justify a day's outing from Tokyo.

Locals are proud of their city's international heritage, and there's definitely a cosmopolitan flavour to the place, with its scattering of Western-style buildings, Chinese temples and world cuisines, and its sizeable foreign community. The upmarket suburb of **Yamate** (also known as "the Bluff") is one of the city's highlights and boasts a splendid museum; the area forms a pleasant contrast with the vibrant alleys, colourful trinket shops and bustling restaurants of nearby **Chinatown**. Near the seafront, the **harbour area** boasts a few grand old Western edifices, in complete contrast to the **Minato Mirai 21** development's high-tech skyscrapers in the distance.

19

Brief history

When Commodore Perry sailed his "Black Ships" into Tokyo Bay in 1853, Yokohama was a mere fishing village of some eighty houses on the distant shore. But it was this harbour, well out of harm's way as far as the Japanese were concerned, that the shogun designated one of the five **treaty ports** open to foreign trade in 1858.

From the early 1860s until the first decades of the twentieth century, Yokohama flourished on the back of raw silk exports, a trade dominated by British merchants. During this period the city provided the main conduit for new ideas and inventions into Japan: the first bakery, photographers', ice-cream shop, brewery and – perhaps most importantly – the first railway line, which linked today's Sakuragichō with Shimbashi in central Tokyo in 1872. The **Great Earthquake** levelled the city in 1923, and it was devastated again in air raids at the end of World War II; the rebuilt city is, however, among the world's largest ports.

Motomachi and Yamate

The narrow, semi-pedestrianized shopping street of **Motomachi** (元町) exudes a faint retro flavour with its European facades. You'll get more of the old Motomachi feel in the two streets to either side, particularly Naka-dōri (仲通り), to the south, with its funky cafés and galleries.

At the northeast end of Motomachi, a wooded promontory marks the beginning of the **Yamate** (山手) district. The panoramic view from **Harbour View Park** is particularly beautiful at night; if you look really hard, just left of the double chimney stacks, you'll see the Tokyo Skytree blinking away.

Yokohama Foreign General Cemetery

外国人墓地, Gaikokujin Bochi • 96 Yamate-chō • March–Dec Sat & Sun noon–4pm • ¥200 donation • ☎ 045 622 1311, ⓦ yfgc-japan.com

Just a few minutes' walk south of the Harbour View Park, you'll likely happen upon the **Yokohama Foreign General Cemetery**, which sits on a west-facing hillside. Over 4500 people from more than forty countries are buried here, the vast majority either British or American.

Yamate Museum

山手博物館, Yamate Hakubutsukan • 254 Yamate-chō • Daily 11am–4pm • ¥200 • ☎ 045 622 1188

The tiny **Yamate Museum** is housed in the city's oldest wooden building, a stunning, fairytale-like structure erected in 1909. Exhibits focus on life in the area during the

YOKOHAMA

metres 0 500

Yokohama Bay Bridge

Harbour View Park

Yokohama Foreign General Cemetery

YAMATE

Motomachi-kōen

Yamate Museum

Doll Museum

Marine Tower

Motomachi-Chūkagai (S)

MOTOMACHI

MOTOMACHI

MAA-DŌRI

Sea Bass Pier

Hikawa-maru

Yamashita-kōen

CHINATOWN

Kantei-byō

Ishikawachō Station

METROPOLITAN EXPRESSWAY

Royal Wing Cruise Terminal

Yokohama International Passenger Terminal

Ōsanbashi

SHŪKAGAI-DŌRI

Yokohama Archives of History

Nihonōdōri (S)

Nihonōdōri

Yokohama Stadium

MINATO DŌORI

Negishi & Sankei-en

Isazaki-chōjamachi (S)

Akarenga

SHINKŌ

Cup Noodle Museum

World Porters

Manyō Club

Cosmo Clock 21

Yokohama Port Museum

Bashamichi (S)

Bashamichi

Kanagawa Prefectural Museum of Cultural History

KANNAI

BASHAMICHI

Kannai Station (S)

ISEZAKICHŌ

METROPOLITAN EXPRESSWAY

Minato Mirai Pukari-sanbashi

Queen's Square

Nippon-maru

Landmark Plaza

Landmark Tower

Sakuragichō Station (S)

Hinodechō Station

Pacifico Yokohama Exhibition Hall

MINATO MIRAI 21 (MM21)

Minato Mirai (S)

Yokohama Museum of Art

Mitsubishi Minatomirai Industrial Museum

JR NEGISHI LINE

Shin Takashima (S)

Tobe Station

Takashimachō Station (S)

Bay Quarter

Sea Bass Pier

Sōgō Department Store

YCAT

Yokohama Station (S)

Shin-Yokohama & Tokyo

Hiranumabashi Station

METROPOLITAN EXPRESSWAY

Yokohama & Tokyo

● EATING
Bairan	4
Café de la Presse	1
Enokitei	5
Manchinrō	2
Shofukumon	2

■ ACCOMMODATION
Daiwa Roynet	2
Hostel Village	3
Royal Park Hotel	1

foreign-settlement period, and include a collection of cartoons from *Japan Punch*, a satirical magazine published in Yokohama for a while in the late nineteenth century. However, it's the building itself that's the main draw.

Chinatown

中華街, Chūka-gai

Founded in 1863, Yokohama's **Chinatown** is the largest in Japan: its streets contain roughly two hundred restaurants and over three hundred shops, while some eighteen million tourists pass through its narrow byways every year; few leave without tasting what's on offer, from steaming savoury dumplings to a full-blown meal in one of the famous speciality restaurants.

Kantei-byō

関帝廟 • 140 Yamashita-chō • Daily 9am–7pm • Free; ¥500 to see main altar

The focus of community life is **Kantei-byō**, a shrine dedicated to Guan Yu, a former general and guardian deity of Chinatown. The building is a bit cramped, but impressive nonetheless, with a colourful ornamental gateway and writhing dragons wherever you look. You can pay to enter the main building to see the red-faced, long-haired Guan Yu, but it's not really worth it.

The harbour

From the eastern edge of Chinatown it's a short hop down to the harbour, which is fronted by **Yamashita-kōen**, a pleasant park – more grass than trees – created as a memorial to victims of the Great Earthquake. Here you can pick up a *Sea Bass* ferry (see p.248) or take a harbour cruise (see box, p.248) from the pier beside the **Hikawa-maru** (see below). The 106m-high **Marine Tower**, built in 1961, is still the focal point of the area after all these years, but it's better to save your money for the Landmark Tower's much higher observation deck (see opposite). Cruise ships pull up at **Ōsanbashi** pier to berth at Yokohama's International Passenger Terminal; a beautifully fluid, low-slung design inspired by ocean waves, it's a skateboarder's dream come true.

Hikawa-maru Museum

日本郵船氷川丸, Nikon Yūsen Hikowe-maru • Off Yamashita-kōen • Tues–Sun 10am–5pm • ¥200 • ☎ 045 641 4362, ⓦ nyk.com/rekishi

The *Hikawa-maru*, a retired passenger liner also known as the *Queen of the Pacific*, was built in 1930 for the NYK line Yokohama–Seattle service, though it was later commandeered as a hospital ship during World War II. It now serves as the **Hikawa-maru Museum**, with the ship done up to look as it did in its prime.

Minato Mirai 21 (MM21)

みなとみらい21 • ⓦ www.minatomirai21.com

Occupying over two square kilometres of reclaimed land and disused dockyards, **Minato Mirai 21**, or **MM21**, is an ever-expanding mini-city of apartment blocks, offices, recreational and cultural facilities.

Yokohama Port Museum

横浜みなと博物館, Yokohama Minato Hakubutsukan • 2-1-1 Minatomirai • Tues–Sun 10am–5pm • ¥600 March–Nov, ¥400 Dec–Feb • ⓦ nippon-maru.or.jp

Built in 1930, the **Nippon-maru** training sail ship saw service up until 1984 (during which time she sailed the equivalent of 45 times round the world) and now forms part of the enjoyable **Yokohama Port Museum**. You can explore the entire vessel, which has plenty of English labelling throughout, and alternating Japanese and English commentary over the loudspeakers.

Landmark Tower

横浜ランドマークタワー • 2-2-1 Minatomirai • **Observation deck** Daily 10am–9pm (Sat until 10pm) • ¥1000 •
Ⓦ yokohama-landmark.jp

You can't miss the awesome, 296m-tall **Landmark Tower** – Yokohama's tallest building
by far, and still ranked second countrywide (Tokyo Tower and the Skytree are mere
towers). The **Sky Garden observation deck** is on its 69th floor, and on clear days, when
Fuji is flaunting her beauty, the superb views more than justify the entry fee. You can
also enjoy a coffee for about the same price in the opulent *Sirius Sky Lounge*, another
floor up in the *Royal Park Hotel*, or splash out on an early evening cocktail as the city
lights spread their magic.

Yokohama Museum of Art

横浜美術館, Yokohama Bijutsukan • 3-4-1 Minatomirai • Daily except Thurs 10am–6pm • ¥500; varying prices for special exhibitions •
Ⓣ 045 221 0300, Ⓦ yokohama.art.museum

The centrepoint of the MM21 area is the splendid **Yokohama Museum of Art**, which is
filled with mostly twentieth-century works of Japanese and Western art. Such refinement
is set off to fine effect by designer Tange Kenzō's cool, grey space, which grabs your
attention as much as the exhibits.

Shinkō island

Between MM21 and Ōsanbashi is **Shinkō** island, which was reclaimed about a hundred
years ago as part of Yokohama's then state-of-the-art port facilities. Sights here include
a huge Ferris wheel, and an even huger spa complex; on the eastern side of the island,
two handsome red-brick warehouses dating from 1911 now form the attractive
Akarenga shopping, dining and entertainment complex.

Cosmo Clock 21

コスモクロック21 • 2-8-1 Shinkō • Mon–Fri 11am–9pm, Sat & Sun 11am–10pm; occasionally closed on Thurs • ¥700

The slowly revolving **Cosmo Clock 21** is one of the world's largest Ferris wheels, with a
diameter of 112m; one circuit takes around fifteen minutes, allowing plenty of time to
take in the view, which is particularly spectacular at night. The clock's changing colours
provide a night-time spectacle in their own right.

Manyō Club

万葉倶楽部, Manyō Kaiabu • 2-7-1 Shinkō • Daily 10am–9pm • ¥2700 • Ⓣ 045 663 4126

Spread over five floors, the **Manyō Club** spa complex offers a variety of hot-spring
baths – the water is trucked in from Atami onsen down the coast – in addition
to massages and treatments, restaurants and relaxation rooms. The rooftop is one
of the best places from which to admire the night-time colour display of the
Cosmo Clock.

Cup Noodle Museum

カップヌードルミュージアム • 2-3-4 Shinkō • Daily except Tues 10am–6pm • ¥500 • Ⓣ 045 345 0825, Ⓦ cupnoodles
-museum.jp

Instant noodles are one of Asia's most important snacks, and the contribution made
since 1971 by the pioneering Japanese Cup Noodle brand is traced in the fun,
beautifully designed **Cup Noodle Museum**. There are all sorts of interactive displays,
though for many the main sources of enjoyment are sampling some of the many Cup
Noodle varieties, and purchasing quirky branded souvenirs.

ARRIVAL AND DEPARTURE   **YOKOHAMA**

On the northwest side of town, Yokohama station functions as the city's main transport hub, offering train, subway and bus
connections, as well as featuring several gargantuan department stores.

19

YOKOHAMA SIGHTSEEING CRUISES

From Yamashita-kōen you can join the *Marine Shuttle* or *Marine Rouge* for a variety of **sightseeing cruises** round the harbour (from ¥1000 for 40min; ⓦ yokohama-cruising.jp); the *Marine Rouge* also offers lunch and dinner cruises (¥2520 plus ¥5500–11,000 for food). In addition, the bigger and more luxurious *Royal Wing* cruise ship (☎ 045 662 6125, ⓦ royalwing.co.jp) runs lunch, tea and dinner cruises from Ōsanbashi pier (¥1500–2500 plus ¥1500–5400 for food).

BY TRAIN

From Shibuya The fast Tōkyū-Tōyoko line (every 5–10min; 30min; ¥270) runs via Nakameguro, calling at Yokohama station before heading off underground to Minato Mirai and terminating at Motomachi-Chūkagai station. Some services actually start life way back in Saitama prefecture as Fukutoshin metro trains, stopping at Ikebukuro and Shinjuku-sanchōme stations before magically switching identity in Shibuya. JR's Shōnan-Shinjuku line runs into Yokohama station from Shibuya and Shinjuku (every 20–30min; 24min; ¥390).

From Tokyo station You can choose from the Tōkaidō or Yokosuka lines (both every 5–10min; 30min; ¥470), or the Keihin-Tōhoku line (every 5–10min; 40min; ¥470). All three are JR lines; the first two terminate at Yokohama station, while the latter continues to Sakuragichō, Kannai and Ishikawachō.

GETTING AROUND

By train Getting around central Yokohama is easy on either the Tōkyū-Tōyoko line or the JR Negishi line (the local name for Keihin-Tōhoku trains). Trains on both lines run every 5min.

By subway A single subway line connects Kannai and stations north to Shin-Yokohama, on the Shinkansen line; services run every 5–15min.

By Akai Kutsu sightseeing bus A retro-style sightseeing bus runs from outside Sakuragichō station's east exit via Minato Mirai, the Akarenga complex, Chinatown and Yamashita-kōen to Harbour View Park, then loops back via Ōsanbashi pier. Services run every 10–15min (¥100 per hop, or ¥300 for a day-pass).

By ferry Perhaps the most enjoyable way of getting about the city is on the *Sea Bass* ferries (ⓦ yokohama-cruising.jp) that shuttle between Yokohama station (from a pier in the Bay Quarter shopping complex) and southerly Yamashita-kōen, with some services stopping at Minato Mirai and Akarenga en route. There are departures every 15min (10am–7.30pm; ¥350–700).

INFORMATION

Tourist information The most useful centre (daily: April–Nov 9am–6pm; Dec–March 9am–7pm; ☎ 045 211 0111, ⓦ yokohamajapan.com) is immediately outside Sakuragichō station's east entrance, but there's also a booth in the underground concourse at Yokohama station (daily 9am–7pm; ☎ 045 441 7300).

ACCOMMODATION

★Daiwa Roynet ダイワロイネットホテル 204-1 Yamashita-chō, Naka-ku ☎ 045 664 3745, ⓦ daiwa roynet.jp. Secure, clean and in a good location, this is a good-value business hotel, where rooms are both cheaper and more stylish than anything else in this category. 📶 **¥10,300**

Hostel Village ホステルヴィレッジ 3-11-2 Matsukage-chō, Naka-ku ☎ 045 663 3696, ⓦ yokohama.hostel village.com. As the name suggests, this hostel is spread across various buildings; the main location is nice and clean, has a fun rooftop area, and holds regular parties and other themed nights. They also do good weekly and monthly deals for those who'll be in Yokohama a while. 📶 Dorms **¥2400**, doubles **¥4700**

Royal Park Hotel ローヤルパークホテル 2-2-1-3 Minato Mirai, Nishi-ku ☎ 045 221 1111, ⓦ yrph.com This hotel occupies the 52nd to 67th floors of the Landmark Tower, so spectacular views are guaranteed. Rooms are fairly spacious and come with good-sized bathrooms. As well as a fitness club and swimming pool (extra charges apply), facilities include a tea ceremony room and the *Sirius Sky Lounge*. 📶 **¥30,000**

EATING

One of Yokohama's highlights is sampling the enormous variety of restaurants and snack-food outlets cramming the streets of **Chinatown**. In fine weather, the casual little eating places on the ground floor of **Akarenga** on Shinkō island (see p.247) are also a good option, if only because you can take your food to the tables outside.

Bairan 梅蘭 133-10 Yamashita-chō ☎045 651 6695, ⓦbairan.jp. Small, unpretentious restaurant tucked in the backstreets and known for its Bairan *yakisoba*, stir-fried noodles served like a sort of pie, crispy on the outside and with various varieties of juicy stuffing (from ¥940). Mon–Fri 11.30am–3pm & 5–10pm, Sat & Sun 11am–10pm.

★**Café de la Presse** カフェドゥラプレス 2F Media Centre Building, 11 Nihon-dōri ☎045 222 3348. Viennese-style café in the corner of one of Yokohama's grand old buildings. Go for a coffee or tea (from ¥480), with a dessert such as macaroons or their utterly delectable crème brûlée (¥600). They also serve croques monsieur (¥800), and other sandwiches and light meals. Tues–Sun 10am–8pm.

Enokitei えの木てい 89-6 Yamate-chō ☎045 623 2288. Set in a venerable Yamate former residence, this cute English-style café serves dainty sandwiches and home-made cakes. Tues–Fri 11am–7pm.

Manchinrō 萬珍樓 153 Yamashita-chō ☎045 681 4004, ⓦmanchinro.com. This famous restaurant has been serving tasty Cantonese cuisine since 1892. Though prices are on the high side, the portions are generous; noodle and fried-rice dishes start at around ¥1200, lunch sets at ¥2200, and evening course menus at ¥5000. The branch behind serves a full range of dim sum. Daily 11am–10pm.

Shōfukumon 招福門 81-3 Yamashita-chō ☎045 664 4141. Multistorey restaurant offering all-you-can-eat dim sum deals for ¥3000, plus fried rice and soup. Mon–Fri 11.30am–10pm, Sat & Sun 11am–10pm.

19

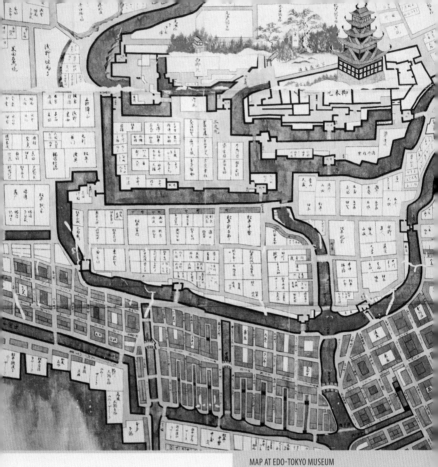

MAP AT EDO-TOKYO MUSEUM

Contexts

History

Although Tokyo's founding date is usually given as 1457, the year when Ōta Dōkan, a minor lord, built his modest castle on a bluff overlooking the Sumida-gawa, there have been people living on the Kantō plain since the Paleolithic period. Today's restless metropolis began life as a humble fishing village called Edo, meaning "river gate", a name granted in the twelfth century by Edo Shigenaga, a member of the Taira clan that held control of the Kantō district at the time.

The beginnings

The earliest archeological finds from the Tokyo area date back to the late Paleolithic period; the stone tools of ancient **hunter-gatherers**, who are believed to have arrived in Japan from Polynesia and mainland Asia, have been found at various sites to the west of today's city centre. The rationale behind their settling on the Kantō plain is clear, for it was, and remains, a strategically important spot at the nexus of sea, river and land routes. The centre of today's Tokyo, however, was under water for much of this time; as the land slowly rose due to tectonic shifts, the waters fell back, providing a boon to the Tokyoites of the time, since the resultant marshland provided an excellent source of food.

During the **Jōmon period** (10,000–3000 BC), the pottery for which Japan is now famed started to be produced in significant quantities, often employing distinctive "rope-cord" patterning. More elaborate techniques began to be used in the **Yayoi period** (300 BC–300 AD), when there were also major advances in wet-rice cultivation and the use of bronze and iron implements. Given the city's modern-day renown in the pottery field, it may come as a surprise to learn that Tokyo was actually nearer the end of the talent line: most advances can be sourced to China, from where they slowly trickled to western Japan (often via Korea), and then finally on to Tokyo and the north. The same can be said for Buddhism, which arrived from Sabi (now Buyeo), contemporary capital of the Korean kingdom of Baekje, around the mid-sixth century AD; and *kanji*, the Chinese characters that remain a hugely important component of Japan's writing system today.

Early dynasties

Tokyo was a mere bit-part player in Japan's early dynastic days. The **Soga clan** (592–645), based out west around Nara, were the first of Japan's non-imperial ruling dynasties; Asakusa's Sensō-ji, apparently built in 628 after local fishermen found a golden bodhisattva statue in their nets, was likely founded during these times. In 645 the **Nakatomi clan** staged a successful coup against the Soga; within the next year they had reorganized their nascent dynasty along a Tang Chinese system of land tenure and taxation (known as the Taika, or "great reforms"), with the area on which Tokyo now

10,000–3000 BC	628 AD	645	1180
Creation of earliest known pottery	Asakusa's Sensō-ji constructed	Nakatomi clan depose Soga in coup, and reform land tenure and taxation	First use of Tokyo's original name, Edo

sits becoming part of Musashi province. It became customary to relocate the royal palace after the death of each emperor, until Japan's first permanent capital, Nara, was founded in 710.

It wasn't long before the capital was on the move again, however; in 784 the Fujiwara court distanced itself from Nara's increasingly influential monks and priests by relocating to nearby Nagaoka, then to Heian (later known as Kyoto) in 794. The colourful Heian era came to a close with the Genpei wars of 1180–85; the victorious **Minamoto clan** chose to base themselves in Kamakura, just west of Tokyo. In fact, Tokyo's original name, **Edo**, meaning "river gate", can be traced back to the beginning of the war; it was first used by Shigenago Edo of the competing Taira clan, who had settled in the area.

The Kamakura and Muromachi eras

The leader of the Minamoto clan, Yoritomo, established his military-based Bakufu, or **"tent government"**, at **Kamakura**, styling himself Sei-i Tai Shogun, the "Barbarian-subduing Great General". Japan settled into a period of semi-feudalism, with peasants allowed tenure of land in return for service to their loyal lord. After Yoritomo's death in 1199, his loyal lieutenant Hōjō Tokimasa, in partnership with Yoritomo's widow Masako, took the helm, assuming the combined roles of military and civil governor, and ushering in the century-long era of the **Hōjō regents** – these regents, rather than the figurehead emperor or shogun, were the real power-holders during this time.

The Mongol invasions of the late thirteenth century – thwarted by typhoons, dubbed the kamikaze or "divine wind" by the Japanese of the time – contributed to the fall of the ineffectual Kamakura government, which in 1333 found itself roundly beaten by the forces of **Emperor Go-Daigo**. Kamakura's Bakufu soon dispatched the warrior **Ashikaga Takauji** to bring Go-Daigo to heel; the wily Takauji initially switched allegiance to the emperor but later turned against him, forcing Go-Daigo to retreat to the mountains of Yoshino. Takauji set up a rival emperor in Kyoto, and for sixty years Japan had two courts; they were reconciled in 1392, by which time the Ashikaga shogunate had established its headquarters in Kyoto's **Muromachi** district, from where they ruled for over two centuries.

In the meantime, things were quietly ticking along in Tokyo (then still named Edo), with its first castle erected in 1457 by Ōta Dōkan, a poet better known as **Ōta Sekenaga**, and now regarded as the founder of modern Tokyo; his battlements formed part of what is now the Higashi Gyoen, which abuts today's Imperial Palace, and it became the precursor to a small wave of nearby temples, shrines and mercantile complexes. Ōta himself came to a sticky end in 1486, killed in Sagami (now Kanagawa) after being falsely accused of traitorship. His death occurred during a period of national strife, with the **Ōnin wars** of 1467–77 effectively relieving the government of authority, and regional *daimyō* (feudal warlords) fighting for dominance – a pattern that continued for over a century.

Reunification

The civil wars ended with the reunification of Japan under a triumvirate of generals of outstanding ability. The first, Oda Nobunaga, achieved dominance of the Kyoto region; however, in 1582 he was betrayed and forced to commit ritual suicide. Toyotomi

1185	1333	1457	1467–77
Minamoto clan victorious in Genpei wars; base themselves in Kamakura	Kamakura government falls	Founding of Tokyo	Ōnin wars result in regional warlords fighting for dominance

Hideyoshi, who had risen from obscurity to become one of Nobunaga's most trusted generals, avenged his death, managing to outmanoeuvre all rivals with a shrewd mix of force and diplomacy. Success went to his head, however, and he embarked on costly excursions into Korea, each time stymied by far smaller forces and the armoured "turtle ships" of modern-day Korean hero General Yi Sun-shin.

In 1590 another ambitious warlord, **Tokugawa Ieyasu**, established his power base in Edo, far from the emperor in Kyoto. The same year, Hideyoshi gained control over the region by defeating the powerful Go-Hōjō family at nearby Odawara castle. Shortly before his death in 1598, Hideyoshi persuaded Ieyasu, now an ally after a period of circumspect confrontation, to support the succession of his son Hideyori. The trust was misplaced: after defeating the remaining western clans at the Battle of Sekigahara in 1600, Ieyasu seized power himself, reuniting the country and taking the title of **shogun** – effectively a military dictator. Though the emperor continued to hold court in Kyoto, Japan's real centre of power would henceforth lie in Edo, at this point still little more than a small huddle of buildings at the edge of the Hibiya inlet.

The Edo era

The **Tokugawa** dynasty set about creating a city befitting its new status, initiating massive construction projects – a trend which has continued to the present day. By 1640, Edo Castle was the most imposing in all Japan, and most probably the largest in the whole world – a sixteen-kilometre perimeter line of defences complete with a five-storey central keep, a double moat and a complex, spiralling network of canals. Drainage work also began on the surrounding marshes, where embankments were raised to protect the nascent city against flooding.

The shogun required his *daimyō* to split the year between their provincial holdings and Edo, where their families were kept as virtual hostages. Maintaining two households with two sets of retainers, travelling long distances and observing prescribed ceremonies on the way left them neither the time nor money to raise a serious threat.

In exchange for their loyalty, *daimyō* were granted prime land to the west of the castle, in the area known as **Yamanote**. Artisans, merchants and others at the bottom of the established order, meanwhile, were confined to **Shitamachi**, a low-lying, overcrowded region to the east. Though less distinct, this division between the "high" and "low" city (see box, p.75) is still apparent today.

Closed Japan

Though the *daimyō* had been cleverly kept in check, the shogun perceived another threat to state security: Christianity. Despite the fact that Ieyasu's advisers had included Englishman Will Adams (whose tale was fictionalized in the novel *Shogun*), heavy restrictions began to be placed on all foreigners residing in Japan; missionaries and Christian converts found themselves persecuted. A policy of national seclusion was introduced in 1639; by this time, an estimated 250,000 Japanese Christians had been executed, imprisoned or forced to apostatize. Thus began the period of *sakoku*, or the **"closed country"**, which lasted more or less continuously until 1853. The only exceptions to the edicts were Korean diplomats, and a handful of Dutch and Chinese traders allowed to operate out of Nagasaki, way out to the west.

1590	1600	1639	1640
Warlord Tokugawa Ieyasu establishes power base in Edo	Ieyasu reunites country, and declares himself shogun	Policy of national seclusion introduced; Christians persecuted	Completion of Edo Castle

FIRE OF THE LONG SLEEVES

Shitamachi's tightly packed streets of thatch and wood dwellings usually suffered worst in the great fires which broke out so frequently that they were dubbed *Edo no hana*, the "flowers of Edo". In January 1657, the **Fire of the Long Sleeves** – so named because it started at a temple where the long-sleeved kimono of women who had recently died were being burnt – laid waste to three-quarters of the district's buildings and killed an estimated 100,000 people. Subsequent precautions included earth firewalls, manned watchtowers and local firefighting teams, who were much revered for their acrobatic skills and bravery. The fires continued, however, and the life expectancy of an Edo building averaged a mere twenty years.

Edo rising

The long period of stability under the Tokugawa, interrupted only by a few peasant rebellions, brought steady economic development. Mid-eighteenth-century Edo was the world's largest city, with a population well over one million, of whom roughly half were squeezed into Shitamachi at an astonishing 70,000 people per square kilometre. Peace gave rise to an increasingly wealthy merchant class, and the arts flourished; in parallel with this ran a vigorous, often bawdy subculture where the pursuit of pleasure was taken to new extremes. In Shitamachi, the arbiters of fashion were the **Edo-ko**, the "children of Edo", with their earthy humour and delight in practical jokes. Inevitably, there was also a darker side to life and the *Edo-ko* knew their fair share of squalor, poverty and violence. Licensed brothels, euphemistically known as "pleasure quarters", in areas such as Shinjuku, flourished, and child prostitution was common.

The arrival of the Black Ships

During Japan's period of seclusion, a small number of Westerners managed to breach the barriers, among them Engelbert Kaempfer, a Dutchman who wrote the first European-language history of Japan in the late seventeenth century. Various British survey vessels and Russian envoys also visited Japan in the early nineteenth century, but the greatest pressure came from the US, whose trading and whaling routes passed to the south of the country. In 1853, Commodore Matthew Perry of the US Navy arrived in Shimoda – at the tip of the Izu peninsula, just west of Tokyo – with a small fleet of **"Black Ships"**, demanding that Japan open at least some of its ports to foreigners. Japan's ruling elite was thrown into turmoil – the shogunate was already fearful of foreign incursions following the British defeat of China in the Opium Wars. However, when the emperor demanded that the foreigners be rebuffed it quickly became clear that Japan's military was no longer up to the task.

American Townsend Harris managed to extract **concessions** in 1858, and similar treaties were soon concluded with other Western nations; certain ports were opened up (including Yokohama), while foreigners were given the right of residence and certain judicial rights in these enclaves. Opponents of such shameful appeasement by the shogunate took up the slogan "revere the emperor, expel the barbarians!"; less reactionary factions could see that Japan was in no state to do this, and that their only hope of remaining independent was to learn from the more powerful nations.

Edo's power was not only being weakened from outside Japan, but from inside as well. Evidence of a westward shift in power came in 1863, when the emperor ordered

1657	1684	1853	1858
Fire lays waste to most of Shitamachi	First sumo tournament held	Matthew Perry arrives with the "Black Ships"	Japan opens up to foreign trade

Shogun Iemochi to Kyoto to explain his conciliatory actions towards the West – the first visit of a shogun to the imperial capital since 1634. To add to the humiliation, Iemochi could only muster a mere 3000 retainers, compared with the 300,000 who had accompanied Ieyasu to Kyoto on the previous occasion.

In 1867 the fifteenth and final shogun, Tokugawa Yoshinobu, formally applied to the emperor to have imperial power restored. The shogunate was terminated, and in December of that year the **Imperial Restoration** was formally proclaimed and 15-year-old Mitsuhito acceded to the throne, ushering in a period dubbed Meiji, or "enlightened rule".

The Meiji era

The first years of **Meiji rule** saw a wave of great changes take place. Far from following the shogunate in a fall from grace, Edo was cemented as the seat of national power; in 1869, the young emperor shifted his court from Kyoto to Edo, renaming it Tokyo, or the "eastern capital". Determined to modernize, Japan embraced the ideas and technologies of the West with startling enthusiasm. Brick buildings, electric lights, trams, trains and then cars all made their first appearance in Tokyo. Within a few decades the castle lost its outer gates and most of its grounds, canals were filled in or built over and the commercial focus shifted to Ginza, while Shitamachi's wealthier merchants decamped for the more desirable residential areas of Yamanote, leaving the low city to sink into slow decline.

Beneath its modern veneer, however, Tokyo remained largely a fragile city of wood. When the **Great Kantō Earthquake** struck at noon on September 1, 1923, half of Tokyo – by then a city of some two million – was destroyed, while 100,000 people lost their lives in the quake itself and in the blazes sparked by thousands of cooking-fires.

World War II and recovery

By the early 1930s Tokyo had rebuilt itself, but before long the city, like the rest of Japan, was gearing up for war. The first US bombs fell on Tokyo in April 1942, and, as the Allied forces drew closer, increasingly frequent raids reached a crescendo in March 1945. During three days of sustained **incendiary bombing** an estimated 100,000 people died, most of them on the night of March 9. The physical devastation surpassed even that of the Great Earthquake: Meiji-jingū, Sensō-ji and Edo Castle were all destroyed, and Shitamachi all but obliterated; from Hibiya it was possible to see clear across the 3km to Shinjuku.

From a prewar population of nearly seven million, Tokyo was reduced to around three million people in a state of near-starvation. Regeneration was fuelled by an influx of American dollars and food aid under the **Allied Occupation** led by General MacArthur. The liveliest sector of the economy during this period was the black market, first in Yūrakuchō and later in Ueno and Ikebukuro.

In 1950 the **Korean War** broke out, and central Tokyo underwent extensive redevelopment on the back of a manufacturing boom partly fuelled by the war, while immigrants flooded in from the provinces to fill the factories. Anti-American **demonstrations** occurred sporadically throughout the decade, and rumbled on into

1867	1869	1881	1923
Meiji restoration	Edo becomes imperial capital; renamed Tokyo ("eastern capital")	Small watch shop called Seikō opens in Ginza	Great Kantō Earthquake strikes, killing over 100,000

the late 1960s (in 1968 the authorities closed Tokyo University for a year). Heavily armed riot police became a familiar sight on the streets, but the situation was never allowed to threaten the major event of the postwar period: on October 10, 1964, Emperor Hirohito opened the eighteenth **Olympic Games**. The first Olympics ever held in Asia, the Games marked Japan's return to economic health and to international respectability.

Boom and bust

Like the rest of the industrialized world, Japan suffered during the oil crisis of the 1970s, but by the following decade its economy was the envy of the world. The late 1980s **boom** saw land prices in Tokyo reach dizzying heights, matched by excesses of every conceivable sort – everything from gold-wrapped sushi to mink toilet-seat covers. Now referred to as the "bubble period", these days were characterized by fast living – the stereotype of salarymen throwing down tens of thousands of yen each night at champagne-and-girlie bars is not all that far off the truth.

Such heady optimism was reflected, too, in a series of ambitious **building projects**. Some came off, like the Metropolitan Government offices in Shinjuku and the Odaiba reclamation in Tokyo Bay, while others were left on the drawing board, among them the X-Seed 400, which remains the largest building ever designed in full: 4km high, larger than Mount Fuji and planned to house half a million.

By 1992, with the stock market rapidly sinking and businesses contracting, it was clear that the economic bubble had burst. This grim situation was compounded by

EDUCATION

"Efficient" is probably the stereotype most readily associated with Japan, and in a land where trains run to the second, you'll see plenty of supporting evidence during your stay. Efficiency, however, is not a word that can really be applied to the country's **educational system**: one of the most conservative elements of one of the world's most conservative countries, it has essentially remained unchanged for decades. For visitors, its problems will be most evident in the low levels of **English-speaking** ability: though all Japanese study the language for up to a decade, only a fraction are able to hold a simple conversation. With private language academies catering to a demand that the government has not been able to sate, this has been a boon to thousands upon thousands of **foreign teachers**, most of whom each cart a substantial chunk of their salary home at the end of their stay.

Then of course, there's the **pressure** on the students themselves. Days can be long, and even on Saturdays and Sundays you'll see plenty of kids walking around in school uniform. All students are required to attend after-school classes; most do sports of some kind, which is great for health, but some students clock up more than 36 hours per week doing extracurricular activities (baseball is said to be the most time-consuming). Though a majority of students go on to university, getting there is no walk in the park: those who want to go to Tokyo University or other high-end establishments have to sit full suites of independent tests (usually multiple-choice, with no room for discussion or debate). Pressure is thus magnified into a few precious hours, and results from previous years of schooling are often overshadowed. In Tokyo, and around the country, there exist lobby groups which demand wholesale change to the system; if change eventually arrives, it's likely to do so slowly.

1942	1945	1964	1973
First bombs fall in World War II	World War II ends; Japan under American occupation	Hosting of Olympic Games	First Family Mart convenience store opens

AFTER THE 'QUAKE

On 11 March, 2011, powerful tremors were felt throughout Tokyo. Foreign journalists sent the regular tweets and filed the regular reports about how their office had shaken; how things had fallen on the floor; how they'd had to evacuate their buildings. It quickly became clear that the situation was far more serious. Tokyo had merely been rattled by the fourth most powerful earthquake ever recorded, its epicentre further north, near the city of Sendai. While relatively few died in the **Tōhoku earthquake** itself, more than 16,000 perished as a result of the giant **tsunami** that inundated the country's eastern shore – helicopter images showed a sickening black wave sweeping across villages, roads and farmland, effortlessly swallowing anything and everything in its path. This included the Fukushima Daiichi nuclear power plant, whose swamped reactors went into meltdown.

The tsunami displaced more than 300,000 people, many of whom were left without power and water for some time. Serious questions were asked about the government's failure to control the situation; it also emerged that details regarding leaks from the power plant had been covered up, and an exclusion zone remains in place around it today. Tokyo's tourism figures also took a tumble, though these have since rebounded: the capital is located a safe distance from the stricken power plant, and its buildings are designed to withstand the powerful earthquakes which will always remain a fact of life in Japan.

revelations of deep-seated political corruption and by the **AUM Shinrikyō** terrorist group releasing deadly sarin gas on Tokyo commuter trains in 1995, leaving twelve dead and thousands injured.

Recession was officially announced in 1998, the same year a manual on how to commit suicide sold an incredible 1.1 million copies; over 30,000 people – the majority middle-aged men facing unemployment – killed themselves that year, followed by a record 33,000 in 1999. The new millennium brought glimmerings of **recovery** – hardly surprising after trillions of yen had been pumped into the economy through various government packages. But Tokyo would never quite be the same, and the blue-tarpaulin tent compounds of the **homeless** remain commonplace in the capital's parks.

To the present day

In 1999, the ultranationalistic **Ishihara Shintarō** was elected Tokyo's governor. Despite frequently going on record with racist and other intemperate remarks, Ishihara proved a popular figure with voters, winning two further mayoral elections.

Under Ishihara's stewardship, Tokyo partly hosted a successful **2002 World Cup** and has boosted itself as the crucible of Japan's "soft power" in areas such as anime, manga, pop music and fashion. Districts from Akihabara to Roppongi have undergone structural makeovers, the latest projects being a huge renovation of Tokyo station and its surrounding area, and the sprucing up of Oshiage around the Tokyo Skytree (see p.78).

One of Ishihara's main aims was to make Tokyo the first Asian city to host the **Olympic Games** twice. The bid for 2016 failed, with the event going to Rio instead; after the Tokyo city reins had been handed over to former journalist **Inose Naoki** in 2012, the 2020 application proved successful, with Tokyo beating off competition from Madrid

1979	1981	Late 1980s	1992
Walkman invented	Mario makes first appearance in Donkey Kong	Boom-time in Tokyo: the "bubble years"	Bursting of economic bubble

and Istanbul. The new National Olympic Stadium will, when finally completed (see box, p.120), be the centre of proceedings; other venues include the Imperial Palace gardens (cycling), and sumo's Ryōgoku Kokugikan (boxing, appropriately).

Tokyo was not physically hit too hard by the gigantic **Tōhoku earthquake** of 2011 (see box, p.257), though tens of thousands of its residents fled for the relative security of western Japan, and many never returned. Unemployment also spiked, but has since eased to around 3 percent, the best rate since 1995. There has also been better news of late regarding Japan's famously low birth rates, which a few years ago had dropped to 1.26 but have now risen to a marginally more nuclear 1.41. However, the looming problem of an ageing population remains one of the biggest challenges facing Tokyo, and Japan as a whole; countries expecting a similar timebomb to go off further down the line will be watching avidly.

1995	2002	2012	2020
Sarin attack on Tokyo subway	Hosting of World Cup	Completion of Tokyo Skytree	Due to host Olympic Games for the second time

Books

A byword for transformation, change and tradition – and even, on occasion, "the Orient" itself – it's no surprise that Tokyo is so well represented on the literary scene. In addition, the overseas popularity of Japanese fiction has ballooned in recent decades, with certain writers now household names abroad. The following publishers specialize in English-language books on Japan, as well as translations of Japanese works: Kodansha (ⓦkodanshausa .com); Charles E. Tuttle (ⓦtuttlepublishing.com); Stonebridge Press (ⓦstonebridge.com); and Vertical (ⓦvertical-inc.com). Note that Japanese authors listed below follow the Japanese convention of placing the family name first. Titles marked with the ★ symbol are particularly recommended.

HISTORY

Ian Buruma *Inventing Japan*. Focuses on the period 1853–1964, during which Japan went from a feudal, isolated state to a powerhouse of the modern world economy. Buruma's *The Wages of Guilt* also skilfully explains how and why Germany and Japan have come to terms so differently with their roles in World War II.

John Dower *Embracing Defeat: Japan in the Aftermath of World War II*. This Pulitzer Prize winner offers an erudite and clear appraisal of the impact of the American occupation on Japan. First-person accounts and snappy writing bring the book alive.

Kawabata Yasunari *The Scarlet Gang of Asakusa*. File this one under historical fiction: serialized in a Tokyo daily newspaper in 1930, Nobel Prize-winner Kawabata brought the seediness of Shitamachi to life with his tales of bingeing, crime, prostitution and other goings-on in 1920s Asakusa.

Stephen Mansfield *Tokyo: A Biography*. This recently published summary of Tokyo's history may veer towards the bombastic, but it's a very decent rundown of what the city has been through over the years, from samurai days to the 2011 'quake, via World War II.

Bill O'Reilly *Killing the Rising Sun*. O'Reilly is not exactly a renowned Japan expert, but for this latest of his "Killing" series (which includes *Killing Jesus*, *Killing Patton* and *Killing Reagan*) he teamed up with Martin Dugard to create this very readable, if extremely one-sided, account of the main acts of World War II's Pacific Theater.

Edward Seidensticker *Tokyo Central: A Memoir*. Though increasingly hard to hunt down, the memoirs of this leading translator of ancient and modern Japanese literature make for fascinating reading.

★ **Paul Waley** *Tokyo: City of Stories*. An intimate, anecdotal history of the capital, delving into Tokyo's neighbourhoods and uncovering some fascinating stories in the process.

ARTS, CULTURE AND SOCIETY

★ **Jake Adelstein** *Tokyo Vice*. With forensic thoroughness and gallows humour Adelstein documents his unsentimental education in crime reporting for the *Yomiuri Shimbun*, Japan's top-selling newspaper. His main scoop is about three *yakuza* heavyweights who sneaked into the US, with FBI approval, to get liver transplants. A true-crime classic.

Edmund de Waal *The Hare with Amber Eyes: a Hidden Inheritance*. The tale of a family heirloom – some netsuke carvings found in his uncle's Tokyo apartment – written by one of Britain's most famous contemporary ceramicists.

Hector Garcia *A Geek in Japan*. A good read for newbie Japanophiles itching to learn more about manga, anime or the eponymous otaku (Japanese geeks); it also includes information about Zen, tea ceremonies and the like, even though they're a bit of a mismatch given the aim at a younger crowd.

Alex Kerr *Dogs and Demons*. A scathing and thought-provoking attack on Japan's economic, environmental and social policies of the past decades, by someone who first came to Japan as a child in the 1960s and has been fascinated by the country ever since. Also worth reading is his earlier book *Lost Japan*.

Gunji Masakatsu *Kabuki*. Excellent introduction to kabuki, by one of the leading connoisseurs of Japanese drama, illustrated with copious annotated photos of the great actors and the most dramatic moments in kabuki theatre.

★ **Donald Richie** *A Lateral View, Partial Views* and *Tokyo Megacity*. Setting a standard other expat commentators can only aspire to, *A Lateral View* and *Partial Views* tackle Tokyo style, avant-garde theatre, pachinko and the Japanese kiss, among many other things. *Tokyo Megacity* uses photos and essays to capture the essence of the city, arrayed in the order in which its neighbourhoods originally developed.

Shinzo Satomi *Sushi Chef Sukiyabashi Jiro*. The titular restaurant rocketed to fame after being featured in 2011 documentary *Jiro Dreams of Sushi*, culminating in a 2014 visit by Barack Obama. In this short book, star chef Ono Jiro talks about sushi, rather than dreaming of it, and his insights are quite absorbing.

Joan Stanley-Baker *Japanese Art*. Highly readable introduction to the broad range of Japan's artistic traditions (though excluding theatre and music), tracing their

development from prehistoric to modern times.

Robert Twigger *Angry White Pyjamas*. The subtitle "An Oxford poet trains with the Tokyo riot police" gives you the gist. Twigger provides an intense forensic account of the daily trials, humiliations and triumphs of becoming a master of aikido.

Robert Whiting *Tokyo Underworld*. This well-researched tale follows the ups and downs of Nick Zapapetti, a larger-than-life Italian-American who arrived with the occupying forces in 1945 and stayed on to become "the king of Roppongi" and Tokyo's Mafia boss. In the process, Whiting also charts the history of the *yakuza* in postwar Japan.

GUIDES AND REFERENCE BOOKS

Enbutsu Sumiko *Old Tokyo: Walks in the City of the Shogun*. Tokyo's old Shitamachi area is best explored on foot, and this guide, illustrated with block prints, helps bring the city's history alive.

Thomas F. Judge and Tomita Hiroyuki *Edo Craftsmen*. Beautifully produced portraits of some of the traditional craftsmen still working in the backstreets of Tokyo. A timely insight into a disappearing world.

Ono Tadashi and Harris Salat *Japanese Soul Cooking*. Cookbook focusing on Japanese comfort food, such as tempura, *tonkatsu*, curry, ramen and more.

Mark Robinson *Izakaya: The Japanese Pub Cookbook*. A beautifully illustrated celebration of some of the author's favourite Tokyo-based *izakaya*, with over sixty recipes for

their rustic food.

Dominic Roscrow *Whisky Japan*. Japanese whisky is gaining an ever-better international reputation (one won the *Whisky Bible*'s prestigious annual award in 2013), and this handy guide will help you sort your Nikka Yoichi from your Yamazaki Single Malts.

Robb Satterwhite *What's What in Japanese Restaurants*. Handy guide to all things culinary from a Tokyo-based epicure; the menus annotated with Japanese characters are particularly useful.

Julian Worrall and Erez Golani Solomon *Twenty-first Century Tokyo: A Guide to Contemporary Architecture*. Relatively up-to-date survey of some of the city's outstanding modern buildings and structures.

JAPANESE FICTION

Kirino Natsuo *Out*. Four women working in a bentō factory just outside Tokyo discover that committing murder is both easier and much more complicated than they could ever have imagined, in this dark, superior thriller that mines a very dark seam of Japan's underbelly. Follow-up

books are *Grotesque*, about the deaths of two Tokyo prostitutes, and *Real World*, a grim thriller about alienated Japanese teenagers.

Mishima Yukio *Spring Snow*. Novelist Mishima sealed his notoriety by committing ritual suicide after leading a failed

HARUKI MURAKAMI

One of Japan's most entertaining and translated contemporary writers, **Haruki Murakami** (ⓦ harukimurakami.com) has been hailed as a postwar successor to the great novelists Mishima, Kawabata and Tanizaki, and talked of as a future Nobel laureate. Many of Murakami's books are set in Tokyo, drawing on his time studying at Waseda University in the early 1970s and running a jazz bar in Kokubunji, a place that became a haunt for literary types and, no doubt, provided inspiration for his jazz-bar-running hero in the bittersweet novella *South of the Border, West of the Sun*.

The de facto introduction to Murakami is *Norwegian Wood*, a book about the tender coming-of-age love of two students, which has sold over five million copies. The truly bizarre *A Wild Sheep Chase* and its follow-up *Dance Dance Dance* are funny but unsettling modern-day fables, dressed up as detective novels. Considered among his best works are *The Wind-Up Bird Chronicle*, a hefty yet dazzling cocktail of mystery, war reportage and philosophy, and the surreal *Kafka on the Shore*, a murder story in which cats talk to people and fish rain from the sky.

After Dark, set in the dead of Tokyo night, has all the usual Murakami trademark flourishes, from quirky characters to metaphysical speculation; while his mega-opus *1Q84*, a complex tale of cults and assassins set in 1984, unravels over three volumes totalling more than 1600 pages.

military coup in 1970, leaving behind a highly respectable body of work, including *After the Banquet, Forbidden Colours* and *The Sea of Fertility*. *Spring Snow* is the most Tokyo-centric of his novels, part of it being set here in 1912.
★**Murakami Haruki** *Norwegian Wood* and *After Dark*. Two Tokyo-based novels from the pen of one of Japan's most famous writers (see box opposite).
★**Murakami Ryū** *Coin Locker Babies* and *In the Miso Soup*. Murakami burst onto Japan's literary scene in the mid-1980s with *Almost Transparent Blue*, a disturbing tale of student life mixing reality and fantasy. *Coin Locker Babies* is his most ambitious work, spinning a revenger's tragedy about the lives of two boys dumped as babies in adjacent coin lockers, while *In the Miso Soup* is a superior thriller along the lines of *American Psycho*, set in Tokyo.
Various *The Book of Tokyo: a City in Short Fiction*. There are few translated anthologies of Japanese short stories, but this is an excellent series of Tokyo-centric shorts from several acclaimed Japanese writers, including Banana Yoshimoto, Hideo Furukawa and Hiromi Kawakami.

TOKYO IN FOREIGN FICTION

★**Alan Brown** *Audrey Hepburn's Neck*. Beneath this rib-tickling, acutely observed tale of a young guy from the sticks adrift in big-city Tokyo are several important themes, including the continuing impact of World War II and the confused relationships between the Japanese and *gaijin*.
William Gibson *Idoru*. Love in the age of the computer chip. Cyberpunk novelist Gibson's sci-fi vision of Tokyo's high-tech future – a world of non-intrusive DNA checks at airports and computerized pop icons (the *idoru* of the title) – rings disturbingly true. The hip thriller *Pattern Recognition* is also partly set in Tokyo.
Jonathan Lee *Who is Mister Satoshi?* By turns intriguing, funny and moving, if occasionally a little clichéd, this novel follows a middle-aged man on a quest to find the addressee on an unexplained package that belonged to his dead mother.
★**David Mitchell** *Ghostwritten* and *number9dream*. Mitchell made a splash with his debut *Ghostwritten*, a dazzling collection of interlocked short stories, a couple of which were set in Japan. *number9dream*, shortlisted for the Booker prize in 2001, conjures up a postmodern Japan of computer hackers, video games, gangsters and violence.
David Peace *Tokyo Year Zero* and *Occupied City*. The first two instalments in Peace's crime trilogy set in Tokyo immediately after the end of World War II. Never an easy read, Peace's novels nonetheless impress with their attention to detail, complex plots and compelling characters.

Film

Dazzlingly colourful, fetchingly otherworldly and indisputably unique, Tokyo has proved an irresistible location and subject matter for film-makers – Japanese and foreign alike – down the ages. Films marked with the ★ symbol are particularly recommended.

Adrift in Tokyo (*Tenten*; Satoshi Miki; 2007). A debt-ridden law student and a loan shark heavy bond in this quirky comedy drama that sees the unlikely pair stroll across the city meeting a cast of oddball characters along the way.

★**Akira** (Ōtomo Katsuhiro; 1988). Still the most Tokyo-centric major anime, this is set in a newly rebuilt Neo-Tokyo during the run-up to the fictional 2019 Olympics (funny, they'd have got the date spot on if they'd looked at the Olympic schedule properly).

Babel (Alejandro González Iñárritu; 2006). The talented Mexican director nails contemporary Tokyo. There's a particularly beautiful sequence filmed at Shibuya club *Womb*. Oscar-nominated Kikuchi Rinko as the mute Chieko and her father, played by veteran actor Yakusho Kōji, are both outstanding.

Godzilla (*Gojira*; Honda Ishirō; 1954). The whole world knows how Tokyo turns out in this classic, which sees the eponymous monster stomp his way through intricately constructed scale models of the city – much of it was filmed on the volcano-island of Ōshima.

House of Bamboo (Samuel Fuller; 1955). Released only a decade after the end of World War II, this American film isn't a great classic, but it acts as a time capsule of a let's-be-friends-again era, perhaps best exemplified by an inter-racial romance that far predates John and Yoko.

Ichi the Killer (*Koroshiya Ichi*; Miike Takashi; 2001). Stand by for graphic depictions of bodies sliced in half in this *yakuza* tale set in Kabukichō, as told by the *enfant terrible* of Japanese cinema. Not for the squeamish.

★**Let's Go!** (Tanuma Yuichi; 1967). Extremely hard to find, this early vehicle for actor Kayama Yūzō (regularly voted Sexiest Man in Japan through at least three decades) provides a lovely dollop of 1960s Japan. Not only does he solve crimes and get the girls, but he's a star football player, and also the singer-songwriter-guitarist of a popular band – take that, James Bond.

Like Someone in Love (Abbas Kiarostami; 2013). A great piece from the famed Iranian director, detailing the life of a young woman selling her body to pay her way through university.

Lost in Translation (Sofia Coppola; 2003). Memorable performances from Bill Murray and Scarlett Johansson in this stylish romantic drama set in and around Shinjuku's *Park Hyatt* hotel. Brilliantly captures what it's like to be a clueless *gaijin* adrift in Tokyo.

Our Little Sister (*Umimachi Daiarii*; Koreeda Hirokazu; 2015). Not set in Tokyo, but the nearby town of Kamakura (see p.233), this beautiful, tender piece tells the story of three sisters and the fallout from the death of their estranged father.

★**Stray Dog** (*Nora Inu*; Kurosawa Akira; 1949). Not the most famous work from Japan's most famous director (who made his name with *Seven Samurai*, which begat *The Magnificent Seven*), but this gritty film noir is still up there with the best, following a cop as he chases a killer around sweaty summertime Tokyo.

Tampopo (Itami Jūzō; 1985). Tampopo, the proprietress of a noodle bar, is taught how to prepare the perfect ramen, in this comedy about Japan's gourmet boom. From the old woman squishing fruit in a supermarket to the gangster and his moll passing a raw egg sexily between their mouths, this is a film packed with memorable scenes.

Tokyo! (Michel Gondry, Bong Joon-ho & Leos Carax; 2009). Two French and one Korean director each provide their own distinctive takes on the shape-shifting megalopolis in this omnibus triptych.

Tokyo Godfathers (Kon Satoshi; 2003). This heart-warming Christmas fairy tale of redemption for three tramps and the baby they discover in the trash is pure anime magic.

Tokyo Sonata (Kurosawa Kiyoshi; 2008). When a father decides to keep it secret from his family that he's lost his job it has all kinds of repercussions in this bleak, satirical drama – a prize winner at Cannes – that's reflective of contemporary Japanese society.

★**Tokyo Story** (*Tōkyō Monogatari*; Ozu Yasujirō; 1954). An elderly couple travel to Tokyo to visit their children and grandchildren. The only person who has any time for them is the widow of their son who was killed in the war. On their return, the mother falls ill and dies. Ozu's themes of loneliness and the breakdown of tradition are grim, but his simple approach and the sincerity of the acting make the film a genuine classic.

Tokyo Tribe (Sion Sono; 2014). As with any other Sion Sono production, you're either going to love or hate this hip-hop *yakuza* opera. Just like *Tommy* or anything similar, the storyline is more incidental than the music, but some will find it a fun watch.

You Only Live Twice (Lewis Gilbert; 1967). A retro look at the city as Sean Connery, in his fifth outing as Bondo-san, grapples with arch-enemy Blofeld and sundry Japanese villains. Cool gadgets include a mini-helicopter in a suitcase (with rocket launchers, of course).

The arts, architecture and design

Tokyo isn't just the contemporary art capital of Japan – it has the biggest art scene of any Asian city (though Beijing is catching up fast). Innumerable galleries provide a window into a fascinating scene that's still relatively little known in the Western world – perhaps bar the manga comics lining the shelves of every convenience store. If the stage is more your thing, there are also plenty of local forms of performance to enjoy, from stylized nō to vibrant kabuki. The city offers a brilliant showcase of contemporary design, too. Concrete-and-glass buildings that double as enormous public sculptures or electronic art screens; fashions, consumer gadgets and household goods that could be – and often are – exhibits in galleries; striking blasts of elegant graphics and eye-grabbing visuals on practically every corner: all are part of the city's dazzling visual appeal.

Visual arts

Some of the oldest evidence of human habitation in Japan is artistic in nature: stylized **pottery** dating back millennia to the Jōmon period (see p.251) can be seen at a number of museums in Tokyo, as well as **ceramics** and **bells** from the Yayoi, who were based in what is now the Japanese capital from around 350 BC. Many of the traditional arts fostered in Japan since then can trace their lineage back to **China**, including Buddhist sculpture, oil paintings and even elements now thought of as quintessentially Japanese, including folding screens and calligraphy.

Shitamachi art

A more local aesthetic emerged from the seventeenth century with the burgeoning popularity of **ukiyo-e** woodblock prints and paintings. Some illustrated historical scenes and folk tales, and others flora and fauna, but perhaps most interesting for visitors to Tokyo are those that depict **Shitamachi** (Tokyo's old working-class quarter), giving an illuminating insight into the birth of sumo, kabuki and other gems spawned by the *hoi polloi* of yore. Whimsical views of **nature** were also popular: Mount Fuji's near-symmetrical cone became a regular *ukiyo-e* feature, and also made a guest appearance in Hokusai's *The Great Wave off Kanagawa*, created circa 1830 and still one of the most famous "Eastern" pictures in the West.

After the restoration

Hokusai's cracking tsunami-like wave did not, however, cause any ripples outside Japan for around thirty years; the country was, at the time, essentially closed to the wider world until the Meiji Restoration of 1868 (see p.255). After Japan's opening up, artists were foremost among those itching for knowledge of **Western culture**, and ideas and styles raced back and forth between Tokyo and Europe; Manet, Monet, van Gogh and Gauguin were among those who came to employ elements of "Japonisme" in their work. Almost inevitably, a chasm developed in Japanese art between European-influenced creators, and those determined to hang onto the traditional forms; with near-equal predictability, many in the latter school (known as **nihonga**) did eventually come to use things like shading and perspective in their work, while keeping things local in style.

ART AROUND TOKYO

Tokyo has long boasted Asia's most vibrant art scene, and galleries in the city are listed throughout the Guide. These include **major venues** such as the National Art Center (see p.100), Mori Art Museum (see p.102) and the Museum of Contemporary Art (see p.84), but it's also fascinating to explore the city's many **commercial galleries**, make a few discoveries of your own and maybe even buy something. Ginza (see box, p.54) and Roppongi (see box, p.99) have the greatest concentrations of galleries.

The **Art Fair Tokyo** (⦿ artfairtokyo.com) takes place each April, and brings together around one hundred galleries, with a strong focus on contemporary work. In between times, check out **Tokyo Art Beat** (⦿ tokyoartbeat.com) for exhibition listings and interesting features on the city's art scene.

To the modern day

This fusion was also evident in the work of the greatest artistic catalyst of recent years: **Murakami Takashi** – often referred to as Japan's own Andy Warhol – who rose to prominence in the 1990s. Famed for creating the "Superflat" genre, his blending of *nihonga* and Western-style pop art isn't to everyone's taste, but it suddenly made the wider world sit up and take notice of Japanese art again – and, perhaps more importantly, inspired a whole legion of local youngsters to give art a go.

Talented artists who have cemented their reputations in recent years include **Haroshi**, a Tokyo skateboarder who uses recycled skateboards to create his sculptures; **Makoto Aida**, who welds together manga, painting, video, sculpture, photography and more; **Jun Inoue**, a street artist who brings elements of ancient calligraphy to his graffiti; **Kusama Yayoi**, a contemporary of Warhol whose polka-dotted designs are now spotted around the world; and **Tabaimo**, who creates interesting video installations that reflect modern life. The art collective **Chim Pom** took part in the 2007 Venice Biennale and have been very active since, sometimes attracting controversy and media attention: examples include their *Erigero* video of a young girl spewing up pink vomit, and the somewhat misjudged pasting of the stricken Fukushima Daiichi power plants into Okamoto Tarō's *Myth of Tomorrow* mural (see p.121). Perhaps by way of apology for the latter, in 2013 the collective staged an exhibition fusing their works with a selection of Tarō's own.

Manga

In Japan all types of cartoons, from comic strips to graphic novels to magazines, are known as **manga**, while animation is called **anime**. International reception of the medium can be clouded by the graphic sexual imagery and violence seen in some manga, compounded by the misconception that the subject matter is exclusively limited to sci-fi and fantasy. In reality, manga covers an enormous range of stories, from cooking to politics, and has many genres – for example, *manga-shi* (magazines) aimed at young people are split into *shōjo* (girls), *shōnen* (boys) and *seinen* (youth) categories.

The bestselling manga **magazine** is *Shūkan Shōnen Jump* (⦿ shonenjump.com/e), which once sold over six million copies a week – in these digital days it's down to a "mere" 2.2 million. Strips from this and other magazines are collected in **graphic-novel** style books (known as *tankōbon*), which come in several volumes. There are also *dōjinshi* – **amateur manga**, often with sexual themes, that are produced by fans. These works sometimes emulate the originals so faithfully that it's hard to tell them apart.

Performing arts

The traditional theatre arts of **nō**, **bunraku**, **kabuki** and **buyō** evolved in the context of broader cultural developments during different periods of Japan's history.

Nō

The oldest – and most difficult to appreciate – type of Japanese theatre is **nō**. This form of masked drama has its roots in sacred Shinto dances, but was formalized six hundred years ago under the patronage of the Ashikaga shoguns and the aesthetic influence of Zen. The bare wooden stage with its painted backdrop, the actors' stylized robes and the fixed expressions of the finely crafted masks create an atmosphere that is both understated and refined. The dramatic contrasts of stillness and sudden rushes of movement, and of periods of silence punctuated by sound, conjure up the essence of the Zen aesthetic.

The comic **kyōgen** interludes in a nō programme provide light relief. As in the main drama, *kyōgen* performers are all male and assume a variety of roles, some of which are completely independent of the nō play, while others comment on the development of the main story. The language used is colloquial (though of sixteenth-century origin) and, compared with the esoteric poetry of nō, far more accessible to a contemporary audience.

Kabuki

Colourful, exuberant and full of larger-than-life characters, **kabuki** is a highly stylized theatrical form which delights in flamboyant gestures and elaborate costumes, make-up and staging effects. While the language may still be incomprehensible to foreigners, the plots themselves deal with easily understood, often tragic themes of love and betrayal.

Kabuki originated in the early 1600s as rather **risqué dances** performed by all-female troupes, but today kabuki actors are predominantly older men, some of whom specialize in performing female roles (*onnagata*). To learn more about kabuki, go to ⓦkabuki21.com and ⓦkabuki-bito.jp/eng.

Bunraku

Japan's puppet theatre, **bunraku**, developed out of the *jōruri* storytelling of travelling minstrels, and was adapted to the stage in the early seventeenth century. Stylized **puppets**, one-half to one-third the size of humans, are worked by three operators, while a chanter tells the story to the accompaniment of *shamisen* (three-stringed guitar) music. The skill of the puppeteers – the result of lengthy apprenticeships – contributes to the high degree of **realism** in the performance, and the stylized movements can result in great drama. To learn more about *bunraku*, go to ⓦbunraku.or.jp.

Buyō

Classical Japanese dance is known as **buyō** and originates from the folk and ritual dances of ancient Japan. Dancers usually wear kimono, and as a result their graceful movements are slow and restricted.

Architecture

There has seldom been much of a grand plan to Tokyo's built environment, which has resulted in the city's cluttered, ad hoc look. However, the capital's great wealth and relative lack of planning restrictions have given architects almost unparalleled freedom to realize their wildest dreams. A fascinating time can be spent tracing the capital's modern evolution through its buildings, many designed by local luminaries. Winners of the Pritzker Prize, the architecture world's most prestigious accolade, include Tange Kenzō and Andō Tadao (see box, p.266, for more on these two), Maki Fumihiko, Sejima Kazuyo and Nishizawa Ryūe (of practice SANAA), Itō Toyō and Shigeru Ban.

Ginza is a prime district to see cutting-edge architecture: **Itō Toyō**'s Mikimoto Ginza 2 building – housing *Mikimoto Lounge* (see p.158) – serves as a good example, as does the LED-covered Chanel building. Ginza is also a local hub of **graphic design**, curated in a collection of small galleries (see box, p.54).

HUNTING DOWN THE STARCHITECTS

Andō Tadao Most of Andō's designs (especially his formative projects) were realized out west in his home region of Kansai, but the architect – famed for his less-is-more decorative aesthetic – has worked on a handful of buildings in Tokyo. As well as designing several ateliers in Shibuya, he landed a major Tokyo project with Omotesandō Hills (see p.118), before collaborating on Tokyo Midtown's 21_21 Design Sight gallery (see p.100) alongside fashion icon Issey Miyake, and product designers Fukasawa Naoto and Satoh Taku.

Kengo Kuma Although recently kept busy in the anything-goes architectural playground of Beijing, Kuma hailed from close to Tokyo, and some of his best work can be seen in the city, including the shrine at Akagi-jinja (see p.141), the acclaimed Nezu Museum (see p.118), the Suntory Museum of Art (see p.100) and Asakusa's quirky Culture and Sightseeing Centre (see p.73).

Tange Kenzō It's incredible how modern and daring Tange's iconic 1960s Yoyogi National Gymnasium (see p.117) and St Mary's Cathedral (see p.139) still look beside his late-career Tokyo Metropolitan Government Building (see p.127) and Fuji TV building (see p.93) – two structures that could have been ripped from the pages of a sci-fi manga. Although he died in 2005, the practice that Tange founded is also responsible for one of Tokyo's most recent "wow" structures: the cool, sleek **Mode Gakuen Cocoon Tower** (see p.128), duly dubbed the 2008 Skyscraper of the Year by the prestigious Emporis (Ⓦemporis.com).

Frank Lloyd Wright Okay, so *Furanku Roido Raito* wasn't Japanese, but a clutch of his buildings live on in Tokyo, most pertinently the Myonichi-kan (see p.135). The *Imperial Hotel* that he designed so lovingly has been replaced with something more modern, but hints survive in the on-site *Old Imperial Bar* (see p.175).

Recent developments have seen the city take a bit of a step back. Locals have been unimpressed by the ugly **Tokyo Skytree** – completed in 2011 along ostensibly "traditional" lines – and the boxy Shibuya Hikarie building which went up the following year. In 2013 protests followed the release of Iraqi-born Zaha Hadid's **2020 Olympic stadium** design (see box, p.120), and the government duly announced its replacement with a cheaper design by Kengo Kuma (see box above).

Design

In Tokyo's **home furnishing** and **interior design** shops you can find iconic products such as Yanagi Sori's butterfly stool and cutlery collection, or Isamu Noguchi's paper lantern lamps, as well as new instant classics by rising local and overseas talents. Also acting as top design galleries are **"select shops"** (boutiques) such as Cibone (see p.203) and Do at the *Claska* hotel (see p.203), or the gift shop of the National Art Center, Tokyo (see p.100), all of which carry a meticulously curated range of items, sometimes with displays highlighting the creators behind each product. If you're in the Tokyo Midtown area, you can browse an upscale branch of homeware and fashion emporium Muji (see p.203),

DESIGNING THE FUTURE

To discover the absolute bleeding edge of Japanese design, time your trip to coincide with **Tokyo Design Week** (Oct/Nov; see p.27), which has been going, and growing, since 1985. Aoyama, Roppongi and the outer grounds of Meiji Jingū are the focus for the annual whirlwind of events, exhibitions and installations that take place in giant tents and container crates as well as galleries and shops. Sampling the future is part of what TDW is all about, which makes for a lot of shows that tend toward the experimental rather than the commercial.

Even more anarchic and colourful are the biannual **Design Festa** events (May & Nov/Dec; see p.26). If you don't happen to be in town for one of them you can get a very good idea of the kinds of bizarre and beautiful things they can throw up by visiting the permanent **Design Festa Gallery** tucked away in Harajuku's backstreets (see p.118).

KINGS AND QUEENS OF THE CATWALK

Together with London and New York, Tokyo forms part of global fashion's holy trinity, acting as a magnet to clothing designers from all over Japan, many of whom have made their name here. Designers from overseas, too, often use Tokyo as an incubator or laboratory for their wilder ideas.

Nicola Formichetti Though he may not sound Japanese, Formichetti was born to a Japanese mother (and Italian father) and raised in Tokyo. He worked as fashion director for Uniqlo (see p.200), and has also been involved with Diesel and *Vogue* – and, of course, was also Lady Gaga's personal stylist.

Toshikazu Iwaya Known for being ahead of the trends, but often employing styles and motifs from yesteryear, you can see some of Iwaya's flamboyant clothing at Dresscamp (see p.200).

Jun Ashida Practical yet elegant, an incredible amount of attention goes into Ashida's designs, which have been worn by members of the royal family, as well as political leaders. His daughter Tae is also busily making a name for herself, and you can browse clothing from both designers at the Jun Ashida flagship store in Daikanyama (see p.200).

Yohji Yamamoto A big name since the 1970s, Yamamoto's designs (see p.201) tend to be timeless black-and-white numbers. He also designs clothing for major ballet companies, and sometimes even the sets themselves.

Kawakubo Rei A Tokyo native, Kawakubo was the driving force behind Comme des Garçons (see p.200), carving out a niche with designs that refused to kowtow to the general notions of body shape. Junya Watanabe, a one-time protégé of hers, has also made it big.

Issey Miyake Still one of the big hitters after all these years, his flagship store in Aoyama (see p.201) has merely acted as the centre of a hub whose nodes have touched on museum exhibitions, theatre work and one of the world's best-selling perfume ranges.

as well as other contemporary Japan-focused interior design stores such as Design Hub (ⓦdesignhub.jp).

Spare a moment also to admire the shopping environment itself. Some of the most eye-catching – and globally influential – **store designs** come courtesy of design agency Wonderwall (ⓦwonder-wall.com). These include Bapexclusive in Aoyama (see p.200), with its sushi-inspired conveyor belt for sneakers, and recycled goods emporium Pass the Baton (see p.203). Other designers reference traditional design in creative new ways – witness the elegant gifts and packaging on display in the retail sections of tea and Japanese sweet café *Higashiya* (see p.159) and its offshoots, which are themselves beautifully designed spaces.

Japan publishes some of the world's most beautiful **design and culture magazines**, and they make for great primers on places you might want to see or things you might want to buy in Tokyo. Don't worry if your Japanese isn't up to scratch: popular titles like *Casa Brutus*, *Brutus*, *PEN* and *Real Design* tend to accentuate the visuals, while others such as *AXIS*, *+81* and *Kateigahō International Edition* (available as a digital magazine at ⓦint.kateigaho.com) are bilingual or fully English.

Lastly, the district of **Akihabara** deserves a special mention as an integral part of the city's contemporary design landscape; its stores are packed with the colourful output of Japan's manga, anime, toy and computer game industries.

Japanese

Picking up a few words of Japanese is not difficult. Pronunciation is simple and standard and there are few exceptions to the straightforward grammar rules. With just a little effort you should be able to read the words spelled out in *hiragana* and *katakana*, Japanese phonetic characters, even if you can't understand them. And any time spent learning Japanese will be amply rewarded by delighted locals, who'll always politely comment on your fine linguistic ability.

However, it takes a very great effort to master Japanese. The primary stumbling block is the thousands of **kanji** characters (Chinese ideograms) that need to be memorized, all of which have at least two pronunciations (often many, many more), depending on the sentence and their combination with other characters. Also tricky is the language's multiple levels of **politeness**, married with different sets of words used by men and women, as well as different **dialects** to deal with, involving whole new vocabularies.

Japanese characters

Japanese is written in a combination of three systems. To be able to read a newspaper, you'll need to know around two thousand *kanji*, much more difficult than it sounds, since what each one means varies with its context.

The easier writing systems to pick up are the phonetic syllabaries, **hiragana** and **katakana**. Both have 46 regular characters (see box opposite) and can be learned within a couple of weeks. *Hiragana* is used for Japanese words, while *katakana*, with the squarer characters, is used mainly for "loan words" borrowed from other languages (especially English) and technical names. **Rōmaji** (see opposite), the roman script used to spell out Japanese words, is also used in advertisements and magazines.

The first five letters in *hiragana* and *katakana* (**a**, **i**, **u**, **e**, **o**) are the vowel sounds (see "Pronunciation", opposite). The remainder are a combination of a consonant and a vowel (eg **ka**, **ki**, **ku**, **ke**, **ko**), with the exception of **n**, the only consonant that exists on its own. While *hiragana* provides an exact phonetic reading of all Japanese words, *katakana* does not do the same for foreign loan words. Often words are abbreviated, hence "television" becomes *terebi* and "sexual harassment" *sekuhara*. Sometimes, they become almost unrecognizable, as with *kakutēru* (cocktail).

Traditionally, Japanese is written in vertical columns and read right to left. However, the Western way of writing from left to right, horizontally from top to bottom is increasingly common (though page-wise, books and magazines are usually read "backwards" from a Western perspective). In the media and on signs you'll see a mixture of the two ways of writing.

Grammar

In Japanese **verbs** do not change according to the person or number, so that *ikimasu* can mean "I go", "he/she/it goes", or "we/they go". **Pronouns** are usually omitted, since it's generally clear from the context who or what the speaker is referring to. There are no **definite articles**, and **nouns** stay the same whether they refer to singular or plural words.

Compared to English grammar, Japanese **sentences** are structured back to front. An English-speaker would say "I am going to Tokyo" which in Japanese would translate directly as "Tokyo to going". Placing the sound "*ka*" at the end of a verb indicates a **question**, hence *Tokyo e ikimasu-ka* means "Are you going to Tokyo?" There are also levels of **politeness** to contend with, which alter the way the verb is conjugated, and

HIRAGANA AND KATAKANA

Hiragana and *katakana* are two phonetic syllabaries represented by the characters shown below. *Katakana*, the squarer characters in the first table, are used for writing foreign "loan words". The rounder characters in the bottom table, *hiragana*, are used for Japanese words, in combination with, or as substitutes for, *kanji*.

KATAKANA

a	ア	i	イ	u	ウ	e	エ	o	オ
ka	カ	ki	キ	ku	ク	ke	ケ	ko	コ
sa	サ	shi	シ	su	ス	se	セ	so	ソ
ta	タ	chi	チ	tsu	ツ	te	テ	to	ト
na	ナ	ni	ニ	nu	ヌ	ne	ネ	no	ノ
ha	ハ	hi	ヒ	fu	フ	he	ヘ	ho	ホ
ma	マ	mi	ミ	mu	ム	me	メ	mo	モ
ya	ヤ			yu	ユ			yo	ヨ
ra	ラ	ri	リ	ru	ル	re	レ	ro	ロ
wa	ワ							wo	ヲ
n	ン								

HIRAGANA

a	あ	i	い	u	う	e	え	o	お
ka	か	ki	き	ku	く	ke	け	ko	こ
sa	さ	shi	し	su	す	se	せ	so	そ
ta	た	chi	ち	tsu	つ	te	て	to	と
na	な	ni	に	nu	ぬ	ne	ね	no	の
ha	は	hi	ひ	fu	ふ	he	へ	ho	ほ
ma	ま	mi	み	mu	む	me	め	mo	も
ya	や			yu	ゆ			yo	よ
ra	ら	ri	り	ru	る	re	れ	ro	ろ
wa	わ							wo	を
n	ん								

sometimes change the word entirely. Stick to the polite *-masu* form of verbs and you should be fine.

The Rough Guide Japanese Phrasebook includes essential phrases and expressions, and a dictionary section and menu reader.

Pronunciation

Japanese words in this book have been transliterated into the standard Hepburn system of romanization, called **rōmaji**. Pronunciation is as follows:

a as in mad
i as in macaroni, or **ee**
u as in you, or oo
e as in bed; pronounced even at the end of a word
o as in not
ae as in the two separate sounds, **ah-eh**
ai as in Thai

ei as in weight
ie as in two separate sounds, **ee-eh**
ue as in two separate sounds, **oo-eh**
g, a hard sound as in girl
s as in mass (never z)
y as in yet

A bar (macron) over a vowel or "ii" means that the vowel sound is twice as long as a vowel without a bar. Only where words are well known in English, such as Tokyo, Kyoto, judo and shogun, have we not used a bar to indicate long vowel sounds. Sometimes, vowel sounds are shortened or softened; for example, the verb *desu* sounds more like *dess* when pronounced, and *sukiyaki* like *skiyaki*. Some syllables are also softened or hardened by the addition of a small ° or " above the character; for example, **ka** (か) becomes **ga** (が) and **ba** (ば) becomes **pa** (ぱ). Likewise a smaller case ya, yu or yo following a character alters its sound, such as **kya** (きゃ) and **kyu** (きゅ). Lastly, double consonants (as in *kippu*, meaning ticket) require a momentary pause similar to a glottal stop; when you see "tch" (as in *matcha*, meaning powdered green tea) pronounce it as a double c.

Useful words and phrases

PERSONAL PRONOUNS

I	Watashi	私
I (familiar, men only)	Boku	ぼく
You	Anata	あなた
You (familiar)	Kimi	きみ
He	Kare	彼
She	Kanojo	彼女
We	Watashi-tachi	私たち
You (plural)	Anata-tachi	あなたたち
They (male/female)	Karera/Kanojo-tachi	彼ら/彼女たち
They (objects)	Sorera	それら

BASIC COMMUNICATIONS

Yes	Hai	はい
No	Iie/Chigaimasu	いいえ/違います
OK	Daijōbu/Ōkē	大丈夫/オーケー
Please (offering something)	Dōzo	どうぞ
Please (asking for something)	Onegai shimasu	お願いします
Excuse me	Sumimasen/Shitsurei shimasu	すみません/失礼します
I'm sorry	Gomen nasai/Sumimasen	ごめんなさい/すみません
Thanks (informal)	Dōmo	どうも
Thank you	Arigatō	ありがとう
Thank you very much	Dōmo arigatō gozaimasu	どうもありがとうございます
What?	Nani?	なに
When?	Itsu?	いつ
Where?	Doko?	どこ
Who?	Dare?	だれ
This	Kore	これ
That	Sore	それ
That (over there)	Are	あれ
How many?	Ikutsu?	いくつ
How much?	Ikura?	いくら
I want (x)	(x) ga hoshii desu	(x)が欲しいです
I don't want (x)	(x) ga irimasen	(x)がいりません
Is it possible …?	… koto ga dekimasu ka	…ことができますか
Is it …?	… desu ka	…ですか
Can you please help me?	Tetsudatte kuremasen ka	手伝ってくれませんか
I can't speak Japanese	Nihongo ga hanasemasen	日本語が話せません
I can't read Japanese	Nihongo ga yomemasen	日本語が読めません
Can you speak English?	Eigo ga dekimasu ka	英語ができますか
Is there someone who can interpret?	Tsūyaku wa imasu ka	通訳はいますか
Could you please speak more slowly?	Motto yukkuri hanashite kuremasen ka	もっとゆっくり話してくれませんか
Could you say that again please?	Mō ichido itte kuremasen ka	もう一度言ってくれませんか
I understand/I see	Wakarimasu/Naruhodo	分かります/なるほど
I don't understand	Wakarimasen	分かりません
What does this mean?	Kore wa dōiu imi desu ka	これはどういう意味ですか

How do you say (x) in Japanese?	Nihongo de (x) o nan-te iimasu ka	日本語で(x)を何て言いますか
What's this called?	Kore wa nan-to iimasu ka	これは何と言いますか
How do you pronounce this character?	Kono kanji wa nan-te yomimasu ka	この漢字は何て読みますか
Please write in English/Japanese	Eigo/Nihongo de kaite kudasai	英語/日本語で書いてください

GREETINGS AND BASIC COURTESIES

Hello/Good day	Konnichiwa	今日は
Good morning	Ohayō gozaimasu	おはようございます
Good evening	Konbanwa	今晩は
Good night (when leaving)	Osaki ni	お先に
Good night (when going to bed)	Oyasuminasai	お休みなさい
How are you?	O-genki desu ka	お元気ですか
I'm fine	Genki desu	元気です
I'm fine, thanks	Okagesama de	おかげさまで
How do you do/Nice to meet you	Hajimemashite	はじめまして
Don't mention it/you're welcome	Dō itashimashite	どういたしまして
I'm sorry	Gomen nasai	ごめんなさい
Just a minute please	Chotto matte kudasai	ちょっと待ってください
What's your name?	Shitsurei desu ga o-namae wa	失礼ですがお名前は
My name is (x)	Namae wa (x) desu	名前は(x)です
Goodbye	Sayonara/Sayōnara	さよなら/さようなら
Goodbye (informal)	Dewa mata/Jā ne	では又/じゃあね

CHITCHAT

Where are you from?	O-kuni wa doko desu ka	お国はどこですか
Britain	Eikoku/Igirisu	英国/イギリス
Ireland	Airurando	アイルランド
America	Amerika	アメリカ
Australia	Ōsutoraria	オーストラリア
Canada	Kanada	カナダ
New Zealand	Nyū Jiirando	ニュージーランド
Japan	Nihon	日本
How old are you?	O-ikutsu desu ka	おいくつですか
I am (x) years old	(x) sai desu	(x)際です
Are you married?	Kekkon shite imasu ka	結婚していますか
I am married/not married	Kekkon shite imasu/imasen	結婚しています/いません
Do you like …?	… suki desu ka	好きですか
I like	… suki desu	…好きです
I don't like	… suki dewa arimasen	…好きではありません
What's your job?	O-shigoto wa nan desu ka	お仕事は何ですか
I work for a company	Kaishain desu	会社員です
I'm a tourist	Kankō kyaku desu	観光客です
Really? (informal)	Hontō	本当
It can't be helped (informal)	Shikata ga nai (formal)/ Shō ga nai (informal)	仕方がない/しょうがない

NUMBERS, TIME AND DATES

There are special ways of **counting** different things in Japanese. The most common first translation is used when counting time and quantities and measurements, with added qualifiers such as minutes (*pun/fun*) or yen (*en*). The second translations are sometimes used for counting objects. From ten, there is only one set of numbers. For four, seven and nine, alternatives to the first translation are used in some circumstances.

Zero	Zero/rei	0/零		
One	Ichi	一	Hitotsu	ひとつ

Two	Ni	二	Futatsu	ふたつ
Three	San	三	Mittsu	みっつ
Four	Yon/Shi	四	Yottsu	よっつ
Five	Go	五	Itsutsu	いつつ
Six	Roku	六	Muttsu	むっつ
Seven	Shichi/Nana	七	Nanatsu	ななつ
Eight	Hachi	八	Yattsu	やっつ
Nine	Kyū	九	Kokonotsu	ここのつ
Ten	Jū	十	Tō	とう
Eleven	Jū-ichi	十一		
Twelve	Jū-ni	十二		
Twenty	Ni-jū	二十		
Twenty-one	Ni-jū-ichi	二十一		
Thirty	San-jū	三十		
One hundred	Hyaku	百		
Two hundred	Ni-hyaku	二百		
Thousand	Sen	千		
Ten thousand	Ichi-man	一万		
One hundred thousand	Jū-man	十万		
One million	Hyaku-man	百万		
One hundred million	Ichi-oku	一億		

TIME AND DATES

Now	Ima	今
Today	Kyō	今日
Morning	Asa	朝
Evening	Yūgata	夕方
Night	Yoru/Ban	夜/晩
Tomorrow	Ashita	明日
The day after tomorrow	Asatte	あさって
Yesterday	Kinō	昨日
Week	Shū	週
Month	Getsu/Gatsu	月
Year	Nen/Toshi	年
Monday	Getsuyōbi	月曜日
Tuesday	Kayōbi	火曜日
Wednesday	Suiyōbi	水曜日
Thursday	Mokuyōbi	木曜日
Friday	Kin'yōbi	金曜日
Saturday	Doyōbi	土曜日
Sunday	Nichiyōbi	日曜日
What time is it?	Ima nan-ji desu ka	今何時ですか
It's 10 o'clock	Jū-ji desu	十時です
10.20	Jū-ji ni-juppun	十時二十分
10.30	Jū-ji han	十時半
10.50	Jū-ichi-ji juppun mae	十一時十分前
AM	Gozen	午前
PM	Gogo	午後

GETTING AROUND

Aeroplane	Hikōki	飛行機
Airport	Kūkō	空港
Bus	Basu	バス
Bus stop	Basu tei	バス停

Train	Densha	電車
Station	Eki	駅
Subway	Chikatetsu	地下鉄
Ferry	Ferii	フェリー
Left-luggage office	Ichiji azukarijo	一時預かり所
Coin locker	Koin rokkā	コインロッカー
Ticket	Kippu	切符
Ticket office	Kippu uriba	切符売り場
One-way	Kata-michi	片道
Return	Ōfuku	往復
Bicycle	Jitensha	自転車
Taxi	Takushii	タクシー
Map	Chizu	地図
Straight ahead	Massugu	まっすぐ
In front of	Mae	前
Right	Migi	右
Left	Hidari	左
North	Kita	北
South	Minami	南
East	Higashi	東
West	Nishi	西

PLACES

Temple	Otera/Odera/-ji/-in	お寺/-寺/-院
Shrine	Jinja/Jingū/-gū/-taisha	神社/神宮/-宮/-大社
Castle	-jō	城
Park	Kōen	公園
River	Kawa/Gawa	川
Street	Tōri/Dōri/Michi	通り/道
Bridge	Hashi/Bashi	橋
Museum	Hakubutsukan	博物館
Art gallery	Bijutsukan	美術館
Garden	Niwa/Teien/-en	庭/庭園/-園
Island	Shima/-jima/-tō	島/-島
Hill	Oka	丘
Mountain	Yama/-san/-take	山/-山/-岳
Hot spring spa	Onsen	温泉
Lake	Mizu-umi/-ko	湖/-湖

ACCOMMODATION

Hotel	Hoteru	ホテル
Traditional-style inn	Ryokan	旅館
Guesthouse	Minshuku	民宿
Youth hostel	Yūsu hosuteru	ユースホステル
Single room	Shinguru rūmu	シングルルーム
Double room	Daburu rūmu	ダブルルーム
Twin room	Tsuin rūmu	ツインルーム
Dormitory	Kyōdō/Ōbeya	共同/大部屋
Japanese-style room	Washitsu	和室
Western-style room	Yōshitsu	洋室
Western-style bed	Beddo	ベッド
Bath	O-furo	お風呂
Do you have any vacancies?	Kūshitsu wa arimasu ka	空室はありますか
I'd like to make a reservation	Yoyaku o shitai no desu ga	予約をしたいのですが

I have a reservation	Yoyaku shimashita	予約しました
I don't have a reservation	Yoyaku shimasen deshita	予約しませんでした
How much is it per person?	Hitori ikura desu ka	一人いくらですか
Does that include meals?	Shokuji wa tsuite imasu ka	食事はついていますか
I would like to stay one night/ two nights	Hitoban/Futaban tomaritai no desu ga	一晩/二晩泊まりたいのですが
I would like to see the room	Heya o misete kudasaimasen ka	部屋を見せてくださいませんか
Key	Kagi	鍵
Passport	Pasupōto	パスポート

SHOPPING, MONEY AND BANKS

Shop	Mise	店
How much is it?	Kore wa ikura desu ka	これはいくらですか
It's too expensive	Taka-sugimasu	高すぎます
Is there anything cheaper?	Mō sukoshi yasui mono wa arimasu ka	もう少し安いものはありますか
Do you accept credit cards?	Kurejitto kādo wa tsukaemasu ka	クレジットカードは使えますか
I'm just looking	Miru dake desu	見るだけです
Foreign exchange	Gaikoku-kawase	外国為替
Bank	Ginkō	銀行
Travellers' cheque	Toraberāzu chekku	トラベラーズチェック
Where is the nearest ATM?	Ichiban chikai ATM wa doko desu ka	一番近いATMはどこですか

INTERNET, POST AND TELEPHONES

Internet	Intānetto	インターネット
Post office	Yūbinkyoku	郵便局
Letter	Tegami	手紙
Postcard	Hagaki	葉書
Stamp	Kitte	切手
Airmail	Kōkūbin	航空便
Telephone	Denwa	電話
International telephone call	Kokusai-denwa	国際電話
Reverse charge/collect call	Korekuto-kōru	コレクトコール
Telephone card	Terefon kādo	テレフォンカード
I would like to call (place)	(place) e denwa o kaketai no desu	(place)へ電話をかけたいのです
I would like to send a fax to (place)	(place) e fakkusu shitai no desu	(place)へファックスしたいのです
Telephone card	Terefon kādo	テレフォンカード

HEALTH

Hospital	Byōin	病院
Pharmacy	Yakkyoku	薬局
Medicine	Kusuri	薬
Doctor	Isha	医者
Dentist	Haisha	歯医者
I'm ill	Byōki desu	病気です

Food and drink

BASICS

Bar	Nomiya	飲み屋
Standing-only bar	Tachinomiya	立ちのみ屋
Café/coffee shop	Kissaten	喫茶店
Cafeteria	Shokudō	食堂
Pub	Pabu	パブ

Pub-style restaurant	Izakaya	居酒屋
Restaurant	Resutoran	レストラン
Restaurant specializing in charcoal-grilled foods	Robatayaki	炉端焼
Breakfast	Asa-gohan	朝ご飯
Lunch	Hiru-gohan	昼ご飯
Dinner	Ban-gohan	晩ご飯
Boxed meal	Bentō	弁当
Set meal	Teishoku	定食
Daily special set meal	Higawari-teishoku	日替り定食
Menu	Menyū	メニュー
Do you have an English menu?	Eigo no menyū wa arimasu ka	英語のメニューはありますか
How much is that?	Ikura desu ka	いくらですか
I would like (a) …	(a)… o onegai shimasu	(a)をお願いします
May I have the bill?	Okanjō o onegai shimasu	お勘定をお願いします
I am a vegetarian	Watashi wa bejitarian desu	私はベジタリアンです
Can I have it without meat?	Niku nashi de onegai dekimasu ka	肉なしでお願いできますか

STAPLE FOODS

Bean curd tofu	Tōfu	豆腐
Bread	Pan	パン
Butter	Batā	バター
Dried seaweed	Nori	のり
Egg	Tamago	卵
Fermented soyabean paste	Miso	味噌
Garlic	Ninniku	にんにく
Oil	Abura	油
Pepper	Koshō	こしょう
Rice	Gohan	ご飯
Salt	Shio	塩
Soy sauce	Shōyu	しょうゆ
Sugar	Satō	砂糖

FRUITS AND VEGETABLES

Fruit	Kudamono	果物
Apple	Ringo	りんご
Banana	Banana	バナナ
Grapefruit	Gurēpufurūtsu	グレープフルーツ
Grapes	Budō	ぶどう
Japanese plum	Ume	うめ
Lemon	Remon	レモン
Melon	Meron	メロン
Orange	Orenji	オレンジ
Peach	Momo	桃
Pear	Nashi	なし
Persimmon	Kaki	柿
Pineapple	Painappuru	パイナップル
Strawberry	Ichigo	いちご
Tangerine	Mikan	みかん
Watermelon	Suika	すいか
Vegetables	Yasai	野菜
Salad	Sarada	サラダ
Aubergine	Nasu	なす
Beans	Mame	豆

Beansprouts	Moyashi	もやし
Carrot	Ninjin	にんじん
Cauliflower	Karifurawā	カリフラワー
Green pepper	Piiman	ピーマン
Green horseradish	Wasabi	わさび
Leek	Negi	ねぎ
Mushroom	Kinoko	きのこ
Onion	Tamanegi	たまねぎ
Potato	Poteto/Jagaimo	ポテト/じゃがいも
Radish	Daikon	だいこん
Sweetcorn	Kōn	コーン
Tomato	Tomato	トマト

FISH AND SEAFOOD DISHES

Fish	Sakana	魚
Shellfish	Kai	貝
Raw fish	Sashlmi	さしみ
Sushi	Sushi	寿司
Serving of sushi rice with topping	Nigiri-zushi	にぎり寿司
Sushi rolled in crisp seaweed	Maki-zushi	まき寿司
Bowl of sushi rice topped with fish, egg and vegetables	Chirashi-zushi	ちらし寿司
Abalone	Awabi	あわび
Blowfish	Fugu	ふぐ
Cod	Tara	たら
Crab	Kani	かに
Eel	Unagi	うなぎ
Herring	Nishin	にしん
Horse mackerel	Aji	あじ
Lobster	Ise-ebi	伊勢海老
Octopus	Tako	たこ
Oyster	Kaki	かき
Prawn	Ebi	えび
Sea bream	Tai	たい
Sea urchin	Uni	うに
Squid	Ika	いか
Tuna	Maguro	まぐろ
Yellowtail	Buri	ぶり

MEAT AND MEAT DISHES

Meat	Niku	肉
Beef	Gyūniku	牛肉
Chicken	Toriniku	鶏肉
Lamb	Ramu	ラム
Pork	Butaniku	豚肉
Breaded, deep-fried slice of pork	Tonkatsu	とんかつ
Chicken, other meat and vegetables grilled on skewers	Yakitori	焼き鳥
Skewers of food dipped in breadcrumbs and deep-fried	Kushiage	串揚げ
Stew including meat (or seafood), vegetables and noodles	Nabe	鍋
Thin beef slices cooked in broth	Shabu-shabu	しゃぶしゃぶ
Thin beef slices braised in a sauce	Sukiyaki	すきやき

OTHER DISHES

Buddhist-style vegetarian cuisine	Shōjin-ryōri	精進料理
Chinese-style noodles	Rāmen	ラーメン
Chinese-style dumplings	Gyōza	ぎょうざ
Fried noodles	Yakisoba/Yakiudon	焼そば/焼きうどん
Stewed chunks of vegetables and fish on skewers	Oden	おでん
Thin buckwheat noodles	Soba	そば
Soba in a hot soup	Kake-soba	かけそば
Cold soba served with a dipping sauce	Zaru-soba/Mori-soba	ざるそば/もりそば
Thick wheat noodles	Udon	うどん
Fried rice	Chāhan	チャーハン
Lightly battered seafood and vegetables	Tempura	天ぷら
Meat, vegetable and fish cooked in soy sauce and sweet sake	Teriyaki	照り焼き
Mild curry served with rice	Karē raisu	カレーライス
Octopus in balls of batter	Takoyaki	たこやき
Pounded rice cakes	Mocihi	もち
Rice topped with fish, meat or vegetables	Donburi	どんぶり
Rice triangles wrapped in crisp seaweed	Onigiri	おにぎり
Savoury pancakes	Okonomiyaki	お好み焼き
Chinese food	Chūka-ryōri/Chūgoku-ryōri	中華料理/中国料理
Japanese-style food	Washoku	和食
Japanese haute cuisine	Kaiseki-ryōri	懐石料理
Korean food	Kankoku-ryōri	韓国料理
"No-nationality" food	Mukokuseki-ryōri	無国籍料理
Western-style food	Yōshoku	洋食

DRINKS

Beer	Biiru	ビール
Black tea	Kōcha	紅茶
Coffee	Kōhii	コーヒー
Distilled liquor	Shōchū	焼酎
Fruit juice	Jūsu	ジュース
Green tea	Sencha	煎茶
Milk	Miruku/Gyūnyū	ミルク/牛乳
Oolong tea	Ūron-cha	ウーロン茶
Powdered green tea	Matcha	抹茶
Sake (rice wine)	Sake/Nihon-shu	酒/日本酒
Water	Mizu	水
Whisky	Uisukii	ウイスキー
Whisky and water	Mizu-wari	水割り
Wine	Wain	ワイン

Glossary

anime Animated movies or TV shows.

banzai Traditional cheer, meaning "10,000 years".

basho Sumo tournament.

bentō Food boxes.

bodhisattva Buddhist who has forsaken nirvana to work for the salvation of all humanity.

bunraku Puppet theatre.

-chō or **machi** Subdivision of the city, smaller than a -ku.

-chōme Area of the city consisting of a few blocks.

dai Big or great.

daimyō Feudal lords.

-dōri Main road.

Edo Pre-1868 name for Tokyo.

furo Traditional Japanese bath.

futon Bedding.

-gawa/kawa River.

gaijin/gaikokujin Foreigner.

geisha Traditional female entertainer accomplished in the arts.

geta Wooden sandals.

hanami Cherry-blossom viewing.

Heian Period when Japan was ruled from Heian-kyō, now Kyoto (794–1185).

izakaya Traditional bar, also serving food.

ji-biiru Beer produced in local microbreweries.

Jizō Buddhist protector of children, travellers and the dead.

JR Japan Railways.

kabuki Traditional theatre.

kaiseki Japanese haute cuisine.

kaiten-zushi Conveyor-belt sushi restaurant.

kampai "Cheers" when drinking.

kanji Japanese script derived from Chinese characters.

Kannon Buddhist Goddess of Mercy.

katakana Phonetic script used mainly for writing foreign words in Japanese.

kimono Literally "clothes" but usually referring to women's traditional dress.

kissaten Traditional, independent café.

kōban Local police box.

-kōen Park.

-ku Principal administrative division of the city, usually translated as "ward".

maid café A café where the waitresses are dressed in costumes and role play.

maiko apprentice geisha.

manga Comics.

matsuri Festival.

Meiji Period named after the Emperor Meiji (1868–1912).

mikoshi Portable shrine used in festivals.

minshuku Family-run lodge, similar to a bed and breakfast, cheaper than a ryokan.

mon Gate.

netsuke Small, intricately carved toggles for fastening the cords of cloth bags.

nō Traditional theatre.

noren Split curtain hanging in shop and restaurant doorways.

obi Wide sash worn with kimono.

okashi Japanese sweets.

omiyage Gift, souvenir.

onsen Hot spring, generally developed for bathing.

otaku Obsessive fan mainly of manga and anime but can refer to other things, too.

pachinko Vertical pinball machines.

rōnin Masterless samurai.

rotemburo Outdoor hot-spring bath.

ryokan Traditional Japanese inn.

ryōtei Restaurant serving *kaiseki*.

sabō Traditional teahouse.

sakura Cherry blossom.

samurai Warrior class who were retainers of the *daimyō*.

sentō Neighbourhood public bath.

shamisen Type of lute.

Shinkansen Bullet train.

Shinto Japan's indigenous animist religion.

Shitamachi Old working-class districts of east Tokyo.

shogun The military rulers of Japan before 1868.

shōji Paper-covered sliding screens used to divide rooms or cover windows.

soaplands Brothel.

soba-ya Noodle bar.

sumi-e Ink paintings.

sumo Japan's national sport, a form of heavyweight wrestling which evolved from ancient Shinto divination rites.

tansu Traditional chest of drawers.

tatami Rice-straw matting, the traditional covering for floors.

torii Gate to a Shinto shrine.

udon-ya Noodle bar.

ukiyo-e Colourful woodblock prints.

washi Japanese paper.

yakuza Professional criminal gangs.

yokochō Market-style area, often focusing on food shacks.

yukata Loose cotton dressing gown.

Small print and index

Rough Guide credits

Editor: Claire Saunders
Layout: Nikhil Agarwal
Cartography: Deshpal Dabas
Picture editor: Phoebe Lowndes
Proofreader: Diane Margolis
Managing editor: Andy Turner
Assistant editor: Divya Grace Matthew

Production: Jimmy Lao
Cover photo research: Marta Bescos
Editorial assistant: Aimee White
Senior DTP coordinator: Dan May
Programme manager: Gareth Lowe
Publishing director: Georgina Dee

Publishing information

This seventh edition published July 2017 by
Rough Guides Ltd,
80 Strand, London WC2R 0RL
11, Community Centre, Panchsheel Park,
New Delhi 110017, India
Distributed by Penguin Random House
Penguin Books Ltd, 80 Strand, London WC2R 0RL
Penguin Group (USA), 345 Hudson Street, NY 10014, USA
Penguin Group (Australia), 250 Camberwell Road,
Camberwell, Victoria 3124, Australia
Penguin Group (NZ), 67 Apollo Drive, Mairangi Bay,
Auckland 1310, New Zealand
Penguin Group (South Africa), Block D, Rosebank Office
Park, 181 Jan Smuts Avenue, Parktown North, Gauteng,
South Africa 2193
Rough Guides is represented in Canada by DK Canada, 320
Front Street West, Suite 1400, Toronto, Ontario M5V 3B6
Printed in Singapore
© Rough Guides, 2017
Maps © Rough Guides

Help us update

We've gone to a lot of effort to ensure that the seventh
edition of **The Rough Guide to Tokyo** is accurate
and up-to-date. However, things change – places get
"discovered", opening hours are notoriously fickle,
restaurants and rooms raise prices or lower standards.
If you feel we've got it wrong or left something out,
we'd like to know, and if you can remember the address,
the price, the hours, the phone number, so much
the better.

Please send your comments with the subject line
"Rough Guide Tokyo Update" to mail@uk.roughguides
.com. We'll credit all contributions and send a copy of the
next edition (or any other Rough Guide if you prefer) for
the very best emails.

A ROUGH GUIDE TO ROUGH GUIDES

Published in 1982, the first Rough Guide – to Greece – was a student scheme that became a
publishing phenomenon. Mark Ellingham, a recent graduate in English from Bristol University,
had been travelling in Greece the previous summer and couldn't find the right guidebook.
With a small group of friends he wrote his own guide, combining a contemporary, journalistic
style with a thoroughly practical approach to travellers' needs.

The immediate success of the book spawned a series that rapidly covered dozens of
destinations. And, in addition to impecunious backpackers, Rough Guides soon acquired a
much broader readership that relished the guides' wit and inquisitiveness as much as their
enthusiastic, critical approach and value-for-money ethos. These days, Rough Guides include
recommendations from budget to luxury and cover more than 120 destinations around the
globe, from Amsterdam to Zanzibar, all regularly updated by our team of roaming writers.

Browse all our latest guides, read inspirational features and book your trip at **roughguides.com**.

ABOUT THE AUTHOR

Martin Zatko started travelling in early 2002, and hasn't really stopped since. Finding that food, shelter and coffee cost money, he started writing guidebooks for a living, and has now written or contributed to almost thirty Rough Guides, including those to Korea, Seoul, China, Beijing, Vietnam, Myanmar, Turkey, Morocco and Europe. A big fan of noodles in general, Tokyo suits him down to the ground, and he finds that the city's unique blend of tame chaos simply never gets boring.

Acknowledgements

Martin Zatko would like to thank the TCVB, the JNTO and the Freshroom team for their kind assistance with his research trip, and Claire Saunders for her careful editing work. He would also like to thank house-mate Pierre Terron for his sterling company in distant Akatsuka; German Serina and Swiss Reto for the karaoke night, convenience-store runs and rooftop drinks; Thomas Clinard and Yoko Yagi for their cameo appearances; Ayano Tamaki for the 2003 time-warp; Rena and Mey for the Godzilla nights in Shinjuku; Nakameguro for barely changing a jot; David Carruth for the loan of his apartment during the write-up; Hyeri Yang for the retro nights during that time; and Y's for all the tsukemen, plus the near-death experience.

Readers' updates

Thanks to all the readers who have taken the time to write in with comments and suggestions (and apologies if we've inadvertently omitted or misspelt anyone's name):

Claire Gulvin, Tim Laslavic, Colin Rowat, A.J. Stidwill, Peter and Margaret Thomson, Yuki Tokui.

Photo credits

Index

Maps are marked in grey

Map index

Listings key

■ Accommodation

● Eating

■ Drinking and nightlife

● Shopping

Map symbols

— · · Provincial boundary	— — Ferry	⧫ Place of interest	♟ Museum
— — — Chapter division boundary	- - - - Path	P Parking	▲ Mountain peak
Motorway	⥱ Bridge	⊞ Hospital	❀ Ferris wheel
Road	✈ Airport	E Embassy	𝄞 Waterfall
Pedestrianized road	Ⓢ Subway station	⊙ Statue	⋀⋀ Onsen
JR line	○ Rail stop	⊠ Gate	Building
Shinkansen line	⛴ Boat	Pagoda	Stadium
Other rail line	⊠ Post office	⛩ Shrine	Cemetery
Monorail	ⓘ Tourist information	🛕 Buddhist temple	Park
- - - - Cable car			

City plan

The **city plan** on the pages that follow is divided as shown:

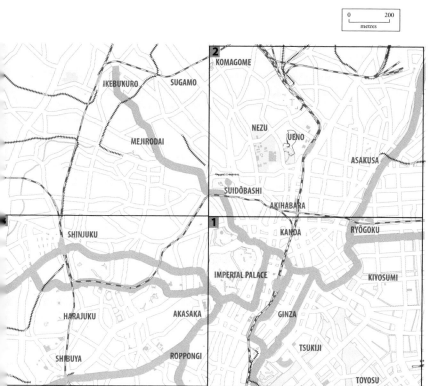

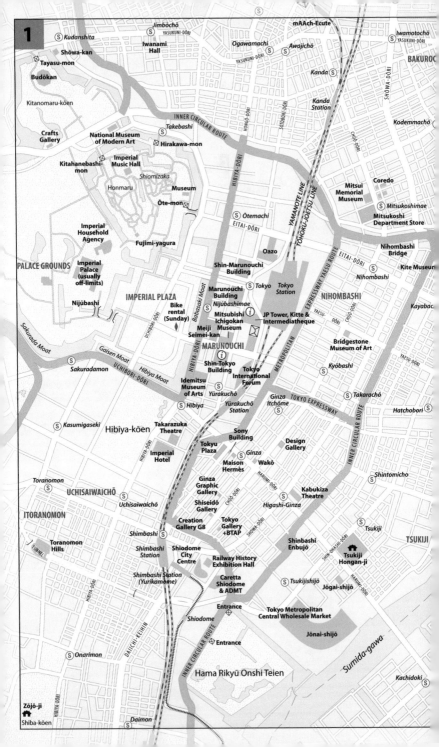

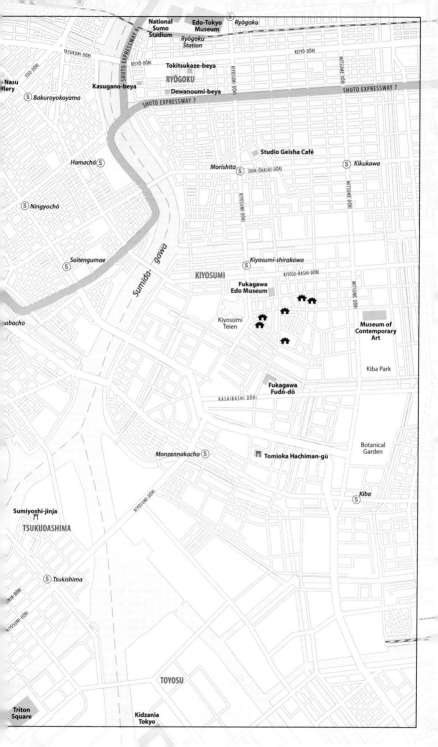

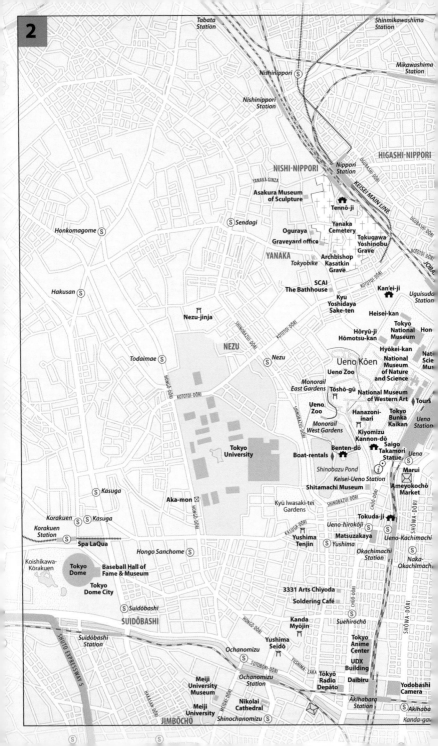

2

Tabata Station

Shinmikawashima Station

Nishinippori ⑤

Mikawashima Station

Nishinippori Station

HIGASHI-NIPPORI

NISHI-NIPPORI

YANAKA GINZA

Nippori Station

KEISEI MAIN LINE

OGUBASHI-DORI

Asakura Museum of Sculpture

✝ Tennō-ji

Honkomagome ⑤

⑤ Sendagi

Yanaka Cemetery

Oguraya

Graveyard office

Tokugawa Yoshinobu Grave

YANAKA

Tokyobike

Archbishop Kasatkin Grave

KOTOTOI-DORI

JOBA

Hakusan ⑤

SCAI The Bathhouse

Kan'ei-ji 卍

Uguisuda Station

Kyu Yoshidaya Sake-ten

KOTOTOI-DORI

Heisei-kan

⛩ **Nezu-jinja**

Hōryū-ji Hōmotsu-kan

Tokyo National Museum

Hon

NEZU

Hyōkei-kan

Nati Scie Mus

Todaimae ⑤

Nezu ⑤

Ueno Kōen

National Museum of Nature and Science

Ueno Zoo

SHINOBAZU-DORI

Monorail East Gardens

Tōshō-gū ⛩

National Museum of Western Art

Ueno Zoo

Hanazono-inari ⛩

Tokyo Bunka Kaikan

♦ Tour

Monorail West Gardens

Kiyomizu Kannon-dō

Ueno Station

HONGO-DORI

KOTOTOI-DORI

Benten-dō 卍

Saigo Takamori Statue

Ueno

Tokyo University

Boat-rentals

Shinobazu Pond

ⓘ

Marui

Keisei-Ueno Station

Shitamachi Museum

Ameyokochō Market

Aka-mon ✉

Kyū Iwasaki-tei Gardens

SHINOBAZU-DORI

SHOWA-DORI

⑤ Kasuga

Tokuda-ji 卍

Korakuen ⑤ ⑤ Kasuga

KASUGA-DORI

Ueno-hirokōji

CHUO-DORI

Ueno-Kachimachi

Korakuen Station

⑤

Spa LaQua

Yushima Tenjin ⛩

Matsuzakaya

⑤ Yushima

Naka-Okachimach

Hongo Sanchome ⑤

Okachimachi Station

Koishikawa-Kōrakuen

Tokyo Dome

Baseball Hall of Fame & Museum

Suehirochō

⑤

Tokyo Dome City

3331 Arts Chiyoda

Soldering Café

⑤ Suidōbashi

SUIDŌBASHI

Tokyo Anime Center

HONGO-DORI

CHUO-DORI

Suidōbashi Station

Kanda Myōjin ⛩

UDX Building

SHITO EXPRESSWAY S

⑤

SOTOBORI-DORI

Yushima Seidō ✝

Daibiru

Ochanomizu

YUSHIMA-ZAKA

Yodobashi Camera

HAKUSAN-DORI

Meiji University Museum

Ochanomizu Station

Tōkyō Radio Depāto

MEIDAI-DORI

Nikolai Cathedral

Akihabara Station

⑤ Akihaba

Meiji University

Shinochanomizu ⑤

JIMBŌCHŌ

Kanda-gav

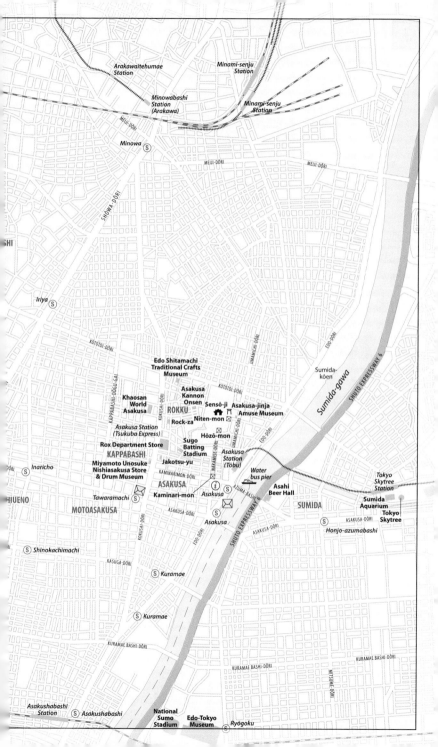

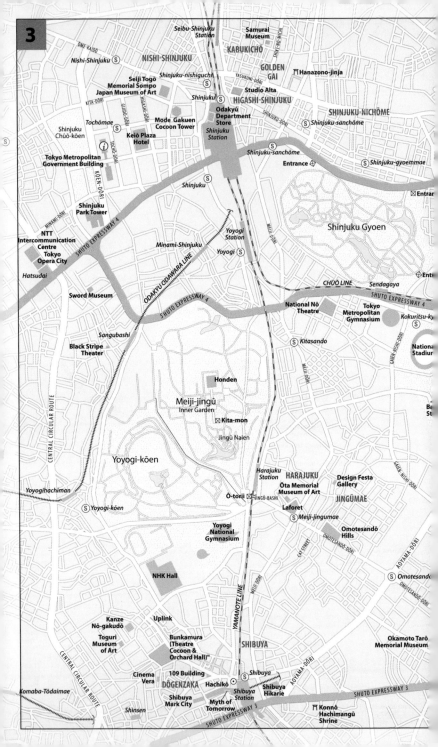

3

Seibu-Shinjuku Station

Samurai Museum

KABUKICHO

OME-KAIDŌ

Nishi-Shinjuku Ⓢ

NISHI-SHINJUKU

Shinjuku-nishiguchi

GOLDEN GAI

⛩ Hanazono-jinja

YASUKUNI-DŌRI

KITA-DŌRI

Seiji Tōgō Memorial Sompo Japan Museum of Art

Studio Alta

HIGASHI-SHINJUKU

SHINJUKU-NICHŌME

Shinjuku Ⓢ

HIGASHI-DŌRI

GUIDO-DŌRI

Shinjuku-sanchōme Ⓢ

Shinjuku-dōri

Tochōmae

Mode Gakuen Cocoon Tower

Odakyū Department Store

Shinjuku Chūō-kōen

ⓘ

Keiō Plaza Hotel

Shinjuku Station

Shinjuku-sanchōme

Shinjuku-gyoemmae Ⓢ

Tokyo Metropolitan Government Building

KŌEN-DŌRI

Entrance ⬦

⊠Entran

MINAMI-DŌRI

Shinjuku Ⓢ

Shinjuku Gyoen

Shinjuku Park Tower

SHUTO EXPRESSWAY 4

Yoyogi Station

NTT Intercommunication Centre Tokyo Opera City

ODAKYU ODAWARA LINE

Minami-Shinjuku

Yoyogi Ⓢ

⊕Entr

Hatsudai

CHŪŌ LINE

Sendagaya

SHUTO EXPRESSWAY 4

Sword Museum

National Nō Theatre

Tokyo Metropolitan Gymnasium

Kokuritsu-ky

S SHUTO EXPRESSWAY 4

Sangubashi

GAIEN-NISHI-DŌRI

Ⓢ Kitasando

Black Stripe Theater

MEIJI-DŌRI

Nationa Stadiur

Honden

Meiji-jingū

Inner Garden

CENTRAL CIRCULAR ROUTE

⊠ Kita-mon

Jingū Naien

Yoyogi-kōen

Ba St

GAIEN-NISHI-DŌRI

Harajuku Station

HARAJUKU

Design Festa Gallery

Ōta Memorial Museum of Art

JINGŪMAE

Ō-torii ⊠JINGŪ-BASHI

Yoyogihachiman

Laforet

Ⓢ Meiji-jingumae

Ⓢ Yoyogi-kōen

Omotesandō Hills

Yoyogi National Gymnasium

CAT STREET

OMOTESANDO-DŌRI

Ⓢ Omotesando

NHK Hall

YAMANOTE LINE

OMOTESANDO-DŌRI

Kanze Nō-gakudō

Uplink

MEIJI-DŌRI

Toguri Museum of Art

Bunkamura (Theatre Cocoon & Orchard Hall)"

SHIBUYA

Okamoto Tarō Memorial Museum

AOYAMA-DŌRI

CENTRAL CIRCULAR ROUTE

Cinema Vera

109 Building

Shibuya Ⓢ

DŌGENZAKA

Hachikō

Shibuya Hikarie

Komaba-Tōdaimae

Shibuya Mark City

Shibuya Station

Myth of Tomorrow

SHUTO EXPRESSWAY 3

Shinsen

⛩ Konnō Hachimangū Shrine

SHUTO EXPRESSWAY 3

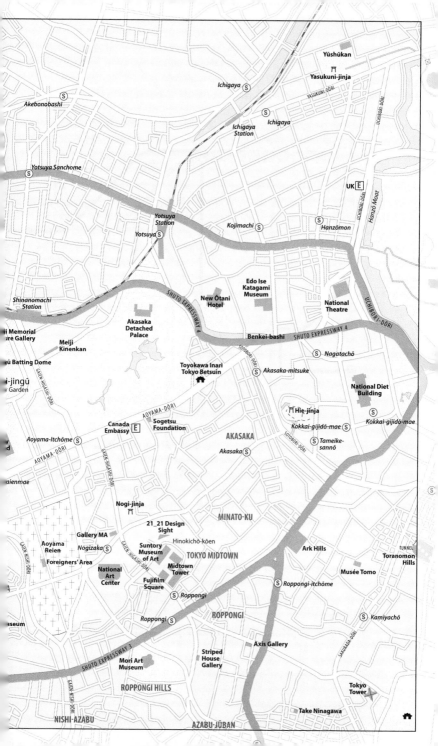

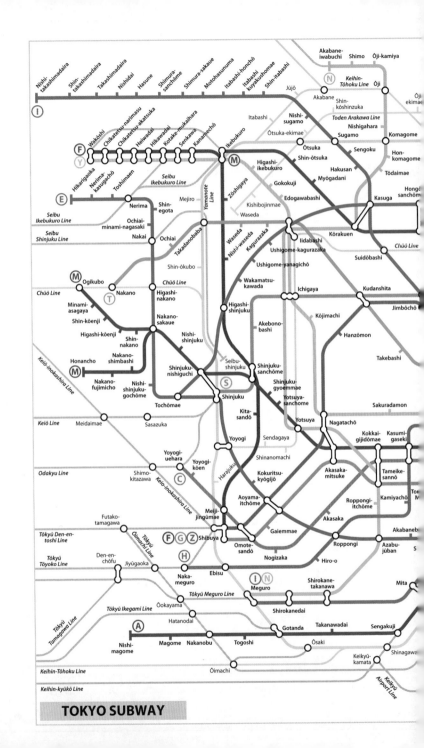

TOKYO SUBWAY

ROUGH GUIDES

ESCAPE THE EVERYDAY

COLOUR THE WORLD
Create beautiful artwork inspired by the greatest places on earth

BEST DAY ON EARTH
THE WORLD'S MOST EXTRAORDINARY EXPERIENCES
FROM DAWN TILL AFTER DARK

1000 ULTIMATE TRAVEL EXPERIENCES
MAKE THE MOST OF YOUR TIME ON EARTH
THIRD EDITION

ADVENTURE BECKONS
YOU JUST NEED TO KNOW WHERE TO LOOK

roughguides.com

Long bus journey?
Phone run out of juice?

1 Denim, the pencil, the stethoscope and the hot-air balloon were all invented in which country?

a. Italy
b. France
c. Germany
d. Switzerland

2 What is the currency of Vietnam?

a. Dong
b. Yuan
c. Baht
d. Kip

3 In which city would you find the Majorelle Garden?

a. Marseille
b. Marrakesh
c. Tunis
d. Malaga

4 What is the busiest airport in the world?

a. London Heathrow
b. Tokyo International
c. Chicago O'Hare
d. Hartsfield-Jackson Atlanta International

5 Which of these countries does not have the equator running through it?

a. Brazil
b. Tanzania
c. Indonesia
d. Colombia

6 Which country has the most UNESCO World Heritage Sites?

a. Mexico
b. France
c. Italy
d. India

7 What is the principal religion of Japan?

a. Confucianism
b. Buddhism
c. Jainism
d. Shinto

8 Every July in Sonkajärvi, central Finland, contestants gather for the World Championships of which sport?

a. Zorbing
b. Wife-carrying
c. Chess-boxing
d. Extreme ironing

9 What colour are post boxes in Germany?

a. Red
b. Green
c. Blue
d. Yellow

10 For three days each April during Songkran festival in Thailand, people take to the streets to throw what at each other?

a. Water
b. Oranges
c. Tomatoes
d. Underwear

For more quizzes, competitions and inspirational features go to **roughguides.com**